Advances in Science, Technology & Innovation

IEREK Interdisciplinary Series for Sustainable Development

Advances in Science, Technology & Innovation (ASTI) is a series of peer-reviewed books based on important emerging research that redefines the current disciplinary boundaries in science, technology and innovation (STI) in order to develop integrated concepts for sustainable development. It not only discusses the progress made towards securing more resources, allocating smarter solutions, and rebalancing the relationship between nature and people, but also provides in-depth insights from comprehensive research that addresses the **17 sustainable development goals (SDGs)** as set out by the UN for 2030.

The series draws on the best research papers from various IEREK and other international conferences to promote the creation and development of viable solutions for a **sustainable future and a positive societal** transformation with the help of integrated and innovative science-based approaches. Including interdisciplinary contributions, it presents innovative approaches and highlights how they can best support both economic and sustainable development, through better use of data, more effective institutions, and global, local and individual action, for the welfare of all societies.

The series particularly features conceptual and empirical contributions from various interrelated fields of science, technology and innovation, with an emphasis on digital transformation, that focus on providing practical solutions to **ensure food, water and energy security to achieve the SDGs.** It also presents new case studies offering concrete examples of how to resolve sustainable urbanization and environmental issues in different regions of the world.

The series is intended for professionals in research and teaching, consultancies and industry, and government and international organizations. Published in collaboration with IEREK, the Springer ASTI series will acquaint readers with essential new studies in STI for sustainable development.

ASTI series has now been accepted for Scopus (September 2020). All content published in this series will start appearing on the Scopus site in early 2021.

Sara Arezki · Mariya Ouaissa · Mariyam Ouaissa ·
Moez Krichen · Anand Nayyar
Editors

Emerging Disruptive Technologies for Society 5.0 in Developing Countries

Challenges and Applications

Springer

Editors
Sara Arezki
Faculty of Sciences and Techniques
Université Hassan 1er
Settat, Morocco

Mariyam Ouaissa
Chouaib Doukkali University
El Jadida, Morocco

Anand Nayyar
School of Computer Science
Duy Tan University
Da Nang, Vietnam

Mariya Ouaissa
Cadi Ayyad University
Marrakech, Morocco

Moez Krichen
Department of Information Technology
Al-Baha University
Alaqiq, Saudi Arabia

ISSN 2522-8714 ISSN 2522-8722 (electronic)
Advances in Science, Technology & Innovation
IEREK Interdisciplinary Series for Sustainable Development
ISBN 978-3-031-63700-1 ISBN 978-3-031-63701-8 (eBook)
https://doi.org/10.1007/978-3-031-63701-8

This Springer imprint is published by the registered company Springer Nature Switzerland AG
The registered company address is: Gewerbestrasse 11, 6330 Cham, Switzerland

Preface

Disruptive technology is a technology that affects the way businesses, consumers, or industries function. This technology generally attracts a limited audience, performance issues, and unproven practical application. Artificial intelligence, virtual/augmented reality, internet of things, blockchain technology, and e-commerce are some of the disruptive technologies significantly influencing the future. Nowadays, these technologies are extensively used in developed countries, but they are still at an early stage in emerging countries. As these countries were more affected by the COVID-19 pandemic, both healthcare-wise and economy-wise, the need to adopt new solutions to sustainable development challenges has become more crucial than ever.

In an age of unparalleled technological innovation and societal evolution, we find ourselves on the cusp of a profound transformation. The book you hold in your hands, *Emerging Disruptive Technologies for Society 5.0 in Developing Countries*, is your gateway to understanding the dynamic interplay between cutting-edge technologies and the reshaping of our societies.

The idea behind this book is to focus on solutions based on disruptive technologies that can face the challenges of the developing countries. We will shed the light on different sectors such as education, agriculture, industry, transportation, environment, energy, and healthcare. We will discuss the challenges that the emerging countries face in these sectors and provide disruptive technologies based solutions to them. This book will also introduce success stories of disruptive technologies based solutions and their impact on the lives of people in developing countries.

This book will be divided into 5 parts. The first part will introduce AI and IoT as actors that can help address the challenges of emerging disruptive technologies for society 5.0. The other parts will go in depth and spot the light on emerging disruptive technologies and their role to play in each of the most important sectors of everyday life. They will also expose how researchers from emerging countries applied emerging disruptive technologies to approach sustainable development challenges taking into consideration the specificities of their own countries.

Part One: AI and Challenges of Emerging Disruptive Technologies for Society 5.0

Here, in the opening part, we set the stage. In First chapter "A Comprehensive Review on Disruptive Emerging Technologies for Society 5.0", we embark on a comprehensive exploration, tracing the origins, key characteristics, advantages, and challenges of Society 5.0. It is a society where technology takes center stage, aimed at sustainability, inclusivity, and the betterment of humankind.

Second chapter "Harnessing Emerging Disruptive Technologies for Society 5.0 in Africa: Advancements in Precision Agriculture, Machine Learning, and IoT" examines the role of digital technology in enhancing product variety in African agriculture. The platform economy serves as a case study, highlighting the transformative potential of digital technology and emerging technologies for Society 5.0 in agriculture.

Third chapter "IoT Based Smart Flood Monitoring System" will monitor the water level at the web application, and the computer will broadcast a warning signal to the people for evacuation so that fast essential steps can be performed. The suggested system with a low price in design is easy to operate.

Fourth chapter "A Machine Learning Approach to Analyze Flight Delays Causal Factors: A Predictive System" presents a case study of the aviation industry. Discover how machine learning algorithms empower us to predict flight delays, mitigating operational shortcomings and enhancing customer satisfaction.

Part Two: Business and Economic Transformation Through Disruptive Technologies

Our journey then takes a deep dive into the business and economic transformation through disruptive technologies. Fifth chapter "Emerging and Disruptive Technologies in Entrepreneurship for Global Societies" shifts the spotlight to entrepreneurship in the digital age. We explore how emerging technologies such as artificial intelligence, blockchain, the Internet of Things, and edge computing are reshaping the entrepreneurial landscape, offering efficiency, decision-making process, and enhanced customer experiences while addressing the challenges of cybersecurity and job displacement.

Sixth chapter "Strategic Imperative of Data Analytics: Empowering Informed Business Decision-Making" closes our exploration with a focus on business transformation. Discover how data analytics, driven by AI, blockchain, IoT, and VR empowers businesses to make informed decisions and thrive in the digital age.

Seventh chapter "Too Big to Fail in Real Estate Development in Saudi Arabia" explores the dynamic world of real estate development in Saudi Arabia. Uncover the critical factors that define success in this ever-evolving sector.

Eighth chapter "An Impact of Sustainable Finance Initiatives on Financial Markets and Economic Stability" scrutinizes sustainable finance initiatives and their implications on financial markets and economic equilibrium. Dive deep into the world of ESG considerations and risk mitigation techniques.

Ninth chapter "Exploring Broadband Adoption amongst Rural Businesses: A Review of the Literature" addresses the digital divide, investigating the drivers and barriers to broadband adoption by rural businesses. These insights are crucial for achieving equitable access to digital resources.

Part Three: Advancements in Education and Social Media

Education, technology, and social media development emerge as focal points. Tenth chapter "Analyzing the Attributes of the Moroccan Educational System: A Phase Prior to the Establishment of a Smart Classroom Based on IoT" scrutinizes Morocco's educational landscape, probing its readiness for IoT-based smart classrooms.

In Eleventh chapter "Critical Analysis of the Efficacy of Servant Leadership and Its Relation to Job Satisfaction and Leader Member Exchange Model (LMX)—A Case Study of Private Higher Education Sector in Kuwait", we explore the transformative potential of servant leadership within the context of Kuwait's private higher education sector. This chapter examines the intricate relationship between leadership, job satisfaction, and leader-member exchange.

In Twelfth chapter "Unleashing IT Innovation in Education Based on Meta Learning Approach in English Language Classroom", we witness the dawn of innovative education driven by IT. Meta learning takes the spotlight, transforming English language education through technology.

Thirteenth chapter "Role of Social Media Data and Social Computing Techniques in Society 5.0" delves into the transformative power of social media data and cutting-edge social computing techniques. This chapter illustrates how these tools, when harnessed effectively, drive societal transformation across governance, education, health, and transportation.

Part Four: Intelligent Systems for Healthcare and Agriculture

In this part, we explore the transformative power of technology in healthcare and agriculture areas. Fourteenth chapter "Healthcare Transformation Through Disruptive Technologies: The Role of Telepresence Robots" offers a glimpse into the future of healthcare delivery. Telepresence robots bridge geographical gaps, revolutionizing patient care.

In Fifteenth chapter "Blockchain-Based Traceability in the Agricultural Sector: A Case Study on the Adoption of FPO", we pivot to the agricultural sector. Traceability takes center stage as we explore how blockchain ensures the integrity of the agricultural supply chain, with a spotlight on the adoption of Farmer Producer Organizations (FPOs).

Sixteenth chapter "Design and Development of an AI Agriculture System" showcases the intersection of technology and agriculture. Discover how the fusion of the Internet of Things and Artificial Intelligence revolutionizes agriculture by optimizing resource use, monitoring soil conditions, and automating irrigation, thus contributing to sustainable food production.

Seventeenth chapter "Blockchain for Collaborative and Integrated Supply Chain" showcases the revolutionary potential of blockchain in supply chain management. Learn how blockchain enhances transparency, security, and traceability, fostering collaboration across supply chain networks.

Part Five: Intelligent Transportation and Engineering Applying to Society 5.0

In the final part we focus on engineering applying in society 5.0. In Eighteenth chapter "Energy Supply Control for a Hybrid Microgrid Using an Artificial Neural Network with Integrating of an EV Charging Station: A Case Study of Smart University in a DC Hybrid Microgrid", we venture into the realm of energy management. Explore how artificial neural networks optimize energy supply within smart university microgrids.

Nineteenth chapter "Chapter IoT System for Smart Electric Car Charging Station Using Micro-CPV Unit" discusses the general performance of two optical components to be utilized in micro concentrator photovoltaic (MCPV) systems for electric car charging stations employing in smart transportation.

Twentieth chapter "The Role of Software-Defined Vehicular Networks in Society 5.0" underscores the pivotal role of Software-Defined Vehicular Networks in reshaping urban mobility. Witness the transformation of our cities as technology empowers us to navigate them more efficiently and sustainably.

Twenty-first chapter "Dilute Magnetic III–V Semiconductors for Spintronic Applications in the Digital Society 5.0 Era" presents the future trend in the microelectronic technologies which is to exploit the fundamental degrees of freedom, spin and charge of electron for enhancing the operational speed, transfer efficiency, and storage capacity of the electronic devices in the digital society 5.0 era.

Settat, Morocco — Sara Arezki
Marrakech, Morocco — Mariya Ouaissa
El Jadida, Morocco — Mariyam Ouaissa
Alaqiq, Saudi Arabia — Moez Krichen
Da Nang, Vietnam — Anand Nayyar

Contents

About the Editors

Sara Arezki is Associate Professor, Ph.D., in University Hassan First and Visiting Professor in several moroccan universities and schools. She is also Computer Science Engineer from University Mohamad V—National School of Informatics and System Analysis in Rabat. She started her professional career as an IT project manager in a Finance sector and then in several others sectors (EDtech, Fintech, etc.). She is Expert in implementing quality projects using referentials and norms (CobiT, CMMI, Cobit, ITIL, and ISO 27001, etc.) in public and private sectors. She has served and continues to serve on technical program and organizer committees of several conferences and events. Prof. Arezki leads several projects related to smart cities such as smart citizen, smart parking and smart waste management. Her main research topics are Digital Transformation, Smart Cities, Quality Assurance, Disruptive technologies. She has published over 15 papers (book chapters, international journals, and conferences/workshops). Prof. Arezki is also Startup Coach and Mentor.

Mariya Ouaissa is currently Professor in Cybersecurity and Networks at Faculty of Sciences Semlalia, Cadi Ayyad University, Marrakech, Morocco. She is a Ph.D. graduated in 2019 in Computer Science and Networks, at the Laboratory of Modelisation of Mathematics and Computer Science from ENSAM-Moulay Ismail University, Meknes, Morocco. She is Networks and Telecoms Engineer, graduated in 2013 from National School of Applied Sciences Khouribga, Morocco. She is Co-Founder and IT Consultant at IT Support and Consulting Center. She was working for School of Technology of Meknes Morocco as Visiting Professor from 2013 to 2021. She is Member of the International Association of Engineers and International Association of Online Engineering, and since 2021, she is "ACM Professional Member". She is Expert Reviewer with Academic Exchange Information Centre (AEIC) and Brand Ambassador with Bentham Science. She has served and continues to serve on technical program and organizer committees of several conferences and events and has organized many Symposiums/Workshops/Conferences as General Chair and also as Reviewer of numerous international journals. Dr. Ouaissa has made contributions in the fields of information security and privacy, Internet of Things security, and wireless and constrained networks security. Her main research topics are IoT, M2M, D2D, WSN, Cellular Networks, and Vehicular Networks. She has published over 40 papers (book chapters, international journals, and conferences/workshops), 12 edited books, and 8 special issue as Guest Editor.

Mariyam Ouaissa is currently Assistant Professor in Networks and Systems at ENSA, Chouaib Doukkali University, El Jadida, Morocco. She received her Ph.D. degree in 2019 from National Graduate School of Arts and Crafts, Meknes, Morocco, and her Engineering Degree in 2013 from the National School of Applied Sciences, Khouribga, Morocco. She is a Communication and Networking Researcher and Practitioner with industry and academic experience. Dr. Ouaissa's research is multidisciplinary that focuses on Internet of Things, M2M, WSN, vehicular communications and cellular networks, security networks, congestion overload problem and the resource allocation management and access control. She is serving as Reviewer for international journals and conferences including as IEEE Access, Wireless

Communications and Mobile Computing. Since 2020, she is Member of "International Association of Engineers IAENG" and "International Association of Online Engineering", and since 2021, she is "ACM Professional Member". She has published more than 30 research papers (this includes book chapters, peer-reviewed journal articles, and peer-reviewed conference manuscripts), 10 edited books, and 6 special issue as Guest Editor. She has served on Program Committees and Organizing Committees of several conferences and events and has organized many Symposiums/Workshops/Conferences as General Chair.

Moez Krichen obtained his HDR (Ability to Conduct Researches) in Computer Science from the University of Sfax (Sfax, Tunisia) in 2018. He obtained his Ph.D. in Computer Science in 2007. He is currently Associate Professor at the University of Al-Baha (KSA) and Member of the Research Laboratory on Development and Control of Distributed Applications—REDCAD (Sfax, Tunisia). His main Research Interest is Model-Based Conformance/Load/Security Testing Methodologies for Real-Time, Distributed, and Dynamically Adaptable Systems. Moreover, he works on applying Formal Methods to several Modern Technologies like Smart Cities, Internet of Things (IoT), Smart Vehicles, Drones, Healthcare Systems, etc. Currently, he is also working on Formal Aspects related to Deep Learning, Data Mining, Block-chain, Smart Contracts and Optimization.

Anand Nayyar received Ph.D. (Computer Science) from Desh Bhagat University in 2017 in the area of Wireless Sensor Networks and Swarm Intelligence. He is currently working in School of Computer Science-Duy Tan University, Da Nang, Vietnam, as Assistant Professor, Scientist, Vice-Chairman (Research) and Director—IoT and Intelligent Systems Lab. He is a Certified Professional with 75+ Professional certificates from CISCO, Microsoft, Oracle, Google, Beingcert, EXIN, GAQM, Cyberoam and many more. Published more than 125+ Research Papers in various High-Quality ISI-SCI/SCIE/SSCI Impact Factor Journals cum Scopus/ESCI indexed Journals, 50+ Papers in International Conferences indexed with Springer, IEEE Xplore and ACM Digital Library, 40+ Book Chapters in various SCOPUS, WEB OF SCIENCE Indexed Books with Springer, CRC Press, Elsevier and many more with Citations: 5400+, H-Index: 38 and I-Index: 138. He is Member of more than 50+ Associations as Senior and Life Member including IEEE, ACM. He has authored/co-authored cum Edited 30+ Books of Computer Science. Associated with more than 500+ International Conferences as Program Committee/Chair/Advisory Board/Review Board member. He has 11 Australian Patents, 7 Indian Design cum Utility Patents, 1 Indian Copyright, 2 Canadian Copyrights and 3 German Patents to his credit in the area of Wireless Communications, Artificial Intelligence, Cloud Computing, IoT and Image Processing. Awarded 33+ Awards for Teaching and Research—Young Scientist, Best Scientist, Young Researcher Award, Outstanding Researcher Award, Excellence in Teaching and many more. He is acting as Associate Editor for *Wireless Networks* (Springer), *Computer Communications* (Elsevier), *International Journal of Sensor Networks* (IJSNET) (Inderscience), *Frontiers in Computer Science*, *PeerJ Computer Science*, *Human Centric Computing and Information Sciences* (HCIS), *IET-Quantum Communications*, *IET Wireless Sensor Systems*, *IET Networks*, *IJDST*, *IJISP*, *IJCINI*, *IJGC*. He is acting as Editor-in-Chief of IGI-Global, USA Journal titled *International Journal of Smart Vehicles and Smart Transportation* (IJSVST). He has reviewed more than 1600+ Articles for various Web of Science Indexed Journals. He is currently researching in the area of Wireless Sensor Networks, IoT, Swarm Intelligence, Cloud Computing, Artificial Intelligence, Drones, Blockchain, Cyber Security, Network Simulation and Wireless Communications.

AI and Challenges of Emerging Disruptive Technologies for Society 5.0

A Comprehensive Review on Disruptive Emerging Technologies for Society 5.0

Indu Bala, Kiran Ahuja, and Maad M. Mijwil

Abstract

In 2016, the Japanese government introduced the idea of Society 5.0 with the objective of building a society that centers on people, is sustainable, and inclusive by incorporating digital technologies. Society 5.0 is recognized as the fifth level in the development of human societies after hunting and gathering, agricultural, industrial, and information societies. This article provides an extensive analysis of the definition, significant characteristics, advantages, obstacles, and forthcoming implications of Society 5.0.

Keywords

Society 5.0 · Challenges, · IoT · Artificial intelligence · Blockchain

1 Introduction

Society 5.0 envisages a future society that integrates digital technologies with society to create a sustainable, inclusive, and human- centered society. It is a concept that envisions a society where digital technologies are used to solve societal challenges, such as aging populations, climate change, and economic inequality (Kuroda 2018). Society 5.0 is built on the idea that technology should be used to serve society and not the other way around. It is a society that values the well-being of its citizens, the environment, and the economy. The pictorial view of key features of society 5.0 and its benefits are shown in (Figs. 1 and 2), respectively.

1.1 Key Features of Society 5.0

The key features of Society 5.0 are important because they reflect a more holistic approach to societal development, emphasizing the importance of solving social problems and enhancing human well-being. The utilization of advanced digital technologies can enable Society 5.0 to establish a future that is more sustainable and inclusive for all individuals (IEEE xxxx; Mavrodieva and Shaw 1893; Skobelev and Borovik 2017; Roblek et al. 2020).

- *Integration of digital technologies*: The Society 5.0 initiative is heavily focused on incorporating digital technologies, including AI, IoT, big data, and blockchain, into our society. This integration is crucial to creating groundbreaking solutions that can tackle a wide range of societal issues.
- *Human-centered approach*: Society 5.0 is built on the idea that technology should be used to serve society and not the other way around. It is a society that values the well-being of its citizens, the environment, and the economy.
- *Sustainability*: Society 5.0 emphasizes creating a society that is inclusive and sustainable. It focuses on developing technologies and solutions that can help mitigate climate change, reduce carbon emissions, and promote sustainable development.
- *Collaboration*: Society 5.0 requires a collaborative approach involving government, industry, academia, and civil society. It promotes partnerships and collaborations

I. Bala (✉)
Lovely Professional University, Phagwara, Punjab, India
e-mail: i.rana80@gmail.com

K. Ahuja
DAV Institute of Engineering and Technology, Jalandhar, Punjab, India

M. M. Mijwil
Computer Techniques Engineering Department, Baghdad College of Economic Sciences University, Baghdad, Iraq
e-mail: mr.maad.alnaimiy@baghdadcollege.edu.iq

S. Arezki et al. (eds.), *Emerging Disruptive Technologies for Society 5.0 in Developing Countries*, Advances in Science, Technology & Innovation, https://doi.org/10.1007/978-3-031-63701-8_1

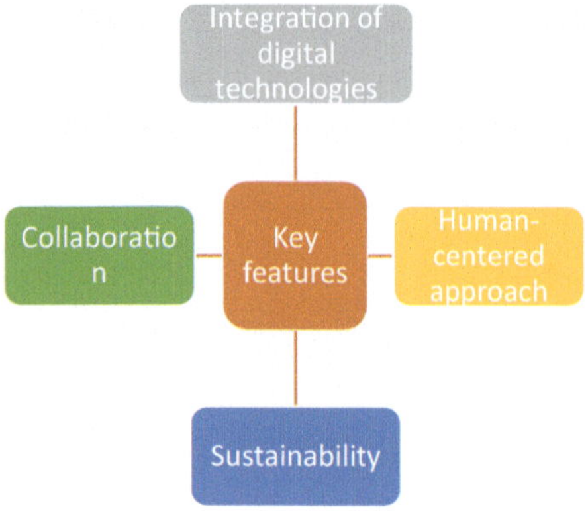

Fig. 1 Key features of society 5.0

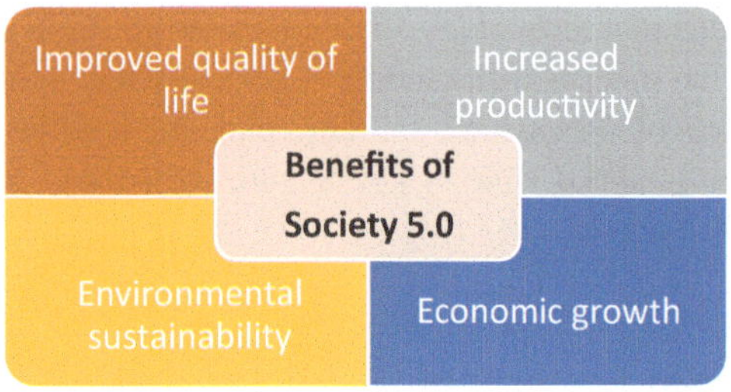

Fig. 2 Benefits of Society 5.0

among these stakeholders to drive innovation and progress towards a more sustainable and inclusive society.

1.2 Benefits of Society 5.0

Society 5.0 promises to create a world that is smarter, safer, and more efficient, while also bringing about greater social inclusion and economic prosperity. The potential benefits of Society 5.0 (Pereira et al. 2020; Deguchi et al. 2020; Opoku 2019; Bala et al. 2022) are vast and far-reaching, and could have a profound impact on our lives and our planet.

- *Improved quality of life*: The vision of Society 5.0 is to utilize technology to enhance the quality of life for citizens in the future. By integrating digital technologies with society, new solutions can be developed that can solve societal challenges, such as aging populations, healthcare, and education.
- *Increased productivity*: Society 5.0 emphasizes the integration of digital technologies with society to create more efficient and productive systems. By using AI, IoT, and big data, businesses and governments can make better decisions, improve processes, and increase productivity.
- *Environmental sustainability*: Society 5.0 focuses on creating a sustainable society that is environmentally friendly. The development of technologies and solutions aimed at mitigating climate change and reducing carbon emissions is crucial to ensuring a sustainable future for future generations.
- *Economic growth*: Society 5.0 emphasizes the integration of digital technologies with society to create new business opportunities and drive economic growth. By promoting entrepreneurship and innovation in sectors such as healthcare, education, and agriculture, society can create more job opportunities and drive economic growth.

1.3 Challenges of Society 5.0

Society 5.0 is a vision for the future that involves incorporating cutting-edge technologies, like AI, IoT, robots, and big data, into all aspects of society. While this vision holds tremendous potential for improving people's lives, it also presents a number of significant challenges that must be addressed. Here are some of the key challenges of Society 5.0 (Ghosh et al. 2021; Narvaez Rojas et al. 2021; Mohan et al. 2021; Bala et al. 2023; Mourtzis et al. 2022; Leng et al. 2022; Fukuyama 2018):

- *Inequality*: The benefits of advanced technologies must be distributed fairly, so that they do not exacerbate existing social and economic inequalities. This requires careful planning and policy-making to ensure that everyone has access to the same opportunities.
- *Privacy and Security*: The integration of advanced technologies into every aspect of society raises serious concerns about privacy and security. There must be robust safeguards in place to protect people's personal information and prevent cyber-attacks.
- *Job Displacement*: The increased automation of many tasks could lead to significant job displacement, particularly in low-skilled industries. This could have serious social and economic consequences and requires careful planning and investment in education and retraining.
- *Ethical Concerns*: The utilization of cutting-edge technologies like automation and artificial intelligence has given rise to various ethical dilemmas. It is vital to guarantee that the creation and application of these technologies conform to moral principles and uphold human values.
- *Infrastructure*: Society 5.0 requires a significant investment in infrastructure, including high-speed internet, advanced transportation systems, and smart cities. This requires significant public and private investment, as well as careful planning and collaboration between different stakeholders.

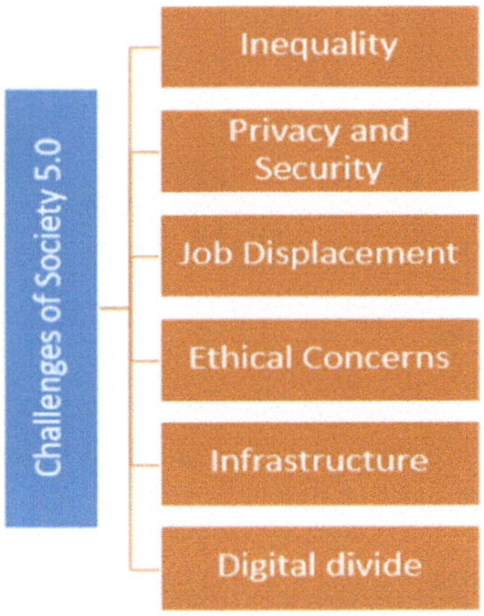

Fig. 3 Challenges related to society 5.0

- *Digital divide*: Society 5.0 requires a skilled workforce with the necessary technical expertise. Governments need to invest in upskilling and reskilling their workforces, particularly in the areas of AI, data analytics, cybersecurity, and digital literacy.

Though Society 5.0 holds tremendous promise, to ensure equitable access and ethical and sustainable use of advanced technologies, it is crucial to address the challenges they present. This will promote the equitable sharing of benefits that these technologies offer. Pictorial view of various challenges is shown in Fig. 3 below.

2 Evolution of Society 5.0

The aim is to establish a community that integrates the technological progressions of Industry 4.0, also referred to as the Fourth Industrial Revolution, with a strong emphasis on human needs and welfare, with the objective of forming a more sustainable, just, and thriving society. Originating in Japan, the idea of Society 5.0 is closely linked to the Japanese government's initiatives to build a highly advanced society that tackles the hurdles presented by environmental sustainability, declining birth rates, and an aging population (Bala and Singh 2019).

Society 5.0 aims to tackle complex societal problems and enhance human capabilities by leveraging cutting-edge technologies like artificial intelligence, the Internet of Things (IoT), and robotics. For example, in a Society 5.0 world, autonomous vehicles could reduce traffic congestion and air pollution, while AI-powered healthcare could improve patient outcomes and reduce costs. The core goal of Society 5.0 is to create a society that revolves around people and uses technology to enhance the well-being of everyone, as well as to address the challenges faced by the world today (Huang et al. 2022).

Society 5.0 marks the latest stage in human societal development, which has undergone significant changes over time. Previously, societies were predominantly based on agriculture, followed by the industrial revolution, which ushered in mass production and mechanization. The digital revolution then brought about the information age, and now, Society 5.0 represents the next evolutionary stage. This stage is characterized by the integration of physical and digital technologies to create a smart, sustainable, and comprehensive society. The primary objective of the concept is to address complex societal issues such as climate change, resource depletion, and an aging population while simultaneously improving the well-being of people. As a result, Society 5.0 represents a significant shift towards a more human-centric approach to technology and innovation, with the objective of enhancing the lives of individuals and creating a better future for all. (Pereira et al. 2020). The evolution of society 5.0 is shown in Fig. 4 and on the basis of some specific parameters is given in Table 1.

Society 5.0 has the potential to bring about several benefits. The primary objective is to use digital technologies to address some of the most crucial social and environmental challenges of our era, such as climate change, resource depletion, and aging populations. AI, IoT sensors, and automation can aid in reducing waste and fostering sustainable practices by being implemented in energy and resource management. Moreover, the integration of digital technologies into the healthcare sector could enhance patient outcomes and lower costs (Tavares et al. 2022).

Another advantage of Society 5.0 is the potential for enhanced connectivity and collaboration. Digital technologies can connect people, organizations, and resources in new ways, enabling the sharing of knowledge and expertise across different sectors and regions. This could lead to more effective problem-solving and innovation, as well as greater efficiency and productivity (Fukuda 2020).

2.1 Society 5.0 and Sustainable Development Goals (SDGs)

Society 5.0 is a term that describes a future society that aims to achieve a balance between economic progress, social integration, and environmental conservation. It aims to achieve sustainable development goals by harnessing the power of digital transformation and innovation to create a society that is smarter, more connected, and more sustainable. Here are some ways in which Society 5.0 can help in attaining sustainable development goals. Figure 5 clears their collaboration between them (Zengin et al. 2021; Costa Tavares and do Carmo Azevedo, G. M. 2021; Salimova et al. 2020; Espina-Romero et al. 2023; Alojaiman 2023; Alimohammadlou and Khoshsepehr 2023).

Fig. 4 Evolution of society 5.0

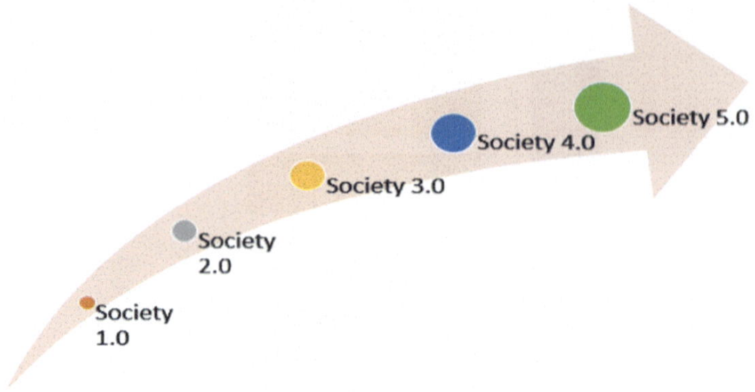

Table 1 Evolution of society 5.0 on the basis diverse parameters

Parameter	Society 1.0	Society 2.0	Society 3.0	Society 4.0	Society 5.0
Economic system	Hunting and gathering	Agriculture and farming	Industrial manufacturing	Information and service	Automation and post-scarcity
Technology	Simple tools and weapons	Domesticated animals, plows	Steam engines, telegraphs	Computers, internet	Robotics, nanotechnology
Energy source	Human and animal power	Wood, water, wind	Fossil fuels	Renewable energy	Advanced fusion power
Social organization	Kinship-based tribes	Hierarchical societies	Bureaucratic institutions	Decentralized networks	Global governance
Political system	Informal leadership	Monarchy, feudalism	Representative democracy	Direct democracy, socialism	Technocracy
Resource ownership	Common property	Personal and communal property	Private property	Intellectual property	Shared commons
Value system	Survival and kinship ties	Property and social hierarchy	Efficiency and productivity	Innovation and individualism	Sustainability and collaboration
Education	Oral tradition, apprenticeships	Formal schools, universities	Compulsory education	Online learning, MOOCs	AI-assisted learning
Work-life balance	Integrated with life, seasonal	Rural agrarian lifestyle, family-based	Urban, regulated working hours	Work from anywhere, remote work	Work-life integration, shorter workweeks
Health and wellbeing	Balanced, traditional medicine	Improved hygiene, public health	Medical advancements, specialization	Personalized medicine, telemedicine	Longevity, life extension

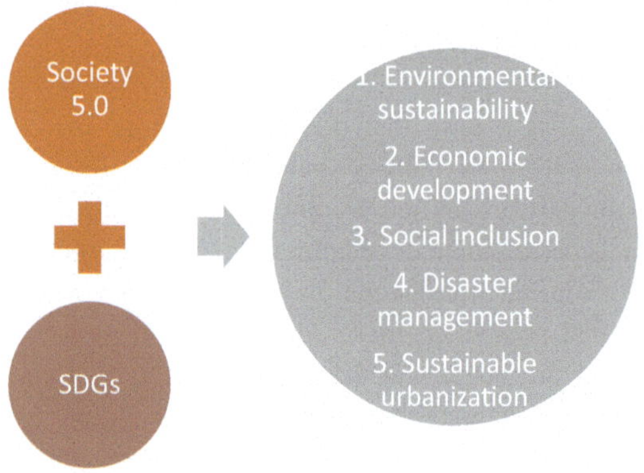

Fig. 5 The combined efforts of society 5.0 and SDGs

- *Environmental sustainability*: Society 5.0 is capable of tackling environmental sustainability challenges by advocating the usage of renewable energy, diminishing carbon emissions, and enhancing resource efficiency by utilizing advanced technologies like IoT and AI.
- *Economic development*: Society 5.0 is capable of tackling environmental sustainability challenges by advocating the usage of renewable energy, diminishing carbon emissions, and enhancing resource efficiency by utilizing advanced technologies like IoT and AI.
- *Social inclusion*: Society 5.0 can help to promote social inclusion by providing access to education and healthcare services through the use of digital technologies, and promoting equal opportunities and diversity.

- *Disaster management*: Society 5.0 can help in managing natural disasters through the use of technology such as AI, big data analytics, and drones to monitor and respond to disasters in real-time.
- *Sustainable urbanization*: Society 5.0 can help in promoting sustainable urbanization by enhancing mobility through the use of autonomous vehicles, reducing traffic congestion and air pollution, and improving public services through the use of smart technologies.

3 Disruptive Technologies for Society 5.0

Society 5.0 is a concept that envisions a future society that leverages advanced technologies to create a sustainable and human-centered society. There are several emerging and disruptive technologies that have the potential to transform Society 5.0 as shown in Fig. 6. Some of them are as follows (Bali et al. 2021; Kasinathan et al. 2022; Carayannis and Morawska-Jancelewicz 2022; Malau 2021; Ahuja et al. 2021):

- *Artificial Intelligence (AI)*: AI has the potential to transform various industries and enable automation, personalization, and decision-making. It can help create intelligent systems that can learn, adapt, and evolve to meet changing societal needs (Bartoloni et al. 2022).
- *Internet of Things (IoT)*: The Internet of Things (IoT) has the potential to link tangible devices to the internet, which can then gather and evaluate data in real-time. This can lead to smarter decision-making, superior resource management, and process optimization (Tyagi et al. 2023).
- *Blockchain*: Blockchain technology is a type of distributed ledger system that eliminates the need for intermediaries in secure and transparent transactions. Its efficient and secure nature makes it a valuable tool in finance and supply chain management (Garg 2022).
- *Augmented and virtual reality (AR/VR)*: AR/VR technologies have the potential to enrich the user experience by creating a highly engaging and participatory environment. They have wide-ranging applications in different sectors, including healthcare, education, and entertainment (Almusaed et al. 2023).

Fig. 6 Disruptive technologies form society 5.0

- *Robotics*: Robotics can help automate various tasks and enable efficient and accurate processing of information. It can also help enhance human capabilities, especially in dangerous or difficult environments.

These advanced technologies have the potential to build a society that is both sustainable and focused on the welfare of its people. Nevertheless, there are certain risks and obstacles linked with their adoption, including privacy issues, loss of jobs, and moral dilemmas. Thus, it is crucial to be cautious while embracing these technologies and ensure that their usage is for the betterment of the community as a whole.

3.1 Applications of Disruptive Technologies in Society 5.0

Disruptive technologies are technologies that fundamentally change the way we do things, creating new markets and transforming industries. In Society 5.0, disruptive technologies play a vital role in enabling the society to become more connected, smarter, and sustainable. Here are some detailed applications (Mukherjee et al. 2023; Srinivasa et al. 2022; Siddesh and Kulkarni 2022; Ciasullo et al. 2022) of disruptive technologies for Society 5.0 in different industries and pictorial represented in Fig. 7:

- *Healthcare*: In healthcare, disruptive technologies such as artificial intelligence, telemedicine, and wearable devices can enable remote monitoring of patients, early detection of diseases, and personalized medicine. AI has the potential to examine medical data and detect trends, which can be used to devise innovative treatments. Additionally, telemedicine enables patients in distant areas to obtain medical care. Wearable devices can also enable continuous monitoring of vital signs and early detection of health issues.
- *Agriculture*: In agriculture, disruptive technologies such as precision agriculture, automation, and the Internet of Things can enable more efficient use of resources, reduce waste, and increase yields. Precision agriculture refers to the practice of utilizing data and analytical tools to enhance crop productivity while reducing wastage. Automation can help in the planting, harvesting, and processing of crops, while IoT can enable farmers to monitor and control their operations remotely.
- *Transportation*: In transportation, disruptive technologies such as autonomous vehicles, electric vehicles, and hyper loops can enable more efficient, sustainable, and safe transportation. Autonomous vehicles can reduce traffic congestion and accidents, while electric vehicles can reduce emissions and dependence on fossil fuels.

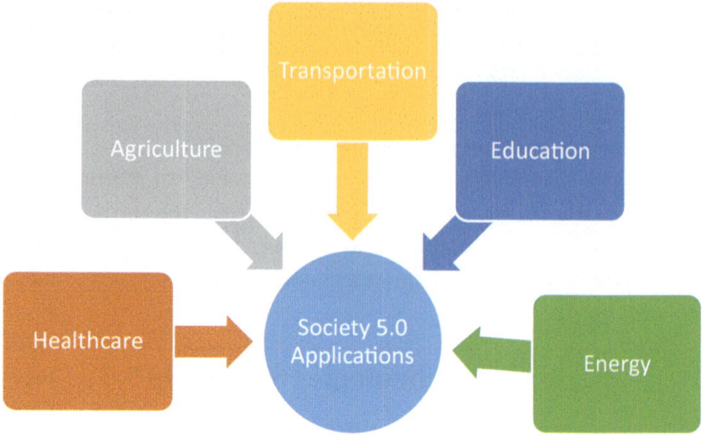

Fig. 7 Diverse applications of society 5.0

Hyper loops can enable high-speed, low-cost transportation of people and goods over long distances.

- *Education*: In education, disruptive technologies such as online learning, gamification, and virtual reality can enable personalized, engaging, and accessible education. Online learning can enable students to access educational resources from anywhere, while gamification can make learning more engaging and motivating. Virtual reality can enable immersive and interactive learning experiences.
- *Energy*: In energy, disruptive technologies such as renewable energy, energy storage, and smart grids can enable a transition to a more sustainable energy system. Renewable sources of energy like solar and wind power are capable of reducing our dependence on fossil fuels. The integration of intermittent renewable energy sources can be made possible with the help of energy storage. Also, the use of smart grids can lead to more efficient energy consumption and improve the reliability of the grid.

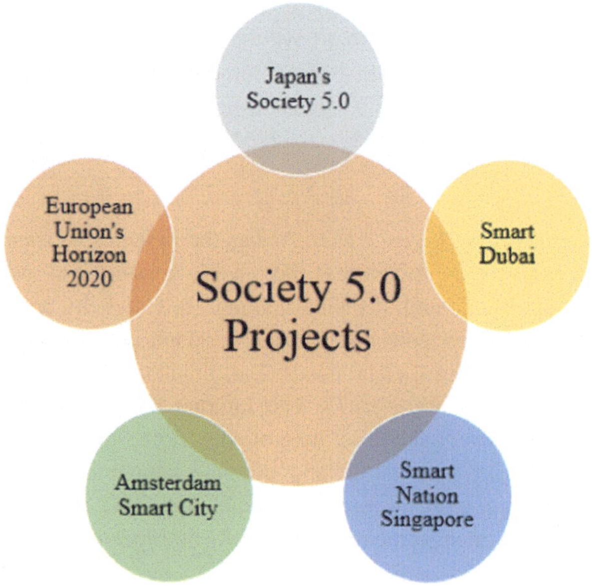

Fig. 8 Latest projects world-wide are going on society 5.0

4 Worldwide Ongoing Projects to Develop Society 5.0

There are several projects worldwide (Sahib 2020; Komninos et al. 2022; Ismagilova et al. 2020; Chauhan et al. 2016) aimed at developing and implementing the Society 5.0 concept. Here are some examples and presented in Fig. 8:

- *Japan's Society 5.0*: Japan has been a pioneer in promoting the Society 5.0 concept and has launched several initiatives to develop smart cities, promote innovation, and improve the quality of life for its citizens. The Japanese government has also launched several research and development programs aimed at developing technologies that can contribute to the realization of Society 5.0, such as robotics, AI, and IoT.
- *Smart Dubai*: Dubai's government has launched an initiative called Smart Dubai, which aims to convert the city into a smart city while promoting sustainability and innovation. The initiative involves the development of smart infrastructure, digital services, and a supportive ecosystem for startups and entrepreneurs.
- *Smart Nation Singapore*: Smart Nation Singapore is a government-led initiative aimed at harnessing the power of technology to create a more connected, efficient, and sustainable society. The initiative involves the development of smart infrastructure, digital services, and a supportive ecosystem for innovation and entrepreneurship.
- *Amsterdam Smart City*: Amsterdam Smart City is a collaboration between public and private sectors with

an objective to foster eco-friendly urban growth and enhance the living standards of the populace. The initiative involves the development of smart infrastructure, digital services, and a platform for collaboration between businesses, government, and citizens.

- *European Union's Horizon 2020*: The Horizon 2020 program by the European Union is a research and innovation initiative that strives to create technological advancements to support the Society 5.0 concept. The program prioritizes important fields including AI, robotics, smart cities, and the Internet of things.

4.1 Ongoing Research Activities on Society 5.0

There are several ongoing research activities (Bartoloni et al. 2022; Ghobakhloo et al. 2022; Hussain et al. 2023; Saniuk et al. 2023; Dwivedi et al. 2023) aimed at developing the Society 5.0 concept. Here are some examples and pictorial presented in Fig. 9:

- *Artificial Intelligence and Robotics*: Researchers are currently conducting studies in the fields of artificial intelligence and robotics with the aim of creating innovative technologies that can support the Society 5.0 concept. Research is focused on developing advanced AI algorithms and robotics systems that can perform complex tasks, interact with humans, and contribute to a more efficient and sustainable society.
- *Internet of Things*: The Internet of Things (IoT) is a crucial technology that can make the vision of Society 5.0 a reality by establishing a network of linked devices and sensors that can gather and exchange data instantly. Continuous studies are dedicated to producing innovative IoT devices and systems that can enhance the effectiveness of diverse sectors, including healthcare, agriculture, transportation, and energy.

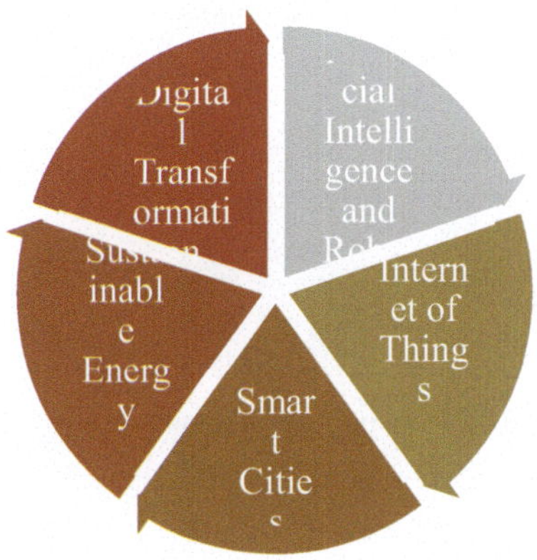

Fig. 9 Ongoing research activities related to society 5.0

- *Smart Cities*: Smart cities play a vital role in realizing the Society 5.0 vision. The research efforts are currently directed towards discovering innovative technologies and systems that can facilitate the establishment of smart cities. Research is focused on developing smart infrastructure, digital services, and platforms for collaboration between government, businesses, and citizens.
- *Sustainable Energy*: Sustainable energy is another key area of research for the Society 5.0 concept. Ongoing research is focused on developing new renewable energy technologies, such as solar and wind, as well as energy storage systems and smart grids that can enable a transition to a more sustainable energy system.
- *Digital Transformation*: The digital transformation of industries and society is a critical enabler of the Society 5.0 vision. The current research endeavors are concentrated on devising fresh digital technologies and frameworks that facilitate the digital revolution of different industries. These technologies aim to encourage novel ways of collaboration and innovation.

These ongoing research activities demonstrate the commitment and focus of the research community on developing the Society 5.0 concept and enabling a more connected, innovative, and sustainable society.

5 Indian Scenario for Society 5.0

Society 5.0 is a futuristic concept that envisions a society powered by digital technologies with a focus on human well-being, sustainability, and inclusivity. This vision is particularly relevant to India given its vast population and growing digital infrastructure. Society 5.0 aims to improve the standard of living for all individuals by utilizing technology. It involves the application of cutting-edge tech, such as Artificial Intelligence, Internet of Things, and Big Data analytics to develop creative business models, enhance healthcare services, and facilitate education accessibility. Furthermore, Society 5.0 seeks to cultivate a culture of innovation and provide support for startups to promote entrepreneurship and innovation. Ultimately, the goal is to establish a sustainable society by promoting renewable energy, reducing carbon emissions, and minimizing waste. With effective implementation, Society 5.0 can transform India into a leading digital economy that prioritizes the well-being of its citizen. The pictorial represented in Fig. 10 (Ghosh et al. 2021, 2022; Mishra and Pandey 2023; Ahuja and Bala 2021; Adel 2022):

- *Digital infrastructure*: Society 5.0 necessitates a strong digital framework to facilitate the implementation of cutting-edge technologies like AI, IoT, and blockchain.

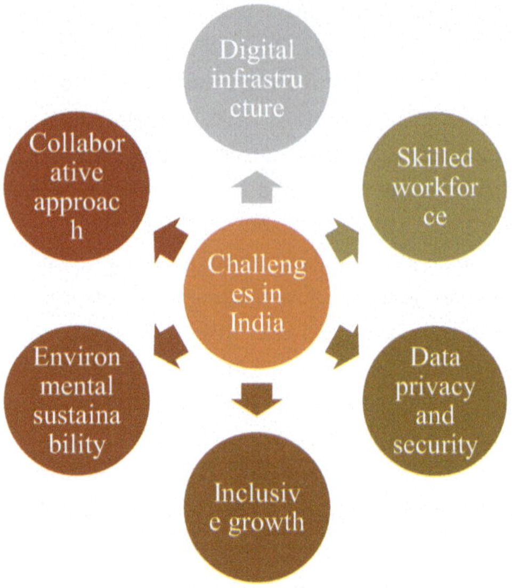

Fig. 10 Challenges in India to develop Society 5.0

India must prioritize constructing a dependable and speedy network, broadening internet accessibility, and closing the gap between urban and rural regions to meet this requirement.

- *Skilled workforce*: Developing and deploying advanced technologies requires a skilled workforce with the necessary technical expertise. India needs to invest in upskilling and reskilling its workforce, particularly in the areas of AI, data analytics, cybersecurity, and digital literacy.
- *Data privacy and security*: With the increasing use of digital technologies, data privacy and security become critical concerns. India should establish strong data protection rules and cybersecurity systems to safeguard the personal information of its citizens against misuse, unauthorized access, and abuse.
- *Inclusive Growth*: Society 5.0 prioritizes the development of an all-encompassing and eco-friendly society. India must ensure that the advancements in technology benefit all members of society, particularly those who are socially and financially marginalized.
- *Environmental Sustainability*: Another key aspect of Society 5.0 is the promotion of environmental sustainability. India needs to focus on developing technologies and solutions that can help mitigate climate change, reduce carbon emissions, and promote sustainable development.
- *Collaborative Approach*: Finally, developing Society 5.0 requires a collaborative approach involving government, industry, academia, and civil society. India needs to promote partnerships and collaborations among these stakeholders to drive innovation and progress towards a more sustainable and inclusive society.

6 Recommendations for the Successful Development of the Society 5.0 in India

There are several recommendations for developing Society 5.0, which emphasizes the integration of digital technology with society to create a more sustainable, inclusive, and human-centered society. Here are some key recommendations and presented in Fig. 11:

- *Foster innovation and entrepreneurship*: Society 5.0 requires innovation and creativity to develop new solutions that can solve societal challenges. Governments, businesses, and educational institutions need to create an environment that fosters innovation and entrepreneurship.
- *Develop digital infrastructure*: It is imperative to have a strong digital foundation to implement cutting-edge technologies like AI, IoT, and blockchain. Therefore, governments must allocate funds towards constructing dependable and fast networks, broadening internet accessibility, and closing the gap between urban and rural regions.
- *Focus on digital literacy*: Society 5.0 requires a skilled workforce with the necessary technical expertise. Governments need to invest in upskilling and reskilling their workforces, particularly in the areas of AI, data analytics, cybersecurity, and digital literacy.
- *Prioritize data privacy and security*: With the increasing use of digital technologies, data privacy and security become critical concerns. Governments should create strong regulations for data protection and cybersecurity to safeguard citizens' personal information from unauthorized access, misuse, and abuse.
- *Promote social and environmental sustainability*: Society 5.0 emphasizes creating a society that is inclusive and sustainable. It is crucial for governments to

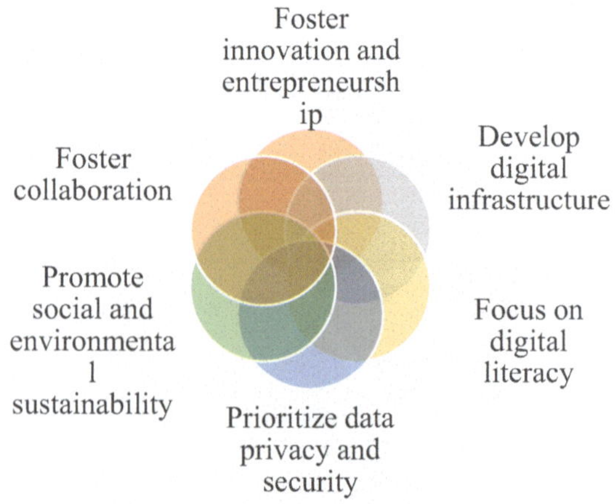

Fig. 11 Recommendation for developing Society 5.0

make sure that advancements in technology are accessible to everyone, especially those who are facing social and economic challenges. Additionally, they should put effort into creating innovative solutions that combat climate change, minimize carbon emissions, and encourage sustainable growth.Foster collaboration: Developing Society 5.0 requires a collaborative approach involving government, industry, academia, and civil society. Governments need to promote partnerships and collaborations among these stakeholders to drive innovation and progress towards a more sustainable and inclusive society. They can also establish a platform for collaboration and knowledge-sharing among stakeholders.

In nutshell, the development of Society 5.0 requires a multidimensional approach that prioritizes innovation, education, digital infrastructure, data privacy and security, social and environmental sustainability, and collaboration.

7 Conclusion

In conclusion, Society 5.0 offers a vision for a more sustainable, inclusive, and human-centered society, where technological innovations are used to solve complex societal challenges. It requires a multidimensional approach that prioritizes innovation, education, digital infrastructure, data privacy and security, social and environmental sustainability, and collaboration among stakeholders. While there are challenges and risks associated with the development of Society 5.0, it presents significant opportunities to create a better future for all. By adopting this vision and working towards its realization, we can create a society where technology is not just a tool for economic growth but also a means to improve the quality of life for all.

References

Adel, A. (2022). Future of industry 5.0 in society: human-centric solutions, challenges and prospective research areas. Journal of Cloud Computing, 11(1), 1–15

Ahuja, K., & Bala, I. (2021). Role of Artificial Intelligence and IoT in Next Generation Education System. Intelligence of Things: AI-IoT Based Critical-Applications and Innovations, 189–208

Ahuja, K., Bala, I., & Nayyar, A. (2021). Advancements and Trends in Green Computing and Communication. Recent Advances in Computer Science and Communications (Formerly: Recent Patents on Computer Science), 14(4), 978–979

Alimohammadlou, M., & Khoshsepehr, Z. (2023). The role of Society 5.0 in achieving sustainable development: a spherical fuzzy set approach. Environmental Science and Pollution Research, 1–25

36. Almusaed, A., Yitmen, I., & Almssad, A. (2023). Enhancing Smart Home Design with AI Models: A Case Study of Living Spaces Implementation Review. Energies, 16(6), 2636

Alojaiman, B. (2023). Technological Modernizations in the Industry 5.0 Era: A Descriptive Analysis and Future Research Directions. Processes, 11(5), 1318

9. Bala, I., Sharma, A., Tselykh, A., & Kim, B. G. (2022). Throughput optimization of interference limited cognitive radio-based Internet of Things (CR-IoT) network. Journal of King Saud University-Computer and Information Sciences, 34(7), 4233–4243

Bala, I., & Singh, G. (2019). Green communication for cognitive cities. In Driving the Development, Management, and Sustainability of Cognitive Cities (pp. 87–110). IGI Global

Bala, I., Ahuja, K., Arora, K., & Mandal, D. (2023). A comprehensive survey on heterogeneous cognitive radio networks. Comprehensive Guide to Heterogeneous Networks, 149–178

Bali, V., Bhatnagar, V., Sinha, S., & Johri, P. (Eds.). (2021). Disruptive Technologies for Society 5.0: Exploration of New Ideas, Techniques, and Tools. CRC Press

Bartoloni, S., Calò, E., Marinelli, L., Pascucci, F., Dezi, L., Carayannis, E., ... & Gregori, G. L. (2022). Towards designing society 5.0 solutions: The new Quintuple Helix-Design Thinking approach to technology. Technovation, 113, 102413

Carayannis, E. G., & Morawska-Jancelewicz, J. (2022). The futures of Europe: Society 5.0 and Industry 5.0 as driving forces of future universities. Journal of the Knowledge Economy, 1–27

Chauhan, S., Agarwal, N., & Kar, A. K. (2016). Addressing big data challenges in smart cities: a systematic literature review. info, 18(4), 73–90.

Ciasullo, M. V., Orciuoli, F., Douglas, A., & Palumbo, R. (2022). Putting Health 4.0 at the service of Society 5.0: Exploratory insights from a pilot study. Socio-Economic Planning Sciences, 80, 101163

Da Costa Tavares, M. D. C., & do Carmo Azevedo, G. M. (2021). Society 5.0 as a contribution to the sustainable development report. In Advances in Tourism, Technology and Systems: Selected Papers from ICOTTS20, Volume 1 (pp. 49–63). Springer Singapore

Deguchi, A.; Hirai, C.; Matsuoka, H.; Nakano, T.; Oshima, K.; Tai, M.; Tani, S. What Is Society 5.0? In Society 5.0: A People-Centric Super-Smart Society; Springer: Singapore, 2020; pp. 1–23. ISBN 9789811529894

Dwivedi, A., Agrawal, D., Jha, A., & Mathiyazhagan, K. (2023). Studying the interactions among Industry 5.0 and circular supply chain: Towards attaining sustainable development. Computers & Industrial Engineering, 176, 108927

Espina-Romero, L., Guerrero-Alcedo, J., Goñi Avila, N., Noroño Sánchez, J. G., Gutiérrez Hurtado, H., & Quiñones Li, A. (2023). Industry 5.0: Tracking Scientific Activity on the Most Influential Industries, Associated Topics, and Future Research Agenda. Sustainability, 15(6), 5554

Fukuda, K. (2020). Science, technology and innovation ecosystem transformation toward society 5.0. International journal of production economics, 220, 107460

Fukuyama, M. (2018). Society 5.0: Aiming for a new human-centered society. Japan Spotlight, 27(5), 47–50

Garg, P. K. (2022). The future healthcare technologies: a roadmap to society 5.0. In Geospatial Data Science in Healthcare for Society 5.0 (pp. 305–318). Singapore: Springer Singapore

45. Ghobakhloo, M., Iranmanesh, M., Mubarak, M. F., Mubarik, M., Rejeb, A., & Nilashi, M. (2022). Identifying industry 5.0 contributions to sustainable development: A strategy roadmap for delivering sustainability values. Sustainable Production and Consumption, 33, 716–737

Ghosh, T., Saha, R., Roy, A., Misra, S., & Raghuwanshi, N. S. (2021). AI-based communication-as-a-service for network management in society 5.0. IEEE Transactions on Network and Service Management, 18(4), 4030–4041

Ghosh, T., Roy, A., & Misra, S. (2022). B2H: Enabling delay-tolerant blockchain network in healthcare for Society 5.0. Computer Networks, 210, 108860

18. Huang, S., Wang, B., Li, X., Zheng, P., Mourtzis, D., & Wang, L. (2022). Industry 5.0 and Society 5.0—Comparison, complementation and co-evolution. Journal of manufacturing systems, 64, 424-428.

Hussain, S., Singh, A. M., Mohanty, P., & Gavinolla, M. R. (2023). Next generation employability and career sustainability in the hospitality industry 5.0. Worldwide Hospitality and Tourism Themes

IEEE. "Society 5.0," n.d. [Online]. Available: https://spectrum.ieee.org/static/society-50

Ismagilova, E., Hughes, L., Rana, N. P., & Dwivedi, Y. K. (2020). Security, privacy and risks within smart cities: Literature review and development of a smart city interaction framework. Information Systems Frontiers, 1–22

Kasinathan, P., Pugazhendhi, R., Elavarasan, R. M., Ramachandaramurthy, V. K., Ramanathan, V., Subramanian, S., ... & Alsharif, M. H. (2022). Realization of Sustainable Development Goals with Disruptive Technologies by Integrating Industry 5.0, Society 5.0, Smart Cities and Villages. Sustainability, 14(22), 15258

42. Komninos, N., Kakderi, C., Mora, L., Panori, A., & Sefertzi, E. (2022). Towards high impact smart cities: A universal architecture based on connected intelligence spaces. Journal of the Knowledge Economy, 13(2), 1169–1197

1. Y. Kuroda, "Society 5.0: Japan's Vision for a New Era of Human-Centered Society," Journal of the Japanese Society for Artificial Intelligence, vol. 33, no. 5, pp. 1–6, 2018

15. Leng, J., Sha, W., Wang, B., Zheng, P., Zhuang, C., Liu, Q., ... & Wang, L. (2022). Industry 5.0: Prospect and retrospect. Journal of Manufacturing Systems, 65, 279–295

Malau, M. (2021, June). Analysis of the Accounting Learning Digital Disruptive in Industrial Revolution 4.0 and Society 5.0. In 2nd Annual Conference on blended learning, educational technology and Innovation (ACBLETI 2020) (pp. 276–281). Atlantis Press.

Mavrodieva, A.V.; Shaw, R. Disaster and Climate Change Issues in Japan's Society 5.0—A Discussion. Sustainable 2020, 12, 1893.

Mishra, K. N., & Pandey, S. C. (2023). Cloud-IoT Technologies in Society 5.0. Springer Nature

Mohan, N., Singla, R., Kaushal, P., & Kadry, S. (Eds.). (2021). Artificial Intelligence, Machine Learning, and Data Science Technologies: Future Impact and Well-being for Society 5.0. CRC Press

Mourtzis, D., Angelopoulos, J., & Panopoulos, N. (2022). A Literature Review of the Challenges and Opportunities of the Transition from Industry 4.0 to Society 5.0. Energies, 15(17), 6276

Mukherjee, A. A., Raj, A., & Aggarwal, S. (2023). Identification of barriers and their mitigation strategies for industry 5.0 implementation in emerging economies. International Journal of Production Economics, 108770

Narvaez Rojas, C., Alomia Peñafiel, G. A., Loaiza Buitrago, D. F., & Tavera Romero, C. A. (2021). Society 5.0: A Japanese concept for a superintelligent society. Sustainability, 13(12), 6567

8. Opoku, A. Biodiversity and the built environment: Implications for the Sustainable Development Goals (SDGs). Resour. Conserv. Recycl. 2019, 141, 1–7

Pereira, A. G., Lima, T. M., & Charrua-Santos, F. (2020). Society 5.0 as a result of the technological evolution: Historical approach. In Human Interaction and Emerging Technologies: Proceedings of the 1st International Conference on Human Interaction and Emerging Technologies (IHIET 2019), August 22–24, 2019, Nice, France (pp. 700–705). Springer International Publishing

Pereira, A.G.; Lima, T.M.; Charrua-Santos, F. Industry 4.0 and Society 5.0: Opportunities and Threats. Int. J. Recent Technol. Eng. 2020, 8, 3305–3308

Roblek, V.; Meško, M.; Bach, M.P.; Thorpe, O.; Šprajc, P. The Interaction between Internet, Sustainable Development, and Emergence of Society 5.0. Data 2020, 5, 80.

Sahib, U. (2020). Smart Dubai: sensing Dubai smart city for smart environment management. Smart environment for smart cities, 437–489

24. Salimova, T., Vukovic, N., & Guskova, N. (2020). Towards sustainability through Industry 4.0 and Society 5.0. International Review, (3–4), 48-54

Saniuk, S., Grabowska, S., & Fahlevi, M. (2023). Personalization of Products and Sustainable Production and Consumption in the Context of Industry 5.0. In Industry 5.0: Creative and Innovative Organizations (pp. 55–70). Cham: Springer International Publishing

Siddesh, G. M., & Kulkarni, A. S. (2022). Introduction to Smart Big Data Analytics and Smart Real-Time Analytics in Society 5.0. In Society 5.0: Smart Future Towards Enhancing the Quality of Society (pp. 35–55). Singapore: Springer Nature Singapore

Skobelev, P. O., & Borovik, S. Y. (2017). On the way from Industry 4.0 to Industry 5.0: From digital manufacturing to digital society. Industry 4.0, 2(6), 307–311

Srinivasa, K. G., Siddesh, G. M., & Manisekhar, S. R. (Eds.). (2022). Society 5.0: Smart Future Towards Enhancing the Quality of Society. Springer Nature Singapore

Tavares, M. C., Azevedo, G., & Marques, R. P. (2022). The Challenges and Opportunities of Era 5.0 for a More Humanistic and Sustainable Society—A Literature Review. Societies, 12(6), 149

Tyagi, A. K., Dananjayan, S., Agarwal, D., & Thariq Ahmed, H. F. (2023). Blockchain—Internet of Things Applications: Opportunities and Challenges for Industry 4.0 and Society 5.0. Sensors, 23(2), 947

Zengin, Y., Naktiyok, S., Kaygın, E., Kavak, O., & Topçuoğlu, E. (2021). An investigation upon industry 4.0 and society 5.0 within the context of sustainable development goals. Sustainability, 13(5), 2682

Harnessing Emerging Disruptive Technologies for Society 5.0 in Africa: Advancements in Precision Agriculture, Machine Learning, and IoT

Fatima Zahra Bassine, Victor Ongoma, Siham Eddamiri, Perez L. K. Kambiet, and Abdelghani Chehbouni

Abstract

Agriculture remains the primary source of livelihood for most Africans despite being challenged by factors such as climate change and limited investment. Overcoming obstacles faced by African farmers is crucial to boost food productivity that can meet the growing food demand. To address these issues, digital technology, including emerging technologies such as machine learning and the Internet of Things (IoT), is being prioritized in Africa. This paper examines the role of digital technology in enhancing product variety in African agriculture. While digital solutions are not standalone remedies, they offer substantial assistance in specific areas. The platform economy serves as a case study, highlighting the transformative potential of digital technology and emerging technologies for Society 5.0 in agriculture. The platform economy revolutionizes the agricultural landscape by effectively matching supply and demand, providing African farmers with increased product variety, income, and livelihood opportunities.

F. Z. Bassine (✉) · V. Ongoma · S. Eddamiri · P. L. K. Kambiet · A. Chehbouni
International Water Research Institute, Mohammed VI Polytechnic University, Lot 660, Hay Moulay Rachid, 43150 Benguerir, Morocco
e-mail: fatimazahra.bassine@um6p.ma

S. Eddamiri
e-mail: siham.eddamiri@um6p.ma

P. L. K. Kambiet
e-mail: perez.kambiet@um6p.ma

A. Chehbouni
e-mail: abdelghani.chehbouni@um6p.ma

A. Chehbouni
Center for Remote Sensing Applications, Mohammed VI Polytechnic University, Lot 660, Hay Moulay Rachid, 43150 Benguerir, Morocco

Keywords

Precision agriculture · Machine learning · Internet of Things (IoT) · Digital technology · Society 5.0

1 Introduction

Agriculture is the backbone of the economies of most African countries and a source of livelihood for most Africans. Agriculture, mainly rain-fed and dominated by smallholder farmers, is challenged by many factors not limited to climate change, land fragmentation and degradation, and limited inputs (Shimeles et al. 2018). This is happening in the wake of the continent's fast-growing population that increases food demand, threatening the realization of the first and second United Nations Sustainable Development Goals on ending poverty and zero hunger, respectively. Thus, there is a need to identify and implement practical and effective strategies to sustain food productivity in Africa.

Digital technology has gained considerable attention due to its immense potential to revolutionize African agriculture. Advanced tools such as remote sensing, drones, machine learning (ML), and the Internet of Things (IoT) present promising solutions for enhancing agricultural practices and diversifying product variety. These cutting-edge technologies offer valuable insights, facilitate precision farming, and optimize resource allocation, thereby transforming the agricultural landscape. Society 5.0 emphasizes integrating cyber-physical systems, artificial intelligence (AI), and big data, providing a framework for sustainable development (Raj et al. 2021a). By embracing digital technologies within the context of Society 5.0, African farmers can seize opportunities to expand their product range, cater to diverse market demands, and capitalize on emerging trends. This research work (Mendes et al. 2022) looks into the role of remote sensing, drones,

S. Arezki et al. (eds.), *Emerging Disruptive Technologies for Society 5.0 in Developing Countries*, Advances in Science, Technology & Innovation, https://doi.org/10.1007/978-3-031-63701-8_2

ML, and IoT in bolstering product variety in African agriculture. While it acknowledges that digital solutions alone are not a panacea, they can be instrumental in addressing specific challenges and driving progress in targeted areas. Product variety is paramount in agriculture, enabling farmers to cater to various market demands, mitigate risks, and strengthen economic resilience. However, African farmers need help developing and diversifying their product offerings due to limited access to information, inadequate resources, and adherence to traditional farming practices. There is a need to overcome these barriers by harnessing the potential of digital technology to enhance product variety within African agriculture. The concept of the platform economy serves as a compelling case study to illustrate the potential impact of digital technology and Society 5.0. The platform economy exemplifies the transformative power of digital technology by facilitating seamless supply–demand matching. This research explores the adoption of digital technology in African agriculture, evaluating the associated benefits, challenges, and implications through a comprehensive analysis. This illustration contributes to understanding digital solutions' role in bolstering product variety and fostering sustainable agricultural development in Africa.

2 Precision Agriculture in Society 5.0

The functional architecture of a precision farming system in agriculture production involves the seamless integration of multiple components and cutting-edge technologies to optimize farming practices. By harnessing satellite imagery, farmers can access valuable data on crop health, vegetation indices, and environmental conditions. This technology enables the monitoring of large agricultural areas and assists in identifying spatial variations that impact crop growth and development (Yang 2018). Equipped with remote sensing devices (Fig. 1), drones play a pivotal role in capturing high-resolution images and collecting data at a finer scale (Bassine et al. 2019). Drones are instrumental in crop scouting, conducting plant health assessments, and identifying areas that require special attention or intervention. Soil sensors provide crucial information about soil health by measuring critical parameters such as moisture content, temperature, pH, and nutrient levels. This data is essential for optimizing irrigation practices, guiding fertilization strategies, and ensuring the overall well-being of the soil. Fertigation, a precision application technique combining irrigation and fertilizer injection systems, precisely delivers fertilizers and irrigation water tailored to the specific needs of crops, fertigation ensuring efficient nutrient uptake and optimal plant growth. The data collected from various sources, including satellite imagery, drones, and soil sensors, is stored and managed in a cloud-based platform. This centralized data storage facilitates easy accessibility, integration with other systems, and seamless data sharing among stakeholders. Precise mapping involves the generation of detailed maps that depict variations in soil, crop health, and other relevant parameters (Almalki et al. 2021). These maps serve as a foundation for making informed decisions regarding crop management, enabling farmers to allocate resources effectively and implement effective interventions. Advanced data analytics techniques are employed to analyze the collected data and extract meaningful information. ML algorithms and statistical models are utilized to

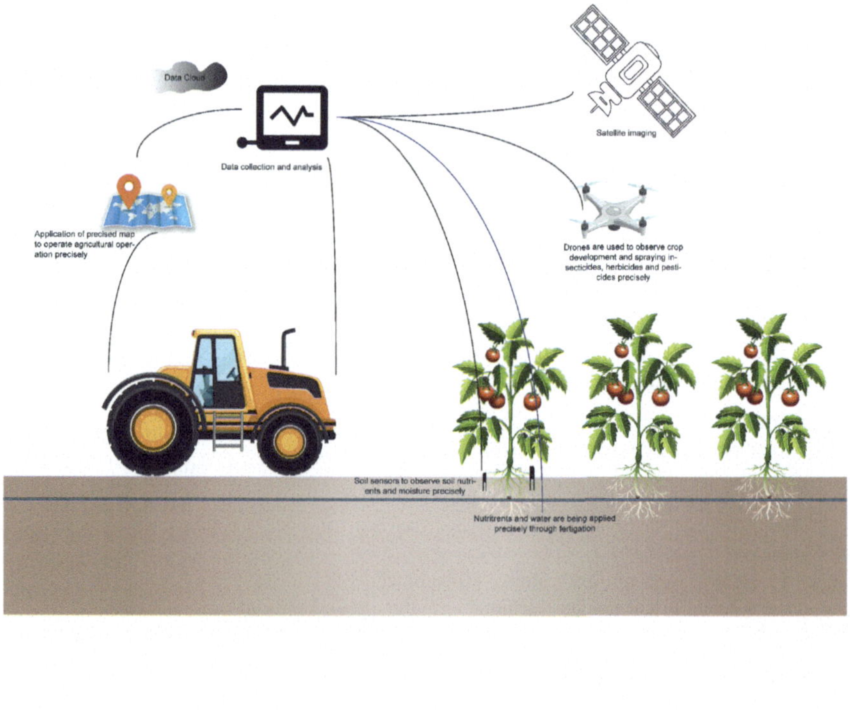

Fig. 1 Functional architecture of precision farming system in agriculture production

identify patterns, predict crop growth, detect anomalies, and optimize farming practices for enhanced productivity and resource efficiency.

2.1 The Role of Precision Agriculture in Enhancing Farming Practices in Africa

Precision agriculture is a transformative paradigm that has gained significant attention in Africa for its potential to revolutionize farming practices. Leveraging advanced technologies, data analytics, and real-time monitoring, precision agriculture offers numerous benefits that contribute to sustainable agricultural development in the region (Tantalaki et al. 2019). Farmers can optimize their farming practices by adopting precision agriculture techniques to achieve higher crop yields. Through the integration of cutting-edge tools such as satellite imagery, drones, and sensor technologies, farmers can monitor crop health, identify areas of stress or nutrient deficiencies, and take targeted actions to address these issues. This holistic approach results in improved crop productivity and increases overall agricultural output. Precision agriculture empowers farmers to make informed decisions regarding allocating vital resources such as water, fertilizers, and pesticides (Sari et al. 2021). The farmers can accurately assess soil moisture levels, nutrient requirements, and pest infestations by harnessing the power of soil sensors, remote sensing technologies, and data analytics. This allows for the precise application of resources, minimizing waste and reducing the environmental impact associated with conventional farming practices. Early detection and effective management of pests and diseases are critical for crop protection. Precision agriculture embraces the utilization of advanced technologies, including drones and sensors, enabling farmers to monitor crop health in real time and swiftly detect signs of pest infestation or disease outbreak. This allows them to take timely actions, implementing targeted interventions and minimizing crop losses, thus safeguarding their harvests.

2.1.1 Climate Resilience

Against the backdrop of the increasing frequency and intensity of weather and climate extremes associated with climate change (Masson-Delmotte et al. 2021), precision agriculture emerges as a groundbreaking and adaptable approach to strengthen farming systems. By harnessing real-time weather data, continuous soil moisture monitoring, and advanced predictive modeling, farmers are equipped with tools to make well-informed decisions regarding irrigation scheduling, crop selection, and risk management. This proactive adaptation to the multifaceted challenges associated with climate change helps farmers to build resilience against impacts on agricultural production, thereby upholding sustainable farming practices and securing the long-term viability of their operations.

2.1.2 Data-Driven Decision-Making

At the very core of precision agriculture lies the power of data analytics, presenting a paradigm shift in decision-making within farming operations. Farmers gain invaluable insights into various facets of their farming practices by meticulously collecting and analyzing vast and diverse datasets derived from different sources such as satellite imagery, sensor networks, and historical records. This data-driven approach helps farmers to make timely and informed decisions about optimal planting strategies, precise resource allocation, and efficient crop management practices. Thus, farmers can attain heightened efficiency, amplified profitability, and ultimately ensure the triumph and resilience of their agricultural pursuits by harnessing the immense potential of data.

2.1.3 Empowerment of Farmers

One of the most remarkable hallmarks of precision agriculture lies in its unwavering commitment to empowering small-scale farmers, often limited by numerous challenges. Precision agriculture bridges the digital divide and levels the playing field for marginalized farmers by facilitating access to cutting-edge technologies, data-driven insights, and innovative farming techniques. Moreover, comprehensive training and support programs are integral to this transformative approach, ensuring farmers acquire the necessary knowledge and skills to leverage these tools adeptly. By empowering small-scale farmers, precision agriculture catalyzes improving livelihoods, augmenting income levels, and fostering sustainable agricultural development at the grassroots level. In doing so, it strengthens the overall resilience and prosperity of the farming community. It amplifies the broader objectives of sustainable agriculture, food security, and socioeconomic advancement in Africa and beyond.

2.2 Applications of Precision Agriculture in Africa

Precision agriculture offers several applications that have proven beneficial for agricultural practices in Africa following its advanced methods and concepts; these applications involve various sensors, including crop, soil, and position sensors, as well as global positioning and remote sensing technologies.

Precision agriculture utilizes sensors to detect and monitor crop stress, variability, and growth patterns. Farmers can identify areas of concern using the data obtained from these sensors. Precision agriculture has become popular by providing soil and crop surface temperature measurements, thermal remote sensing has the potential to be used for a wide range of applications, including monitoring crop stress, crop disease, plant health, soil water stress, planning irrigation, and harvesting activities. Precision agriculture employs soil sensors to monitor soil properties, including moisture levels, nutrient content, and pH. This information allows farmers to tailor their soil management practices, such as fertilization and irrigation, to specific areas of their fields (Khanal et al. 2017). Utilizing available technologies such as GPS, remote sensing, yield monitoring, and soil sampling generally makes map-based approaches easier to implement. This approach requires grid sampling of fields and conducting laboratory analysis of soil samples. Precision agriculture techniques aid in the early detection and management of weeds and diseases (Zhang et al. 2002). Sensors and remote sensing technologies help identify weed-infested areas and detect signs of diseases in crops. Farmers can implement targeted weed control strategies and apply appropriate treatments to minimize crop losses with this information. Precision agriculture utilizes machine controls and computer-based systems to automate and optimize farming operations. These systems enable precise machinery control based on real-time data, such as planting and spraying equipment (Raj et al. 2021b). Automation improves accuracy and efficiency, leading to cost savings and increased productivity. Precision agriculture plays a vital role in improving water and nutrient use efficiency. By monitoring soil moisture levels and plant nutrient requirements, farmers can optimize irrigation and fertilization practices (Raimi et al. 2021); this leads to more efficient resource utilization, reduced water and fertilizer waste, and improved water and nutrient management. Further, precision agriculture reduces environmental pollution and degradation; by applying fertilizers and agrochemicals, farmers can minimize their usage, resulting in less ground and surface water pollution. This promotes environmental sustainability and the conservation of natural resources.

Notable examples of African precision agriculture applications are FruitLook and the Chameleon, Wetting Front Detector Sensors, SoilScan, Yield Prophet, and AgriEdge. FruitLook (Nhamo et al. 2023), used by farmers in the Western Cape of South Africa, provides state-of-the-art information technology for water-efficient and climate-smart farming in the deciduous fruit and grape industry. The Chameleon and Wetting Front Detector Sensors have significantly enabled small-scale farmers in Mozambique, Tanzania, and Zimbabwe to reduce irrigation frequency and double productivity (Ncube et al. 2018). SoilScan (Kelly et al. 2022) from Kenya, is a remarkable soil sensor capable of measuring moisture, nutrient levels, and pH, offering valuable insights for precision agriculture. The Yield Prophet yield monitoring system, developed in Nigeria, uses GPS technology to track crop yields at various field locations, enabling farmers to make informed decisions about crop management strategies (MacCarthy et al. 2018). AgriEdge Morocco offers data collection services that use sensors and tools to gather vital information, helping agriculturalists make informed crop management decisions (Overview: Priorities to make digitalisation work for all in Africa. 2021). In addition, AgriEdge provides data analysis and software solutions that enable farmers to optimize their operations, striving to improve productivity.

These examples demonstrate the diverse applications of precision agriculture already accessible in Africa.

3 Machine Learning for Agricultural Advancements

In the growing adoption of smart farming, applying a robust ML framework is poised to revolutionize agricultural practices. This will happen by enabling the assessment and analysis of data across various stages of the farming process. Spanning from pre-harvesting to harvesting and post-harvesting, the integration of ML algorithms empowers farmers with data-driven decision-making capabilities that drive efficiency and optimize outcomes. During the pre-harvesting stage, ML techniques delve into many factors, including assessing soil composition, evaluating seed quality, analyzing environmental parameters, precisely detecting pests and diseases, and intelligent irrigation management. These algorithms derive predictive insights on optimal irrigation schedules, disease identification and classification, pesticide optimization, soil analysis, and crop yield prediction. During harvesting, ML models leverage soil, meteorological, and satellite data to analyze crop quality, maturity assessment, size estimation, color analysis, firmness evaluation, fruit identification, and growth observations. These models, including Support Vector Machine SVM, XGBoost, LightGBM, and deep learning algorithms like Convolutional Neural Network CNN and Deep Neural Network DNN, enable farmers to classify produce, determine fruit quality and firmness, monitor crop growth, and accurately count harvested yield. In the post-harvest phase (Fig. 2), ML algorithms continue monitoring storage conditions, ensuring optimal fruit quality, accurate classification, grading, and detecting anomalies (Benos et al. 2021). Integrating diverse data sources and ML algorithms enhances decision-making and minimizes losses in agriculture. By harnessing the power of ML across the entire agricultural spectrum, farmers are empowered to make informed decisions, precisely allocate resources, and ultimately elevate productivity, leading to the embrace of sustainable practices, the delivery of impeccable crop

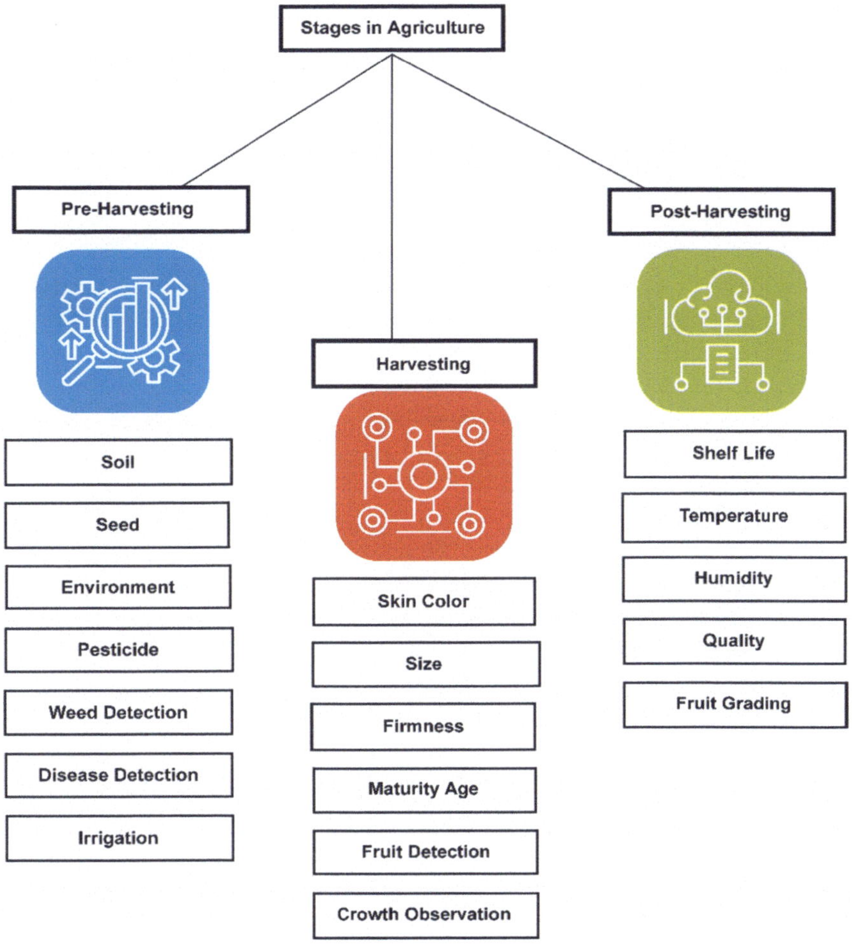

Fig. 2 Machine learning framework for assessing agricultural data in smart farming

quality, and the realization of heightened profitability in the dynamic realm of intelligent farming.

3.1 Benefits of Machine Learning in Agricultural Systems

ML, big data technologies, and high-performance computing have triggered a transformative revolution in the agricultural domain. This comprehensive review examines the diverse applications where ML showcases its prowess in agricultural production systems, unraveling a myriad of benefits that it brings forth.

Crop management, an essential facet of agriculture, experiences the power of ML. Accurate yield prediction becomes possible, empowering farmers with valuable insights for informed decision-making. Disease detection algorithms prove their mettle by identifying crop diseases at their nascent stages, enabling timely intervention and effective disease management. ML techniques also aid in weed detection, facilitating targeted and efficient control measures and mitigating the adverse impact on crop yields (Vitali et al. 2021). Assessing crop quality becomes more efficient with ML, ensuring adherence to high standards and bolstering market competitiveness. Furthermore, the ability of ML algorithms to recognize various plant species contributes to easy crop identification and robust management practices.

In livestock management, ML emerges as a game-changer. Animal welfare monitoring improves as ML algorithms analyze sensor data to identify signs of distress or health issues, enabling swift intervention and improved animal well-being. Livestock production optimization becomes a reality as ML techniques scrutinize data encompassing feed composition, environmental conditions, and animal behavior, enhancing productivity and streamlining operations (Liakos et al. 2018).

Water management, a pressing concern in agriculture, benefits a lot from ML applications. ML algorithms optimize irrigation practices by harnessing data from sensors, satellite imagery, and other sources, minimizing water wastage by increasing water use efficiency. Real-time insights and recommendations provided by ML facilitate irrigation scheduling and resource management, empowering farmers to make data-driven decisions and conserve this precious resource (Sun and Scanlon 2019).

Soil management which is an essential aspect of sustainable agriculture embraces ML. By analyzing data from soil sensors, ML algorithms evaluate soil quality and predict nutrient deficiencies, enabling farmers to fine-tune fertilizer applications and bolster soil health. ML also lends its expertise by recommending appropriate soil management practices based on comprehensive data analysis, reducing soil degradation and promoting long-term soil health (Motia and Reddy 2021).

The fusion of ML and agriculture empowers farmers to navigate complex challenges, enhance productivity, and embrace sustainability. Precision agriculture has become a reality driven by the transformative capabilities of ML techniques, paving the way for a more efficient, productive, and sustainable agricultural landscape.

3.2 Use Cases and Applications of ML in Africa

The slow growth of Africa has been partly attributed to limited investments and expertise (Anyanwu 2014). The emerging technologies present an opportunity for the continent to use its underutilized resources to spur its socio-economic growth. Accurate and comprehensive measurements of economic well-being at a local level are crucial for research and policymaking. However, such measures are often limited in many parts of the world, including Africa. Deep learning models have been trained to predict asset wealth estimates using publicly available multispectral satellite imagery in approximately 20,000 African villages to address this gap. The results are remarkable, as these models can explain up to 70% of the variation in ground-measured village wealth in countries where the model was not trained initially. This outperforms previous benchmarks using high-resolution imagery. Additionally, comparisons with independent wealth measurements from censuses indicate that satellite estimates are similar to errors in existing ground data (Raj et al. 2021a).

Satellite-based wealth estimates also prove valuable in explaining up to 50% of the variation in district-aggregated changes in wealth over time. Daytime imagery, in particular, plays a significant role in this task. These findings demonstrate satellite-based estimates' utility in research and policy domains. The scalability of this approach is evident, as a wealth map for Africa's most populous country has been created using ML techniques and satellite imagery. This highlights the potential for widespread implementation across the continent, especially to increase access to financial services and products to rural communities.

By leveraging ML and satellite data, these applications offer valuable insights into local economic well-being and provide a scalable approach to measuring wealth. ML can significantly enhance research and policy efforts in Africa, enabling more targeted interventions and fostering evidence-based decision-making for sustainable development (Yeh et al. 2020).

4 Internet of Things (IoT) in Agricultural Systems

4.1 Understanding IoT in Agriculture

The functional architecture of an IoT system in agriculture production encompasses various components and capabilities, including farm management data, auto spreading, field monitoring, yield analysis, fertility rate, cumulative farm data, server, cloud, and mobile phone integration (Fig. 3).

At its core, the IoT system in agriculture utilizes interconnected devices and sensors to collect and transmit farm management data. This data includes soil conditions, weather patterns, crop growth, and nutrient levels. The IoT system enables the automated and precise distribution of fertilizers and pesticides based on real-time data, optimizing resource utilization and minimizing environmental impact through auto spreading. Field monitoring is a crucial aspect of the IoT system, utilizing sensors to continuously monitor parameters such as temperature, humidity, and soil moisture levels. This real-time monitoring enables farmers to make informed irrigation scheduling and crop health management decisions. Yield analysis is another critical feature facilitated by the IoT system. By collecting data on crop yield, quality, and growth patterns, farmers can gain insights into the performance of different crops and optimize their cultivation practices. The system also tracks fertility rates, allowing farmers to monitor and adjust nutrient levels for optimal crop growth and health. The IoT system utilizes servers and cloud infrastructure to store and process the vast amount of data generated. This enables secure storage, efficient data analysis, and access to cumulative farm data over time. Farmers can access and manage this data through mobile phone applications, providing real-time insights and decision-making support (Tantalaki et al. 2019).

4.2 Enhancing Agricultural Efficiency and Sustainability with IoT

The adoption of IoT technology in agriculture has significantly enhanced efficiency and sustainability within the industry. By leveraging IoT, farmers can optimize their farming practices, improve resource management, and achieve higher yields while minimizing environmental impact.

One key aspect of IoT in agriculture is the utilization of various sensors. These sensors play a crucial role in collecting essential data for decision-making. For example,

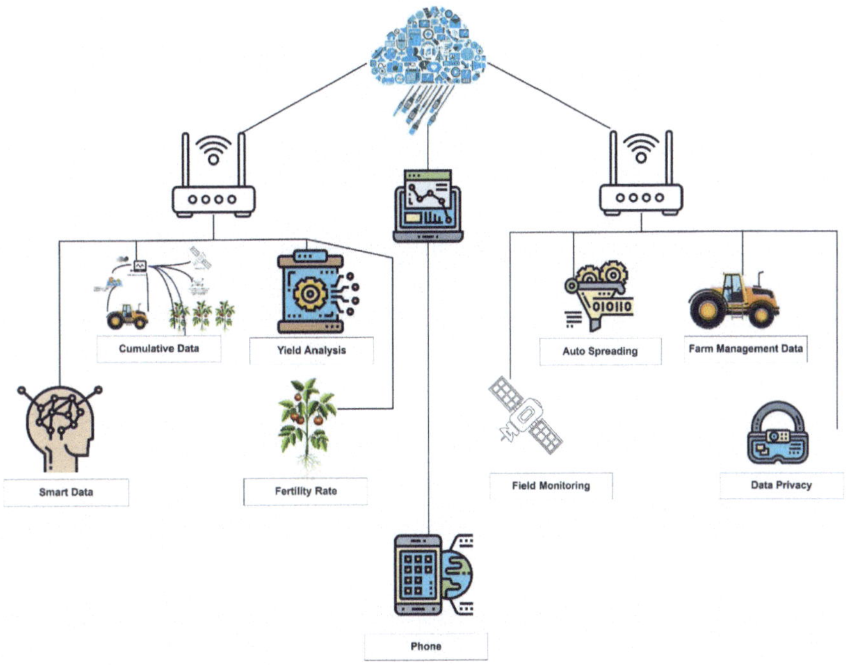

Fig. 3 The functional architecture of IoT system in agriculture production

sensors such as electrical capacitance and electrical conductivity provide valuable insights into soil moisture, ambient humidity, and soil health, enabling farmers to make informed decisions regarding irrigation management and environmental monitoring (Antony et al. 2020). Load cells facilitate accurate measurement of harvested crop weight, leading to more precise yield estimation and reduced crop waste. Electrochemical sensors help quality control by detecting ethylene concentration in crop storage, monitoring greenhouse CO_2 levels, and facilitating beehive monitoring (Yong et al. 2016). Optical sensors offer a wide range of applications, including crop height measurement, livestock, and predator monitoring, volume estimation of harvested grain, plant mapping, plant disease detection, and soil composition analysis, enabling precision farming and early detection of issues. In addition, thermocouples and thermistors assist in monitoring seed and crop storage conditions, greenhouse parameters, and soil and water temperature and contribute to effective water management.

Another critical aspect of IoT in agriculture is the choice of communication protocols for IoT devices. These protocols determine the efficiency and reliability of data transmission. For instance, protocols like Zigbee and Z-Wave provide mesh network solutions that enable efficient communication within short to medium ranges. LoRa (Long Range) protocol offers long-range, low-power communication capabilities, making it well-suited for agricultural applications. Based on IEEE 802.11 standards, WiFi provides broad device support and easy setup. At the same time, Bluetooth Low Energy (BLE) is known for its low power consumption and compatibility with various devices. SigFox, a low-power wide area network (LPWAN) solution, offers cost-effective connectivity managed in the cloud. Cellular networks, available globally, provide broad device support, although network traffic can sometimes lead to bandwidth limitations (Antony et al. 2020; Zamora-Izquierdo et al. 2019).

4.3 IoT Implementation in African Agricultural Context

Precision farming practices have been adopted by farmers like Jozeph du Plessis, a grain producer in the Northwest province of South Africa. Du Plessis has been using satellite imagery, yield monitors, and precision software to optimize his dryland crops since 2001(Soeker et al. 2021; Zhou and Rompaey 2009). Through soil mapping, monitoring, and analysis, he has made informed decisions about crop rotation, soil nutrient levels, and water management, increasing maize yields and efficient water usage.

The growing adoption of IoT and cloud-based services in South Africa has increased demand for broadband and reliable connectivity across sectors. Adequate internet bandwidth and economic infrastructure are crucial for successful IoT implementation. Therefore, African governments need to invest in infrastructure that supports IoT solutions. However, it is essential to acknowledge that South African farmers still face challenges rooted in historical institutionalized racial discrimination from the Apartheid era, which is reflected in the distribution of agricultural land among racial minorities in commercial farming. While the benefits of IoT in agriculture are evident, it remains to be seen whether the farming sector in South Africa is fully prepared to adopt and leverage this technology (Maloku 2020).

Addressing the readiness of the agricultural sector in South Africa to implement IoT requires a comprehensive approach that considers infrastructure development, policy support, and addressing social and historical inequalities. By overcoming these challenges, African countries can harness the transformative potential of IoT in agriculture, paving the way for increased productivity, sustainability, and economic growth in the sector.

5 Successful Implementation of Emerging Disruptive Agricultural Mobile/Web Applications in Africa

GeoFarmer app (Eitzinger et al. 2019) facilitates communication among farmers and experts. It enables farmers to share their experiences, learn from others, and improve their yield and risk management. It offers cost-effective offline usage and real-time data services (Singh and Sobti 2022). The Pix Fruit project offers several advantages in the estimation of crop yield. Utilizing advanced modeling software and fruit-recognition technology provides a more accurate crop count, minimizing the margin for error that exists with traditional estimation methods. Smartphones and automated fruit-recognition technology streamline the process, enhancing efficiency and saving time for farmers. Moreover, the project's databank, compiled with the help of drones, includes valuable information on climate, soil, and administrative constraints, allowing for better risk assessment. This enables wholesalers and price negotiators to make more informed decisions, considering the potential market glut or undersupply risk. The Pix Fruit system also helps farmers negotiate fair prices for their produce, maximizing profitability and avoiding potential losses from inaccurate estimations. However, there are challenges to consider, such as the technological requirements and associated costs of implementing the system. Furthermore, the accuracy of the crop estimation relies on the quality and reliability of the data used, and the adaptability of the technology to different crops may require further research and development. Despite these considerations, the Pix Fruit project showcases the potential of advanced technologies in revolutionizing crop estimation and benefiting the agricultural industry.

TruTrade, an innovative and transformative initiative, seeks to revolutionize the lives of smallholder farmers in Kenya and Uganda by addressing the challenges they encounter in unorganized staple food markets (Subramanian et al. 2022). These farmers often need more transportation options, a lack of financing for aggregation, and a disconnection between producers and buyers, resulting in low prices, unreliable supply chains, and limited rural employment opportunities. TruTrade aims to overcome these obstacles and integrate smallholder farmers into sustainable supply chains by introducing their Trade Transparency Service (TTS) to bring visibility to supply chain transactions. The advantages of TruTrade's approach are diverse and significant. TruTrade facilitates collaborative supply chain management via a mobile-enabled trading and payment platform by establishing networks comprising village agents equipped with the TTS. This empowers farmers by granting them the authority to set prices, monitor the entire journey of their produce from collection to delivery, and receive payments directly on their mobile devices upon verification. Furthermore, TruTrade offers trade finance to ensure timely payment upon delivery and covers transaction costs associated with transporting the produce to buyers. By conducting market analyses, identifying potential buyers, and managing supplier relationships, TruTrade opens up market access, enabling farmers to secure fair prices and establish long-term partnerships with buyers.

Nevertheless, it is essential to note the challenges that accompany TruTrade's model. Limited access to reliable network coverage and technological resources in remote rural areas can impede effective participation. Farmers may need help with smartphone availability or technological literacy, potentially limiting their full engagement with the platform. Additionally, while TruTrade endeavors to provide fair prices and equitable profit-sharing, the commission-based service charge could impact farmers' overall income. Continuous monitoring and evaluation of these charges are essential to ensure they do not unduly burden the farmers and undermine the intended benefits of the initiative. For example, the SPGT App (Reporter 2023) introduces an innovative solution encompassing two integral parts, offering many advantages to farmers. The first component revolves around a network of interconnected sensors crucial in monitoring and optimizing greenhouse conditions. These sensors include a moisture sensor that diligently tracks the soil quality, a humidity sensor that accurately measures the moisture levels in potatoes and an intelligent irrigation sensor that facilitates the efficient distribution of water throughout the greenhouse. By harnessing the power of these sensors, farmers can achieve climate resilience and combat food insecurity through intelligent and automated irrigation practices.

The second facet of the SPGT App revolves around seamless data transmission. Leveraging cutting-edge technology, this component ensures that greenhouse managers receive timely notifications, alerts, and remote monitoring information directly on their mobile devices. This real-time flow of data empowers managers to stay updated on the status of their greenhouse operations, enabling them to make informed decisions promptly and effectively. Furthermore, the SPGT App goes beyond its primary functionalities by enhancing security systems within the greenhouse. Equipped with sound and motion sensors, as well as automated digital cameras, the app provides an advanced surveillance mechanism to deter theft attempts. Whenever unauthorized activity is detected, these sensors swiftly capture and transmit images to the mobile phones of greenhouse managers, enabling swift intervention and safeguarding agricultural assets. The benefits offered by the SPGT App are manifold. Developed to address food insecurity and promote agricultural sustainability, the app equips farmers with invaluable tools to optimize greenhouse operations. By seamlessly integrating sensor technology, real-time data transmission, and enhanced security systems, the SPGT App revolutionizes how farmers approach greenhouse management, ultimately contributing to their productivity, profitability, and resilience in environmental challenges.

Rwanda, a landlocked country in East Africa, has diverse agroecological zones and varying climatic conditions. Understanding the spatial variation of soil nutrient balance is crucial for sustainable agricultural practices. This case study presented in Table 1 aimed to assess the nutrient inputs and outputs in different cropping systems and predict soil nutrient depletion across the country.

The nutrient inputs varied among cropping systems, with rice receiving the highest average inputs of nitrogen (98.4 kg/ha/yr), phosphorus (34.7 kg/ha/yr), and potassium (41.3 kg/ha/yr). Soybeans had the lowest nutrient inputs. The annual mean nutrient deposition was also determined. Soil erosion, rainfall, soil texture, nutrient content, and elevation significantly influenced soil nutrient depletion. Depletion increased from the southeast to the northwest of the country, corresponding to variations in soil nutrient content, rainfall, and elevation. This study demonstrated the applicability of ensemble ML models in mapping the spatial variation of soil nutrient balance in Rwandan croplands. The findings emphasized the importance of soil erosion control and nutrient management practices to mitigate soil nutrient depletion. The identified predictors can guide targeted interventions to address nutrient imbalances and promote sustainable agriculture.

Using ML models and relevant predictors, this study revealed that a significant portion of Rwandan croplands experienced nitrogen depletion. The spatial patterns indicated variations in nutrient balance across different agroecological zones. These findings highlight the need for tailored soil nutrient management strategies to optimize agricultural productivity and sustainability. Further research and interventions should focus on improving soil fertility

Table 1 Data table summarizing the materials and methods used in the study (Uwiragiye et al. 2022)

Parameter	Description
Study location	Rwanda
Area	26,338 km^2
Latitude range	1°4′ S to 2°51′ S
Longitude range	28°45′ E to 31°53′ E
Elevation range	918 m–4501 m above sea level
Climate	Sub-equatorial climate
Mean annual temperature (MAT)	15–25 °C (varies with altitude)
Average annual precipitation	827–1413 mm
Data sources	Lewis et al. (1988), Verdoodt and Ranst (2003)
Cropping systems analyzed	Rice, Soybeans
Nutrient inputs	Rice: 98.4 kg N, 34.7 kg P, 41.3 kg Kha^{-1} yr^{-1} Soybeans: 21.5 kg N, 20.7 kg P, 3.20 kgKha^{-1} yr^{-1}
Nutrient deposition	Annual mean: 4.60 kg N, 0.80 kg P, 3.18 kg Kha^{-1} yr^{-1}
Analysis techniques	Ensemble ML, spatial analysis, and soil erosion assessment
Predictors	Soil erosion, Mean annual precipitation (MAP), soil texture, soil nutrient content, Digital elevation model (DEM)
Soil properties analyzed	Cation Exchange Capacity (CEC), Organic C, Total N, Exchangeable K, Extractable P, Bulk Density, Clay, Sand, Silt
Agro-ecological zones	10
Nutrient depletion	56.1% of croplands experienced N depletion ranging from 30.0 to 237 kg N ha^{-1} yr^{-1}. 27.4% of croplands lost 0 to 30 kg N ha^{-1} yr^{-1}

and nutrient management practices in the identified regions with higher nutrient depletion rates.

5.1 Case Study: Implementation of IoT for Smallholder Agriculture in Kenya

This case study aims to investigate the implementation of IoT technologies in smallholder agriculture in Kenya. The study utilized a mixed-method approach, combining literature reviews, expert interviews, web-based surveys, and site visits to gather data (Foster et al. 2023; McCampbell et al. 2023; Moon MJ Searching for Inclusive Artificial Intelligence for Social Good: Participatory Governance and Policy Recommendations for Making AI More Inclusive and Benign for Society xxxx). The study categorized sensor and communication technology applications into five categories: climate, livestock, plant, soil, and water. Each category included measurable parameters that influence agricultural performance. Standard sensor types and their applications in agriculture were identified, including electrical capacitance and conductivity sensors for soil moisture measurement, optical sensors for crop mapping and disease detection, thermocouples for temperature monitoring, and radio frequency identification (RFID) technology (Voulodimos et al. 2010) for livestock tracking, among others. Data transmission protocols were also evaluated, considering range, data rate, and power consumption factors. In Kenya, the study (Antony et al. 2020) identified active IoT for agriculture cases with the following characteristics:

Lodwar Basin Aquifer project: Electrical current sensors were installed on solar-electric borehole pumps to monitor water usage. The data was transmitted via cellular or satellite networks to a web server and dashboard, allowing government officials to monitor pump functionality and reduce maintenance costs. ML algorithms were utilized to predict failures and improve system uptime. The Kenya RAPID project involved a well-coordinated team, including the supplier of IoT technology, resulting in clear roles and efficient implementation. The IoT implementation demonstrated clear value and utility to government officials, reducing maintenance costs and increasing pump uptime. They were relying on grant funding risks project sustainability, highlighting the need for long-term financial planning. This case study examined the implementation of IoT for smallholder agriculture in Kenya. The analysis revealed the current state of IoT applications, highlighted successful implementation cases and identified key factors contributing to the success and associated risks. The findings can serve as a valuable reference for policymakers, researchers, and stakeholders interested in leveraging IoT technologies to enhance agricultural practices in similar contexts.

6 Benefits and Challenges of Harnessing Emerging Disruptive Technologies in Society 5.0

6.1 Advantages and Opportunities of Adopting Emerging Technologies

Integrating cutting-edge technologies in African agriculture presents a transformative landscape, yielding several advantages and opportunities. By harnessing the power of data-driven decision-making, businesses can gather real-time data, employing advanced analytics and ML algorithms to extract valuable insights. This empowers organizations to make informed decisions, optimize operations, and unearth untapped growth potentials. Adopting emerging technologies such as the IoT and automation revolutionize efficiency, streamlining processes, reducing manual labor, and bolstering productivity across sectors like agriculture, manufacturing, and logistics. Moreover, the implementation of new technologies drives cost reduction through various means. Automation and robotics mitigate the need for extensive manual work, ultimately minimizing operating costs. Furthermore, the advent of predictive maintenance facilitated by IoT averts costly equipment failures by accurately forecasting maintenance requirements. This proactive approach reduces expenses and enhances overall operational efficiency (Blackmore 2003; Finger et al. 2019; Fastellini and Schillaci 2020). Innovation and gaining a competitive edge are intrinsic outcomes of leveraging novel technologies within African agriculture.

AI and ML empower businesses to create groundbreaking products, services, and business models, revolutionizing traditional markets. Additionally, integrating immersive technologies like augmented reality (AR) and virtual reality (VR) enriches customer experiences, while chatbots and virtual assistants provide immediate and personalized customer support. Beyond innovation and competitiveness, adopting new technologies promotes sustainable practices across industries. The IoT enables implementing intelligent energy management systems, optimizing resource consumption, and contributing to environmental conservation. Furthermore, renewable energy technologies like solar and wind power can seamlessly integrate into the energy grid, reducing reliance on fossil fuels and fostering a greener future.

The proliferation of technological advancements expands market reach, enabling businesses to transcend geographical boundaries through e-commerce platforms, digital marketing strategies, and social media connectivity. This unprecedented global connectivity facilitates enhanced customer engagement, empowering African agricultural enterprises to tap into new markets and diversify revenue streams. Embracing new technologies also empowers small businesses, leveling the playing field and granting access to tools and resources previously accessible only to larger organizations. Cloud computing, mobile applications, and digital marketing platforms empower small enterprises to compete effectively, bolstering their growth trajectory and economic impact. While concerns persist regarding job displacement, introducing new technologies simultaneously creates novel employment opportunities. Industries like data science, cybersecurity, and AI demand specialized skills, fostering job creation, upskilling, and career development within the workforce (Tzounis et al. 2017). African agriculture stands poised to unlock its full potential, driving economic growth, sustainability, and increased competitiveness by embracing these revolutionary technological advancements. Integrating data-driven decision-making, automation, and innovative technologies enhances operational efficiency and cost savings, propels innovation, expands market reach, and empowers businesses of all sizes. Through this transformative journey, African agriculture can harness its inherent strengths, cultivate sustainable practices, and thrive in the digital age.

6.2 Challenges and Limitations in Implementing Emerging Technologies

The implementation of emerging technologies in agriculture poses several challenges and limitations that necessitate careful consideration. One of the primary obstacles is the cost associated with acquiring and maintaining these technologies, which can be prohibitive for small-scale farmers with limited financial resources. To overcome this barrier, it is crucial to develop accessible and affordable technology solutions and provide financial support to enable wider adoption. Furthermore, successfully utilizing these technologies requires technical expertise among farmers and agricultural workers, necessitating training programs and ongoing support to enhance their digital literacy and skill sets in data analytics and software management.

Connectivity and infrastructure limitations, particularly in rural areas, must be addressed to effectively implement emerging technologies. Access to reliable internet connectivity and robust digital infrastructure is essential for seamless data transmission and real-time monitoring (Sharma et al. 2020). Addressing these infrastructure gaps is crucial to ensure that technology solutions can reach all farmers, regardless of geographic location.

Data privacy and security concerns are critical considerations in adopting emerging technologies. Safeguarding agricultural data, such as crop yields, soil quality, and weather patterns, is imperative to protect farmers' proprietary information and ensure responsible use of data. Implementing robust data protection measures and complying with privacy regulations is essential to build trust and confidence among farmers.

Compatibility and interoperability issues between different technology platforms and systems present further challenges. Integration and seamless data exchange between various technologies, such as sensors, drones, and farm management software, require standardized protocols and interfaces. Overcoming these interoperability barriers will enable the seamless flow of data and enhance the overall effectiveness of technology solutions. Addressing adoption barriers is crucial to ensure successful implementation. Resistance to change and skepticism among farmers and agricultural communities can hinder the adoption of emerging technologies. Effective communication strategies, awareness campaigns, and showcasing tangible benefits are essential to overcome these barriers and foster a culture of innovation and acceptance. Ethical considerations should also be at the forefront of implementing emerging technologies in agriculture. Equitable benefit distribution, environmental sustainability, and responsible use of resources are essential to ensure that technology-driven advancements contribute positively to society and the environment.

7 Implications for Society 5.0 and Future Directions

7.1 Impact of Emerging Technologies on Society 5.0 Objectives

The impact of emerging technologies on Society 5.0 objectives in agriculture is significant. Society 5.0 aims to create a human-centric society that combines economic progress with social development and sustainability. Emerging technologies are crucial in aligning the agricultural sector with these objectives. They enable sustainable farming practices by optimizing resource utilization and minimizing environmental impact. Precision agriculture techniques, powered by technologies like IoT and AI, allow for precise monitoring and management of crops, promoting the efficient use of water, fertilizers, and pesticides. These technologies also enhance productivity by employing AI, robotics, and automation, increasing efficiency and reducing labor requirements. Additionally, emerging technologies improve food safety and quality by ensuring transparency and traceability through blockchain and monitoring critical parameters during storage and handling. They empower farmers by providing access to real-time information and decision-support tools, facilitating informed decision-making and direct market access. Furthermore, these technologies bridge the digital divide and promote inclusivity in rural areas, supporting rural development and economic growth. In summary, emerging technologies have a transformative impact on agriculture, enabling sustainable practices, boosting productivity, ensuring food safety, empowering farmers, and driving rural development in alignment with the objectives of Society 5.0.

7.2 Recommendations for Policy, Research, and Adoption of Emerging Technologies

It is imperative to establish robust policy support mechanisms to facilitate the successful adoption of emerging technologies in agriculture. Policymakers should devise and enforce policies that incentivize and endorse the integration of new technologies across diverse sectors, particularly in agriculture. This necessitates the formulation of regulatory frameworks that streamline technology implementation while safeguarding data privacy and security. Moreover, fostering collaborations between public and private entities can fuel innovation and cooperation. Multiple research projects demonstrate relatively higher prospects in using ML algorithms than conventional statistics (Mosaffa et al. 2022; Elavarasan et al. 2018). One such project in Morocco is the imaging4Agriculture known as 'Yield Gap project' implemented by Mohammed VI Polytechnic University in partnership with Fransh institution (CESBIO) and other Sub-Saharan African institutions (Senegal). The project seeks to combine several approaches (ML, Statistics, Experimentation, RS, and Digital Applications) in yield gap predictions, ultimately leading to the effective formulation and execution of policies and initiatives to close the gap.

Investing in research and development assumes paramount significance in comprehending the applications and ramifications of emerging technologies in agriculture. Allocating resources to research institutes and universities enables comprehensive studies on technology adoption's potential advantages and challenges. Encouraging interdisciplinary research becomes pivotal in addressing the multifaceted nature of technological advancements in agriculture. Furthermore, comprehensive assessments of emerging technologies' societal and environmental impacts are crucial for responsible and sustainable implementation.

Enhancing digital infrastructure, particularly in rural areas, is necessary to facilitate the widespread adoption of emerging technologies. This entails prioritizing the development of robust digital networks such as high-speed internet and mobile phone connectivity to ensure equitable access to digital technologies. Promoting the utilization of cloud computing and data analytics can harness the potential of emerging technologies, enabling efficient data management and analysis.

Strengthening extension services assumes paramount importance in effectively disseminating information about emerging technologies to farmers. Investing in the training and capacity building of agricultural extension personnel ensures their proficiency in educating farmers about the benefits and practicalities of adopting new technologies. Embracing farmer-centered approaches that involve the active participation of farmers in the planning and implementation of extension programs can yield higher adoption rates. Leveraging virtual networks and information and communication technologies can enhance advisory services and facilitate knowledge sharing among farmers, extension agents, and experts.

By implementing these and related strategies, policymakers and stakeholders can foster an enabling environment for adopting emerging technologies in agriculture, stimulating innovation, sustainability, and enhanced productivity within the sector.

8 Conclusion

In conclusion, the integration of advanced technology in African farming has the potential to revolutionize agricultural practices in the region, addressing challenges and driving sustainable development. African farmers can overcome obstacles and unlock numerous benefits by embracing precision farming techniques, ML, and the IoT.

Adopting these technologies empowers farmers to work more efficiently, optimize resource utilization, and protect the environment. Through precision farming, farmers can make informed decisions based on real-time data through precision farming can make informed decisions based on real-time data, ensuring optimal crop health, efficient resource allocation, and improved yield predictions. This translates into increased productivity, minimized environmental impact, and reduced waste. However, the implementation of new technologies in African farming has its challenges. Small-scale farmers face hurdles such as limited access to technology and a need for more technical know-how. The difficulties are compounded by the cost of acquiring and implementing these tools and the need for more necessary infrastructure. Thus, there is a need for concerted efforts to provide training and support to small farmers, enabling them to leverage technology effectively. Initiatives should focus on making these technologies affordable, accessible, and tailored to the specific needs of African farmers. Moreover, the development of supportive policies and infrastructure is critical to foster technology adoption and integration. Africa's farms can use new technology better if they get help from policies, research, and adopting new methods. This will help farmers grow more crops and manage their resources sustainably for the socio-economic development of Africa.

References

African Union Commission (2021) Overview: Priorities to make digitalisation work for all in Africa

Almalki FA, Soufiene BO, Alsamhi SH, Sakli H (2021) A low-cost platform for environmental smart farming monitoring system based on IoT and UAVs. Sustainability 13:5908

Antony AP, Leith K, Jolley C, Lu J, Sweeney DJ (2020) A review of practice and implementation of the internet of things (IoT) for smallholder agriculture. Sustainability 12:3750

Anyanwu JC (2014) Factors affecting economic growth in Africa: are there any lessons from China? African Development Review 26:468–493

Bassine FZ, Errami A, Khaldoun M (2019) Vegetation recognition based on UAV image color index. IEEE, pp 1–4

Benos L, Tagarakis AC, Dolias G, Berruto R, Kateris D, Bochtis D (2021) Machine learning in agriculture: A comprehensive updated review. Sensors 21:3758

Blackmore S (2003) Precision farming: a dynamic process. American Society of Agronomy, pp 84–104

Eitzinger A, Cock J, Atzmanstorfer K, Binder CR, Läderach P, Bonilla-Findji O, Bartling M, Mwongera C, Zurita L, Jarvis A (2019) GeoFarmer: A monitoring and feedback system for agricultural development projects. Computers and electronics in agriculture 158:109–121

Elavarasan D, Vincent DR, Sharma V, Zomaya AY, Srinivasan K (2018) Forecasting yield by integrating agrarian factors and machine learning models: A survey. Computers and Electronics in Agriculture 155:257–282

Fastellini G, Schillaci C (2020) Precision farming and IoT case studies across the world. In: Agricultural internet of things and decision support for precision smart farming. Elsevier, pp 331–415

Finger R, Swinton SM, El Benni N, Walter A (2019) Precision farming at the nexus of agricultural production and the environment. Annual Review of Resource Economics 11:313–335

Foster L, Szilagyi K, Wairegi A, Oguamanam C, de Beer J (2023) Smart farming and artificial intelligence in East Africa: Addressing indigeneity, plants, and gender. Smart Agricultural Technology 3:100132

Kelly C, Wynants M, Patrick A, Taylor A, Mkilema F, Nasseri M, Lewin S, Munishi L, Mtei K, Ndakidemi P (2022) Soils, Science and Community ActioN (SoilSCAN): a citizen science tool to empower community-led land management change in East Africa. Environmental Research Letters 17:085003

Khanal S, Fulton J, Shearer S (2017) An overview of current and potential applications of thermal remote sensing in precision agriculture. Computers and Electronics in Agriculture 139:22–32

Lewis LA, Clay DC, Dejaegher YMJ (1988) Soil loss, agriculture, and conservation in Rwanda: toward sound strategies for soil management. Journal of Soil & Water Conservation 43:418–421

Liakos KG, Busato P, Moshou D, Pearson S, Bochtis D (2018) Machine learning in agriculture: A review. Sensors 18:2674

MacCarthy DS, Kihara J, Masikati P, Adiku SG (2018) Decision support tools for site-specific fertilizer recommendations and agricultural planning in selected countries in sub-Sahara Africa. Improving the Profitability, Sustainability and Efficiency of Nutrients Through Site Specific Fertilizer Recommendations in West Africa Agro-Ecosystems: Volume 2 265–289

Maloku D (2020) Adoption of precision farming technologies: USA and EU situation. SEA–Practical Application of Science 8:7–14

Masson-Delmotte V, Zhai P, Pirani S, Connors C, Péan S, Berger N, Caud Y, Chen L, Goldfarb M, Scheel Monteiro PM (2021) Ipcc, 2021: Summary for policymakers. in: Climate change 2021: The physical science basis. contribution of working group i to the sixth assessment report of the intergovernmental panel on climate change

McCampbell M, Adewopo J, Klerkx L, Leeuwis C (2023) Are farmers ready to use phone-based digital tools for agronomic advice? Ex-ante user readiness assessment using the case of Rwandan banana farmers. The Journal of Agricultural Education and Extension 29:29–51

Mendes JAJ, Carvalho NGP, Mourarias MN, Careta CB, Zuin VG, Gerolamo MC (2022) Dimensions of digital transformation in the context of modern agriculture. Sustainable Production and Consumption 34:613–637

Moon MJ Searching for Inclusive Artificial Intelligence for Social Good: Participatory Governance and Policy Recommendations for Making AI More Inclusive and Benign for Society. Public Administration Review

Mosaffa H, Sadeghi M, Mallakpour I, Jahromi MN, Pourghasemi HR (2022) Application of machine learning algorithms in hydrology. In: Computers in Earth and Environmental Sciences. Elsevier, pp 585–591

Motia S, Reddy S (2021) Exploration of machine learning methods for prediction and assessment of soil properties for agricultural soil management: a quantitative evaluation. IOP Publishing, p 012037

Ncube B, Mupangwa W, French A (2018) Precision agriculture and food security in Africa. Systems analysis approach for complex global challenges 159–178

Nhamo L, Mpandeli S, Liphadzi S, Hlophe-Ginindza S, Kapari M, Molwantwa J, Mabhaudhi T (2023) Advances in water research: Enhancing sustainable water use in irrigated agriculture in South Africa. In: Progress in Sustainable Development. Elsevier, pp 233–248

Raimi L, Panait M, Sule R (2021) Leveraging Precision Agriculture for Sustainable Food Security in Sub-Saharan Africa: A Theoretical Discourse. Shifting Patterns of Agricultural Trade: The Protectionism Outbreak and Food Security 491–509

Raj M, Gupta S, Chamola V, Elhence A, Garg T, Atiquzzaman M, Niyato D (2021) A survey on the role of Internet of Things for adopting and promoting Agriculture 4.0. Journal of Network and Computer Applications 187:103107

Raj EFI, Appadurai M, Athiappan K (2021) Precision Farming in Modern Agriculture. In: Choudhury A, Biswas A, Singh TP, Ghosh SK (eds) Smart Agriculture Automation Using Advanced Technologies: Data Analytics and Machine Learning, Cloud Architecture, Automation and IoT. Springer, Singapore, pp 61–87

Reporter S (2023) Young Rwandan lady develops mobile app to enhance potato production. In: Farmers Review Africa. https://farmersreviewafrica.com/young-rwandan-lady-develops-mobile-app-to-enhance-potato-production/. Accessed 3 Aug 2023

Sari MYA, Hassim YMM, Hidayat R, Ahmad A (2021) Monitoring Rice Crop and Paddy Field Condition Using UAV RGB Imagery. JOIV: International Journal on Informatics Visualization 5:469–474

Sharma R, Kamble SS, Gunasekaran A, Kumar V, Kumar A (2020) A systematic literature review on machine learning applications for sustainable agriculture supply chain performance. Computers & Operations Research 119:104926

Shimeles A, Verdier-Chouchane A, Boly A (2018) Introduction: understanding the challenges of the agricultural sector in Sub-Saharan Africa. Building a resilient and sustainable agriculture in sub-Saharan Africa 1–12

Singh DK, Sobti R (2022) Long-range real-time monitoring strategy for Precision Irrigation in urban and rural farming in society 5.0. Computers & Industrial Engineering 167:107997

Soeker I, Lusinga S, Chigona W (2021) Readiness of the South African Agricultural Sector to Implement IoT. arXiv preprint arXiv:210810081

Subramanian K, Bozzola M, Nugent A (2022) The role of ICT adoption in promoting livelihoods in Eastern Africa: Evidence from Uganda

Sun AY, Scanlon BR (2019) How can Big Data and machine learning benefit environment and water management: a survey of methods, applications, and future directions. Environ Res Lett 14:073001. https://doi.org/10.1088/1748-9326/ab1b7d

Tantalaki N, Souravlas S, Roumeliotis M (2019) Data-driven decision making in precision agriculture: The rise of big data in agricultural systems. Journal of agricultural & food information 20:344–380

Tzounis A, Katsoulas N, Bartzanas T, Kittas C (2017) Internet of Things in agriculture, recent advances and future challenges. Biosystems engineering 164:31–48

Uwiragiye Y, Ngaba MJY, Zhao M, Elrys AS, Heuvelink GB, Zhou J (2022) Modelling and mapping soil nutrient depletion in humid highlands of East Africa using ensemble machine learning: A case study from Rwanda. Catena 217:106499

Verdoodt A, Van Ranst E (2003) Land evaluation for agricultural production in the tropics. A large-scale land suitability classification for Rwanda. Ghent University. Laboratory of Soil Science

Vitali G, Francia M, Golfarelli M, Canavari M (2021) Crop management with the iot: An interdisciplinary survey. Agronomy 11:181

Voulodimos AS, Patrikakis CZ, Sideridis AB, Ntafis VA, Xylouri EM (2010) A complete farm management system based on animal identification using RFID technology. Computers and electronics in agriculture 70:380–388

Yang C (2018) High resolution satellite imaging sensors for precision agriculture. Frontiers of Agricultural Science and Engineering 5:393–405

Yeh C, Perez A, Driscoll A, Azzari G, Tang Z, Lobell D, Ermon S, Burke M (2020) Using publicly available satellite imagery and deep learning to understand economic well-being in Africa. Nature communications 11:2583

Yong JY, Klemeš JJ, Varbanov PS, Huisingh D (2016) Cleaner energy for cleaner production: modelling, simulation, optimisation and waste management. Journal of Cleaner Production 111:1–16

Zamora-Izquierdo MA, Santa J, Martínez JA, Martínez V, Skarmeta AF (2019) Smart farming IoT platform based on edge and cloud computing. Biosystems engineering 177:4–17

Zhang N, Wang M, Wang N (2002) Precision agriculture—a worldwide overview. Computers and electronics in agriculture 36:113–132

Zhou H, Van Rompaey A (2009) Detecting the impact of the "Grain for Green" program on the mean annual vegetation cover in the Shaanxi province, China using SPOT-VGT NDVI data. Land Use Policy 26:954–960

IoT Based Smart Flood Monitoring System

Younas Aziz, Hanif Ur Rahman, Muhammad Ejaz, Adeel Ahmed Abbasi, Anbar Hussain, Inayat Ur Rahman, and Aasim Danish

Abstract

Flood is among the natural catastrophes which can be avoided. A lot of people and things get destroyed in a short amount of time. Before this, almost all present structures were only focused on specific regions. Additionally, most people need access to information and data regarding the weather, making it impossible to monitor and predict when a flood will occur. Every problem with the current system can be remedied by installing an Internet of Things (IoT) based Smart Surveillance System for Flood Monitoring. In both urban and rural settings, the proposed approach will work well. Furthermore, if the audience has internet connectivity, they may monitor what is happening or anticipate any oncoming flood at the web server. The suggested system with a low price in design is easy to operate. This work will monitor the water level at the web application, and the computer will broadcast a warning signal to the people for evacuation so that fast essential steps can be performed.

Keywords

Smart surveillance system · Flood monitoring · IoT and warning signal

1 Introduction

Since June 14th, 2022, 1481 persons have been killed by flooding in Pakistan. Extreme heat waves and the melting of glaciers have been connected to climate change, contributing to floods. There has not been a flood of this magnitude elsewhere since the South Asian rains in 2017. (Akhtar et al. 2023) On August 25th, Pakistan declared a state of emergency because of flooding. By August 29th, Pakistan's Minister of Climate Change said around one-third of the country is under water, affecting 33 million people. The government of Pakistan estimated a loss of US $30 Billion so far from flooding across the country.

Climate change poses a real threat to people, places and livelihoods. To mitigate those threats, a person, community or society must protect and decontaminate the environment in their respect. Overpopulation, deforestation and burning coal, oil and gas are some of the causes of global warming. Due to global warming, glaciers are melting, and sea levels are rising, causing floods and disasters. Combined with biodiversity and ecosystem loss, the scale and impact of climate change are unprecedented. Adapting to these changes will be difficult in the future; therefore, substantial actions are required now.

Both natural and manmade causes contribute to flooding. The early people of Pakistan settled along the banks of the peninsula's major rivers, giving them a long association with the waterways. Heavy monsoon rainfall, severe convective rain storms, poor drainage, and other local variables have made flooding a regular occurrence for many people in Pakistan. Floods are extremely harmful and can completely wipe out a town or neighborhood. In addition to the human

Y. Aziz · M. Ejaz · A. A. Abbasi · A. Hussain
Department of Computer Science and Engineering, Central South University, Changsha 410000, Hunan, China
e-mail: younas.maidan@gmail.com

M. Ejaz
e-mail: m.ejaz@csu.edu.cn

H. U. Rahman (✉)
Department of Computer Science, Abdul Wali Khan University, Mardan 23200, Khyber Pakhtoonkhawa, Pakistan
e-mail: hanif.maidan@gmail.com

I. U. Rahman · A. Danish
Department of Geo-Sciences and Info Physics, Central South University, Changsha 410000, Hunan, China

S. Arezki et al. (eds.), *Emerging Disruptive Technologies for Society 5.0 in Developing Countries*, Advances in Science, Technology & Innovation, https://doi.org/10.1007/978-3-031-63701-8_3

and material costs, floods can be catastrophic. When this happens, ordinarily dry terrain is flooded beneath the water, causing a natural calamity. Some floods are sudden and happen extremely quickly. Wood has sharp edges that could potentially cut someone.

The whirling objects have injured some people. It is crucial to have a flood early warning system to inform locals of the dangers they face before a flood occurs. It is possible to plan and stay safe with the help of various technologies. Most people in the country probably have access to electronic devices like tablets and smartphones. The Intelligent Tracking Device Large contributions are made by flood monitoring systems during floods, with the most efficient systems allowing governments and societies to better manage the plight of flood victims and lessen the impact of disasters. In order to properly inform society as soon as possible, this system must be made simpler, easier to operate, and more cost-effective. The proposed system will provide an easy-to-use interface for monitoring, ample information on flood levels, and the ability to predict future water levels in the short term.

1.1 Project Background

Climate change poses a real threat to people, places and livelihoods. To mitigate those threats, a person, community or society must protect and decontaminate the environment in their respect. Overpopulation, deforestation and burning of coal, oil and gas are some causes of global warming. The melting of glaciers and the subsequent rise in sea levels directly result from human-caused global warming (Akhtar et al. 2023). Combined with biodiversity and ecosystem loss, the scale and impact of climate change is unprecedented. Adapting to these changes will be difficult in the future; therefore, substantial actions are required now.

1.2 Problem Statement

The major setback to the environment is the loss of agricultural lands. Every year, thousands of acres of land are destroyed by the supply of sewage water to them. Although water coming from rivers, groundwater reservoirs, and canals is clean, industrial and household waste disposal makes it dirty. As a result, the crops are exposed to contaminated water with many pollutants. The poisonous water affects the quality and yield of the crops (Noar and Kamal 2017). The sewage water is destroying agricultural lands, and aquatic life is in danger. Oceans receive a large number of sewage waste because the coasts are densely populated. Most of the waste comes from residential and Industrial areas, while some come from other sources. Even though sewage treatment plants are installed to decontaminate the water, partly treated or untreated water can enter the seas. Factors include improper infrastructure, facility breaks down or heavy rainfalls, which burden the treatment plants (Akhtar and Khan 2019). Torrential rains can cause sewage channels to overflow and mix with clean water sources, polluting the ecosystem. Moreover, excessive rains and floods can significantly affect city life. Floods can occur when there are blockages in the sewage channels, or they might also occur due to the lack of available infrastructure to handle them (Bande and Shete 2017). Similarly, there is another problem of gas explosions that hap- pen in underground sewage channels. The explosions take place when the gases inside these channels get trapped. Blasts resulting from this can be very catastrophic and even result in casualties (Khan et al. 2016). Sewer gas is a mixture of methane, hydrogen sulfide, carbon monoxide, ammonia and many more. Gases like these are highly inflammable and, if not properly managed, can cause huge explosions (Lin et al. 2006; Mishra et al. 2020).

1.3 Scope of the Project

The effects of climate change combined with Population growth are everywhere. Cities which received less rainfall are now receiving more which affects their infrastructure. Urbanization of cities mostly in Asia, like Karachi, Delhi, Dhaka, etc., has resulted in contamination of fresh water and pollution (Goyal et al. 2020; Sroor et al. 2021). Take the example of Karachi, where untreated wastewater goes into the sea directly and causes harm to aquatic life. In addition to this, there is also room for improvement in the city's underground sewage mechanism. A recent blast killed more than 10 people and destroyed many buildings (Khan et al. 2016).

The systems already designed to decontaminate the sewage water include treatment plants. The sewage water from industries and households goes into the wastewater channels, then routed to the treatment facilities. The major problem in this regard is that the treatment plants are located at the last points meaning the wastewater has to go through the whole passage before reaching its destination. During the journey, it becomes a source of pollution, affecting air quality and the general environment.

The proposed solution includes two segments. The first is sewage waste monitoring, and the other is storm-water monitoring. The waste channels are filled with trash, harmful chemicals and gases; therefore, sensors are used at multiple locations to monitor these channels for blockages and the amount and type of harmful chemicals and gases. The benefit of installing sensors at multiple locations is that the locations can be narrowed down where there is a considerable amount of contamination in the water and then take measures to minimize the effect at the source rather than the destination.

The second portion of our proposed project includes storm-water monitoring. It is related to the first part in a way that if there are blockages in the sewage channels, the excess water from rains will cause floods. However, it is not limited to just this. Excessive rains can cause floods even without blockages (Rani et al. 2020). By installing speed sensors, the water flow rate can be checked, and if the critical rate is touched, it can alert the user.

1.4 Significance of the Project

The proposed project can help a great deal to the environment. There are several benefits involved in using the proposed system. The agricultural lands can be saved by providing them with clean water, which would not only increase the yield and quality of the crop but will also help reduce the diseases caused by taking unhealthy food.

As a second point, marine life can benefit significantly from a decrease in the discharge of dangerous compounds into the sea. Greek, Italian, and Spanish economies take a yearly hit of about $329 million due to algal blooms' pollution of seafood, which in turn leads to significant health problems, according to research even by the European Environment Agency (EEA, 2005) (Basnyat et al. 2020). Moreover, monitoring the underground water ways can minimize the risk of explosions, thus saving precious human lives.

2 Related Work

Many researchers have worked hard on a flood warning system that can track and warn of impending stream surges in real-time and for areas likely to be affected. This review focuses on the warning system's location and early warning alarm that alerts neighborhood residents of impending flood events (Akhtar and Khan 2019). A method for determining the extent of flooding has been devised by Mohd Sabre et al. (Bande and Shete 2017), which considers variables such as water depth, water pressure, and precipitation totals. The data is first sent to a microcontroller for processing, then transmitted to a server over Wi-Fi, where it can be shared over the internet. The system's efficacy resulted from the collaboration of its operational components, which allowed for the efficient monitoring, processing, and communication of a wide range of background concerns (Akhtar and Khan 2019). Abhijeet A. Pasi et al. (Khan et al. 2016) implemented a system that uses cutting-edge sensing technologies to keep tabs on current water levels in real-time to detect and predict floods. We will implement the sensor network in remote areas where there is no existing network infrastructure. The far-flung burrows are in charge of the communication system. The sensors collect data on water conditions, while the processing and transmission modules prepare the data for storage and transmission to the database and application server. This program was developed, allowing residents to view both real-time and historical water data through a database and application server. The application server can also notify the proper people in an emergency. Uyioghosa B. Iyekekpolo et al. (Lin et al. 2006) developed a system that is an enhanced version of preexisting sensor networks that provides individuals with warnings via constant monitoring of water flow and rainfall totals. As a result of gathering the necessary data from the sensors existing in the networks, regular checks of the flood were performed, and the information was fed to the end users. The final consumers also received an alert from this mechanism. Brindha. D et al. (Mishra et al. 2020) created a model that effectively reduced the likelihood of flooding caused by the rapid release of excess water from a barrage. Since the water from the barrage is discharged gradually, the plain surfaces are safe from flooding. Here, the writers have chosen to analyze using a minimum number of parameters. A model to predict the likelihood of flooding in low-lying locations was proposed by Tejaswitha et al. (Goyal et al. 2020). Wireless sensor networks track the weather and river levels to ensure safety during floods. Sensors and wireless connectivity protocols were utilized to generate a database, and the resulting massive amounts of data were saved on a server. We need to do something useful with the massive amounts of stored data. For the GSM module to function properly, the network's signals must be consistently accessible. A novel method developed by Luz Estella Torres Molina et al. (Sroor et al. 2021). Moreover, based on the utilization of water levels in hydrological assessments and, in particular, a flood alert system in a parking monitoring system has been implemented. DigiMesh protocol was applied for this approach, and it was used to transmit surge alerts to the renter zones for critical activity via SMS caution. Thanks to its broad capabilities, it may be expanded to cover a wider area. Eventually, this will be used in areas with an especially high risk of flooding, such as those that get flash surges or have roads predisposed to floods. Data collection and transmission in real-time from far river stations to a central database server was proposed by Sandeep Shiravale et al. (Rani et al. 2020), who utilized a variety of sensor nodes and WSN technology. This system was designed to monitor flooding and send out SMS warnings to residents so that they can take the appropriate measures if a flood is detected. Indira Priyadarshinee et al. (Basnyat et al. 2020) proposed three primary sensor nodes to perform tasks such as measuring water levels, processing the data, and uploading it to a central server. There, sensors measure the water level and send that information to a central computer. The sensing node, located some distance from the barrage, measures the height and velocity of the water flowing over the barrage. The system's EXCEL-formatted database was stored as a history graph in the Blynk application. This early warning has been issued as a buzzer and can be viewed on the LED. At the height of a field test, the water level is between the mini- mum required depth of 66.1 cm and the maximum required depth of 75.2 cm. If you live in a neighborhood near the lake, this is the highest water level considered safe (Narayanan et al. 2014). Etebong et al. (Kadir et al. 2019) responded to the emerging issue of low-cost and low-power operation of control and wireless networks. Various sensors, including ones for measuring temperature, rainfall, humidity, and water level, collect signals or data and then send them to the Microcontroller. Because the information being transmitted is analogue, an Analog–Digital converter built within the Microcontroller is required. The Zigbee module picked up the transmission from its radio and relayed it to the central processing unit. The sensor unit could transmit data packets to the processing unit through Zigbee. Thus, it could be broadcast and received by the other nodes. The microcontroller unit also instructed the Zigbee module, which set up the network. The proposed system, developed by Maligi et al. (Sivabalakrishnan et al. 2021), uses WSN and Monitoring technology. Sensor data from many sources, including water level, heat, and LDR, is processed by the PIC16F877A Microcontroller. The data collected by the sensors is transmitted to the controller unit, and every three minutes, the controller unit randomly sends commands to each segment based on the signals' current states. The control part of the Microcontroller receives a complete report from all sensors once every three minutes. The control web host is used to update the ESP8266 database. Moreover, the data transfer is accomplished via the GSM cellular communication protocol. In order to limit the amount of data that needed to be broadcast to the base station, Hossam et al. (El-Bendary et al. 2013) devised a system in which optimizations were performed. Pre-analyzed data from the sensors were used to issue timely warnings to the affected populations. The process of creating the system has just begun.

A web-based BRBES method for flood forecasting was created by Raihan et al. (Yuan et al. 2022). The suggested system required much processing power, using more run-the-program bases and the flexibility afforded by moving to a web-based setup. The authors recommend a BRBES system with multiple levels for flood prediction. Machine learning methods, including Artificial Neural Networks, were also compared. Several approaches have been utilized to create the system, according to works in the same field. Based on the findings of this study (Noar and Kamal 2017), we employ the'Things- peak' platform, a web-based monitoring system with open API services that stores and retrieves data from sensors and presents the data in graphical form. Sensors are employed in this project's Monitoring System Operation to collect data on environmental factors such as temperature, humidity, light intensity, precipitation, air quality, barometric pressure, and sea level pressure. Then, in the method proposed in Bande and Shete (2017), one Arduino served as the brains of the operation. It connects to a GSM modem and a pressure sensor. A pressure sensor reads the water level, and the Arduino then uses Pascal's Law to determine the height of the water. After determining the water level, it will be compared to the predetermined limit. A microcontroller is programmed to send an SMS to the home if the water rises above a certain point. Each member of the Arduino family comes with its own set of advantages and disadvantages. In contrast to the Mbed platform's usage of ARM Cortex microcontrollers, the Arduino family's microcontrollers are typically sluggish, have little memory, and offer few features. It is advised that ARM platforms be used for projects needing more excellent memory or processing speed.

3 Methodology

Information-gathering methods and public policy deliberation are the subject of discussion in the field of methodology. The creation of a Smart Flood Monitoring System still needs some refinement. The emphasis here is on the electronic parts of the system being built. The project's planning process will be outlined in full.

Synthetic artificial neural networks (ANN) that simulate brain activity. This method significantly improves our ability to spot flooding as soon as it begins. Furthermore, Linear Regression and SVM-based regression (based on a Support Vector Machine) were implemented.

This regression-based machine learning method is also quite effective. Muhammad et al. (Azid et al. 2015) devised a system based on a probability-based algorithm to automatically compare observed values with the threshold value and identify the flood disaster. If the monitored values exceed a certain level, the persons would be notified via the Global System for Mobile (GSM) Communication.

In (Jamali and Giman 2021), Tibin et al. devised a low-cost real-time monitoring of flood detection utilizing Wireless Sensor Networks. The system offered reliable, low-cost connectivity provided by the guarantee. CMOS image sensors are utilized as sensor nodes to take pictures that are then sent through Zigbee and GSM networks to a remote monitoring device. The remote device would issue an alert based on the data it received. The methods for predicting disasters like tsunamis, floods, and earthquakes that have been reviewed thus far in this literature review take a slightly different tack. The proposed system answers the problems encountered by the previously mentioned methods.

3.1 Block Diagram

Regarding the functional block diagram shown, an ultrasonic HC-SR04 modules sensor will be utilized to measure river levels. The micro-controller NXP LPC1768 microcontroller will collect all data in this system. The data will be updated on the online server, and a buzzer will sound to inform the public and authorities of an impending flood. LCD LEDs are used for displaying and indicating the water level.

Based on a flowchart in Fig. 1, Smart Mechanism for Keeping an Eye on Things, the purpose of the Flood Surveillance System is to provide warning to residents in the event of an impending flood. Ultrasonic river level measurement kicks off the procedure. The information gleaned from the sensors is sent to the microcontroller, which sends the information to the web server. Information will then be compared and analyzed. Each user has wireless access to the motor driver and buzzer. Intense flood warnings will be issued once such information has been compiled. The status of the water level will be shown on the LCD and the web server. The water level will be displayed through a lit LED. In addition, the stepper motor will activate for the passage of extreme flood when it reaches the highest threshold value, and the alarm will sound quickly to warn the public. So, people will be ready to evacuate well before a flood is expected to hit their area.

The Smart Monitoring system operates following the diagram shown in Fig. 1. The Flood Surveillance System's purpose is to warn residents in the event of an impending flood. Ultrasonic river level measurement kicks off the procedure. The information gleaned from the sensors is sent to the microcontroller, which sends the information to the web server. Information will then be compared and analyzed. Each user has wireless access to the motor driver and buzzer. Intense flood warnings will be issued once such information has been compiled. The status of the water level will be shown on the LCD and the web server. The water level will be displayed through a lit LED. In addition, the stepper motor will activate for the passage of extreme flood when it reaches the highest threshold value, and the alarm will sound quickly to warn the public. This way, people will be ready to evacuate their homes before a flood.

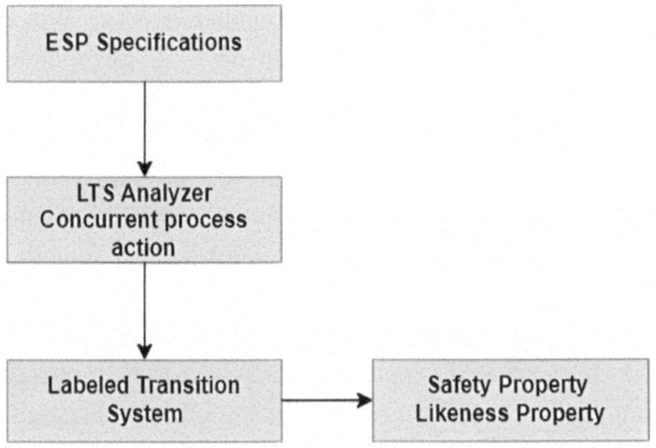

Fig. 1 Flow diagram

3.2 The Art of Building Structures

During this stage, the SoS moves from a high-level design to a more specific structural architecture (including its components and interfaces). It also shows how the components depend on one another and how they communicate with one another via interfaces. The SoS's underlying architecture can be seen as a component diagram. Figure 4 displays flood experimental tested results. For ease of comprehension, the red areas represent the external interfaces used to communicate with the autonomous parts.

3.3 Big Picture: System Architecture at a High

System elements are presented at an abstract level in a high-level architecture. It provides a clear breakdown of the components of SoS and how they work together. The Smart Flood Detection SoS's high-level architecture is depicted in Fig. 3 shows Device shutdown coloring. Elements crucial to flood monitoring are gathered from Data Sources. Rainfall, snowfall, water level, water flow, and structure reports are all parameters. These actions are communicated to Data Storage in response to a request from Communications Controller 1. This information about storms and floods might take several forms. Diagrams, models, and tables may accompany documents. The collected data undergo additional analysis in this stage to yield conclusions and predictions. When a flood warning is expected, alerts are produced and sent to far-flung areas through communication. Emergency personnel, locals, and outsiders all fall into this category of far-flung observers. Remote data, such as queries, aid measures, damage reports, and verification results, are also received and stored by central data collection, storage, analysis, and distribution centers. This information is utilized to assess the efficiency of individual parts and, ultimately, the system's effectiveness. The second communication controller helps keep in touch with faraway places.

System-of-Systems (SoS) simplifies the process of creating elaborate systems. Rather than being centralized, it consists of a network of autonomous systems spread out worldwide that can adapt to new conditions over time. These are autonomous systems, both in terms of function and management. Integrated systems use their combined strengths to perform tasks that would be impossible to accomplish using any of them alone. According to Blanchard and Fabrycky et al. (Noar and Kamal 2017), a system of systems (SoS) is"a coordinated effort involving pieces that are typically managed separately and located in different physical locations in order to achieve a common goal."

3.4 Colored Petri-Nets

To verify synchronizations in concurrent and distributed systems, a powerful tool is coloured Petri nets (CPN), a high-level extension of Petri-Nets. A system's executable model can be created in this language, which is formal, mathematical, and pictorial. Jensen introduced CPNs and their uses in system modelling in Goyal et al. (2020). Constructing CPN models subject to time constraints is now possible thanks to CPN Tools (Sroor et al. 2021). This instrument can also perform state space analysis verification and system behaviour simulation (Rani et al. 2020). Standard qualities such as boundedness, home, liveness, and fairness can be analysed using CPN Tools' state space analysis.

Correctness: Properties of safety and vitality It is invariant that"something terrible does never happen" or that the system always remains in a desirable state. A characteristic guaranteeing that the temperature inside a nuclear power plant's reactor never rises above 100 degrees Celsius is only one example. In (Kramer and Magee 2007), Magee and Kramer define safety real estate S = a1, a2 as a predetermined process stating that S. acknowledges a trace of the behaviour in the letters of S Like exceptional cases, ERROR situations highlight unrequired criteria. The qualities of safety in complex systems are established by outlining the necessities. The" something nice happens" when a system exhibits the liveness quality, which describes the possible system states that a particular agent can induce. To ensure that multi-agent-oriented robotic systems are accurate, the researchers have employed LTS.

The Labelled Transition System (LTS) is a toolkit for automating the formal verification of concurrent systems with a finite state machine. It comprises interconnected FSMs and their attributes and uses compositional analysis to thoroughly probe for failures to meet specified conditions. Each part of a design is detailed in LTS, which includes all of the states and transitions that part can take.

3.4.1 ARM

IoT (Monitoring system) solutions built on the Mbed Arm Mbed device platform include an OS and many cloud services. The Smart Monitoring for Floods utilizes an Mbed LPC1768 with an application board as its microprocessor. These are members of the LPC176x microcontroller family. The board is modelled after a USB drive, and the software development kit is accessible online.

3.4.2 Hardware

Structure and Methodology for Design and Development, and Production, The connected parts of the circuit are depicted in Fig. 6 and describes the mean participation. The ARM microcontroller is linked to the ultrasonic sensor, stepping motor, Wi-Fi modules, LED, LCD, and buzzer. Even though the Wi-Fi module only needs 3.3v, the ultrasonic sensor and stepper motor need at least 5 V. To generate data. The driver module is attached to the PWM pin on the ARM microcontroller, allowing the motor to communicate with the controller. The ESP8266 Wi-Fi device also has a serial peripheral (SPI) RX TX pin interface. An overabundance of water that usually floods dry areas can be considered a natural wonder. However, the massive devastation it wreaks on people and their communities makes it more of a social disaster than a marvel. Predicting and warning of floods is crucial today due to the devastating effects that flooding may have on coastal communities and their inhabitants. In the recent monsoon season, high unexpected rain caused devastating floods inside the Indian state of Kerala, which had never happened before in the last century. A total of 373 individuals have been killed, and 83% of the reservoirs in the state have been opened up in that time. As a result, it is essential to regularly assess the risk of flooding.

Consequently, a Wireless Sensor Network-based warning system is essential for saving people's lives in high-risk locations (WSN). This paper presents a system for real-time surge checking and discovery using Wireless Sensor Networks. This system uses sensor hubs transported to specific surges and vulnerable areas. Considering how quickly and easily data might be gathered using Wireless Sensor Networks [WSN], they can be used in other real-time projects. The sensor node comprises a collection of sensors with limited data and transmission capacities, such as a temperature sensor, ultrasonic sensor, and rain sensor. The microprocessor receives the data from the sensors so it may be processed. The processed data is sent to the cloud using a LoRA (Long Range) module. Because smartphones are so convenient and can spread news quickly, an app has been created to send out early warnings to people in the impacted areas. As a result, cutting-edge tools like sensor networks will be utilized to ascertain the precise level of flooding, and mobile phones linked to this technology will disseminate the forecasted information to the impacted folks to avert needless loss.

4 Discussion

Each year, millions of people all over the world are impacted by natural dis- asters. Many people and animals perish in these calamities, and many crops, buildings, and possessions are destroyed or damaged. Consequently, having a profound effect on the economy, particularly for a developing nation like Pakistan. Repeatedly, the catastrophic power of rushing water has been on full display in Pakistan's most common hydrological disaster: floods. Since the 1970s, floods have been the leading cause of property loss worldwide. An evacuation plan might be made in advance when flooding is expected, such as when heavy rains are forecasted. However, also there are flash floods, which occur suddenly. The primary causes of flooding in our region are: 1. Low floods are made more dangerous by the massive, haphazard, and unlawful construction of structures and highways along riverbanks. Because of this, less land is available to soak up rain that falls in excess. 2. clogged flood-draining channels. Maintenance of these waterways is a recurring responsibility. 3. Deforestation contributes to landslides and flooding. 4. Levee failure or dam damage. Periodic upkeep is required for these levees and dams. Heavy monsoon rains are a yearly occurrence thanks to Pakistan's cyclical weather pattern. When flood warnings turn into actual floods, homes and businesses are wiped out, and people are displaced, often leaving them to deal with the consequences of water-borne illnesses. The regional economy is impacted. Moreover, over 20 million people were impacted by a flood in 2010. There were nearly 2000 fatalities recorded. Many people were displaced, and crops and homes were destroyed (Akhtar et al. 2023). However, the destruction could have been minimized by taking precautions against flooding and taking alternative routes. The massive dam's levees also have a role. Flood risk and severity can be accurately predicted using cutting-edge computer forecasts and projections based on meteorological and flood-related data.

Smart Flood Detection SoS monitors floods and sends alerts to helpers and people in danger. Text messages (SMS), television and radio broadcasts, email, and a website portal are all used to disseminate these flood alerts to the impacted communities. Direct, dedicated high-speed links keep emergency responders in the loop. It updates those affected by the floods on the status of essential services like food, shelter, new highway plans, electricity and gas, healthcare, and rescue operations. They also help individuals stay in touch with one another in the aftermath of a catastrophe. After the disaster strikes, communication systems must continue to function normally. Even if the communications cables and towers are knocked out of commission by a calamity, such as flooding, a backup plan is in place to ensure that communication will continue normally. As such, we have designed a Smart Flood Detection SoS to keep tabs on flooding and the response of rescue and emergency personnel when a flood has occurred. Our SoC has relay stations outfitted with booster balloons to guarantee constant transmission. All communication systems, including broadcast media, landlines, and mobile phones, may continue operating thanks to these balloons. Technology like this helps people stay in touch with one another and also facilitates analyses for better decision-making.

Tsunamis, floods, and earthquakes are all natural disasters that can strike with little warning and significantly negatively impact human society. Therefore, it is necessary to develop novel approaches based on the learned tactics to record the happening signals with minimal interference. Wireless sensor networks, which can swiftly respond to abrupt types of information and convey the collected data to an info examination center in the zones via a wireless connection, are discussed as an essential and relevant technology to handle the concerns (Akhtar et al. 2023). Satellite imagery combined with RADAR's weather forecasting capabilities allows for accurate flood warnings and real-time preventative measures. It is achieved through constant monitoring of the stream, precipitation level, and water level, as well as the need for critical decisions regarding the continuation of aid (Noar and Kamal 2017). Additionally, with the rapidly altering climatic conditions, many researchers have recently shown interest in water level monitoring of the water bodies. Monitoring and measuring water levels provide helpful information for weather forecasting and estimating the likelihood of flooding. In order to assess the likelihood of flooding, target values have been established for the amounts of water in the rivers, which are then compared with the actual values. New wireless technologies and communication protocols within predetermined ranges are used to facilitate the development of natural check frameworks equipped with low-cost, low-power, integrated-functional sensors (Noar and Kamal 2017). The standard operating procedure for information monitoring and detection is integrating several sensors at a single out-of-the-control-supply monitoring station. This structure needs to be placed in the water and will monitor data for as long as you need it (Akhtar et al. 2023).

The data is sent over when the allotted time has elapsed to be analyzed and the predetermined procedures carried out. In this research, we implement an intelligent flood monitoring system with a robust network of sensors. A literature review is presented in section II, followed by descriptions of current and future systems.

5 Results

Efficient flood monitoring and forecasting depend on multiple factors performed in a sequence: correct data gathering, practical data analysis and timely result notifications. This paper proposes a three-layer architecture to cover all these factors, as shown in Fig. 5. These factors depend on the outputs of previous factors, which encouraged to proposal of an architecture of layered structure. Figure 2 shows the hexagonal classification results.

Three layers of the proposed architecture are lower most layer, known as IoT middle layer, known as Data Analysis Layer (DAL) and upper most layer, known as Presentation Layer (PL). Each layer performs certain set of actives independent of other layers and provides outputs to higher layers (Figs. 3, 4, 5 and 6).

IL is responsible for the installation of IoT devices and data collection from installed IoT devices. DAL is responsible for analyzing collected data to effectively forecast floods in any geographical area. PL is responsible for timely distributing information generated from DAL through RSS feeds, emails, messages, alerts and notifications. Each layer

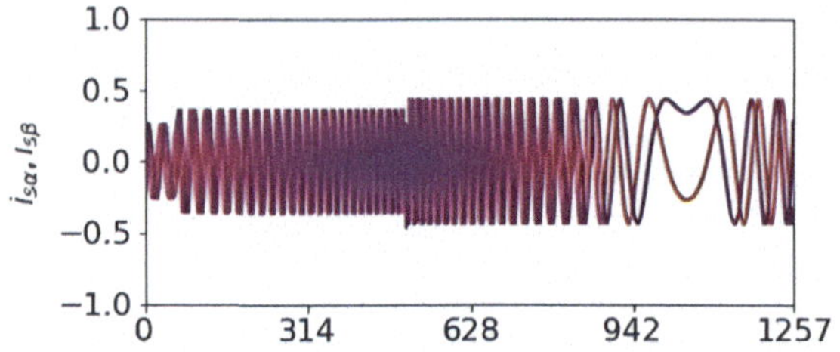

Fig. 2 Hexagonal classification

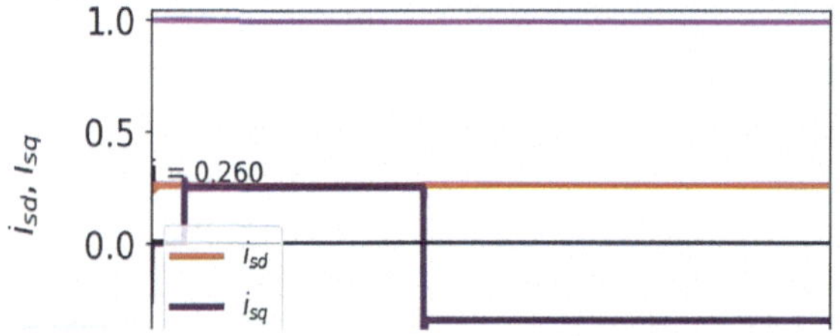

Fig. 3 Device shutdown coloring

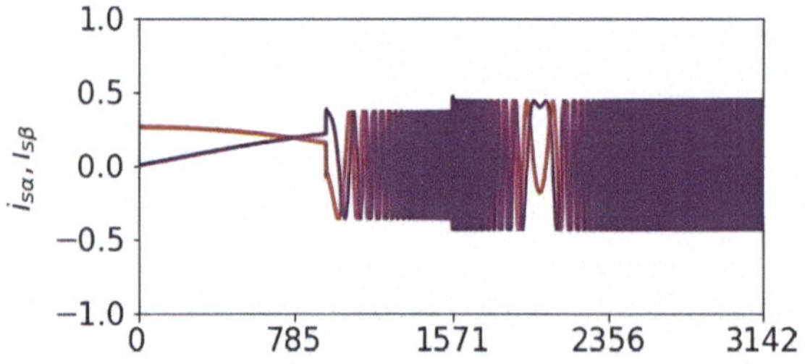

Fig. 4 Flood experimental tested

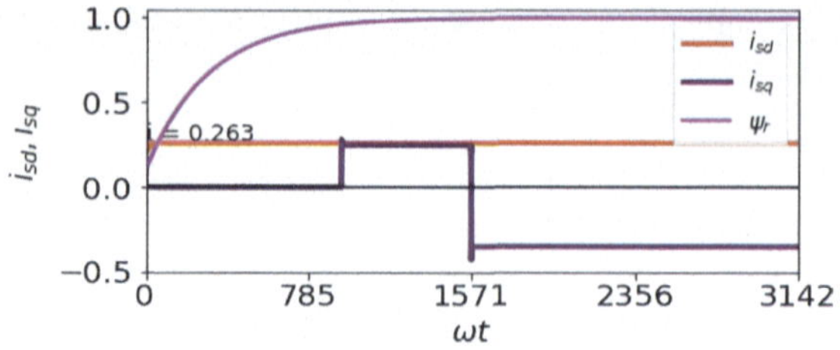

Fig. 5 Three layered architecture

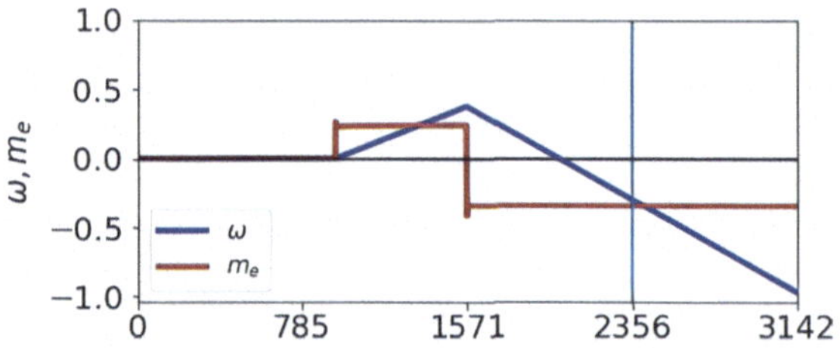

Fig. 6 Mean precipitation

is explained in detail ahead. The preliminary examination of the data revealed the ability to predict floods in real-time, and simulation results demonstrated that the data size exhibits significant improvement utilizing this method. The amount of data sent to the base station is the sole topic of this research. Power evaluation of sensor nodes is outside the scope of this simulation and would require a separate simulation.

The functionalities of this layer are flood attribute selection, geographical classification in the form of hexagonal structures, social collaboration of IoT devices, and energy saving of IoT devices. All these functionalities are explained in detail ahead.

5.1 Flood Attributes

Flood attributes can be classified into two main categories: Flood Causing Attributes (FCAs) and Flood Preventing Attributes (FPAs). FCAs are dynamic and often change with time, providing the current flood state. FPAs help prevent the flood spread rate, which is static for longer. These attributes are used to monitor and forecast any flood for geographical location. To remove the sudden fluctuations in flood parameters, they are also sorted into five different clusters; the study's results on wireless sensors reveal their efficiency and low cost in monitoring real-world phenomena like traffic and billiard courts. Figure 7 shows flood velocity of the catchment results.

Most of the time, the WSN will be used to predict and avert environmental disasters because of the convenience of its easy spread of sensor nodes and the speed and accuracy with which its computations can be performed.

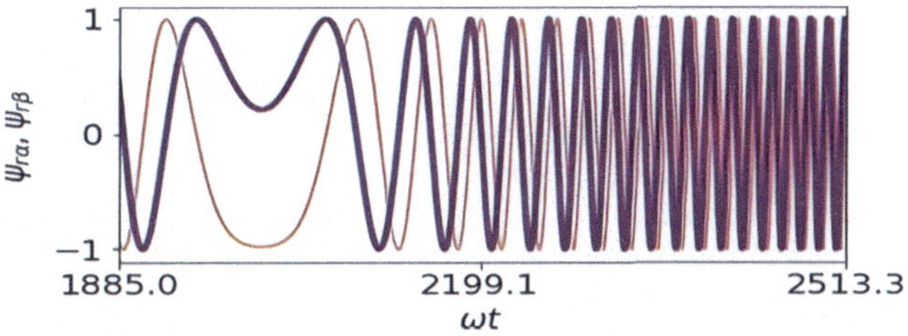

Fig. 7 Flood velocity of the catchment

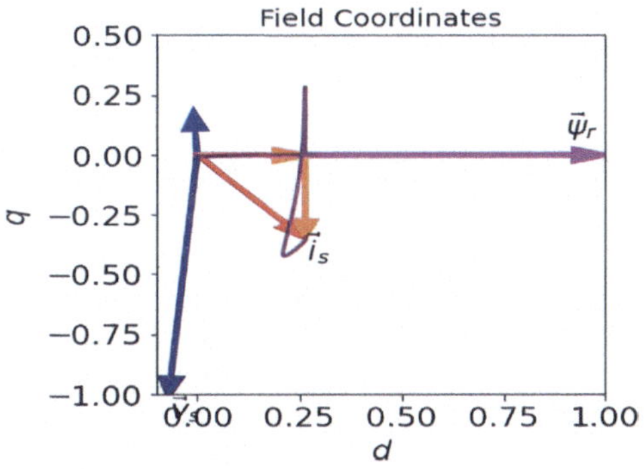

Fig. 8 Flood results from SVD

In this study, we use a wireless sensor network (WSN) that employs energy-saving methods to keep track of the flow and level of water regularly. Each sensor node in the proposed system is equipped with a variety of sensors (including temperature, ultrasonic, and rain sensors), a microcontroller unit (for processing data), and a transceiver unit (for communicating with other nodes). Figure 8 shows the flood results on SVD.

The microcontroller receives the gathered environmental data and processes it. The sensing unit measures all three of these factors—temperature, water level, and water flow. Multiple transmissions of real-time data are made available to examine the flood level at the river's location. Wireless sensor nodes positioned strategically along the coast can track subtle sea-level changes. These sensor nodes are installed on riverbanks and are used to monitor the river's water level in real-time. The data collected by the sensor after sensing and monitoring are then saved for further use. Potentially useful for ongoing evaluation and for making future choices.

A PSU supplies energy to the nodes. Every so often, the nodes in the network check in on the sensors' current state thanks to some programming. Employing the LoRA long-range communication protocol, the acquired data will be transmitted from the processor to the server for long-term storage. A mobile application has been created to notify the public when the water level hits a predetermined threshold. This model employs the fewest possible analytical parameters. Energy optimization could also reduce the drain on the sensor nodes' power supplies. Because of its low cost and high effectiveness, the proposed system is being implemented in developing countries to help them fight floods.

The produced framework is performed to screen the disparities in water levels at rivers, and the values obtained are put away occasionally in the program cloud and servers for assistance evaluation. When a flood is detected, authorities will be notified immediately so they can take the necessary precautions. LoRa communicates and transmits the signals for an extended distance range compared to the prevailing modules like Wi-Fi and RF modules; thus, the provided techniques may efficiently over- come to the constraint of the existing system, such as connection and continuous monitoring. Esp8266 Wi-Fi D1R2 is a 32-bit microcontroller with a Wi-Fi module and can communicate with additional modules through an expansion bus. It is where all the information collected by the various sensors, like, a level sensor, which is positioned in the river, measures water speed via the engines attached to it; an ultrasonic sensor attempts to measure the water level via sound navigation, such as an echoing process, at regular intervals; a humidity and temperature sensor measures the humidity and temperature of the sur- rounding environment. The microcontroller interfaces with provides satellite over the available internet, and the sensors are wired directly to it. The thrust values have been predetermined, and the real-time values have been gathered via the sensor network and sent to the processing element for comparison. If the measured values are less than the thrust, the situation is under control; if the measured values are more significant than the thrust, an alert is sent to the locals.

References

Akhtar, Z., Qazi, U., Sadiq, R., El-Sakka, A., Sajjad, M., Ofli, F., & Imran, M. (2023, April). Mapping Flood Exposure, Damage, and Population Needs Using Remote and Social Sensing: A Case Study of 2022 Pakistan Floods. In Proceedings of the ACM Web Conference 2023 (pp. 4120–4128)

Akhtar, N., & Khan, S. (2019). Formal architecture and verification of a smart flood monitoring system-of-systems. Int. Arab J. Inf. Technol., 16(2), 211–216

Azid, S. I., Sharma, B. N., Raghuwaiya, K., Chand, A., Prasad, S., & Jacquier, A. (2015). SMS based flood monitoring and early warning system. ARPN Journal of Engineering and Applied Sciences, 10(15), 6387–6391

Bande, S., & Shete, V. V. (2017, August). Smart flood disaster prediction system using IoT & neural networks. In 2017 International Conference On Smart Technologies For Smart Nation (SmartTechCon) (pp. 189–194). Ieee

Basnyat, B., Singh, N., Roy, N., & Gangopadhyay, A. (2020, September). Design and deployment of a flash flood monitoring IoT: Challenges and opportunities. In 2020 IEEE International Conference on Smart Computing (SMARTCOMP) (pp. 422–427). IEEE

El-Bendary, N., Fouad, M. M. M., Ramadan, R. A., Banerjee, S., & Hassanien, A. E. (2013). Smart environmental monitoring using wireless sensor networks. K15146_C025. indd

Goyal, H. R., Ghanshala, K. K., & Sharma, S. (2020). Role of IoT devices in Flood Monitoring System using Social Networking Sites. Int. J. Innov. Technol. Explor. Eng., 9, 1986–94

Jamali, A., & Giman, J. P. (2021, August). Performance Analysis of IOT based Flood Monitoring Framework in Sub-urban. In 2021 IEEE 7th International Conference on Smart Instrumentation, Measurement and Applications (ICSIMA) (pp. 99–104). IEEE

Kadir, E. A., Siswanto, A., Rosa, S. L., Syukur, A., Irie, H., & Othman, M. (2019, April). Smart sensor node of WSNs for river water pollution monitoring system. In 2019 International Conference on Advanced Communication Technologies and Networking (CommNet) (pp. 1–5). IEEE

Khan, S., Anwar, M., & Akhtar, N. (2016). ANALYSIS, DESIGN, ARCHITECTURE SPECIFICATION, AND FORMAL VERIFICATION OF A SMART FLOOD MONITORING SYSTEM-OF-SYSTEMS. Science International, 28(1)

Kramer, J., & Magee, J. (2007, May). Self-managed systems: an architectural challenge. In Future of Software Engineering (FOSE'07) (pp. 259–268). IEEE

Lin, Y. B., Lai, J. S., Chang, K. C., & Li, L. S. (2006). Flood scour monitoring system using fiber Bragg grating sensors. Smart materials and Structures, 15(6), 1950

Mishra, B. K., Thakker, D., Mazumdar, S., Neagu, D., Gheorghe, M., & Simpson, S. (2020). A novel application of deep learning with image cropping: a smart city use case for flood monitoring. Journal of Reliable Intelligent Environments, 6, 51–61

Narayanan, R., Lekshmy, V. M., Rao, S., & Sasidhar, K. (2014, July). A novel approach to urban flood monitoring using computer vision. In Fifth International Conference on Computing, Communications and Networking Technologies (ICCCNT) (pp. 1–7). IEEE

Noar, N. A. Z. M., & Kamal, M. M. (2017, November). The development of smart flood monitoring system using ultrasonic sensor with blynk applications. In 2017 IEEE 4th international conference on smart instrumentation, measurement and application (ICSIMA) (pp. 1–6). IEEE

Rani, D. S., Jayalakshmi, G. N., & Baligar, V. P. (2020, March). Low cost IoT based flood monitoring system using machine learning and neural networks: flood alerting and rainfall prediction. In 2020 2nd International Conference on Innovative Mechanisms for Industry Applications (ICIMIA) (pp. 261–267). IEEE

Sivabalakrishnan, R., Dineshkumar, M., Sharon, B. P., Naveenkumar, P., & Vignesh, S. (2021). Design and Fabrication of 3D-Printed Acrylonitrile Butadiene Styrene (ABS) Dam Automation Structure with Integrated Flood Monitoring System Using Data Analysis and Computation Techniques. In Advances in Materials Research: Select Proceedings of ICAMR 2019 (pp. 137–145). Springer Singapore

Sroor, M. M. Y., Ngah, R., Din, J., Othman, N., Loung, V. Y. K., & Nawawi, Z. (2021, August). Wideband MIMO Antenna for Smart Flood Monitoring System. In 2021 IEEE Symposium on Wireless Technology & Applications (ISWTA) (pp. 71–76). IEEE

Yuan, F., Fan, C., Farahmand, H., Coleman, N., Esmalian, A., Lee, C. C., ... & Mostafavi, A. (2022). Smart flood resilience: Harnessing community-scale big data for predictive flood risk monitoring, rapid impact assessment, and situational awareness. Environmental Research: Infrastructure and Sustainability, 2(2), 025006

A Machine Learning Approach to Analyze Flight Delays Causal Factors: A Predictive System

Hajar Alla, Sara Arezki, Lahcen Moumoun, and Youssef Balouki

Abstract

Recently, air traffic demand has been increasing rapidly which creates saturation, congestion and queues issues. Flight delays put an immense load on transportation networks, resulting in operational shortcomings, higher economic losses for airlines and complaints and non-satisfaction for their customers. For this reason, aviation authorities, academics and researches become more interested in taking preventive actions in order to minimize the effect of flight delays. In this paper and based on a questionnaire distributed among pilots, air traffic controllers, airport administrators, airport staff, and travelers, we proposed a predictive model in order to forecast traffic delays for United States domestic flights. Four effective Machine Learning algorithms such as feed-forward Neural Network, Gradient Boosting, Decision Trees and Random Forest were employed on a data from 1st January to 31st December, 2018. We extracted from the dataset the traditional features that are contributing to flight delays. To enhance the precision of the suggested model, we created and proposed new features that, the best of our knowledge, were never treated in existing researches. Hence, the model was capable to predict flight delays with a higher coefficient of determination of 98.70% in the case of feed-forward neural network with a lower error value when both traditional and suggested features were utilized.

Keywords

Machine learning algorithms • Air transportation • Flight delay estimation • Neural networks • Random forest • Decision trees • Gradient boosting

1 Introduction

Nowadays, air travel is regarded as the most favorable mode of transportation due to its enhanced safety, time efficiency, suitability for covering long distances, and cost-effectiveness. Furthermore, it plays a crucial role in providing medical aid, contributing to the expansion of the aviation sector and a surge in demand. Flight delays cause problems for carriers, airports, travellers, and transportation administrators. Flight delays can be attributed to a multitude of factors, ranging from elevated air traffic levels and congested airports to inclement weather, difficulties during boarding or disembarking procedures, security protocols, and various operational challenges on the ground. These operational challenges encompass aspects such as aircraft maintenance, staff availability, baggage management, refueling processes, aircraft cleaning, equipment availability, and more.

The Federal Aviation Administration (FAA) (2023) has identify many reasons of delays comprising bad weather conditions effect, volume and congestion, equipment failure, closed runways and other causes according to Fig. 1.

The Bureau of Transportation Statistics (BTS) (2023) has considered air Carrier, aircraft arriving late, security delay, National Aviation System (NAS) and extreme weather as the most important causes of delay as highlighted in Fig. 2.

In order to normalize the flight delay reporting procedure, The International Air Transport Association (IATA) (2023) implemented codes that explain the cause of each delay.

H. Alla (✉) · S. Arezki · L. Moumoun · Y. Balouki
Laboratory of Mathematics, Computer and Engineering sciences, Faculty of Science and Techniques, Hassan First University of Settat, 26000 Settat, Morocco
e-mail: h.alla@uhp.ac.ma

S. Arezki
e-mail: sara.arezki@gmail.com

L. Moumoun
e-mail: lahcen.moumoun@uhp.ac.ma

Y. Balouki
e-mail: youssef.balouki@uhp.ac.ma

S. Arezki et al. (eds.), *Emerging Disruptive Technologies for Society 5.0 in Developing Countries*,
Advances in Science, Technology & Innovation, https://doi.org/10.1007/978-3-031-63701-8_4

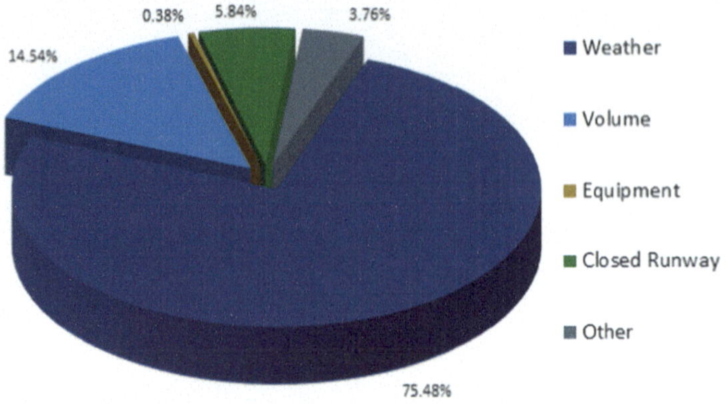

Fig. 1 FAA delays by cause. *Source* FAA (2023) OPSNET standard report

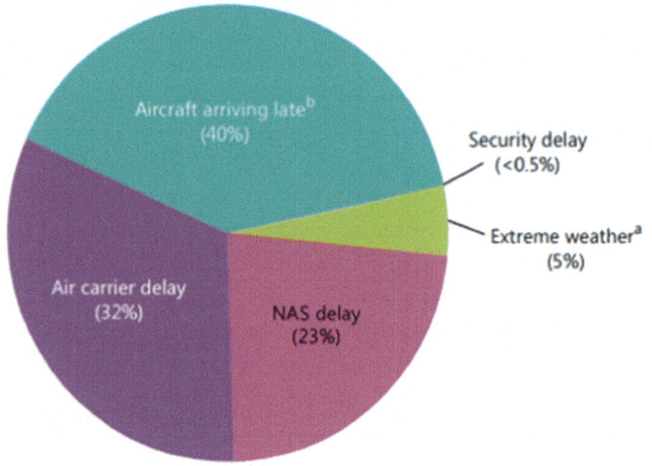

Fig. 2 BTS causes of delays. *Source* U.S. Department of Transportation, BTS (2023), Office of airline information

The European Organisation for the Safety of Air Navigation (Eurocontrol) (2023) established a programme that offers all-causes delay, punctuality, and cancellation records based on flight data from airspace users through the Central Office for Delay Analysis. The Free Route Airspace (FRA),[1] is a new concept that allows users to freely plan a path between a specified entrance point A and a specified exit point C without necessarily passing through an intermediate point B. This procedure encourages direct routes which reduces flight duration and then the possibility for flight delays.

In this research, a survey was developed and distributed to air users such as pilots, air traffic controllers, terminal employees, airport managers and passengers in order to assess the importance of reducing flight delays. The effects of flight delays go beyond affecting passengers, airlines, and airports - they also have an impact on the environment by leading to increased fuel consumption and elevated gas emissions. To alleviate these consequences, airlines can proactively address the impact of flight delays by investing in cutting-edge technology, optimizing organizational efficiency, and putting in place robust contingency plans.

In response to this issue, researchers from various corners of the globe have undertaken numerous investigations aimed at identifying remedies for traffic delays. This particular study introduces a forward-looking classification model designed to forecast airline delays within the context of the United States. The model employs four potent Machine Learning algorithms-Neural Network, Gradient Boosting, Decision Trees, and Random Forest. To fuel the study, data pertaining to both punctual and delayed flights in the year 2018 were sourced from the BTS database (2023). Because of the unequal distribution in the data, we implemented a dual strategy involving both oversampling and undersampling through the utilization of the SMOTE-Tomek technique. The approach of SMOTE-Tomek integrates the over-sampling technique of SMOTE (Synthetic Minority Over-Sampling Technique) with the under-sampling method of Tomek, leading to enhanced results (Kotb and Ming 2021).

To the best of our knowledge, this is the first work dealing with new aspects that impact flight delays such as the season in which the flight was performed, whether it was a holiday or not, whether the airports of departure and arrival are hubs and whether the day on which the flight took place is a weekday or a weekend day. The distance of the flight is also an important factor to include in this study.

[1] https://www.eurocontrol.int/concept/free-route-airspace.

The rest of the paper is organized as follows. Section 2 reviews the researches conducted in the field of flight delays and flight time prediction. Section 3 discusses the methodology proposed in this paper as well as all the features considered in order to enhance the efficiency of the model. The experimental results of the suggested method and the comparison with other existing studies from literature are described in Sect. 4. Conclusion, perspectives and future works are described in Sect. 5.

2 Literature Review

In the pursuit of optimal air traffic operations, improved customer satisfaction, and minimized financial losses for airlines, a multitude of inquiries have approached the subject of flight delays from a wide array of viewpoints.

Ding (2017) suggested an approach for modeling incoming flights to address the challenge of predicting flight delays using multiple linear regression. The results were compared with Naive-Bayes and C4.5 approach. The best model reached approximately 80% of the accuracy. Authors in Zoutendijk and Mitici [2021] applied both Mixture Density Networks and Random Forest regression to estimate traffic delays at an European airport. The experimental results showed that the Mean Absolute Error for the proposed model was less than 15 min. Utilizing a variety of sampling strategies, Authors in Henriques and Feiteira [2018] employed the multilayer perceptron (MLP), decision trees and random forest in conjunction to predict flight delays. The MLP, achieving an accuracy rate of 85%, emerged as the top-performing model. Utilizing the Gradient Boosted Decision Tree model, flight delay prediction was carried out by Manna et al. (2017) considering six crucial features. The study's findings indicate that this model achieved the biggest Coefficient of Determination R^2 of 92.3185% for arrival data and an even higher 94.8523% for departure data. Authors in Nigam and Govinda [2017] developed a logistic regression model in order to predict departure delays of flights. They incorporated weather data encompassing variables like temperature, humidity, precipitation, and dew point, in conjunction with the airport-related information, so as to enhance the accuracy of the suggested method. The model was able to achieve a flight delay prediction with precision and recall rates exceeding 50%. The research conducted by Yi et al. (2021) introduces a flight delay prediction classification technique utilizing the Stacking method. The initial level of learning incorporated Decision Trees, Random Forest, Logistic Regression, Gaussian Naive Bayes, and KNN, while the secondary level of learning employed Logistic Regression. The findings explain that the Stacking algorithm was able to enhance the prediction accuracy and maintain a great stability. In their work, authors in Pamplona et al. (2018) opted for Artificial Neural Network (ANN) to construct a prediction model for air delays on the Sao Paulo to Rio de Janeiro route. They employed the Random Search technique for network hyperparameterization, leading to results that demonstrated a remarkable accuracy exceeding 90%. In the study established by researchers in Ebenezer and Brahmaji Rao [2018], U.S. flights and weather data were employed combined with data sampling techniques so as to forecast flight delays in the United States. The predictive system has obtained satisfying results. Authors in Hatıpoğlu et al. (2022) performed a three up-to-date methods namely, XGBoost, LightGBM, and CatBoost based on Gradient Boosting algorithm in order to predict delayed flights. Bayesian method and SMOTE technique were respectively used for hyper-parameter tuning and data balancing. XGBoost outperformed the other algorithms with a testing accuracy of 96.20% with SMOTE technique. ANN, logistic regression and Decision tree classifiers were implemented by Kuhn et al. (2017) to forecast flight arrival delays in the United States for the year 2015. Remarkably, all three classifiers achieved an accuracy of 91%. In their study, researchers in Dalmau et al. [2021] created a model utilizing an ANN with a feed-forward approach so as to estimate the progression of delay for a particular regulated flight. The proposed model successfully anticipated the delay with a precision level of 75%. Xu et al. (2007) presented a stochastic Bayesian Network model designed to examine the connections among delay variables and the underlying causes of delays. The methodology was illustrated through a case study focused on analyzing the relationship between Chicago O'Hare International Airport (ORD) and Hartsfield-Jackson Atlanta International Airport (ATL), as well as between LaGuardia Airport (LGA) and ATL airport. The experiments show satisfying outcomes. In the study conducted by Liu et al. (2008) and directed towards an important airport, distinct models for arrival delay and delay propagation were individually constructed using Bayesian Networks (BN). Following the training of these models with actual data, estimates were made for both the arrival delay and the propagation delay within and emanating from that airport. Alla et al. (2022) utilized Four Machine Learning classifiers namely Random Forest, Decision Trees, K-Nearest Neighbors and Naïve Bayes in order to forecast the arrival time of United States flights. The experimental outcomes demonstrated that the suggested system achieved the highest accuracy in predicting flight arrival delays, with a remarkable score of 0.9356 using the Random Forest model. Authors in AYAYDIN and AKCAYOL [2022] proposed a predictive model in order to estimate flight delays. The evaluation encompassed the effectiveness of Deep Recurrent Neural Network (DRNN), Long-Short Term Memory (LSTM), and Random Forest (RF) models using authentic data from 368 airports around the globe. Researchers in Gopalakrishnan and Balakrishnan [2017] tried several methods to anticipate delays in air traffic networks well in advance, possibly spanning several hours or even a day. The findings illustrated that the ANN excelled beyond the other methods, achieving an impressive accuracy rate of 94%. In the prediction of cancellations, flight arrival, and flight departure delays at London Heathrow Airport, Lambelho et al. (2020) utilized numerous approaches. Significantly, the LightGBM decision-trees demonstrated exceptional performance in contrast to the other models, achieving an accuracy level of 0.79 or greater.

3 Proposed Methodology

3.1 Problem Description

The importance of predicting flight delays extends beyond passengers and airlines to encompass all stakeholders in the aviation and transportation networks. Creating a highly precise predictive model for air traffic delays would enable airlines to proactively alert passengers to possible delays and provide options, including the opportunity to easily book new tickets for alternative flights. Customer satisfaction and loyalty will be improved then and the economic losses for airports and airlines will be minimized.

In order to assess and examine the assumptions and experiences of different air users, a survey[2] was produced and shared with pilots and crew members, air traffic controllers, passengers and airport personnel from different countries. According to the responses of the target population, the most common reasons of delays are personnel strikes, bad weather conditions and congestion due to the rush hour. As a consequence, the passengers are annoyed for missing connecting flights. Most of the answers voted for flight disruption, flight cancellations, reactionary delays generated by previous delays, getting late to appointments, meetings or exams as the worst effects of flight delays. Pilots and cabin crew suffer from stress and fatigue, not being able to fly next sectors and having extra unpaid duty time. Also, when there are more traffic delays, the circulation in the airports and the sky will be dense and congested leading to an increased workload for air traffic controllers and airport personnel.

From the survey, it is important to fight against delays in order to better promote air transportation, gain passengers trust and satisfaction , and also for the passengers, pilots and airport personnel comfort. Many collaborators can participate in flight delays optimization, air traffic units by allowing short-cuts and direct routes in the sky, passengers by showing up early to the airport and boarding quickly, airlines and pilots by ensuring turnaround efficiency, airport personnel by minimizing strikes and protests, researchers and academics by proposing models and applications for flight delays prediction and estimation.

[2] https://tinyurl.com/3pcu8ycr.

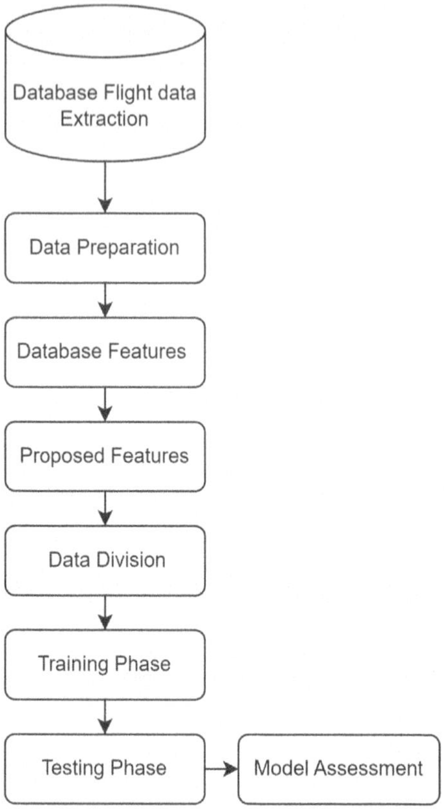

Fig. 3 The overview of the suggested method

The aim of our study is to identify all potential factors contributing to flight delays. Some were extracted from the dataset used, the others were created and proposed for the first time in this research to the best of our knowledge. Data were prepared and split. Due to the imbalance in the data, we employed a combined approach of oversampling and undersampling using the SMOTE-Tomek method. Efficient machine learning algorithms were utilized to train the model. We tested and evaluated the performance of the suggested model. Figure 3 describes the overview of the proposed method.

3.2 Data Collection

Data for U.S domestic flights for the year 2018 were extracted from BTS (2023). BTS is a U.S. Federal Organization in charge of collecting, analyzing, and distributing transportation information and statistics.

Data for the world's airports used as airline hubs were obtained from Wikipedia,the free encyclopedia. Information about the federal holidays for the year 2018 in the U.S. were taken from the online calendar of holidays in the United States (U.S. Federal Holidays Calendar 2023).

3.3 Data Preparation

In order to produce accurate outcomes and models, it is necessary to ensure that the data is accurate, consistent, and reliable. For this, cleaning and preprocessing techniques have been performed before the training phase. The size of the dataset has been reduced by removing unnecessary variables, missing values and duplicates. All errors and mistakes have been corrected and data normalized.

3.4 Database Features

We extracted relevant information about each flight from BTS database and summarized it in Table 1. The FAA FAA [2023] considers an aircraft to be delayed if it departs or arrives 15 min later than planned.

3.5 Proposed Features

While the traditional features remain pertinent to modeling flight delays, they are limited and lack novelty. Therefore, it becomes imperative to incorporate more significant and influential attributes into the investigation. Consequently, novel features were formulated and introduced in this study, which, as far as our understanding goes, have not been explored in prior research. The details outlining these suggested attributes are presented in Table 2.

Distance: Longer flights are more likely to experience delays because they may involve more transfers, more complicated flight routes, and more potential spots of congestion. Moreover, increased flight distances can substantially contribute to higher occurrences of napping behavior, extended wakefulness durations, sleep deficiency, and heightened levels of sleepiness (Lowden and Åkerstedt 1999).

Flight Duration: Longer flights across time zones called long-haul flights are accompanied by jet lags. The severity and extent of jet lag are affected by the flight direction and the number of time zones crossed (Silverman and Gendreau 2009).

Hub: Flight delays are more likely to occur at major airports because any interruption to one flight can have an ongoing effect on other flights. For example, if a flight landing at a hub airport is delayed, travellers may miss connecting flights, causing additional and reactionary delays.

Holiday: In holidays, the percentage of flights increases especially because of the high demand. It results in an air and ground density and congestion which causes flight delays.

Table 1 Description of database features

Feature	Description	Example
Date of Flight	The date of the trip	2018-05-02
Flight code	IATA [2023] identification of the flight	AS2103 (Alaska Airlines)
Departure airport	The airport of departure	JFK (John F. Kennedy International Airport)
Arrival airport	The airport of arrival	LAX (Los Angeles International Airport)
Est_DEP	The estimated time of departure	13:16
Real_DEP	The actual departure of time	13:26
delay_DEP	The delay of departure	10.00 (10 min)
Est_ARR	The estimated time of arrival	20:20
delay_ARR	The delay of arrival in minutes	09.00 (9 min)

Table 2 Description of proposed features

Feature	Description	Example
Distance	The distance of the flight in nautical miles (NM)	300 NM
Flight duration	The elapsed time between departure and arrival at the destination in minutes	44.00 (44 min)
Hub	1 if the airport of departure or destination is a Hub 0 if not	1 if the airport of departure or arrival is San Francisco International Airport (SFO) for example which is a hub in the U.S.
Holiday	1 if the date of the flight is a holiday	1 if the date is 04-07-2018 which is the Independence day in the U.S. 0 if not
Season	The season in which the flight was performed ("Summer", "Autumn", "Winter" or "Spring")	Winter
Weekend	Binary	1 if the date of the flight is a weekend 0 if not

Season: Seasons have an impact on flight delays. In winter for example, flights light be delayed or cancelled due to bad weather conditions. In spring and summer, more people tend to travel because of the nice and calm weather in these seasons which result in a peak travel period, congestion and then traffic delays.

Weekend: Weekends, like holidays and seasons, can be an increasingly common period for travel, resulting in congested airports and more extended waiting times for security, luggage processing and boarding.

3.6 Proposed Model Algorithms

3.6.1 Decision Trees

A decision tree is a method that is useful in the classification of an event or the prediction of variable output values. It has a root and internal nodes that reflect characteristics and branches (outcomes) (Alla et al. 2021). The decision tree has the benefit of adjusting to the data collected, having a fast classification speed, good accuracy, and dealing with independent, binary, and continuous features (Osisanwo et al. 2017). The advantages of Decision Tree are as follows (Song and Ying 2015):

- It divides original input variables into meaningful subgroups to simplify complicated interactions between input variables and target variables.
- It is simple to comprehend and interpret.
- It is a non-parametric technique that makes no distributional assumptions.
- It is simple to handle missing values without resorting to imputation.
- It handles heavily inaccurate information without the requirement for data transformation.
- It is resistant to outliers.

3.6.2 Random Forest

Random Forest is a method developed by Leo Breiman in the 2000s for the construction of a prediction ensemble using a group of decision trees that grow in randomly chosen data subspaces (Biau 2012). It has become recognized for dealing with data imbalances, particularly with big datasets. Random forest classifier is quicker than other literature classifiers due to its parallel architecture (Paul et al. 2018).

The advantages of Random Forest are as follows (Cutler et al. 2012):

- It copes with both regression and classification tasks.
- It is relatively easy and quick to train and predict.
- It relies on only one or two tuning parameters.
- It can be applied for high-dimensional problems.
- It is simple to implement in parallel.

3.6.3 Gradient Boosting

Gradient Boosting stands out as a potent technique within the realm of machine learning, delivering state-of-the-art results across a diverse array of real-world challenges. For an extended period, it has remained the predominant choice for tackling learning tasks characterized by diverse attributes, noisy data, and intricate associations, as highlighted by Dorogush (2018). The primary approaches in gradient boosting revolve around employing decision trees as fundamental predictors. These strategies amalgamate the outcomes of numerous uncomplicated predictors to craft a resilient ensemble that surpasses the performance of individual elements (Biau et al. 2019).

3.6.4 Artificial Neural Network

ANN introduces a range of potent novel approaches to address pattern recognition, data processing, and control challenges. It encompasses several distinct attributes, including rapid processing speeds and the ability to acquire the correct problem-solving approach from a sequence of instances. Operating as a nonlinear mathematical function, it converts input variables into corresponding output variables. The specific form of this transformation is determined by a set of parameters called weights, which can be computed using a collection of instances that map to the desired output (Bishop 1994). Neural networks are adept at identifying intricate non-linear connections between independent and dependent variables, as well as potential associations among predictors (Alla et al. 2021).

4 Results and Discussion

4.1 Evaluation Metrics

MAE (Mean Absolute Error)

MAE is the average of all test case deviations between anticipated and actual values. It represents the average prediction error (Patil et al. 2010). The MAE is determined using Eq. 1.

$$MAE = \frac{1}{n}\sum_{i=1}^{n}|R_i - E_i| \quad (1)$$

where E_i is the estimated value of the i-th sample, R_i is the corresponding real value and n is the number of samples.

RMSE (Root Mean Squared Error)

RMSE is one of the most often used measurements of success for numeric prediction. It is determined by taking the average of the squared differences between each expected and correct value (Patil et al. 2010). Simply said, it is the square root of the mean-squared-error according to Eq. 2.

$$RMSE = \sqrt{\frac{1}{n}\sum_{i=1}^{n}(R_i - E_i)^2} \quad (2)$$

where E_i is the estimated value of the i-th sample, R_i is the corresponding real value and n is the number of samples.

Median Absolute Error

It is referred as the mean of all absolute variations between the objective and predicted outcomes. It assesses the adaptability of a method against sample variability (Wong et al. 2017). It is calculated by Eq. 3.

$$Median(R_i, E_i) = median(|R_1 - E_1|, \ldots, |R_n - E_n|) \quad (3)$$

where E_i is the estimated value of the i-th sample, R_i is the corresponding real value and n is the number of samples.

Coefficient of determination R^2

It represents the proportion of the variability in a response variable that can be accounted for by a model. It measures how effectively the model minimizes error when compared to simply taking the mean as an estimate. It can be understood as the ratio of the predictable variance in the dependent variable attributed to the independent variables (Chicco et al. 2021). It is computed using Eq. 4.

$$R^2 = 1 - \frac{\sum (z_i - \hat{z}_i)^2}{\sum (z_i - \bar{z})^2} \quad (4)$$

where z_i are the observed data, $\hat{z}_i$ the predicted values and $\bar{z}$ is the mean of the observed data.

4.2 Experimental Results

We examined approximately 800,000 samples of aviation data from the United States in 2018. We used the 70/30 ratios plit with Scikitlearn and Python to split the data. We used an combined oversampling and undersampling procedure with SMOTETomek method since the data were not balanced. For the architecture of the feedforward neural network model, we chose 3 layers, one as the input , one as the hidden and the third one as the output. The hidden layer has 50 neurons. We selected the solver Adam, the activation function Relu and the alpha 10^{-2}. Figure 4 represents the architecture of the feed forward neural network using only traditional features from the dataset and Fig. 5 the architecture with both traditional and proposed features.

We evaluated our model using assessment metrics, including R^2, RMSE, Median and MAE. To demonstrate the effectiveness of the newly introduced features compared to the traditional ones in the dataset, we present the training outcomes using only traditional attributes in Table 3 and the results incorporating both traditional and suggested features in Table 4.

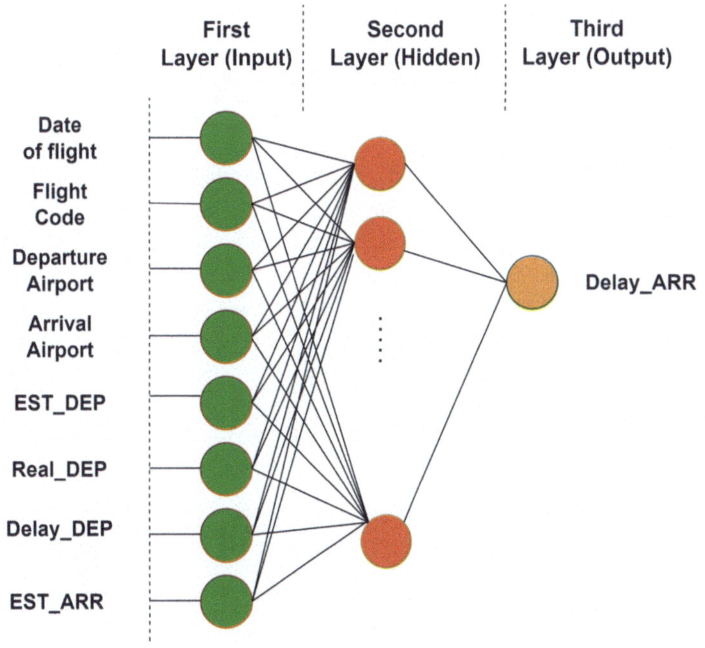

Fig. 4 ANN architecture incorporating traditional features

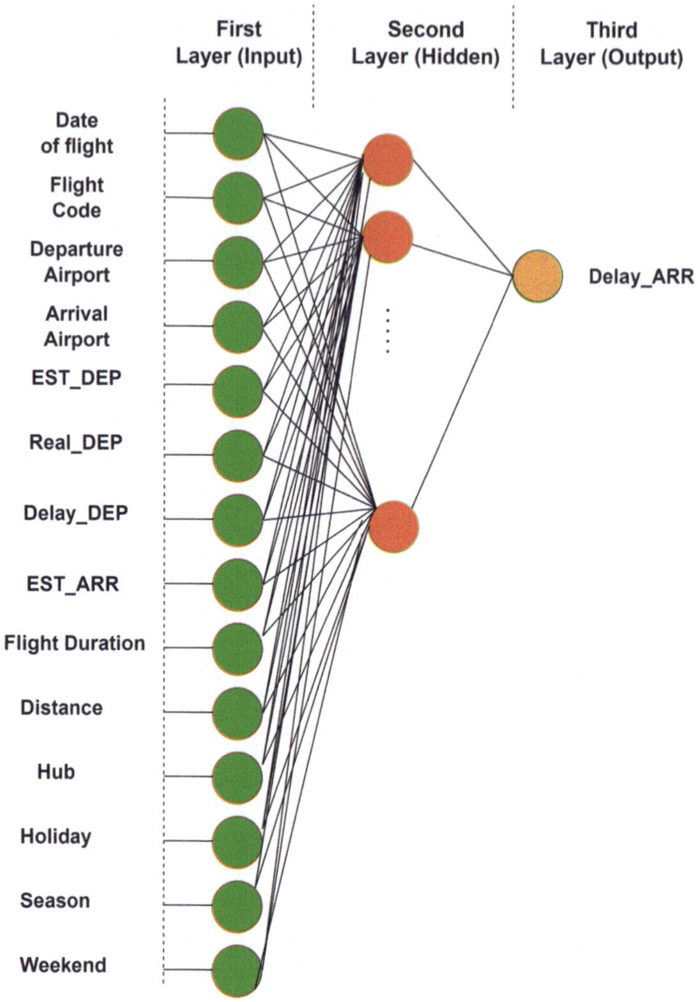

Fig. 5 ANN architecture incorporating traditional and suggested features

From the tables, it is evident that the proposed features significantly influenced the performance of the trained model across all utilized algorithms. Notably, the feed-forward neural network demonstrated superior performance compared to other models, achieving the highest R^2 of 98.70% and median absolute error of 01.09.

In order to establish the reliability of the proposed approach, we conducted a comparison of its performance against that of previously conducted studies documented in the literature. The results presented in Table 5 indicate that the proposed model exhibits a higher level of accuracy when compared with the methodologies employed by other researchers.

The results show the importance of analyzing all the factors and attributes, that have an impact on flight delays, in order to achieve an optimal prediction.

5 Conclusion

Flight delays have consistently remained a paramount concern for airlines, passengers, and airport management, necessitating the allocation of additional resources like fuel, materials, and personnel, which consequently incurs heightened expenses and costs for airline companies. As a result, aviation authorities, scholars, and researchers are actively striving to

Table 3 Evaluation metrics using traditional features

Algorithm	R^2 (%)	RMSE	Median	MAE
ANN	95.10	16.04	08.24	09.40
RF	93.01	18.13	09.02	11.13
DT	90.2	20.12	11.02	13.17
GB	89.14	28.23	12.33	15.11

Table 4 Evaluation metrics using traditional and proposed features

Algorithm	R^2 (%)	RMSE	Median	MAE
ANN	98.70	08.80	01.09	04.23
RF	96.14	11.14	07.25	10.44
DT	94.22	20.98	10.04	13.02
GB	92.33	21.19	11.14	14.55

Table 5 Benchmarking of the proposed method with studies present in the existing literature

Methods	Suggested	Ayaydin and Akcayol (2022)	Gopalakrishnan and Balakrishnan (2017)	Henriques and Feiteira 2018	Lambelho et al. (2020)	Dalmau et al. (Dalmau et al. [2021])
Accuracy (%)	98.70	96.50	94.00	85.00	79.00	75.00

formulate innovative and advanced models aimed at analyzing and mitigating flight delays. This study introduces novel attributes, particularly flight distance, flight duration, hub location, seasonal variations, and weekends, which play a pivotal role in air traffic delays. The model's training involved the utilization of four supervised machine learning algorithms: Neural Networks, Random Forest, Decision Trees, and Gradient Boosting. Data balancing using a SMOTE-tomek technique was performed by combining oversampling and undersampling strategies. The model's performance underwent rigorous testing using both conventional features sourced from the database and the newly proposed attributes. Among the algorithms, Neural Networks emerged as the most effective, achieving the highest accuracy rate of 98.70% and demonstrating reduced error when leveraging the suggested new features. To gauge the reliability and effectiveness of the proposed model, we conducted a comparative analysis, juxtaposing our findings with outcomes previously documented in the literature. The presented system holds potential advantages for various stakeholders, including air traffic control units, airport management, airlines, and operators. Its potential lies in optimizing the allocation of ground personnel and resources through the formulation of effective strategies and proactive measures to streamline schedules and alleviate congestion. Equally significant is its impact on passenger experience, as it offers the foresight of potential delays well in advance, preventing last-minute disruptions. In the future, we envisage the augmentation of features, the choice of more efficient algorithms, and the use of more coherent datasets in order to enhance the precision of the predictive system.

References

Alla H, Moumoun L, Balouki Y. A multilayer perceptron neural network with selective-data training for flight arrival delay prediction. Scientific Programming. 2021:1–2. 2021 Jun 14.

Alla H, Moumoun L, Balouki Y. Flight arrival delay prediction using supervised machine learning algorithms. In Intelligent Systems in Big Data, Semantic Web and Machine Learning. pp. 231–246. Cham: Springer International Publishing. 2021 May 29.

Alla H, Moumoun L, Balouki Y. Impact of Aircraft Performance and Time of the Day on Flight Arrival Delays Prediction in the United States: a Machine Learning Classification. In ITM Web of Conferences 2022 (Vol. 48, p. 03005). EDP Sciences.

AYAYDIN A, AKCAYOL MA. Deep Learning Based Forecasting of Delay on Flights. Bilişim Teknolojileri Dergisi.15(3):239–49. 2022 Jul 7.

Biau G. Analysis of a random forests model. The Journal of Machine Learning Research. 13:1063-95. 2012 Apr 1.

Biau G, Cadre B, Rouvìère L. Accelerated gradient boosting. Machine learning. 108:971–92. 2019 Jun 15.

Bishop CM. Neural networks and their applications. Review of scientific instruments. 65(6):1803–32. 1994 Jun 1.

Bureau of Transportation Statistics, BTS Transtats. http://www.transtats.bts.gov/. Accessed: 2023-01-04.

Chicco D, Warrens MJ, Jurman G. The coefficient of determination R-squared is more informative than SMAPE, MAE, MAPE, MSE and RMSE in regression analysis evaluation. PeerJ Computer Science. 7:e623. 2021 Jul 5.

Cutler A, Cutler DR, Stevens JR. Random forests. Ensemble machine learning: Methods and applications. 157–75. 2012.

Dalmau R, Genestier B, Anoraud C, Choroba P, Smith D. A machine learning approach to predict the evolution of air traffic flow management delay. In Proceedings of the 14th ATM Research and Development Seminar, Virtual Online. pp. 14–17. 2021 Jun.

Ding Y. Predicting flight delay based on multiple linear regression. In IOP conference series: Earth and environmental science. Vol. 81, No. 1, p. 012198. IOP Publishing. 2017 Aug 1.

Dorogush AV, Ershov V, Gulin A. CatBoost: gradient boosting with categorical features support. arXiv preprint arXiv:1810.11363. 2018 Oct 24.

Ebenezer K, Brahmaji Rao KN. Machine learning approach to predict flight delays. Int. J. Comput. Sci. Eng. 6. pp. 231–4. 2018.

U.S. Federal Holidays Calendar. https://usafederalholidays.com. Accessed: 2023-01-05.

Gopalakrishnan K, Balakrishnan H. A comparative analysis of models for predicting delays in air traffic networks. ATM Seminar. 2017.

Hatıpoğlu I, Tosun Ö, Tosun N. Flight delay prediction based with machine learning. LogForum. 18(1). 2022.

Henriques R, Feiteira I. Predictive modelling: flight delays and associated factors, Hartsfield-Jackson Atlanta International airport. Procedia computer science 138. pp.638–645. 2018 Jan 1.

Kotb MH, Ming R. Comparing SMOTE family techniques in predicting insurance premium defaulting using machine learning models. International Journal of Advanced Computer Science and Applications. 2021;12(9).

Kuhn N, Jamadagni N. Application of machine learning algorithms to predict flight arrival delays. CS229. 2326-9865. 2017.

Lambelho M, Mitici M, Pickup S, Marsden A. Assessing strategic flight schedules at an airport using machine learning-based flight delay and cancellation predictions. Journal of air transport management. 82:101737. 2020 Jan 1.

Liu YJ, Cao WD, Ma S. Estimation of arrival flight delay and delay propagation in a busy hub-airport. In2008 Fourth International Conference on Natural Computation 2008 Oct 18 (Vol. 4, pp. 500–505). IEEE.

Lowden A, ÅKERSTEDT T. Eastward long distance flights, sleep and wake patterns in air crews in connection with a two-day layover. Journal of sleep research. 8(1):15–24. 1999 Mar.

Manna S, Biswas S, Kundu R, Rakshit S, Gupta P, Barman S. A statistical approach to predict flight delay using gradient boosted decision tree. In2017 International conference on computational intelligence in data science (ICCIDS). pp. 1–5. IEEE. 2017 Jun 2.

Nigam R, Govinda K. Cloud based flight delay prediction using logistic regression. In 2017 International Conference on Intelligent Sustainable Systems (ICISS). pp. 662–667. IEEE. 2017 Dec 7.

Osisanwo FY, Akinsola JE, Awodele O, Hinmikaiye JO, Olakanmi O, Akinjobi J. Supervised machine learning algorithms: classification and comparison. International Journal of Computer Trends and Technology (IJCTT). 48(3):128–38. 2017 Jun.

Pamplona DA, Weigang L, de Barros AG, Shiguemori EH, Alves CJ. Supervised neural network with multilevel input layers for predicting of air traffic delays. In 2018 International Joint Conference on Neural Networks (IJCNN). pp. 1–6. IEEE. 2018 Jul 8.

Patil BM, Joshi RC, Toshniwal D. Impact of K-Means on the performance of classifiers for labeled data. In International Conference on Contemporary Computing. pp. 423–434. Berlin, Heidelberg: Springer Berlin Heidelberg. 2010 Aug 9.

Paul A, Mukherjee DP, Das P, Gangopadhyay A, Chintha AR, Kundu S. Improved random forest for classification. IEEE Transactions on Image Processing. 27(8):4012–24. 2018 May 10.

Silverman D, Gendreau M. Medical issues associated with commercial flights. The Lancet. 373(9680):2067-77. 2009 Jun 13.

Song YY, Ying LU. Decision tree methods: applications for classification and prediction. Shanghai archives of psychiatry. 27(2):130. 2015 Apr 4.

The European Organisation for the Safety of Air Navigation. Eurocontrol. https://www.eurocontrol.int. Accessed: 2023-01-04.

The Federal Aviation Administration (FAA). https://www.faa.gov. Accessed: 2023-01-07.

The International Air Transport Association (IATA). https://www.iata.org. Accessed: 2023-01-04.

Wong PK, Wong ML, Leung KS. Long-short term memory network for RNA structure profiling super-resolution. In International Conference on Theory and Practice of Natural Computing. pp. 255–266. Cham: Springer International Publishing. 2017 Nov 19.

Xu N, Laskey KB, Chen CH, Williams SC, Sherry L. Bayesian network analysis of flight delays. In Transportation Research Board 86th Annual Meeting, Washington, DC. 2007 Jan 25.

Yi J, Zhang H, Liu H, Zhong G, Li G. Flight delay classification prediction based on stacking algorithm. Journal of Advanced Transportation. 2021:1. 2021 Aug 17.

Zoutendijk M, Mitici M. Probabilistic flight delay predictions using machine learning and applications to the flight-to-gate assignment problem. Aerospace. 8(6):152. 2021 May 28.

Business and Economic Transformation Through Disruptive Technologies

Emerging and Disruptive Technologies in Entrepreneurship for Global Societies

Naman Mishra and Vandana Sharma

Abstract

Entrepreneurship is an evolving and changing concept, which is complemented by the new disruptive technologies. This chapter focuses on the emerging and disruptive technologies that are shaping the future of entrepreneurship for global societies. Through this we delve deeper into the various emerging and disruptive technologies that are transforming the entrepreneurial landscape, including artificial intelligence, blockchain, the Internet of Things, and edge computing. The chapter highlights the potential benefits of these technologies, including increased efficiency, improved decision-making, and enhanced customer experiences. It also explores the potential challenges and risks associated with the adoption of these technologies, such as cybersecurity threats and the displacement of jobs. It shows how the consumer mindset is evolving with the new technologies and how the behavior will be impacted with the changing environment especially targeted ads and AI driven business insights. Overall, this chapter provides insights into the role of emerging and disruptive technologies in shaping the future of entrepreneurship for global societies, and highlights the need for entrepreneurs to be aware of these technologies and their potential impacts on business and society.

Keywords

Artificial intelligence · Edge computing · Entrepreneurship · Blockchain · Consumer behavior

N. Mishra (✉)
FS University, Shikohabad, India
e-mail: mnaman225@gmail.com

V. Sharma
Chirst (Deemed to be University), Delhi, NCR, India

1 Introduction

To get an insight how technology would change entrepreneurship, it becomes important for us to first understand what entrepreneurship means and what it means to become one. In simple terms we define it as the activity when a person sets us a business with the hopes of making a profit by trading or manufacturing, and thus generally the person who is involved in such a task and spearheads the same is termed to be an entrepreneur. Through the ages many prominent authors have contributed to this field by improving upon the definition of entrepreneurs, a few of them are as follows, according to Cantillon(Murphy 1986), any person who groups certain means of produc tion into a product and sells them at some price above his buying price is termed as an entrepreneur. For Cantillon, an entrepreneur is simply put a dealer, which undertakes some risk to group various means of production into sellable product. A better insight into the thinking and creative capabilities of an entrepreneur were highlighted by Peter Drucker, (Drucker 2014) who defined that an entrepreneur is a person who is always on the lookout for any abnormality, makes use of it and then converts into profitable ventures. He also said that innovation is a tool for such a person and that he uses any source and coverts into a resource which is useful. Sara Sarasvathy, Failed 2008) pointed out that entrepreneurs are not necessarily risk-takers, they are individuals who have the ability to identify and pursue opportunities in situations where others see chaos and confusion. All these definitions tell us that entrepreneurs are people who are calculative, make informed decisions to make their business grow. Technology as inseparable part of the world today and such technology has been an involved in entrepreneurship as well, they both have been closely intertwined and many successful business are reliant on technology to sustain themselves. The up- ward trend in technology has led to a new type of term being coined the Technology entrepreneurship, one which refers to the process of creating as

S. Arezki et al. (eds.), *Emerging Disruptive Technologies for Society 5.0 in Developing Countries*, Advances in Science, Technology & Innovation, https://doi.org/10.1007/978-3-031-63701-8_5

well as developing businesses which are primarily focused around the new innovative technologies. It is an intricate balance between the technical expertise and business sense which makes this a possibility, with the entrepreneur focusing on the new technologies, identifying their use cases, their applications as well as developing new strategies to implement them in their daily routine. This new type of entrepreneurship has many characterises attributed to it which can be listed as follows:

- Innovation—with the help of technology, the new entrepreneurs, can easily develop new products and services which can be made more economically and are more customer friendly.
- Disruption—Technology entrepreneurship often involves disrupting traditional business models and industries, by introducing new products or services that are more efficient, cost-effective, or provide a better user experience.
- Collaboration: Technology entrepreneurship often requires collaboration between technical experts, business leaders, investors, and other stakeholders.
- Risk-taking: Technology entrepreneurship involves taking risks, such as investing in new technologies, developing new products or services, and entering new markets.
- Scalability: Technology entrepreneurship often involves developing products or services that have the potential to scale quickly and reach a global market.

The current trend in technology has made certain impact on entrepreneurship with the inclusion of network connectivity and the internet, the major use cases of these technologies are discussed further.

1.1 Mobile Phones and Smartphone Technology

The growth of mobile devices and connectivity technologies of smartphones has made India change its consumer behaviour as well as change the ways of entrepreneurs conducting their businesses. Mobile phones are no longer a luxury but an essential tool which allow for entrepreneurs to run their business more effectively and efficiently, they act as a fast and convenient way to communicate with customers, suppliers, partners, and employees. It allows them to be in touch with their business even when they are on the go, mobile phones are not just limited to communication but also to the access of information at any point of time, using the internet. The computers have been gradually replaced by mobiles for the small screen users which make use of this technology to access their emails, work reports or even engage in marketing loops. The various marketing channels like, Instagram, apps, Facebook ads have all been heralded by mobile phones, creating the sense of brands for the businesses. In the financial sector Mobile phones allow entrepreneurs to accept payments from customers using mobile payment systems, such as mobile wallets or card readers that plug into the phone. This makes it easy for entrepreneurs to process transactions and accept payments on the go. Such advancements in technology has changed the perspective of the consumers as well as the business owners as well as instigating the fire of innovation and competition in them.

1.2 E-commerce

With the advent of technology, we see that internet has attracted a credible boost to the existing businesses and has changed the way these businesses are being carried out, one such major change is the use of ecommerce. Simply put ecommerce is the moving the existing business or creating a new business on the online platforms with the help of the internet to provide services to the customer. In India with the cost of Internet continuously declining making it the fifth lowest in the world, the status of ecommerce has been booming (Kalia et al. 2018), the young generation which is now the target audience is more attracted to online shopping and this feature has been exploited by the entrepreneurs. The benefits of ecommerce are expansive in nature and thus it was rapidly adopted by the businesses to expand their business, the key positives being eliminating the need of having a physical base. The foremost point of attraction is the fact that the new businesses are reliant on the low or no start-up cost as the need for physical presence is eliminated as well as it optimizes the current pitfalls such as the inventory management, logistical issues and cutting the cost by inclusion of technology. Ecommerce as a platform has also helped business expand their consumer base and have access to the global market, another benefit adding to this list the ability of convenience and flexibility. In this new age business can be handled from any part of the world, which is connected to the internet, thus allowing for entrepreneurs to handle their business as per their convenience and reach. These very benefits of ecommerce have revolutionized the way that entrepreneurs create and grow their businesses, providing a platform for innovation, growth, and global expansion (Fig. 1).

From the above Fig. 1, we see the boom of ecommerce (Mishra 2023) in India and the predictions for the same for the upcoming ages, the contribution to the same being coupled by the new disruptive technologies. All these technologies show how entrepreneurship has been growing and the potential that it has in the future to come and thus it is imperative for us to understand the implications of these

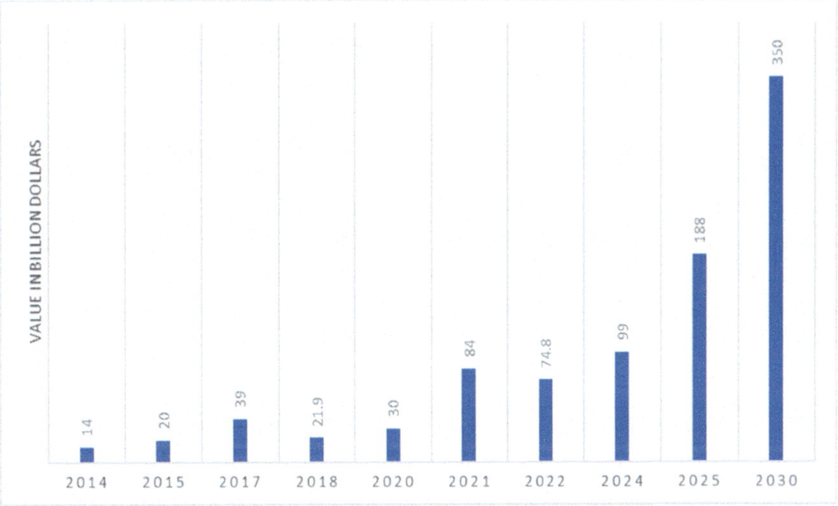

Fig. 1 The growing market of ecommerce

technologies as well as how they would change the workings of the current run businesses coupled with the consumer behavior.

2 Artificial Intelligence

Before understanding how business are impacted with inception of Artificial Intelligence, understanding the different fundamentals of the same which present them- selves as use cases becomes imperative. Typically, any computer system which can efficiently and effectively perform tasks which require human intelligence can be termed as an AI. These smart AI does away with the need of human intervention in the day-to-day task. These are generally set of algorithms which are used to analyse data, identify patterns, and then make decisions backed by them. In general terms there are usually two different types of AI namely the weak AI and the strong AI. Weak AI are the systems which are used for specific tasks such as speech recognition or image recognition while on the other hand strong AI is the one which can perform any task which a human can. These two types of AI are both changing the way how business owner conduct their businesses (Enholm et al. 2022) which can been seen by the wide use of chatbots. In any business the customer journey is imperative to let the consumer attached and a better way to accomplish this is by guiding the customer through the various steps and helping them whenever required. This task was facilitated by the use of customer support but with the growing number of users, this kind of one-to-one support becomes hectic to be maintained and as such AI helps by developing virtual assistants and chatbots. These chatbots (Selamat and Windasari 2021) makes the use of natural language processing to understand what the user is trying to say and thus guide them accordingly, these chatbots have moved ahead from a bunch of if-else statements to understand how things work and thus more effectively help the consumers. These assistants have helped the entrepreneurs to reduce the work load as well as make the consumer experience more personalized and engaging.

The use of chatbot is just a simple implementation of AI other tasks such an the redundant tasks of data entry, scheduling and operations management are all handled by automating the task with AI, this way the entrepreneurs are freed from excessive workload and even the cost of maintaining the overheads. This benefit helps to boost the business, by letting the entrepreneurs focused more on the planning, development as well as innovation. With the humongous growth of data of any business and the ability of AI to produce meaningful predictions from the haystack, a new ability of AI is identified. AI can be used to analyse data and make predictions about future trends and customer behavior. AI can be used to analyse customer data and predict customer behavior, such as which products or services they are most likely to purchase, when they are most likely to make a purchase, and how much they are likely to spend. This can help businesses to optimize their marketing and sales strategies, and tailor their offerings to meet the needs and preferences of their customers. These predictive algorithms can be used to analyse market trends and predict future changes in the market, such as how the preferences of any consumer changes, the popularity of any particular product, or the threat of any technology which would change the dynamics of the market. In turn this allows for the businesses to be always ahead of the growing competition as well as change their strategies to capitalize on emerging opportunities. AI is not just limited to understanding the consumer but also helps the internals workings of the business by predicting financial performance, such as revenue, profits, and cash flow, based on historical data and other factors such as market trends, customer behaviour, and economic indicators. This allows entrepreneurs to better manage their finances, make informed investment decisions, and optimize their operations for growth.

On the security side AI can be used to predict and mitigate risks, such as supply chain disruptions, cybersecurity threats, or financial losses. By using AI to identify potential risks and vulnerabilities, businesses can take counter measures to mitigate the ill effect of these changes and ensure the continuity of their operations. These regulatory changes present themselves as a powerful tool for entrepreneurs and can help businesses of all sizes operate more efficiently, improve the customer experience, and stay ahead of the competition.

3 Blockchain

While discussing disruptive technologies and their implications on the global societies in terms of Entrepreneurial development, it is important to take note of the recent developments in the field of blockchain and how it aims to changes the current era of businesses. In general terms Blockchain is a decentralized, distributed ledger technology that allows for secure, transparent, and tamper-proof record-keeping of transactions. In a blockchain network, transactions are grouped together in blocks, which are linked together in chronological order to form a chain of blocks. Each block contains a unique cryptographic code called a"hash," as well as a reference to the previous block in the chain. The decentralized nature of blockchain means that there is no central authority or intermediary controlling the network. Instead, each participant in the network has a copy of the entire blockchain, and all participants work together to validate and verify new transactions. In the context of businesses, blockchain technology can be used to improve various aspects of opera tions, such as supply chain management, financial transactions, digital identity, and more. Blockchain facilitates the business to keep a record of how and where their goods are being moved throughout the supply chain, allowing for a more transparent delivery process. This can help businesses to identify inefficiencies, reduce waste, and improve their supply chain operations. Another way that blockchain can be used is that it facilitates faster, more secure, and more cost-effective financial transactions. By using blockchain to process payments, businesses can reduce transaction fees, eliminate intermediaries, and streamline the payment process. The concept of digital identities is also facilitated by the development of blockchain technology, allowing businesses to verify the identity of customers, partners, and employees. By using blockchain to create a trusted digital identity system, businesses can reduce fraud, increase security, and streamline their operations.

Another important feature which is the basis of blockchain technology are the smart contracts and the impact which is has on streamlining and optimizing the current operations of a business are great. Smart contracts can automate complex processes and eliminate intermediaries, reducing the time and costs associated with traditional contract execution, allowing for businesses to streamline their operations and increase efficiency. One of the primary security risk of businesses is the potential for fraud and this issue can easily be mitigated with the help of smart contracts. The ability of smart contracts to be tamper-proof and operate according to predefined rules, ensuring that the terms of the contract are executed accurately and transparently. There are many evidence which share that blockchain would be the beneficial, in a report by the World Economic Forum (World Economic Forum 2019) estimates that by 2025, blockchain could generate over $1.5 trillion in new trade value globally. The report also suggests that blockchain technology could help to reduce trade costs by 20 to 25%, resulting in cost savings of up to $500 billion per year. In another report by Accenture (Accenture 2016), the consulting firm estimated that blockchain could save eight of the world's ten largest investment banks up to $12 billion per year by 2025. In the supply chain industry, blockchain has the potential to reduce costs by improving efficiency and reducing fraud. Even the World Trade Organization and the World Food Program (World Trade Organization World Food Programme 2019), blockchain-based solutions could reduce global food supply chain costs by $100 billion per year (Naman 2022). In all, the potential economic benefits of blockchain in business are significant, and many companies are exploring the technology to drive innovation, improve efficiency, and unlock new revenue streams.

4 Industrial Internet of Things

Another important disruptive technology is the Internet of things which is a system of connected devices, sensors, and machines that communicate with each other over the internet. The Industrial Internet of Things (IIoT) is a subset of the broader IoT concept, focused specifically on industrial applications. It refers to the use of connected devices, sensors, and machines in industrial settings to collect, analyze, and act on data in real-time. IIoT is aimed at improving efficiency, productivity, and safety in industrial environments such as factories, refineries, power plants, and warehouses. By connecting machines and devices to the internet, IIoT enables companies to monitor and control operations remotely, optimize processes, and reduce costs. IIoT has many different benefits which include but are not limited to predictive maintenance: by monitoring machines and devices in real-time, IIoT can help companies to predict when maintenance will be needed, reducing downtime and extending the lifespan of equipment. Quality control: IIoT can be used to monitor production processes and detect defects or quality issues in real-time, enabling companies to take corrective action before products are shipped to customers. Supply chain management: IIoT can be used to track inventory levels, monitor shipping and receiving, and optimize logistics, reducing costs and improving efficiency. Energy management: IIoT can be used to monitor and optimize energy usage in industrial settings, reducing energy costs and improving sustainability.

These said benefits are very useful in enabling business grow and change the way of conducting their business. From the perspective of the entrepreneurs IIoT can enable entrepreneurs to collect and analyse data from their operations in real-time. This helps them to identify inefficiencies in their processes and optimize them for maximum efficiency. On the operations side IIoT devices can help entrepreneurs detect potential issues with their equipment and machinery in real-time, enabling them to perform predictive maintenance and prevent unexpected downtime. These benefits can be coupled to increase the productivity of the business, by using IIoT devices to monitor their production processes, entrepreneurs can identify and correct bottlenecks that are slowing down production. In terms of the safety point of view the IIoT devices can be used to monitor the safety of workers in industrial settings. By collecting data on the environment, equipment, and workers, IIoT can help entrepreneurs identify potential safety hazards and take corrective action to prevent accidents (Fig. 2).

Zhang et al. (2021) provides a comprehensive review of the enabling technologies, architecture, and applications of IIoT. It discusses the growth of IIoT Fig. 2 and its potential to transform various industries, such as manufacturing, transportation, and energy. Another research (Biswas et al. 2021) provides a review of research trends related to IoT and its industrial applications, including IIoT. It discusses the growth of IIoT and its potential to improve productivity, reduce costs, and enable new business models in various industries. (Strassner et al. 2021) discusses the security challenges associated with IIoT and the need for secure and reliable communication between devices. It highlights the growth of IIoT and the potential for security solutions to enable new business models and improve productivity in various industries. In all we see that there is potential to transform various industries, improve productivity, and enable new business models.

5 Edge Computing

We all have heard about cloud computing and the various benefits that it adds to the computational and storage power of any infrastructure but it comes with its fair share of disadvantages and as such the concept of edge computing has be developed.

Edge computing is a computing facility that enables data transmission, relaying and analysis to occur closer to the source of data, such as on IoT devices or edge servers located in proximity to the devices. Edge computing architecture involves processing data at some point which is situated at the edge of the designated place and not relying on transmitting the data to a the cloud servers. The aim of edge computing is to reduce data latency and network congestion, improve the efficiency of data transfer and response time, and enhance security and privacy by keeping sensitive data closer to its source.

The most significant benefit of edge computing is attributed to the fact that it can reduce latency. In traditional cloud computing architectures, data is sent from a device to a data center for processing and analysis. This can result

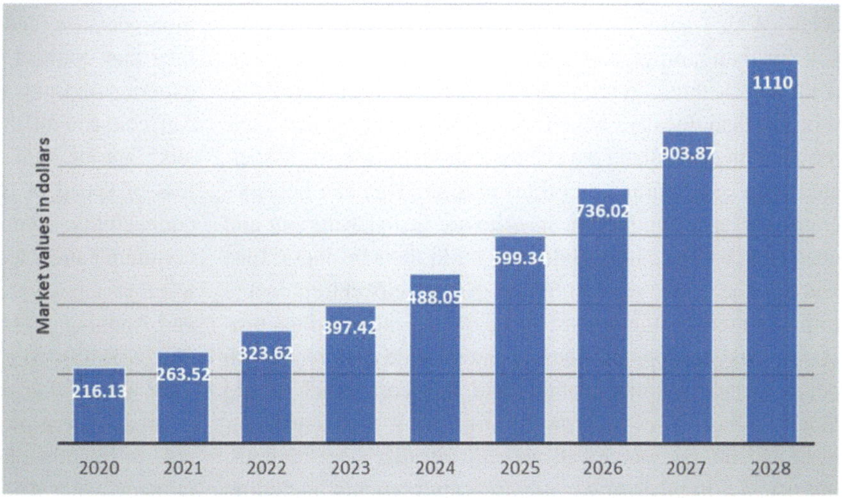

Fig. 2 The predicted growth of IoT in industry

in significant delays, especially when dealing with real-time data, such as that generated by IoT devices. Since the data is stored and maintained at a relatively close by location, entrepreneurs can reduce the amount of time it takes for data to be analyzed and acted upon. This can be especially beneficial in industries such as healthcare, where even a few seconds can make a significant difference in patient outcomes.

Edge computing also offers enhanced security benefits for entrepreneurs. In a cloud-based architecture, sensitive data is transmitted from devices to data centers, which can make it vulnerable to interception and unauthorized access. With edge computing, sensitive data can be processed locally, without ever leaving the device or edge server. This can significantly reduce the risk of data breaches and unauthorized access, which is especially important in industries such as finance and healthcare. Scalability is another benefit of edge computing. With traditional cloud computing, businesses must rely on centralized data centers to process and store data. This can limit scalability, as businesses are often limited by the capacity of their data center. With edge computing, businesses can process data at the edge of the network, which means they can scale their infrastructure as needed to accommodate changes in demand. This can be especially useful for entrepreneurs in industries such as manufacturing, where production volumes can fluctuate significantly. Another advantage of edge computing is the ability to perform analytics in real-time. With traditional cloud computing, data is sent to a data center for processing and analysis. This can result in significant delays, especially when dealing with real-time data. With edge computing, entrepreneurs can perform real-time analytics on the data as it is generated, which can help them identify patterns and trends quickly. This can be especially useful in industries such as retail, where businesses can use real-time data to optimize their supply chain and improve their customer experience.

Edge computing can also help entrepreneurs reduce costs. With traditional cloud computing, businesses must pay for data storage and processing resources in a centralized data center. With edge computing, businesses can process data locally, which means they can reduce their reliance on centralized data centers and reduce costs associated with data storage and transmission. This can be especially useful for entrepreneurs who are just starting out and need to keep costs low while they build their business. Last but not the least, edge computing can help entrepreneurs improve their customer experience. With real-time data processing and analysis, businesses can provide customers with personalized recommendations and services; which would help the businesses to grow by improving their consumer base and interaction. At all we can say that edge computing offers a number of benefits for entrepreneurs, including improved latency, enhanced security, and greater scalability. With real-time data processing and analysis, entrepreneurs can gain insights into their business operations and improve their customer experience.

6 5G Connectivity

5G is the latest mobile communication technology that is being deployed around the world. It promises to deliver faster speeds, lower latency, and greater capacity compared to the previous generation of mobile communication technologies. For entrepreneurs, 5G (Shivsharan et al. 2021) brings a number of benefits that could help them transform the way they do business.

Firstly, 5G offers much faster download and upload speeds. This means that entrepreneurs can download and upload large files much more quickly than before. For instance, an entrepreneur can upload a high-resolution video of a product demon- station in seconds, allowing potential customers to view the video instantly. This can help entrepreneurs to better engage with their customers and reach a wider audience. Secondly, 5G offers much lower latency than previous generations of mobile communication technologies. Latency (Li et al. Oct. 2020) refers to the delay that is present when data is transmitted from one location to another. With 5G, latency can be as low as 1 ms (ms), compared to 20–30 ms with 4G. This means that entrepreneurs can offer real-time services, such as video conferencing, without any noticeable de- lays. For instance, an entrepreneur can conduct a virtual meeting with customers, suppliers, or partners without any delays, which can help to save time and increase productivity. Thirdly, 5G offers greater bandwidth compared to previous generations of mobile communication technologies. The maximum amount of data which can be relayed over the network in a set period of time is defined as bandwidth. With the increase of the same, entrepreneurs can support more devices and users simultaneously. This means that they can connect multiple devices to the internet without experiencing any slowdowns. For instance, an entrepreneur can connect all their devices, including smartphones, tablets, laptops, and IoT devices, to the internet without any loss of speed or quality. Fourthly, 5G offers more reliable connectivity compared to previous generations of mobile communication technologies. This is because 5G networks use a variety of technologies, such as beamforming (Kumar and Anpalagan Oct. 2020) and multiple-input multiple-output (MIMO), to provide better coverage and connectivity. This means that entrepreneurs can connect to the internet in areas where previous technologies would not have been able to provide a reliable connection. For instance, an entrepreneur can work from remote locations or during travel, without worrying about losing connectivity. Fifthly, 5G offers enhanced security compared to previous generations of mobile communication technologies. With 5G, data is encrypted and transmitted through secure channels, making it more difficult for hackers to intercept and steal data. This means that entrepreneurs can safely transmit sensitive business data over the internet without worrying about security breaches. (Yao et al. 2021) For instance, an entrepreneur can send confidential business plans, financial data, and customer information over the internet without any risk of data theft or hacking. Sixthly, 5G offers new opportunities for entrepreneurs to innovate and create new products and services. With faster speeds, lower latency, and greater capacity, entrepreneurs can develop new applications and services that were not possible with previous generations of mobile communication technologies. For instance, an entrepreneur can develop new IoT devices, such as smart sensors, that can provide real-time data to help optimize business operations. They can also develop new virtual and augmented reality applications that can enhance the customer experience. Lastly, 5G offers new opportunities for entrepreneurs to collaborate and work together. With faster speeds, lower latency, and greater capacity, entrepreneurs can work together in real-time, even if they are in different locations. For instance, they can collaborate on a project, share files and data, and communicate with each other seamlessly. This can help to improve teamwork, increase productivity, and reduce the time and cost associated with travel.

In conclusion, 5G offers a range of benefits for entrepreneurs that can help them transform the way they do business. With faster speeds, lower latency, greater capacity, enhanced security, and new opportunities for innovation and collaboration.

7 Augmented Reality and Virtual Reality

Technology has been advancing and this has heralded new technologies which aim to change the way we interact with the data and the virtual environments, the major contribution to this field is given by Augmented reality and virtual reality. Augmented Reality (AR) overlays digital information, graphics, and other content onto the real world. AR uses cameras, sensors, and other technology to track the user's position and orientation, and then superimposes virtual content onto the real-world view. AR can be experienced through smartphones, tablets, smart glasses, and other devices. Virtual Reality (VR), on the other hand, creates a fully immersive digital environment that the user can interact with using specialized VR headsets and other equipment. VR replaces the real-world environment with a simulated one, often with highly realistic graphics and audio. Users can interact with the virtual environment using handheld controllers, hand gestures, or other input devices.

One of the biggest benefits of AR for entrepreneurs is the ability to offer a more engaging and interactive experience for customers. With AR, entrepreneurs can create immersive experiences that allow customers to interact with their products or services in a more meaningful way. For example, a furniture retailer could use AR to create a virtual showroom where customers can see how their furniture would look in their home before making a purchase. AR can also be used to improve employee productivity and training. With AR-enabled devices, employees can access real-time information, instructions, and guidance in their field of view. This can improve their efficiency and accuracy in completing tasks, leading to better overall performance. Another benefit of AR for entrepreneurs is the ability to gain insights into customer behavior and preferences. AR-enabled devices can collect data on customer interactions, such as what products they view or how they interact with digital overlays. This data can be used to make informed decisions on marketing strategies, product development, and overall business operations. AR can also be used to create new revenue streams for entrepreneurs. For example, a travel company could use AR to create virtual tours of popular destinations, offering customers a unique and immersive experience. Entrepreneurs can also use AR to create new advertising and sponsorship opportunities, such as creating interactive advertisements that customers can engage with. Furthermore, AR can be used to reduce costs and improve efficiency in various industries. For example, AR-enabled devices can be used to provide remote assistance to technicians, reducing the need for on-site visits and potentially costly downtime. AR can also be used to improve supply chain management by providing real-time visibility into inventory and logistics operations.

The benefits of VR for entrepreneurs is that it provides them with a more immersive and interactive way to design and develop their products. With VR, entrepreneurs can create virtual prototypes and test them in a simulated environment before producing the final product. VR allows entrepreneurs to evaluate the functionality, design, and user experience of their products without the need for costly physical prototypes. VR technology can also help entrepreneurs reduce business costs. For instance, it can be used to create virtual events, eliminating the need for physical venues and reducing event costs. VR technology can also reduce travel costs, as team members can attend virtual meetings and events without the need to travel physically. VR technology offers significant benefits to entrepreneurs, including enhancing product development, improving employee training, enhancing customer experience, enabling remote collaboration, reducing business costs, and providing a competitive advantage.

8 NFT

NFT, or non-fungible token, is a type of digital asset that is stored on a blockchain, which is a decentralized digital ledger. NFTs are unique and cannot be replaced or exchanged for something else of equal value, unlike fungible assets like cryptocur- rency. NFTs can represent various types of digital content, such as artwork, music, videos, and other forms of media. NFTs have numerous applications in entrepreneur- ship that can bring benefits to both businesses and consumers. NFTs can be used to represent digital art and collectibles, creating a new market for artists and collectors to exchange unique digital assets. By assigning a digital asset a unique identifier on the blockchain, artists can prove ownership and authenticity of their digital work. This has opened up new opportunities for artists to monetize their work in a way that was not possible before. Entrepreneurs can create marketplaces and platforms that facilitate the exchange of NFTs, providing a new revenue stream for both artists and the platform. NFTs can be used to represent in-game items and virtual real estate, allowing players to trade and sell unique virtual assets. This has opened up new opportunities for game developers to create revenue streams beyond traditional in-game purchases. Entrepreneurs can create marketplaces for players to buy, sell, and trade NFTs, creating a new ecosystem for gaming and virtual real estate. In the case of events and ticketing NFTs can be used to represent event tickets and experiences, creating a new way for event organizers to sell and distribute tickets. By assigning a unique NFT to each ticket, event organizers can prevent ticket fraud and create a secondary market for reselling tickets. Entrepreneurs can create platforms and marketplaces for buying and selling NFT tickets, creating a new revenue stream for both event organizers and the platform owners. It can also be used to represent loyalty program points and rewards, providing a more secure and transparent way for businesses to manage their loyalty programs. By assigning a unique NFT to each point or reward, businesses can prevent fraud and provide customers with a secure and transparent way to track their rewards. Entrepreneurs can create plat- forms and marketplaces for buying and selling loyalty program points and rewards, creating a new ecosystem for loyalty programs. NFTs have numerous applications in entrepreneurship that can bring benefits to both businesses and consumers. By leveraging blockchain technology, entrepreneurs can create new marketplaces and ecosystems that were not possible before, providing new revenue streams for busi- nesses and unique opportunities for consumers. As the technology continues to evolve, we can expect to see even more use cases for NFTs in entrepreneurship.

9 Effects of Technology on the Consumer Behaviour

The widespread adoption of new technologies such as smartphones, social media, e-commerce platforms, and the internet of things (IoT) has made profound changes in the interactions between people, as well as the interactions of the masses with the products and services. In this section, we will discuss the impact of Industry 4.0 on consumer behavior, exploring how technological advancements have changed the way people shop, consume, and engage with brands. One of the most significant changes in consumer behavior brought about by Industry 4.0 is the shift to digital channels for shopping and consumption. The growth of e-commerce platforms such as Amazon, Alibaba, and Flipkart has transformed the retail landscape, allowing consumers to shop from the comfort of their homes, and access a wide range of products and services. This trend is particularly pronounced in emerging economies such as India, where the growth of e-commerce platforms has been explosive in recent years.

The growth of digital channels (Fig. 3) has not only changed the way people shop but also their expectations from brands. Consumers now expect a seamless and personalized experience across all touchpoints, from social media to websites to mobile apps. Brands that fail to deliver on these expectations risk losing customers to competitors who offer a more seamless experience. This has led to the rise of technologies such as artificial intelligence (AI) and machine learning, which enable brands to personalize their offerings and provide a more immersive experience. Another significant impact of Industry 4.0 on consumer behavior is the rise of social media and its influence on purchasing decisions. Platforms such as Facebook, Instagram, and Twitter have become a crucial channel for brands to engage with their customers and build brand loyalty. Social media has also enabled consumers to share their experiences and opinions with a global audience, giving rise to a new form of consumer activism. Brands that fail to engage with their customers on social media risk losing credibility and relevance in the eyes of their target audience.

Growing IIoT is another important driver of change in consumer behavior. IoT enabled devices such as smart homes, wearables, and connected cars are transforming the way people interact with their environment and with each other. For example, smart homes enable consumers to control their appliances, lights, and security systems remotely, while wearables such as fitness trackers enable them to monitor their health and fitness in real-time. The rise of connected cars is also transforming the way people commute, with features such as autonomous driving

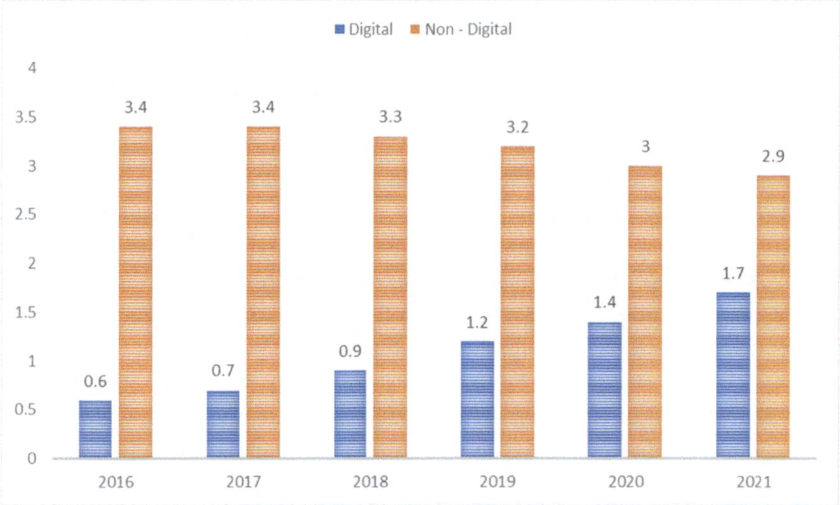

Fig. 3 The growth of targeted ads

and predictive maintenance becoming increasingly common. Industry 4.0 has also led to a significant increase in the amount of data available on consumers, enabling brands to gain deeper insights into their behavior and preferences. This has led to the rise of data-driven marketing, where brands use analytics and machine learning to personalize their offerings and target their marketing efforts more effectively. However, this also raises concerns about privacy and data security, with consumers becoming increasingly aware of the risks associated with sharing their personal data with brands. We can also say that Industry 4.0 has had a profound impact on consumer behavior, transforming the way people shop, consume, and engage with brands. The growth of e-commerce platforms, social media, IoT, and data analytics has enabled brands to provide a more personalized and immersive experience, while also raising concerns about privacy and data security. Brands that fail to adapt to these changes risk losing relevance and credibility in the eyes of their target audience, highlighting the importance of staying ahead of the curve in an era of rapid technological change.

10 Case Studies at Global Level

There are numerous startups that have utilized AI (Cao et al. 2020) to create innovative solutions and drive growth in various industries. The following are some case studies of AI startups: Cognitivescale: CognitiveScale is a company that develops industry-specific AI systems. They have created AI systems for healthcare, financial services, and retail industries. The company's software provides customer engagement solutions and personalized product recommendations. Their solutions are powered by cognitive computing and machine learning algorithms that enable businesses to provide more intelligent customer service.

AIBrain is a startup that creates natural language processing (NLP) technol-ogy that enables machines to understand human language. They have developed AI technology that can understand and respond to spoken commands, allowing for the creation of intelligent personal assistants. Their technology has been used to create a personal assistant called "Robin" that can assist users with scheduling, messaging, and other tasks. Nauto is an AI startup that has developed technology for autonomous vehicles. Their technology enables vehicles to detect and respond to traffic situations in real-time, allowing for safer driving. Their system uses machine learning algorithms to analyze data from sensors and cameras, allowing the vehicle to make decisions based on its environment. SoundHound is an AI startup that has created a voice recognition and search engine platform. Their technology can recognize and interpret human voice commands, allowing for the creation of intelligent personal assistants and voice-activated devices. Their platform has been integrated into devices such as smartphones, smart speakers, and automobiles.

These AI startups have achieved significant success through their innovative use of AI technology. According to a study published in the Journal of Business Research (Bandyopadhyay and Sen 2020), AI startups are more likely to achieve high growth rates and financial success compared to startups that do not use AI technology. The study also found that AI startups are more likely to attract venture capital funding and achieve higher valuations. Another study published in the International Journal of Information Management found that AI startups can improve operational efficiency and increase customer satisfaction through the use of AI technology. The study also found that AI startups are more likely to be successful when they focus on specific industry applications, such as healthcare or financial services. In all we can say that AI startups have demonstrated the potential of AI technology to revolutionize various industries and drive growth. Through their innovative use of AI, these startups have achieved financial success, attracted venture capital funding, and improved operational efficiency. These case studies serve as examples of the potential of AI technology for entrepreneurs to create disruptive solutions and drive growth in their respective industries.

There are many startups that are actively leveraging edge computing to create products and services that solve critical problems and deliver significant value to their customers. In this section, we will explore some of the most promising edge computing startups and their use cases. Foghorn Systems is a startup that provides edge intelligence and analytics solutions for industrial IoT. Its flagship product, Lightning, enables organizations to process and analyze data at the edge, reducing the need for cloud computing and enabling real-time insights. SWIM AI is a startup that provides edge intelligence and analytics solutions for real-time applications. Its flagship product, SWIM EDX, enables organizations to process and analyze data at the edge, reducing the need for cloud computing and enabling real-time insights. MachineMax is a startup that provides edge computing solutions for the construction and mining industry. Its product enables equipment owners to optimize equipment utilization, monitor machine health, and reduce equipment downtime. Saguna Networks is a startup that provides edge computing solutions for mobile networks. Its product enables mobile network operators to improve the quality of service for their customers, reduce network latency, and reduce network congestion. AlefEdge is a startup that provides edge computing solutions for 5G networks. Its product enables organizations to create and deploy applications that require low latency and high bandwidth, such as augmented reality and virtual reality.

These startups are just a few examples of how edge computing is being leveraged to create innovative solutions for a variety of industries. With the boom of technology and the wide rate of acceptance we might see the rise of many computing startups emerge, each with their own unique value proposition and use cases. The research papers cited in this section provide valuable insights into the market trends and growth potential of edge computing, making them essential resources for entrepreneurs looking to capitalize on this emerging technology.

11 Conclusion

Emerging and disruptive technologies have changed the face of entrepreneurship, and have presented new opportunities and challenges for researchers and practitioners in the field. The growing use of technology in various fields has ushered the creation of new types of products as well as changed the traditional ways of the business models. This has resulted in an increased interest in understanding the role of technology in entrepreneurship, and how it can be used to enhance and transform businesses. The emergence of new technologies such as blockchain, artificial intelligence, the internet of things, edge computing, and 5G has transformed the entrepreneurial land- scape. These technologies have opened up new avenues for entrepreneurs to develop and scale their businesses, and have enabled them to reach customers in previously untapped markets. One of the main benefits of emerging and disruptive technologies in entrepreneurship is that they provide entrepreneurs with a competitive edge. By leveraging technology, entrepreneurs can develop innovative products and services, streamline their operations, and gain insights into customer behavior that can be used to improve their offerings. For instance, the use of artificial intelligence in marketing can help entrepreneurs understand their customers better, and develop more effective marketing strategies. Another important benefit of emerging technologies in entrepreneurship is the ability to increase efficiency and reduce costs. For example, edge computing can help entrepreneurs reduce latency and increase data processing speeds, resulting in faster decision-making and reduced costs. The use of blockchain technology can help entrepreneurs reduce the costs associated with intermediaries, and streamline their supply chains. Moreover, these technologies can help entrepreneurs reach new markets and customers. For example, the use of the internet of things can enable entrepreneurs to gather data on customer behavior in previously untapped markets, and use this data to develop products and services tailored to the needs of these markets. Similarly, the use of 5G technology can help entrepreneurs reach customers in remote areas with limited access to high-speed internet. Furthermore, emerging and disruptive technologies can help entrepreneurs enhance collaboration and communication within their organizations. For example, the use of artificial intelligence in project management can help entrepreneurs monitor progress, predict potential problems, and improve communication between team members. Despite the benefits of emerging technologies in entrepreneurship, there are also challenges that need to be addressed. One of the main challenges is the need for entrepreneurs to keep up with the pace of technological change, and to continually update their skills and knowledge. This can be particularly challenging for entrepreneurs who operate in industries that are not traditionally associated with technology. Another challenge is the need to ensure the security and privacy of data. Emerging technologies such as blockchain and the internet of things generate large amounts of data, which need to be stored and protected from cyber threats. Entrepreneurs need to invest in robust security measures to prevent data breaches and ensure the safety of their customers' data. In conclusion, emerging and disruptive technologies have transformed the entrepreneurial landscape, presenting new opportunities and challenges for researchers and practitioners in the field. These technologies have the potential to provide entrepreneurs with a competitive edge, increase efficiency, reduce costs, reach new markets, and enhance collaboration and communication. However, entrepreneurs need to address challenges such as the need to continually update their skills and knowledge, and the need to ensure the security and privacy of data. Researchers and practitioners in entrepreneurship need to continue to study and understand the impact of these technologies on businesses and society, and develop strategies to help entrepreneurs harness their potential for growth and innovation.

References

Accenture. (2016). Banking on blockchain: A value analysis for investment banks. Retrieved from https://www.accenture.com/_acnmedia/PDF-22/Accenture-Banking-on-Blockchain.pdf

Bandyopadhyay, D., & Sen, J. (2020). AI-based entrepreneurial innovation: Insights from Indian startups. Journal of Business Research, 118, 311–326 https://doi.org/10.1016/j.jbusres.2020.08.001

Biswas, A., Gope, N., Hossain, M. S., & Muhammad, S. (2021). Internet of Things and its Industrial Applications: A Review of Research Trends. IEEE Access, 9, 22519–22541 https://doi.org/10.1109/ACCESS.2021.3060833

Cao, X., Wei, S., & Su, Q. (2020). Research on the application of AI in entrepreneurship education. Journal of Physics: Conference Series, 1670(1), 012021 https://doi.org/10.1088/1742-6596/1670/1/012021

Drucker, Peter. Innovation and entrepreneurship. Routledge, 2014

Enholm, I. M., Papagiannidis, E., Mikalef, P., & Krogstie, J. (2022). Artificial intelligence and business value: A literature review. Information Systems Frontiers, 24(5), 1709–1734

Kalia, Prateek, Navdeep Kaur, and Tejinderpal Singh. "E-Commerce in India: evolution and revolution of online retail." Mobile commerce: Concepts, methodologies, tools, and applications. IGI Global, 2018. 736–758

K. Kumar and A. Anpalagan, "5G wireless networks: A survey on technologies, applications and research challenges," Journal of Network and Computer Applications, vol. 159, pp. 102–117, Oct 2020. https://doi.org/10.1016/j.jnca.2020.06.005

Y. Li, Y. Li, C. Li, X. Li, and X. Li, "Towards energy-efficient and sustainable 5G networks: A survey," Journal of Network and Computer Applications, vol. 180, pp. 1-19, Oct. 2020 https://doi.org/10.1016/j.jnca.2020.102505

Mishra, N. (2023.). The current era of Ecommerce and its contribution to the digital economy. International Research Journal of Economics and Management Studies IRJEMS

Murphy, Antoin E. Richard Cantillon: entrepreneur and economist. Oxford University Press, 1986

Naman, M. (2022). The Effect of Changing Population and Inflation on the Indian GDP. International Journal of Trend in Scientific Research and Development, 6(5), 1573–1576

Sarasvathy, Saras D. "Effectuation: Elements of entrepreneurial expertise." Effectuation. Edward Elgar Publishing, 2008

Selamat, M. A., & Windasari, N. A. (2021). Chatbot for SMEs: Integrating customer and business owner perspectives. Technology in Society, 66, 101685

S. S. Shivsharan, B. S. Karki, and R. K. Gupta, "5G network slicing: A survey on architecture, components, and applications," Journal of Network and Computer Applications, vol. 186, pp. 1–21, Feb. 2021 https://doi.org/10.1016/j.jnca.2020.102833

Strassner, J. T., Kakkonda, M. V. K., Henze, M., Pahl, C., Banerjee, A., & Oertel, C. (2021). Securing the Industrial Internet of Things: A Review of Current Trends, Challenges, and Solutions. IEEE Internet of Things Journal, 8(3), 1917–1941 https://doi.org/10.1109/JIOT.2020.3044565

World Economic Forum. (2019). TradeLens: Building a global trade digitalization platform. Retrieved from https://www.weforum.org/reports/tradelens-building-a-global-trade-digitalization-platform

World Trade Organization & World Food Programme. (2019). Blockchain and supply chain: A catalyst for change. Retrieved from https://www.wto.org/english/res_e/booksp_e/blockchainrev18_e.pdf

Y. Yao, J. Liu, Y. Huang, H. Zhang, and Y. Xiao, "5G vehicular networks: A survey on architecture, challenges, and solutions," IEEE Communications Surveys and Tutorials, vol. 23, no. 2, pp. 1216–1251, 2021 https://doi.org/10.1109/COMST.2020.3034751

Zhang, H., Al-Shyoukh, M., & Zhang, L. (2021). Industrial internet of things: A review of enabling technologies, architecture, and applications. IEEE Internet of Things Journal, 8(1), 299–323 https://doi.org/10.1109/JIOT.2020.3024388

Strategic Imperative of Data Analytics: Empowering Informed Business Decision-Making

Muhammad Hilal, Sumbal, and Muhammad Imad

Abstract

The continuous evolution of technology is forcing companies in varying fields to keep pace and adapt accordingly. To stay competitive, businesses must successfully integrate new technologies into their strategies rather than just staying up to date with them. The present study investigates the revolutionary potential of nascent technologies and offers valuable perspectives on how commercial enterprises can efficiently exploit these technologies to attain a competitive advantage. This study investigates the transformative influence of several key emerging technologies, namely artificial intelligence (AI), blockchain, Internet of Things (IoT), and virtual reality (VR), on various business functions such as operations, marketing, customer experience, and supply chain management. Additionally, the text emphasizes the significance of taking a proactive stance towards integrating technology and offers pragmatic suggestions for entities to optimize the advantages of emerging technologies while minimizing the accompanying risks. Organizations that incorporate transformative technologies into their strategic framework can distinguish themselves as industry leaders and tap into innovative avenues for expansion.

Keywords

Business strategy · Emerging technologies · Artificial intelligence (AI) · Virtual reality (VR) · Blockchain · Internet of Things (IoT)

1 Introduction

How businesses operate and make informed decisions has undergone a significant shift due to the rise of digital technologies and the rapid expansion of data in recent times. The emergence of big data analytics has transformed the business terrain by presenting organizations with unprecedented chances to obtain valuable insights, promote creativity, and attain a competitive edge. This opening section summarises the historical backdrop of big data analytics in the corporate world, accentuates the value of decision-making based on data, and outlines the objectives and boundaries of the study (Arruda and Madhavji 2017).

The emergence of digital technologies and the exponential growth of data has brought about a remarkable transformation in how businesses function and make well-informed judgments. Big data analytics has revolutionised the business landscape, supplying organizations with unique opportunities to glean valuable insights, foster innovation, and achieve a significant advantage (Sharma et al. 2014). The initial segment of this text provides an overview of the past events leading to the emergence of big data analytics in the business industry, highlights the significance of making informed decisions supported by data, and delineates the researchs goals and limitations (Petrova et al. 2022).

In contemporary business, employing data-driven decision-making techniques has been recognized as a crucial determinant for achieving success. Conventional methods of decision-making, which rely on subjective judgments, prior expertise, and insufficient datasets are increasingly being supplanted by evidence-based practices informed by

M. Hilal (✉)
Institute of Management Science Peshawar, Peshawar, Pakistan
e-mail: Hilalakbar123@gmail.com

Sumbal
Shaheed Benazir Bhutto Women University Peshawar, Peshawar, Pakistan

M. Imad
Abasyn University Peshawar, Peshawar, Pakistan

S. Arezki et al. (eds.), *Emerging Disruptive Technologies for Society 5.0 in Developing Countries*, Advances in Science, Technology & Innovation, https://doi.org/10.1007/978-3-031-63701-8_6

rigorous data analysis (Barham 2017). Using big data analytics techniques enables organizations to arrive at informed decisions based on empirical evidence, thereby lessening uncertainty and augmenting the probability of accomplishing desired outcomes. Furthermore, the utilization of data-driven decision-making empowers organizations to reveal concealed patterns, recognize emergent trends, and leverage unexploited opportunities amid a highly dynamic and fiercely competitive market (Alsghaier 2017).

The present study aims to delve into the utilization of big data analytics in business and examine its capacity to produce valuable insights, foster data-informed decision-making, and promote innovation across diverse functional domains, including but not limited to marketing, operations, and finance. The studys objective is to offer a thorough insight into the essential principles, methodologies, and practical implementations of big data analytics in the domain of commerce. This investigation endeavors to determine the difficulties, prospects, and tactics necessary to efficiently integrate big data analytics within organizational settings by scrutinizing concrete instances and exemplars of the industrys paramount procedures. Moreover, the investigation will elucidate forthcoming patterns and ramifications related to big data analytics, augmenting the current intellectual repository within this swiftly progressing domain.

2 Big Data Analytics: Concepts and Techniques

The concept of big data pertains to datasets of remarkable size, complexity, and heterogeneity, which prove resistant to conventional modes of data management, processing, and analysis. The nomenclature "big data" is recognized for its three salient attributes: volume, velocity, and variety. The term "volume" pertains to a substantial quantity of information that originates from diverse origins, involving organized data such as databases, unorganized data such as text, images, and videos, and partially organized data such as XML and JSON. Velocity corresponds to the rate at which information is produced, accumulated, and analyzed on time, either immediately or in close proximity. The concept of variety pertains to the wide spectrum of data formats, sources, and structures, necessitating the utilization of adaptable strategies for managing data (Saleh et al. 2019).

The phenomenon of big data presents a set of distinctive features, including veracity, variability, and value. Veracity pertains to the quality and reliability of the data, whereas variability denotes the tendency of the data to exhibit inconsistent patterns. Finally, the value reflects the potential insights and benefits that can be derived from data analysis. Comprehending the traits mentioned earlier is indispensable for proficiently controlling and deriving valuable perceptions from voluminous datasets (Ebbers 2013).

2.1 Overview of Big Data Analytics Techniques

Big data analytics methodologies are used to extract discriminative intelligence, trends, and associations from voluminous datasets (Journal 2022). The methodologies employed in examining and analysing data can be classified into three distinct categories: descriptive analytics, predictive analytics, and prescriptive analytics (Fig. 1).

2.1.1 Descriptive Analytics

Predictive analytics utilizes statistical modelling, machine learning algorithms, and data mining techniques to forecast future outcomes, trends, and behaviours based on historical and real-time data. Predictive analytics enables organizations to make informed predictions and anticipate future events by analysing patterns and correlations in the data. This includes techniques such as regression analysis, time series forecasting, classification, and clustering.

2.1.2 Predictive Analytics

Predictive analytics utilizes statistical modelling, machine learning algorithms, and data mining techniques to forecast future outcomes, trends, and behaviours based on historical and real-time data. Predictive analytics enables organizations to make informed predictions and anticipate future events by analysing patterns and correlations in the data.

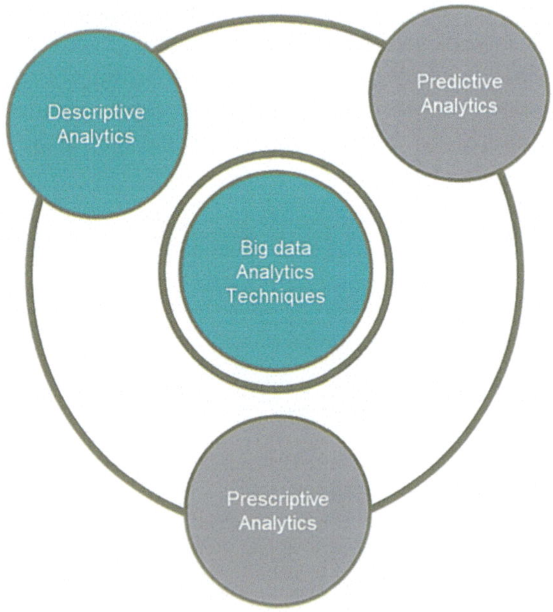

Fig. 1 Big data analytics techniques

This includes techniques such as regression analysis, time series forecasting, classification, and clustering.

2.1.3 Prescriptive Analytics

Prescriptive analytics goes beyond descriptive and predictive analytics by providing recommendations and insights on optimal courses of action. It leverages advanced optimization algorithms, simulation modeling, and decision analysis to generate actionable insights. Prescriptive analytics assists organizations in making data-driven decisions by evaluating different scenarios, identifying trade-offs, and recommending the most favorable strategies (Huang 2016).

2.2 Role of Machine Learning and Artificial Intelligence in Big Data Analytics

The utilization of machine learning (ML) and artificial intelligence (AI) has emerged as a consequential element in the analysis of large-scale data, thereby providing organizations with the means to extract significant insights and automate decision-making procedures. Machine learning algorithms assimilate patterns from data and enable predictions or actions to be carried out without explicit programming intervention. Artificial Intelligence (AI) has made significant advances due to the utilization of various techniques such as natural language processing, computer vision, and deep learning. These techniques have allowed machines to imitate various cognitive functions typical of humans and reach sound, often complex, decision-making levels.

The domain of big data analytics employs machine learning (ML) and artificial intelligence (AI) algorithms to accomplish a range of tasks, including but not limited to data classification, clustering, anomaly detection, recommendation systems, sentiment analysis, and predictive modelling. The algorithms can manage vast amounts of data, detect recurring patterns, and produce precise prognostications or discernments (Zhou et al. 2017).

3 Big Data Sources and Collection Methods

Big data can be categorized into three main types based on its structure and format (Arena and Pau 2020):

3.1 Structured Data

Structured data refers to data with a predefined format that fits into traditional databases. It is organized, easily searchable, and represented in tabular or relational formats. Examples of structured data include sales transactions, customer profiles, financial records, and inventory data.

3.2 Unstructured Data

Unstructured data refers to data that does not have a predefined format and does not fit neatly into traditional databases. It includes textual data, such as emails, social media posts, customer reviews, documents, and multimedia data, such as images, videos, and audio files. Unstructured data is typically more challenging to analyze due to its lack of structure, but it holds valuable insights that can be extracted through text mining, natural language processing, and image recognition techniques.

3.3 Semi-Structured Data

Semi-structured data lies between structured and unstructured data. It has some organizational structure but does not adhere to a strict schema. Examples of semi-structured data include XML files, JSON files, and log files. Semi-structured data often requires preprocessing and transformation before analysis.

3.4 Data Collection Methods

Organizations collect big data from various internal and external sources to gain a comprehensive view of their operations and the external environment (Harwood and Vang 2009). Some common data collection methods include (Fig. 2):

3.4.1 Internal Data

Internal data refers to the data generated within an organizations systems and processes. It includes transactional data, customer data, employee data, financial data, and operational data. Internal data is typically structured and stored in databases or data warehouses. Organizations can extract valuable insights from internal data by performing data mining, statistical analysis, and other data analytics techniques.

3.4.2 External Data

External data comes from sources outside the organization. It includes publicly available data, such as government databases, public APIs, market research reports, and industry benchmarks. External data can provide valuable context and external benchmarks for analysis. Organizations can integrate external and internal data to gain a broader perspective and make more informed decisions.

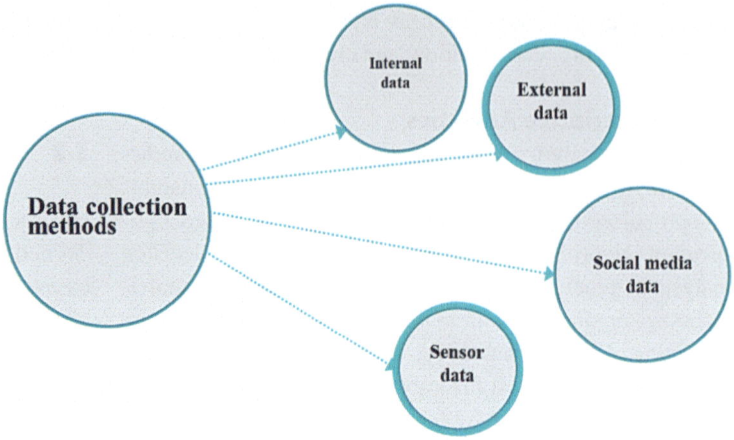

Fig. 2 Data collection sources

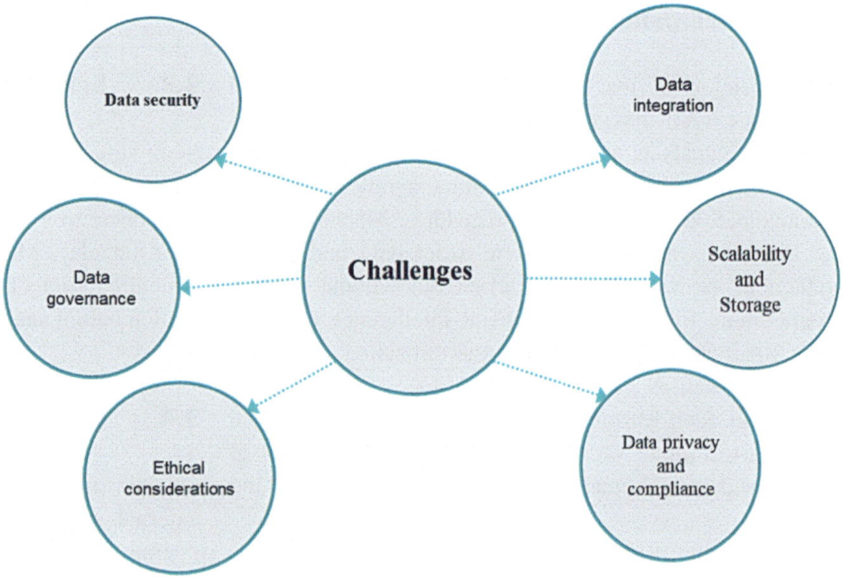

Fig. 3 Challenges and considerations in data collection

3.4.3 Social Media Data

Social media platforms generate vast amounts of data in posts, comments, likes, shares, and user profiles. Social media data provides valuable insights into customer sentiments, preferences, and trends. Organizations can collect social media data using APIs from platforms like Twitter, Facebook, and Instagram. Text mining and sentiment analysis techniques can be applied to social media data for brand monitoring, customer feedback analysis, and market research purposes.

3.4.4 Sensor Data

With the proliferation of Internet of Things (IoT) devices, organizations can collect data from various sensors embedded in physical objects. Sensor data includes information from temperature sensors, GPS devices, accelerometers, and RFID tags. This data can be used to monitor and optimise processes, predict maintenance needs, and improve operational efficiency (Ramírez-Gallego et al. 2017).

3.5 Challenges and Considerations in Data Collection and Preprocessing

Collecting and preprocessing big data pose several challenges and require careful considerations, as mentioned in Fig. 3:

3.5.1 Data Quality and Reliability

Big data sources may contain errors, missing values, duplicates, and inconsistencies. Ensuring data quality and reliability is crucial to obtain accurate insights. Data cleansing techniques, such as data deduplication, data validation, and outlier detection, are employed to address data quality issues.

3.5.2 Data Integration

Integrating data from various sources with different formats and structures can be complex. Data integration involves mapping and transforming data from different sources into a unified format, enabling seamless analysis. Data integration techniques, such as data merging, transformation, and normalization, are applied to ensure compatibility and consistency across datasets.

3.5.3 Scalability and Storage

Big data is characterized by volume, and storing and processing large datasets can be challenging. Organizations need to invest in scalable storage systems and computing infrastructure capable of handling the volume and velocity of data. Cloud computing platforms and distributed storage systems, such as Hadoop and Spark, are commonly used to address scalability requirements.

3.5.4 Data Privacy and Compliance

Collecting and analyzing big data must comply with relevant privacy regulations and ethical considerations. Organizations must ensure that data collection methods and processes align with privacy policies, obtain necessary consent when dealing with personal data, and anonymize or encrypt sensitive information to protect privacy.

3.5.5 Data Security

Big data poses security risks, and organizations must implement robust security measures to protect data from unauthorized access, breaches, and cyber threats. Encryption, access controls, secure data transfer protocols, and regular security audits are essential to maintain data security.

3.5.6 Data Governance

Establishing effective data governance practices is crucial for managing big data. Organizations need to define data ownership, data stewardship roles, data governance policies and establish processes for data management, data quality assurance, and data lifecycle management.

3.5.7 Ethical Considerations

Organizations should consider ethical implications when collecting and analyzing big data, such as potential biases, discrimination, and unintended consequences. Ethical frameworks and guidelines can help organizations ensure responsible and ethical use of data throughout the analytics process (Fan et al. 2021).

4 Big Data Analytics Applications in Marketing

Big data analytics has revolutionized the marketing field by enabling organizations to gain deeper insights into customer behavior, preferences, and sentiments. Here are three key applications of big data analytics in marketing (Research on the Application of Big Data Analytics in Corporate Marketing 2022):

4.1 Personalization and Targeted Marketing

The utilization of big data analytics empowers organizations to customize marketing activities and disseminate focused messages to individual consumers. Establishments can establish intricate customer profiles through comprehensive analysis of vast quantities of customer data, encompassing previous transactions, browsing patterns, demographics, and engagements with the brand. These profiles facilitate the identification of distinct customer requirements, inclinations, and predilections, empowering organizations to customize marketing communications, propositions, and suggestions that cater to individual customers. The implementation of personalized marketing strategies has been observed to impact customer engagement levels positively, significantly increase the rate of conversion, and serve to develop stronger customer loyalty over time (Erevelles et al. 2016).

4.2 Customer Segmentation and Behaviour Analysis

Implementing big data analytics facilitates efficient segmentation of organizational customer bases, while affording valuable insights and a comprehensive understanding of individual customer segments. By scrutinising consumer data, organizations can discern recurring attributes, inclinations, and conduct amongst particular sections. Segmentation assists organizations in formulating precise marketing strategies by allowing them to customize their products, services, and promotional activities to cater to the distinct requirements of each segment. Analyzing customer behaviour, specifically examining purchase patterns, product preferences, and responsiveness to marketing campaigns, facilitates comprehension of customer motivations and enables organizations to optimize their marketing endeavours (Choi et al. 2017).

4.3 Sentiment Analysis and Social Media Analytics

The utilization of big data analytics enhances the ability of organizations to conduct an in-depth analysis of customer sentiments and opinions conveyed through various channels such as social media platforms, online reviews, and other forms of customer feedback. Sentiment analysis methodologies, such as those employed in natural language processing and text mining, facilitate an organizations capacity to ascertain the prevailing customer sentiment regarding its brand, merchandise, or amenities, delineating whether this is favourable, unfavourable, or neutral. Through integrating social media monitoring tools and analysing sentiment trends, entities can effectively detect and address emerging matters, cater to customer inquiries, and take preemptive measures to maintain a positive perception of their brand. Social media analysis enables organizations to gain valuable insights regarding customer predilections, trends, and influencers, thus enabling them to modify their marketing strategies and maintain a competitive edge (Ge et al. 2022).

5 Big Data Analytics Applications in Operations

Big data analytics has significant applications in optimizing operations and improving efficiency in various industries. Here are three key applications of big data analytics in operations (Grefen et al. 2021):

5.1 Supply Chain Optimization

Through big data analytics, organizations can optimize their supply chain operations by analyzing extensive amounts of information from various sources. Organizations may acquire real-time visibility into their supply chain processes by integrating data from suppliers, logistics providers, and proprietary systems. The enhanced level of visibility facilitates more precise demand projection, efficient inventory control, and effective logistics strategizing. Implementing big data analytics can equip organizations to detect patterns, trends, and bottlenecks in the supply chain. This, in turn, facilitates informed decision-making founded on data-driven insights, intending to decrease costs, enhance delivery times, and heighten the overall effectiveness of the supply chain (Lee and Mangalaraj 2022).

5.2 Predictive Maintenance and Asset Management

The utilization of big data analytics is of utmost importance in predictive maintenance and asset management, particularly in industries that involve intricate machinery and equipment. Organizations can identify equipment malfunctions or maintenance requirements by analyzing the information gathered from sensors, machine logs, and past maintenance records. This is achieved by detecting patterns and anomalies. The use of predictive analytics algorithms helps organizations anticipate equipment failure or maintenance needs, allowing them to plan for maintenance and reduce unexpected downtime proactively. This strategy enhances the efficiency of asset usage, curtails the expenses of maintenance, and betters the overall functioning proficiency.

5.3 Quality Control and Process Optimization

By utilizing big data analytics, organizations can upgrade their quality control procedures and maximize the efficiency of their manufacturing and operational processes. By gathering and examining diverse data sources such as sensors, production records, and quality control checkpoints, entities can pinpoint elements that influence both the caliber of their products and the effectiveness of their processes. Employing big data analytics methods including statistical process control, root cause analysis, and anomaly detection, facilitates the prompt recognition of defects, variances, and ineffectiveness. By utilizing data, organizations can effectively make decisions supported by evidence, resolve any problems, enhance their operations, and maintain the quality of their products at a constant level (Liu et al. 2020).

6 Big Data Analytics Applications in Finance

Big data analytics has revolutionized the finance industry by providing powerful tools and techniques to analyze large volumes of financial data. Here are three key applications of big data analytics in finance:

6.1 Fraud Detection and Risk Management

The finance industry depends heavily on big data analytics for detecting fraud and managing risks effectively. By examining extensive financial transactions, customer information, and external data sources, businesses can detect signs of fraudulent behaviour by recognizing trends and unusual occurrences. Sophisticated analytics methods, including utilising machine learning algorithms and detecting unusual patterns, enable companies to identify and avert dishonest transactions promptly. By examining past data, market tendencies, and other pertinent elements, big data analytics aids corporations in evaluating and curtailing hazards. Organizations can mitigate financial losses and safeguard assets by anticipating potential risks and implementing preventive measures (Tekaya et al. 2020).

6.2 Financial Forecasting and Predictive Analytics

Big data analytics enables organizations to leverage historical financial data, market data, and other relevant factors to perform accurate financial forecasting and predictive analytics. Organizations can develop predictive models that forecast financial performance, market trends, and customer behavior by analysing historical trends and patterns. This enables organizations to make informed investment strategies, capital allocation, and financial planning decisions. Big data analytics also helps in scenario analysis and stress testing, allowing organizations to assess the potential impact of different market conditions and adjust accordingly (Eltweri and Khassawneh 2021).

6.3 Customer Analytics and Cross-Selling Opportunities

Implementing big data analytics allows financial organizations to obtain extensive insights into their clienteles behaviour, preferences, and requirements. By analysing diverse customer data sources, such as transactional records, demographic information, and online behavioral patterns, organizations can aptly partition their customer base and detect opportunities for cross-selling. Comprehending consumers necessities and inclinations enables institutions to tailor their products and promotional initiatives, resulting in enhanced customer contentment and augmented potential for cross-selling and upselling. The implementation of big data analytics empowers businesses to enhance customer retention by identifying customers who are at a higher risk of churn and deploying increasingly tailored retention strategies (Nobanee 2021).

In light of the points mentioned earlier, it can be affirmed that the utilization of big data analytics has brought about a substantial alteration in the finance sector by providing potent apparatuses and methodologies dedicated to the identification of fraudulent activities, mitigation of risks, projection of financial trends as well as analysis of customer behaviour. Using big data enables organizations to make informed decisions, reduce risks, optimize operational efficacy, and augment customer experiences within the finance domain (Khan 2019).

7 Challenges and Limitations of Big Data Analytics

While big data analytics offers immense potential and benefits, organisations must address several challenges and limitations. Here are three key challenges associated with big data analytics (Gomathy 2023):

7.1 Data Privacy and Security Concerns

The increasing quantity and diversity of data being amassed engender notable apprehensions regarding the privacy and security of data. Organizations must implement adequate measures to safeguard sensitive information against unauthorized access, breaches, and misuse. The upholding of privacy regulations, notably the GDPR (General Data Protection Regulation), is paramount in fostering confidence amongst customers and stakeholders. Organizations must adopt rigorous data security measures encompassing encryption, access controls, and secure data transfer protocols, to ensure the confidentiality and integrity of sensitive data.

7.2 Ethical Considerations in Data Usage

Big data analytics raises ethical considerations related to the use of data, potential biases, and unintended consequences. Organizations must be mindful of the ethical implications of their data analytics activities and ensure responsible and ethical use of data. This includes addressing issues of data bias, discrimination, and transparency. Establishing ethical frameworks, guidelines, and governance processes can help organizations navigate these ethical challenges and ensure data analytics is conducted ethically and responsibly.

7.3 Scalability and Infrastructure Requirements

Big data analytics requires significant computational power and infrastructure to handle the volume, velocity, and variety of data. Organizations must invest in scalable storage systems, high-performance computing resources, and data processing technologies to effectively handle big data. Cloud computing platforms and distributed storage systems like Hadoop and Spark can help address scalability requirements. However, building and maintaining the necessary infrastructure can be costly and complex, requiring expertise and ongoing investment.

7.4 Data Quality and Data Integration

The efficacy of big data analytics is contingent on the high caliber of the data subject to analysis. Ensuring data quality, encompassing precision, entirety, and uniformity, presents a formidable obstacle in light of vast datas heterogeneous and intricate aspects. Combining data from various sources, encompassing structured, unstructured, and semi-structured formats, can present a formidable challenge, necessitating the implementation of techniques such as cleansing, transformation, and normalization to ensure the integrity of the resulting dataset. Implementing data governance practices, data quality assurance mechanisms, and data integration strategies is imperative for organizations to confront these obstacles and guarantee dependable and precise analyses.

8 Strategies for Successful Implementation of Big Data Analytics

Implementing big data analytics effectively requires a strategic approach and organizational support. Here are three key strategies for the successful implementation of big data analytics (Al-Sai et al. 2019):

8.1 Building a Data-Driven Culture Within Organizations

Creating a data-driven culture is essential for successfully implementing big data analytics. It fosters a mindset where data is valued and data-driven decision-making is embraced across all levels of the organization. To build a data-driven culture, organizations should:

8.2 Talent Acquisition and Training for Data Analytics

Acquiring and developing the right talent is crucial for successfully implementing big data analytics. Organizations should focus on:

8.3 Data Governance and Data Quality Management

Data governance and data quality management are fundamental for the success of big data analytics initiatives. Organizations should:

Define policies, procedures, and guidelines for data management, access, usage, and security. This ensures data is properly managed, protected, and compliant with relevant regulations.

Implement data quality management practices, including data cleansing, validation, and integration processes. This helps ensure the accuracy, consistency, and reliability of the data used for analysis.

Develop a robust data infrastructure that supports data storage, integration, and processing capabilities to handle large volumes of data effectively. By building a data-driven culture, acquiring and training the right talent, and implementing robust data governance and quality management practices, organizations can lay a strong foundation for the successful implementation of big data analytics. These strategies will enable organizations to effectively leverage data analytics to drive informed decision-making, gain competitive advantage, and achieve business goals.

9 Conclusion

In conclusion, the strategic imperative of data analytics in empowering informed business decision-making is undeniable. Big data analytics has revolutionized the business landscape, providing organizations unprecedented opportunities to extract valuable insights, drive innovation, and gain a competitive advantage. Throughout this research, we have explored various aspects of big data analytics, including its background, concepts, techniques, and applications in different functional areas of business.

The utilization of big data analytics exhibits a wide range of applications in functional areas such as marketing, operations, and finance, which facilitate personalization, optimization, and risk management. The successful implementation of big data analytics necessitates undertaking various challenges, including data privacy, ethical considerations, and the scalability of infrastructures.

In conclusion, utilising big data analytics offers significant prospects for organizations to leverage data as a fundamental strategic resource. Organizations can fully leverage the potential of big data analytics and advance informed business decision-making in a progressively data-driven world by adopting a data-centric strategy, dedicating resources to talent development and infrastructure enhancement, and proactively deliberating ethical implications. Ongoing advancement in research and development within this domain shall result in enhanced comprehension and utilization of big data analytics, culminating in ingenious resolutions and better commercial and business outcomes.

References

Z. A. Al-Sai, R. Abdullah, and M. H. Husin, "Big Data Impacts and Challenges: A Review," in 2019 IEEE Jordan International Joint Conference on Electrical Engineering and Information Technology (JEEIT), Amman, Jordan: IEEE, Apr. 2019, pp. 150–155. https://doi.org/10.1109/JEEIT.2019.8717484.

H. Alsghaier, "The Importance of Big Data Analytics in Business: A Case Study," AJSEA, vol. 6, no. 4, p. 111, 2017, https://doi.org/10.11648/j.ajsea.20170604.12.

F. Arena and G. Pau, "An overview of big data analysis," Bulletin EEI, vol. 9, no. 4, pp. 1646–1653, Aug. 2020, https://doi.org/10.11591/eei.v9i4.2359.

D. Arruda and N. H. Madhavji, "The Role of Big Data Analytics in Corporate Decision-making:," in Proceedings of the 6th

International Conference on Data Science, Technology and Applications, Madrid, Spain: SCITEPRESS - Science and Technology Publications, 2017, pp. 28–37. https://doi.org/10.5220/0006402300280037.

H. Barham, "Achieving Competitive Advantage Through Big Data: A Literature Review," in 2017 Portland International Conference on Management of Engineering and Technology (PICMET), Portland, OR: IEEE, Jul. 2017, pp. 1–7. https://doi.org/10.23919/PICMET.2017.8125459.

T.-M. Choi, H. K. Chan, and X. Yue, "Recent Development in Big Data Analytics for Business Operations and Risk Management," IEEE Trans. Cybern., vol. 47, no. 1, pp. 81–92, Jan. 2017, https://doi.org/10.1109/TCYB.2015.2507599.

M. Ebbers, Addressing data volume, velocity, and variety with IBM InfoSphere Streams V3.0, 1st ed. United States: IBM, International Technical Support Organization, 2013.

Eltweri, A. Faccia, and O. Khassawneh, "Applications of Big Data within Finance: Fraud Detection and Risk Management within the Real Estate Industry," in 2021 3rd International Conference on E-Business and E-commerce Engineering, Sanya China: ACM, Dec. 2021, pp. 67–73. https://doi.org/10.1145/3510249.3510262.

S. Erevelles, N. Fukawa, and L. Swayne, "Big Data consumer analytics and the transformation of marketing," Journal of Business Research, vol. 69, no. 2, pp. 897–904, Feb. 2016, https://doi.org/10.1016/j.jbusres.2015.07.001.

C. Fan, M. Chen, X. Wang, J. Wang, and B. Huang, "A Review on Data Preprocessing Techniques Toward Efficient and Reliable Knowledge Discovery From Building Operational Data," Front. Energy Res., vol. 9, p. 652801, Mar. 2021, https://doi.org/10.3389/fenrg.2021.652801.

L. Ge, T. Du, C. Li, Y. Li, J. Yan, and M. Rafiq, "Virtual Collection for Distributed Photovoltaic Data: Challenges, Methodologies, and Applications," Energies, vol. 15, no. 23, p. 8783, Nov. 2022, https://doi.org/10.3390/en15238783.

Department of Information technology, SCSVMV, Kanchipuram and Dr. C. K. Gomathy, "A Survey on Big Data Analytics: Challenges, Open Research Issues and Tools," IJSREM, vol. 07, no. 01, Jan. 2023, https://doi.org/10.55041/IJSREM16959.

P. Grefen, A. Wilbik, F. Kuitems, and M. Blanken, "Outcome-Based Business Design in IoT-Enabled Digital Supply Chain Transformation," in 2021 IEEE International Conference on Internet of Things and Intelligence Systems (IoTaIS), Bandung, Indonesia: IEEE, Nov. 2021, pp. 28–34. https://doi.org/10.1109/IoTaIS53735.2021.9628770.

E. M. Harwood and P. Vang, "Data Collection Methods Series: Part 1: Define a Clear Purpose for Collecting Data," Journal of Wound, Ostomy & Continence Nursing, vol. 36, no. 1, pp. 15–20, Jan. 2009, https://doi.org/10.1097/01.WON.0000345172.28246.7a.

J. Huang, "Cloud Services Platform based on Big Data Analytics and its Application in Livestock Management and Marketing," in Proceedings of The fourth International Conference on Information Science and Cloud Computing — PoS(ISCC2015), Guangzhou, China: Sissa Medialab, Feb. 2016, p. 063. https://doi.org/10.22323/1.264.0063.

Journal, "BIG DATA ANALYTICS: A LITERATURE REVIEW PAPER," IJSREM, vol. 06, no. 06, Jun. 2022, https://doi.org/10.55041/IJSREM14243.

M. Khan, "Challenges with big data analytics in service supply chains in the UAE," MD, vol. 57, no. 8, pp. 2124–2147, Sep. 2019, https://doi.org/10.1108/MD-06-2018-0669.

Lee and G. Mangalaraj, "Big Data Analytics in Supply Chain Management: A Systematic Literature Review and Research Directions," BDCC, vol. 6, no. 1, p. 17, Feb. 2022, https://doi.org/10.3390/bdcc6010017.

J. Liu, M. Chen, and H. Liu, "The role of big data analytics in enabling green supply chain management: a literature review," J. of Data, Inf. and Manag., vol. 2, no. 2, pp. 75–83, Jun. 2020, https://doi.org/10.1007/s42488-019-00020-z.

H. Nobanee, "A Bibliometric Review of Big Data in Finance," Big Data, vol. 9, no. 2, pp. 73–78, Apr. 2021, https://doi.org/10.1089/big.2021.29044.edi.

M. Petrova, P. Popova, V. Popov, K. Shishmanov, and K. Marinova, "Potential of Big Data Analytics for Managing Value Creation," in 2022 International Conference on Communications, Information, Electronic and Energy Systems (CIEES), Veliko Tarnovo, Bulgaria: IEEE, Nov. 2022, pp. 1–6. https://doi.org/10.1109/CIEES55704.2022.9990882.

S. Ramírez-Gallego, B. Krawczyk, S. García, M. Woźniak, and F. Herrera, "A survey on data preprocessing for data stream mining: Current status and future directions," Neurocomputing, vol. 239, pp. 39–57, May 2017, https://doi.org/10.1016/j.neucom.2017.01.078.

"Research on the Application of Big Data Analytics in Corporate Marketing," acccm, vol. 4, no. 4, 2022, https://doi.org/10.23977/acccm.2022.040409.

S. H. Saleh, R. Ismail, Z. Ibrahim, and N. Hussin, "Issues, Challenges and Solutions of Big Data in Information Management: An Overview," IJARBSS, vol. 8, no. 12, p. Pages 1382–1393, Jan. 2019, https://doi.org/10.6007/IJARBSS/v8-i12/5240.

R. Sharma, S. Mithas, and A. Kankanhalli, "Transforming decision-making processes: a research agenda for understanding the impact of business analytics on organisations," European Journal of Information Systems, vol. 23, no. 4, pp. 433–441, Jul. 2014, https://doi.org/10.1057/ejis.2014.17.

B. Tekaya, S. E. Feki, T. Tekaya, and H. Masri, "Recent applications of big data in finance," in Proceedings of the 2nd International Conference on Digital Tools & Uses Congress, Virtual Event Tunisia: ACM, Oct. 2020, pp. 1–6. https://doi.org/10.1145/3423603.3424056.

L. Zhou, S. Pan, J. Wang, and A. V. Vasilakos, "Machine learning on big data: Opportunities and challenges," Neurocomputing, vol. 237, pp. 350–361, May 2017, https://doi.org/10.1016/j.neucom.2017.01.026.

Too Big to Fail in Real Estate Development in Saudi Arabia

Rahul Deo Gupta, Liza Gernal, and Abhijit Ganguly

Abstract

Having a good strategy by itself does not guarantee the success of an Organisation in achieving its strategic objectives without the successful execution of the strategy (Srivastava and Sushil in Int. J. Product. Perform. Manag. 66:1043–1063, 2017). The challenge faced by business executives is not in formulating a strategy but in executing it (Blahová in Sci. Pap. Univ. Pardubice Ser. Fac. Econ. Adm. (16):26–31, 2010) which has been recognised as a major challenge for many organisations (MacLennan and Markides in Calif. Manage. Rev. 63:89–122, 2021). Research shows that 67% of organisations failed during strategy execution (Carucci in Executives Fail to Execute Strategy Because They're Too Internally Focused. https://hbr.org/2017/11/executives-fail-to-execute-strategy-because-theyre-too-internally-focused) and up to 75% of large organisations have faced problems during strategy execution (Sull et al. in Why Strategy Execution Unravels—and What to Do About It. https://hbr.org/2015/03/why-strategy-execution-unravel-sand-what-to-do-about-it) resulting in significant opportunity costs (Safdari Ranjbar et al. in J. Strategy Manag. 7:127–154, 2014) and Real estate development organisations in Saudi Arabia are not an exception to this. There is a literature gap as no literature is available on strategy implementation or the study of strategy execution failures in real estate development organisations in Saudi Arabia. This research was conducted using a quantitative methods approach using surveys. Participants from 20 (out of 123) real estate development organisations (Real Estates Companies—Business Directory. http://www.eyeofriyadh.com/directory/category/14_real-estates-companies) were approached using expert sampling followed by snowball sampling to gather survey data from 184 participants. Results were analysed using descriptive and inferential analysis with the aid of online using DataTab.net. This research was conducted using surveys. Participants from 20 (out of 123) real estate development organisations (Real Estates Companies—Business Directory. http://www.eyeofriyadh.com/directory/category/14_real-estates-companies) were approached using expert sampling followed by snowball sampling to gather survey data from 184 participants. The findings of the survey confirmed that the nine strategy execution hurdles were applicable to the real estate development organisations in Saudi Arabia and the implementation of the Balanced Scorecard Management System could help these industries to overcome these hurdles. Considering the gap in the body of knowledge, the researcher's original contribution to knowledge is the finding that there are nine strategy execution hurdles applicable to industries and geographies across the globe which apply to the real estate development organisations in Saudi Arabia. The nine strategy execution hurdles fall into three categories: Category 1—Related to Planning: (1) Non-involvement of the workforce, (2) Unclear strategic choices/ objectives, and (3) Rigid plan; Category 2—Related to Execution: (4) Misalignment, (5) Poor communication, (6) Ineffective initiatives management, and (7) Unclear responsibilities and accountabilities; and Category 3—Related to Enablers: (8) Improper change management, and (9) No strategy management framework.

Keywords

Strategy · Strategy execution · Execution hurdles · Real estate development · Saudi Arabia

R. D. Gupta (✉)
UCAM, Murcia, Spain
e-mail: rahul_deo_gupta@yahoo.com

L. Gernal · A. Ganguly
Westford University College, Sharjah, UAE

S. Arezki et al. (eds.), *Emerging Disruptive Technologies for Society 5.0 in Developing Countries*,
Advances in Science, Technology & Innovation, https://doi.org/10.1007/978-3-031-63701-8_7

1 Introduction

Organisations are known to formulate good strategies. However, many organisations have failed during strategy execution (Carucci 2017; Sull et al. 2015) resulting in significant opportunity costs (Safdari Ranjbar et al. 2014). Employees become disheartened, leadership loses credibility, and the company may be put in jeopardy when an organisation is unable to execute (Richard Panico 2019).

Strategy planning is a complex process but implementing it is even more challenging. Implementing the planned strategy is harder for many organisations (Harandi and Fatemi 2020) as strategy execution requires the organisations to dedicate more time and effort as compared to strategy planning (Blahová 2010) making it more difficult than the planning process (Lawrence 2005). It is thus important to understand the strategy execution hurdles so that they can be addressed to reap the full benefits of strategy execution.

The research was conducted with two objectives: 1) Assess the reasons for strategy execution failure and 2) Appraise the extent of strategy execution failure in real estate development in Saudi Arabia.

2 Literature Review

The literature review was conducted keeping in mind the positivist deductive approach (Crowther and Lancaster 2012) of this research with the aim of exploring research objective 1 (Assess the reasons for strategy execution failure).

The importance of understanding the strategy execution hurdles can be understood by the fact that the hurdles not only hamper the strategy execution on their own, but they can interact with each other and form dynamic and complex interrelated systems reinforcing each other and developing blockage chains. Strategy implementation hurdles play a vital role in affecting strategy execution as they are a result of internal and external events that impact strategy execution by either modifying or impeding the execution of the initial strategic intent of an organisation. The hurdles may modify the original intent of the strategy causing it to be partially implemented as planned or they may totally prevent the strategic intent to be implemented. The strategy execution hurdles impact strategy execution by (1) accumulation of the hurdles by hurdles that are independent and unrelated; (2) individual hurdles interaction with each other by hurdles that coexist concurrently and reinforce themselves; and (3) creating other new hurdles by hurdles which occur in time but are related through some function or some logic (Sharma and Sharma 2022). Cândido and Santos (2015) observe that many managers are of the opinion that strategy implementation is far more difficult than strategy planning. They state that 73% of the managers think that strategy implementation is more difficult, 82% believe that the time taken for strategy implementation is more, and 82% admit that strategy execution is the part of strategy over which they have the least control.

Strategy execution is a very crucial, complicated, and complex process in all organisations and many fail during execution even when they have been planned well which calls for an additional push from the management to make it a success (Sharma and Sharma 2022). They state that strategy execution is affected by many environmental factors, both from within and outside. They further note that the attention of the experts has seen a shift to focus on the organisation's internal environment as a factor that influences a firm's ability to execute strategy.

This research focuses on the business context of real estate development organisations in Saudi Arabia. There are different forms of real estate development. Mixed-use development is one of the popular and efficient strategies for real estate development in urban redevelopment programmes or high-density city development. Mixed-use projects have helped high-density cities use land efficiently in recent decades. Vertical mixed-use construction, in which different uses are vertically dispersed inside the same building, is gaining popularity. Mixed-use development refers to horizontal or form-based zoning where the planning agency combines land uses in one administrative area. Commercial and residential zones are planned in the same district allowing residents to shorten their commutes. A district comprising retail and residential establishments can boost its accessibility and desirability with some zones having flexible land use. In these zones, the developer can predetermine land use proportions based on market conditions (Zhong and Hui 2021).

The word strategy owes its origin to the Greek word strategía or strategiké. The word refers to the art or the skills mastered by the general who would practice strategy. Strategy is a concerted action plan that develops a business' competitive advantage while compounding it further and calls for an all-encompassing dedication and commitment from everyone in an organisation (Henderson 1989). Business strategy is something unique to an organisation for achieving a set of objectives that cannot be attained only through the daily activities of a manager (Ansoff 1965). It is a part of the organisation's hard management (Waterman et al. 1980), and is a continuous process that is one of the basic building blocks of strategy management (Kant et al. 2008). Work on strategy by Michael Porter in the 1980s gives a further clear and accepted definition of strategy.

Concepts of strategy were addressed in the latter half of the twentieth century with much scholarly research being carried out on strategy formulation. However, commensurate knowledge about executing the strategy and reaping the full benefits from the implementation of the strategy is limited (Pella et al. 2013).

A good strategy is essential; however, it does not guarantee the success of an organisation in achieving its objectives unless it is executed (Srivastava and Sushil 2017). Strategy execution is considered to be one of the major problems faced by businesses, and the challenge for most executives is not in formulating a strategy but in executing it (Blahová 2010). Industries recognise strategy execution as a major challenge for organisations (MacLennan and Markides Aug. 2021).

Although the creation of a strategic plan and policies is a complicated process, it is even more challenging and harder to implement (Harandi and Fatemi 2020). Strategy execution generally requires more time than strategy planning (Blahová 2010) thus making it more difficult than planning itself (Lawrence 2005).

Research shows that many strategies (67% in 2016) often failed during execution (Carucci 2017) and 67–75% of large organisations face problems during strategy execution (Sull et al. 2015). Since the strategic objectives of an organisation cannot be achieved without effective strategy execution, poor execution can result in significant opportunity costs (Safdari Ranjbar et al. 2014).

Research by Cândido and Santos (2015), details that the failure rates of strategy implementation have a wide variation from 7 to 90%. They explain that the variation in the study by different authors can be attributed to factors such as overestimating the strategy outcome, varying environmental factors of the organisations, the definition of success by the organisations, and the methodologies used by the researchers. The variations in the failure rates are also attributed to the different research objectives of the researchers. They warn against the use of the high failure rate estimated at 70–90% for designing or taking action either managerially or academically as the standards of measuring true strategy execution failures are not established.

The test of the strategy is in the results delivered against the organisational strategic objectives and goals through its execution. Thus, it is important to understand the reasons for the failure during strategy execution and take countermeasures.

The literature review concluded that the factors impeding effective and required strategy execution can be broadly classified into three buckets: (1) Planning, (2) Execution, and (3) Enablers as shown in Fig. 1.

Each of these factors has been discussed below.

2.1 Non-Involvement of the Workforce

The phases of strategic management that are devoted to the creation and execution of strategies are distinct from one another. In a manner consistent with logic, formulation comes before implementation; one cannot implement anything before that something already exists. But the formulation and execution of a plan are also interdependent on one another, and together they form part of the larger process of planning, executing, and adapting. Because of this connection, having the planners and those who execute together can increase the likelihood of successful execution. Knowledge transfer, dedication to the outcomes that are desired, and the entire process of implementation are all put in jeopardy when individuals responsible for execution are not included in the planning phase (Blahová 2010).

The general practice of most organisations is to conduct strategic planning by the top management with minimal involvement of the workforce at all levels. In doing so, the top management ignores the interdependency between strategy planning and execution, as the people responsible for the strategy execution are not involved during the planning process. Not involving the people responsible for strategy execution mars the knowledge transfer and commitment of

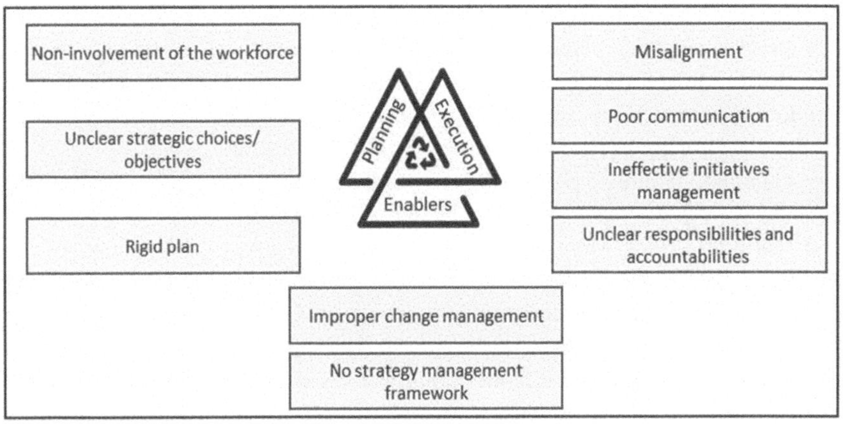

Fig. 1 Factors impacting strategy. *Source* processed information from literature review

the workforce, which eventually jeopardizes the entire strategy execution (Lawrence 2005). Strategy planning requires data and if the workforce at all levels is not involved during the planning process; the data received at the top is filtered at different levels resulting in improper information reaching the top for planning purposes (Blahová 2010). The strategy thus planned will suffer from inaccurate assumptions and strategic hypotheses.

Many organisations use consultants to construct strategic plans instead of thinking and listening to the workforce. The consultants advise the organisation (their client) based on the assumption of what is good for the client and what their understanding is about what the client is capable and willing to do (Blahová 2010). However, effective strategy execution requires the involvement of managers at all hierarchical levels (Lawrence 2005) and middle management who run business-critical functions (Sull et al. 2015). The rich knowledge specific to the organisation is often lost in the process which the consultants cannot be aware of. Some of the top management rushes to finish the strategic planning through a limited-time workshop (often a half-day session) involving a handful of team members and creating communication maps to be given to the workforce the next day. Sometimes it's unrealistic to include many individuals in a workshop. However, developing a strategy execution plan is not a one-time event, but a sequence of interactions over a period of time (MacLennan and Markides 2021). This approach to strategic planning limits the opportunity for participation of the required workforce.

2.2 Unclear Strategic Choices/Objectives

Many strategies do not see the light of execution and fail because the strategies do not portray some clear set of choices made by the organisation (Vermeulen 2017). Many organisational senior leaders mistake goals for strategy which are vague and not clearly articulated strategic choices.

One key component of a strategy is the ability of the management to make strategic choices. The strategy plan is non-functional if the top management is unable to identify the organisation's playing field and how they intend to win in the said playing field. The combination of both is required, however, they are often overlooked resulting in ineffective strategy execution (Blahová 2010). While strategy planning, failure to make strategic trade-offs and set strategic priorities cause execution failures (MacLennan and Markides 2021). More often than not chief executives are internally focused while making strategic choices which causes them to fail during strategy execution (Carucci 2017). Scanning the business environment while making strategic choices and trade-offs are required for successful strategy formulation and subsequent execution.

Organisations are required to take a holistic view and orchestrate a strategy that encompasses the strategic choices including the business model, and the competitive positioning incorporating implementation processes that are adaptive enough to adapt to the constantly changing business environment (Collis 2021). Without clear strategic objectives and choices, it becomes difficult to link the day-to-day objectives at various levels and locations within the organisation which leads to strategy execution failure (Lawrence 2005). Clear strategic choices are the cornerstone for the allocation of the strategic budget and other resources vital for not only the day-to-day running of the business but also for executing the strategy.

2.3 Rigid Plan

For a long time, many top managements have been hit hard by the notion that execution is sticking to the plan, and deviation from the plan is thought of as indiscipline which may even hamper execution. Lack of clarity of the execution hurdles during planning adds uncertainty to the entire process (MacLennan and Markides 2021). However good the strategic plan may be, no organisation can anticipate all the developments that may either positively or negatively impact the execution during the planning stage itself (Sull et al. 2015). Today's businesses is characterised by events changing in the environment attributed mainly to the changes due to changes in technology in a blink of an eye. This requires the strategic plan to be flexible and agile enough to accommodate real-time changes.

Control systems, using feedback from market developments, should be used by the management to adjust the plan accordingly. A dynamic adaptive execution process capable of adjusting to unanticipated events can bring the strategy execution on track (Blahová 2010). Adaptation of the plan while executing the strategy based on the iterative process of using hypothesis, conducting experimentation, learning in the process, and taking action is required for successful strategy execution (Collis 2021).

However, managers should not go astray to pick up on every opportunity that comes their way as an excuse of being agile (Sull et al. 2015) and adaptive.

2.4 Misalignment

Alignment of organisational structures, enterprise processes, and systems to support the strategy execution is important during the execution of the strategy. Alignment is effective when the high-level organisational strategy is cascaded to business units, departments, and individuals (Rohm et al. 2013). Although the alignment of the strategy seems obvious and straightforward, research points to many companies failing to link the business and the shared services units to the divisional and the corporate level strategy (Kaplan and Norton 2001). Organisation structure, a key component of strategic alignment is often designed in isolation from the strategic goals and is not aligned with the strategy (Gorzelany 2020).

On the other hand, many executives believe that alignment is sufficient for execution. They believe that converting strategy into objectives, cascading these objectives down the organisation, measuring progress thereof, and rewarding those who perform is enough for strategy execution. However, this process does not take into consideration the trust factors across teams for the strategy execution. A study by Sull et al. (2015) shows that 84% of managers stated that they can rely on their team and their members for commitment toward a common goal. However, merely 9% of managers stated that they could rely on the commitment of colleagues from other functions and units.

Misalignment in the organisation fails to link strategy to the process and actions within an organisation (Sull et al. 2015). Alignment of the strategic decisions to the relationships between various units and departments within the organisation is required to achieve the desired level of strategic performance through the corporate structure and processes (Srivastava and Sushil 2017). The misalignment, thus, often leads to the organisation performing well in some metrics and doing miserably badly in others (Kaplan and Norton 2001) which is not good for the organisational strategy execution.

Strategy execution requires decisions that are aligned towards the choice of opportunities to pursue, the quantum of value an organisation can create and capture, and how to create long-term sustainability and success through continuous value creation (Collis 2021). MacLennan and Markides (2021) observe that vision and strategy are seen as abstract by most of the workforce, but the strategic alignment through mapping is seen and understood by all and the workforce can see how their work contributes to the success of the organisation.

Alignment is not just a top-down percolation of the strategic direction. Alignment is a sophisticated interplay between the top-down strategic direction and bottom-up enablement of the teams to identify initiatives within the set strategic choices. Top management should allow the team to organically choose the initiatives and not be tempted to pick up the initiatives themselves (Vermeulen 2017).

2.5 Poor Communication

Communication of strategic objectives and goals is important and is recognised as one of the main problems in strategy execution. Employees can contribute to strategy execution only after they understand strategy, targets, and initiatives through effective communication. However, communication of strategy down the organisation to the workforce and across various functions and departments is always a challenge (Lawrence 2005). Poor communication leads to poor knowledge dissemination among functions and departments leading to inadequate coordination during strategy execution between them (Blahová 2010).

Nonspecific and indistinct communication by the top management creates ambiguity and confusion—something acknowledged as problematic in strategy execution (MacLennan and Markides 2021). Most of the time, the planners believe that communication can be achieved through a simple formal announcement to the workforce, but this is not likely in reality as the workforce is not fully aware of the hypothetical nitty–gritty and the intricacies leading to the strategy development and strategic objectives (Harandi and Fatemi 2020). Communication should make the workforce understand both the "know-how" along with the "know-why".

Organisational management should not only clearly communicate the strategic choices made by the organisation but also explain to the workforce the logic working behind the choice (Vermeulen 2017). To add to this, the use of ambiguous language including phrases and buzzwords which are vague adds to the confusion leaving doubts regarding the interpretation of these (MacLennan and Markides 2021). Successful communication is characterised by simplification of communication making it easy to understand without doubts of interpretation so that it is understood by all.

2.6 Ineffective Initiatives Management

Strategic initiatives are a collection of time-bound projects and programmes, carried outside the regular operations of an organisation, which overcome the organisational inertia and resistance to change, in order to successfully implement the strategy (Kaplan and Norton 2008).

A significant reason for not achieving strategic objectives is that top management does not put in the same extent of time, energy, and resources in the management of the execution of the strategy through initiatives as they do in formulating the strategy (Safdari Ranjbar et al. 2014).

Successful strategy execution requires the protection of the long-term strategic initiatives from short term suboptimization which may creep in due to the annual budgeting process. Effective initiatives management requires the organisation to consider a separate strategy budget along with the annual operational budget (Kaplan and Norton 2001). Initiatives identification is different from budget formulation (Rohm et al. 2013). However, it was found that 50% of the organisations do not link initiative to budget (Kaplan and Norton 2008).

Identification of initiatives is a crucial phase in initiatives management as many organisations fall into the trap of coming up with a laundry list of too many initiatives (Niven 2012). To bring in focus and proper alignment initiatives have to be chosen to give the maximum impact to the organisation so that the strategic objectives are met (Rohm et al. 2013). Various criteria to check the impact and importance of initiatives can be used for their selection and allocating resources to them. Initiatives management is the main building block for the success of strategy implementation as identification of initiatives solves the problem of culling ideas for improvement and shorting the ideas laundry list to a manageable shortlist which can be allocated with the limited resources for delivering impactful strategic results (Rohm et al. 2013).

2.7 Unclear Responsibilities and Accountabilities

Balancing agility and control are required by organisations which can be achieved by giving the required authority to experiment with new initiatives and concepts to the workforce and at the same time investing in building the capabilities needed for the success and sustainability of the organisation in the future. While unclear responsibility and accountability during the execution of the strategy execution activities and decisions is one of the causes which negatively impact strategy execution (Collis 2021).

Strategy execution requires ownership across the organisation from the top management to the managers at all levels and the people concerned must own the process and commit their actions to them for effective execution. Although the tasks and actions required at different levels vary, they are all interconnected, interdependent, and important for strategy execution (Lawrence 2005). Strategy execution is not a spectator sport but a full-contact sport where all the team members have a role to play (Flander 2012).

Strategy execution is the main responsibility of managers across levels with clearly defined responsibility and accountability (Lawrence 2005).

2.8 Improper Change Management

Hrebiniak (2008) observes that strategy execution often requires a change in structure, incentives, controls, people, objectives, and responsibilities which can be perceived as threatening by the people involved. It is extremely important to manage change well for effective strategy implementation. Ineffective change management to handle resistance to new strategic execution choices or initiatives can create deterrent effects to effective strategy execution efforts. Organisations should make concerted efforts towards change management for the success of strategy execution (Blahová 2010) in achieving the organisational strategic objectives. Change management calls for change in behaviour and strategy execution often fails when people are rewarded for the wrong behaviour (Lawrence 2005). Employees in general and managers, in particular, are involved in projects that require change and adaption of business processes and not a one-time change management program to execute a different strategy, making the change management process still difficult (Collis 2021). Failure to hire and retain the right talent as part of the change management and the inability to facilitate them to do what they are best at spells disaster for strategy execution (Ming-Jer Chen 2020).

The organisation which does not recognise that change and transformation are the fundamental rules for the success of strategy execution and does not take change as a way of revitalising and renewing the organisation spirit is heading towards execution failure for certain (Rohm et al. 2013).

2.9 No Strategy Management Framework

The specifics of the business's offerings and services, its processes and resources, its human capital, and almost everything else about the organisation, are the constituents of strategy implementation. Without a doubt, getting the details accurate is immensely significant for effective strategy implementation. Frameworks for thinking through these issues, circumventing probable reasons of failure for facilitating to get the details accurate, are immensely helpful (Blahová 2010).

Numerous hindrances can derail strategy implementation. However, using the timing and methods, coupled with strategy management frameworks may help to minimise or reduce the impact of such causes (Blahová 2010). Sull et al. (2015) found that many executives do not execute the strategy as a full system and fall into the trap of cherry-picking strategy execution pieces often based on the trends in the market. Marr (2005) also argues that even some organisations that claim to use the strategy management framework such as the Balanced Scorecard use only some parts or incomplete versions of it, making it less effective and unreliable. Creating and implementing a strategy is both an art and a science (Rohm et al. 2013). The art part is characterised by innovation and creativity which is enabled by using a management system that aids in bringing focus to the most important things, enhances decision-making, and enhances operational efficiency and organisational effectiveness. Managing communication and change management is also integral part of art. Strategic thinking to develop and link the necessary elements into an integrated system for planning and strategic management forms the science part. A strategy management system is required to facilitate all of these.

3 Research Methodology

The research used a positivist philosophy with a deductive approach to theory development. Survey was used as the quantitative data collection strategy. A cross-sectional time horizon was chosen. The quantitative data collected was analysed online using datatab.net.

3.1 Research Strategy

The theory for this research was based on the approach that entails modifying or expanding existing theories to account for a new situation or context (Bhattacherjee 2012). This deductive method effectively develops new theories by expanding upon old ones by drawing on the extensive body of social science hypotheses created by earlier theorists.

The research was conducted by considering the existing theories which indicate that there are 9 factors impeding strategy implementation (discussed in Sect. 2.1 through 2.9). These theories were expanded to test the extent to which they negatively impact strategy execution in Real Estate Development Organisations in Saudi Arabia.

The theoretical framework used for the research is depicted in Fig. 2.

The theoretical framework consists of Strategy Planning (independent variable) which is the input and is translated into strategy execution (dependent variable). However, strategy execution is negatively impacted by strategy execution hurdles (negatively moderating variables). The framework studied the impact of moderating variables on the dependent variables keeping the independent variable constant.

The details of the variables are enumerated in Table 1.

The Quantitative Study for this research was conducted following the steps as follows:

1. Questionnaire development
2. Questionnaire validation
3. Sample selection using Snowball technique
4. Survey using Google forms
5. Statistical Analysis using datatab.net
6. Interpretation and findings

3.2 Research Methods

3.2.1 Survey Research Questionnaire Design

The questionnaire for this research was designed in two parts: Part 1 was to address the moderating variables for strategy execution hurdles based on the outcome of the literature review (Sect. 2); Part 2 was to study the impact of moderating variable on dependent variable (strategy execution). The questionnaire linkage to the relevant sections of the literature review and categories are shown in Table 2.

3.2.2 Survey Research Questionnaire Validation

The questionnaire developed for this research was validated by six experts from real estate development organisations in Saudi Arabia. Two of them had DBA degrees and all six had engineering degrees and all of them had over 15 years of experience in the industry. Three of them held the positions of departmental heads and the other three were Chiefs in their respective organisations. The panel of experts was competent to comment and score the questionnaire to test the validity during pretesting. The questionnaire pretesting form was shared with the experts through WhatsApp and received back from them. Validity indices were calculated following the procedure indicated by Polit and Beck (2006). The indices as shown in Table 3 conclude that questionnaire has the required content validity Table.

The pretested survey questionnaire was administered to 30 participants working in real estate development organisations in Saudi Arabia. The responses were analysed online using DataTab.net for validity with acceptable scores of Cronbach's Alpha / Pearson correlation (Bhattacherjee 2012; Saunders 2019) as indicated in Table 4. Cronbach's

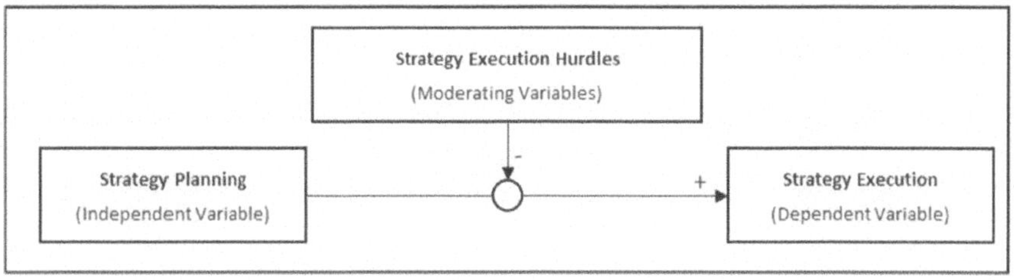

Fig. 2 Theoretical framework. *Source* Researcher's own construction

Table 1 Theoretical framework variables

Variable type	Variable group	Impact	Variable description
Independent variable	Strategy planning	Input/initiating	• Strategy planning
Dependent variable	Strategy execution	Output/effect	• Strategy execution
Moderating variables	Strategy execution hurdles	Negative impact	• Non-involvement of the workforce
			• Unclear strategic choices/ objectives
			• Rigid plan
			• Misalignment
			• Poor communication
			• Ineffective initiatives management
			• Unclear responsibilities and accountabilities
			• Improper change management
			• No strategy management framework

Source Researcher's own creation based on literature review

Alpha value of 0.7–0.8 is acceptable for questionnaires to be used as an instrument of measurement (Field 2017). Questions which were direct measures (9.1 EPMO_OSM and DV_ EXC_STG) were not tested.

3.2.3 Survey Administration

The population for this research was the employees working in real estate development organisations in Saudi Arabia. Saudi Arabia has 123 real estate development companies with 98 in Riyadh, 8 in Jeddah, 7 in Khobar, and the rest in other cities (Real Estates Companies—Business Directory 2022). Public information about the employees in these organisations was not available. Thus, 30 employees in 20 organisations (representing 16.5% of the real estate development organisation population) known to the researcher were approached initially to answer the questionnaire and they were requested to forward the questionnaire to employees within their organisation. The sample size was more that the recommended 10% of the population (Creswell 2012).

The questionnaire was hosted on the cloud in Google forms and the questionnaire links were sent to 30 employees in 20 organisations through WhatsApp. The initial 30 participants were requested to send the self-administered survey questionnaire to the employees within their organisation. Expert sampling followed by snowball sampling was thus used to reach the participants (Bhattacherjee 2012; Saunders 2019). The questionnaire is available in Table 2.

The questionnaire was kept open for receiving responses for two weeks. A total of 184 responses were received by the end of the second week. The received responses were downloaded from Google forms to MS excel sheet and coded for quantitative analysis. The values for the response on the Likert scale were coded as follows: Strongly Disagree = 1; Somewhat Disagree = 2; Neutral = 3; Somewhat Agree = 4; and Strongly Agree = 5 to facilitate quantitative data analysis (Bhattacherjee 2012; Saunders 2019).

Descriptive and inferential analysis of the survey respondents was done online using DataTab.net.

4 Findings

184 participants from real estate development organisations (question No. 30) which were operating from within Saudi Arabia (question No. 31) responded to the survey questionnaire. Since snowball sampling method was used the response rate could not be ascertained. The profile of the survey participants is summarized in Table 5 which shows that the participants are a representative sample of the population of employees in the real estate development organisations in Saudi Arabia.

Descriptive analysis of the survey responses was done as summarized in Table 6.

A multiple linear regression analysis was performed to examine the influence of the moderating variables on the dependent variable. The regression model showed that the moderating variables explained 70.19% of the variance from the dependent variable. An ANOVA test found that the effect was significantly different from zero, $F = 13.6$, $p = <0.001$, $R2 = 0.7$.

Table 2 Survey questionnaire

Category	Literature review section	Question	Code	Scale
Planning	2.1 Non-involvement of the workforce	1. My inputs are taken into account during strategy planning	1.1 IP_TKN	Likert
		2. My organisation uses the help of consultants for strategy formulation	1.2 CON_USD	Likert
		3. I attend strategic Initiatives review sessions	1.3 ATND_REV	Likert
	2.2 Unclear strategic choices/ objective	4. I am aware of my organisation's strategic objectives	2.1 AWR_SO	Likert
		5. My organisation has clearly stated the areas in which it will operate	2.2 OPR_YES	Likert
		6. I am aware of the areas where my organisation does not want to operate	2.3 OPR_NO	Likert
		7. My daily activities help my organisation to achieve its strategy	2.4 DAL_ACT-STG	Likert
	2.3 Rigid plan	8. My organisation periodically reviews the strategy plan	3.1 STG_PLN_ REV	Likert
		9. I am aware of the changes made to my organisation's strategy in the last 6 months	3.2 STG_CNG _AWR	Likert
		10. The COVID-19 pandemic caused the strategy of my organisation to be altered	3.3 STG_CNG_ COVID	Likert
Execution	2.4 Misalignment	11. My company's organisation structure is aligned with the strategy	4.1 ORG_STR _ALIGN	Likert
		12. The hiring in my organisation is driven by the organisation's strategy	4.2 HIR_STR_ ALIGN	Likert
		13. The processes that I follow are aligned with the organisation's strategy	4.3 PROCESS_ STR_ALIGN	Likert
		14. I can trust my team members for carrying out our daily tasks	4.4 TRST_OWN	Likert
		15. I can trust the team members from other departments for support in carrying out our daily tasks	4.5 TRST_OTH	Likert
		16. I know what decisions to take in case I encounter conflicting situations	4.6 DEC_ CONFLT	Likert
	2.5 Poor Communication	17. The management of my organisation periodically communicates the strategy with the workforce	5.1 COMM_STG	Likert
		18. I am aware of why I am doing the work that I have to do	5.2 WHY_WORK	Likert
		19. The strategic message I receive is the same from all the management team members	5.3 SAME_MSG	Likert
	2.6 Ineffective initiatives	20. The management team dedicates sufficient time while planning for strategic projects/ initiatives	6.1 PLG_TIME	Likert
		21. My organisation provides a separate budget for each strategic project/ initiative	6.2 BUDG_ INITIATIVE	Likert
		22. I have annual sessions with my manager to prioritise the strategic projects/ initiatives for the department	6.3 PRIORITY_I NITIATIVE	Likert
	2.7 Unclear responsibilities and accountabilities	23. I have the signed and documented KPIs/ measures for the whole year for myself	7.1 KPIs_SIGN	Likert
		24. I have clarity on my roles and responsibilities	7.2 ROLE_ CLRTY	Likert

(continued)

Table 2 (continued)

Category	Literature review section	Question	Code	Scale
Enablers	2.8 Improper change management	25. The management explains to the workforce any change taking place within the organisation	8.1 EXPLN_CHNG	Likert
		26. The changes in the organisation are adjusted with proper training for the workforce	8.2 TRG_CHNG	Likert
	2.9 No Strategy management framework	27. My organisation has a department dedicated to coordinating strategy implementation (e.g. EPMO, office of Strategy Management, etc.)	9.1 EPMO_OSM	Likert
		28. Has your organisation implemented any other strategy management system such as MBO, OKR, Hosin Kanri, etc.?	9.3 MBO_OKR	Bipolar (Yes/No)
Strategy Execution	Not Applicable Dependent Variable	29. My organisation has executed/ implemented the organisation's strategy effectively	9.2 BSC	Likert
	Not Applicable (demographic information)	30. Which of the following best describes the industry in which your organisation operates in? (Real Estate Development, Asset Operations and Maintenance, Others)	9.4 SMS_STG _IMPL	Single choice
	Not Applicable (demographic information)	31. Where is your organisation located? (Saudi Arabia, outside Saudi Arabia)	LOCATION	Single choice
	Not Applicable (demographic information)	32. For how long are you working with your current organisation? (less than or equal to 1 year, More than 1 year to less than or equal 5 years. More than 5 years to less than or equal 10 years, More than10 years)	TENURE	Single choice
	Not Applicable (demographic information)	33. What is your reporting structure within your organisation? (I report to the Board of Directors/ Chairperson, I report to the CEO/ MD, I report to C-Suite (other than CEO), I report to Department Head/ Unit Head, Others)	REPORT	Single choice
	Not Applicable (demographic information)	34. How many full-time employees work in your organisation? (Less than 50 employees, more than 50 employees and less than 250 employees, more than 250 employees and less than 500 employees, more than 500 employees and less than 1,000 employees, more than 1,000 employees)	EMP_CNT	Single choice

Source Researcher's own creation

Table 3 CVI

Index	Description	Achieved value
I-CVI	Expert proportion agreeing to individual items	0.98
S-CVI/ UA	Proportion of Item scales agreed by all experts	0.98
S-CVI/ Ave	Average of I-CVIs for all scales	0.98

Source researcher's processed data

5 Discussion

The reasons for strategy execution failures were studied through existing literature and the literature review concluded that there are nine factors impeding strategy execution. The nine factors impeding strategy execution are:

(1) Non-involvement of the workforce (Sect. 2.1)
(2) Unclear strategic choices/ objectives (Sect. 2.2)
(3) Rigid plan (Sect. 2.3)
(4) Misalignment (Sect. 2.4)
(5) Poor communication (Sect. 2.5)
(6) Ineffective initiatives management (Sect. 2.6)
(7) Unclear responsibilities and accountabilities (Sect. 2.7)
(8) Improper change management (Sect. 2.8), and
(9) No strategy management framework (Sect. 2.9).

The research analysis suggested that these factors are applicable to real estate development organisations in Saudi Arabia as well. The applicability of these are summarized in Table 7 and discussed in details below.

Table 4 Survey questionnaire validation

1. Non-involvement of the workforce		
Cronbach's Alpha	Number of Items	
0.82	3	
	Corrected Item-Total Correlation	Cronbach's Alpha if Item Deleted
1.1 IP_TKN	0.85	0.54
1.2 CON_USD	0.48	0.91
1.3 ATND_REV	0.74	0.68
2. Unclear strategic choices/objectives		
Cronbach's Alpha	Number of Items	
0.77	4	
	Corrected Item-Total Correlation	Cronbach's Alpha if Item Deleted
2.1 AWR_SO	0.59	0.71
2.2 OPR_YES	0.56	0.73
2.3 OPR_NO	0.63	0.68
2.4 DAL_ACT-STG	0.53	0.73
3. Rigid plan		
Cronbach's Alpha	Number of Items	
0.83	3	
	Corrected Item-Total Correlation	Cronbach's Alpha if Item Deleted
3.1 STG_PLN_REV	0.60	0.88
3.2 STG_CNG_AWR	0.82	0.62
3.3 STG_CNG_COVID	0.70	0.78
4. Misalignment		
Cronbach's Alpha	Number of Items	
0.71	6	
	Corrected Item-Total Correlation	Cronbach's Alpha if Item Deleted
4.1 ORG_STR_ALIGN	0.53	0.64
4.2 HIR_STR_ALIGN	0.52	0.64
4.3 PROCESS_STR_ALIGN	0.28	0.71
4.4 TRST_OWN	0.15	0.73
4.5 TRST_OTH	0.60	0.61
4.6 DEC_CONFLT	0.53	0.63
5. Poor communication		
Cronbach's Alpha	Number of Items	
0.74	3	
	Corrected Item-Total Correlation	Cronbach's Alpha if Item Deleted
5.1 COMM_STG	0.66	0.53
5.2 WHY_WORK	0.37	0.84
5.3 SAME_MSG	0.70	0.47

(continued)

Table 4 (continued)

6. Ineffective initiatives management		
Cronbach's Alpha	Number of Items	
0.76	3	
	Corrected Item-Total Correlation	Cronbach's Alpha if Item Deleted
6.1 PLG_TIME	0.67	0.60
6.2 BUDG_INITIATIVE	0.60	0.68
6.3 PRIORITY_INITIATIVE	0.54	0.75
7. Unclear responsibilities and accountabilities		
	r	p (2-tailed)
7.1 KPIs_SIGN and 7.2 ROLE_CLRTY	0.53	0.002
A Pearson correlation was performed to test whether there was an association between 7.1 KPIs_SIGN and 7.2 ROLE_CLRTY. The result of the Pearson correlation showed that there was a significant association between 7.1 KPIs_SIGN and 7.2 ROLE_CLRTY, $r(28) = 0.53$, $p = 0.002$		
8. Improper change management		
	r	p (2-tailed)
8.1 EXPLN_CHNG and 8.2 TRG_CHNG	0.63	<0.001
A Pearson correlation was performed to test whether there was an association between 8.1 EXPLN_CHNG and 8.2 TRG_CHNG. The result of the Pearson correlation showed that there was a significant association between 8.1 EXPLN_CHNG and 8.2 TRG_CHNG, $r(28) = 0.63$, $p \leq 0.001$		

Source researcher's processed data

Table 5 Survey participants' profile

Organisation's size (No of employees)	Participant's tenure (years)	Participant's reporting line			Total
		CEO or MD	C-Suite	Department or Unit Head	
<50					9 (5%)
	<1	-	-	-	
	1–5	3 (2%)	-	6 (3%)	
	5–10	-	-	-	
	>10	-	-	-	
50 to 250					156 (85%)
	<1	2 (1%)	-	3 (2%)	
	1–5	27 (25%)	36 (20%)	48 (26%)	
	5–10	8 (4%)	11 (6%)	19 (10%)	
	>10	-	1 (1%)	1 (1%)	
250 to 500					19 (10%)
	<1	-	-	-	
	1–5	-	2 (1%)	12 (7%)	
	5–10	2 (1%)	1 (1%)	2 (1%)	
	>10	-	-	-	
Total		42 (23%)	51 (28%)	91 (49%)	184 (100%)

Source researcher's processed data

5.1 Non-Involvement of the Workforce

The study suggests that the problem of non-involvement of the workforce as measured by the three variables applies to real estate development organisations in Saudi Arabia. The findings correlate with the literature review discussed in Sect. 2.1.

The implication of non-involvement of the workforce could result in a negative impact on the knowledge transfer and commitment of the workforce, which eventually

Table 6 Descriptive analysis of the survey responses (N = 184)

Item	Mean	Median	SD	Variance	Skew	Kurtosis
1.1 IP_TKN	1.98	2.0	1.06	1.12	1.04	0.31
1.2 CON_USD	2.93	3.0	0.82	0.68	0.13	− 1.51
1.3 ATND_REV	1.76	1.0	0.99	0.97	1.34	0.77
2.1 AWR_SO	3.11	3.0	1.06	1.13	− 0.48	− 0.98
2.2 OPR_YES	3.89	4.0	0.76	0.57	− 1.03	1.75
2.3 OPR_NO	2.35	3.0	1.06	1.11	− 0.04	− 1.30
2.4 DAL_ACT-STG	3.76	4.0	0.89	0.80	− 0.10	− 0.86
3.1 STG_PLN_REV	2.27	3.0	1.10	1.20	0.07	− 1.33
3.2 STG_CNG_AWR	1.59	1.0	0.98	0.95	1.58	1.24
3.3 STG_CNG_COVID	2.48	2.0	0.74	0.55	1.18	− 0.14
4.1 ORG_STR_ALIGN	2.09	2.0	1.02	1.03	0.62	− 0.32
4.2 HIR_STR_ALIGN	1.66	1.0	1.01	1.01	1.56	1.64
4.3 PROCESS_STR_ALIGN	3.53	4.0	0.92	0.85	− 1.24	1.19
4.4 TRST_OWN	4.51	5.0	0.59	0.35	− 1.08	1.86
4.5 TRST_OTH	2.58	3.0	1.16	1.35	0.08	− 1.20
4.6 DEC_CONFLT	1.81	1.5	1.02	1.04	1.14	0.13
5.1 COMM_STG	1.63	1.0	1.01	1.02	1.53	1.04
5.2 WHY_WORK	3.21	4.0	1.10	1.21	− 0.73	− 0.51
5.3 SAME_MSG	1.71	1.0	1.01	1.03	1.37	0.67
6.1 PLG_TIME	2.28	3.0	1.02	1.03	− 0.02	− 1.04
6.2 BUDG_INITIATIVE	2.27	2.0	1.07	1.15	0.21	− 0.94
6.3 PRIORITY_INITIATIVE	1.36	1.0	0.86	0.75	2.66	6.60
7.1 KPIs_SIGN	2.39	2.0	1.35	1.84	0.57	− 1.14
7.2 ROLE_CLRTY	3.56	4.0	0.94	0.89	− 1.02	0.38
8.1 EXPLN_CHNG	1.46	1.0	0.75	0.57	1.88	3.45
8.2 TRG_CHNG	1.25	1.0	0.58	0.34	2.72	7.97
9.1 EPMO_OSM	1.22	1.0	0.63	0.40	4.10	19.93
9.2 BSC	1.00	1.0	0.00	0.00	N/A	N/A
9.3 MBO_OKR	1.00	1.0	0.00	0.00	N/A	N/A
9.4 SMS_STG_IMPL	1.88	2.0	0.33	0.11	− 2.36	3.63
DV_ EXC_STG	2.08	2.0	1.06	1.11	0.77	− 0.37

Source researcher's processed data

jeopardizes the entire strategy execution (Lawrence 2005). Also, the data received at the top could be filtered at different levels resulting in improper information reaching the top for planning purposes (Blahová 2010). The advice of consultants assumes what is good for the client and what their understanding is about what the client is capable and willing to do (Blahová 2010) which again could impact the strategy planning itself being started with wrong assumptions. The effectiveness of strategy execution is impacted by the involvement of managers at all hierarchical levels (Lawrence 2005) and middle management who run business-critical functions (Sull et al. 2015). Hence, the real estate development organisations in Saudi Arabia could be susceptible to all these impacts during strategy execution.

5.2 Unclear Strategic Choices/Objectives

The study suggests that the problem of unclear strategic choices/ objectives as measured by the four variables applies, but not fully, to the real estate development organisations in Saudi Arabia. The findings do not correlate fully with the literature review discussed in Sect. 2.2.

However, not being aware of the strategic objectives is a major problem (Lawrence 2005). This may result in the real estate development organisations failing to see the light of strategy execution and failing as they do not seem to portray some clear set of choices made by the organisation (Vermeulen 2017). The probable cause could be that while strategy planning, the organisations fail in making strategic

Table 7 Factor Applicability to real estate development organisation in Saudi Arabia

Category	Literature review section	Question	Remarks
Planning	2.1 Non-involvement of the workforce	• My inputs are taken into account during strategy planning • My organisation uses the help of consultants for strategy formulation • I attend strategic Initiatives review sessions	Cronbach's Alpha = 0.79
	2.2 Unclear strategic choices/ objectives	• I am aware of my organisation's strategic objectives • My organisation has clearly stated the areas in which it will operate • I am aware of the areas where my organisation does not want to operate • My daily activities help my organisation to achieve its strategy	Cronbach's Alpha = 0.74
	Rigid plan	• My organisation periodically reviews the strategy plan • I am aware of the changes made to my organisation's strategy in the last 6 months • The COVID-19 pandemic caused the strategy of my organisation to be altered	Cronbach's Alpha = 0.83
Execution	2.4 Misalignment	• My company's organisation structure is aligned with the strategy • The hiring in my organisation is driven by the organisation's strategy • The processes that I follow are aligned with the organisation's strategy • I can trust my team members for carrying out our daily tasks • I can trust the team members from other departments for support in carrying out our daily tasks • I know what decisions to take in case I encounter conflicting situations	Cronbach's Alpha = 0.74
	2.5 Poor communication	• The management of my organisation periodically communicates the strategy with the workforce • I am aware of why I am doing the work that I have to do • The strategic message I receive is the same from all the management team members	Cronbach's Alpha = 0.74
	2.6 Ineffective initiatives management	• The management team dedicates sufficient time while planning for strategic projects/ initiatives • My organisation provides a separate budget for each strategic project/ initiative • I have annual sessions with my manager to prioritise the strategic projects/ initiatives for the department	Cronbach's Alpha = 0.81
	2.7 Unclear responsibilities and accountabilities	• I have the signed and documented KPIs/ measures for the whole year for myself • I have clarity on my roles and responsibilities	Pearson correlation: $r(182) = 0.37$ and $p = <0.001$
Enablers	2.8 Improper change management	• The management explains to the workforce any change taking place within the organisation • The changes in the organisation are adjusted with proper training for the workforce	Pearson correlation: $r(182) = 0.74$ and $p = <0.001$
	2.9 No strategy management framework	• My organisation has a department dedicated to coordinating strategy implementation (e.g., EPMO, Office of Strategy Management, etc.) • Has your organisation implemented any other strategy management system such as MBO, OKR, Hosin Kanri, etc.?	NA as all the responses were "No"

Source researcher's processed data

trade-offs and setting strategic priorities to clarify the strategic objectives (MacLennan and Markides 2021). Also, without clear strategic objectives and choices, it becomes difficult to link the day-to-day objectives at various levels and locations within the organisation which leads to strategy execution failure (Lawrence 2005).

5.3 Rigid Plan

The study suggests that the problem of the rigid plan measured by the three variables applies to real estate development organisations in Saudi Arabia. The findings correlate with the literature review discussed in Sect. 2.3.

Having an inflexible rigid plan can stop the real estate organisations from adapting the plan while executing the strategy based on the iterative process of using hypothesis, conducting experimentation, learning in the process, and taking action is required for successful strategy execution (Collis 2021) and adjust the business to unanticipated events and bring the strategy execution on track (Blahová 2010) whenever required. A flexible plan is important because however good the strategic plan may be, no organisation can anticipate all the developments that may either positively or negatively impact the execution during the planning stage itself (Sull et al. 2015).

5.4 Misalignment

The study suggests that the problem of misalignment measured by the six variables applies to real estate development organisations in Saudi Arabia. The findings correlate with the literature review discussed in Sect. 2.4.

Alignment for strategy execution is characterised by the alignment of organisational structures, enterprise processes, and systems to support the strategy execution is important during the execution of the strategy. Alignment allows all employees to understand what the organisation is trying to accomplish and guides them to make decisions and take actions that are aligned with the strategy (Rohm et al. 2013). Misalignment in real estate development organisations in Saudi Arabia aligns with the previous research pointing to many companies failing to link the business and the shared services units to the divisional and the corporate level strategy (Kaplan and Norton 2001). The research also aligns with the study by Sull et al. (2015) which shows that 84% of managers stated that they can rely on their team and their members for commitment toward a common goal, and merely 9% of managers stated that they could rely on the commitment of colleagues from other functions and units.

5.5 Poor Communication

The study suggests that the problem of poor communication measured by the six variables applies to real estate development organisations in Saudi Arabia. The findings correlate with the literature review discussed in Sect. 2.5.

Communication of strategy down the organisation to the workforce and across various functions and departments is always a challenge (Lawrence 2005) and the study suggests improper communication is prevalent within the real estate development organisations in Saudi Arabia. This can lead to poor knowledge dissemination among functions and departments leading to inadequate coordination during strategy execution (Blahová 2010). Nonspecific and indistinct communication by the top management was also discovered within the real estate development organisations in Saudi Arabia which can again lead to ambiguity and confusion—something acknowledged as problematic in strategy execution (MacLennan and Markides 2021).

5.6 Ineffective Initiatives Management

The study suggests that the problem of ineffective initiatives management measured by the three variables applies to a great extent to the real estate development organisations in Saudi Arabia. The findings correlate to a great extent with the literature review discussed in Sect. 2.6.

The study suggests that planning for strategic initiatives is not given enough time. Planning for the initiatives is the starting point for strategy execution and a significant reason for not achieving strategic objectives is that top management does not put in the same extent of time, energy, and resources in the management of the execution of the strategy as they do in formulating the strategy (Safdari Ranjbar et al. 2014).

Also, even though the study suggests that the initiatives have a budget, initiative identification is different from budget formulation (Rohm et al. 2013) and organisations do not link initiative to budget (Kaplan and Norton 2008) leading to strategy execution failure.

Again, the problem of not prioritizing initiatives can lead to organisations falling into the trap of coming up with a laundry list of too many initiatives (Niven 2012) making them dilute focus leading to ineffective resource utilization and failure in strategy execution.

5.7 Unclear Responsibilities and Accountabilities

The study suggests that the problem of unclear responsibilities and accountabilities measured by the two variables applies to real estate development organisations in Saudi Arabia. The findings correlate with the literature review discussed in Sect. 2.7.

The absence of signed and documented KPIs coupled with the unclear roles and responsibilities is an indicator of the problem of unclear responsibilities and accountabilities in real estate development organisations in Saudi Arabia which can adversely impact strategy execution (Blahová 2010). Also, although the tasks and actions required at different levels vary, they are all interconnected, interdependent and important for strategy execution (Lawrence 2005), and the absence of clear responsibilities and accountabilities can thus negatively impact the strategy execution.

5.8 Improper Change Management

The study suggests that the problem of improper change management measured by the two variables applies to real estate development organisations in Saudi Arabia. The findings correlate with the literature review discussed in Sect. 2.8.

The absence of change management could impact the strategy execution adversely as organisations that do not recognize change management as a vital requirement for strategy execution and implement the change management system will be heading towards execution failures (Rohm et al. 2013).

Change management calls for change in behaviour (Lawrence 2005) and the failure of the management to explain and train the employees for change could be a recipe for execution failure.

5.9 No Strategy Management Framework

The study suggests that the problem of no strategy management system applies to real estate development organisations in Saudi Arabia. The findings correlate with the literature review discussed in Sect. 2.9.

The specifics of the business's offerings and services, its processes and resources, its human capital, and almost everything else about the organisation, are the constituents of strategy implementation. Getting the details accurate is immensely significant for effective strategy implementation. Thus, the absence of strategy management frameworks takes away the opportunity for organisations to use a tool that helps in thinking through this issue and circumventing probable reasons for failure (Blahová 2010).

Strategy implementation is both an art and a science. The art part of the implementation is facilitated using strategy management frameworks (Rohm et al. 2013).

Thus, not implementing a strategy management system deprives an organisation of using a tool to enhance the chances of strategy execution.

6 Conclusion and Recommendations

The researcher's original contribution to knowledge is the finding that there are nine strategy execution hurdles applicable to industries and geographies across the globe which apply to the real estate development organisation in Saudi Arabia.

The strategy of the real estate development organisations in Saudi Arabia can face the nine strategy execution hurdles which may derail them from achieving their strategic goals. The real estate development organisations can consider implementing strategy management systems such as the balanced scorecard management system to minimize the effects of the strategy execution hurdles. The implementation of the Balanced Scorecard Management system can help them not only to execute the strategy better but also to reap the benefits of better financial results along with increasing exploitative innovation (Malagueño et al. 2018). The organisation becomes better equipped to achieve superior targets, great results, create a pipeline of future leaders, and develop immunity for business sustainability (Muthuraman and Jayaraman 2014).

7 Limitations of the Study

The survey data was collected using the snowball technique. Thus, the sample population for the survey was not under the control of the researcher.

References

H. I. Ansoff, *Corporate Strategy: an Analytic Approach to Business Policy for Growth and Expansion*, Later Printing edition. McGraw-Hill, 1965.

Anol Bhattacherjee, University of South Florida, Scholar Commons, and Open Textbook Library, *Social science research: principles, methods, and practices*. 2012. Accessed: Sep. 02, 2021. [Online]. Available: https://open.umn.edu/opentextbooks/BookDetail.aspx?bookId=79

Michaela Blahová, 'Why do ceos fail while translating strategy into action?', *Sci. Pap. Univ. Pardubice Ser. Fac. Econ. Adm.*, no. 16, pp. 26–31, 2010.

Carlos J F Cândido and Sérgio P Santos, 'Strategy implementation: What is the failure rate?', *J. Manag. Organ.*, vol. 21, no. 2, pp. 237–262, Mar. 2015, https://doi.org/10.1017/jmo.2014.77

Ron Carucci, 'Executives Fail to Execute Strategy Because They're Too Internally Focused', *Harvard Business Review*, Nov. 13, 2017. Accessed: May 06, 2021. [Online]. Available: https://hbr.org/2017/11/executives-fail-to-execute-strategy-because-theyre-too-internally-focused

Ming-Jer Chen, Y. P. Chan, and Charles Tucker, 'The Culture–Strategy–Execution Trio: A How-To Guide', *Asian Case Res. J.*, vol. 24, no. 1, pp. 1–12, Jun. 2020, https://doi.org/10.1142/S021892752010001X.

David J. Collis, 'Why Do So Many Strategies Fail?', *Harv. Bus. Rev.*, vol. 99, no. 4, pp. 82–93, Aug. 2021.

J. W. Creswell, *Educational research: planning, conducting, and evaluating quantitative and qualitative research*, 4th ed. Boston: Pearson, 2012.

D. Crowther and G. Lancaster, *Research Methods*. Routledge, 2012.

Andy Field, *Discovering statistics using IBM SPSS statistics*, 5th edition. Thousand Oaks, CA: SAGE Publications, 2017.

Jereon De Flander, *Strategy execution heroes: business strategy implementation and strategic management demystified : a practical performance management guidebook for the successful leader*. Brussels, Belgium: Performance Factory, 2012.

Julia Gorzelany, 'Integration of Structure, Culture and Strategy in Designing a Management System', *Sci. Pap. Silesian Univ. Technol. Organ. Manag. Zesz. Nauk. Politech. Slaskiej Ser. Organ. Zarzadzanie*, no. 144, pp. 115–124, May 2020, https://doi.org/10.29119/1641-3466.2020.144.9.

Ata Harandi and Zahra Fatemi, 'Identifying the Restrictive Factors of Strategic Plan's Execution of Technology in Order to Modelling', *Proc. Eur. Conf. Innov. Entrep.*, pp. 280–289, Jan. 2020, https://doi.org/10.34190/EIE.20.211.

B. D. Henderson, 'The Origin of Strategy', *Harvard Business Review*, Nov. 01, 1989. Accessed: May 11, 2021. [Online]. Available: https://hbr.org/1989/11/the-origin-of-strategy

I. Kant, M. Weigelt, and M. Muller, *Critique of Pure Reason*, Revised edition. London: Penguin Classics, 2008.

R. S. Kaplan and D. P. Norton, 'Transforming the Balanced Scorecard from Performance Measurement to Strategic Management: Part I', *Account. Horiz.*, vol. 15, no. 1, pp. 87–104, Mar. 2001, https://doi.org/10.2308/acch.2001.15.1.87.

Robert S. Kaplan and David P. Norton, *The execution premium: linking strategy to operations for competitive advantage*. Boston, Mass: Harvard Business Press, 2008.

Lawrence G. Hrebiniak, *Making strategy work: leading effective execution and change*. Upper Saddle River, N.J: Wharton School. Pub, 2005.

Lawrence Hrebiniak, 'Making strategy work: overcoming the obstacles to effective execution', *Ivey Bus. J.* Online, vol. 72, no. 2, p. N_A, Apr. 2008

A. F. MacLennan and C. C. Markides, 'Causal Mapping for Strategy Execution: Pitfalls and Applications', *Calif. Manage. Rev.*, vol. 63, no. 4, pp. 89–122, Aug. 2021, https://doi.org/10.1177/00081256211019799.

Ricardo Malagueño, Ernesto Lopez-Valeiras, and Jacobo Gomez-Conde, 'Balanced scorecard in SMEs: effects on innovation and financial performance', *Small Bus. Econ.*, vol. 51, no. 1, pp. 221–244, Jun. 2018, https://doi.org/10.1007/s11187-017-9921-3.

Bernard Marr, 'Business performance measurement: an overview of the current state of use in the USA', *Meas. Bus. Excell.*, vol. 9, no. 3, pp. 56–62, 2005, https://doi.org/10.1108/mbe.2005.26709caf.006

B Muthuraman and R Jayaraman, '*Driving Business Strategy through BSC in Large Organizations*', *Vikalpa J. Decis. Mak.*, vol. 39, no. 1, pp. 1–20, Jan. 2014, https://doi.org/10.1177/0256090920140101.

Paul R. Niven, Ed., *Balanced Scorecard Evolution: A Dynamic Approach to Strategy Execution*, 1st ed. Hoboken, New Jersey: Wiley, 2012. https://doi.org/10.1002/9781119197287.

Muh. Darmin Ahmad Pella, Ujang Sumarwan, Arief Daryanto, and Kirbrandoko, 'Factors Affecting Poor Strategy Implementation', *Gadjah Mada Int. J. Bus.*, vol. 15, no. 2, pp. 183–204, May 2013, https://doi.org/10.22146/gamaijb.5702.

D. F. Polit and C. T. Beck, 'The content validity index: are you sure you know what's being reported? Critique and recommendations', *Res. Nurs. Health*, vol. 29, no. 5, pp. 489–497, Oct. 2006, https://doi.org/10.1002/nur.20147.

'Real Estates Companies—Business Directory', *eyeofriyadh.com*. http://www.eyeofriyadh.com/directory/category/14_real-estates-companies (accessed Oct. 25, 2022).

C. Richard Panico, 'To transform your organization, start by transforming your strategy executionTo transform your organization, start by transforming your strategy execution', *Healthc. Financ. Manage.*, vol. 73, no. 11, pp. 34–37, Nov. 2019.

Howard Rohm, David Wilsey, Gail Stout Perry, and Dan Montgomery, *The Institute Way: Simplify Strategic Planning and Management with the Balanced Scorecard*, 1st edition. The Institute Press, 2013.

Mostafa Safdari Ranjbar, Mohsen Akbarpour Shirazi, and Mojtaba Lashkar Blooki, 'Interaction among intra-organizational factors effective in successful strategy execution: An analytical view', *J. Strategy Manag.*, vol. 7, no. 2, pp. 127–154, 2014, https://doi.org/10.1108/JSMA-05-2013-0032.

M. N. K. Saunders, Philip Lewis, and Adrian Thornhill, *Research methods for business students*, Eighth Edition. New York: Pearson, 2019.

Manoj Kumar Sharma and Sonali Sharma, 'Role of Organizational Culture as an Internal Business Factor in Successful Strategy Execution: A Review', *IUP J. Manag. Res.*, vol. 21, no. 2, pp. 7–28, Apr. 2022.

Amit Kumar Srivastava and Sushil, 'Alignment: the foundation of effective strategy execution', *Int. J. Product. Perform. Manag.*, vol. 66, no. 8, pp. 1043–1063, 2017, https://doi.org/10.1108/IJPPM-11-2015-0172.

Donald Sull, Rebecca Homkes, and Charles Sull, 'Why Strategy Execution Unravels—and What to Do About It', *Harvard Business Review*, Mar. 01, 2015. Accessed: May 06, 2021. [Online]. Available: https://hbr.org/2015/03/why-strategy-execution-unravelsand-what-to-do-about-it

Freek Vermeulen, 'Many Strategies Fail Because They're Not Actually Strategies', *Harvard Business Review*, Nov. 08, 2017. Accessed: Jan. 09, 2022. [Online]. Available: https://hbr.org/2017/11/many-strategies-fail-because-theyre-not-actually-strategies

R. H. Waterman, T. J. Peters, and J. R. Phillips, 'Structure Is Not Organization', *Bus. Horiz.*, vol. 23, no. 3, p. 14, Jun. 1980.

Jiawei Zhong and Eddie C. M. Hui, 'Real option and vertical mixed-use development', *Int. J. Strateg. Prop. Manag.*, vol. 25, no. 5, pp. 382–395, Jun. 2021, https://doi.org/10.3846/ijspm.2021.15059.

An Impact of Sustainable Finance Initiatives on Financial Markets and Economic Stability

Muhammad Hilal, Sumbal, and Muhammad Imad

Abstract

Sustainable finance initiatives have become a pivotal force in shaping the international financial arena, aiming to incorporate environmental, social, and governance (ESG) considerations into investment decision-making procedures. This investigation analyzes the ramifications of these undertakings on monetary markets and economic equilibrium, imparting scholarly discernment into the advantages, difficulties, and ramifications of sustainable financing. By meticulously examining the dynamic relationships between sustainable finance and the broader economy, this study scrutinizes the incorporation of environmental, social, and governance (ESG) considerations, alterations in investment approaches, risk mitigation techniques, and the resultant economic repercussions. This research endeavor advances a more profound comprehension of the function of sustainable finance in shaping financial markets and fostering economic stability amidst urgent global impediments. This paper undertakes a meticulous and exhaustive analysis of the available literature to discern inadequacies and insufficiencies in current knowledge, thereby underscoring the imperative for subsequent inquiry. The current study utilizes a mixed-methods design, consisting of both quantitative analysis and qualitative interviews, to present empirical evidence on the financial implications of sustainable investments and evaluate the efficacy of sustainable finance initiatives. This work presents significant contributions to policymakers, investors, and financial institutions by providing valuable insights into the potential benefits and challenges accompanying initiatives related to sustainable finance.

Keywords

Business strategy · Financial markets · Economic stability · Sustainable finance

1 Introduction

Sustainable finance has emerged as a critical driver in the global financial landscape, responding to the pressing need for environmentally and socially responsible investment practices. Sustainable finance initiatives have gained significant momentum due to increasingly recognizing climate change, resource depletion, and social inequalities as urgent issues (Zielińska-Lont 2020). The aforementioned initiatives aim to incorporate environmental, social, and governance (ESG) elements into investment decision-making procedures, thereby catalysing a significant alteration towards a more sustainable and equitable economy (Ivanitsk and Petrenko 2021).

The present research investigates the ramifications of sustainable finance initiatives on financial markets and economic stability. An analysis of the interdependence between sustainable finance and pivotal constituents of the economic apparatus can furnish us with valuable discernments pertaining to the plausible advantages, impediments and ramifications of such endeavors.

The fundamental purpose of sustainable finance initiatives is to amalgamate fiscal aims with enduring sustainability targets. Various methodologies and structures have been adopted, including the assimilation of environmental, social, and governance (ESG) considerations, the establishment of eco-friendly bonds and sustainable indices, and the

M. Hilal (✉)
Institute of Management Science, Peshawar, Pakistan
e-mail: Hilalakbar123@gmail.com

Sumbal
Shaheed Benazir Bhutto Women University, Peshawar, Pakistan

M. Imad
Abasyn University, Peshawar, Pakistan

S. Arezki et al. (eds.), *Emerging Disruptive Technologies for Society 5.0 in Developing Countries*,
Advances in Science, Technology & Innovation, https://doi.org/10.1007/978-3-031-63701-8_8

advancement of ethical investment approaches. The initiatives as mentioned earlier typify a collaborative undertaking among financial establishments, governing bodies, and parties invested in a common cause aimed at channeling financial resources towards endeavors that yield favorable ecological and societal results (Srivastava et al. 2022).

By conducting a thorough analysis of the incorporation of Environmental, Social, and Governance (ESG) factors, alterations in investment approaches, practices related to risk management, and implications on the economy, our study aims to evaluate the contribution of sustainable finance initiatives towards enhancing the durability and sustainability of financial markets, while simultaneously promoting prolonged economic stability. By investigating the interdependencies between sustainable finance and the larger economy, the present study aims to furnish insightful knowledge to policymakers, investors, and financial institutions striving to comprehend the potential advantages and hurdles linked with sustainable finance initiatives. This analysis is expected to provide valuable insights regarding the influence of sustainable finance on the configuration of financial markets and the facilitation of economic stability amid the current disruptive global circumstances.

2 Literature Review

In recent years, there has been a noteworthy rise in the importance of sustainable finance, largely prompted by the necessity to tackle environmental and social issues. The present section endeavors to thoroughly comprehend the current state of knowledge in this area through a comprehensive review of existing literature, to draw attention to any areas that require further investigation.

2.1 Sustainable Finance: Concepts, Theories, and Frameworks

The rapidly expanding field of sustainable finance comprises diverse concepts, theories, and frameworks. The concept combines environmental, social, and governance (ESG) considerations with investment decision-making procedures (Kuhn 2022). The literature highlights the development of sustainable finance, which has transitioned from conventional financial frameworks to encompass a more expansive range of aspects, including responsible investment approaches and endeavors toward realizing sustainable development objectives. Regulatory frameworks and guidelines, including but not limited to the United Nations Principles for Responsible Investment and the European Union Sustainable Finance Action Plan, have facilitated the advancement and execution of sustainable finance initiatives (Neto and Fontgalland 2023).

2.2 Sustainable Finance and Financial Markets

The integration of sustainable finance in financial markets bears significant outcomes. According to extant research, including Environmental, Social, and Governance (ESG) issues in investment decisions results in alterations in investment methodologies and the distribution of assets. According to the extant literature, sustainable investments influence asset pricing and valuation. This is due to their ability to reflect the enduring risks and opportunities that arise from environmental and social factors over a prolonged period (Kashi and Shah 2023). Empirical research has brought attention to sustainable investments' performance and risk ramifications. The body of evidence reveals that portfolios incorporating sustainability factors present the potential for delivering comparable, or even more favorable, returns when juxtaposed with conventional investments while maintaining a lower degree of risk exposure. The conduct of investors has been subject to the influence, as evinced by a swelling trend of solicitation for sustainable financial commodities and amenities (Kölbel et al. 2020).

2.3 Sustainable Finance and Economic Stability

Analyzing the correlation between sustainable finance and economic stability is a significant topic requiring thorough investigation. The empirical evidence suggests that sustainable finance endeavors effectively augment evaluating and mitigating environmental and social hazards. Financial institutions that incorporate environmental, social, and governance (ESG) considerations into their operations have been observed to exhibit greater resilience, leading to an overall improvement in systemic stability. Sustainable investments are deemed to have a positive correlation with economic benefits, as they stimulate economic growth and pave the way for job creation (Folqué et al. 2021).

2.4 Impact of Empirical Studies on Sustainable Finance

Empirical studies have provided valuable insights into the impact of sustainable finance initiatives. Numerous studies have examined the financial market implications of sustainable investments, including asset pricing, stock performance, and portfolio diversification. Additionally, case studies of successful sustainable finance initiatives have demonstrated real-world outcomes, such as increased renewable energy investments or the financing of sustainable infrastructure projects. These empirical studies contribute to understanding sustainable finance's potential benefits and challenges (Nizam et al. 2019).

3 Sustainable Finance Initiatives and Financial Markets

3.1 Green Bonds

Green bonds are a specific financial instrument used to raise capital for projects with environmental benefits. This subsection defines green bonds and highlights their key characteristics, such as using proceeds for eligible green projects. The analysis focuses on green bonds' growth and issuance trends, assessing the market size and the increasing interest from both issuers and investors. Furthermore, the impact of green bonds on capital markets and investor demand is evaluated, examining how they contribute to sustainable investment practices and shape market dynamics (Akomea-Frimpong et al. 2022) (Fig. 1).

3.2 Sustainable Investment Funds

Sustainable investment funds are investment vehicles that integrate environmental, social, and governance (ESG) factors into their investment strategies. This subsection overviews sustainable investment funds and their objectives, emphasizing their role in promoting sustainable finance. The analysis includes an assessment of the growth and performance of sustainable investment funds, examining trends in assets under management and financial performance. Additionally, the strategies and approaches used by sustainable investment funds are evaluated to understand how they align with sustainability goals. The impact of sustainable investment funds on investment flows and market dynamics is also examined (Chen and Zhao 2021).

Apart from green bonds and sustainable investment funds, various other sustainable finance initiatives contribute to integrating sustainability into financial markets. This subsection reviews additional initiatives, such as social impact bonds, green indices, and sustainability-linked loans. The analysis focuses on their implementation in financial markets and their contribution to sustainable investment practices. This includes evaluating their effectiveness in driving positive environmental and social outcomes and their impact on investment decision-making and market behavior (Yeow and Ng 2021).

3.3 Impact on Investment Patterns, Asset Allocation, and Risk Management Strategies

This subsection examines the impact of sustainable finance initiatives on investment patterns.

3.3.1 Investment Patterns

It explores the shift in investment preferences and behaviors, highlighting the growing demand for sustainable assets and investment vehicles. The analysis investigates the factors influencing investment decisions, including

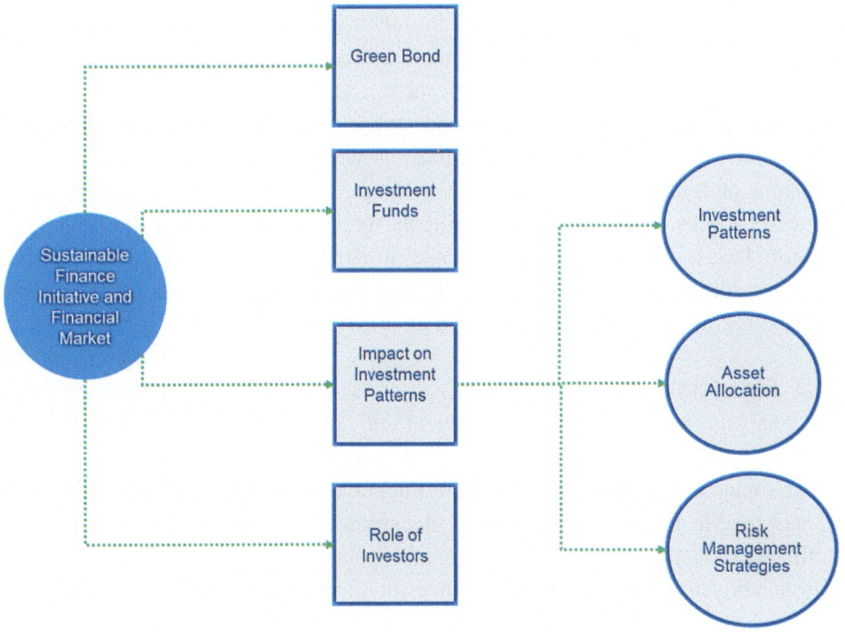

Fig. 1 Sustainable finance initiatives and financial markets

incorporating ESG factors and sustainability goals. Additionally, it evaluates the impact of sustainable investments on investment diversification and portfolio composition, exploring the extent to which investors allocate their assets toward sustainable assets (Kashi and Shah 2023).

3.3.2 Asset Allocation

The impact of sustainable finance initiatives on asset allocation strategies is assessed in this subsection. It analyzes how integrating sustainability considerations affects the allocation of investments across different asset classes and sectors. The analysis explores sectoral allocation trends and preferences in sustainable investments, highlighting the sectors that receive significant funding and have a positive environmental or social impact. Furthermore, the risk-return profiles of sustainable assets are evaluated, comparing them to traditional assets and assessing their attractiveness to investors (Popescu et al. 2021).

3.3.3 Risk Management Strategies

The analysis assesses the effectiveness of risk measurement models for sustainable investments, exploring whether incorporating ESG factors enhances risk management practices. Additionally, it considers the development of sustainable finance-specific risk frameworks and methodologies to manage environmental and social risks effectively (Akala et al. 2022).

3.4 Role of Investors, Financial Institutions, and Regulatory Bodies

The investors in promoting sustainable finance initiatives are evaluated in this subsection. It assesses investor motivations for incorporating sustainability into their investment decisions, considering risk management, ethical considerations, and the desire for long-term value creation. The analysis explores the role of institutional investors, such as pension funds and sovereign wealth funds, as well as asset managers and individual investors in driving sustainable finance practices. Additionally, it highlights the challenges investors face in implementing sustainable investment strategies, including data availability, measurement methodologies, and regulatory constraints (Zioło et al. 2021).

3.4.1 Financial Institutions

The analysis assesses the development of sustainable finance products, such as green loans and sustainability-linked financial instruments, and their impact on financing sustainable projects. Additionally, it explores the role of financial institutions in providing ESG-related information and advisory services to investors, facilitating the mainstream adoption of sustainable finance practices (Pavláková Dočekalová and Kocmanová 2018).

3.4.2 Regulatory Bodies

The effects of regulatory measures, namely the obligations to make disclosures and the implementation of Environmental, Social, and Governance (ESG) reporting frameworks, on stakeholders in financial markets have an impact. Furthermore, the present study delves into the commendable contribution of regulatory entities toward promoting transparency, accountability, and market integrity concerning sustainable finance. The efficacy of regulatory measures aimed at promoting the uptake of sustainable finance practices and alleviating the prevalence of greenwashing is subject to evaluation (Ioannou and Serafeim 2011).

4 Economic Stability and Sustainable Finance

This comprehensive understanding of the relationship between sustainable finance and economic stability explores the potential effects of sustainable finance initiatives on key economic indicators, such as GDP growth, employment, and inflation. Furthermore, it examines the influence of sustainable finance on long-term economic resilience and risk mitigation (Lester 2020) (Fig. 2).

4.1 Relationship Between Sustainable Finance and Economic Stability

Furthermore, it examines the influence of sustainable finance on long-term economic resilience and risk mitigation.

4.1.1 Theoretical Framework

Theoretical frameworks play a significant role in explicating the interplay between sustainable finance and economic stability. A multitude of theoretical frameworks have been posited to elucidate this association. An eminent framework known as the Triple Bottom Line posits that initiatives geared toward achieving sustainable finance objectives should consider not only financial performance but also the social and environmental impacts. Sustainable finance aims to facilitate favorable societal, environmental, and economic outcomes by incorporating sustainability principles into financial decision-making processes (Durusu-Ciftci et al. 2017).

An additional pertinent theoretical framework consists of the Sustainable Development Goals (SDGs) conceived

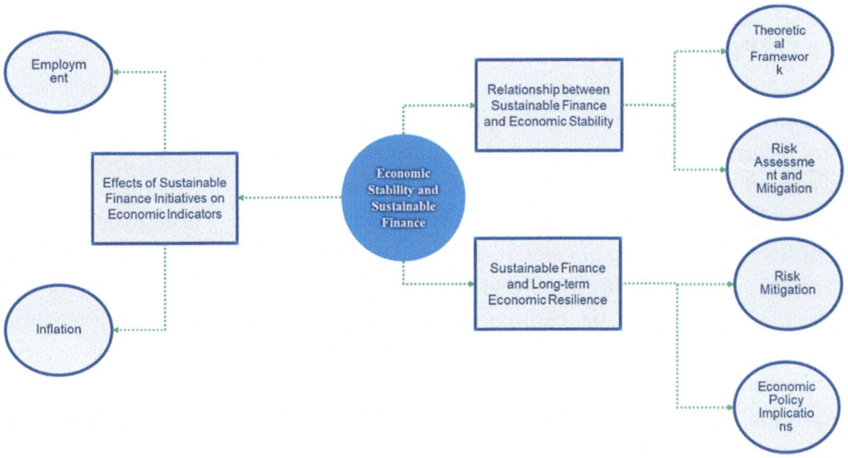

Fig. 2 Relationship between economic stability and sustainable finance

by the United Nations. The Sustainable Development Goals (SDGs) constitute a comprehensive framework for comprehensively addressing global challenges. These challenges encompass multifaceted issues, including but not limited to poverty, inequality, climate change, and environmental degradation. Sustainable development is supported through sustainable finance initiatives, which direct financial investments toward projects and enterprises that promote sustainable development. Sustainable finance can potentially augment economic stability by prioritizing social and environmental welfare through economic pursuits (Manu et al. 2011).

4.1.2 Risk Assessment and Mitigation

An essential aspect of economic stability is effective risk assessment and mitigation. Sustainable finance initiatives contribute by integrating environmental and social risks into economic decision-making. Traditional financial models often overlook these risks, significantly affecting long-term economic stability. By incorporating sustainability factors, such as climate change, resource scarcity, and social inequality, into risk assessment frameworks, sustainable finance enhances the understanding and management of potential risks. This, in turn, strengthens the stability and resilience of the financial system (Panel on Measuring Medical Care Risk in Conjunction with the New Supplemental Income Poverty Measure 2012).

4.2 Effects of Sustainable Finance Initiatives on Economic Indicators

Sustainable finance initiatives can influence Gross Domestic Product (GDP) growth by guiding investments toward sustainable sectors and undertakings. Investments in renewable energy, energy efficiency, sustainable infrastructure, and other environmentally friendly industries have the potential to promote and facilitate economic growth. The industries frequently necessitate significant allocations of resources towards research and development initiatives, consequently driving technological advances and fostering ingenuity. Furthermore, sustainable finance fosters enduring economic expansion by effectively addressing the predicaments arising from the depletion of resources, environmental degradation, and climate change (Verdoliva and Vigne 2022).

4.2.1 Employment

Sustainable finance initiatives can have significant implications for employment by creating new job opportunities and transforming labor markets. Investments in sustainable sectors, such as clean energy, green technologies, and sustainable agriculture, can generate employment across various skill levels. The transition to a low-carbon economy and adopting sustainable practices in existing industries can lead to the development of green jobs. However, it is essential to consider potential challenges associated with workforce transitions and ensure equitable access to sustainable job opportunities (Mahesh et al. 2022).

4.2.2 Inflation

The influence of sustainable finance on inflation dynamics is a critical examination area. Sustainable finance initiatives can impact inflation through various channels. Investments in sustainable sectors may change production costs, energy prices, and consumer preferences. Additionally, adopting sustainable practices can influence the pricing mechanisms and cost structures of goods and services. Understanding the potential effects of sustainable finance on inflation is important for policymakers and central banks in managing inflation rates and maintaining price stability (Linnenluecke et al. 2016).

4.3 Sustainable Finance and Long-Term Economic Resilience

Sustainable finance initiatives are pivotal in driving the sectoral transformation towards sustainability. By directing investments towards sustainable business models and practices, sustainable finance supports the development of green industries and adopting of circular economy principles. This transformation promotes long-term economic resilience by reducing dependency on carbon-intensive industries and fostering the sustainable use of resources. Furthermore, sectoral transformations driven by sustainable finance contribute to job creation, technological innovation, and increased competitiveness (Kovács 2020).

4.3.1 Risk Mitigation

One of the key contributions of sustainable finance to economic stability is long-term risk mitigation. Sustainable finance initiatives help address environmental and social risks, such as climate change, natural resource depletion, and social inequality. By integrating sustainability considerations into investment decision-making, financial institutions and investors can identify and manage risks associated with these factors. This approach leads to more resilient and sustainable investment portfolios, reducing the potential negative impacts of such risks on the economy (Tariqullah Khan 2019).

4.3.2 Economic Policy Implications

Incorporating sustainable finance within economic policy frameworks presents considerable ramifications for the economy's stability. Policymakers have the potential to devise and execute supportive frameworks aimed at fostering sustainable finance initiatives. These frameworks encompass a diverse range of approaches, which may entail regulatory measures, fiscal incentives, and programs aimed at enhancing individual or collective capacities. The governance entities are pivotal in furnishing supervision and direction to secure the efficiency and authenticity of sustainable fiscal policies. Policymakers must confront many potential challenges, including establishing relevant metrics and standards, aligning global frameworks, and facilitating collaboration amongst multiple stakeholders (Melo Pimentel and Ramírez Hunter 2021).

This discourse underscores the significance of incorporating sustainability principles into financial decision-making. Additionally, it brings to the fore the possible gains of sustainable finance in bolstering enduring economic stability and resilience.

5 Discussion

The research reveals a noteworthy influence of sustainable finance endeavors on financial markets and economic stability, thus corroborating earlier studies in the area. The outcomes of the empirical investigation demonstrate an unequivocal realignment of investment tendencies directed towards sustainable investments, prompted by the escalating request for financially viable products that conform to social responsibility and environmental preservation. The present discovery aligns with the expanding collection of literature underscoring the significance of sustainable finance as a key driver for encouraging responsible investment practices and tackling environmental and social issues (Korytsev and Morozov 2022).

Moreover, the analysis findings reveal that sustainable finance initiatives have a constructive impact on implementing risk management strategies within financial institutions. Including environmental, social, and governance (ESG) factors in risk assessment and mitigation approaches substantially fortifies the durability of financial establishments and contributes to the generation of enduring value. This determination is corroborated by antecedent scholarly investigations underscoring the significance of integrating sustainability factors within risk management frameworks.

The investigation discloses that sustainable financial products and instruments demonstrate analogous or superior market performance relative to customary financial products. This discovery is consistent with research that posits a favorable association between sustainability performance and financial performance. The augmentation in investors' recognition of the prospect for both monetary returns and affirmative societal and ecological influences has generated an escalator exigency for sustainable investments (Nizam et al. 2019).

Furthermore, the investigation underscores the significance of sustainable finance in advancing economic equilibrium. Sustainable investments augment the Gross Domestic Product (GDP) by stimulating employment opportunities, fostering innovation and development, and supporting sustainable industries. This discovery highlights the potential of sustainable finance in fostering alignment between economic development and environmental and societal aspirations, with the ultimate objective of reinforcing long-term economic stability.

The study significantly explains how sustainable finance initiatives impact the industry. Nonetheless, acknowledging its limitations and potential biases remains crucial. Primarily, the analysis is contingent upon accessible data sources that may possess inherent limitations and probable biases. Striving for data reliability and representation was undertaken; however, potential limitations, such as data lacunae or incongruities, may have impacted the produced findings.

Furthermore, the empirical analysis utilized in this study is founded upon particular assumptions and methodological approaches. The applied analytical techniques exhibit inherent limitations, while alternative methodologies possess the potential to generate different outcomes. Moreover, utilizing sample selection criteria might give rise to sampling biases, thereby imposing restrictions on the extent to which the findings can be extrapolated.

Notwithstanding, the present investigation constitutes a valuable contribution to the extant scholarship on sustainable finance, as it furnishes tangible and verifiable evidence regarding its effects. Subsequent investigations ought to endeavor to address the recognized restrictions, amplify the sample size and extent, and assimilate supplementary variables to advance our comprehension of the interdependence between sustainable finance, financial markets, and economic stability (Fulton et al. 2012).

In order to enhance comprehension of sustainable finance and its ramifications on financial markets and economic steadiness, forthcoming research ought to delve into several crucial domains. Initial research indicates that additional thorough examinations are required to evaluate the enduring effects of sustainable finance endeavors on the resilience and stability of economies. Longitudinal investigations have the potential to yield comprehensive insights regarding the prolonged and efficacious implementation of sustainable financial strategies.

Subsequent inquiry is necessary to grasp sustainable finance endeavors' societal ramifications comprehensively. This encompasses evaluating the impact of sustainable investments on societal benefits, including but not limited to the amelioration of impoverishment, the enhancement of educational access, and the achievement of gender parity. It is crucial to comprehend the wider societal implications of sustainable finance in order to actualize its complete potential (Fowler and Hope 2007).

Consequently, future academic inquiry must focus on assessing the efficaciousness of regulatory frameworks and policy interventions for fostering sustainable finance. Evaluating the enactment and consequences of regulations and incentives can offer valuable discernment into the policy mechanisms that effectively steer sustainable financial practices.

6 Conclusion

The research underscores the notable influence of sustainable finance endeavors on financial markets and the economy's stability. The present empirical investigation illustrates a discernible alteration in investment tendencies towards sustainable investments, primarily due to the mounting demand from investors for financial products that adhere to social responsibility and ecological friendliness. This alteration advocates for conscientious investment strategies and affirms a commitment to the progression of environmental and societal goals. Moreover, the analysis indicates that sustainable finance initiatives benefit the implementation of risk management strategies within financial institutions. Incorporating environmental, social, and governance (ESG) considerations into risk evaluation and intervention techniques augments financial institutions' durability and fosters enduring value. This underscores the criticality of incorporating sustainability criteria within financial decision-making processes.

Furthermore, the analysis indicates that sustainable financial products and instruments demonstrate equivalent or even enhanced market performance compared to traditional financial products. This discovery posits that investors have the potential to realize favorable financial gains alongside encouraging social and environmental outcomes through integrating sustainability considerations into their investment methodologies. The significance of these findings carries substantial implications. The transition towards sustainable finance can revolutionize financial markets, as it facilitates the diversion of capital towards environmentally sustainable and socially responsible projects. Furthermore, the integration of sustainable finance practices into the operations of financial institutions has the potential to elevate their risk management capabilities and bolster their resilience, thereby mitigating the possibility of systemic risks.

Sustainable finance initiatives possess a profound significance in their capacity to harmonize economic advancement with environmental and societal aspirations. By aligning financial decision-making processes with sustainability considerations, sustainable finance principles can facilitate the transition toward a more sustainable and socially inclusive economy. It holds paramount importance when tackling urgent worldwide issues, including but not limited to climate change, social disparity, and depletion of resources.

Sustainable finance endeavors are also increasingly incorporated into regulatory structures and policy agendas. Governments and regulatory bodies have acknowledged the significance of encouraging sustainable financial practices to effectively address environmental and social objectives without compromising financial stability. The burgeoning policy backing could serve as an additional catalyst in expediting the widespread integration of sustainable finance.

References

C. S. Akala, T. Neuhaus, and I. O. Leary-Govender, "A Systematic Review of Sustainable Investment Approaches," IJEF, vol. 14, no. 12, p. 72, Nov. 2022, https://doi.org/10.5539/ijef.v14n12p72.

I. Akomea-Frimpong, D. Adeabah, D. Ofosu, and E. J. Tenakwah, "A review of studies on green finance of banks, research gaps and future directions," Journal of Sustainable Finance & Investment, vol. 12, no. 4, pp. 1241–1264, Oct. 2022, https://doi.org/10.1080/20430795.2020.1870202.

Y. Chen and Z. J. Zhao, "The rise of green bonds for sustainable finance: global standards and issues with the expanding Chinese market," Current Opinion in Environmental Sustainability, vol. 52, pp. 54–57, Oct. 2021, https://doi.org/10.1016/j.cosust.2021.06.013.

D. Durusu-Ciftci, M. S. Ispir, and H. Yetkiner, "Financial development and economic growth: Some theory and more evidence," Journal of Policy Modeling, vol. 39, no. 2, pp. 290–306, Mar. 2017, https://doi.org/10.1016/j.jpolmod.2016.08.001.

M. Folqué, E. Escrig-Olmedo, and T. Corzo Santamaría, "Sustainable development and financial system: Integrating ESG risks through sustainable investment strategies in a climate change context," Sustainable Development, vol. 29, no. 5, pp. 876–890, Sep. 2021, https://doi.org/10.1002/sd.2181.

S. J. Fowler and C. Hope, "A Critical Review of Sustainable Business Indices and their Impact," J Bus Ethics, vol. 76, no. 3, pp. 243–252, Oct. 2007, https://doi.org/10.1007/s10551-007-9590-2.

M. Fulton, B. M. Kahn, and C. Sharples, "Sustainable Investing: Establishing Long-Term Value and Performance," SSRN Journal, 2012, https://doi.org/10.2139/ssrn.2222740.

I. Ioannou and G. Serafeim, "The Consequences of Mandatory Corporate Sustainability Reporting," SSRN Journal, 2011, https://doi.org/10.2139/ssrn.1799589.

V. Ivanitsk and L. Petrenko, "Development of responsible investment within the concept of sustainable finance," *Journal of New Economy*, vol. 21, no. 4, pp. 63–78, Jan. 2021, https://doi.org/10.29141/10.29141/2658-5081-2020-21-4-4.

A. Kashi and M. E. Shah, "Bibliometric Review on Sustainable Finance," Sustainability, vol. 15, no. 9, p. 7119, Apr. 2023, https://doi.org/10.3390/su15097119.

J. F. Kölbel, F. Heeb, F. Paetzold, and T. Busch, "Can Sustainable Investing Save the World? Reviewing the Mechanisms of Investor Impact," Organization & Environment, vol. 33, no. 4, pp. 554–574, Dec. 2020, https://doi.org/10.1177/1086026620919202.

M. A. Korytsev, S. A. Morozov, and Southern Federal University, "Institutional Development of Sustainable Finance: its Potential and Current Limitations," JER, vol. 13, no. 4, pp. 125–137, Dec. 2022, https://doi.org/10.17835/2078-5429.2022.13.4.125-137.

A. F. Kovács, Green Financial Perspectives - Proceeds of the Central European Scientific Conference on Green Finance and Sustainable Development, October 2020. Corvinus University of Budapest, 2021. https://doi.org/10.14267/978-963-503-890-9.

B. M. Kuhn, "Sustainable finance in Germany: mapping discourses, stakeholders, and policy initiatives," Journal of Sustainable Finance & Investment, vol. 12, no. 2, pp. 497–524, Apr. 2022, https://doi.org/10.1080/20430795.2020.1783151.

S. Lester, "Creating conditions for sustainable degree apprenticeships in England," HESWBL, vol. 10, no. 5, pp. 701–714, Jul. 2020, https://doi.org/10.1108/HESWBL-04-2020-0062.

M. K. Linnenluecke, T. Smith, and B. McKnight, "Environmental finance: A research agenda for interdisciplinary finance research," Economic Modelling, vol. 59, pp. 124–130, Dec. 2016, https://doi.org/10.1016/j.econmod.2016.07.010.

M. K. Mahesh, P. S. Aithal, and S. K. R. S., "Impact of Sustainable Finance on MSMEs and other Companies to Promote Green Growth and Sustainable Development," IJAEML, pp. 60–76, Feb. 2022, https://doi.org/10.47992/IJAEML.2581.7000.0120.

L. P. Manu, C. K. D. Adjasi, J. Abor, and S. K. Harvey, "Financial stability and economic growth: a cross-country study," IJFSM, vol. 5, no. 2, p. 121, 2011, https://doi.org/10.1504/IJFSM.2011.041920.

B. Melo Pimentel and G. A. Ramírez Hunter, "Sustainable Finance and its Sustainability," SSRN Journal, 2021, https://doi.org/10.2139/ssrn.3884907.

J. J. D. M. Neto and I. L. Fontgalland, "The BRICS in the sustainable agenda: Performance analysis of ESG indices in the financial markets in Brazil, China, India and South Africa," 62, vol. 10, no. 1, pp. 1–11, Mar. 2023, https://doi.org/10.18488/62.v10i1.3325.

E. Nizam, A. Ng, G. Dewandaru, R. Nagayev, and M. A. Nkoba, "The impact of social and environmental sustainability on financial performance: A global analysis of the banking sector," Journal of Multinational Financial Management, vol. 49, pp. 35–53, Mar. 2019, https://doi.org/10.1016/j.mulfin.2019.01.002.

Panel on Measuring Medical Care Risk in Conjunction with the New Supplemental Income Poverty Measure, M. J. O'Grady, and G. S. Wunderlich, Eds., Medical care economic risk: measuring financial vulnerability from spending on medical care. Washington, D.C: National Academies Press, 2012.

M. Pavláková Dočekalová and A. Kocmanová, "Comparison of Sustainable Environmental, Social, and Corporate Governance Value Added Models for Investors Decision Making," Sustainability, vol. 10, no. 3, p. 649, Feb. 2018, https://doi.org/10.3390/su10030649.

I.-S. Popescu, C. Hitaj, and E. Benetto, "Measuring the sustainability of investment funds: A critical review of methods and frameworks in sustainable finance," Journal of Cleaner Production, vol. 314, p. 128016, Sep. 2021, https://doi.org/10.1016/j.jclepro.2021.128016.

A. K. Srivastava, M. Dharwal, and A. Sharma, "Green financial initiatives for sustainable economic growth: A literature review," *Materials Today: Proceedings*, vol. 49, pp. 3615–3618, 2022, https://doi.org/10.1016/j.matpr.2021.08.158.

T. K. Tariqullah Khan, "Reforming Islamic Finance for Achieving Sustainable Development Goals," JKAU Islamic Econ, vol. 32, no. 1, pp. 3–21, Jan. 2019, https://doi.org/10.4197/Islec.32-1.1.

V. Verdoliva and S. A. Vigne, "An introduction to the special issue on Green Finance and sustainability," Financ Manag Account, vol. 33, no. 3, pp. 379–382, Oct. 2022, https://doi.org/10.1111/jifm.12149.

K. E. Yeow and S.-H. Ng, "The impact of green bonds on corporate environmental and financial performance," MF, vol. 47, no. 10, pp. 1486–1510, Oct. 2021, https://doi.org/10.1108/MF-09-2020-0481.

K. Zielińska-Lont, "Sustainable finance initiatives and their impact on financial stability," *FLR*, vol. 20, no. 4, pp. 118–133, 2020, https://doi.org/10.4467/22996834FLR.20.024.13096.

M. Zioło, I. Bąk, K. Cheba, A. Spoz, and P. Niedzielski, "Sustainable financial systems toward sustainability in finance. Institutional and managerial approach," Procedia Computer Science, vol. 192, pp. 4237–4248, 2021, https://doi.org/10.1016/j.procs.2021.09.200.

Exploring Broadband Adoption amongst Rural Businesses: A Review of the Literature

Sayed Abdul Majid Gilani, Liza Gernal, Rommel Sergio, Ansarullah Tantry, Peter Duncan, and Anne Smith

Abstract

Broadband has revolutionized how businesses operate. Research has demonstrated the importance of broadband adoption by smaller businesses to ensure growth as they make up over 90% of all businesses worldwide. This is especially for rural-based smaller businesses as limited innovation for them may lead to social exclusion between rural and urban areas. Research has identified a lag in the take-up of broadband by rural businesses in comparison to other businesses. Investigating broadband adoption by rural businesses may inform solutions to improving the rural economy. Therefore, the purpose of this paper is to review literature related to investigating drivers and barriers to broadband adoption by rural businesses to identify solutions for improving broadband take-up amongst rural businesses. Through a systematic literature review (SLR), this paper reviews studies from 2000 to 2023. A thematic analysis identifies drivers and barriers to broadband adoption, however, size, sector, frequency of broadband adoption and level of rurality for the businesses are not clarified. The review identified limited primary research in regions like South America, the United Kingdom (UK) and Australia. Findings inform the development of a conceptual framework. Infrastructure highlighted as a barrier may inform policymakers. Findings may also inform the take-up of broadband by other businesses.

Keywords

Barriers · Drivers · Broadband · Internet · Rural

1 Introduction

Broadband has revolutionized lives around the world in terms of retail as well as everyday services like banking, medical and communication since its inception at the end of the twentieth century (Castells 2021, Allardyce 2017). Like individuals, businesses have greatly benefitted from marketing and selling products as well as communicating with suppliers and clients online via broadband (Allardyce 2017). In terms of business sizes, large multi-national businesses have profoundly benefitted from the adoption of broadband for their business operations by integrating the use of technology into their business strategies and operations, e.g., online marketing and online shops which led to lower costs than the traditional methods. However, compared to larger enterprises, broadband adoption among smaller businesses seems to be lagging, particularly in rural areas (Young and Miles 2015).

Smaller businesses make up over 90% of all businesses worldwide, which highlights their significant impact on

S. A. Gilani (✉)
School of Business, Birmingham City University, Birmingham B15 3TN, UK
e-mail: majidgilanii@hotmail.com

L. Gernal
School of Business, Westford University College, 61110 Sharjah, United Arab Emirates
e-mail: liza.g@westford.org.uk

R. Sergio
Faculty of Business, Canadian University Dubai, City Walk, Dubai, United Arab Emirates
e-mail: rommel@cud.ac.ae

A. Tantry
Department of Psychology, Westford University College, 61110 Sharjah, United Arab Emirates
e-mail: ansarullah.t@westford.org.uk

P. Duncan · A. Smith
School of Business, Law and Society, Glasgow Caledonian University, Glasgow G4 0BA, UK
e-mail: p.b.duncan@gcu.ac.uk

A. Smith
e-mail: anne.smith@gcu.ac.uk

S. Arezki et al. (eds.), *Emerging Disruptive Technologies for Society 5.0 in Developing Countries*, Advances in Science, Technology & Innovation, https://doi.org/10.1007/978-3-031-63701-8_9

national economic growth and job creation (Castells 2021). Gilani et al. (Abdul et al. 2023) highlight the importance of broadband/innovation adoption by smaller businesses in isolated areas as it ensures a minimum digital divide and social exclusion between such businesses and their urban counterparts, and it enhances their prospects of survival and growth due to the related benefits to business operations from broadband adoption (Young and Miles 2015). As smaller businesses make up over 90% of all businesses worldwide and there have been benefits highlighted for businesses adopting broadband, then there is a need to identify solutions to improve the lag in broadband taken up by rural businesses (Allardyce 2017). In addition to supporting the rural economy, such solutions may eliminate the possibility of depopulation in rural areas, hence, leading to the preservation of local rural cultures and identities (Battisti et al. 2013).

Therefore, the purpose of this paper is to investigate the drivers and barriers related to broadband adoption/use by rural businesses to understand why such businesses are lagging in broadband adoption and implementation. The purpose will be based on the following objectives:

What are the drivers and barriers to broadband adoption by rural businesses?
What is the role of government in supporting broadband adoption by businesses?

The term "Rural" has always been linked with large open green fields, smaller populations, and a perceived simplicity in living with limited reliance on ongoing technological trends (Delalić and Oruč Mar. 2014). The definition of rural has varied from sources around the world. Rural, defining as a complex process where multiple factors need to be considered to effectively clarify the level of rurality in each region (Chuabsamai 2016). Therefore, Gilani et al. (Abdul et al. 2023) developed dimensions for defining rurality (Table 1) based on the rural definitions from the United States of America (Chuabsamai 2016), and the United Kingdom (Bourreau et al. 2017).

Dimension 1 addresses the population number and population density in each area. The travel distance between a given area and the nearest recognised urban area is represented by Dimension 2. Dimension 3 evaluates the development of an area in terms of things like resources and infrastructure. The culture within a given area is the fourth dimension identified by Gilani et al. (Abdul et al. 2023). The social perception related to identifying rural areas is addressed in Dimension 5. Therefore, the rural dimensions developed by Gilani et al. (Abdul et al. 2023) will inform this research study's understanding of the rurality of locations for businesses in the reviewed studies.

Table 1 Dimensions for defining rural areas

Dimension	Focus
Dimension 1	Population and population density
Dimension 2	Proximity to urban areas
Dimension 3	Development
Dimension 4	Culture
Dimension 5	Social perception

2 Methodology

A systematic literature review (SLR) was adopted which involved identifying and reviewing broadband adoption-related studies conducted from 1999 to 2023. The year 1999 was established as the starting point for selecting studies as broadband became globally available for public use from 1999 onwards (Burnett and Danson Jan. 2017, C. University 2019). The key terms of 'broadband', 'internet', 'broadband/internet adoption/take up', 'remote-rural micro-businesses and 'remote-rural Scotland' are being inputted into the search engines of Google, Google Books and Google Scholar in different combinations. The prerequisites for studies to be included in this research are outlined in Table 2.

As specified in Table 1, 'Step 2' determines whether the study was conducted during 2000–2023. Through a thematic analysis, the arrangement of collected literature review data was reported in alphabetical as well as chronological order; key themes/patterns identified amongst the reviewed studies; the age of the research study and geographic relevance of each study to the focus of this paper. Along with the Google/Google books/Google Scholar searches regular visits were made to different journals through email notifications to check for any recent research produced in the "broadband adoption/use by rural business" area.

Studies relevant to this paper's focus were identified by checking their abstract, methodology and conclusion sections. For example, the sections were checked to verify whether a given study was related to the paper's focus and how the information could be adopted to support the research related to the paper. The thematic analysis was based on the criteria in Table 3.

Table 2 Pre-requisites informing the inclusion of each study in the systematic review

Step 1	Does the research purpose investigate the take-up of innovations/technology by rural businesses?
Step 2	Was the study conducted during the period 2000–2023?
Step 3	Are rural businesses included in the studies?

Table 3 Criterion for the template analysis

Criterion
Year
Geography
Business size
Business sector
Level of rurality of business location
Level/degree of broadband adoption

The year of studies was adopted as a criterion to ensure that the research was not dated. The criteria of geography allowed this study to identify the level of existing research investigating broadband adoption by rural businesses. The criteria of business size and sector allowed the research to determine if existing literature factored in business size and sector with broadband adoption. The rurality of businesses included in the reviewed studies allowed the researchers with the aid of the rural dimensions (Abdul et al. 2023) to determine if businesses' level of isolation was not factored in studies while investigating innovation adoption. The final criterion investigating the degree of broadband adoption by enterprises in the reviewed studies allowed the study to identify whether existing literature has addressed the frequency of broadband adoption by rural businesses.

A thematic analysis was also adopted in the review of innovation/technology adoption theories to inform the development of a theory related to investigating broadband adoption by rural businesses. The theories of the Bass Diffusion Model, Technological Acceptance Model (TAM), Diffusion of Innovations (DoI) theory, and the TOE (Technological Organizational and Environmental) framework were included in the review as they were involved in previous broadband adoption-related studies. The purpose of the review was to identify a theory which can investigate initial broadband adoption as well as the frequency of broadband adoption by a business. A summary of the strengths and weaknesses of each reviewed theory is provided in Table 4.

The review of the theories highlighted the suitability of the TOE and DoI frameworks as being suitable theories for inclusion in research related to investigating initial broadband adoption and frequency of broadband adoption by rural businesses. The TOE can investigate broadband adoption by businesses (Aljowaidi 2015) and the DoI can investigate the frequency of broadband adoption through the Innovation Decision Process (IDP) (Singeh et al. 2020).

3 Literature Review

In this paper, the following definitions for drivers and barriers to broadband adoption/use have been adopted:

Driver: Something that promotes or encourages broadband take up and broadband use thereafter.

Barrier: Something that limits/completely stops broadband takeup (Horberry and Regan 2014, Lima et al. 2018).

The identified broadband adoption/use drivers from the review of worldwide studies are presented in Table 5. The table presents the drivers in alphabetic order where locations are presented in alphabetic order for each driver and author names are arranged in alphabetic order for each location.

Table 4 Summary of strengths and weaknesses for each theoretical framework/model

Theoretical framework /model	Advantages	Weaknesses	Source
Bass	Flexibility to be combined with another framework/model and can be included in all types of methodologies and contexts	Reliability issues due to parameter bias, and inability to measure innovation diffusion factors	Cosguner et al. (2018)
DoI	Flexibility to be combined with another framework/model and can be included in all types of methodologies and contexts	Does not consider disruptive technologies	Choudrie and Middleton (2013), Singeh et al. (2020)
TAM 1/2/3	Flexibility to be combined with another framework/model and can be included in all types of methodologies and contexts	Rigidness	Koichu and Keller (2017)
TOE	Allows an explanation of inter/intra-firm adoption for innovation/technology; the ability to look at innovation/technology adoption through multiple contexts; the flexibility to be combined with another framework/model and can be included in all types of methodologies and contexts	No clarification on the impact of business size on innovation/technology adoption; studying the adoption of inter-organizational procedures and systems from the perspective of a single business over multiple businesses; limited to yes or no regarding innovation/technology adoption	Aljowaidi (2015)

Table 5 Summary of broadband adoption/use drivers identified in the review

Drivers	Location	Author (s)
Access to business information	Asia	Srinivas et al. (2014)
	Scotland, UK	Deakins et al. (2004, White et al. (2016)
Affordability (cost)	Africa	Groves-Phillips (2023, Masita-Mwangi et al. 2012)
	Europe	Doherty (2012)
	New Zealand	Clark and Douglas (2011)
	North America	Kuhn et al. (2016)
Communication	Africa	Finbarr (2015)
	Asia	Srinivas et al. (2014, Bagchi (2013)
	Australia	Beacom and Nanere (2023)
	Scotland, UK	Townsend et al. (n.d.)
	Wales, UK	C. University (2019)
Confidence/training	Europe	Doherty (2012, Glance (2017)
	United Arab Emirates (UAE)	Gilani et al. (2023)
Culture (growth-driven business)	Africa	Finbarr (2015)
	Asia	Srinivas et al. (2014, S. V. 'Ofa (2018)
	England, UK	Bosworth and Salemink (2014, Warren (2004) Wilson et al. (2018)
	Australia	Glance (2017)
	New Zealand	Fabling et al. (n.d.)
	North America	Passerini et al. (2012)
	Scotland, UK	Townsend et al. (n.d.)
	Wales, UK	C. University 2019)
Environmentally friendly	Scotland, UK	Steiner and Atterton Mar. (2014)
Improved income for businesses	Asia	S. V. 'Ofa (2018)
	England, UK	Wilson et al. (2018)
	New Zealand	Fabling et al. (n.d.)
	Scotland, UK	Townsend et al. (n.d.)
	Wales, UK	Cardiff University (2019)
Infrastructure, eg satisfactory broad-band quality and speed	Australia	Glance (2017)
	England, UK	Wilson et al. (2018)
	New Zealand	Fabling et al. (n.d.)
	Scotland, UK	Gilani and Faccia (2022)
	Wales, UK	Davies (2014)
Marketing/Promotion	Africa	Finbarr (2015)
	Asia	Kriechbaumer and Christodoulidou Aug. (2014)
	Scotland, UK	Townsend et al. (n.d.)
	Wales, UK	Cardiff University (2019)
Support towards daily operations (Planning)	Africa	Ojanji (2013)
	Asia	S. V. 'Ofa (2018)
	UAE	Gilani et al. (2023)
	England, UK	Wilson et al. (2018)
	New Zealand	Clark and Douglas (2011)
	Scotland, UK	Galloway and Kapasi (2014)

As shown in Table 5, the main drivers identified from the literature review are 'communication', 'culture' in the business, 'infrastructure', 'marketing' and 'planning'. In Table 5, the main barriers are identified as 'lack of government support' and 'poor infrastructure'. It should be noted that these drivers and barriers have been identified as the main drivers and barriers for broadband adoption/use based on the number of studies identifying each driver and barrier. It should be noted that culture is defined as a driver for businesses adopting broadband due to the dated culture of the local rural society or the more traditional culture of the businesses included in the review (Cardiff University 2019; Warren 2004; Wilson et al. 2018). An explanation for each of the identified broadband adoption drivers is provided in Table 6.

Table 7 presents the barriers related to broadband adoption/use for rural businesses. These findings are presented in terms of barriers, authors, and location. Table 7 presents the barriers in alphabetic order where locations are presented in alphabetic order for each barrier and author names are arranged in alphabetic order for each location.

Culture is defined as a barrier for businesses adopting broadband due to the dated culture of the local rural society or the more traditional culture of the businesses included in the review (Burnett and Danson Jan. 2017; Townsend et al. (n.d.); Olukayode et al. 2014). The definitions for each of the identified barriers are provided in Table 8.

Table 6 Broadband adoption/use drivers identified in the literature review and their definitions

Drivers	Definitions
Access to business information	Such information informs owner-managers purchase of stock and revision of policies and strategies related to the daily running of the business
Affordability (cost)	Daily costs for operations like banking and marketing are reduced through online banking and e-marketing where owner-managers also save money through online price comparison sites for stock and equipment
Communication	Communication with consumers, employees and suppliers through email or social media
Confidence/ Training	Confidence from a good understanding and training in using broadband
Culture	The business' ambition along with the beliefs, religions, rituals and virtues of the local population
Environmentally friendly	All operations completed online are paperless which has a positive impact on the environment
Improved income for businesses	An online presence allows businesses to have visibility amongst a larger customer base where products through online shopping lead to a higher probability of sales, therefore, increasing the chances of an improved income for the business
Infrastructure	Up-to-date infrastructure for broadband will lead to consistent broadband connectivity within the business which then allows the business to operate without disruptions that are normally caused by an intermittent broadband service
Marketing/ Promotion	Promoting the business through a website or social media
Planning	Support towards daily operations, such as time saved and convenience in tasks like market research, accounting, stocking ordering and recruitment

Table 7 Summary of broadband adoption/use barriers identified in the review

Barriers	Author (s)	Location
Confidence/ training	Marlin and Bruce (2006)	Canada, North America
	Young and Miles 2015, (White et al. (2016)	Scotland, UK
	Davies (2014)	Wales, UK
	Gilani et al. (2023)	UAE
Cost	Marlin and Bruce (2006)	Canada, North America
	Bourreau et al. (2017)	Europe
	Wilson et al. (2018)	England, UK
	Townsend et al. (n.d.)	Scotland, UK
Culture	Olukayode et al. (2014)	Asia
	Marlin and Bruce (2006)	Canada, North America
	Battisti et al. (2013)	New Zealand
	Burnett and Danson (2017; Townsend et al. (n.d.)	Scotland, UK
Lack of government support (awareness)	Srinivas et al. (2014)	Asia
	Choudrie and Middleton (2013)	Australia
	Marlin and Bruce (2006)	Canada, North America
	Wilson et al. (2018)	England, UK
	Bourreau et al. (2017)	Europe
	Hill et al. (2016)	Scotland, UK
Poor infrastructure	Finbarr 2015)	Africa
	Srinivas et al. (2014), S. V. 'Ofa (2018)	Asia
	Choudrie and Middleton (2013)	Australia
	Marlin and Bruce (2006)	Canada, North America
	Wilson et al. (2018), Cowie et al. (2013)	England, UK
	Burnett and Danson (2017; Gilani and Faccia (2022) Ogston (2017)	Scotland, UK
	Cardiff University (2019)	Wales, UK
Security/Level of trust	Townsend et al. (n.d.)	Scotland, UK

Table 8 Broadband adoption/use barriers identified in the literature review and their definitions

Barriers	Definitions
Confidence/Training	Owner-managers are under the impression that they cannot effectively use broadband for different operations
Cost	The initial cost of buying the equipment along with paying for a subscription
Culture	The business' ambition along with the beliefs, religions, rituals and virtues of the local population
Lack of government support	Lack of awareness campaigns regarding broadband training and availability
Poor infrastructure	Inability to access a level of service which allows owner-managers to carry out online-based operations
Security/Level of trust	Possibility of online fraud and a lack of uncertainty related to not meeting customers/manufacturers/suppliers face to face

In addition to the identified drivers and barriers for broadband adoption/use by rural businesses, the study identified that there was limited clarity provided on the size and sector of the included businesses along with the rurality of their locations. These findings highlight an opportunity for future primary research involving businesses with clearly defined sectors, sizes, and rurality of location. The SLR also highlighted a lack of discussion among the reviewed studies regarding the frequency of broadband adoption where only Deakins et al. (Deakins et al. 2004), Galloway (Galloway 2007) and Galloway and Kapasi (Galloway and Kapasi 2014) have addressed this discussion.

4 Discussion

A summary of the drivers and barriers to broadband adoption by rural businesses in the review is provided in Table 9.

As identified earlier, the TOE and the IDP feature from DoI can be combined to investigate initial broadband adoption and frequency of broadband adoption by rural businesses.

It should be noted that there is the Unified Theory of Acceptance and Use of Technology (UTAUT) which can investigate initial broadband adoption and frequency of broadband adoption (Venkatesh 2003). The rationale behind developing a new theory rather than simply adopting the UTAUT was justified by this research looking to get a detailed breakdown of social constructs in terms of drivers and barriers for broadband adoption/use by rural businesses. Therefore, there was a need to develop a framework that exclusively investigates drivers and barriers to broadband adoption and the frequency of broadband adoption by rural businesses. Additionally, the conceptual framework will distinguish between broadband adoption by all users (users with access to urban or rural infrastructure) and broadband adoption by users with access to rural-based infrastructure due to the development of the conceptual framework being informed by broadband adoption/use drivers and barriers for businesses in a rural context. The characteristics of TOE incorporated in the conceptual framework are illustrated in Fig. 1.

The IDP feature that will be included in the conceptual framework is illustrated in Fig. 2.

The drivers and barriers for broadband adoption/use identified in Table 9 are mapped against the TOE framework's contexts in Table 10.

The content in Figs. 1 and 2 and Table 10 was combined to form the Broadband Adoption Framework (BAF) which is illustrated in Fig. 3.

As shown in Fig. 3, the drivers, and barriers for broadband adoption/use are organised under the technological, organisational, and environmental contexts from TOE. The words and lines labelled with **D** represent drivers; words

Table 9 Drivers and barriers of broadband adoption/use by rural businesses

	Access to business information		Cost
	Affordability (cost)		Confidence/training
	Communication		Culture (business/local area)
Drivers	Confidence/training	**Barriers**	Lack of government support (awareness)
	Environmentally friendly		Poor Infrastructure
	Growth-driven business (culture)		Security/Level of trust
	Improved income for businesses		
	Infrastructure, e.g., satisfactory broadband quality and speed		
	Marketing/Promotion		
	Planning (Support towards daily operations)		

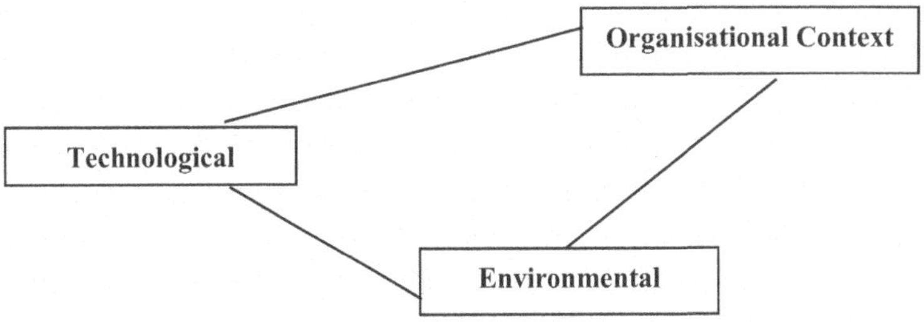

Fig. 1 Outline shell of TOE
Source (Aljowaidi 2015)

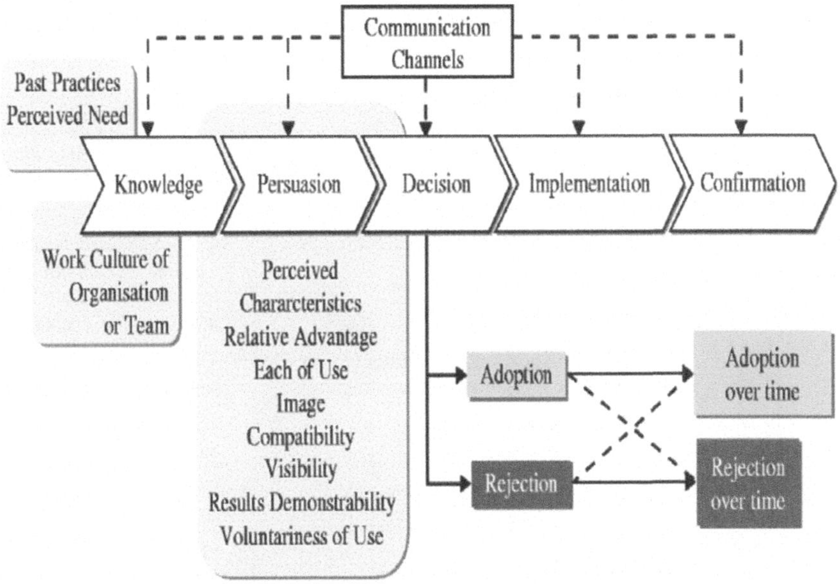

Fig. 2 The IDP from DoI theory
Source (Singeh et al. Jun. 2020)

and lines labelled with **B** represent barriers; words labelled **D/B** represent both drivers and barriers. The single arrows in the lines labelled with **D** and **B** are respectively represented by drivers leading to broadband adoption/use, and barriers leading to non-broadband adoption/use and the interconnectivity between the contexts of technology, organisation and environment are represented by the double arrowed black lines. Knowledge is represented by 'K', Persuasion is represented by 'P', Decision is represented by 'D', Implementation is represented by 'I' and Confirmation is represented by 'C'. Additionally, Adoption is represented by 'A' and Rejection is represented by 'R'.

5 Conclusion and Recommendations

An investigation of the drivers and barriers related to broadband adoption by rural businesses was established as the purpose of this paper. From the findings, the paper was looking to understand why such businesses are lagging in broadband adoption and implementation. Earlier, the paper established that broadband adoption by businesses aids their growth, especially for businesses based in isolated locations which are subject to a higher probability of social exclusion and the digital divide. Based on the findings, the paper was looking to establish directions towards developing solutions to overcome the problem of lagging broadband adoption amongst rural businesses as this may aid the rural economy, preservation of rural cultures, job creation and economies through the survival and growth of rural businesses. The purpose of the paper was established on 2 objectives. The realization of the objectives is explained below.

1. *What are the drivers and barriers to broadband adoption by rural businesses?*

The identified drivers and barriers to broadband adoption by rural businesses from the SLR are identified in Table 11.

2. *What is the role of government in supporting broadband adoption by businesses?*

As shown in Table 11, 'Good Infrastructure' was identified as a driver for broadband adoption, however, 'Poor Infrastructure' and 'Lack of government support' were

Table 10 Drivers and barriers categorised in terms of TOE contexts

Contexts	Drivers/barriers	Explanation
Technological	**Infrastructure** Good/bad infrastructure due to location	The situation with the infrastructure for broadband in each location is a technological factor that influences a business
	Culture (Innovation driven by business (internal)/ local area (external) culture)	Innovation is within technology as it is related to experimenting with or adopting technologies which may be new to the business
Organisational	**Access to business information**	This allows businesses to stay informed regarding customer demand for their products, whether that may affect stock delivery, government regulations or to learn from other industry rivals
	Culture (the ambition of growth driven by the business' internal culture)	A level of ambition is set by the owner-manager along with employees within a business. Therefore, it belongs in the organisational context
	Communication	Broadband can be used as a tool through sites like Skype or WhatsApp for employers or employees to either communicate with each other, suppliers, and customers
	Cost The cost saved/incurred	Cost either saved or incurred from broadband adoption/use directly impacts the business itself. Therefore, the cost saved/incurred is within organisational
	Culture Cultural and family/Cultural issues	Culture and beliefs can affect an owner-manager or employees within a business in adopting broadband. For example, traditional background managers would not be too keen on using broadband; however, family members may encourage employers or managers to adopt broadband
	Confidence/Knowledge/Training (eg confidence driven by the level of knowledge/training)	The level of training of owner-managers and employees within a business may encourage or discourage broadband adoption/use
	Environmentally friendly	The positive or negative effects of using broadband may influence a business' take up of the service
	Improved income for business	Broadband allows businesses to gain a larger customer base and an additional method to sell their products, e.g., online business
	Marketing	Figures from within a business can use broadband to market business products
	Planning	Business-related information based online can advise an owner-manager to plan future steps in terms of pricing, buying materials and so on
	Security/Level of trust	The increase in online fraud and the quick/efficient transfer of valuable documents can influence broadband takeup
Environmental	**Cost**	Costs incurred through creating/maintaining a competitive edge against rivals. There are also costs incurred to ensure that the business is operating within government guidelines and the adjustment of pricing to retain/attract customers
	Culture (Influenced by beliefs, values, virtues, or religion)	The local culture can affect a business owner in adopting broadband for daily operations, e.g., if locals are not happy booking a dinner reservation online then adopting an online booking system is ineffective
	Environmentally friendly	The paperless nature of performing online tasks such as sending out electronic receipts, booking confirmations and promotions may encourage the local community in using the business due to the environmentally friendly nature of the operations
	Infrastructure Good/bad infrastructure due to location	Infrastructure is an external factor which impacts the business owner's decision to adopt broadband for daily operations. For example, poor broadband will discourage adoption and strong broadband will encourage adoption
	Government policy/support	Government policy is an external factor which can improve broadband adoption/use within a business. For example, government policy to improve broadband infrastructure will encourage greater adoption amongst businesses
	Marketing/Promotion Marketing received by customers	Customers need to be using broadband to see the online promotion of business services where customers can use broadband for online communication with the business owner or employees
	Planning Planning to compete better against rivals	Business-related information based online can allow a business to gain an advantage in running operations at greater efficiency over competitors not adopting broadband

Fig. 3 The BAF

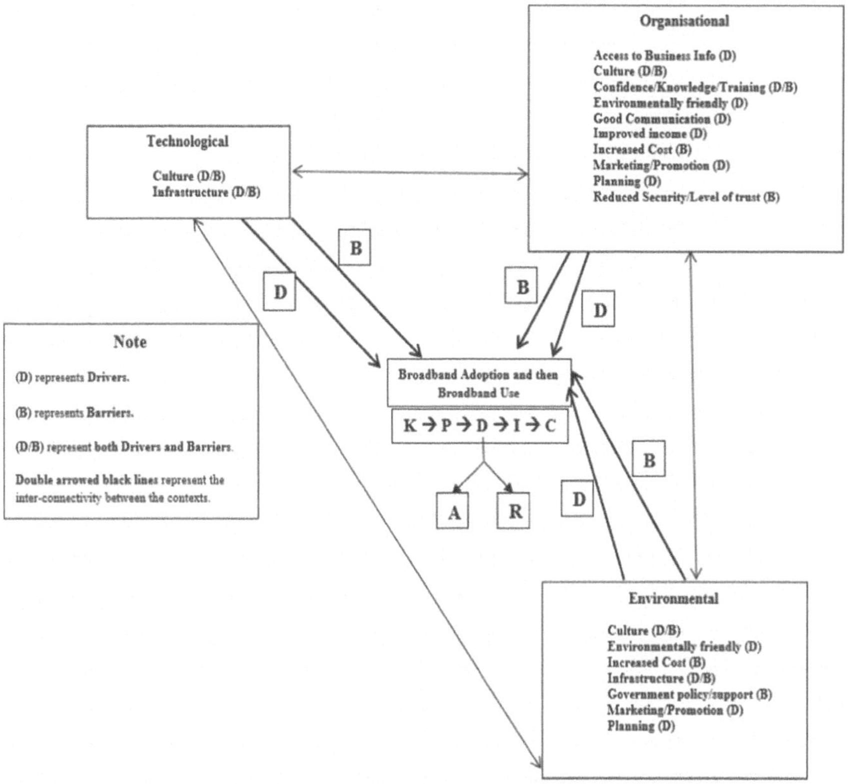

Table 11 Drivers and barriers of broadband adoption/use by rural businesses

	Access to business information		Cost
	Affordability (cost)		Confidence/ training
	Communication		Culture (business/local area)
Drivers	Confidence/training	**Barriers**	Lack of government support (awareness)
	Environmentally friendly		Poor Infrastructure
	Growth-driven business (culture)		Security/Level of trust
	Improved income for businesses		
	Infrastructure, e.g., satisfactory broadband quality and speed		
	Marketing/Promotion		
	Planning (Support towards daily operations)		

identified as barriers against broadband adoption. These identified drivers and barriers highlight that there is scope for a greater level of involvement by the government to improve broadband-related infrastructure and raise awareness regarding broadband-related benefits in rural communities which may improve broadband adoption by rural businesses.

a. policy-based contributions

The findings related to infrastructure and a lack of government support as barriers against broadband adoption may inform policymakers in developing policies related to the improvement of broadband infrastructure and campaigns promoting the benefits of broadband adoption which may improve broadband adoption amongst rural businesses and communities. Therefore, in the process eliminate social exclusion and the digital divide between rural and urban business communities.

b. Practice-based contributions

The findings from this research may better inform non-broadband adopting business owners on the benefits related to broadband adoption which may encourage a higher level of broadband adoption amongst such populations. The findings may also encourage existing broadband-adopting business owners to further integrate broadband-driven processes into their business operations.

c. Theoretical-based contributions

The findings of this research informed the development of the BAF which can investigate initial broadband adoption and the frequency of broadband adoption amongst rural businesses in terms of drivers and barriers. The BAF may inform or act as a template for future related studies in developing theories that may vary in terms of geography, business sectors and business size.

6 Future Directions

The authors of this study advise future research investigating broadband adoption by businesses with established sectors, sizes, rurality of their location and the frequency of their adoption as in the SLR these areas were highlighted to be explored at a limited capacity.

References

S. Abdul, S. A. M. Gilani, N. Yasin, and A. M. J. Smith, "What is Remote-Rural and Why is it Important?," *Inderscience*, May 24, 2023. https://www.researchgate.net/publication/370995457_What_is_Remote-Rural_and_Why_is_it_Important (accessed Aug. 03, 2023)

M. Aljowaidi, "A study of e-commerce adoption using TOE framework in Saudi retailers: firm motivations, implementation and benefits," Doctoral dissertation, RMIT University, 2015. [Online]. Available: https://researchbank.rmit.edu.au/view/rmit:161568

J. Allardyce, "'Marginalisation' risk for the 20% who stay offline," *The Sunday Times*, Jun. 24, 2017. Accessed: Aug. 02, 2023. [Online]. Available: https://www.thetimes.co.uk/article/marginalisation-risk-for-the-20-who-stay-offline-glv5f20h9 M. Fornefeld, G. Delaunay, and D. Elixmann, "Columbia Institute for Tele-Information (CITI)," *Columbia Business School*, 2021. https://www8.gsb.columbia.edu/citi/sites/citi/files/Panel%203.Martin%20Fornefeld%20paper.pdf (accessed Aug. 03, 2023)

S. Bagchi, "Rural India yet to reap true benefits of the Internet." http://www.cxotoday.com/story/taking-internet-opportunity-to-rural-india/http://www.cxotoday.com/story/taking-internet-opportunity-to-rural-india/ (accessed 2013) G. Jason Paolo; Whalley, "Fibre to the countryside: A comparison of public and community initiatives in the UK"

M. Battisti, D. Deakins, and M. Perry, "The sustainability of small businesses in recessionary times," *International Journal of Entrepreneurial Behavior & Research*, vol. 19, no. 1, pp. 72–96, Jan. 2013, https://doi.org/10.1108/13552551311299260

M. Beacom and M. Nanere, "The Impact of Internet Technologies and E-business applications on Tourism Enterprises: A Case Study from central Victoria, Australia." http://www.afbe.biz/main/wp-content/uploads/AFBEConfPapers2010.pdf#page=526 (accessed Aug. 03, 2023)

G. Bosworth and K. Salemink, "Investigating community-led broadband initiatives as a model for neo-endogenous development," Jan. 2014

M. Bourreau, R. Feasey, and S. Hoernig, "Demand-Side Policies to Accelerate the Transition to Ultrafast Broadband," 2017. https://www.cerre.eu/sites/cerre/files/171212_CERRE_BroadbandDemand_FinalReport.pdf

K. A. Burnett and M. Danson, "Enterprise and entrepreneurship on islands and remote rural environments," *The International Journal of Entrepreneurship and Innovation*, vol. 18, no. 1, pp. 25–35, Jan. 2017, https://doi.org/10.1177/1465750316686237

C. University, "Superfast Broadband Business Exploitation Project Digital technologies and future opportunities for rural businesses and areas in Wales January," https://www.cardiff.ac.uk/__data/assets/pdf_file/0008/1438802/Horizon-scanning_rural-opportunities-03.pdf, 2019

M. Castells, "The Impact of the Internet on Society: A Global Perspective," *OpenMind*, 2021. https://www.bbvaopenmind.com/en/articles/the-impact-of-the-internet-on-society-a-global-perspective/ (accessed Jun. 20, 2023)

J. Choudrie and C. Middleton, *Management of Broadband Technology and Innovation*. Routledge, 2013. Accessed: Aug. 03, 2023. [Online]. Available: https://doi.org/10.4324/9780203754184 K. Miri Lavassani, B. Movahedi, and G. Parry, "Broadband Internet adoption challenge," *Transforming Government: People, Process and Policy*, vol. 8, no. 4, pp. 620–644, Oct. 2014, https://doi.org/10.1108/tg-11-2013-0050

T. Chuabsamai, "'Alarming' disparity in broadband connectivity within Asia-Pacific, UN regional study finds," *UN News*, Aug. 19, 2016. https://news.un.org/en/story/2016/08/536972-alarming-disparity-broadband-connectivity-within-asia-pacific-un-regional-study (accessed Jun. 14, 2023)

D. N. Clark and H. Douglas, "Information and communication technology adoption and diffusion in micro-enterprises: the case of techno-savvy home-based businesses," *International Journal of Entrepreneurship and Small Business*, vol. 14, no. 3, p. 349, 2011, https://doi.org/10.1504/ijesb.2011.042758

K. Cosguner, S. Seetharaman, and C. Wu, "Dynamic Pricing for New Products: Utility-Based Generalization of the Bass Diffusion Model," 2018. https://www.researchgate.net/publication/328736172_Dynamic_Pricing_for_New_Products_Utility-Based_Generalization_of_the_Bass_Diffusion_Model (accessed Jun. 10, 2023)

P. Cowie, N. Thompson, and F. Rowe, "Honey Pots and Hives: Maximising the potential of rural enterprise hubs," 2013

R. Davies, "An Investigation into Methodologies for Measuring the Effect of Varying Broadband Quality on Economic Impact in SMEs," 2014

D. Deakins, R. Mochrie, and L. Galloway, "Rural business use of information and communications technologies(ICTs): a study of the relative impact of collective activity in rural Scotland," *Strategic Change*, vol. 13, no. 3, pp. 139–150, May 2004, https://doi.org/10.1002/jsc.683

S. Delalić and N. Oruč, "Determinations of Firm Growth: A Study of Rural SMEs in Bosnia-Herzegovina," *Journal of Economic and Social Studies*, vol. 4, no. 1, pp. 5–23, Mar. 2014, https://doi.org/10.14706/jecoss11411

E. Doherty, "Broadband adoption and diffusion : a study of Irish SMEs," Jan. 01, 2012. http://ethos.bl.uk/OrderDetails.do?uin=uk.bl.ethos.567099 (accessed Aug. 03, 2023)

R. Fabling and A. Grimes, "[PDF] Picking up Speed: Does Ultrafast Broadband Increase Firm Productivity?," *ERN: Productivity (Topic)*

B. Finbarr, "Will Africa take the lead in the Internet of Things?" 2015. https://discover.gcu.ac.uk/discovery/fulldisplay?docid=proquest1654891980&context=PC&vid=44GLCU_INST:44GLCU_VU2&lang=en&search_scope=MyInst_and_CI&adaptor=Primo%20Central&tab=Everything&query=any,cont (accessed Aug. 03, 2023)

L. Galloway, "Can broadband access rescue the rural economy?" *Journal of Small Business and Enterprise Development*, vol. 14, no. 4, pp. 641–653, Oct. 2007, https://doi.org/10.1108/14626000710832749. A. Phippen and H. Lacohée,

"Defining the Research Context," *Springer International Publishing*, Jan. 01, 2017. http://link.springer.com/chapter/https://doi.org/10.1007/978-3-319-47554-7_2 (accessed Aug. 03, 2023)

L. Galloway and I. Kapasi, "Rural home-based businesses and their contribution to rural lives: an exploratory study," 2014

S. A. M. Gilani, A. Copiaco, L. Gernal, N. Yasin, G. Nair, and I. Anwar, "Savior or Distraction for Survival: Examining the Applicability of Machine Learning for Rural Family Farms in the United Arab Emirates," *Sustainability*, vol. 15, no. 4, p. 3720, Feb. 2023, https://doi.org/10.3390/su15043720

D. Glance, "Three charts on Australia's growing appetite for fast broadband," *The Conversation*, Apr. 11, 2017. https://theconversation.com/three-charts-on-australias-growing-appetite-for-fast-broadband-75780 (accessed Aug. 03, 2023)

S.-J. Groves-Phillips, "In-migration and economic activity in rural areas of Wales." http://eprints.uwe.ac.uk/20050/ (accessed Aug. 03, 2023)

A. Hill, Joan Scott, D. Moyes, and R. Smith, "Supporting knowledge exchange in rural business—A case story from Dumfries and Galloway, Scotland," *Local Economy: The Journal of the Local Economy Policy Unit*, vol. 31, no. 7, pp. 812–824, Oct. 2016, https://doi.org/10.1177/0269094216669110

T. Horberry, M. Regan, and Stevens, "Book Review: Driver Acceptance of New Technology - Theory, Measurement and Optimisation," *International Journal of Business and Technology Management*, Mar. 2014, https://doi.org/10.55057/ijbtm.2023.5.1.2. http://www.ncl.ac.uk/cre/publish/researchreports/Honey%20Pots%20and%20HivesFINAL.pdf (accessed Jun. 16, 2023)

B. Koichu and N. Keller, "Implementation enterprise through the lens of a theory of diffusion of innovations: A case of online problem-solving forums," *Archive ouverte HAL*, Feb. 01, 2017. https://hal.archives-ouvertes.fr/hal-01950521/ (accessed Aug. 03, 2023)

F. Kriechbaumer and N. Christodoulidou, "SME website implementation factors in the hospitality industry," *Worldwide Hospitality and Tourism Themes*, vol. 6, no. 4, pp. 328–351, Aug. 2014, https://doi.org/10.1108/whatt-01-2014-0006

K. Kuhn, T. Galloway, and M. Collins-Williams, "Near, far, and online: small business owners' advice-seeking from peers," *Journal of Small Business and Enterprise Development*, vol. 23, no. 1, pp. 189–206, Feb. 2016, https://doi.org/10.1108/jsbed-03-2015-0037

E. Lima *et al.*, "Drivers for precision livestock technology adoption: A study of factors associated with the adoption of electronic identification technology by commercial sheep farmers in England and Wales," *PLOS ONE*, vol. 13, no. 1, Jan. 2018, https://doi.org/10.1371/journal.pone.0190489

S. A. Majid Gilani and A. Faccia, "Broadband Connectivity, Government Policies, and Open Innovation: The Crucial IT Infrastructure Contribution in Scotland," *Journal of Open Innovation: Technology, Market, and Complexity*, vol. 8, no. 1, p. 1, Mar. 2022, https://doi.org/10.3390/joitmc8010001

A. Marlin and D. Bruce, "Transforming a Rural Society: Impacts of Broadband Adoption and Use in Rural New Brunswick Institutions," 2006. https://www.mta.ca/research/rstp/Amanda_ICSpaper.doc O. Evans, "Connecting the poor: the internet, mobile phones and financial inclusion in Africa," *Digital Policy, Regulation and Governance*, vol. 20, no. 6, pp. 568–581, Sep. 2018, https://doi.org/10.1108/dprg-04-2018-0018

M. Masita-Mwangi, K. Mwakaba, and J. Impio, "Taking micro-enterprise online: the case of Kenyan businesses," *ACM Digital Library*, 2012. http://dl.acm.org/citation.cfm?id=2212815 (accessed Aug. 03, 2023)

S. V. 'Ofa, "Drivers of Broadband Connectivity in Asia-Pacific Developing Economies," 2018. https://papers.ssrn.com/sol3/papers.cfm?abstract_id=3274554 (accessed Jun. 13, 2023)

G. Ogston, "Villagers dig in for their broadband network," 2017. http://www.bbc.co.uk/news/uk-Scotland-tayside-central-39692030

N. B. Ojanji, "The Effect of Mobile Money Uptake on Financial Performance of Non-governmental Organizations in Kenya," Oct. 01, 2013. http://erepository.uonbi.ac.ke/handle/11295/59304 (accessed Aug. 03, 2023)

O. M. Olukayode, W. R. S. Osman, H. Abdulhameed Hussein, A. N. Ismael, A. A. Masoud, and A. G. Mansor, "Rural Small and Medium Enterprise: Information and Communication Technology as Panacea," *IOSR Journal of Computer Engineering*, vol. 16, no. 3, pp. 28–31, 2014, https://doi.org/10.9790/0661-16362831

K. Passerini, E. Tarabishy, and K. Patten, "SMEs and Information Technologies in the Broadband Economy. USA: Springer. pp1–18," USA: Springer International Publishing, 2012, pp. 1–18

F. W. Singeh, A. Abrizah, and K. Kiran, "Bringing the digital library success factors into the realm of the technology-organization-environment framework," *The Electronic Library*, vol. 38, no. 3, pp. 659–675, Jun. 2020, https://doi.org/10.1108/EL-08-2019-0187

Y. Srinivas, N. Venkatanarayana, A. Sreeram, J. Vijayasekhar, G. Yugandhar, and M. Reddy, "Information Technology in Rural India," *International Journal of Modern Engineering Research*, vol. 4, no. 1, pp. 217–211, 2014

A. Steiner and J. Atterton, "The contribution of rural businesses to community resilience," *Local Economy: The Journal of the Local Economy Policy Unit*, vol. 29, no. 3, pp. 228–244, Mar. 2014, https://doi.org/10.1177/0269094214528853

L. Townsend, C. Wallace, A. Smart, and T. Norman, "Building Virtual Bridges: How Rural Micro-Enterprises Develop Social Capital in Online and Face-to-Face Settings," *Sociologia Ruralis*, vol. 56, no. 1, pp. 29–47, https://doi.org/10.1111/soru.12068

Venkatesh, Morris, Davis, and Davis, "User Acceptance of Information Technology: Toward a Unified View," *MIS Quarterly*, vol. 27, no. 3, p. 425, 2003, https://doi.org/10.2307/30036540

M. Warren, "Farmers online: drivers and impediments in the adoption of the Internet in UK agricultural businesses," *Journal of Small Business and Enterprise Development*, vol. 11, no. 3, pp. 371–381, Sep. 2004, https://doi.org/10.1108/14626000410551627

G. R. T. White, P. Jones, and P. Beynon-Davies, "The Strategic Impact of Information Technology Deployment, Part II," *Strategic Change*, vol. 25, no. 1, pp. 3–5, Jan. 2016, https://doi.org/10.1002/jsc.2043

B. Wilson, J. Atterton, J. Hart, M. Spencer, and S. Thomson, "Unlocking the digital potential of rural areas across the UK," 2018

W. Young and C. F. Miles, "A spatial study of parking policy and usage in Melbourne, Australia," *Case Studies on Transport Policy*, vol. 3, no. 1, pp. 23–32, Mar. 2015, https://doi.org/10.1016/j.cstp.2014.07.003. L. Philip and F. Williams, "Remote rural home-based businesses and digital inequalities: Understanding needs and expectations in a digitally underserved community," *Journal of Rural Studies*, vol. 68, pp. 306–318, May 2019, https://doi.org/10.1016/j.jrurstud.2018.09.011

Analyzing the Attributes of the Moroccan Educational System: A Phase Prior to the Establishment of a Smart Classroom Based on IoT

Zahra Oughannou, Ibtissame Kandrouch, Nour El Houda Chaoui, and Habiba Chaoui

Abstract

Integrating smart campuses into education will make universities smart. This Campus is essentially based on the IoT technology that has made our lives connected. To successfully design and implement a Smart Classroom project, a preliminary study of the main socio-economic or cultural characteristics in the field of education in Morocco is required. Thus, we conducted this study in Morocco to investigate if there is a positive reaction toward the installation of a smart university in this North African context. In other words, we searched via this survey to assess the role of the solutions offered by Information and Communication Technologies for Education (ICT). To achieve our goals, we prepared two questionnaires: i) the first, containing questions about the familiarization of rural students with the Internet; and i) the second questioner about was destined for teachers of primary, secondary and higher. The obtained results show that there is no correlation between the age of the teacher and the use of instructional technology and between the use of technology and the type of work environment. In contrast, there is a significant association between the use of information technology and teaching level, and the use of information technology increases with the level of teaching. Equally, the online school experience during confinement had a positive impact on the future engagement of teachers in the project of a possible smart school ($p<0.005$). On the other hand, no association between the presence of disabilities in the classroom and the use of information technologies in teaching practice ($p>0.005$). Generally, we received a favorable opinion to set up a smart classroom, based on criteria that must be respected and that are adapted to the Moroccan context. However, more advanced studies are needed to enlarge the investigated samples.

Keywords

Empirical study · Data analysis · Smart campus · Smart classroom

1 Introduction

The digital classroom is merely one part of a larger digital ecosystem created by this homo numericus, a stage in the evolution of humanity when Man is organized around technologies and digital tools. After all, it is the digital age (Compiègne, I.: Chapitre V. 2010; Mhlanga and Moloi 2020). Currently, it is tough that "Our hyper connected societies can no longer do without digital systems (Vermesan et al. 2022). However, the importance of digital connection varies depending on country ranking, education level, and geographical location (Abad-Segura et al. 2020). In fact, the digital classroom in more developed in North American and European countries when compared to Asian and African contexts (Wu and Chen 2020).

In the Moroccan context, digital ecosystems, considered as new way of life, is taking hold and experiencing more and more success (Maaroufi et al. 2022). This is mostly a result of the country's growing telecommunications and technological infrastructure (Ghita et al. 2020). In this regard, the numbers supplied by ANRT1 in its 2017 report show that Morocco had the highest Internet penetration rate on the African continent at 64% of the population at the end of 2017; 60% of Moroccan households had laptops or

Z. Oughannou (✉)
Ibn Zohr University, Agadir, Morocco
e-mail: oughannou.zahra@gmail.com

I. Kandrouch · N. E. H. Chaoui · H. Chaoui
Ibn Tofail University, Kenitra, Morocco
e-mail: Ibtissame.Kandrouch@uit.ac.ma

S. Arezki et al. (eds.), *Emerging Disruptive Technologies for Society 5.0 in Developing Countries*, Advances in Science, Technology & Innovation, https://doi.org/10.1007/978-3-031-63701-8_10

tablets (ANRT 2022). For the Moroccan school, this current development represents a real opportunity to succeed in the digital transition in this sector (Laamraoui and Grine 2022). In general, the digital school has a number of benefits over the traditional school (Kalolo 2019). Indeed, the employment of digital technology in the classroom makes communication simple, significant, and time-saving. (Szymkowiak et al. 2021). Similarly, parents and students also gain in terms of costs related to the purchase of paper books, printing, registering in libraries, transport costs (Szymkowiak et al. 2021).

In the latest decades, No one can dispute the importance that technological advancement has had in the creation and dissemination of knowledge (Roberts 2000; Stehr et al. 2020). Information and communication technologies (ICT), in particular, are crucial for learning and acquiring new knowledge (Espino-Díaz et al. 2020). Indeed, ICT makes it easier to quickly gather, collect, store, and disseminate data, which makes it easier to produce and spread knowledge (Abdalla et al. 2022). The smart school fits perfectly into this dynamic. This concept, which remains relatively new, has been the subject of numerous research works (Bai and Zhang 2020, Saini and Goel 2019, Song et al. 2014, Temkar et al. 2016). While circumstances may differ between nations, the implementation of Information and Communication Technology (ICT) can profoundly enhance learning and the exchange of knowledge (Espino-Díaz et al. 2020). However, in order to properly plan and implement a smart school project, it is crucial to do a preliminary analysis of the key socio-economic and cultural aspects of Moroccan education. Thus, one could not develop this type of project without understanding the features of the Moroccan educational system. As such, this work aims to identify the main criteria that must be respected and especially taken into account when designing the solution of a smart school in the Moroccan context.

The objective of this research is to assess for the first time the contribution of information and communication technology solutions to education (ICTE) in Morocco. This study involved teachers, students and their parents, which constitute the principal segment of the Moroccan school. In our survey, the Smart Classroom is suggested to enhance the effectiveness of the Moroccan educational system.

2 Review and Motivation

The term "smart" was first used exclusively to describe cell phones before spreading to other fields. The IoT-based Smart Campus is found in the context of smart buildings (Dong et al. 2020). So, in educational field, to make universities smart, we need to integrate a Smart Campus (Min-Allah and Alrashed 2020). Universities are made up of a variety of venues, including lecture halls, labs, open areas, etc. (Radja et al. 2020). As IoT advances, all of these spaces can be managed automatically by making them into "smart classrooms" (Mohamad et al. 2020).

2.1 The National Telecommunications Regulatory Agency

In this context, several research works were treated and used. To deliver services in the education sector, such as the contact between students, parents, and faculty, the (Vinod et al. 2017) built intelligent platforms based on IoT tools. Equally, An IoT and cloud-based system was proposed by the (Faritha Banu et al. 2020) to control an intelligent application for communication between various components of the educational system. In other study, (AchenkunjuJohn and Kumar 2020) proposed an IoT-based biometric attendance system to mark the presence of students which is very simple to implement. The most used methods are the Fingerprint scanner and Iris scanner. A magnetic door lock was the foundation of a scheme created by Mohamad et al. (2020) to automatically control access to the lecture hall. This control is provided by an application that is based on a smartphone with a Wi-Fi connection. For the university campus, (Sharma and Suryakanthi 2015) developed an IoT-based system to improve energy consumption and examine how all electrical and electronic equipment is used. Further, IoT's contribution to an intelligent educational process and the (Abdel-Basset et al. 2019)'s definition of successful decision-making. In another study, To make the learning environment intelligent, (Al-Malah et al. 2020) researched key IoT aspects.

To demonstrate the effectiveness of switching to smart education, studies are carried out to collect student interactions after the deployment of the smart classroom (Khoroshko et al. 2021; Kiryakova et al. 2018). Recently, many authors conducted their investigations to clarify the importance of using both teaching methods (traditional and smart) to diversify teaching styles (Marcellus and Ghrayeb 2002). For example, (Petchamé et al. 2021a) used a variety of techniques to get student feedback on smart classrooms. The ability to access recorded class sessions, which enables them to save time, was viewed favorably by the students as a benefit of Smart Classroom. Therefore, thanks to Smart Classroom, they will not have to go to school (Distance Education) (Kwet and Prinsloo 2020). In another study, (Petchamé et al. 2021b) A study was conducted to find out how students perceive different approaches differently during the lockdown. The usage of a Smart Classroom and online instruction received positive feedback from the students, who felt they provided practical answers to the mobility issues brought on by the epidemic and allowed for time savings on excursions to the university.

In this regard, we conducted our study, which is the first of its kind, with the goal of evaluating the contribution that the solutions provided by Information and Communication Technologies for Education (ICTE). In our survey, the Smart Classroom, make to the enhancement of the effectiveness of the Moroccan educational system. The study's objective is to offer data and information that as closely resembles reality as possible so that our project, which entails the creation of a "Smart Classroom based on IoT," can begin. To put it another way, we wished for the creation of the smart classroom solution to be founded on the actual realities of the Moroccan educational system.

3 Theoretical and Problematic Framework

Starting out, the smart school is a multifaceted idea created by David Perkins in 1990 (Fig. 1). It is a space for learning, acquisition and exchange of skills, knowledge, and communication (MacGilchrist et al. 2004). These elements in their turn give great importance to different types of intelligence, whether individual or collective. while the aim is to allowing better adaptation to economic, environmental, educational, technological, economic, social and cultures that are induced by globalization and by the effects of new information and communication technologies (Guemmache and Hammouche Maroua 2021).

The smart school is based on an active and collaborative methodology of Information and Communication Technology resources (henceforth ICT). It is therefore impossible to speak of a smart school without the deployment of the solutions offered by ICT (connection, camera, computers, software, etc.) (Saini and Goel 2019). A smart school is a confined environment dedicated to the facilitation of teaching and learning. It represents a crucial component of the educational structure. Its main task, therefore, is to enable knowledge to be transferred quickly and easily from an educator to a group of students or pupils, while taking advantage of the possibilities of technological advancement. The domains of signal processing, web technology, hardware, and software. Smart schools or smart classrooms are designed on the principle of reducing the disparity among students and teachers, simplifying it for teachers to teach more effectively, and most importantly, improving the conditions for learning and teaching (Díaz León et al. 2016).

For (Roberts 2000; Roberts 2000; Díaz León et al. 2016) ICTs make it possible, through the increased use of images, videos, text and data, to facilitate the collection of information, recording, storage and the rapid dissemination of data, which contributes to improving learning and updating knowledge. According to Laurent et al. (2021), the "smart classroom" concept covers classes with different functionalities: a smart classroom for the purposes of distance education; a class where information from an interactive whiteboard is disseminated; classes equipped with computers and interconnected whiteboards, allowing the tracing of student activity by the teacher, in the form of dashboards or classes tracing characteristics related to teacher-student interactions are built and tested.

It appears from the previous developments that the smart classroom takes different forms. In the context of our research, it is the intelligent class based on ICT and for the purposes of distance education that attracts our attention more. More specifically, it is the study of the characteristics of the key elements of the Moroccan education system that can impact the design and implementation of an intelligent class that fuels our desire to do this research work.

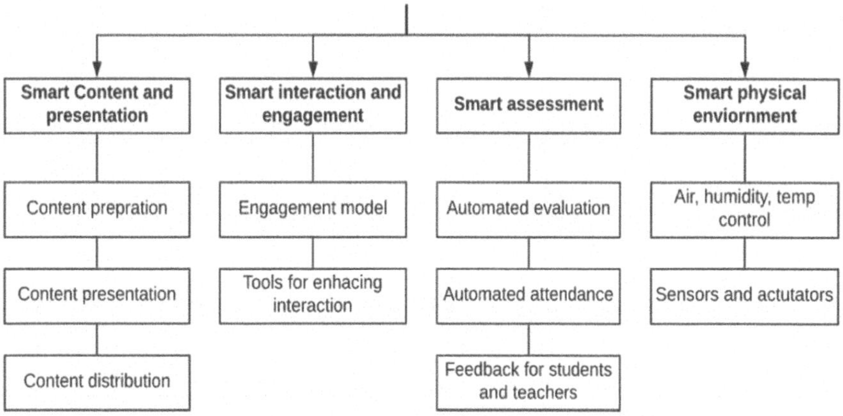

Fig. 1 Areas covered by the smart school (Saini and Goel 2019)

4 Methodology

4.1 Empirical Study

To clarify the primary elements affecting the use of ICT in Moroccan schools, we conducted this study using two questionnaires. The development of the two questionnaires was made on the basis of 13 items each, which were relate to the main individual characteristics (i.e. specific to the respondents) and those related to ICT. We therefore tried to find out whether the main individual characteristics of teachers (age, work environment, etc.) and students (parents' financial situation, class, etc.) have a link with whether or not they use ICT.

4.2 Participants

In order to provide answers to the objective of the study, we conducted a survey using two questionnaires with the two most representative parts of the Moroccan education system, namely the teachers (questionnaire n°1: teacher category) who's the number of participants is 218 teachers and the students (questionnaire n°2: student category) whose number is 161 responses. The two tables below (Tables 1 and 2) summarize the characteristics of the two samples required.

As for the questionnaire for teachers, it was developed using the "Google Forms" solution and distributed online via the social networks x which allowed the participation of 218 teachers whose characteristics are summarized in Table 3. The questionnaire for students is made up of 30 questions. In the space of a few days, we were able to collect 161 responses in the field from qualifying secondary school students. Respondent characteristics are shown in the table below:

Table 1 Attributes of the interviewed teachers

Attributes	Modalities	Pourcentage (%)
Gender	Male	46.6
	Female	53.4
Age	Between the ages of 18 and 30	30.1
	Between the ages of 30 and 50	61.6
	Over 50 years old	8.2
Middle of the work	Urban	55.3
	Rural	44.7
Seniority	Between 1 and 5 years	34.7
	Between 6 and 10 years	26.5
	Between 11 and 20 years	21.0
	Over 20 years	17.8
Taught level	Primary	22.8
	college	18.7
	qualifying	44.3
	higher	14.2

Source study results

Table 2 Characteristics of the students interviewed

Characteristics	Modalities	Pourcentage (%)
Gender	Male	57,50
	Female	41,88
Age	Between the ages of 15 and 16	23.11
	Between the ages of 17 and 18	40.63
	Between the ages of 19 and 20	25
	Over 20 years old	11.25
class	Common	24.38
	1st year baccalaureate	31.25
	2nd year baccalaureate	44.38
Internal	Yes	48.13
	No	51.86

Source study results

4.3 Measurement Tool and Statistics

The two questionnaires were designed to collect a number of important information on pupils and teachers, enabling the link between the use of ICT in education and socio-economic aspects of said population. The collected responses were imported on SPSS, coded and analyzed through the study of associations between the different constituted variables (contingency table and Chi-square test) (Table 3).

4.4 Analysis

4.4.1. Presentation of the qualitative variables constituted.

5 Results

Analysis of the findings obtained focused on the search for associations between the various dimensions taken and the utilization of Information and Communication Technology in instructional practices.

5.1 Category of Teachers

The analysis findings of the correlation between the age of teachers and the use of teaching technologies are shown in Table 4. According to statistical research, there

Table 3 Qualitative variables constituted

	Category of teachers		Category of students		
	Variables	Modalities		Variables	Modalities
1	Gender	Male; female	1	Gender	Boy; girl
2	Age	Age	2	Age	Range
3	Work environment	Urban; rural	3	Class	Common Core; First year baccalaureate; second year baccalaureate
4	Seniority	Between 1 and 5 years; Between the ages of 11 and 20 Between the ages of 6 and 10 Over 20 years old	4	Financial situation of parents	Poor; means; wealthy
5	Level taught	Primary; college secondary; secondary qualifying; higher	5	Kindergarten	Yes; No
6	Number of pupils	Band	6	School repetition	Yes; no
7	Presence of disabilities	Yes; No	7	School dropout	Yes, No
8	Use of ICT	Yes; No	8	Computer tools	Yes; No
9	ICT during confinement	Fairly important; Unimportant; Not important; Very important	9	Access to internet connection	Yes; No
10	Generalization of online courses	Yes; Nope	10	Online courses	Very important; Quite important; Unimportant; Not important
11	ICT is the future of school	Yes; No	11	Preferred mode for attending classes	Face Remote
12	Disadvantage of the smart classroom	Connection; lack of control; technological dependence	12	Advantages of the smart school	Internet connection; weak interaction; technological dependence
13	Engagement in smart school	Yes; Nope	13	Engagement in smart school	Yes; Nope

Table 4 Analysis of the association between "age of teachers" and "use of ICT" with Chi-square test

Chi-square tests			
	Value	df	Asymptotic significance (2-sided)
Pearson Chi-square	1.619[a]	2	0.445
Likelihood ratio	1 552	2	0.460
Linear-by-linear association	1 519	1	0.218
N of valid cases	218		

a. 1 cells (16, 7%) have expected count less than 5
The minimum expected count is 2.56

is no correlation between instructors' ages and the usage of teaching technologies in teachers' teaching practices ($p = 0.445$).

The analysis findings of the correlation between the usage of technologies and the characteristics of the workplace are shown in Table 5. According to Chi-Square test analysis, there is no correlation between participants' use of technologies and the type of workplace.

In Table 6, the findings of the correlation between "level taught" and "use of ICT" are shown. The Chi-square test results revealed a positive correlation between the variables "level taught" and "use of ICT" in participant replies. The crosstab indicated that as levels of instruction climb, so does the use of information technology.

The result of the relationship between "online school experience during confinement" and "commitment to smart Classroom success" is presented in Table 7. The findings of the Chi-square test indicated that the two variables in question are related ($p = 0.001$). In other words, the online learning experience while imprisoned had a favorable effect on teachers' future involvement in the concept of a potential smart school.

The result of the relationship between "presence of disabilities in the classroom" and "use of ICT in teaching practice" is presented in Table 8. The Chi-square test findings revealed that among the subjects who were examined, there is no relationship between the two variables ($p = 0.255$).

Table 5 Chi-square test analysis of the relationship between technology use and the work environment's nature

Chi-square tests

	Value	df	Asymptotic significance (2-sided)	Exact sig. (2-sided)	Exact sig. (1-sided
Pearson Chi-square	0.741[a]	1	0.389		
Continuity correction[b]	0.443	1	0.505		
Likelihood ratio	0.737	1	0.391		
Fisher's exact test				,438	,252
Linear-by-linear association	0.738	1	0.390		
N of valid cases	218				

a. 0 cells (0, 0%) have expected count less than 5. The minimum expected count is 13.79
b. Computed only for a 2 × 2 table

Table 6 Association between "level taught" and "use of ICT" analysed with Chi-Square test

Chi-square tests

	Value	df	Asymptotic Significance (2-sided)
Pearson Chi-square	16.490[a]	3	0.001
Likelihood ratio	18.919	3	0.000
Linear-by-linear association	15.622	1	0.000
N of valid cases	218		

a. 1 cells (12, 5%) have expected count less than 5
The minimum expected count is 4.41

Table 7 Relationship between "online school experience during confinement" and "commitment to smart Classroom success" analyzed with Chi-square test

Chi-square tests

	Value	df	Asymptotic significance (2-sided)
Pearson Chi-square	16.099[a]	3	0.001
Likelihood ratio	15 322	3	0.002
Linear-by-linear association	1 871	1	0.171
N of valid cases	218		

a. 0 cells (0, 0%) have expected count less than 5
The minimum expected count is 8.39

5.2 Results for Pupils' Category

The result of the relationship between "Parents' financial situation" and "Availability of IT tools" is presented in Table 9. There is no correlation between the parents' financial status and their access to IT resources (such as a mobile phone or computer), according to the Chi-square test results ($p = 0.288$).

In this part, we investigated the relationship between "parents' financial situation" and "access to internet connection" and the results are presented in Table 10. The p-value of Chi-Square test equals to 0.002, which is under the level of 5% chosen. Therefore, we can conclude that there is a link between the parents' financial situation and availability of internet connectivity among tested participants.

In this part, we investigated the relationship between "course mode" and "access to internet connection" and the results are presented in Table 11. The chi-square test measuring the association involving these two variables showed that there is a link between the continuation of courses during Covid and the connection disposition of the Internet ($p = 0.000$).

In this part, we investigated the relationship between "internet connection disposition" and "smart class fame" and the results are presented in Table 12. The chi-square test has a p-value of 0.000, which is below the 5% criterion that was selected. This indicates that there is a meaningful correlation between the fame of the smart classroom and the access to the internet connection. Thus, 86.6% of students who have the internet connection know the principle of the smart classroom.

In this part, we investigated the relationship between "engagement in the smart class" and "fame of the smart class" and the findings are displayed in Table 13.

The results obtained clearly demonstrate that these two variables are significantly dependent ($p = 0.000$). In our results, 98.5% of students who are going to engage in CI solutions know its principles, which indicates a great dependency between tested variables among participants.

Table 8 Relationship between "presence of disabilities in the classroom" and "use of ICT in teaching practice " analyzed with Chi-square test

Chi-square tests

	Value	df	Asymptotic significance (2-sided)	Exact sig. (2-sided)	Exact Sig. (1-sided)
Pearson Chi-square	1.298[a]	1	0.255		
Continuity correction[b]	0.848	1	0.357		
Likelihood ratio	1239	1	0.266		
Fisher's exact test				0.278	0.177
Linear-by-linear association	1292	1	0.256		
N of valid cases	218				

a. O cells (0, 0%) have expected count less than 5. The minimum expected count is. 8, 39
b. Computed only for a 2 × 2 table

Table 9 Relationship between "Parents' financial situation" and "Availability of IT tools" analyzed with Chi-Square test

Chi-square tests

	Value	df	Asymptotic significance (2-sided)	Exact sig (2-sided)	Exact sig (1-sided)
Pearson Chi-square	1.127[a]	1	0.288		
Continuity correction[b]	0.721	1	0.396		
Likelihood ratio	1 166	1	0.280		
Fisher's exact test				0.396	0.199
Linear-by-linear association	1 120	1	0.290		
N of valid cases	160				

a. 0 cells (0, 0%) have expected count less than 5. The minimum expected count is 10.50
b. Cells (0, 0%) have expected count less than 5. The minimum expected count is 10.50
c. Computed only for a 2 × 2 table

Table 10 Relationship between "parents' financial situation" and "access to internet connection" analyzed with Chi-Square test

Chi-square tests

	Value	df	Asymptotic significance (2-sided)	Exact sig. (2-sided)	Exact sig. (1-sided)
Pearson Chi-square	10.075[a]	1	0.002		
Continuity correction[b]	9 042	1	0.003		
Likelihood ratio	10 387	1	0.001		
Fisher's exact test				0.002	0.001
Linear-by-linear association	10 012	1	0.002		
N of valid cases	160				

a. 0 cells (0, 0%) have expected count less than 5. The minimum expected count is 24.50
b. Cells (0, 0%) have expected count less than 5. The minimum expected count is 24.50
c. Computed only for a 2 × 2 table

Table 11 Relationship between "course mode" and "access to internet connection" analyzed with Chi-Square test

Chi-square tests

	Value	df	Asymptotic significance (2-sided)	Exact sig. (2-sided)	Exact sig. (1-sided)
Pearson Chi-square	148.047[a]	1	0.000		
Continuity correction[b]	144 158	1	0.000		
Likelihood ratio	189 620	1	0.000		
Fisher's exact test				0.000	0.000
Linear-by-linear association	147 122	1	0.000		
N of valid cases	160				

a. 0 cells (0, 0%) have expected count less than 5. The minimum expected count is 30.19
b. Computed only for a 2 × 2 table

Table 12 Relationship between "internet connection disposition" and "smart class fame" analyzed with Chi-Square test

Chi-square tests

	Value	df	Asymptotic significance (2-sided)	Exact sig. (2-sided)	Exact sig. (1-sided)
Pearson Chi-square	43.052[a]	1	0.000		
Continuity correction[b]	40 958	1	0.000		
Likelihood ratio	46 703	1	0.000		
Fisher's exact test				0.000	0.000
Linear-by-linear association	42 782	1	0.000		
N of valid cases	160				

a. 0 cells (0, 0%) have expected count less than 5. The minimum expected count is 29.31
b. Computed only for a 2 × 2 table

Table 13 Relationship between "engagement in the smart class" and "fame of the smart class" analyzed with Chi-Square test

Chi-square tests

	Value	df	Asymptotic significance (2-sided)	Exact sig. (2-sided)	Exact sig. (1-sided)
Pearson Chi-square	16.495[a]	1	0.000		
Continuity correction[b]	14 723	1	0.000		
Likelihood ratio	20 831	1	0.000		
Fisher's exact test				0.000	0.000
Linear-by-linear association	16 392	1	0.000		
N of valid cases	160				

a. 0 cells (0, 0%) have expected count less than 5. The minimum expected count is 10.05
b. 0 cells (0, 0%) have expected count less than 5. The minimum expected count is 10.05
c. Computed only for a 2 × 2 table

6 Discussion

This research highlighted for the first time the primary factors that can impact the exploitation of information and communication technologies in Moroccan schools. Our results defined the main elements to consider when developing a smart school IT solution, which are suggested to facilitate the integration of ICT in Moroccan school for smart and harmonic functioning.

The investigation into the connection between teachers' age and their utilization of ICT in teaching practice unveiled an absence of correlation between these two variables.

Similar results were mentioned during the aftermath of the COVID-19 pandemic in Morocco, when teachers used the distance learning in their school (Bachiri and Sahli 2020). In our case, the lack of correlation between teachers' age and the utilization of ICT means that the age of the teachers should not be taken as an explanatory variable of the use or not of ICT.

In the same sense, our results showed that the work environment, whether urban or rural, does not impact the utilization of Information and Communication Technology (ICT) in their instructional methodologies. The same issue was investigated currently by Ismaili (2020) when they evaluated the role of information and communication technology in educational initiatives for intermediate and secondary schools. In our case, the results could be explained by the effort made either by the teachers themselves or by the State to provide schools with the necessary computer equipment, especially in rural areas, where this equipment are less available. In other words, this conclusion is very important for the implementation of the intelligent school initiative.

In previous studies related to ICT in Morocco, the link between the level taught and the use of ICT in educational instruction was neglected (Benhima and Benabderrazik 2020; Collis and Jung 2004; Ilahiane and Sherry 2008). However, in this study, the link between the level taught and the use of ICT in teaching was verified. In results, more the level taught is higher, more the use of ICTs is greater. Further, a positive link was demonstrated between the experience of online courses during the period of confinement due to Covid-19 and the commitment of teachers in the success of the implementation of a smart school. This relationship could be explained by the role that ICT played in maintaining courses during the last health crisis, as mentioned currently in Medical Education, in in Marrakesh, Morocco (Sebbani et al. 2021). Furthermore, the inquiry into the presence of disabilities within the classroom does not influence teachers' selection of ICT solutions in their instructional methods. In other words, having disabilities in the classroom does not change anything in terms of the tools used: it is not because we have disabilities in the classroom that we use ICT or not.

7 Conclusion

The incorporation of Smart Campus into the education sector will lead to the transformation of universities into intelligent entities. This campus primarily relies on IoT technology, which has interconnected our lives. Before integrating this concept in the Moroccan educational system, we are supposed to carry out this empirical study based on a questionnaire survey of a population formed by public education teachers on one side and by secondary school students on the other hand. The purpose of the survey is to allow our project, which consists in the development of a Smart Classroom, to start from data and information that reflect as much as possible the image closer to reality. In other words, we wanted the advancement of intelligent classroom environments and smart university solution to be adapted to the Moroccan context. After the analysis of the results obtained, we received a positive response for establishing a smart classroom. Indeed, as perspectives we will propose our model of Smart Classroom, and we will realize a feasibility study to implement our model, citing the necessary technologies to design our Smart Classroom.

References

4.Abad-Segura, E., González-Zamar, M.-D., Infante-Moro, J.C., Ruipérez García, G.: Sus-tainable Management of Digital Transformation in Higher Education: Global Research Trends. Sustainability. 12, 2107 (2020). https://doi.org/10.3390/su12052107.

Abdalla, W., Renukappa, S., Suresh, S.: Managing COVID-19-related knowledge: A smart cities perspective. Knowledge and Process Management. 1–23 (2022). https://doi.org/10.1002/kpm.1706.

28.Abdel-Basset, M., Manogaran, G., Mohamed, M., Rushdy, E.: Internet of things in smart education environment: Supportive framework in the decision-making process. Concur-rency and Computation: Practice and Experience. 31, e4515 (2019). https://doi.org/10.1002/cpe.4515.

26.AchenkunjuJohn, A., Kumar, P.V.: A New concept of Smart Universities Using Internet of Things (IoT). 9, 5 (2020).

Al-Malah, D., Jinah, H., Alrikabi, H.: Enhancement of Educational Services by Using the Internet of Things Applications for Talent and Intelligent Schools. Periodicals of Engi-neering and Natural Sciences (PEN). 8, 2358–2366 (2020). https://doi.org/10.21533/pen.v8i4.1744.

ANRT: Rapport annuel, https://www.anrt.ma/publications/rapport-annuel, last accessed 2022/06/06.

40.Bachiri, H., Sahli, R.: The Need of Distance Learning in the Wake of COVID-19 in Mo-rocco:: Teachers' Attitudes and Challenges in the English Foreign Language Instruction. International Journal of Language and Literary Studies. 2, 240–256 (2020).

Bai, H., Zhang, Q.: English smart classroom teaching system based on 5 network and in-ternet of things. Microprocessors and Microsystems. 103421 (2020).

Benhima, M., Benabderrazik, Y.: The Role of Using Information Communication Tech-nology in the Motivation of Moroccan English Department Students during COVID-19 Quarantine. The Journal of Quality in Education. 10, 22–47 (2020). https://doi.org/10.37870/joqie.v10i16.226.

Collis, B., Jung, I.: Uses of information and communication technologies in teacher educa-tion. In: Teacher education through open and distance learning. pp. 187–208. Routledge (2004).

Compiègne, I.: Chapitre V. Qui est l'homo numericus ? In: La société numérique en question(s). pp. 59–70. Éditions Sciences Humaines, Auxerre (2010).

Díaz León, C.A., Hincapié Montoya, E.M., Guirales Arredondo, E.A., Moreno López, G.A.: Design and Development of an Interaction System in Order to be Implemented in a Smart Classroom. Revista EIA. 95–109 (2016).

20.Dong, Z.Y., Zhang, Y., Yip, C., Swift, S., Beswick, K.: Smart campus: definition, framework, technologies, and services. IET Smart Cities. 2, 43–54 (2020). https://doi.org/10.1049/iet-smc.2019.0072.

Espino-Díaz, L., Fernandez-Caminero, G., Hernandez-Lloret, C.-M., Gonzalez-Gonzalez, H., Alvarez-Castillo, J.-L.: Analyzing the Impact of COVID-19 on Education Profession-als. Toward a Paradigm Shift: ICT and Neuroeducation as a Binomial of Action. Sustain-ability. 12, 5646 (2020). https://doi.org/10.3390/su12145646.

Faritha Banu, J., Revathi, R., Suganya, M., NR, G.M.: IoT based Cloud Integrated Smart Classroom for smart and a sustainable Campus. Procedia Computer Science. 172, 77–81 (2020).

7.Ghita, M., Siham, B., Hicham, M., Abdelhafid, A., Laurent, D.: Digital twins: develop-ment and implementation challenges within Moroccan context. SN Appl. Sci. 2, 885 (2020). https://doi.org/10.1007/s42452-020-2691-6.

Guemmache, A., Hammouche Maroua, M.: Conseption et réalisation d'une application mobile pour une école intelligente. https://dspace.univ-bba.dz:443/xmlui/handle/123456789/1862, (2021).

44.Ilahiane, H., Sherry, J.: Joutia: street vendor entrepreneurship and the informal economy of information and communication technologies in Morocco. The Journal of North African Studies. 13, 243–255 (2008). https://doi.org/10.1080/13629380801996570.

41.Ismaili, J.: Evaluation of information and communication technology in education pro-grams for middle and high schools: GENIE program as a case study. Educ Inf Technol. 25, 5067–5086 (2020). https://doi.org/10.1007/s10639-020-10224-1.

10.Kalolo, J.F.: Digital revolution and its impact on education systems in developing coun-tries. Educ Inf Technol. 24, 345–358 (2019). https://doi.org/10.1007/s10639-018-9778-3.

Khoroshko, L.L., Vikulin, M.A., Khoroshko, A.L.: Experience in Smart e-Learning Sys-tem Application When Switching to Distance Education to the Fullest Extent: The Case of the Moodle LMS. In: Uskov, V.L., Howlett, R.J., and Jain, L.C. (eds.) Smart Educa-tion and e-Learning 2021. pp. 89–96. Springer, Singapore (2021). https://doi.org/10.1007/978-981-16-2834-4_8.

31.Kiryakova, G., Angelova, N., Yordanova, L.: The potential of augmented reality to trans-form education into smart education. TEM Journal. 7, 556 (2018).

34.Kwet, M., Prinsloo, P.: The 'smart' classroom: a new frontier in the age of the smart uni-versity. Teaching in Higher Education. 25, 510–526 (2020). https://doi.org/10.1080/13562517.2020.1734922.

Laamraoui, S.-E., Grine, A.: Digital transformation in the Moroccan public sector: Litera-ture review, state of the art and perspectives. Revue Française d'Economie et de Gestion. 3, (2022).

Laurent, R., Dessus, P., Vaufreydaz, D.: Apprendre en toute éthique dans les salles de classe intelligentes. (2021).

Maaroufi, M.M., Stour, L., Agoumi, A.: Sustainable Mobility Model for Fez City (Moroc-co). In: Motahhir, S. and Bossoufi, B. (eds.) Digital Technologies and Applications. pp. 91–102. Springer International Publishing, Cham (2022). https://doi.org/10.1007/978-3-031-02447-4_10.

MacGilchrist, B., Reed, J., Myers, K.: The intelligent school. Sage (2004).

Marcellus, R., Ghrayeb, O.: Effects Of Smart Classrooms On Learning And Teaching Effectiveness: The Students' Point Of View. Presented at the June 16 (2002).

2.Mhlanga, D., Moloi, T.: COVID-19 and the Digital Transformation of Education: What Are We Learning on 4IR in South Africa? Education Sciences. 10, 180 (2020). https://doi.org/10.3390/educsci10070180.

21.Min-Allah, N., Alrashed, S.: Smart campus—A sketch. Sustainable Cities and Society. 59, 102231 (2020). https://doi.org/10.1016/j.scs.2020.102231.

Mohamad, E., Tee, K., Chew, C.C., Faizan, O., Rahim, R., Mohamad, M.: Energy smart saving classroom with IoT based. IOP Conference Series: Materials Science and Engineer-ing. 917, 012086 (2020). https://doi.org/10.1088/1757-899X/917/1/012086.

Petchamé, J., Iriondo, I., Villegas, E., Fonseca, D., Romero Yesa, S., Aláez, M.: A Quali-tative Approach to Help Adjust the Design of Management Subjects in ICT Engineering Undergraduate Programs through User Experience in a Smart Classroom Context. Sen-sors. 21, 4762 (2021). https://doi.org/10.3390/s21144762.

Petchamé, J., Iriondo, I., Villegas, E., Riu, D., Fonseca, D.: Comparing Face-to-Face, Emergency Remote Teaching and Smart Classroom: A Qualitative Exploratory Research Based on Students' Experience during the COVID-19 Pandemic. Sustainability. 13, 6625 (2021). https://doi.org/10.3390/su13126625.

Radja, A.M., Wikantari, R., Harisah, A.: Characteristic of Student Informal Gathering Space (SIGS) Faculty of Engineering Hasanuddin University at Gowa Campus. IOP Conf. Ser.: Mater. Sci. Eng. 875, 012010 (2020). https://doi.org/10.1088/1757-899X/875/1/012010.

12.Roberts, J.: From know-how to show-how? Questioning the role of information and communication technologies in knowledge transfer. Technology analysis & Strategic man-agement. 12, 429–443 (2000).

17.Saini, M.K., Goel, N.: How smart are smart classrooms? A review of smart classroom technologies. ACM Computing Surveys (CSUR). 52, 1–28 (2019).

45.Sebbani, M., Adarmouch, L., Mansouri, A., Mansoury, O., Michaud, S., ElAdib, A.R., Bouskraoui, M., Amine, M.: Implementation of Online Teaching in Medical Education: Lessons Learned from Students' Perspectives during the Health Crisis in Marrakesh, Mo-rocco. Education Research International. 2021, e5547821 (2021). https://doi.org/10.1155/2021/5547821.

27.Sharma, K., Suryakanthi, T.: Smart System: IoT for University. (2015). https://doi.org/10.1109/ICGCIoT.2015.7380720.

Song, S., Zhong, X., Li, H., Du, J., Nie, F.: Smart classroom: From conceptualization to construction. In: 2014 International Conference on Intelligent Environments. pp. 330–332. IEEE (2014).

Stehr, N., Adolf, M., Mast, J.L.: Knowledge Society, Knowledge-Based Economy, and Innovation. In: Carayannis, E.G. (ed.) Encyclopedia of Creativity, Invention, Innovation and Entrepreneurship. pp. 1536–1541. Springer International Publishing, Cham (2020). https://doi.org/10.1007/978-3-319-15347-6_440.

11.Szymkowiak, A., Melović, B., Dabić, M., Jeganathan, K., Kundi, G.S.: Information tech-nology and Gen Z: The role of teachers, the internet, and technology in the education of young people. Technology in Society. 65, 101565 (2021). https://doi.org/10.1016/j.techsoc.2021.101565.

19.Temkar, R., Gupte, M., Kalgaonkar, S.: Internet of things for smart classrooms. Interna-tional research journal of engineering and technology. 3, 203–207 (2016).

Vermesan, O., Friess, P., Guillemin, P., Serrano, M., Bouraoui, M., Freire, L.P., Kall-stenius, T., Lam, K., Eisenhauer, M., Moessner, K.: IoT digital value chain connecting re-search, innovation and deployment. In: Digitising the Industry Internet of Things Connecting the Physical, Digital and VirtualWorlds. pp. 15–128. River Publishers (2022).

Vinod, M., Vinay, H.S., Prathap, M.: Smart school. In: 2017 International Conference On Smart Technologies For Smart Nation (SmartTechCon). pp. 1424–1427 (2017). https://doi.org/10.1109/SmartTechCon.2017.8358599.

5.Wu, J., Chen, D.-T.V.: A systematic review of educational digital storytelling. Computers & Education. 147, 103786 (2020). https://doi.org/10.1016/j.compedu.2019.103786.

Critical Analysis of the Efficacy of Servant Leadership and Its Relation to Job Satisfaction and Leader Member Exchange Model (LMX)—A Case Study of Private Higher Education Sector in Kuwait

Nourhan El-Bayaa

Abstract

The practice of servant leadership has given rise to a leadership revolution, and those who practice it are a revolutionary group who have exploited and completely flipped upside down the traditional power of leadership. Servant leadership aggressively creates and aligns an employee's feeling of purpose with the organization's goal, going beyond transactional management. This research investigates and examines the efficacy of servant Leadership and Its relation to job satisfaction and leader member exchange model among employees in Kuwait's private universities by conducting a closed-ended survey, which was administered to 240 employees from personnel in Kuwait's two private higher education institutions. For data analysis, exploratory factor analysis (EFA), reliability test, and person correlation have been used to explore the relationship between the variables. The results revealed that there was significant positive correlation between servant leadership dimensions and job satisfaction, likewise servant leadership dimensions and LMX among employees.

Keywords

Servant leadership (SL) · Job satisfaction (JS) · Servant leadership dimensions · Leader-member exchange theory (LMX) · Private higher education sector · Kuwait

1 Introduction

Greenleaf coined the terminology "servant leadership" in 1970, setting the phenomenal definition and meaning of servant leadership by first serving, not leading. Likewise, servant leaders aim to form and 'construct' the followers "to grow healthier, wiser, freer, more autonomous, and more likely themselves to become servants" (Greenleaf 1977) (p 60). Hence, the latter points out that the most significant notion and idea of servant leadership stands on "to serve first, and then aspire to lead". In (Dierendonck 2011, Parris and Peachey 2013), and (Stone Gregory et al. 2004) views, servant leaders seek to operate on a superior level, as well as their prime incentive in leadership is their drive and yearn to serve others. The two dimensions serving and leading of servant leadership have major significance in the success and growth of the organization (Ragnarsson et al. 2018). Therefore, correspondingly, the hallmark of such leadership style (in comparison to the other styles) is that leaders take the time and consideration to, both, hold followers first and care for them (Dierendonck 2011). While the primary focus in the other leadership styles is to achieve organizational standards and goals, the servant leadership approach places first and foremost the follower's needs, with organizational goals being fulfilled as a direct unambiguous result of the follower's needs being accommodated (Liden et al. 2014). As this study takes on a critical analysis of the efficacy of Servant Leadership in creating better job satisfaction, it is foremost important to investigate and identify the key characteristics, aspects and variables that lead to better job satisfaction, constructive, and positive work performances. The correlation between Servant Leadership and job satisfaction within organizations has long been proven and endorsed by several previous research ((Amussah 2020), (Saleem et al. 2020)). Likewise, participatory leadership adopts a positive relation with workers'

N. El-Bayaa (✉)
Faculty of Economics and Administrative Sciences, Istanbul Aydin University, Istanbul, Turkey
e-mail: nourhanelbayaa@aydin.edu.tr

UCAM Universidad Católica San Antonio de Murcia, Av. de los Jerónimos, 135, 30107 Guadalupe de Maciascoque, Murcia, Spain

S. Arezki et al. (eds.), *Emerging Disruptive Technologies for Society 5.0 in Developing Countries*, Advances in Science, Technology & Innovation, https://doi.org/10.1007/978-3-031-63701-8_11

job satisfaction and engagement (Dahleez et al. 2022). Correspondingly, the theme of job satisfaction is significant for employees in organizations, as the servant leadership style embraces the entire aspects of the constitution, both externally and internally (Hasanuddin et al. 2021). Job satisfaction is deliberated as the outcome of a person's assessment towards the working environment, life, and job achievement (Mahdavi and Fazlollahtabar 2012). The most significant attribute in job satisfaction stands to be the leader's attention since it increases organizational performance and productivity. Hence, employees' job satisfaction is pivotal for a company or an organization in account of how crucially it influences the productivity and outcome of organizations (Abbas et al. 2022).

The research gap of this study is a prevalent challenge that is often lodged, and yet mainly neglected in such line of study research is failing to account the potential and possible indignity matters (An et al. 2019), the ideal leadership style to be adopted in a toxic higher education sector work environment is servant leadership, and the job satisfaction of the employees in higher educational institutions are areas that have not been explored enough or in depth, and there is limited empirical studies about work satisfaction within the private higher education sectors (Wilkins et al. 2017), this study exhibits importance in its key findings and recommendations; it investigates Servant Leadership's correlation with the private higher educational sectors' outcomes within a non-western field (State of Kuwait), since most researches focus on such subject matter and its consequences and significances within the western settings, as also when the local culture is factored in, the outcomes and conclusions in non-western nations will change (Abbas et al. 2020).

2 Research Background

2.1 Servant Leadership

In 1970, Robert Greenleaf proposed and pioneered the notion of the leader as a servant, concentrating on human capital ((Northouse 2007), (Spears 2005)). Greenleaf developed the concept of servant leadership after working in large corporations and reading Herman Hesse's novel Journey to the East (Spears 2005). Greenleaf determined that a strong leader would be one who serves others first after reading Journey to the East and reflecting on his own experiences (Kumar 2020). Greenleaf's initial work in 1977 was based on his own experiences with and views of various organizations, rather than on research (Greenleaf 1977). A functioning model of this idea, as well as an agreed-upon set of features, has been tried via research on the topic. While most leadership styles aim for organizational success with individual achievement as a result, servant leadership prioritizes individual success by creating secure and strong connections that foster commitment and dependability, such characteristics particularly important is a higher education organization where there is a flexible mix between authority on the one hand and flexibility and independence of thinking on the other, ultimately leading to organizational success. SL is frequently associated with transformational and real leadership, as well as the LMX concept and leadership skills and behaviors (Al-Asfour et al. 2022). Though they all have leadership as a common thread, their definitions of what leadership is and how it is displayed differ slightly. Each of these styles has a similar leadership concept and foundation, but each is defined by a minor difference (El-Bayaa and Elsaman 2022).

The most recent model for measuring servant leadership asserts that it is the only valid and reliable instrument that gives a succinct scale capturing the main features of servant leadership within a multi-dimensional framework directly tied to Greenleaf's principles (Dierendonck and Nuijten 2011). Van Dierendonck and Nuijten's model of servant leadership is built on eight dimensions: empowerment, accountability, standing back, humility, authenticity, courage, forgiveness, and stewardship, which has been used in this work. They claimed that a leader is effectively practicing servant leadership when these aspects are evident in their actions.

2.2 Leader-Member Exchange

Developed by Graen and Uhl-Bien (1995), LMX theory suggests that leaders do not take advantage of the same style in dealing with all subordinates, but rather create a distinct type of association or exchange with every follower (Liden and Maslyn 1998). SL, LMX, and JS are significant features when establishing an organization's goals and objectives and its achievements. From the Perspective of servant leadership and leader member exchange theory LMX, leaders do not deal with followers in a similar style, instead they build a distinctive form of exchange. LMX, and JS are all essential components when setting an organization's goals and objectives and achieving success.

A great relationship as a group is acclaimed by superior levels of support, communication, cooperation, trust, and recompenses, formal and informal ones. A leader that has more attentiveness to a subordinate and his/her interests has an advantage from the relationship. On the other hand, a dull or an inferior relationship is defined by "high task orientation and mistrust" ((Akdol and Arikboga 2017), p 529). LMX of great quality is developed by servant leadership while sympathizing with subordinated, constructing social trust, and concentrating on employees' needs to be developed (Heriyadi et al. 2020). Servant leaders foster powerful supporting relationships with every follower. Additionally, in high leader member exchange leaders foster trusting and reciprocally favorable relationships with subordinates (Dierendonck 2011). Consequently, followers appreciate better independence and attention to their tasks and most possibly meet the necessities of their responsibilities; furthermore, perceived as an idol, a follower's identity is impacted by the servant leader. As an equal substitution, subordinates adopt the servant leaders' ethics and principles, pursue, and attain acclaim and credits from their leaders (Aggarwal et al. 2021).

2.3 Job Satisfaction

Several research on work satisfaction have been undertaken, revealing elements that affect how someone perceives a worker's job Satisfaction. (Ireri 2016) discovered that an employee's degree of satisfaction is influenced by motivating variables. According to Kalifa et al. (2016), if an employee has worked for a firm for a long period, they are less likely to quit. Employees who are satisfied in their present occupations are more likely to stay with the company and not look for another job, as opposed to those who are unsatisfied with their workplace. As a result, managers in the casualty insurance industry must grasp the influence of job satisfaction on employee retention so that employees do not seek alternative jobs.

The study of Latif et al. (2021) explored the direct and mediated effects of servant leadership on job satisfaction to better understand how it contributes to life fulfillment through self-administered surveys and information gathered from Spain, China, and Pakistan. Results from the entire sample showed that servant leadership had a favorable and significant impact on both career and life satisfaction. In the three samples, these associations were likewise determined to be significant. Additionally, both the overall sample and sub-sample results showed a direct, favorable, and substantial relationship between professional happiness and life contentment. In both the general sample and the sub-samples, career satisfaction was found to be a major mediating factor in the association between servant leadership and life satisfaction (Latif et al. 2021). Recently, it has become more difficult for leaders to establish positive relationships with their followers. Researchers used to think that leaders were more authoritarian, but now they think that leaders are more democratic. According to the findings of the study of Boyum (2012), the elements of servant leadership are defined by the commander and subordinates and grow over time. This leads to a relational engagement between the servant leader and his staff that is characterized by fairness.

2.4 Servant Leadership in Higher Education Sector

As (Greenleaf 1977) cared about universities, colleges, and students' growth, the latter found that these institutions and their leaders should build campuses in ways that they value service. When it comes to adopting the servant leadership approach in the higher education institutions, (Wheeler 2012) noted that most of the current leadership models and approaches in higher education institutions are unsuitable, short-termed, and unsuccessful models, notably when it comes to the individuals' involvements in the institutions. Furthermore, (Aboramadan et al. 2020) also examined the aspect of job satisfaction in the correlation between servant leadership and educational performance in the context of higher education institutions in Palestine, and identified that job satisfaction completely facilitated this association, which shows that servant leadership affects job satisfaction, which sequentially improves the educational performances of educational institutions such universities and schools. Shafai 2020) examined servant leadership in relation to higher education in the Kingdom of Saudi Arabia in terms of the Gulf Countries. It also looked at the power that administrators in higher education wield as a crucial aspect of servant leadership. According to this study, Saudi Arabia, the largest gulf nation, strives to generate more effective leaders who meet the demands of the populace on a basic level without abusing their position of authority. When evaluating servant-leadership techniques in higher education, there are currently no studies that fully capture what Saudi higher educational leaders do in terms of defining and providing service (Shafai 2020).

In the matter of Kuwait, it is observed that its educational system undergoes various challenges, which include a centralized system of education (AlShammari 2010). Therefore, there is immediate need to improve and develop the ongoing administrative reform endeavors in the different sectors in the country Kuwait, notably at higher education levels. It was demonstrated by Ghareeb (2010) that long administrative procedures and bureaucracy are the main hurdles that face higher education institutions in Kuwait (such as Kuwait University). Furthermore, (Abedeen 2015) disclosed that the centralized management adopted at applied and tertiary educational academies in Kuwait has ignored staff's desires and needs, as also deprived them from expressing their opinions and feelings about the various challenges faced (Aldaihani 2019).

3 Research Model and Hypotheses Development

The objective of this study is to examine the relationship between SL dimensions and JS, and the relationship between SL dimensions and LMX (Fig. 1).

3.1 Relationship Between Servant Leadership and Job Satisfaction (H1)

There are several studies in literature that show a link between overall servant leadership and work satisfaction ((Failed 2022), (Huning et al. 2020), (Ramma et al. 2022)). However, there have been few research that look at the link between the 6 dimensions of servant leadership and JS as distinct entities. In this study, the first link is the 6 factors of servant leadership as independent variables (Empowerment, Standing Back, Accountability, Authenticity, Humility, and Stewardship) and the dependent variable which is job satisfaction. The two survey instruments were used to examine the correlation between comprehension of servant leadership style effect and employee satisfaction: the first is the 28-item servant leadership instrument that was conceived and developed by Liden et al. (2005). The second is the Job Satisfaction Scale (MCMJSS) by Mohrman et al. (1978). Therefore, we formulated and proposed the following hypothesis on the links between the 6 dimensions of servant leadership and job satisfaction based on the literature review.

- H1a: There is significant correlation between servant leadership and JS.
- H1o: There is no significant correlation between servant leadership and JS.
- H1.1a: There is significant correlation between Empowerment and JS.
- H1.1o: There is no significant correlation between Empowerment and JS.
- H1.2a: There is a significant correlation between Accountability and JS.
- H1.2o: There is no significant correlation between Accountability and JS.
- H1.3a: There is significant correlation between Humility and JS.
- H1.3o: There is no significant correlation between Humility and JS.
- H1.4a: There is a significant correlation between Stewardship and JS.
- H1.4o: There is no significant correlation between Stewardship and JS.
- H1.5a: There is significant correlation between Authenticity and JS.
- H1.5o: There is no significant correlation between Authenticity and JS.
- H1.6a: There is significant correlation between Standing Back and JS.
- H1.6o: There is no significant correlation between Standing Back and JS.

3.2 Relationship Between Servant Leadership and Leader Member Exchange (H2)

SL is reputed to produce a high level of LMX by focusing on followers' desires for personal growth and developing interpersonal trust with them (Dierendonck 2011). Through reciprocal trust and benefit, this strategy aids in building long-lasting relationships between servant leaders and their followers. The empathy, morality, and acceptance of servant

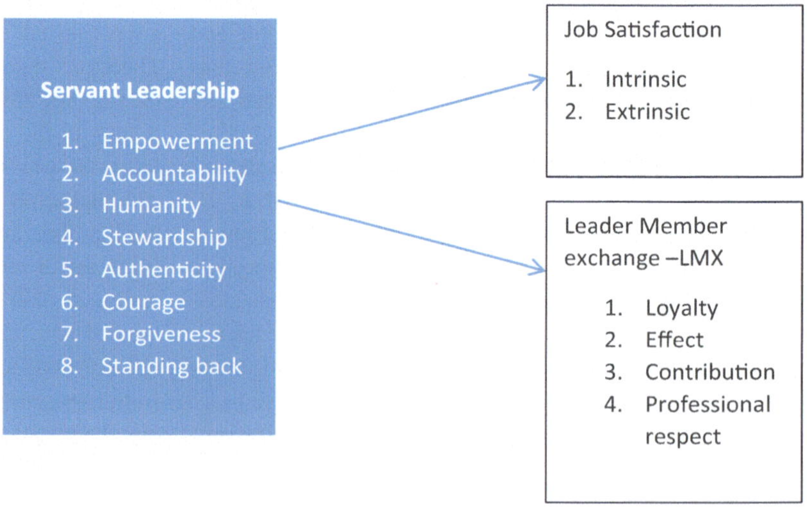

Fig. 1 Research conceptual framework model

leaders have been shown to positively link with LMX for a few reasons, including how they build followers' trust (El-Bayaa and Elsaman 2022). Servant leaders can forge lasting bonds with their followers by empowering their staff and giving them a level of responsibility that is appropriate for their needs and talents. As a result, followers could accept the servant leader's values and work to win their favor (Mohrman et al. 1978). In this study, the second link is between the 6 factors of servant Leadership (Empowerment, Standing Back, Accountability, Authenticity, Humility, Stewardship) as independent variable and leader member exchange LMX. Therefore, we formulated and proposed the following hypothesis on the links between the 6 dimensions of servant leadership and LMX based on the literature review.

- H1a: There is significant correlation between servant leadership and JS.
- H1o: There is no significant correlation between servant leadership and JS.
- H1.1a: There is significant correlation between Empowerment and JS.
- H1.1o: There is no significant correlation between Empowerment and JS.
- H1.2a: There is significant correlation between Accountability and JS.
- H1.2o: There is no significant correlation between Accountability and JS.
- H1.3a: There is significant correlation between Humility and JS.
- H1.3o: There is no significant correlation between Humility and JS.
- H1.4a: There is significant correlation between Stewardship and JS.
- H1.4o: There is no significant correlation between Stewardship and JS.
- H1.5a: There is significant correlation between Authenticity and JS.
- H1.5o: There is no significant correlation between Authenticity and JS.
- H1.6a: There is a significant correlation between Standing Back and JS.
- H1.6o: There is no significant correlation between Standing Back and JS.

4 Research Method

4.1 Research Process

In this study, Kuwait was chosen as a non-western nation to explore and evaluate how servant leadership improves employee job satisfaction for this reason. This study provides empirical data on the correlation between servant leadership and employee job satisfaction in Kuwait's private higher education sector and how they are related to each other. Using a thorough survey, the data collecting stage was completed in one step, classified, and coded. Furthermore, the deductive approach and survey-based quantitative data analysis strategy was adopted in this study and found appropriate for examining the relationship among SL, JS, and LMX. This approach allows for the testing of established hypotheses and the analysis of numerical data using statistical techniques. It enables the researchers to collect a large amount of data from participants using validated scales and enhances the validity and reliability of the study findings. Qualitative data analysis or case studies may not be suitable for this study due to the lack of sufficient data or generalizability (Elsaman et al. 2022). Therefore, it is appropriate in the context of this research to follow the quantitative method in the hypothetico-deductive model of the research and to prove the validity of the research model in the HEIs in Kuwait.

4.2 Participants

Out of 15 private higher education institutions in Kuwait, and this is as per the universities list web page on the Private Universities Council——Kuwait (PUC) official website (http://puc.edu.kw/UniversityListPage.aspx), only two institutions agreed to participate in this study. While this limited the number of institutions involved, it was essential to ensure that the study could be carried out effectively. The two institutions were selected because they were the only accessible ones that agreed to participate in the survey. The total population of the two institutions is approximately 410, with university 1 having 190 employees and university 2 having 220 employees. This was confirmed by the HR departments of both universities. To ensure that the study was conducted using an appropriate sampling method, the research adopted the random sampling procedure for selecting the participant institutions, as recommended by Krejcie and Morgan (1970). This method allowed for the selection of participants in an unbiased manner and ensured that each member of the population had an equal chance of being selected for the study. As a result, the study could generate reliable and accurate data that could be used to draw valid conclusions about the relationship among SL, JS, and LMX in the private higher education institutions in Kuwait.

The questionnaire was sent to 240 employees who are working full-timers (working 32 h per week), and 216 survey questionnaires were received. Out of the 216, the number of survey questionnaires that were valid for data analysis was 205. This ensured that the study was based on a sufficient sample size and that the data collected were reliable and could be used to draw meaningful conclusions about the relationship among SL, JS, and LMX in the private higher education institutions in Kuwait ((Krejcie and Morgan 1970), (Hair et al. 2003)). The questionnaire was given to a worker in a leadership position who is responsible for managing or leading a group of people. Executives and managers were considered. Three groups of employees were established. Heads of departments and assistant managers form the first Manager Group. Executive roles, which include department heads, are the second category. Finally, they have a third category of personnel, which consists of supervisors, team leaders, and other employees. All of them are working in different departments in the 2 private universities that participated in the survey.

4.3 Data Analytical Approach

In this study, the dataset computed by using the Statistical Package for Social Science (SPSS) version 21.0 was utilized for data analysis. Initial screening and missing data analysis were performed on the survey data. To evaluate the factor structure, an exploratory factor analysis (EFA) was done since (Liden et al. 2005)'s servant leadership measure has been extensively used and has demonstrated connection with other servant leadership measures, such as those presented by Dierendonck and Nuijten (2011). At this stage, six SL factors as IV were extracted related to one factor of JS as DV and one factor of LMX has been extracted as DV. After that Cronbach's alphas were calculated to ensure that each factor was reliable to run the correlation analysis to test the hypothesis of the study. Then, Pearson's correlation coefficients Matrix shown in Table 1, used to describe the relationship between the variables of this study proposed to test in the hypothesis of relationships. The correlation analysis was used to assess the strength of the relationship among the variables. A significance level of 0.05 was set for the correlation analysis (Hair et al. 2003).

Table 1 Pearson correlation coefficients

Pearson's r	Indication
Between ± 0.80 and ± 1.00	High correlation
Between ± 0.60 and ± 0.79	Moderately high correlation
Between ± 0.40 and ± 0.59	Moderate correlation
Between ± 0.20 and ± 0.39	Low correlation
Between ± 0.01 and ± 0.19	Negligible correlation

4.4 Measures

In terms of the questionnaire survey's design, three survey instruments were utilized to collect data following the guidelines developed by Tsang et al. (2017). Servant Leadership (Liden et al. 2005), Job Satisfaction Scale (MCMJSS) (Mohrman et al. 1978), and Leader-Member Exchange LMX-7 scale items by Graen and Uhl-Bien (1995) are the three survey tools. These three tools were utilized to gain a better and more in-depth knowledge of the link between servant leadership and job satisfaction among employees. Regarding the survey, there are three components to this survey. The first was about gathering information on followers' gender, education, and age, as well as how long they'd been with their present group. The survey's second section included 28 questions regarding the servant leadership approach. The third set of questions focused on work satisfaction. The last segment includes seven questions to gather information on the correlation of LMX with servant leadership. (Liden et al. 2005) 28-item scale were one of the scales used to judge SL style. This scale assesses followers' views and understandings of their direct leaders who employ a servant leadership style, based on eight primary dimensions which called 8-dimensions of servant leadership: accountability, humility, empowerment, forgiveness, courage, authenticity, stewardship, and Standing Back.

The MCMJSS scale is used to examine and quantify job satisfaction in this study. The purpose of the study was to investigate and assess eight different factors of employee job satisfaction. Four of the aspects measured intrinsic job satisfaction, while the other four measured extrinsic job satisfaction. The survey methodology comprised a 5-point Likert-type scale, with 1 being the lowest score and 5 representing the greatest for employee job satisfaction. There are several aspects that contribute to intrinsic job satisfaction, including self-esteem/respect, professional progression and personal development, accomplishments, and expectations. Extrinsic work satisfaction, on the other hand, is determined by elements such as respect and fairness, being informed, the kind and quantity of supervision available to the employee, and the individual's ability to participate in and achieve the organization's goals (McKee 1990).

After being used with various measures by researchers, the Leader-Member Exchange LMX has recently become increasingly popular with a new formulation. The 7-item LMX scale with Cronbach alpha developed by Graen and Uhl-Bien (1995), is the most frequent and widely used type of LMX, and its dependability is always good (El-Bayaa and Elsaman 2022). For instance, in a study by Liden et al.

(1997), they employed LMX7 and found that the dependability was.90. The LMX-7 is extracted from the main LMX 4-dimenssions theory, and it is made up of seven items that describe various facets of the supervisor-subordinate relationship, four of them are the main 4-dimenssions of LMX theory which is effect, loyalty, contribution, and professional respect. The other 3 items are: understanding of job problems and needs, recognition of potential, and willingness to support the other (Graen and Uhl-Bien 1995).

5 Findings

5.1 Factor Analysis of Servant Leadership

Principal components factor analysis with varimax rotation was performed to investigate interrelationship among the items used in the proposed measures of servant leadership. Factor analysis has been conducted and (Liden et al. 2005) 28-item were the scale used to judge SL style along with servant leadership 8-dimensions for the overall total 2 private higher education organizations in Kuwait with a total of 205 respondents in this study. 6 factors were extracted with eigenvalues of 3.8, 3.7, 3.3, 2.9, 2.8, and 2.4 for the Empowerment, Accountability, Humility, Stewardship, Authenticity, and Standing Back respectively, which means, not all the 8 dimensions of SL is applicable in the context of private HEIs in Kuwait only the 6 dimensions that have been extracted are applicable in the context of private HEIs in Kuwait. The percentage of variance explained is 13.9 %, 13.2 %, 11.9 %, 10.39 %, 10.34 %, and 8.69 % respectively for a total of 68.52 %. The factor loading is shown in Table 2 and variance and rotation sums of squared loadings explained in Table 3.

Based on factor 1 items and its loadings, which is contains 6 items out of SL (Liden et al. 2005) 28-items with factor loadings (0.599, 0.56, 0.714, 0.822, 0.788, 0.75), it is concluded that in private higher education institutions, it is highly likely and recommended that servant leader should care about followers' career goals, career development, improving and progressing in their career, and to care about their needs. This factor was labeled as Empowerment in this study with an eigenvalue of 3.894. Factor 2 contains in total 5 items out of Liden et al. (2005) 28-items with factor loadings (0.562, 0.721, 0.705, 0.665, 0.563). These 5 items show the ability of the servant leader to think outside of the box and to solve hard work problems in a creative and effective way. Also, the leader should notify the followers is there anything going wrong. This factor was labeled as Accountability in this study with an eigenvalue of 3.71. Based on factor 3 and its 4 items with factor loadings (0.703, 0.698, 0.844, 0.78), it's important for the servant leader to show the importance of giving back and help people in the community and to emphasize and encourage the followers to involve and volunteer in community activities. This factor was labeled as Humility in this study with an eigenvalue of 3.33.

Factor 4 contains 4 items out of Liden et al. (2005) 28-items with factor loadings (0.676, 0.771, 0.813, 0.615). These 4 items show the ability of servant leader to delegate the tasks to followers and let them to be responsible by handling important work decisions. This factor was labeled as Stewardship in this study with an eigenvalue of 2.91. Factor 5 contains 4 other items out of Liden et al. (2005) 28-items with factor loadings (0.686, 0.719, 0.671, 0.79). These 4 items show the importance of holding servant leader in HEI high ethical moral standards, and the servant leader should prefer telling the truth more than profits (money). This factor was labeled as Authenticity in this study with an eigenvalue of 2.898. The last factor, which is factor 6, contains 4 items with factor loadings (0.596, 0.603, 0.767, 0.622). These 4 items explain the importance of caring about employee's personal well-being by the servant leader in HEI and pay attention to the employee's personal problems. This factor was labeled as Standing Back in this study with an eigenvalue of 2.435. (Table 4).

5.2 Factor Analysis of Job Satisfaction

Factor analysis with varimax rotation was used to analyze the interrelationships among the items utilized in the proposed Job Satisfaction measures. Factor analysis was performed, and the Mohrman-Cooke-Mohrman Job Satisfaction Scale (MCMJSS) was utilized to judge JS for the overall total of 2 private higher education institutions in Kuwait, with a total of 205 respondents in this study. For job satisfaction, one factor was identified with an eigenvalue of 4.652, indicating that intrinsic and extrinsic JS are both essential for employees working at private HEIs in Kuwait. The percentage of variance explained is 58.155 percent, for a total of 58.155 percent. Table 5 shows the factor loading, while Table 6 explains the variation.

Only 1 factor was extracted with eigenvalue of 4.652 for the job satisfaction and it contains eight items in total, where four items from intrinsic satisfaction (IS1, IS2, IS3, IS4) with factor loadings (0.816, 0.734, 0.790, 0.791) respectively, and four other items from extrinsic satisfaction (ES5, ES6, ES7, ES8) with factor loadings (0.783, 0.767, 0.808, 0.586) respectively, were loaded with eigenvalue of 4.652. The labeling of this factor, however, was problematic in the sense that eight of the items were equally distributed between intrinsic and extrinsic job satisfaction. It appears that intrinsic and extrinsic job satisfaction are

Table 2 The factor loading-servant leadership rotated component matrix

Variables	Component					
	Empowerment	Accountability	Humility	Stewardship	Authenticity	Standing back
LS1						0.596
LS2						0.603
LS3						0.767
LS4						0.622
LS5			0.703			
LS6			0.698			
LS7			0.844			
LS8			0.78			
LS9		0.562				
LS10		0.721				
LS11		0.705				
LS12		0.665				
LS13				0.676		
LS14				0.771		
LS15				0.813		
LS16				0.615		
LS17	0.599					
LS18	0.56					
LS19		0.563				
LS20	0.714					
LS21	0.822					
LS22	0.788					
LS23	0.75					
LS24						
LS25					0.686	
LS26					0.719	
LS27					0.671	
LS28					0.79	

Table 3 Variance and rotation sums of squared loadings

Variable	Total	(%) of variance	Cumulative (%)
Empowerment	3.894	13.907	13.907
Accountability	3.715	13.267	27.174
Humility	3.334	11.908	39.082
Stewardship	2.911	10.395	49.476
Authenticity	2.898	10.349	59.825
Standing back	2.435	8.696	68.521

equally essential for employees working in Kuwaiti higher education institutions HEIs, reflecting that in reacting to feelings of self-esteem or self-respect, the possibility for personal progress in the profession, The sense of success, the expectations when the employee first started, the level of respect and fair treatment the employee receives from the leader, the sense of being informed about the employee's task, Finally, the opportunity for participation in the determination of methods, procedures, and goals must be considered to ensure that leaders working in higher education institutions HEIs are aware of their employees' needs in order to achieve better employee outcomes (Table 7).

5.3 Factor Analysis of Leader Member Exchange LMX

To study the interrelationships among the items included in the proposed Leader Member Exchange LMX measures, principal components factor analysis with varimax rotation

Table 4 Reliability scores of servant leadership—The 28-item of Liden et al., (2005)

Variables	No. of items	Reliability score
Empowerment	6	0.895
Accountability	5	0.789
Humility	5	0.894
Stewardship	4	0.815
Authenticity	4	0.836
Standing back	4	0.766

Table 5 Job satisfaction factor loading and component matrix

Variables	Job satisfaction
IS1	0.816
IS2	0.734
IS3	0.790
IS4	0.791
ES5	0.783
ES6	0.767
ES7	0.808
ES8	0.586

Table 6 Extraction variance sums of squared loadings of job satisfaction

Variable	Total	% of Variance	Cumulative %
Job satisfaction (JS)	4.652	58.155	58.155

Table 7 Reliability scores of job satisfaction—MCMJSS-job satisfaction—Year 1978

Variables	No. of items	Reliability score
Job satisfaction	8	0.890

Table 8 LMX factor loading and component matrix

Variables	Job satisfaction
LMX1	0.768
LMX2	0.844
LMX3	0.818
LMX4	0.780
LMX5	0.669
LMX6	0.827
LMX7	0.832

was used. The performed factor analysis did support Leader Member Exchange LMX in investigating its link and its effect on servant leadership SL for the entire sum of 2 private higher education institutions in Kuwait with a total of 205 respondents in this study. For the LMX, 1 factor was identified with an eigenvalue of 4.403. The percentage of variance explained is 62.894 percent, for a total of 62.894 percent. Table 8 shows the factor loading, and Table 9 explains the variation.

As shown in Table 9, only 1 factor was extracted with factor loadings (0.768, 0.844, 0.818, 0.780, 0.669, 0.827, 0.832) and with eigenvalue of 4.403 for the LMX and it contains seven items in total, these items have been contributed into four factors which are the 4-dimensions/factors of LMX: affect, loyalty, contribution, and professional respect which need all of them to be taken into consideration to ensure that leaders working in higher education institutions HEIs must also know about their employees' needs by using the 4-diminsions of LMX theory and to achieve better employee job satisfaction by adopting servant leadership style. As shown in Table 10, all these seven items were loaded with eigenvalue of 4.403. This factor was labeled as Leader Member Exchange (LMX) for this study (Fig. 2).

5.4 Correlation Hypothesis Servant Leadership SL and Job Satisfaction JS

In this study, Pearson correlation analysis was utilized to see whether there is a significant association between Job satisfaction and the six factors of servant leadership that are extracted from the factor loading which are: Empowerment (EMP), Accountability (ACC), Humility (HUM), Stewardship (STW), Authenticity (AUT), and Standing Back (STB). The intensity of relationships between the dependent and independent variables of the study are described using the scale suggested by Hair et al. (2003), as shown in Table 11, this study is performed to determine whether there is a relationship between the six servant leadership factors and the aspect of job satisfaction.

Table 9 Extraction sums of squared loadings of LMX

Variable	Total	% of variance	Cumulative %
LMX leader-member exchange	4.403	62.894	62.894

Table 10 Reliability scores of LMX—Graen and Uhl-Bien (1995)—LMX 7-scale items

Variables	No. of Items	Reliability scores
LMX	7	0.90

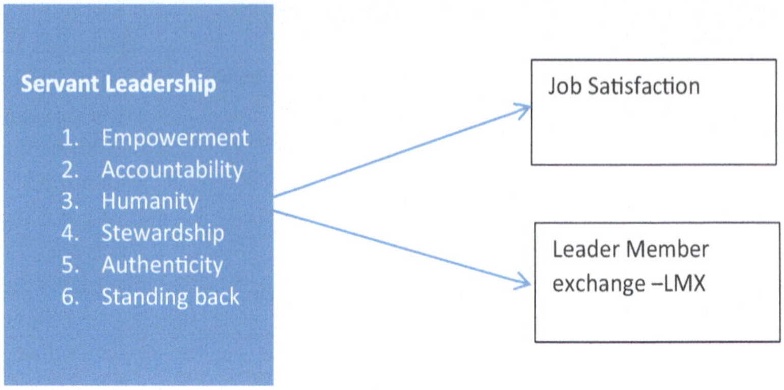

Fig. 2 Research results model

Table 11 The correlation hypothesis of the six factors of servant leadership with job satisfaction

Variable		EMP	ACC	HUM	STW	AUT	STB
Job satisfaction (SJ)	Pearson correlation	0.632**	0.615**	0.509*	0.465**	0.568**	0.424**
	Sig. (2-tailed)	0.000	0.000	0.000	0.000	0.000	0.000
	N	205	205	205	205	205	191

For this final hypothesis, an average summated score has been computed where all six factors of SL were considered to provide an overall score. The JS then tested for the correlation and the following Table 12 shows the finding of an overall relationship between job satisfaction and servant leadership. According to the findings of this research, and as shown in Table 12, this study found out that there is a positive relationship between overall Servant Leadership SL and Job Satisfaction JS. The research found out that the correlation between Servant Leadership SL with its 6 factors and Job Satisfaction JS related to the finding of Pearson correlation with $r=0.715^{**}$ has moderately high correlation with significant P value=0.000<0.05 which approved the alternative hypothesis H1a and rejected H10 null hypothesis.

5.5 Correlation Hypothesis Servant Leadership SL and Job Satisfaction JS

In this study, Pearson correlation analysis was utilized to see whether there is a significant association between Leader Member Exchange LMX and the six factors of servant leadership which are: Empowerment (EMP), Accountability (ACC), Humility (HUM), Stewardship (STW), Authenticity (AUT), and Standing Back (STB). The intensity of correlation between the dependent variable which is LMX and the independent variable of this study which is Servant Leadership are described using the scale suggested by Hair et al. (2003), as shown in Table 13, This study is performed to determine whether there is a correlation between the six servant leadership factors and the aspect of LMX.

Table 12 Overall correlation between job satisfaction and servant leadership

Variable		SL
Job satisfaction (SJ)	Pearson correlation	0.715**
	Sig. (2-tailed)	0.000
	N	205

For this final hypothesis, an average summated score has been computed where all six factors of SL were considered to provide an overall score. The LMX then tested for the correlation and the following Table 14 shows the finding of an overall relationship between LMX and servant leadership. According to the findings of this research, this study found out that there is a positive relationship between Servant Leadership SL and LMX. The research found out that the correlation between Servant Leadership SL and LMX related to the finding of Pearson correlation with $r=0.734^{**}$ has moderately high correlation with significant P value=0.000<. 05, which approved the alternative hypothesis H2a and rejected H20 null hypothesis.

6 Discussion

In this study, literature has highlighted the relevance of servant leadership and its impact on employee job satisfaction in higher education enterprises. The initial level of statistical analysis started with exploratory factor analysis (EFA) which is conducted to evaluate and examine the relationship between the variables. (Liden et al. 2005)'s servant leadership measure, Mohrman-Cooke-Mohrman

Table 13 The correlation hypothesis of the six factors of servant leadership with LMX

Variable		EMP	ACC	HUM	STW	AUT	STB
Leader member exchange (LMX)	Pearson correlation	0.639**	0.564**	0.535**	0.520**	0.548**	0.518
	sig. (2-tailed)	0.000	0.000	0.000	0.000	0.000	0.000
	N	205	205	205	205	205	191

Table 14 Overall correlation between Leader Member Exchange LMX and Servant Leadership SL

Variable		SL
LMX leader-member exchange	Pearson correlation	0.734**
	sig. (2-tailed)	0.000
	N	205

job satisfaction measure, and LMX 7-itms scale have been extensively used and have demonstrated connection with other servant leadership measures, such as the 8-dimensions of servant leadership presented by van (Dierendonck and Nuijten 2011). At this stage, six SL factors out of 8 were extracted as IV related to one factor of JS as DV and one factor of LMX has been extracted as DV. After that Cronbach's alphas were calculated to ensure that each factor was reliable, Pearson's correlation coefficients test has been conducted to discuss and explain if there is a significant association between the variables. The second level of the statistical analysis focused on the link between servant leadership dimensions and job satisfaction. The third level of the study focused on the relationship between servant leadership and LMX theory.

In two ways, the findings of this study add to the validity of the 28-item servant leadership instrument, the Mohrman-Cooke-Mohrman Job Satisfaction Scale (MCMJSS), and the 7-item LMX scale by Graen and Uhl-Bien (1995), as well as theories on leadership, job satisfaction and LMX. This study verifies and extends the validity of the three measuring instruments indicated before. In this paper, Hypothesis 1 focused on the relationship between the 6 factors of servant leadership that have been extracted from EFA test (empowerment, accountability, stewardship, humility, authenticity, and standing back) and job satisfaction. (From H1.1 to H1.6) as shown in the Pearson correlation Table 11.

After explaining and discussing the relationship between servant leadership and job satisfaction, the third level of the statistical analysis focused on the correlation between the 6 factors of servant leadership that have been extracted from EFA test and leader member exchange model LMX which presented in hypothesis 2 with its sub-hypothesis. (From H2.1 to H2.6) as shown in the Pearson correlation Table 13.

6.1 Implications

According to the findings of this research, this study found out that there is a positive relationship between Empowerment and JS. The research found out that the correlation between Empowerment and JS related to the finding of Pearson correlation with $r = 0.632^{**}$ is moderately high correlated with *P* value $= 0.000 < 0.05$ which approved the alternative hypothesis H1.1a and rejected H1.10 null hypothesis. Based on the literature, the importance of empowerment within general management has increased over the last few years. Providing staff members with considerable autonomy to set their own priorities and levels of authority allows them to contribute their entire skill set to the bigger picture objectives of the company, which is generally encouraged. It is simpler to establish a cohesive, excellent workplace where exceptional products and services are offered when people are empowered. If the banking industry wants to improve, management must actively participate in empowering their workers. This is done by cultivating autonomy, exchanging knowledge, and creating self-managed teams. As a result, the results of this concept are congruent with some earlier research (Kahreh et al. 2011).

For H1.2, according to the findings of this research, this study found out that there is a strong significant positive relationship between Accountability and JS. The research found out that the correlation between Accountability and JS related to the finding of Pearson correlation with $r = 0.615^{**}$ is moderately high correlated with P value $= 0.000 < 0.05$ which approved the alternative hypothesis H1.2a and rejected H1.20 null hypothesis. Based on the literature, institutions of higher learning are examples of organizations that need their employees to perform responsibly since they are social systems (Katz and Kahn 1978). Certain kinds of accountability, like role systems theory, emphasize the importance of interpersonal expectations, highlight the results of compliance, and link duties and activities to specific persons (Beu and Buckley 2001). For H1.3, The idea of humility has received more attention in organizational study in recent years. In the light of recent corporate crises that have been connected to the unbridled ego, hubris, feeling of entitlement, and self-importance of the corporate leaders involved, humility is now seen as being more crucial to the character of persons who lead and function within corporations (Owens et al. 2013). Humility is one of the cores "organizational virtues" that is said to create the moral foundation of organizational environments (Wang et al. 2018). Theorists argue that leaders need to be humbler as they lead their firms through increasingly dynamic and turbulent times (Owens et al. 2013). The current study found out that there is a positive relationship between Humility and JS. The research found out that the correlation between Humility and JS related to the finding of Pearson correlation with $r=0.509^{**}$ has moderate correlation with significant *P* value $=0.000<0.05$ which approved the alternative hypothesis H1.3a and rejected H1.30 null hypothesis.

For H1.4, this study found out that there is a positive relationship between Stewardship and JS. The research found out that the correlation between Stewardship and JS related to the finding of Pearson correlation with $r=0.465^{**}$ has moderate correlation with significant *P* value $=0.000<0.05$ which approved the alternative hypothesis H1.4a and rejected H1.40 null hypothesis. Based on previous literature, and according to Kelly (2001), the four pillars of stewardship are reciprocity, responsibility, reporting, and relationship nurturing. The first component, reciprocity, requires companies to communicate gratitude to their viewers for their efforts. Expressing gratitude for their involvement is one way to appreciate stakeholders and their contributions to the organization. (Gouldner 1960), a sociology pioneer, stated that "those whom you have benefitted from having an obligation to support you" (p. 173). Businesses can show their appreciation for their employees by expressing gratitude and doing acts of appreciation. For H1.5, Managers' level of authenticity reflects their capacity to balance their commitments to themselves, their followers, and the public to create collaboration both inside and outside of a business. As a result, leaders who are more authentic will have followers who are more motivated to go above and beyond in their work to repay their leader's highly valued ties (Penger and Černe 2014). The current study found out that there is a positive relationship between Authenticity and JS. The research found out that the correlation between Authenticity and JS related to the finding of Pearson correlation with $r=0.568^{**}$ has moderate correlation with significant *P* value $=0.000<0.05$ which approved the alternative hypothesis H1.5a and rejected H1.50 null hypothesis.

Finally, for H1.6, which is related to standing back as one of the 6 factors of SL that extracted from EFA test, previous research found out that a leader who stands back defers credit to others while keeping a low profile and abstaining from seeking recognition or rewards for the things they do on behalf of others. The extent to which a leader prioritizes the needs of subordinates and provides them with the necessary encouragement and appreciation for a job well done is an important factor to consider (Huning et al. 2020). The current study found out that there is a positive relationship between Standing Back and JS. The research found out that the correlation between Standing Back and JS related to the finding of Pearson correlation with $r=0.424^{**}$ has moderate correlation with significant *P* value $=0.000<0.05$ which approved the alternative hypothesis H1.6a and rejected H1.60 null hypothesis.

In conclusion and based on the literature and findings, there is a positive relationship between Servant Leadership SL and Job Satisfaction JS as overall result. The research found out that the correlation between Servant Leadership SL and Job Satisfaction JS related to the finding of Pearson correlation with $r=0.715^{**}$ has moderately high correlation with significant *P* value $=0.000<0.05$ which approved the alternative hypothesis H1a and rejected H10 null hypothesis. The findings demonstrate that Job satisfaction rises when leaders are less concerned with accumulating power and instead focus on empowering followers, prioritizing subordinates' interests, and helping. Additionally, the findings demonstrate that work satisfaction rises when leaders are following Accountability, Humility, Stewardship, Authenticity and Standing Back towards their followers.

For hypothesis 2, and according to the findings of this research, this study found out that there is a positive relationship between Empowerment and LMX. The research found out that the correlation between Empowerment and LMX related to the finding of Pearson correlation with $r=0.639^{**}$ is moderately high with significant *P* value $=0.000<0.05$ which approved the alternative hypothesis H2.1a and rejected H2.10 null hypothesis. For the sub-hypothesis H2.2, this study found out that there is a positive relationship between Accountability and LMX. The research found out that the correlation between Accountability and LMX related to the finding of Pearson correlation with $r=0.564^{**}$ has moderate correlation with significant *P* value $=0.000<0.05$ which approved the alternative hypothesis H2.2a and rejected H2.20 null hypothesis. For H2.3, this study found out that there is a positive relationship between Humility and LMX. The research found out that the correlation between Humility and LMX related to the finding of Pearson correlation with $r=0.535^{**}$ has moderate correlation with significant *P* value $=0.000<0.05$ which approved the alternative hypothesis H2.3a and rejected H2.30 null hypothesis.

For the sub-hypothesis H2.4, this study found out that there is a positive relationship between Stewardship and LMX. The research found out that the correlation between Stewardship and LMX related to the finding of Pearson correlation with $r=0.520^{**}$ has moderate correlation with significant *P* value $=0.000<0.05$ which approved the alternative hypothesis H2.4a and rejected H2.40 null hypothesis. For H2.5, this study found out that there is a positive relationship between Authenticity and LMX. The research found out that the correlation between Authenticity and LMX related to the finding of Pearson correlation with $r=0.548^{**}$ has moderate correlation with significant P value $=0.000<0.05$ which approved the alternative hypothesis H2.5a and rejected H2.50 null hypothesis. For the sub-hypothesis H2.6, this study found out that there is a positive relationship between Standing Back and LMX. The research found out that the correlation between Standing Back and LMX related to the finding of Pearson correlation with $r=0.518^{**}$ has moderate correlation with significant P value $=0.000<0.05$ which approved the alternative hypothesis H2.6a and rejected H2.60 null hypothesis.

In conclusion, and according to the findings of this research, this study found out that there is a positive relationship between 6 dimensions of Servant Leadership and LMX. The research found out that the correlation between Servant Leadership SL and LMX related to the finding of Pearson correlation with $r=0.734^{**}$ has moderately high correlation with significant P value $=0.000<0.05$ which approved the alternative hypothesis H2a and rejected H20 null hypothesis. Therefore, the findings demonstrate a stronger link between the leader, the followers, and improved LMX when using the SL approach. This outcome is in line with other research that looked at the connection between SL and LMX and demonstrated that SL had a favorable impact on LMX (e.g., (Mostafa and El-Motalib 2019), (Salie 2008)). Leaders who defer credit to others, maintain a low profile, and refrain from seeking recognition or rewards for their accomplishments on others' behalf may see a decline in employee satisfaction levels (Abbas et al. 2022). The best LMX encounters might be supported by SL since they place a high value on their followers' personalized thoughtfulness and relationship-building (Aggarwal et al. 2021).

According to the findings of this study, there is a clear and significant link between servant leadership and Leader Member Exchange Theory LMX. Building trust, affection, and mutual respect at the LMX stage of personalized relationships leads to the formation of stronger links between leaders and followers. According to the results, the study proposes an expansion of their knowledge basis in higher education when it comes to empowerment since it increases their effectiveness, capability, and competence. Including higher education non-faculty administrative staff, this research study was highly significant since it was not widely investigated previously. The study's outcomes serve as the stimulus for the examination and advancement of higher education staff and their capability of decision-making, which is a domain still understudied (Aldaihani 2019).

6.2 Limitations

Several limitations were to be acknowledged throughout the study. The biggest one is the fact that not all academic institutions and their faculties and departments in Kuwait were picked for this study investigation, which could have been effective for further and stronger representativeness, Another restriction of this investigation, this study concentrated mostly on the non-faculty and administration group, the sample size of the examined population, as well as the cohort of higher education institutions' members and employees, may not be an adequate picture of the extensive population. Moreover, because of the study's inclusion of two private higher education institutions located in a specific geographical area, the findings and results obtained from this research's sample will not be applicable to other places. Data and results from various geographical locations may vary and differ from those of this study.

7 Conclusions

Case in point, this study sought to examine and understand how servant leadership affects employees' job satisfaction's level in the context of the private higher education institutions in Kuwait and the correlation between servant leadership and leader member exchange model LMX, through a critical analysis within higher education contexts. EFA, Reliability Test, and Pearson correlation have been conducted to assess the following hypotheses that were formulated on the links between servant leadership and job satisfaction, plus, servant leadership and LMX based on the literature review and the conceptual research model established from a literature analysis and the following research hypothesis, to bridge this elusive gap in theory. Servant leadership and job satisfaction (H1), and servant leadership and LMX are the key findings of this study, which has been operationalized on two levels (H2).

The practice of servant leadership has given rise to a leadership revolution, and those who practice it are a revolutionary group who have exploited and completely flipped upside down the traditional power of leadership. Advocates of servant leadership assert that their efforts will be rewarded in a variety of ways. When employees feel empowered, they will work with a lot of creativity and ingenuity. The organization has higher retention and lower turnover costs because of its employees' increased engagement and sense of purpose. Employees who have received quality training and have earned trust continue to develop into potential leaders, assuring the organization's long-term viability.

References

Abbas, A., Saud, M., Usman, I., and Ekowati, D. (2020). "Servant leadership and religiosity: An indicator of employee performance in the education sector," International Journal of Innovation, Creativity and Change, vol. 13, pp. 391–409.

Abbas, A., Saud, M., Suhariadi, F., Usman, I., and Ekowati, D. (2022). "Positive leadership psychology: Authentic and servant leadership in higher education in Pakistan," Current Psychology, vol. 41, pp. 5859-5871.

Abedeen, F. (2015). Exploration of ESP teacher knowledge and practices at tertiary and applied colleges in Kuwait: implications for pre- and in-service ESP teacher training.

Aboramadan, M., Albashiti, B., Alharazin, H. and Dahleez, K.A., 2020. Human resources management practices and organizational commitment in higher education: The mediating role of work engagement. International Journal of Educational Management, 34(1), pp.154–174.

Aggarwal, A., Nobi, K., Jaisinghani, D., and Sharma, G. (2021). "Analyzing the mediating effect of leader-member exchange on the relationship between servant leadership and organizational commitment," International Journal of Economics and Business Research, vol. 21, pp. 287–303.

Akdol, B., and Arikboga, F. S. (2017). "Leader member exchange as a mediator of the relationship between servant leadership and job satisfaction: A research on Turkish ICT companies," International Journal of Organizational Leadership, vol. 6, pp. 525–535.

Al-Asfour, A., Charkasova, A., Rajasekar, J., and Kentiba, E. (2022). "Servant leadership behaviors and the level of readiness to covid-19 pandemic: evidence from USA higher education institutions," International Journal of Leadership in Education, vol. https://doi.org/10.1080/13603124.2022.2108505, pp. 1–18.

Aldaihani, S. (2019). Distributed leadership applications in high schools in the State of Kuwait from teachers' viewpoints. International Journal of Leadership in Education. Vol. 23. pp. 1 16.

AlShammari, I. (2010). High school principals 'attitudes toward the implementation of e-administration in Kuwait's public schools. Indiana State University, IN.

Amussah, A. (2020). "Leadership styles and its impact on employee performance," School of Social Sciences, Near East University. Nicosia.

An, S.H., Meier, K.J., Bøllingtoft, A. and Andersen, L.B., 2019. Employee perceived effect of leadership training: Comparing public and private organizations. International Public Management Journal, 22(1), pp.2–28.

Beu, D., and Buckley, M. R. (2001). The hypothesized relationship between accountability and ethical behavior. Journal of Business Ethics, 34(1), 57–73.

Boyum, V.S., 2012. A model of servant leadership in higher education. University of Minnesota.

Dahleez, K., and M. Aboramadan, M. (2022). "Servant leadership and job satisfaction in higher education: the mediating roles of organizational justice and organizational trust," International Journal of Leadership in Education, vol. https://doi.org/10.1080/13603124.2022.2052753, pp. 1-22.

El-Bayaa, N., and Elsaman, H. A. (2022). "The efficacy of adopting servant leadership to improve employee engagement and job satisfaction. Empirical Study of Higher Education Sector in Kuwait," Journal of Positive School Psychology, vol. 6, pp. 10261–10265.

Elsaman, H.A., El-Bayaa, N. and Kousihan, S., 2022. Measuring and Validating the Factors Influenced the SME Business Growth in Germany—Descriptive Analysis and Construct Validation. Data, 7(11), p.158.

Ghareeb, N. (2010). Academic freedom of faculty members at Kuwait University: Issues of understanding and freedom of research and publishing. University of Cardiff: Cardiff.

Gouldner, A. W. (1960). The norm of reciprocity. American Sociological Review, 25, 165–167.

Graen, G. B., and Uhl-Bien, M. (1995). "Relationship-based approach to leadership: Development of leader-member exchange (LMX) theory of leadership over 25 years: Applying a multi-level multi-domain perspective," The leadership quarterly, vol. 6, pp. 219-247.

Greenleaf, R.K. (1977). Servant Leadership: A Journey into the Nature of Legitimate Power and Greatness. Paulist Press; NJ.

Hair JF, Anderson RE, Tatham RL, Black WC (2003). Multivariate Data Analysis (5th Ed.). Pearson Education: India.

Hasanuddin, B., Mustainah, M., and Buntuang, P. (2021). "The influence of servant leadership on job satisfaction with individual character as a moderating variable," Problems and Perspectives in Management, vol. 19, pp. 445–455.

Heriyadi, H., Tjahjono, H. K., and Rahayu, M. K. P. (2020). "Improving organizational citizenship behavior through job satisfaction, leader-member exchange, and work-life balance," Binus Business Review, vol. 11, pp. 97–104.

Huning, T. M., Hurt, K. J., and Frieder, R. E. (2020). The effect of servant leadership, perceived organizational support, job satisfaction and job embeddedness on turnover intentions: An empirical investigation. In Evidence-Based HRM: A Global Forum for Empirical Scholarship. Emerald Publishing Limited.

Ireri, K., 2016. High job satisfaction despite low income: A national study of Kenyan journalists. Journalism and mass communication quarterly, 93(1), pp.164–186.

Kahreh, M. S., Ahmadi, H., and Hashemi, A. (2011). Achieving competitive advantage through empowering employees: An empirical study. Far East Journal of Psychology and Business, 3(2), 26–37.

Kalifa, T., Ololo, S., and Tafese, F. (2016). "Intention to leave and associated factors among health professionals in jimma zone public health centers, Southwest Ethiopia," Open Journal of Preventive Medicine, vol. 6, pp. 31–41.

Katz, D., and Kahn, R.L., 1978. Organizations and the system concept. Classics of organization theory, 80, p.480.

Kelly, K. S. (2001). Stewardship: The missing step in the public relations process. In R. L. Heath (Ed.), Handbook of public relations. Thousand Oaks, CA: Sage.

Krejcie, R. V., & Morgan, D. W. (1970). Determining sample size for research activities. Educational and Psychological Measurement, 30, 607–610.

Kumar, A. M. (2020). "Servant Leadership in Indian NGOs," Thesis Abstract. 2013. Department of Business Administration.

Latif, K.F., Machuca, M.M., Marimon, F. and Sahibzada, U.F., 2021. Servant leadership, career, and life satisfaction in higher education: A cross-country study of Spain, China, and Pakistan. Applied Research in Quality of Life, 16, pp.1221-1247.

Liden, R. C., and Maslyn, J. M. (1998). "Multidimensionality of leader-member exchange: An empirical assessment through scale development," Journal of management, vol. 24, pp. 43–72.

Liden, R. C., Wayne, S. J., Zhao, H. and Henderson, D., 2005. Servant leadership: Development of a multidimensional measure and multi-level assessment. The Leadership Quarterly., 19(2), pp. 161–177.

Liden, R.C., Wayne, S.J., Liao, C. and Meuser, J.D., 2014. Servant leadership and serving culture: Influence on individual and unit performance. Academy of management journal, 57(5), pp.1434–1452.

Liden, R.C., Sparrowe, R.T and Wayne, S.J. (1997), Leader-member exchange theory: The past and potential for the future. In Gerald R Ferris, editor, Research in personnel and human resources. Pp. 47–118.

Mahdavi, I. and Fazlollahtabar, H. (2012). Design of a Fuzzy Job satisfaction Matrix with Dynamic Performance Criteria. pp. 1173–1179.

McKee, J., 1990. Relationship between community college presidents' leadership styles and faculty job satisfaction. Clearwater Beach, FL., Paper presented at the Annual Conference of the Eastern Educational Research Association.

Mohrman Jr, A. M., Cooke, R. A., and Mohrman, S. A. (1978). "Participation in decision making: A multidimensional perspective," Educational Administration Quarterly, vol. 14, pp. 13–29.

Mostafa, A. M. S., and El-Motalib, E. A. A. (2019). "Servant leadership, leader–member exchange and proactive behavior in the public health sector," Public Personnel Management, vol. 48, pp. 309–324.

Northouse, P. G. (2007). Leadership: Theory and practice (4th ed.). Thousand Oaks, CA: Sage.

Owens, B. P., Johnson, M. D., and Mitchell, T. R. (2013). Expressed humility in organizations: Implications for performance, teams, and leadership. Organization Science, 24(5), 1517–1538.

Parris, D.L. and Peachey, J.W., 2013. A systematic literature review of servant leadership theory in organizational contexts. Journal of business ethics, 113(3), pp.377–393.

Penger, S., and Černe, M. (2014). Authentic leadership, employees' job satisfaction, and work engagement: A hierarchical linear modelling approach. Economic research-Ekonomska istraživanja, 27(1), 508–526.

Ragnarsson, S., Kristjánsdóttir, E.S. and Gunnarsdóttir, S., 2018. To be accountable while showing care: The lived experience of people in a servant leadership organization. Sage Open, 8(3), p.2158244018801097.

Ramma, Y., Patiro, S. P. S., and Daud, A. (2022). "The influence of servant leadership on motivation and job satisfaction employees at the ministry of religious affairs of merauke regency: The mediation role of trust in leaders," Budapest International Research and Critics Institute-Journal (BIRCI-Journal), vol. 5, pp. 20779–20794.

Saleem, F., Zhang, Y. Z., Gopinath, C., and Adeel, A. (2020). "Impact of servant leadership on performance: The mediating role of affective and cognitive trust," Sage Open, vol. 10, p. 2158244019900562.

Salie, A. (2008). Servant-minded leadership and work satisfaction in Islamic organizations: A correlational mixed study: University of Phoenix.

Shafai, A. A. (2020). "Servant-leadership in higher education in Saudi Arabia," in Global Servant-Leadership: Wisdom, Love, and Legitimate Power in the Age of Chaos, P. Mathew, J. Song, S. R. Ferch, and L. C. Spears, Eds., ed Lexington Books, London, United Kingdom: The Rowman & Littlefield Publishing Group, Inc., pp. 253–276.

Spears, L.C., 2005. THE UNDERSTANDING AND PRACTICE OF SERVANT LEADERSMP. The International Journal of Servant-Leadership, 1(1), pp.29–45.

Stone Gregory, A., Patterson, K and Russell, R.F. (2004). Transformational versus servant leadership: A difference in leader focus. Leadership and Organization Development Journal. Vol. 25(4). pp. 350–361.

Tsang, S., Royse, C. F., and Terkawi, A. S. (2017). "Guidelines for developing, translating, and validating a questionnaire in perioperative and pain medicine," Saudi journal of anaesthesia, vol. 11, p. 80.

Van Dierendonck, D. (2011). "Servant leadership: A review and synthesis," Journal of management, vol. 37, pp. 1228–1261.

Van Dierendonck, D., and Nuijten, I. (2011). "The servant leadership survey: Development and validation of a multidimensional measure," Journal of business and psychology, vol. 26, pp. 249–267.

Vrcelj, N., Bevanda, V., and Bevanda, N. (2022). "Servant leadership: Influence of job satisfaction and organizational commitment," Management: Journal of Sustainable Business and Management Solutions in Emerging Economies, vol. https://doi.org/10.7595/management.fon.2022.0009.

Wang, L., Owens, B.P., Li, J.J. and Shi, L., 2018. Exploring the affective impact, boundary conditions, and antecedents of leader humility. Journal of Applied Psychology, 103(9), p.1019.

Wheeler, D., 2012. Servant leadership for higher education: Principles and practices. s.l.: John Wiley and Sons.

Wilkins, S., Annabi, C. and Butt, M.M. (2017). The effects of employee commitment in transnational higher education: the case of international branch campuses. Journal of Studies in International Education. Vol. 21(4). pp. 294–315.

Unleashing IT Innovation in Education Based on Meta Learning Approach in English Language Classroom

Muthmainnah Muthmainnah, Ahmad Al Yakin, Souvik Ganguli, and Ahmed J. Obaid

Abstract

There has been a lack of both educational focus on computational thinking (CT) and research into effective methods of assessing CT competence. Today, there have been dramatic changes in how, what, and when students learn. The impact of the COVID-19 pandemic and artificially assisted digitalization promise more conscious, independent, and intrinsically driven learning by changing the learning environment and providing the potential for transformative learning experiences according to the learning needs of generation Z. Through a metacognition lens, this article seeks to explore virtual reality as an implication of meta-learning and characterizing the level of meta-learning in universities. Next, the feasibility of using virtual reality technology to investigate how this technology influences meta-learning is investigated. This paper aims to explore the perceptions of college students regarding student-centred approaches to Virtual Reality technology as possible predictors of academic achievement. A student-centered digital technology approach is designed in faculty computer English classes. A total of 350 population and 64 students were deliberately selected to be involved in this study. Following a mixed methods approach, quantitative data were collected from student questionnaires, and qualitative data explored the results of interviews with students learning English in virtual reality. The findings of this paper provide support for the use of an active learning environment where students are actively engaged during learning, and this paper also presents students' perceptions in tertiary institutions as a new theoretical framework for meta-learning supported by smart gadgets that will enable meta-learning-future foreign language learners, or rather meta thinkers, to go beyond the ordinary level of knowledge and to higher and more advanced levels of intelligence. Given the important role of technology and metalearning in learning, this paper recommends a new English language education policy and curriculum.

Keywords

Education · Information technology · Meta learning · Virtual reality · English language

M. Muthmainnah (✉)
Teacher Training and Education Faculty Indonesian Language Study Program, Universitas Al Asyariah Mandar, Polewali Mandar, Indonesia
e-mail: muthmainnahunasman@gmail.com

A. Al Yakin
Teacher Training and Education Faculty Civic Education Study Program, Universitas Al Asyariah Mandar, Polewali Mandar, Indonesia

S. Ganguli
Department of Electrical and Instrumentation Engineering, Thapar Institute of Engineering and Technology, Patiala, Punjab 147004, India
e-mail: souvik.ganguli@thapar.edu

A. J. Obaid
Faculty of Computer Science and Mathematics, University of Kufa, Kufa, Iraq
e-mail: ahmedj.aljanaby@uokufa.edu.iq

1 Introduction

Meta-learning is a process by which students proactively construct and control their own mental models of the learning process. The highest level of understanding, called meta-comprehension or higher order thinking skills, is achieved by meta-learning, which requires a progressive and hierarchical altered set of meta skills (Drigas et al. 2023). Meta-learning is a type of learning that focuses on improving the learning process itself. In other words, it is a learning approach that involves gaining knowledge and skills related to learning, studying and managing

S. Arezki et al. (eds.), *Emerging Disruptive Technologies for Society 5.0 in Developing Countries*, Advances in Science, Technology & Innovation, https://doi.org/10.1007/978-3-031-63701-8_12

information. Meta-learning teaching is a teaching method that is focused on teaching students how to learn effectively (Vilalta et al. 2010).

In meta-learning teaching, the focus is on developing the student's metacognitive abilities such as self-awareness, reflection, and self-regulation. Teachers using this teaching method help students understand their own learning styles and preferences, and teach them how to adapt their learning strategies based on their individual needs. Some examples of meta-learning teaching techniques include goal-setting, reflecting on one's learning process, organizing information and creating note-taking systems, practicing self-evaluation and reflective thinking in learning (Padmanabha 2020). Overall, the goal of meta-learning teaching is to empower students to become more independent and effective learners (Winters 2011; Colthorpe et al. 2015).

In the field of meta learning in teaching, technology-enhanced language learning, virtual reality (VR) is becoming increasingly popular due to the authentic and immersive learning environment it provides (Parmaxi 2023; Wu et al. 2023; Castaneda et al. 2023). Virtual reality (VR) has enormous potential to be integrated into language instruction in order to create contextualised and interactive learning experiences by mimicking a strong illusion of presence. The development of virtual reality (VR) has accelerated since its inception in the 1960s. Modern virtual reality (VR) tools are far more advanced and engaging than their text-based internet predecessors, featuring 3D virtual spaces and user-created avatars (Peterson 2016).

Along with enhancing student learning in a fun way (Chiu et al. 2023; Matovu et al. 2023), mobile or laptop game-based learning has become a common topic in recent literature (Oberer et al. 2023; Daungcharone et al. 2019). According to Troussas et al. (2020) this practice is recommended because it has the potential to generate unique experiences for students, which in turn influences their level of immersion, participation and involvement in game-based learning environments. Supporting constructivism theory, according to which individuals construct their own knowledge through hands-on experience and reflection, game-based learning such as virtual reality has proven to be an efficient student-centered learning method. As technology advances, virtual reality (VR) has found more and more applications outside its original gaming and entertainment context (Kozinets 2023). Many studies over the last few decades have looked at the possibilities of virtual reality in the classroom. According to Vesisenaho et al. (2019) one of the greatest benefits of using virtual reality in the classroom is the increased sense of presence and immersion it provides students.

To better prepare their students for the future technological revolution, educational institutions around the world are looking for new, creative approaches (Chiao et al. 2018). Moreover, for quite some time, the rigid and non-innovative learning of English has developed into fun learning and motivating the rest of learning efficiently with the help of IT. The purpose of this study was to investigate students' opinions using the Co Space Edu virtual reality (VR) game-based English learning platform with a meta learning approach as teaching materials. The purpose of learning English with this meta learning approach includes increasing students' self-confidence so that they can have international competitiveness and workers in the workplace.

Various studies have investigated the usefulness and acceptability of the meta learning approach in learning (Colthorpe et al. 2018) found that students' attitudes toward learning can be influenced by meta-learning assignments, (Chacón-Díaz 2023) meta learning which can provide opportunities for introspection, refinement of learning techniques, and increased academic achievement, all of which contribute to growing students' capacities for lifelong learning, and stimulate students autonomous in learning (Merchie and Keer 2016). However, little research has been conducted on VR immersion-assisted meta-learning in English classes. Therefore, this study looks at how well the VR application-assisted meta learning approach creates experiences for learners for second language acquisition. In addition the purpose of this study was to investigate meta learning approach assisted virtual reality based on computer science students perspective. Therefore, the research question in this study as follows: are meta-learning approaches assisted virtual reality affecting the students interest in learning English?

1.1 Meta Learning in Language Class

Learning about learning is the focus of meta-learning. "Sub-processes of metacognition that apply specifically to learning and learning processes in institutional settings," as defined by Biggs (1985). That's when students know that they are learners and actively choose and use the appropriate method for their learning. Developing students' abilities to reflect and adapt their learning strategies is important to help them succeed as their academic workload increases, as well as to promote their growth as independent students (Bayless 2023; Cameron and Rideout 2022).

Meta-learning abilities have been argued to be teachable and malleable by a number of scholars, (Bartolotta et al. 2023) gain students soft skill and knowledge to learn, (Lee 2023) pedagogical benefit and the performance of human way of learning (Shen et al. 2023). While others argue that meta-learning can be honed through introspection in problem-solving situations (Vallance and Towndrow 2016). Besides that, reflection is encouraged in situations where one's existing pool of information, assumptions, and experiences is questioned. Critical thinking helps students become more self-aware when planning, monitoring, and assessing their own learning English language (Ma and Liu 2023; Zhang 2022).

To better understand this meta learning, (Tarricone 2011) developed a comprehensive taxonomy of metacognition which divides the construct into two parts: awareness and regulation of one's cognitive processes. There are three different types of knowledge with respect to cognition; these are declarative knowledge, procedural knowledge, and conditional knowledge. People's awareness of themselves and the things that influence their cognitive processing abilities is known as declarative metacognition. Personal knowledge (recognizing one's own characteristics, other people's characteristics, and universal human characteristics in learning), task knowledge (recognizing the nature of tasks and their demands, and their implications), and strategy knowledge (recognizing ways, processes, or what actions tend to achieve what ends in what types of situations) are all included here. Procedural metacognitive knowledge is the second subcategory, and it refers to information about the different steps involved in the thinking process and the proper sequence for doing them.

Using metacognition as a tool to get students interested in and taking charge of their own science education for reasons other than just grades. The skills developed through metacognitive practices can be put to use in a variety of unavoidable real-world contexts. In this situation, students adopt a growth mind set, they "learn to learn" by effectively acquiring and processing new information. The term "learning how to learn" (or "meta-learning") has been used interchangeably with "learning" in previous studies. Meta-learning, as defined by Biggs (1985), is "a sub process of metacognition that applies specifically to learning and study processes in institutional contexts, and more particularly, students' awareness of their motives, and control over the strategy selection and deployment" provides a definition of meta-learning that, like that of metacognition, expands the scope of learning beyond traditional classrooms to account for the widespread availability of knowledge thanks to technological advancements.

Finally, knowing when and why to adopt a particular strategy is a type of metacognitive knowledge that enables one to evaluate the needs of a given cognitive task and choose among a range of possible approaches. Planning, monitoring, and assessing are all executive processes that make up the metacognitive control taxonomy. Pre-activity planning includes the stages of metacognitive processing including deciding the best approach to take and allocating time and energy for the factors that will impact performance. Online testing, iterating, and reorganizing one's strategies for approaching cognitive tasks are all part of the monitoring process. Ultimately, one measures the success of a strategic move by how well it is accomplished (Gunawardena 2019).

The coding system used to understand student statements about their own learning is depicted in Fig. 1.

While meta-learning may be most beneficial in a formal learning setting, it has practical applications beyond the classroom as well. In addition, meta-learning necessitates the ability to evaluate knowledge through reflection and to resolve (when provided) conflicting ideas (Bartos and Lederman 2014). Dewey's ideas on learning via reflection are consistent with reflective practice. Learning, problem solving, and behaviour modification are all enhanced through introspection (Biggs 1985). To enable our current and future generations engage in learning and make educated judgments, meta-learning will be a discipline that outlives the current pandemic. Learners in a meta-learning environment are responsible for monitoring and adjusting their own study habits. Learners who engage in self-regulated learning are in charge of their own academic processes and can tailor their methods to meet their individual needs. This independence requires the student to take an active role in their education; hence, motivation is essential for meta-learning. In order to apply and synthesize new material, learners must engage in more complex cognitive procedures. Learning also causes one to alter one's behaviour after the acquisition of new information.

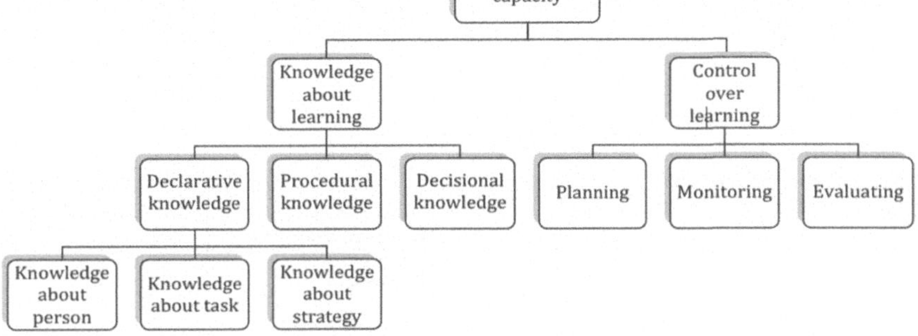

Fig. 1 Coding scheme the role of meta learning adopt from Gunawardena (2019)

To keep up with the ever-changing state of scientific understanding, one must be flexible in their approach to problem-solving (Bartos and Lederman 2014). By absorbing the aforementioned pedagogical methods and traits. Lifelong learning strategies like meta-learning are useful for keeping up with the ever-changing nature of knowledge and taking appropriate action based on what one has learned. The similarities between the scientific method and the process of lifelong learning are made clear by combining meta-learning with the principles of the nature of science and scientific reasoning. The distinction between scientific knowledge and the process from which it develops was first established by Bartos and Lederman (2014). These ideas have useful implications for the metacognitive and metalearning processes.

In this context, the learner engages in meta-learning in science by becoming cognizant of and investigating not only scientific practices/processes but also scientific information. At times of crisis and beyond, the following steps outline a meta-learning method for doing so Fig. 2.

1.2 Enhancing Virtual Reality as Teaching Material in EFL

To our knowledge, the link between the virtual reality assisted meta-learning approach in this study is that engaging students more deeply and critically in their own learning (metacognition) makes them more likely to take responsibility for their education and succeed. Because previous studies have mostly focused on the phenomenon "feeding" teachers are overseeing current English language education (TEFL). The term "tablespoon" refers to a teaching method in which students are expected to passively pick up large amounts of knowledge from the teacher in a short period of time without engaging in critical thinking or practicing what they have learned, and students receive everything that is given by the teacher (Chacón-Díaz 2023). There are three major problems with teaching communications today (Mitchell 2010):

1. Due to a lack of intuition, students who only rely on textbooks or two-dimensional (2D) images may have difficulty understanding the structure of using English in the context of real life. They only focus on textual language.
2. Language teaching (TEFL) is a course that places equal emphasis on theory and practise; therefore, a lack of practise is counterproductive. Students often lack adequate practical experience, leading to a disconnect between theory and practise, as most students feel that their practise is not valued, and the emphasis is on using perfect, native-like language.
3. Third, there is not much student-to-student interaction in English courses because most of the material is given through textbooks or slides, and the teacher talks more about the lessons, does not construct students' knowledge, and requires minimal hours of practise.

Engaging students in VR immersion, interaction, and imagination has been shown to enhance teaching and learning (Mitchell 2010). Virtual reality (VR) applications used in the classroom are sometimes referred to as "serious games". Virtual reality (VR) serious play has been shown to improve learning outcomes in a number of ways, including students' motivation, curiosity, and problem-solving abilities. One of the reasons some academics doubt the potential of serious virtual reality (VR) games for use in the classroom is that it is unclear how much students can actually learn from them (Mauri Medrano et al. 2023). In addition, teachers are hesitant to put in the extra time and effort needed to integrate serious VR games into pre-packaged curricula due to the difficulty of accessing the necessary technology.

However, most academics are still optimistic about the potential of serious virtual reality (VR) gaming in the classroom. Several studies (Morélot et al. 2021; Dimitriadou et al. 2021; Checa and Bustillo 2020) found that students are more involved and retain more information when they are exposed to serious VR games than traditional slide-based demonstrations. (Shi et al. 2021) states there are two main types of VR hardware that can run serious VR games: desktop VR (DVR) and immersive VR (IVR). DVRs are the cheapest option, but they also provide the most immersive experience since users can only interact with the 3D virtual world via a monitor and a standard keyboard and mouse. However, DVRs serve an important purpose by making classroom instruction more accessible to students. According to Zhu et al. (2022) for example, DVRs can generate virtual worlds on computers, meaning that industrial educators can incorporate this cutting-edge technology into their curricula and build a solid foundation for innovative study. (Hamilton et al. 2021) found that using 3D computer

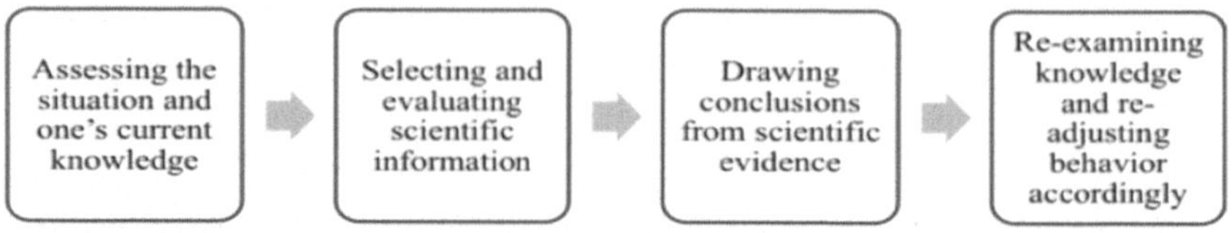

Fig. 2 Meta learning stages process (Bartos and Lederman 2014)

models in the classroom increased students' understanding of complex building systems and their constituent parts. By providing a project-based pedagogical approach in simulated and virtual environments, (Ausburn and Ausburn 2004) suggest a new method for virtual interactive construction education.

Immersive VR technology is garnering attention for its potential application in English language (Glick et al. 2012) when compared to DVR, IVR's visuospatial perspective allows students to learn through action in a high-fidelity environment and increases confidence in their abilities. IVR's natural interactions can increase student engagement and interaction in the classroom, which is important because interactivity is seen as the most fundamental part of effective learning (Goedert and Rokooei 2016). There are now several educational applications of IVR, foreign language teaching (Araiza-Alba et al. 2021), and psychology education (Martirosov and Kopecek 2017).

However, there is little research on the use of IVR in English language education (TEFL) and none on the use of IVR in teaching contexts describing places in English. As far as the author is aware, incorporating IVR into teaching describing places in English can help students understand and recognise the surroundings of the place from an overall perspective and also enable students to experience the components of describing places in English and the process of writing story scripts in an immersive way, all with the goal of increasing student motivation in learning and teaching communication (Peixoto et al. 2021). Rapid production of scenes for training or virtual teaching is one of the five potential goals for VR-related education in knowledge construction techniques identified by Kamińska et al. (2019).

Technology-assisted enhanced language learning has seen an increase in the use of virtual reality (VR) due to the authentic and immersive learning environment it provides (Mukasheva et al. 2023). Virtual reality (VR) has enormous potential to be integrated into language teaching to create contextual and interactive learning experiences by emulating the powerful illusion of presence. Since its inception in the 1960s, virtual reality (VR) has experienced tremendous development. Modern virtual reality (VR) tools are far more sophisticated and engaging than their text-based internet predecessors, featuring 3D virtual spaces and user-generated avatars (Lin and Lan 2015). Low immersion virtual reality (LiVR) and high immersion virtual reality (HiVR) (Kaplan-Rakowski and Gruber 2019) can be broadly categorized despite debates about the definition and classification of VR. The difference between "computer-generated three-dimensional virtual space experienced through standard audio-visual equipment, such as a desktop computer with a two-dimensional monitor", and "computer-generated 360° virtual space that can be experienced as realistic space, due to the high immersion afforded by head-mounted device". The quality of virtual reality content and the equipment used to experience the content has a significant impact on the level of immersion.

2 Method

This study used a mixed-methods research design to investigate students' perceptions and interest in the VR-assisted meta-learning approach as an IT innovation in English teaching. The population of this study includes 350 students enrolled in the 2022–2023 academic year. Purposive sampling was used, with the target group including those enrolled in the English II course. Sophomore students were selected to demonstrate their ability to articulate positive or negative sentiments about their meta-learning approach assisted with VR. A total of 64 students voluntarily took part in this study from English Course 2 became the research sample. In addition, researchers collected information through interviews and questionnaires. Twenty-three items filled out the questionnaire on VR impact to their English.

2.1 Participants

Students in computer science courses in Indonesia in their second semester who agreed to take part in this research were recruited. This first year student has listened to a lecture on describing places in English. The virtual reality (VR) group has 64 students. This research was conducted according to the regular class schedule.

2.2 Meta Learning Intructional Model

Methods from Reeves (2006) design-based research framework were used for this study. Practical problem analysis, solution creation, testing, and refining were included in the processes, as well as self-reflection. Instructional teaching model assisted virtual reality in TEFL class was exposed to material for 45 min using the Co Space Edu platform computer-based. VR distribution system used in the lab (Fig. 3) and the viewing platform accessed through the edu. cospaces link installed on the computer to facilitate VR learning.

1. Students are asked to listen to material regarding describing places in English for each meeting first meeting covering airports from checking in to flying to the destination country, describing zoos, describing cafes, and describing castles.

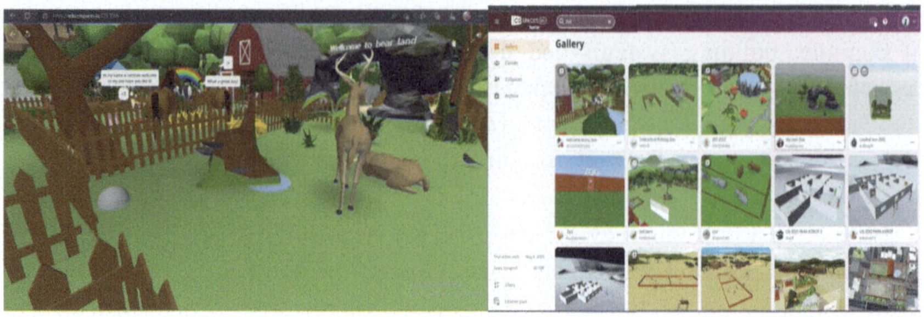

Fig. 3 Describing place in English, welcome to my zoo in edu.cospaces platform https://edu.cospaces.io/Universe

2. After observing VR accounts, playing, analysing, and noting important points in describing places in English, they and their group mates begin to design and write their own versions of describing places, for example, describing zoos and designing stories about zoos according to their own versions on the edu.cospaces platform (Fig. 4).
3. Students are asked to present the results of the description of the place, tell their experiences, and upload them on their respective YouTube accounts.
4. Lecturers provide feedback on student projects and provide corrections and suggestions for improving design and dialogue (grammar, vocabulary, describing content, and story content). The VR video describing place in English produced by students is part of the development of teaching materials for material describing place in English, including writing, speaking, and reading. Scenarios are played out on the edu.cospaces platform, and there is a five-minute instructional chapter from the student's point of view. Students and lecturers can witness first-hand how each student spreads and pollutes their surroundings through the use of interactive visualisations. In addition, VR provides explanations on how to change a person's behaviour through voiceover, text, images, and videos (Fig. 5).
5. The students were given a post-quiz questionnaire to fill out.

2.3 Instrument

Students were given a questionnaire in which they were asked to rate their learning experience on a numerical scale (Likert Scale) based on how well they learned the English course for the describing place. In the Table 1, the Likert scale is used.

Fig. 4 Students design their story in virtual reality https://edu.cospaces.io/Studio/Space/CcUri8vOW4yc0dQp

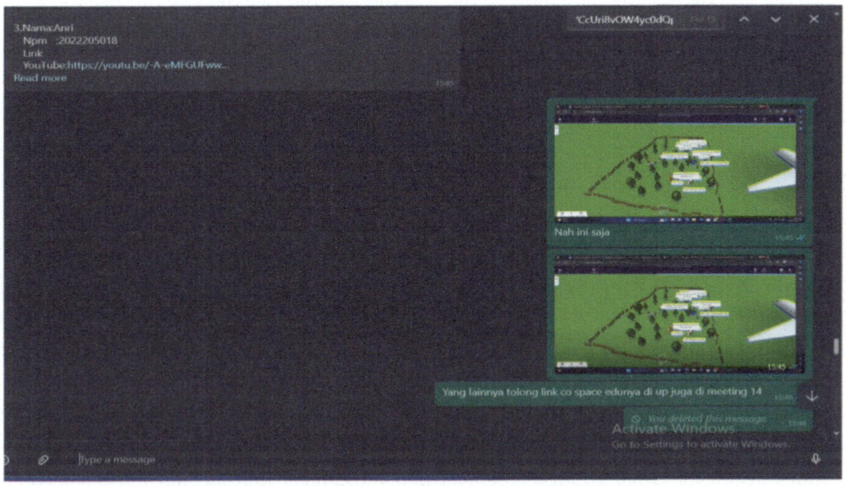

Fig. 5 Teacher feedback

Table 1 Likert scale and classification score (Sugiyono and Kuantitatif 2009)

No.	Statement	Scale	Classification	Score
1	Strongly agree	5	Very interested (very good)	101–120
2	Agree	4	Interested (good)	84–101
3	Fairly	3	Moderate (fairly)	66–83
4	Disagree	2	Uninterested (low)	48–65
5	Strongly disagree	1	Very uninterested (Very low)	30–47

2.4 Research Procedure

This study has three parts: the planning stage and the actual implementation. The following is a brief overview of how the research was conducted.

Input phase. To get a handle on the phenomenon of the research problem to be studied, it is necessary to conduct field studies and literature studies during the preparatory stage. After the research problem is defined, the research equipment must be prepared. The validity and reliability tests were successful for the finished instrument. Content validity and empirical validity were used in the validity test. The validity of the content of the English test was checked by expert opinion on the accuracy of the test's measurement. After receiving expert feedback, the instrument was revised and piloted with separate groups of students. This evaluation is an attempt to test the practical usability and reliability of the device. Research can be started once the instrument is deemed valid and reliable.

Process phase. Finding people to research is part of the process of conducting research. The management of research permits has now been handed over to the competent authorities. Researchers observed English classrooms and computer labs and interviewed educators to select study participants. After study participants were recruited, they carried out pre- and post-test tests before and after the learning therapy was implemented.

Output phase. Distributing Google forms and conducting interviews regarding students' opinions after learning Output phase English with the meta learning approach assisted by virtual reality and how VR affects their English learning.

2.5 Data Analysis

In addition, quantitative and qualitative analyzes were carried out on the data in this study. The experimental results explain how the effectiveness of virtual reality relates to students' motivation to learn English for English II course. Researchers use SPSS version 22 for Windows to store, organize, and analyze research data. Interview data were analyzed using descriptive method.

3 Results and Discussions

3.1 Questionnaire and Interview Results of Meta Learning Approach Assisted Virtual Reality

The purpose of this study was to determine the impact of meta learning approach assisted Virtual Reality to learn language in higher education institution. The following describes the results of quantitative and descriptive statistical analysis related students perceptions to answer the research question. The results obtained are presented in Fig. 6 as follows.

According to the results on Fig. 6 distributing from students answer in the questionnaire, a total 64 respondents met the criteria for analysis since they were willing to share their responses on their meta learning approach assisted virtual reality in learning English language. The students responses was to grade and their scores from questionnaire mention on Fig. 6, it is evidents that 10 students/ respondents, or 15.62% of respondents thought that meta learning approach assisted virtual reality in learning English at has very good category, 15 students 23.4%2, thought that meta learning approach assisted virtual reality in learning English at has good category, 12 respondents 18.75% at has a fairly category, 19 students or 29.64% at has a low category and students or 12.5% at has a very low category.

Based on the data displayed in histogram graph as shown above, which demonstrate that overall the respondents has positive response of meta learning approach assisted virtual reality as IT innovation in learning English.

Based on Fig. 7 the statement about students interest in meta learning approach assisted Virtual Reality, the analysis shows on the statement easy to learn English through Virtual Reality there ara 12.7% respondents took strongly agree, 20.6% respondents states agree category, 34.9% has at fairly category, 19% respondents took disagree and 12.7 states strongly disagree. There are 21.7% respondents who states negative statement or difficult to learn English assisted virtual reality. The second statement asked about fun and enjoyable learning assisted Virtual Reality, it is evident that 20.6% respondents thought that using Virtual Reality at has very fun and enjoyable and 22.2% respondents also in agree category with this statement. Of 25.4% took fairly, there are 25.4% took negative response or disagree category and 6.3% has at strongly disagree category. The students thought that they strong believe meta learning

Fig. 6 Students response

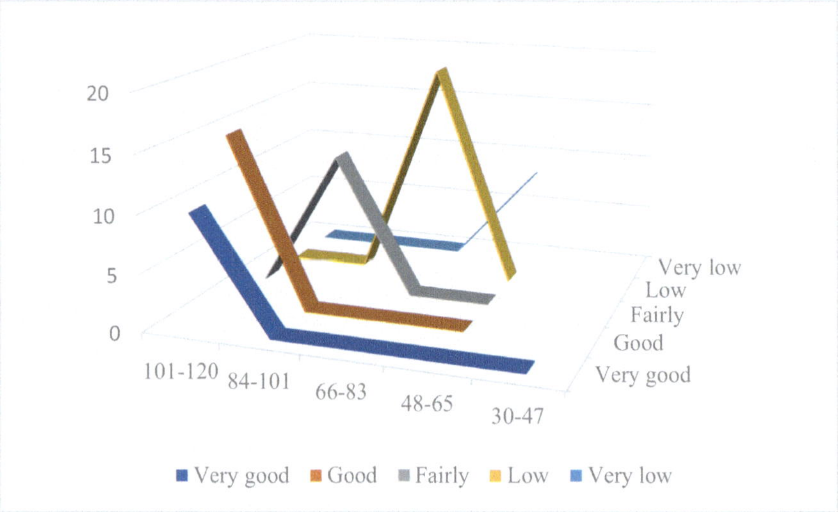

Fig. 7 Students interest in learning through meta learning approach assisted virtual reality

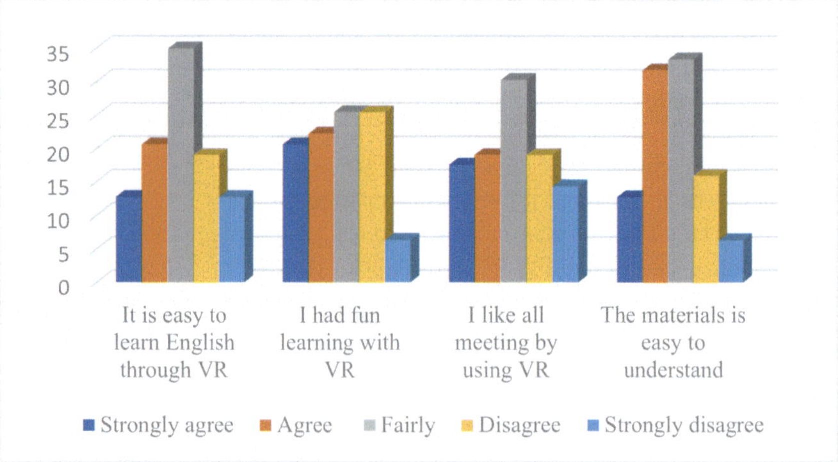

assisted Virtual Reality will be interesting for all English meetings, 33.3% respondent there are in negative statements (Disagree and strongly disagree category) and 66.7% respondents they are took positive statements. The last statement asked about the material easier to understand, 22.2% respondents states the materials difficult to understand and mostly respondents has at positive statement or 77.8 took this category.

As aforementioned on Fig. 8, it is describe that 19% respondents has at very good category with the statement about the opportunity of the students to design their story in Virtual Reality platform, 23% of respondents has at good category, 33.3% took fairly and negative statements are 17.5% disagree (low) and 6.3% chose strongly disagree (very low) position. They are also have to describing place in Virtual Reality platform, 15.9% respondents thought that the Virtual Reality platform, 22.3% respondents also support this statement, 31.7% has at fairly category and there are 30.1% respondents unable to design their story in Virtual Reality platform. Overall, in remembering the lesson and very good feedback from lecturer most of respondents has to chose positive statements.

The Fig. 9 above clearly demonstrates that out of 64 respondents, 14% respondents strongly recommendent Virtual Reality as teaching materials, 28.6% respondents has at agree, 28.6 has at fairly, 22.2% respondents had disagree category and 6.3% strongly disagree category using Virtual reality as teaching materials. The second statement asked about they are learn a lot from Virtual Reality, 22.2% respondents had strongly agree, 19% of respondents had agree, 31.7% of respondents took fairly category and 22.2% had disagree category, 6.3% respondents had strongly disagree category. Students believe that the material is easy to understand, 11.1% of respondents had strongly agree

Fig. 8 Interactiveness

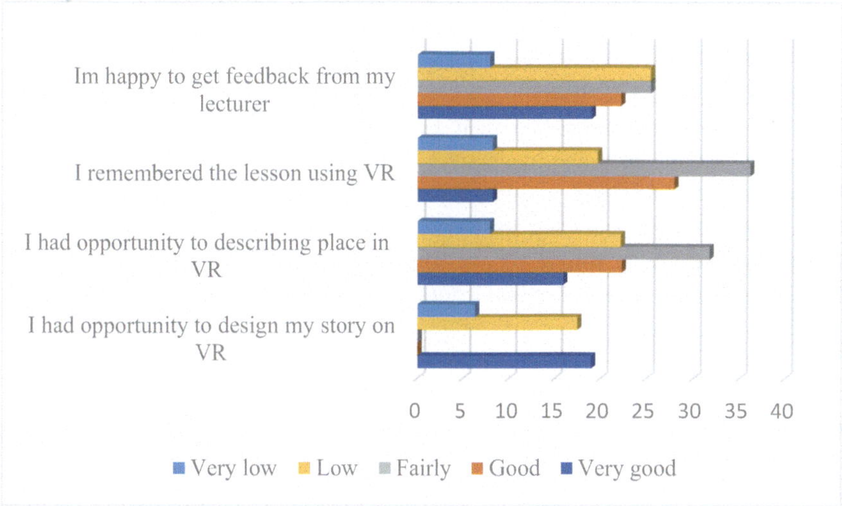

Fig. 9 Retention

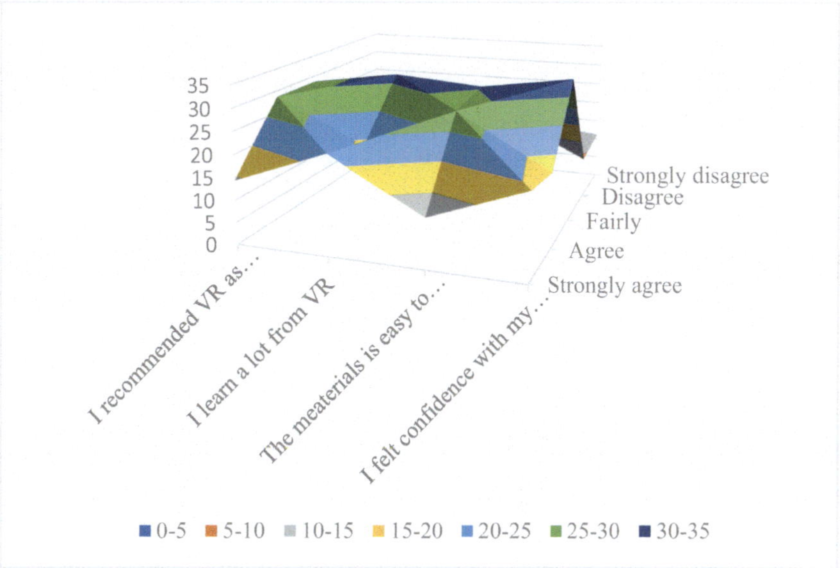

Table 2 Descriptive statistics of the student's response

Descriptive statistics					
	N	Minimum	Maximum	Mean	Std. deviation
Meta learning assisted VR	64	23.00	115.00	73.0159	22.80739
Valid N (listwise)	64				

category, 28.6% of respondents were in agree category, of 30.2% of respondents chose fairly, and negative statement were 21.1% of respondents took this category. In addition, most of the students felt that their English were in good category than before treatment using Virtual Reality, 19% of respondents were strongly agree, 17% of respondents had agree category, 33.3% of respondents fairly position and 21.6% of respondents who are took negative statement (disagree and strongly disagree) (Table 2).

Based on the result of statistic analysis calculations using SPSS, the results of the students mean score response in this study 73.0159 or it is in interval 66–83 they were in fairly category. On the meta learning approach assisted Virtual Reality as well have impact to their English competence, technology competence and interactively in good category. Furthermore, the semi-structured interview session was held to support the data regarding the meta learning approach assisted virtual reality toward the students interest in learn English as IT innovation for hybrid learning environment.

Extract 1 (15th April 2023).

According to one code 1 student, "a factor that can affect my interest in learning English is when learning is designed in a comfortable classroom atmosphere, the material being taught is not boring (lecture method) or just dictating in class and besides that, strategies that used by lecturers in class, it uses virtual reality I am very enthusiastic about."

Extract 2 (15th April 2023).

In the words of one student: "…you know, this Virtual Reality platform is the first time I've come across a learning approach with this platform, I feel learning and playing is a great thing in my class, I enjoy the learning process, I learn English with feeling happy, challenged, curious I enjoy this class".

Extract 3 (15th April 2023).

> "... in my opinion, integrating technology to learn English I did not expect it to be extraordinary by including Virtual Reality in presenting the material, we are all involved in learning and are increasingly curious about the next material"

Extract 4 (15th April 2023).

"eeeeee… in my opinion, learning English with a hybrid system using a virtual reality application is fun, but the campus should pay attention to the computer equipment in the laboratory, because during learning we use Quota which should be facilitated by the university. The laboratory room is hot and not well organized, we hope that the university will pay maximum attention to the needs of internet infrastructure. We want a learning environment that supports our maximum learning comfort'.

Extract 5 (15th April 2023).

hmmmmm….. I think learning English with virtual reality applications is very easy, the only difficulty we experience is the unattractive infrastructure environment… I think this virtual reality platform can be used on smartphones, but running on smartphones is not maximum. However, learning with virtual reality is very helpful in understanding the use of English according to the target of smooth communication, designing stories, thinking critically and making the material easy to remember.

Extract 6 (15th April 2023).

In my perception, the lecturer's instructions are very clear, the material is very accessible, the lecturer gives great feedback during the lesson which causes us to be excited to learn English, excited to get to know virtual reality and excited to design stories'.

3.2 Discussion

The majority of students felt that engaging in meta-learning tasks helped them learn better since they required them to engage in self-regulatory activities like planning and reflection. We observed that students were just as likely to modify their study habits between semesters as they were to maintain them. According to Section Fig. 6, when searching for digital resources for English language education, a lot of information is found about the importance of integrating IT as an innovation in the learning process that can reveal maximum interest in learning with the help of this virtual reality. After careful consideration, most students think that it is not too difficult to implement Virtual reality in a hybrid classroom. The reason is based on the results of this study in Fig. 7 it is known that students are interested in learning English with a meta learning approach assisted by Virtual Reality.

Even though there were around 33.3% of respondents who stated that they were unpleasant due to the class conditions (computer laboratory) the class atmosphere was not optimal (interview with student 4), none of them did not fully meet the criteria to operate this Virtual Reality platform. The learning model that is presented accurately represents the use of English in accordance with the context of daily needs where this virtual reality application presents a simulation of places such as airports or zoos that are realistically similar to their real life environment. Material connectivity is used in accordance with the instructional pilot found on the Virtual Reality platform, while others still fail in designing stories in Virtual Reality as their home work projects because 30.1 (Fig. 8) percent of respondents do not have a laptop, the quality of the internet network must be adequate. This last need is very important to attract and maintain student interest from the start.

Most of the learning technology resources available for teaching English are included in meta learning approach projects (online dictionaries or YouTube) because there is rarely Virtual Reality content of sufficient quality and detail to be included in the curriculum. Therefore, we have to use the help of an online dictionary to accompany the implementation of Virtual Reality in the classroom. This finding is in line with researchers in Radianti et al. (2020) investigating virtual reality (VR) for educational purposes, focusing on the factors that make technology useful and effective in the classroom. The authors identified 24 virtual reality features, including user interaction, immersive interfaces, motion, animation, and simulated worlds. It found that while "immersion interfaces" are commonly used in general education for learning through "hands-on experience" that is closer to reality, the "movement" aspect is especially important in topics like medicine to learn about one's bodily reactions. In addition to the benefits of virtual reality, including increased learning outcomes, more realistic experiences, increased interest and aptitude for learning, and increased abilities; however, in some fields, including psychology, no learning effect was observed.

The results of this study it was found that, current immersive virtual reality research, identified IT innovation research trends, fundamental theoretical foundations, and methods used in previous studies on immersive technology to make class atmosphere comfortable and fun as described in Figs. 7 and 8. In terms of the current study, in line with the findings (Papanastasiou et al. 2019). We can identified four main sectors leveraging immersive technology: teaching and learning, arts and entertainment, health, and promotion. This research also finds two main factors of the importance of using Virtual Reality. First, this research discusses how the 3D elements of immersive systems affect users and their experiences. Second, we investigated immersive technologies improving user performance in various areas including learning and teaching, task completion time, and maximum recall of lessons (Fig. 8).

The results of this study highlighted a positive impact of instructional design principles for VR-based instruction with a meta learning approach contrary to a study conducted by Merchant et al. 2014, where they noted that games produce better learning outcomes than simulations and virtual worlds which contradicts the findings of this study. Interaction with the virtual world really helps them to describe places they have never visited before (eg airports, zoos and palaces). This is reinforced by the results of interviews with students 1, 2 and 3. The number of treatment sessions has a positive correlation with improving learning outcomes and they do not lose ground when using cyberspace for education.

As instructors, we can attest to the fact that students prefer a more hands-on approach to learning over memorization (result of interview with student no 1. Educators who have had positive experiences using virtual reality in the classroom might be able to take advantage of cutting-edge software to shift their focus from theory to practice. Our analysis of the relationship between design features and educational outcomes reveals that the program features the highest density of design components. This raises the bar for the development of such applications and suggests that educators and students can benefit from having a seamless virtual reality (VR) experience more in advance to apply it effectively. Also, shifting emphasis from teaching declarative information to more practice-oriented content could require complex curriculum revisions. However, we believe that the real promise of virtual reality lies not in improving the delivery of pure declarative knowledge, or proper instructional instruction but rather on facilitating the kind of "learning by doing" which until recently was notoriously difficult to incorporate into lectures in English classes.

Despite sharing an interest in VR experiences, the findings of this study are different from other research where this research uses Virtual Reality as teaching material in English courses, the immersive domain used also involves students designing stories according to their version based on the features contained in Virtual Reality accounts. This. Although this study did not show pre- and post-test learning outcomes, in the items in Fig. 9, it was found that respondents felt confident that their English in the field of communication would be better and able to build their confidence to practice their English to the fullest.

This research is also leveraging VR to teach people how to build stories with basic interaction features, users can collect and sort virtual objects, and as a feedback mechanism, they can be rewarded for doing so. The effect on behavior is one measure of improved ecological stewardship as carried out by researchers (Paszkiewicz et al. 2021; Kamińska et al. 2019) creating two virtual reality (VR) demos for use in the industrial sector, such as for the introduction of equipment, tools, and safety protocols. In this virtual reality setting, students can simulate the process of designing stories by picking up virtual tools and experiencing various physical interactions with them. The work presented here aims to change people's habits in such a way that they become more aware and knowledgeable about the importance of knowing how to describe places and become tutorials for students in the real world (eg how to check in at the airport to fly to the destination country).

Overall the results of this study by designing virtual reality as learning content with behavioural implications for learning include a section that tries to change the thoughts, feelings, and behaviour of students learning English as a means in which Virtual Reality can be used to teach programming, logic, computational thinking, thinking. critical and communication. As a form of visual programming, users can choose characters or characters, settings, plots to produce new stories. They can also view virtual self-avatars placed together which can mimic their surroundings (plot), look around in virtual worlds, and feel a high level of presence, all by using a drag and drop interface for various gestures or steps such as walking forwards, backwards., squat, and jump. By showing people that learning languages with Virtual Reality is fun, we can change their attitude towards English to a more positive one.

The data available in this study are insufficient to inform recommendations for the most effective design features that will achieve certain learning goals in virtual reality (VR) applications aimed at improving grammar, computational thinking, pronunciation and writing. After reviewing our results and study objectives, we realize that the current level of knowledge does not allow us to provide a comprehensive list of suggestions or even a best practice directory. However, the first suggestion to the professor can be made. This will help them determine when and why virtual reality is useful, as well as what technological measures or teaching model to adopt.

Virtual reality is undoubtedly a hot topic of interest in learning for the Gen Z generation. Teachers can benefit from this momentum, and the likelihood of early adopters making a meaningful contribution is high. Educators who are considering using virtual reality into their lessons should not be tentative, they must consider supporting technological infrastructure, clean and comfortable classrooms, good classroom atmosphere temperatures and creative teachers. It seems inconceivable that non-technologists will be able to build arbitrary virtual worlds from scratch any time soon; instead, they should be empowered to choose purchasing applications, work with industry, and set requirements.

İn closing, these findings recommend that writers in this field further identify flow theory, conceptual blending theory, cognitive load theory, Physiological theory, wellbeing theory, constructive learning theory, experiential theory, motivation theory, presence theory, situated cognition theory, media richness theory, stimulus-organism-response model, 21th century theory, and technology acceptance model as a theoretical foundation used in existing immersive technology studies. Experimental, survey, and mixed methods study designs are commonplace in this study.

4 Conlcusions

This article presents the results of research looking at how the Virtual Reality assisted meta learning approach is used in colleges or universities. The latest research on Virtual Reality applications in this study is by looking at technology as a learning innovation in the digital era, which of course wants learning materials and story design features used in this program. This research has adopted this technology for use in the classroom, the findings of the review show that students are very interested in learning English with the help of Virtual Reality technology and can significantly motivate them to learn English more optimally. The author believes that VR as a valuable educational tool for universities, but its application is still lacking. Most students believe that with VR their learning outcomes can improve and of course we also recommend that the use of virtual reality not only in English courses but can be applied to all existing courses.

These factors can slow down the widespread use of virtual reality (VR) systems in the classroom, namely inadequate internet, inadequate speed of computer equipment, hot atmosphere in computer laboratory rooms, and suboptimal instructions. We realize that virtual reality (VR) applications have been widely used not only to teach computer skills, but to teach students to construct their own knowledge and teach them to think creatively and innovatively. This study identified important gaps that could be used as springboards for future higher education curriculum and teacher advancements.

References

Araiza-Alba, P., Keane, T., Chen, W. S., & Kaufman, J. (2021). Immersive virtual reality as a tool to learn problem-solving skills. *Computers & Education*, *164*, 104121.

Ausburn, L. J., & Ausburn, F. B. (2004). Desktop virtual reality: A powerful new technology for teaching and research in industrial teacher education. *Journal of Industrial Teacher Education*, *41*(4), 1–16.

Bartolotta, S., Gaggioli, A., & Riva, G. (2023). The META-Learning Project: Design and Evaluation of an Experiential-Learning Intervention in the Metaverse for Soft Skills Improvement. *Cyberpsychology, Behavior, and Social Networking*, *26*(3), 221–224.

Bartos, S. A., & Lederman, N. G. (2014). Teachers' knowledge structures for nature of science and scientific inquiry: Conceptions and classroom practice. *Journal of Research in Science Teaching*, *51*(9), 1150–1184.

Bayless, S. (2023). Challenges and tensions for student academic engagement practices in contemporary UK higher education. *Advancing Student Engagement in Higher Education: Reflection, Critique and Challenge. Abingdon: Routledge*.

Biggs, J. B. (1985). The role of metalearning in study processes. *British journal of educational psychology*, *55*(3), 185–212.

Cameron, R. B., & Rideout, C. A. (2022). 'It's been a challenge finding new ways to learn': first-year students' perceptions of adapting to learning in a university environment. *Studies in Higher Education*, *47*(3), 668–682.

Castaneda, L. M., Bindman, S. W., & Divanji, R. A. (2023). Don't forget to assess: How teachers check for new and deeper learning when integrating virtual reality in the classroom. *Journal of Research on Technology in Education*, *55*(2), 210–229.

Chacón-Díaz, L. B. (2023). A framework for meta-learning in science education for a time of crisis and beyond. *Cultural Studies of Science Education*, 1–11.

Checa, D., & Bustillo, A. (2020). A review of immersive virtual reality serious games to enhance learning and training. *Multimedia Tools and Applications*, *79*, 5501–5527.

Chiao, H. M., Chen, Y. L., & Huang, W. H. (2018). Examining the usability of an online virtual tour-guiding platform for cultural tourism education. *Journal of Hospitality, Leisure, Sport & Tourism Education*, *23*, 29–38.

Chiu, M. C., Hwang, G. J., & Hsia, L. H. (2023). Promoting students' artwork appreciation: An experiential learning-based virtual reality approach. *British Journal of Educational Technology*, *54*(2), 603–621.

Colthorpe, K., Zimbardi, K., Ainscough, L., & Anderson, S. (2015). Know thy student! Combining learning analytics and critical reflections to develop a targeted intervention for promoting self-regulated learning. *Journal of Learning Analytics*, *2*(1), 134–155.

Colthorpe, K., Sharifirad, T., Ainscough, L., Anderson, S., & Zimbardi, K. (2018). Prompting undergraduate students' metacognition of learning: implementing 'meta-learning'assessment tasks in the biomedical sciences. *Assessment & Evaluation in Higher Education*, *43*(2), 272–285.

Daungcharone, K., Panjaburee, P., & Thongkoo, K. (2019). A mobile game-based C programming language learning: results of university students' achievement and motivations. *International Journal of Mobile Learning and Organisation*, *13*(2), 171–192.

Dimitriadou, A., Djafarova, N., Turetken, O., Verkuyl, M., & Ferworn, A. (2021). Challenges in serious game design and development: Educators' experiences. *Simulation & Gaming*, *52*(2), 132–152.

Drigas, A., Mitsea, E., & Skianis, C. (2023). Meta-Learning: A Nine-Layer Model based on Metacognition and Smart Technologies. Sustainability 2023, 15, 1668.

Glick, S., Porter, D., & Smith, C. (2012). Student visualization: Using 3-D models in undergraduate construction management education. *International Journal of construction education and research*, *8*(1), 26–46.

Goedert, J. D., & Rokooei, S. (2016). Project-based construction education with simulations in a gaming environment. *International Journal of Construction Education and Research*, *12*(3), 208–223.

GUNAWARDENA, M. (2019). Thinking skills and creativity in second language education: Case studies from international perspectives. In *Thinking Skills and Creativity in Second Language Education: Case Studies from International Perspectives* (pp. 42–57). Routledge.

Hamilton, D., McKechnie, J., Edgerton, E., & Wilson, C. (2021). Immersive virtual reality as a pedagogical tool in education: a systematic literature review of quantitative learning outcomes and experimental design. *Journal of Computers in Education*, *8*(1), 1–32.

Kamińska, D., Sapiński, T., Wiak, S., Tikk, T., Haamer, R. E., Avots, E., ... & Anbarjafari, G. (2019). Virtual reality and its applications in education: Survey. *Information*, *10*(10), 318.

Kaplan-Rakowski, R., & Gruber, A. (2019, November). Low-immersion versus high-immersion virtual reality: Definitions, classification, and examples with a foreign language focus. In *Conference Proceedings. Innovation in Language Learning 2019*.

Kozinets, R. V. (2023). Immersive netnography: a novel method for service experience research in virtual reality, augmented reality and metaverse contexts. *Journal of Service Management*, *34*(1), 100–125.

Lee, S. M. (2023). The effectiveness of machine translation in foreign language education: a systematic review and meta-analysis. *Computer Assisted Language Learning*, *36*(1–2), 103–125.

Lin, T. J., & Lan, Y. J. (2015). Language learning in virtual reality environments: Past, present, and future. *Journal of Educational Technology & Society*, *18*(4), 486–497.

Ma, L., & Liu, N. (2023). Teacher belief about integrating critical thinking in English teaching in China. *Journal of Education for Teaching*, *49*(1), 137–152.

Martirosov, S., & Kopecek, P. (2017). Virtual reality and its influence on training and education-literature review. *Annals of DAAAM & Proceedings*, *28*.

Matovu, H., Ungu, D. A. K., Won, M., Tsai, C. C., Treagust, D. F., Mocerino, M., & Tasker, R. (2023). Immersive virtual reality for science learning: Design, implementation, and evaluation. *Studies in Science Education*, 1–40.

Mauri Medrano, M., Lafarga Ostáriz, P., Del Barrio Aranda, L., & Soler Costa, R. (2023). Mobile learning and communication: educational change?; a systematic review. *Education+ Training*, *65*(2), 193–209.

Merchant Z., Goetz E.T., Cifuentes L., Keeney-Kennicutt W., Davis T.J. Effectiveness of virtual reality-based instruction on students' learning outcomes in k-12 and higher education: A meta-analysis. Computers & Education, 70 (2014), pp. 29–40, https://doi.org/10.1016/j.compedu.2013.07.033

Merchie, E., & Van Keer, H. (2016). Mind mapping as a meta-learning strategy: Stimulating pre-adolescents' text-learning strategies and performance?. *Contemporary Educational Psychology*, *46*, 128–147.

Mitchell, I. (2010). The relationship between teacher behaviours and student talk in promoting quality learning in science classrooms. *Research in science education*, *40*, 171–186.

Morélot, S., Garrigou, A., Dedieu, J., & N'Kaoua, B. (2021). Virtual reality for fire safety training: Influence of immersion and sense of presence on conceptual and procedural acquisition. *Computers & Education*, *166*, 104145.

Mukasheva, M., Kornilov, I., Beisembayev, G., Soroko, N., Sarsimbayeva, S., & Omirzakova, A. (2023). Contextual structure as an approach to the study of virtual reality learning environment. *Cogent Education*, *10*(1), 2165788

Oberer, B., & Erkollar, A. (2023). Education 5.0: The Effectiveness of Game Based Learning Strategies on Post-pandemic Educational Competences. In *Towards Industry 5.0: Selected Papers from ISPR2022, October 6–8, 2022, Antalya* (pp. 243–254). Cham: Springer International Publishing.

Padmanabha, C. H. (2020). Metacognition: conceptual framework. *Journal on Educational Psychology*, *14*(1), 1–11.

Papanastasiou, G., Drigas, A., Skianis, C., Lytras, M., & Papanastasiou, E. (2019). Virtual and augmented reality effects on K-12, higher and tertiary education students' twenty-first century skills. *Virtual Reality*, *23*, 425–436.

Parmaxi, A. (2023). Virtual reality in language learning: A systematic review and implications for research and practice. *Interactive learning environments*, *31*(1), 172–184.

Paszkiewicz, A., Salach, M., Dymora, P., Bolanowski, M., Budzik, G., & Kubiak, P. (2021). Methodology of implementing virtual reality in education for industry 4.0. *Sustainability*, *13*(9), 5049.

Peixoto, B., Pinto, R., Melo, M., Cabral, L., & Bessa, M. (2021). Immersive virtual reality for foreign language education: A PRISMA systematic review. *IEEE Access*, *9*, 48952–48962.

Peterson, M. (2016). Virtual worlds and language learning: An analysis of research. *The Routledge handbook of language learning and technology*, 308–319.

Radianti, J., Majchrzak, T. A., Fromm, J., & Wohlgenannt, I. (2020). A systematic review of immersive virtual reality applications for higher education: Design elements, lessons learned, and research agenda. *Computers & Education*, *147*, 103778.

Reeves, T. C. (2006). Design research from the technology perspective. JV Akker, K. Gravemeijer, S. McKenney ve N. Nieveen (Eds.), Educational design research içinde (86–109).

Shen, M., Chen, D., & Ren, T. (2023). Meta-learning Based Tasks Similarity Representation for Cross Domain Lifelong Learning. *IEEE Access*.

Shi, R., Liang, H. N., Wu, Y., Yu, D., & Xu, W. (2021). Virtual reality sickness mitigation methods: A comparative study in a racing game. *Proceedings of the ACM on Computer Graphics and Interactive Techniques*, *4*(1), 1–16.

Sugiyono, M. P. P., & Kuantitatif, P. (2009). Kualitatif, dan R&D, Bandung: Alfabeta. *Cet. Vii.*

Tarricone, P. (2011). *The taxonomy of metacognition*. Psychology press.

Troussas, C., Krouska, A., & Sgouropoulou, C. (2020). Collaboration and fuzzy-modeled personalization for mobile game-based learning in higher education. *Computers & Education*, *144*, 103698.

Vallance, M., & Towndrow, P. A. (2016). Pedagogic transformation, student-directed design and computational thinking. *Pedagogies: an international journal*, *11*(3), 218–234.

Vesisenaho, M., Juntunen, M., Häkkinen, P., Pöysä-Tarhonen, J., Fagerlund, J., Miakush, I., & Parviainen, T. (2019). Virtual reality in education: Focus on the role of emotions and physiological reactivity. *Journal of Virtual Worlds Research*, *12*(1).

Vilalta, R., Giraud-Carrier, C., & Brazdil, P. (2010). Meta-learning-concepts and techniques. *Data mining and knowledge discovery handbook*, 717–731.

Winters, T. (2011). Facilitating meta-learning in art and design education. *International Journal of Art & Design Education*, *30*(1), 90–101.

Wu, J. G., Zhang, D., & Lee, S. M. (2023). Into the Brave New Metaverse: Envisaging Future Language Teaching and Learning. *IEEE Transactions on Learning Technologies*.

Zhang, Y. (2022). The research on critical thinking teaching strategies in college English classroom. *Creative Education*, *13*(4), 1469–1485.

Zhu, K., Zhang, Q., He, B., Huang, M., Lin, R., & Li, H. (2022). Immersive Virtual Reality–Based Cognitive Intervention for the Improvement of Cognitive Function, Depression, and Perceived Stress in Older Adults With Mild Cognitive Impairment and Mild Dementia: Pilot Pre-Post Study. *JMIR Serious Games*, *10*(1), e32117.

Role of Social Media Data and Social Computing Techniques in Society 5.0

Muhammad Bilal

Abstract

This chapter examines the significance of social media data and the application of cutting-edge social computing techniques in the context of Society 5.0. An analysis of existing literature is carried out to investigate the impact of social media integration and advanced computing techniques on societal transformation. Massive amounts of social media data have created both opportunities and challenges. Researchers have introduced a wide range of social computing techniques, such as social network analysis (SNA), natural language processing (NLP), and recommendation systems, to collect and analyze such massive amounts of social media data. The integration of social media data and social computing techniques is critical to achieving Society 5.0 objectives. It aids in solving societal problems in a variety of areas such as governance, education, health, and transportation. This chapter also discusses the challenges posed by information overload and disinformation in the context of Society 5.0, as well as the need for ethical considerations to address these issues.

Keywords

Social media data • Social computing • Society 5.0 • Social network analysis • Recommendation systems • Urban planning

M. Bilal (✉)
Department of Software Engineering, National University of Computer and Emerging Sciences, 44000 Islamabad, Pakistan
e-mail: mbilal.csit@gmail.com

1 Introduction

Nowadays, technology is advancing at a rapid pace in almost every aspect of society, resulting in several major changes in daily living activities, as well as changes in working styles and the way people communicate or interact with one another (Newman et al. 2022). The recent COVID-19 pandemic has also contributed significantly to technological advancements and has compelled people to participate in technological shifts (Jose and Carmen 2021). Social media has a significant impact on society because it has infiltrated individuals' daily lives and gained widespread popularity (Kai et al. 2022). Social computing tends to understand societal patterns and interactions occurring on social media (Lazer et al. Lazer et al. [2009]). A new concept known as "Society 5.0" has emerged, which employs cutting-edge technology to integrate the real and virtual worlds and present a data-driven human-centered society in order to address existing societal challenges (Salgues 2018). Social media data and social computing techniques are critical to achieving Society 5.0 goals. This chapter covers the importance and role of social media data and social computing techniques in Society 5.0, as depicted in Fig. 1.

In 2016, the Japanese government introduced the Society 5.0 paradigm, which envisions the development of a human-centric super-smart society through the integration of cyber and physical space. This integration aims to create an autonomous and decentralised society, which accurately aligns with the goal of this new concept (Holroyd 2022). The previous stages of human society, including Hunter-Gatherer (Society 1.0), Agrarian (Society 2.0), Industrial (Society 3.0), and Information (Society 4.0), serve as the fundamental foundations for the evolution towards a highly intelligent and technologically advanced Super-Smart (Society 5.0). The changes introduced at all stages of the society have significantly improved human life in a variety of ways. Society 5.0 aims to utilize the potential of cutting-edge technologies such as artificial intelligence (AI), the Internet of Things (IoT),

S. Arezki et al. (eds.), *Emerging Disruptive Technologies for Society 5.0 in Developing Countries*, Advances in Science, Technology & Innovation, https://doi.org/10.1007/978-3-031-63701-8_13

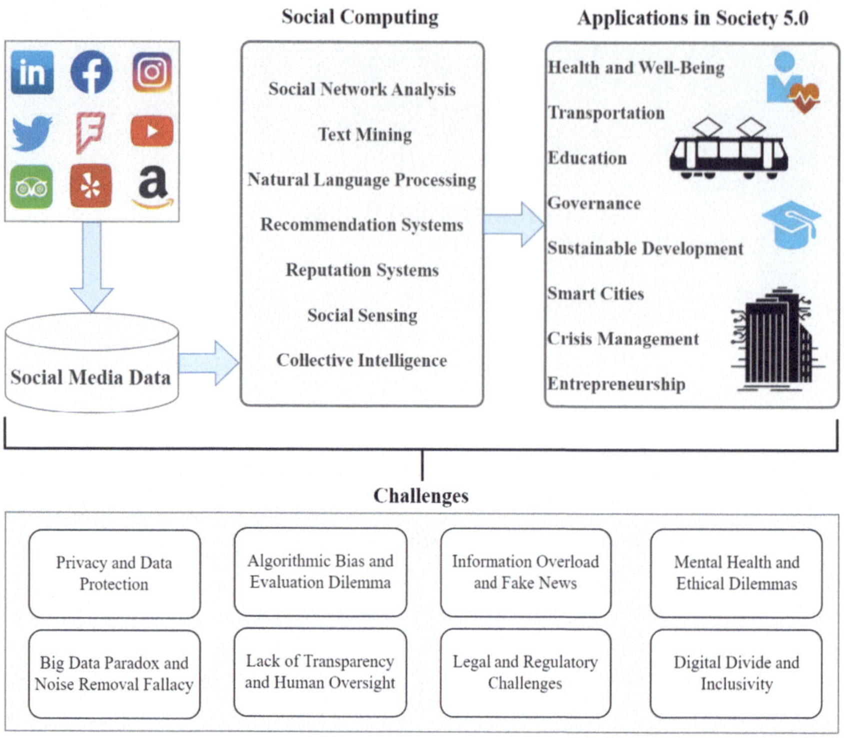

Fig. 1 Intersection of society 5.0, social media data and social computing techniques

big data analytics, robotics, and augmented reality (AR) to improve human lifestyle and promote sustainable development. Human values and technology can coexist as this version of society focuses on integration, inclusivity, privacy, and ethical concerns (Atsushi et al. 2020).

The fundamental aim of Society 5.0 is to give importance to the advancement of human empowerment and well-being. The utilization of advanced technology is aimed towards enhancing the standard of living, alleviating prevalent socio-cultural problems, and creating equal opportunities for the individuals (Vojko et al. 2020). Society 5.0 facilitates proactive involvement and engagement of heterogeneous stakeholders, including government entities, commercial organizations, academic institutions, and individual actors. This utilization of a collaborative approach not only promote the expansion of innovative solutions to diverse challenges by incorporating different perspectives and expertise. The Society 5.0 paradigm supports the adoption of sustainable practices aimed at protecting the environment, optimizing resource utilization, and reducing carbon emissions (Atsushi et al. 2020). Society 5.0 prioritizes a collaborative approach to attain a balance between economic advancement and ecological sustainability, with the ultimate objective of fostering harmonious existence of both humanity and the nature (Dimitris et al. 2022).

Society 5.0 brings along a huge number of implications for almost every aspect of society (Maria et al. 2022). It also stresses on the need to develop ethical AI standards, privacy protection and data security to maintain societal trust as the technology is penetrating in every aspect of society. Society 5.0 mandates the acquisition of new skills and the enhancement of existing skills among the workforce in order to prosper in the digital age. It also emphasizes the importance of lifelong learning, while also anticipating a transformation in the nature of jobs that require technological skills. This also endangers the employment opportunities, therefore a special support mechanism is needed for the efficient transition (Ratri et al. 2023). Huge volume of shared data is a key towards informed decision making. Hence a data governance framework is required that ensures the data protection, privacy, accessibility and accountability. Society 5.0 surpasses the national boundaries and calls for collective international efforts to address common problems by introducing technological standards. It also acknowledges the pressing need to effectively address climate change and environmental issues by adopting sustainable technologies (Elias and Joanna 2022).

The widespread use of social media has completely changed how people interact, communicate, and share information online. Users can create, share, and access information instantly through social media with little to no restriction, which generates enormous amounts of user-generated content (UGC) (Jean et al. 2019). Social media data contains useful information about people's interests, opinions, feelings, and behaviours. Social media data analytics is the process of mining social media data to find hidden patterns and trends. The methods used by researchers to analyse social media data belong to the social computing domain, which combines ideas from various fields like computer science, psychology, and sociology (Norjihan et al. 2019). Social computing techniques including NLP, sentiment analysis, SNA etc. are being used by researchers for a wide range of tasks to extract and interpret social media data for better decision making. There are unlimited applications of social media data and social computing techniques. Existing studies have been using social media data for a variety of tasks including user preferences (Sun et al. 2020), social profiling (Bilal et al. 2019), influence maximization (Li et al. 2020), healthcare communication (Iqra et al. 2023) and crisis management (Fan et al. 2021).

This chapter aims to explore the role of social media data and social computing techniques in achieving goals of Society 5.0. The rest of the chapter is organized in different sections. Section 2 provides understanding of social media data, its characteristics and discusses its relevance in Society 5.0. A brief overview of social computing techniques is provided in Sect. 3. Section 4 provides the real-life applications of social media data and social computing techniques in Society 5.0. The challenges and opportunities are covered in Sect. 5, while the conclusion is provided in Sect. 6.

2 Social Media Data in Society 5.0

In the digital era social media has emerged as a popular and powerful tool that has transformed the way of people's interaction and engagement. The social media landscape has greatly changed in a short span of the last few years. The wide range of popular social media platforms such as Facebook, Twitter, Instagram, YouTube and LinkedIn serve different purposes such as personal vs professional use. The number of registered users on social media platforms are increasing day by day due to accessibility for individuals all around the globe without any geographical boundaries. Social media platforms are categorized as social networking sites, microblogging platforms, media sharing sites, discussion forums, blogs and social bookmarking platforms based on the nature of the platform. Social media has five unique characteristics including participation, openness, conversation, community, and connectedness that can pose significant impact to social interactions. The participation nature encourages publishing UGC, while openness allows individuals to share their own perspectives and opinions. The conversation allows individuals to make new connections that provide a sense of society where they can stay connected virtually. All these characteristics play a very crucial role in making social media data relevant for achieving aims of Society 5.0 (Reza et al. 2014).

Every time an individual posts something on social media, like a Facebook status, Twitter tweet, or Instagram photo, it creates some information called a data point. The collection of these data points generated by individuals as a result of social media interaction from a single or multiple social media platforms is referred to as social media data. The size of social media data is continually increasing at an extreme pace resulting in a huge volume of UGC that also makes it challenging to collect, analyze and interpret it. Social media data has great importance for business and researchers to utilize it for various purposes such as understanding emotions and behavior. The social media data is mainly classified into "structured" and "unstructured" data. When the information is stored in some predefined way, it refers to structured data such as demographics and quantitative measures. While on the other hand unstructured data mainly include the text, videos and pictures shared by individuals that did not necessarily need to follow any predefined standard. Extracting and analyzing information from unstructured data is a challenging task that requires application of different social computing techniques (Yingcai et al. 2016).

Social media data can be broadly categorized into five distinct categories, namely textual data, image and video data, social interaction data, location-based data, and network data. The predominant form of social media data is textual in nature that is mostly generated by status updates, comments, tweets, blog posts etc. The examination of textual data can provide valuable insights into the emotions, and preferences of individuals. The ubiquity of smartphones equipped with advanced imaging technology has significantly changed the nature of social media platforms, prompting them to adopt an emphasis on a visually-centered approach. Presently, the practice of regularly disseminating photographs and videos has become common, leading to the creation of an extensive repository of visual data. Social media platforms serve as a channel through which users may engage in a range of interactions such as likes, post comments, share posts,post reactions, and private messages. In this particular context, the interactions give rise to significant data that has the potential to reveal patterns of involvement and social connections. Several social media platforms provide location-based services that facilitate users to share their geographical coordinates and activities. On social media platforms individuals are interlinked in a form of network. The network data contains information about the nature of relationships such as friend, follower, etc. (Norjihan et al. 2019).

Furthermore, social media data can be categorized into two categories: "public" and "private" data (Gruzd and Hernández-García 2018). Public social media data pertains to data that is openly accessible and visible to all users of the platform. It comprises various forms of publicly-shared content, including but not limited to, posts, comments, and user interactions. Collecting and analyzing publicly available data is a common practice among individuals, researchers, and businesses for several purposes that range from trend monitoring to market research and public sentiment tracking. It is important to note that despite the fact that the data is publicly accessible, ethical considerations and privacy policies must be duly observed while utilizing and disseminating this data. Private social media data refers to the information that is communicated by social media users, while simultaneously restricting its visibility to a considerably reduced audience. This type of data includes direct messages exchanged through private channels, as well as contents disseminated within private groups or accounts. Private data is commonly protected by privacy measures and remains inaccessible to the general public. Respect for the privacy settings of users and adherence to legal regulations is imperative when handling private social media data.

Social media data has distinct characteristics such as volume, velocity, variety, veracity, variability, and value. One of the most important aspects of social media data is its enormous volume. With billions of active users on various social media platforms, a massive volume of data is constantly generated. Every post, comment, like, share, and interaction contributed to this ever-increasing volume. The speed with which information is created and shared on social media is also a unique characteristic of social media data. Data from social media exists in different types and formats as users are able to share text-based posts, pictures, recordings, sound clips, and combinations of different types. Veracity refers to the precision, quality, and reliability of social media data. Social media data shows inconsistency in terms of its structure and setting. The data captured by different platforms, such as Twitter, Facebook, Instagram, or LinkedIn, may have particular characteristics and purpose of usage. Social media data holds huge value because it is a rich source of real-time user related data that provides insights on user preferences and behaviors (Reza et al. 2014). The ethical issues and concerns related to social media data as well as future directions are discussed in detail in Sect. 5. Society 5.0 may utilize the power of social media data to create a more inclusive, sustainable, and highly advanced society.

3 Social Computing Techniques in Society 5.0

During this era of technological advancement, social computing has appeared as an effective and disruptive technology that has shaped the ways of interactions and connectivity. The concept of social computing refers to the convergence and integration of social behavior and computational systems. This phenomenon involves the utilization of advanced technology to enhance and facilitate interpersonal interactions. This field comprises a varied range of methodologies and techniques, with the overarching aim of comprehensively understanding, critically evaluating, and enhancing human social practices across a broad spectrum of virtual and real settings (Manoj and Andrew 2007). The domain of social computing systems includes a wide-ranging collection of components that mainly comprise social networking platforms, online communities, crowd sourcing mechanisms, and collaborative filtering algorithms. The primary aim of these systems is to facilitate genuine social interactions and encourage the dissemination of relevant information among individuals. The field of social computing has substantial implications for diverse domains in contemporary society, with regards to promoting connectivity and collaboration for easy exchange and spread of information (Wang et al. 2021). The proliferation of social media platforms, including Facebook, Twitter, and Instagram, has drastically transformed communication patterns due to no physical and geographical constraints, thereby facilitating a rapid and seamless flow of information on a global scale.

Social computing has significantly transformed the operational dynamics of businesses, introducing novel prospects for engaging customers, marketing, and fostering innovation. In present business practices, enterprises employ social media analytics as a means of comprehending customer preferences, engaging with their desired audience, and customizing their offerings to meet the demands of targeted audiences. Social computing has emerged as a catalyst for the sharing economy, exemplified by the emergence of Uber, Airbnb, and TaskRabbit as platforms that enable collaborative consumption and peer-to-peer interactions. One of the prominent features of social computing centers on the huge list of cutting-edge technologies and platforms that facilitate social interactions (Manoj and Andrew 2007). The utilization of crowdsourcing platforms enables the consolidation of the intellectual resources of a large community of individuals, thus providing the means to devise solutions to overcome challenges by generating novel solutions. These platforms harness the collective intelligence of a group of people, exploiting their heterogeneous perspectives and competences to achieve objectives that would otherwise pose challenges for an individual or a group. The integration of social computing technologies into various aspects of modern communication and interaction has had a significant impact on society and culture. In recent times, social computing has received considerable attention owing to the escalating prominence of social media platforms and the ever-growing accessibility of extensive social data (Wang et al. Wang et al. [2021]). A brief overview of the various prominent social computing techniques is provided in respective sections below.

3.1 Social Network Analysis

SNA is one of the core techniques being used in the field of social computing. SNA provides a mechanism that helps to examine and understand the influence and connections in the form of social networks. A wide range of real-time social network examples exist like friendship network on Facebook, professional network on LinkedIn. The investigation of social networks can be viewed from the perspective of both structural and dynamic analysis. The structural perspective involves a systematic analysis of various network attributes, including centrality measures and clustering coefficients, in order to identify similarities between networks and the communities that exist within them. Dynamic network analysis techniques offer a comprehensive exploratory study of the trajectories and progressions exhibited by social networks across diverse temporal domains. Dynamic analysis focuses on temporal dimensions of relationships, the formation and termination of connections, information diffusion, and maximizing influence within a network. The implementation of advanced analysis techniques necessitates the utilization of longitudinal data. The utilization of dynamic SNA methodologies have the potential to enhance the understanding of the dynamic progression of social networks, enabling the forecasting and interpretation of link prediction over an extended period of time. SNA has exhibited a remarkable degree of adaptability across multiple fields, such as marketing, organizational behavior, epidemiology, and virtual social networks (David and Song 2019).

3.2 Text Mining and Natural Language Processing

NLP focuses on the interaction of computers with human language. NLP facilitates the comprehension, interpretation, and generation of human language by machines, thus becoming a crucial technique of Text Mining within the field of social computing. NLP employs computational algorithms to scrutinize textual data, extract semantic information, and execute a diverse range of functions such as identifying expressions of opinion, identifying entities by name, and converting language from one to another. Advanced statistical and machine learning methods, particularly deep learning, are prevailing over traditional rule-based methodologies for NLP (Anne and Steve 2007). Sentiment analysis is a sub-discipline within the field of NLP which strives to identify and analyze the emotional tone or sentiment conveyed within a particular text corpus. The procedure involves the automated classification of written material into three discrete affective states, namely positive, negative, or neutral. Sentiment analysis methodologies utilize machine learning algorithms, lexicon-based techniques, or a hybrid approach, to detect and distinguish the polarity of emotional expression. These technique exhibits a wide range of applications, including the monitoring of brands, reputation management, market research, and analysis of public opinion. By scrutinizing social media content, feedback from customers, and internet-based conversations, sentiment analysis provides valuable perspective into the opinions and dispositions of individuals. The utilization of text mining and NLP is essential for understanding user-generated content, identifying misinformation or fake news, and conducting social media monitoring and analysis. These tools play a vital role in interpreting textual data and extracting meaningful insights from large volumes of unstructured data (Medhat et al. 2014).

3.3 Recommendation Systems

Recommendation systems have a primary objective of delivering tailored recommendations and content to users based on their preferences, interests, and behaviors. These systems utilize cutting-edge techniques to scrutinize and make meaningful deductions from large amounts of user data, including browsing history, previous interactions, and perceived reactions, for the generation of accurate recommendations. Within the field of social computing, recommendation systems are commonly observed across diverse domains inclusive of social media platforms, e-commerce websites, and content streaming services. One prominent example is the use of recommendation systems by social media platforms like Facebook. These platforms use such systems to select and display posts and content that are likely to captivate users and cater to their interests. E-commerce platforms such as Amazon use recommendation systems to recommend merchandise predicated based on the purchasing history and browsing behaviors of consumers, to improve customer experience and sales. Recommendation systems can be categorized into two main types: content-based and collaborative filtering. Content-based recommendation systems analyze the attributes or characteristics of items or content to generate recommendations. For instance, a content-based recommendation system for movies might recommend movies with similar genres or themes to those a user has previously enjoyed. Collaborative filtering recommendation systems, on the other hand, leverage user behavior and preferences to find patterns and similarities among users, recommending items that are favored by users with similar attributes (Reza et al. 2014).

3.4 Reputation Systems

Reputation systems serve as a mechanism to evaluate and establish trust among users within online communities. They are designed to assess the reliability, credibility, and expertise of individuals based on their past actions, contributions, and interactions. By assigning reputation scores or rankings users, these systems create a measure of social capital that influences how users are perceived and interacted with in the community. eBay, an internet-based commercial platform is a well-known example of a reputation system. Currently, individuals are permitted to evaluate and provide feedback on their interactions with buyers and sellers. Hence, enabling the development of a comprehensive reputation score for each party involved. The current reputation rating serves as an indicator of dependability and reliability for imminent actions, allowing users to make informed decisions about participating in e-commerce activities. However, building effective reputation systems is not without challenges. For instance, reputation manipulation or fake reviews can undermine the integrity of these systems. Careful design and robust algorithms are necessary to mitigate such issues and ensure the accuracy and reliability of reputation systems (Hendrikx et al. [2015]). In Society 5.0, trust systems can help build trust among individuals and organizations, particularly in areas such as peer-to-peer sharing economies, decentralized networks, and community-driven initiatives. Trust systems can promote responsible behavior, reduce transactional risks, and facilitate collaboration in a digitally connected society.

3.5 Social Sensing and Collective Intelligence

The concept of "social sensing" refers to a methodical approach of collecting, analyzing, and comprehending data from social media platforms and online communities for the purpose of gaining insights into real-world events and phenomena. The effectiveness of this methodology is predominantly dependent on the massive size of UGC, that includes tweets, posts, and comments, which facilitate the detection and analysis of prevailing social patterns. In contrast, social sensing offers a more comprehensive and enhanced strategy for the acquisition of data. In natural disasters or emergency situations, social sensing plays a vital role in the identification of impacted locations, evaluating the severity of the disaster, and disseminating critical information to emergency response units. The utilization of social sensing techniques involves the application of sophisticated data mining methodologies, natural language processing approaches, and machine learning algorithms to detect and extract significant patterns and insights from the data obtained through various social media platforms (Wang 2019). Social sensing has the potential to offer valuable insights for marketing initiatives, policy formulation, and public opinion mining by comprehending public sentiment, identifying influencers, and analyzing social networks. Digital communities such as Wikipedia, Stack Overflow, and GitHub are examples of the vast potential of collective intelligence. These platforms facilitate collaborative knowledge creation and management, encourage the sharing of expertise, and support collective problem-solving efforts (Nicolas and Djouvas 2019).

4 Integration of Social Media Data and Social Computing Techniques in Society 5.0

The utilization of social media data and social computing techniques exhibits significant potential for the transformation of different fields such as marketing, healthcare, and public-opinion analysis, through their collaborative interaction. The utilization of social media data provides a huge amount of data points regarding user tendencies and interests, with social computing approaches facilitating the identification and interpretation of consequential findings from the available data. Through the integration of social media data and social computing techniques, organizations and researchers can extract crucial insights, implement data-centric solutions, and improve their understanding of societal events. This section explores and highlights the interactions and the potential applications areas associated with the utilization of social media data and social computing techniques within the context of Society 5.0.

4.1 Health and Well-Being

In the healthcare domain, social computing techniques are playing a transformative role as they facilitate the collection and analysis of copious quantities of health-related data, thereby resulting in enhanced diagnostic precision, tailored treatment strategies, and preemptive disease mitigation. Moreover, wearable devices and mobile applications integrated with social computing techniques can monitor the health indicators of individuals and provide immediate feedback, facilitating the adoption of healthier lifestyles and nurturing self-care practices. The incorporation of social computing methodologies into healthcare and well-being services has the potential to reshape the way individuals approach the management of their health. Online communities provide patients with the opportunity to engage with others who are experiencing similar health conditions (Garg 2023). This facilitates peer support and promotes the exchange of knowledge among the patients. The use of social media platforms for healthcare communication and well-being is rapidly expanding. Researchers have been using social media data to analyze topics being discussed and identify disease outbreaks (Chiara et al. 2022).

4.2 Transportation

The integration of social computing methodologies into transportation systems has resulted in improved effectiveness, resolved congestion, and advanced user engagement. Furthermore, the acquisition of real-time traffic information from multiple sources including social media platforms and GPS-enabled gadgets empowers predictive analytics and proactive management of traffic. Social computing facilitates the seamless integration of various transportation modes, thereby promoting multi-mode traveling via public transport and decreasing reliance on private vehicles (Farman et al. 2021). In the existing literature, a number of frameworks have been proposed that use social sensing to detect abnormal traffic conditions. The sharing of location-based social network data by individuals is critical for detecting abnormal traffic patterns. The framework Social sensing based abnormal traffic geolocalization (SAT-Geo) uses Twitter data to detect abnormal traffic flow. The evaluations conducted using real-world Twitter datasets for three cities demonstrated the SAT-Geo's effectiveness in successfully identifying abnormal traffic (Shang et al. 2022). Similarly, a study examined tweets in order to identify traffic accidents. When the results were compared to actual traffic data, it was discovered that Twitter has a great potential for identifying traffic-related problems (Suat-Rojas et al. 2022).

4.3 Education

The utilization of social computing in online learning platforms and massive open online courses (MOOCs) provides interactive and engaging educational settings. Collaboration amongst students, feedback from teachers, and access to vast educational resources are all available means of enhancing student learning. Social media platforms present significant prospects for teachers to interact with students beyond the boundaries of the classroom, distribute educational materials, and encourage the formation of virtual learning communities (Shen and Kuo 2015). Social media has transformed higher education by facilitating resource sharing, collaborative learning, and interaction with academicians. It has been discovered that using social media for educational purposes increases students' creativity and provides a better learning experience (Jamal and Nawab 2020). The significance of education in the context of Society 5.0 is of great importance, as the integration of social computing techniques can augment learning endeavors and facilitate initiatives for continuous learning and development.

4.4 Governance

In the context of Society 5.0, social computing serves a key role in enabling democratic governance, enhancing the participation of citizens, and fostering transparency. Electronic government platforms facilitate citizen access to government services, active involvement in decision-making processes, and effective communication of policy feedback. Furthermore, social computing techniques like sentiment analysis and social network analysis can be used effectively to analyze public sentiment and provide meaningful insights into the process of policy-making. The utilization of social computing techniques holds the potential to substantially influence civic participation as well as governance within the paradigm of Society 5.0. The incorporation of social computing methodologies can potentially enhance the effectiveness of electronic voting systems (Bindu et al. 2019). This is due to the fact that it can provide citizens with a secure and convenient avenue to express their preferences, thereby creating a more robust democratic infrastructure. The utilization of social computing techniques also plays an important role in public safety, promoting crime prevention and mitigating cyberbullying incidents (Samia et al. 2022). Social media monitoring is an effective tool enabling the identification of possible threats or suspicious activities, thereby enhancing the ability to identify potential threats at an early stage and provide proactive measures in response. The implementation of SNA facilitates the identification of patterns and interconnections that exist among individuals who participate in criminal activities. Furthermore, the utilization of mobile applications and online reporting platforms provide people with the capability to report incidents, exchange information, and engage in community policing programs.

4.5 Sustainable Development and Smart Cities

The utilization of social computing methods within Society 5.0 could potentially make a valuable contribution towards the advancement of sustainable and smart cities. Citizens can participate in environmental monitoring, urban planning, and resource management through crowdsourcing and collective intelligence platforms. The implementation of social computing techniques plays a significant role in the establishment of smart cities by enabling the use of instantaneous data collection and analysis. This allows for more efficient resource distribution, sophisticated transportation arrangements, and optimized metropolitan infrastructure, resulting in improved quality of life and environmental sustainability. Social computing techniques are currently being utilized to tackle environmental challenges and advance sustainable practices. Crowdsourcing platforms facilitate the participation of individuals in data contribution pertaining to environmental concerns, such as air quality and waste management. Social media campaigns serve as effective tools in promoting awareness and advocacy towards sustainable behaviors and fostering collective action. Within the framework of Society 5.0, the utilization of social media data along with social computing methodologies plays a vital role in the effective planning and management of smart cities. Incorporating social media data and social computing techniques into smart city planning facilitates the quick and consistent monitoring of urban challenges like traffic congestion, air quality, and public sentiment. This data provides policymakers with the ability to make informed decisions and develop measures that improve urban living standards (Muhammad et al. 2020).

4.6 Disaster Response and Crisis Management

Social media platforms function as instantaneous channels of communication, enabling individuals to disseminate information, seek aid, and extend assistance. Emergency response agencies are able to use social computing techniques to monitor public sentiment, detect impacted regions, and effectively allocate resources. Crowdsourcing platforms and online communities play a critical role in emergency situations by mobilizing volunteers and facilitating the efficient coordination of relief efforts. Social media data has been extremely useful for disaster management because it contains four key dimensions: space, time, content, and network. It enables researchers to mine real-time data that can provide critical situational awareness insights to response units. It has been observed that existing disaster management studies have conducted analyses using both single and multiple dimensions (Saroj and Pal 2020). The relationship between social media platforms and emergency situations has also been studied in the literature from the perspective of emergency situation, methods to extract and process disaster-related data, and finally assisting rescue teams in responding effectively. Social media platforms have emerged as an effective means of disseminating flood, storm, and earthquake alerts that can reach the audience in a matter of seconds (Bilal et al. 2018; Wang and Ye 2018).

4.7 Economic Empowerment and Entrepreneurship

The use of social computing techniques has empowered individuals to participate in the digital economy and actively cultivate the entrepreneurial spirit. E-commerce platforms and online marketplaces have facilitated the expansion of small businesses and independent entrepreneurs by providing access to a worldwide customer base. Social media marketing is a highly effective strategy that enables the customization of advertising plans and promotes active customer engagement, ultimately driving brand development and boosting sales performance. Furthermore, crowdfunding platforms offer prospects for individuals to procure funds and endorse entrepreneurship initiatives. Within the context of Society 5.0, social media data and social computing techniques are promoting social innovation and entrepreneurship. Startups and social entrepreneurs effectively use social media platforms as a means of engaging with their desired audience and collecting feedback (Abdus-Samad et al. 2020). The utilization of social computing techniques enable entrepreneurs to effectively utilize UGC, NLP, and SNA in order to improve marketing strategies and improve business growth.

5 Challenges and Opportunities in Society 5.0

The incorporation of social media data and social computing techniques into Society 5.0 offers considerable advantages. However, proper consideration must be given to the key challenges related to ensuring the responsible and ethical use of these technologies. This section highlights and discusses some of the most prominent challenges associated with the utilization of social media data and social computing techniques within the context of Society 5.0. By overcoming these challenges, Society 5.0 will be able to leverage the potential of social media data and social computing methodologies to create a future marked by greater inclusivity, equity, and sustainability.

5.1 Privacy and Data Protection

One of the principal implications for privacy in Society 5.0 relates to the huge collection and use of user related personalized data. The proliferation of interconnected and pervasive technologies has resulted in a significant increase in the volume of data generated by individuals through their online activities, and use of smart devices. This commonly includes confidential details such as individual preferences, medical reports, and geographical data (Reza et al. 2014). The personal data can be either used by malicious users or for intrusive profiling and surveillance purposes. The vulnerability to exploitative behavior and unauthorized access to individual data poses an imminent threat to the domain of confidentiality within the context of Society 5.0. Furthermore, Society 5.0 heavily relies on advanced technologies that necessitate access to extensive datasets to operate with optimal efficiency. The imperative for obtaining data access raises concerns about data ownership and regulation. The degree of transparency and control that individuals have over the collection, storage, analysis, and dissemination of their data by various entities within the framework of Society 5.0 may be limited. The lack of regulatory oversight creates an asymmetry in authority, in which individuals become increasingly reliant on technology providers and corporations that retain ownership of their data, increasing the likelihood of exploitation and manipulation. Nonetheless, the deployment of resilient data safeguarding protocols can alleviate the data privacy and protection issues

(Bilal et al. 2019). This can be accomplished by implementing strong legal frameworks, privacy by design principles, transparent data practices, and user control mechanisms.

5.2 Big Data Paradox and Noise Removal Fallacy

The rise of social media networks has resulted in massive amounts of UGC that exhibit all of the characteristics of big data. This abundance of data not only provides numerous opportunities for analysis, but it also poses a paradoxical challenge. The massive amount of data can potentially overwhelm researchers, making it difficult to extract meaningful insights. This big data issue is concerned with the effective management, processing, and analysis of large amounts of data in order to gain useful insights. The emergence of large and complex datasets necessitates the use of advanced methods and tools capable of effectively managing and extracting meaningful insights from massive amounts of data, thereby reducing noise. The noise removal fallacy refers to the mistaken belief that completely eliminating noise will result in cleaner data and better analysis. Despite this, complete noise elimination is frequently impossible and may result in the loss of critical information. To achieve optimal data quality, researchers must attain a balance between removing noise and preserving relevant information (Reza et al. 2014).

5.3 Algorithmic Bias and Evaluation Dilemma

Social media platforms and social computing techniques rely heavily on computational algorithms to customize content presentation, recommend products, and make informed decisions. Nonetheless, it should be noted that these algorithms are still vulnerable to biases that may be inherent in the data on which they are trained. Biased algorithms have the potential to create and reinforce social, cultural, and racial prejudices, resulting in prejudiced treatment and discriminatory actions. To ensure algorithmic equity and reduce bias, it is critical to have a thorough understanding of the data used to train algorithms, as well as to deploy robust methods that can detect and correct inequities (David et al. 2020). The use of social media data faces unique challenges in social computing. Unlike surveys or experiments, social media data is derived from the unprompted self-expression and behavior of a diverse and frequently unregulated user population rather than from controlled sampling methodologies. The researchers face a number of challenges, including the complexities of selection bias, privacy concerns. The evaluation of the effectiveness and influence of social media campaigns, interventions, or policies is a difficult and time-consuming task. Social media analytics frequently address complex and dynamic systems, making establishing causality a difficult task. The challenge is in developing appropriate assessment criteria and techniques that effectively capture the multidimensional aspects of social media (Reza et al. 2014). During the design of evaluation studies, it is critical to consider the ethical implications of user privacy and consent.

5.4 Lack of Transparency and Human Oversight

An overarching concern in algorithmic decision-making is the lack of transparency regarding the algorithms that serve as the foundation for such decision-making. Many algorithms, particularly those based on machine learning, operate in an opaque manner, making it difficult to understand the decision-making process. Individuals who have been impacted by algorithmic decisions are rendered incapable of comprehending or contesting the underlying reasoning behind such decisions in the absence of transparency. Inadequate transparency is a formidable barrier to detecting and correcting potential biases, inaccuracies, or discriminatory measures that may be deeply embedded in algorithms. It is critical to ensure transparency and explain the mechanics of these techniques so that users understand how their data is used and the implications of the insights that have been generated. Transparent systems have the potential to foster trust and enable users to make wise decisions by giving them access to critical information (Grimmelikhuijsen and Meijer 2022). Algorithm-based automated decision-making systems have the potential to function with insufficient human supervision. Although algorithms are capable of efficiently processing massive amounts of data and making quick decisions, they may be limited in their ability to consider contextual details or use judgment in complex situations. Excessive reliance on algorithmic decision-making, which operates without human supervision, can lead to inaccurate or inequitable outcomes. Human involvement is required in accountability mechanisms in order to assess, supervise, and correct decisions made by algorithms as needed (Leila et al. 2021).

5.5 Information Overload and Fake News

The exponential growth of social media networks has resulted in an overload of information available to individuals (Muhammad et al. 2019). The information overload problem presents a significant barrier in distinguishing trustworthy and precise information from dubious and fake news. Social media platforms have become a viable source for the spread of rumors, fake news, and disinformation. The development of capable algorithms and techniques to filter and authenticate information is critical in combating the spread of fake news and promoting the accessibility of reliable information within the context of the Society 5.0 paradigm. The prevalence of misinformation and disinformation on social media platforms has emerged as a prominent concern. The application of social computing techniques is critical in the detection and mitigation of false information through pattern analysis, misinformation detection, and the promotion of credible sources. It is critical to ensure the integrity of data used in these techniques because it serves as a critical means to prevent the dissemination of false information, maintain public trust, and promote ethical information exchange (Botambu et al. 2021).

5.6 Legal and Regulatory Challenges

The rapid development of algorithmic decision-making has surpassed the development of legal and regulatory frameworks required to monitor their use. Algorithms present unique challenges that may not be fully addressed by current legal and regulatory frameworks, making it difficult to enforce algorithmic accountability. Furthermore, the widespread use of the internet and data transmission makes it difficult to establish consistent regulatory structures across diverse legal jurisdictions. Achieving a balance between promoting innovation and protecting individuals' interests necessitates the implementation of comprehensive legal and regulatory structures that refer to the field of algorithmic decision-making. The incorporation of social media data and social computing techniques into Society 5.0 necessitates accountability and governance in order to promote responsible usage, protect individuals' fundamental rights, and prevent potential abuses (Brkan 2019). The creation of comprehensive legal frameworks, regulatory bodies, and guidelines is a viable strategy for mitigating the legal and regulatory challenges associated with social media data and social computing techniques in Society 5.0.

5.7 Mental Health and Ethical Dilemmas

The widespread use of social media, as well as the repeated exposure to idealized depictions of people's lives, can have a negative impact on personal mental health and overall well-being. On social media platforms, comparisons to others, low self-esteem, and cyberbullying are all frequently observed. Furthermore, the addictive qualities of social media platforms have the potential to result in excessive periods of screen engagement and social detachment. The promotion of digital well-being, the adoption of healthy online behavior, and the dissemination of knowledge on the potential drawbacks and benefits associated with the use of social media are all required for the effective resolution of the current issues confronting Society 5.0 (John et al. 2020). Using algorithms in healthcare to allocate limited medical resources raises ethical concerns about the criteria to be used in prioritizing patients, such as age, current medical status, and probability of survival. In these circumstances, it is critical to implement accountability mechanisms to ensure that verdicts conform to societal norms, adhere to equity principles, and protect individual liberties (Formosa et al. 2022).

5.8 Digital Divide and Inclusivity

Social media platforms and social computing techniques have the potential to improve human connectivity and community empowerment. However, a significant digital divide hinders equality in both access and participation. The exclusion of certain populations from fully experiencing the benefits of modern technologies is due to socioeconomic disparities, insufficient internet connectivity, and disparities in technological literacy. To achieve the goals of bridging the digital divide and promoting inclusivity, it is critical to take a collaborative approach that includes equitable access to technology, enhancement of digital literacy skills, and reduction of the persistent societal inequalities that form the underlying causes of this divide. The integration of digital technologies into all aspects of society, as envisioned by Society 5.0, has raised concerns about the possibility of a technological divide (Sophie et al. 2022). Individuals have unequal access to digital platforms and inadequate proficiency in utilizing social media data and social computing techniques. It is critical to build a bridge across this divide in order to achieve parity in the distribution of benefits and avoid worsening prevailing social inequalities.

6 Conclusion

This chapter discussed the significance of social media data and social computing techniques in the context of the Society 5.0. Social media platforms have facilitated the generation and dissemination of huge quantities of data by users, exerting significant impact on opinions and interactions at a societal level. The utilization of social media data has recently gained recognition as a significant resource in analysis of human behavior, opinions, sentiments, and collective intelligence. The fusion of social media data and social computing techniques presents substantial opportunities for resolving current social problems from the perspective of Society 5.0. The ability to analyze massive volumes of UGC in conjunction with advanced computational techniques provides unparalleled insight into individual preferences, community dynamics, and societal complexities. Moreover, the utilization of social computing techniques has expedited the development of innovative applications and platforms that support collective problem solving. The emergence of crowdsourcing, social sensing, and citizen management has provided individuals with the opportunity to play an active role in addressing current societal challenges, consequently narrowing the gap between government bodies and the general public.

In today's society, social media has become a critical enabler of social transformation, particularly by amplifying the influence of various groups, fostering communal mobilization, and initiating advocacy campaigns. It is critical to recognise that the use of social media data and social computing techniques raises ethical, privacy, and security challenges. Responsible data collection, analysis, and application should prioritize the protection of individuals' rights, privacy, and the practice of informed consent. Furthermore, the elimination of algorithmic biases, the assurance of transparency, and the advancement of digital literacy are critical towards the promotion of an equitable and inclusive Society 5.0. In the future, the incorporation of social media data and social computing methodologies will keep influencing and change the direction of Society 5.0. The imperative for optimal societal collective benefit from social media data and social computing necessitates collaborative efforts among academia, industry, policymakers, and citizens. A prominent topic in Society 5.0 is the multifaceted and transformative function of social media data and social computing techniques. While providing unparalleled opportunities for comprehension, cooperation, and resolution, it is critical to expertly navigate the associated ethical implications to ensure that these technologies are used for the betterment of society as a whole. It is possible to cultivate a more interconnected, engaged, and accountable society by integrating social media data and social computing, which prioritizes the needs and goals of its citizens.

References

Abdus-Samad Temitope Olanrewaju, Mohammad Alamgir Hossain, Naomi Whiteside, and Paul Mercieca. Social media and entrepreneurship research: A literature review. *International Journal of Information Management*, 50:90–110, 2020.

Anne Kao and Steve R Poteet. *Natural language processing and text mining*. Springer Science & Business Media, 2007.

Atsushi Deguchi, Chiaki Hirai, Hideyuki Matsuoka, Taku Nakano, Kohei Oshima, Mitsuharu Tai, and Shigeyuki Tani. What is society 5.0. *Society*, 5:1–23, 2020.

Anatoliy Gruzd and Ángel Hernández-García. Privacy concerns and self-disclosure in private and public uses of social media. *Cyberpsychology, Behavior, and Social Networking*, 21(7):418–428, 2018.

Anita Saroj and Sukomal Pal. Use of social media in crisis management: A survey. *International Journal of Disaster Risk Reduction*, 48:101584, 2020.

Botambu Collins, Dinh Tuyen Hoang, Ngoc Thanh Nguyen, and Dosam Hwang. Trends in combating fake news on social media–a survey. *Journal of Information and Telecommunication*, 5(2):247–266, 2021.

Bruno Salgues. *Society 5.0: industry of the future, technologies, methods and tools*. John Wiley & Sons, 2018.

Carin Holroyd. Technological innovation and building a 'super smart' society: Japan's vision of society 5.0. *Journal of Asian Public Policy*, 15(1):18–31, 2022.

Chiara Pomare, Janet C Long, Kate Churruca, Louise A Ellis, and Jeffrey Braithwaite. Social network research in health care settings: design and data collection. *Social networks*, 69:14–21, 2022.

Chao Fan, Cheng Zhang, Alex Yahja, and Ali Mostafavi. Disaster city digital twin: A vision for integrating artificial and human intelligence for disaster management. *International Journal of Information Management*, 56:102049, 2021.

Chien-wen Shen and Chin-Jin Kuo. Learning in massive open online courses: Evidence from social media mining. *Computers in Human Behavior*, 51:568–577, 2015.

David Knoke and Song Yang. *Social network analysis*. SAGE Publications, 2019.

David MJ Lazer, Alex Pentland, Duncan J Watts, Sinan Aral, Susan Athey, Noshir Contractor, Deen Freelon, Sandra Gonzalez-Bailon, Gary King, Helen Margetts, et al. Computational social science: Obstacles and opportunities. *Science*, 369(6507):1060–1062, 2020.

David Lazer, Alex Pentland, Lada Adamic, Sinan Aral, Albert-László Barabási, Devon Brewer, Nicholas Christakis, Noshir Contractor, James Fowler, Myron Gutmann, et al. Computational social science. *Science*, 323(5915):721–723, 2009.

Dimitris Mourtzis, John Angelopoulos, and Nikos Panopoulos. A literature review of the challenges and opportunities of the transition from industry 4.0 to society 5.0. *Energies*, 15(17):6276, 2022.

Dong Wang, Boleslaw K Szymanski, Tarek Abdelzaher, Heng Ji, and Lance Kaplan. The age of social sensing. *Computer*, 52(1):36–45, 2019.

Elias G Carayannis and Joanna Morawska-Jancelewicz. The futures of Europe: Society 5.0 and industry 5.0 as driving forces of future universities. *Journal of the Knowledge Economy*, pages 1–27, 2022.

Farman Ali, Amjad Ali, Muhammad Imran, Rizwan Ali Naqvi, Muhammad Hameed Siddiqi, and Kyung-Sup Kwak. Traffic accident detection and condition analysis based on social networking data. *Accident Analysis & Prevention*, 151:105973, 2021.

Ferry Hendrikx, Kris Bubendorfer, and Ryan Chard. Reputation systems: A survey and taxonomy. *Journal of Parallel and Distributed Computing*, 75:184–197, 2015.

Iqra Javed, Uzair Iqbal, Muhammad Bilal, Basit Shahzad, Tae-Sun Chung, Muhammad Attique, et al. Next generation infectious diseases monitoring gages via incremental federated learning: Current trends and future possibilities. *Computational Intelligence and Neuroscience*, 2023.

Jamal Abdul Nasir Ansari and Nawab Ali Khan. Exploring the role of social media in collaborative learning the new domain of learning. *Smart Learning Environments*, 7(1):1–16, 2020.

Jean M Twenge, Brian H Spitzberg, and W Keith Campbell. Less in-person social interaction with peers among us adolescents in the 21st century and links to loneliness. *Journal of Social and Personal Relationships*, 36(6):1892–1913, 2019.

Jianxin Li, Taotao Cai, Ke Deng, Xinjue Wang, Timos Sellis, and Feng Xia. Community-diversified influence maximization in social networks. *Information Systems*, 92:101522, 2020.

John A Naslund, Ameya Bondre, John Torous, and Kelly A Aschbrenner. Social media and mental health: benefits, risks, and opportunities for research and practice. *Journal of technology in behavioral science*, 5:245–257, 2020.

Jose M Barrutia and Carmen Echebarria. Effect of the covid-19 pandemic on public managers' attitudes toward digital transformation. *Technology in Society*, 67:101776, 2021.

Joshua Newman, Michael Mintrom, and Deirdre O'Neill. Digital technologies, artificial intelligence, and bureaucratic transformation. *Futures*, 136:102886, 2022.

Kai Tai Chan. Emergence of the 'digitalized self' in the age of digitalization. *Computers in Human Behavior Reports*, 6:100191, 2022.

Ke Sun, Tieyun Qian, Tong Chen, Yile Liang, Quoc Viet Hung Nguyen, and Hongzhi Yin. Where to go next: Modeling long-and short-term user preferences for point-of-interest recommendation. In *Proceedings of the AAAI Conference on Artificial Intelligence*, volume 34, pages 214–221, 2020.

Leila Methnani, Andrea Aler Tubella, Virginia Dignum, and Andreas Theodorou. Let me take over: Variable autonomy for meaningful human control. *Frontiers in Artificial Intelligence*, 4:737072, 2021.

Lanyu Shang, Yang Zhang, Christina Youn, and Dong Wang. Sat-geo: A social sensing based content-only approach to geolocating abnormal traffic events using syntax-based probabilistic learning. *Information Processing & Management*, 59(2):102807, 2022.

Manoj Parameswaran and Andrew B Whinston. Social computing: An overview. *Communications of the association for Information Systems*, 19(1):37, 2007.

Maja Brkan. Do algorithms rule the world? algorithmic decision-making and data protection in the framework of the gdpr and beyond. *International journal of law and information technology*, 27(2):91–121, 2019.

Maria C Tavares, Graça Azevedo, and Rui P Marques. The challenges and opportunities of era 5.0 for a more humanistic and sustainable society-a literature review. *Societies*, 12(6):149, 2022.

Muhammad Bilal, Abdullah Gani, Muhammad Ikram Ullah Lali, Mohsen Marjani, and Nadia Malik. Social profiling: A review, taxonomy, and challenges. *Cyberpsychology, Behavior, and Social Networking*, 22(7):433–450, 2019.

Muhammad Bilal, Abdullah Gani, Mohsen Marjani, and Nadia Malik. A study on detection and monitoring of water quality and flow. In *2018 12th International Conference on Mathematics, Actuarial Science, Computer Science and Statistics (MACS)*, pages 1–6. IEEE, 2018.

Muhammad Bilal, Mohsen Marjani, Ibrahim Abaker Targio Hashem, Akibu Mahmoud Abdullahi, Muhammad Tayyab, and Abdullah Gani. Predicting helpfulness of crowd-sourced reviews: A survey. In *2019 13th International Conference on Mathematics, Actuarial Science, Computer Science and Statistics (MACS)*, pages 1–8. IEEE, 2019.

Muhammad Bilal, Raja Sher Afgun Usmani, Muhammad Tayyab, Abdullahi Akibu Mahmoud, Reem Mohamed Abdalla, Mohsen Marjani, Thulasyammal Ramiah Pillai, and Ibrahim Abaker Targio Hashem. Smart cities data: Framework, applications, and challenges. *Handbook of smart cities*, pages 1–29, 2020.

Muskan Garg. Mental health analysis in social media posts: A survey. *Archives of Computational Methods in Engineering*, pages 1–24, 2023.

N Bindu, C Prem Sankar, and K Satheesh Kumar. From conventional governance to e-democracy: Tracing the evolution of e-governance research trends using network analysis tools. *Government Information Quarterly*, 36(3):385–399, 2019.

Nestor Suat-Rojas, Camilo Gutierrez-Osorio, and Cesar Pedraza. Extraction and analysis of social networks data to detect traffic accidents. *Information*, 13(1):26, 2022.

Nicolas Tsapatsoulis and Constantinos Djouvas. Opinion mining from social media short texts: Does collective intelligence beat deep learning? *Frontiers in Robotics and AI*, page 138, 2019.

Norjihan Abdul Ghani, Suraya Hamid, Ibrahim Abaker Targio Hashem, and Ejaz Ahmed. Social media big data analytics: A survey. *Computers in Human Behavior*, 101:417–428, 2019.

Paul Formosa, Wendy Rogers, Yannick Griep, Sarah Bankins, and Deborah Richards. Medical ai and human dignity: Contrasting perceptions of human and artificially intelligent (ai) decision making in diagnostic and medical resource allocation contexts. *Computers in Human Behavior*, 133:107296, 2022.

Ratri Wahyuningtyas, Ganjar Disastra, and Risris Rismayani. Toward cooperative competitiveness for community development in economic society 5.0. *Journal of Enterprising Communities: People and Places in the Global Economy*, 17(3):594–620, 2023.

Reza Zafarani, Mohammad Ali Abbasi, and Huan Liu. *Social media mining: an introduction*. Cambridge University Press, 2014.

Samia Aziz, Muhammad Usman, Awais Azam, Farwa Ahmad, Muhammad Bilal, and Adeel Ashraf Cheema. Analysing machine learning techniques for cyberbullying detection: A review study. In *2022 17th International Conference on Emerging Technologies (ICET)*, pages 247–252. IEEE, 2022.

Sophie Lythreatis, Sanjay Kumar Singh, and Abdul-Nasser El-Kassar. The digital divide: A review and future research agenda. *Technological Forecasting and Social Change*, 175:121359, 2022.

Stephan Grimmelikhuijsen and Albert Meijer. Legitimacy of algorithmic decision-making: six threats and the need for a calibrated institutional response. *Perspectives on Public Management and Governance*, 5(3):232–242, 2022.

Vojko Potočan, Matjaž Mulej, and Zlatko Nedelko. Society 5.0: balancing of industry 4.0, economic advancement and social problems. *Kybernetes*, 50(3):794–811, 2020.

Zheye Wang and Xinyue Ye. Social media analytics for natural disaster management. *International Journal of Geographical Information Science*, 32(1):49–72, 2018.

Wenxi Wang, Huansheng Ning, Feifei Shi, Sahraoui Dhelim, Weishan Zhang, and Liming Chen. A survey of hybrid human-artificial intelligence for social computing. *IEEE Transactions on Human-Machine Systems*, 52(3):468–480, 2021.

Walaa Medhat, Ahmed Hassan, and Hoda Korashy. Sentiment analysis algorithms and applications: A survey. *Ain Shams Engineering Journal*, 5(4):1093–1113, 2014.

Yingcai Wu, Nan Cao, David Gotz, Yap-Peng Tan, and Daniel A Keim. A survey on visual analytics of social media data. *IEEE Transactions on Multimedia*, 18(11):2135–2148, 2016.

Intelligent Systems for Healthcare and Agriculture

Healthcare Transformation Through Disruptive Technologies: The Role of Telepresence Robots

Fawad Naseer, Muhammad Nasir Khan, and Abdullah Addas

Abstract

This chapter discusses the transformative potential of disruptive technologies in the developing world's healthcare sector. The integration and impact of telepresence robotics, an innovation that transcends geographical and logistical barriers to healthcare access, are explicitly emphasised. As digital avatars, telepresence robots enable healthcare professionals to interact with, diagnose, and in some cases treat patients remotely, thereby bridging the healthcare gap in remote regions. It explores how these robots, equipped with advanced features such as real-time audio-visual communication, patient monitoring, and even medical data analysis, redefine patient care by delivering timely, effective, and high-quality healthcare services. In addition, this chapter explains the hurdles associated with deploying telepresence robots, including infrastructure requirements, policy regulations, and social acceptability. Through case studies and empirical evidence, this chapter emphasises the potential of telepresence robots to reduce healthcare disparities and improve healthcare outcomes in developing nations. In the end, this chapter proposed that adopting such disruptive technologies is essential for ushering in a new era of healthcare delivery consistent with the principles of Society 5.0.

Keywords

Telepresence robot · Healthcare · Disruptive technologies · Healthcare transformation

1 Introduction

The issue of healthcare disparities in developing nations is complex and multifaceted, affecting millions of people worldwide. The fundamental right of every individual to access quality healthcare, regardless of socioeconomic status or location. However, despite significant advancements in medical technologies and health policies, this right is still unavailable to a substantial proportion of the global population.

The World Health Organization (WHO) defines health as "a state of complete physical, mental, and social well-being and not merely the absence of disease or infirmity". However, for several individuals in developing nations, achieving this level of well-being is frequently impeded by several challenges. These obstacles are often the result of systemic problems, such as economic instability, inadequate infrastructure, poor health literacy, and a shortage of adequately trained healthcare professionals.

Traditionally, establishing robust and accessible healthcare systems in developing countries has been fraught with different hurdles. Frequently, colonial legacies, civil unrest, and economic instability have impeded the establishment

F. Naseer (✉)
Electrical Engineering Department, The University of Lahore, Lahore, Pakistan
e-mail: fawad.naseer@bic.edu.pk

F. Naseer
Computer Science and Software Engineering Department, Beaconhouse International College, Faisalabad 38000, Pakistan

M. N. Khan
Electrical Engineering Department, Government College University Lahore, Lahore, Pakistan
e-mail: dr.ir.mnkhan@gcu.edu.pk

A. Addas
Department of Civil Engineering, College of Engineering, Prince Sattam Bin Abdulaziz University, Alkharj 11942, Saudi Arabia
e-mail: a.addas@psau.edu.sa

A. Addas
Landscape Architecture Department, Faculty of Architecture and Planning, King Abdulaziz University, P.O. Box 80210, Jeddah 21589, Saudi Arabia

S. Arezki et al. (eds.), *Emerging Disruptive Technologies for Society 5.0 in Developing Countries*, Advances in Science, Technology & Innovation, https://doi.org/10.1007/978-3-031-63701-8_14

of a stable healthcare infrastructure. The result is a healthcare system that is fragmented and frequently inaccessible, leaving many without access to essential healthcare services. The current data reveals an enormous gap between developed and developing nations regarding healthcare access and outcomes. According to data from the WHO Global Health Observatory, the life expectancy at birth in low-income countries in 2019 was significantly lower than the 81.3 years observed in high-income countries (Alsalem et al. 2020). Similarly, the mortality rate among children under five was approximately 14 times higher in low-income countries than in high-income countries. These disparities highlight the persistent health challenges in developing countries.

Moreover, within developing nations, access to healthcare frequently varies significantly based on geographical location, with rural areas often lagging urban centres. Diverse economic, social, and political structures are typically at the root of these disparities. For example, rural areas frequently face a shortage of healthcare facilities and professionals and logistical obstacles such as inadequate transportation and communication infrastructure. In addition, the rural population is commonly characterised by higher rates of poverty and lower levels of education, which can hinder their access to and utilisation of healthcare services.

In addition to these geographical differences, social determinants of health play an important role in determining health outcomes. Gender, ethnicity, and socioeconomic standing can significantly impact an individual's access to quality healthcare. In many developing nations, women face unique health challenges, such as high maternal mortality rates and limited access to reproductive health services. Similarly, marginalised ethnic and social groups are frequently subjected to discrimination and stigma, which can restrict their access to healthcare services.

Inequities in healthcare are not only a matter of social justice; they also pose substantial economic challenges. The World Bank estimates that between 2011 and 2025, the economic cost of premature death (World Bank Group 2022) and disability due to noncommunicable diseases (NCDs) in low- and middle-income countries could reach $7 trillion. In addition, these disparities can exacerbate poverty, as families frequently face substantial financial hardship due to high out-of-pocket healthcare costs. While the challenges are significant, it is essential to acknowledge the progress made in recent years. Global initiatives such as the Millennium Development Goals and, more recently, the Sustainable Development Goals have brought international attention to health disparities and substantially improved areas such as child mortality and HIV/AIDS. However, there is still much work to be done.

As we progress through this chapter, we will investigate the transformative potential of disruptive technologies, particularly telepresence robots, in addressing healthcare disparities in developing nations. Through case studies and empirical evidence, we will examine how these technologies can overcome barriers to healthcare access, enhance the quality of care, and ultimately contribute to the development of more equitable healthcare systems per the principles of Society 5.0.

Even though disruptive technologies hold immense promise, their successful deployment requires a thorough understanding of each region's unique challenges and contextual factors. This chapter begins with a nuanced examination of healthcare disparities for this reason. To address healthcare disparities, implementing advanced technology is not sufficient. Understanding the sociocultural dynamics, financial constraints, health literacy, and infrastructure capacities that define healthcare in developing regions is essential. It involves recognising the need for technologically advanced, culturally sensitive, economically viable, and user-friendly solutions.

The introduction of telepresence robots into the healthcare industry presents an exciting opportunity to overcome some of these obstacles. These devices can provide healthcare services in inaccessible locations, assist overworked healthcare professionals, and allow real-time patient monitoring and interaction. However, their successful deployment also necessitates addressing several challenges, such as ensuring reliable internet connectivity, training healthcare professionals and patients on using these devices and establishing appropriate regulatory frameworks.

This chapter will provide a balanced perspective on the potential of telepresence robots, addressing both their transformative potential and the implementation challenges. Through this discussion, we hope to shed light on how disruptive technologies can be utilised to address healthcare disparities in developing nations and contribute to developing a more equitable and inclusive society. 5.0. The ultimate objective is to spark a discussion about how technological innovation can be utilised to transform healthcare delivery in developing regions. With the right combination of technology, policy, and community engagement, achieving equitable healthcare is well within reach.

2 Disruptive Technologies in Healthcare

The emergence of disruptive technologies has had widespread effects on the healthcare industry, providing innovative solutions to some of the most persistent challenges in accessing and delivering healthcare services. As shown in Fig. 1, these technologies, including artificial intelligence

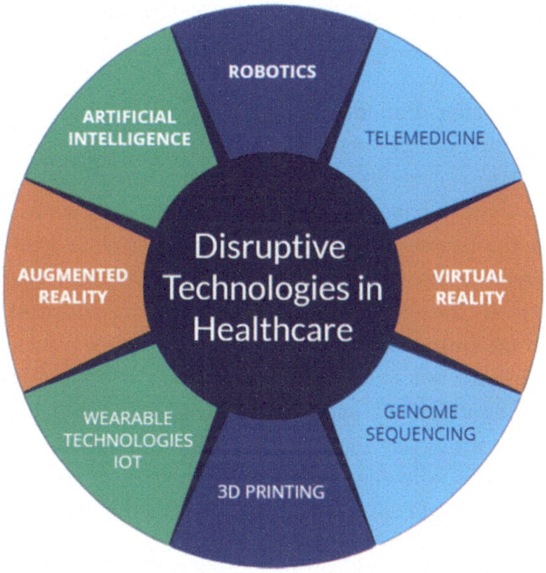

Fig. 1 Different disruptive technologies in healthcare

(AI), telemedicine, blockchain, telepresence robots, and others, have the potential to revolutionise healthcare, particularly in resource-constrained situations in developing nations.

AI can be utilised to enhance diagnostics, individualise treatment, streamline administrative tasks, and predict disease outbreaks. For instance, AI algorithms are currently being used to interpret radiology images with accuracy comparable to or exceeding that of human radiologists. This could be invaluable in regions with a shortage of such specialists. AI is one of the most transformative technologies in the healthcare industry (Nagar et al. 2021a; Mbunge et al. 2021; Jo 2023; Herencsar 2023). According to a 2023 report by the McKinsey Global Institute, AI has the potential to add between $3.5 and $5.8 trillion annually to a variety of industries, with healthcare being one of the primary beneficiaries.

Telemedicine has become crucial for addressing healthcare disparities, particularly in underserved and remote areas (Putrino et al. 2023; Pathania et al. 2022; Ray et al. 2022; Chaudhry 2020). The WHO's 2022 report on digital health emphasises how telemedicine can overcome geographical barriers by facilitating remote consultation, diagnosis, and treatment. This technology can be instrumental in developing nations with large rural populations and inadequate healthcare infrastructure.

Blockchain is frequently associated with financial transactions, but it also has great potential in healthcare (Bass et al. 2021; Biesecker and Biesecker 2019; Huang and Foysal 2021; Kunchur et al. 2021; Singh et al. 2023; Berseneva et al. 2023). The decentralised and secure nature of blockchain can enhance patient data security, allow for the secure sharing of health records, and increase supply chain transparency. BIS Research predicts that the global blockchain in the healthcare market will reach $5.61 billion by 2025, demonstrating its growing significance.

Telepresence robots may be one of the most promising disruptive technologies in healthcare. These devices, which enable healthcare providers to interact with patients remotely, have the potential to be a game-changer in addressing workforce shortages and improving access to care. Telepresence robots can assist with chronic disease management, mental health care, and surgery. Meticulous Research projects that the telehealth market, which includes telepresence, will grow at a compound annual growth rate (CAGR) of 23.0% between 2022 and 2027, reaching $20.25 billion by 2027. Genome sequencing technologies, such as next-generation sequencing (NGS), enable us to comprehend the molecular basis of disease. These technologies allow personalised medicine by identifying disease-causing genetic mutations. For instance, Illumina's genome sequencing machines are widely used in clinical and research settings to understand genetic diseases.

Wearable devices (Iqbal 2021; Wearable Device for Health Monitor 2020; Surantha et al. 2021; Srivastav 2021; Morais et al. 2023; ThameezDeen and Sudhakaran 2022) can be worn on the body and typically contain intelligent sensors and Internet connectivity. They can monitor the health and fitness of the individual wearing them. Fitbit devices, smartwatches that track heart rate and activity levels, and glucose monitoring devices for people with diabetes are some examples.

Using 3D printing technology, physical objects can be created from a digital model (Sheng 2022; Pacheco et al. 2023; Li and Xiong 2022; Saunders 2022). It has been used in healthcare to develop prosthetics, customised implants, and even synthetic skin. Companies such as Organovo are experimenting with 'bio-printed' organs created via 3D printing.

Virtual reality (VR) technology is increasingly employed in healthcare (Augmented and Virtual Reality Environments for Healthcare 2020; Emmelkamp and Meyerbröker 2021; Rogozovs and Meirans 2020) for therapeutic and educational purposes. The use of VR therapy to treat post-traumatic stress disorder (PTSD) and anxiety disorders has shown promise. In addition, virtual reality is used to create realistic simulations for medical training, allowing students to practice procedures in a safe, supervised environment. Medical training and education are utilising augmented reality, which superimposes digital information onto the physical world. It enhances the learning experience by allowing medical students to practice procedures on virtual patients or models.

Despite the enormous potential of these technologies, implementing them in developing nations is not without obstacles. Significant obstacles must be overcome, including deficient digital infrastructure, low digital literacy rates, regulatory hurdles, and data privacy and security concerns. In addition, to ensure that these technologies do not exacerbate existing inequalities, it is essential to adopt a health equity approach when deploying them, ensuring they are accessible, affordable, and relevant to the populations they serve.

Moreover, disruptive technologies can improve healthcare access and delivery, but they are not a silver bullet. They must be integrated into broader health system strengthening efforts, complementing, and enhancing the human touch that is so integral to healthcare rather than replacing it.

Each of these technologies exemplifies how disruptive innovation has the potential to revolutionise healthcare delivery. By leveraging these technologies, we can make healthcare more accessible, efficient, individualised, and cost-effective, especially in developing nations with the greatest need for such innovation. The following sections will examine the potential, challenges, and applications of telepresence robots for transforming healthcare in developing countries. As we delve deeper into the use of telepresence robots (Naseer et al. 2023; Anupama et al. 2021; Naseer et al. 2023a, 2023b; Harikrishnan et al. 2020; Altalbe et al. 2023, 2023) in the subsequent sections, we will examine these challenges and opportunities in greater detail, providing insights into how this technology can be utilised to improve healthcare in developing nations. The lessons learned can also be applied to adopting other disruptive technologies, paving the way for a more equitable and efficient healthcare system.

2.1 Potential for Transformation in Healthcare

Disruptive technologies offer unprecedented opportunities to reshape care delivery, enhance patient outcomes, and reduce costs. Below is the detailed investigation of how these technologies could radically alter the healthcare industry.

Access to Care Democratisation: Disruptive technologies can democratise healthcare by increasing access. Telemedicine and telepresence robots, for instance, enable remote patient monitoring and consultation, thereby reaching rural or underserved patients. This could revolutionise healthcare in developing nations with limited medical professionals and facilities access.

Improving Capabilities for Diagnosis and Treatment: Artificial intelligence and machine learning algorithms can analyse vast amounts of data, identifying patterns and making predictions that would be impossible for humans. This could improve diagnostic accuracy, disease progression prediction, and individualised treatment. Similarly, genome sequencing could enable precision medicine by facilitating the development of treatments based on an individual's genetic makeup.

Enhancing Patient Engagement: Technologies such as wearable devices and mobile health applications enable patients to manage their health actively. Patients can monitor their health metrics, adhere to medication schedules, and adopt healthier lifestyles due to the real-time feedback they receive. This could be especially useful in managing chronic diseases necessitating ongoing self-management.

Streamlining Health Systems: Disruptive technologies have the potential to streamline health systems, thereby enhancing efficiency and lowering costs. AI can automate administrative tasks such as scheduling, billing, and record maintenance, allowing healthcare providers more time to focus on patient care. Blockchain could facilitate the secure and transparent exchange of health records, streamlining coordination among healthcare providers and minimising errors.

Research and Innovation Facilitation: Disruptive technologies can accelerate medical research and innovation. AI can analyse vast datasets and generate research-guiding insights. 3D printing can potentially create customised medical devices, revolutionise prosthetics, and even bioprint organs.

Enhancing Health Monitoring and Response: Artificial intelligence and big data analytics can improve disease surveillance by providing real-time insights into disease outbreaks and facilitating a swift response. This could be especially important in managing pandemics and other public health emergencies.

Despite the immense potential of disruptive technologies to transform healthcare, it is important to note that their adoption comes with obstacles, such as data privacy and security concerns, ethical considerations, and the risk of aggravating health inequalities. For these technologies to reach their full potential, they must be implemented responsibly, fairly, and in a manner that respects patient rights. Additionally, efforts to improve the health system must go hand in hand with technological innovation to guarantee that everyone, including the most vulnerable and marginalised populations, can benefit from these technologies. The following sections will examine these issues in greater depth, using telepresence robots as an example.

2.2 Current Global Trends and Applications

Due to the introduction and widespread adoption of disruptive technologies, the healthcare landscape is undergoing rapid change. Different global trends and applications are currently shaping the future of healthcare, with its description and examples explained in Table 1.

Table 1 Trend description with examples

Trend/application	Description	Examples
AI-powered predictive analytics	Healthcare systems use AI to forecast patient outcomes, disease progression, and potential healthcare crises	DeepMind's AI system (Lu 2019) that predicts acute kidney injury up to 48 h in advance
Expansion of telehealth	Telehealth has become an essential service due to the COVID-19 pandemic and is used for various purposes such as routine checkups to mental health counselling	Telehealth platforms such as Teladoc and Doctor On Demand (Whole-Person Care Delivered Virtually 2023)
Telepresence robots for remote care	Telepresence robots are used for remote care, particularly in rural and underserved areas	InTouch Health's telepresence robots (Virtual Care Solutions for Hospitals Health Systems 2023)
Personalised medicine through genomics	Genomic medicine is used to facilitate personalised treatment strategies for disease prevention, diagnosis, and treatment	Companies like 23andMe (DNA Genetic Testing For Ancestry Traits—23ans Me International 2023) and AncestryDNA (AncestryDNA® 2023) that provide personal genomic information
Wearable devices for continuous monitoring	Wearable health monitoring devices are used for real-time monitoring of various health metrics	Devices such as Fitbit watches (Offizielle Website von Fitbit für Aktivitäts-Tracker und mehr 2023) and Apple Watch ("Watch" 2023)
3D printing for customized medical solutions	3D printing is used in healthcare for the creation of customised prosthetics, surgical instruments, and organ tissues	Companies like Formlabs ("High Resolution SLA and SLSD Printers for Professionals" 2023) that produce 3D printers for medical applications
Data-driven public health	Big data and AI are used to monitor and forecast public health trends	IoT-enabled medical equipment, such as connected insulin pens and remote patient monitoring tools by Propeller Health ("Home" 2023)
Virtual reality (VR) & augmented reality (AR) in treatment and training	VR is used in healthcare treatment and training methods, including pain management and mental health therapy	Companies like Amelia, formerly Psious VR (VR 2023) that provide VR for mental health treatments
Nanotechnology for targeted treatments	Nanotechnology is used to deliver drugs directly to cancer cells	Nanobiotix's ("Building new cancer therapies atom by atom | Nanobiotix" 2023) NBTXR3 for treatment of various cancers
Robot-assisted surgery	Surgeon-guided surgical robots are used to perform complex procedures	Intuitive Surgical's da Vinci Surgical System (Intuitive | Maker of Da Vinci Ion Robotic Systems 2023)
Healthcare Analytics	Healthcare analytics are used to gain insights into treatment outcomes, patient satisfaction, and operational efficiency	Companies like IBM Watson Health (IBM Watson Health is now Merative 2023)

These global trends demonstrate the transformative potential of disruptive healthcare technologies. However, it is essential to remember that their successful implementation requires overcoming obstacles such as the digital divide, privacy concerns, and regulatory barriers. As we examine telepresence robots in the subsequent sections, we will delve deeper into these obstacles and opportunities.

3 Telepresence Robots: Bridging the Healthcare Gap

Telepresence robots are innovative tools with the potential to bridge significant gaps in healthcare delivery, especially in regions with limited access to quality care. By bringing medical professionals to virtually any location, these robots can assist in overcoming geographical isolation, a lack of healthcare professionals, and infectious disease-related health risks.

3.1 Definition and Explanation of Telepresence Robots

Telepresence robots are remote-controlled, wheeled devices with a display that enables video chat and conferencing, providing the controller a virtual presence at the robot's location. These robots surpass traditional video conferencing by providing an experience that is more interactive and immersive. They allow the controller to remotely navigate the environment, interact with people, and perform tasks, simulating the experience of being physically present.

Telepresence robots result from numerous technological developments, including robotics, artificial intelligence, information and communication technology (ICT), and the Internet of Things. They represent the merging of physical and digital spaces, resulting in a hybrid reality that facilitates remote interaction and collaboration.

Telepresence robots can play a transformative role in the healthcare industry, particularly in contexts with significant barriers to access, such as geographic isolation, a shortage of healthcare providers, and situations requiring isolation due to infectious diseases. By enabling healthcare professionals to interact with patients remotely, these robots can provide access to quality care regardless of geographic location.

3.2 Technological Features of Telepresence Robots

Telepresence robots are outfitted with numerous technological features that make them suitable for healthcare applications.

- Mobility: Telepresence robots are typically mobile, equipped with wheels or tracks for navigating various environments. They can be moved remotely around a hospital, clinic, or patient's home, allowing healthcare professionals to interact with multiple patients without being physically present.
- Video Conferencing: Telepresence robots are equipped with a screen, a camera, and a microphone for video conferencing. This enables healthcare providers to see, hear, and communicate in real time with patients.
- Sensors and Cameras: These robots are frequently outfitted with various environmental sensors and cameras. For instance, they may contain depth sensors for navigation, cameras for video conferencing, and possibly additional sensors for measuring vital signs or other health parameters.
- Autonomous Navigation: Some telepresence robots include autonomous navigation capabilities. This means they can navigate an environment autonomously, avoiding obstacles and moving to predetermined locations without human intervention.
- Integration with Medical Equipment Telepresence robots may be integrated with various medical equipment, allowing healthcare professionals to monitor patients' health remotely. This may include devices for measuring vital signs, imaging equipment, and even surgical instruments for remote procedures.

3.3 Role in Healthcare Delivery

Telepresence robots can play various roles in healthcare delivery, providing solutions to a number of the challenges faced by global healthcare systems. Access to specialists is limited in many parts of the world, particularly in rural and remote areas. Using telepresence robots, specialists can provide consultations and even perform procedures remotely, bridging this gap. This improves access to care and reduces the distance that patients must travel for specialist appointments. Numerous nations face a shortage of healthcare professionals, a problem that is expected to worsen as the world's population ages. Telepresence robots can effectively increase the capacity of the healthcare workforce by allowing healthcare providers to care for patients remotely, thereby addressing this issue. As the global population ages, there is a growing demand for solutions that enable older adults to age in place, i.e., to remain in their homes while receiving the necessary care. Telepresence robots can assist in this endeavour by providing remote monitoring and care, reducing the need for hospitalisation or institutional care.

Telepresence robots can play a crucial role in situations with a risk of infection, such as during an outbreak of an infectious disease. They can minimise the risk of

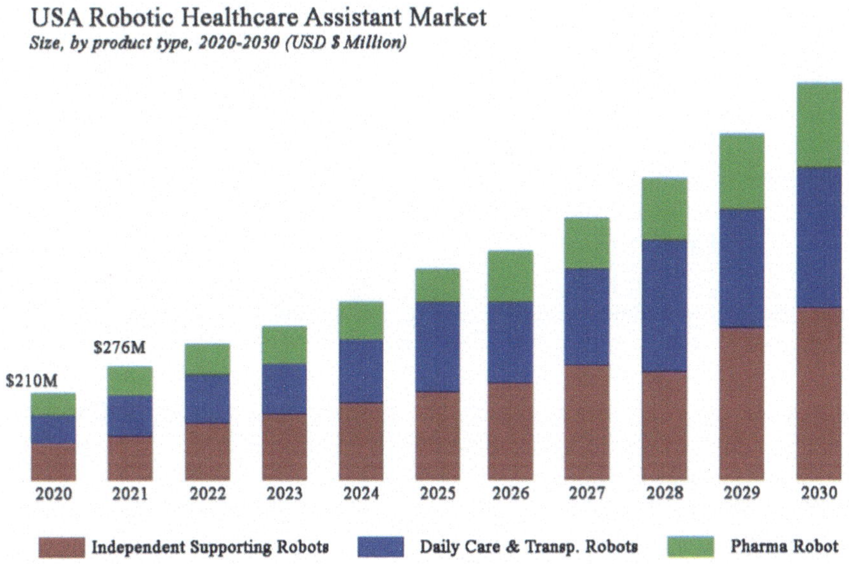

Fig. 2 Prediction of robotics usage by CAGR

transmission by reducing the need for healthcare providers to be physically present with a patient. During the COVID-19 pandemic, telepresence robots were used to communicate with patients in isolation, deliver food and medicine, and even perform hospital cleaning tasks. To enhance healthcare education and training, telepresence robots may also be employed for educational and training purposes. They can allow medical students and professionals to remotely observe and participate in patient care, thereby enhancing their educational opportunities. Using a telepresence robot, for instance, a specialist could guide a less experienced provider through a procedure while providing real-time instruction and feedback. Increasingly, it is acknowledged that healthcare is a team effort involving professionals from various fields. Telepresence robots can facilitate this collaboration by allowing remote team members to participate in patient consultations and discussions.

The use of telepresence robots in healthcare has produced promising results, particularly in enhancing remote access to care, according to a study by the National Institute of Health published in 2022. Nonetheless, the study identifies the need for additional research into the benefits and limitations of this technology. The WHO recognises the potential of telepresence robots in healthcare, especially given the global shortage of healthcare professionals. In its "Global Strategy on Human Resources for Health: Workforce 2030" report, the WHO emphasises the need for innovative solutions, such as telepresence robots, to combat this problem.

Telepresence robots are a promising technology that can significantly revolutionise healthcare delivery. By enabling remote interaction and collaboration, they can help bridge the healthcare gap, especially in settings with limited access to care. However, the successful implementation of these robots in healthcare will necessitate addressing technical issues, user acceptance, and regulatory concerns, among others. In addition, it will be crucial to ensure that these robots do not exacerbate existing health disparities but rather contributes to more equitable access to healthcare.

The global market for robotic nurse assistants was anticipated to be worth USD 1 billion in 2022. As shown in Fig. 2, it is expected to increase at a CAGR of 14.8% from 2023 to 2030 (Robotic Nurse Assistant Market Size & Growth Report 2030). The rising global elderly population drives this growth, increasing the demand for robotic assistance in daily care activities. By 2030, according to the WHO, one out of every six people will be over 60. The global senior population is projected to double by 2050, reaching 4.1 billion people.

Additionally, between 2020 and 2050, the population of people aged 80 and older is projected to triple, reaching 426 million. An additional factor contributing to the growth of the market for robotic nurse assistants is the increase in research and development expenditures aimed at developing technologically advanced robots for healthcare settings. This is anticipated to increase the future demand for robotic nursing.

4 Benefits of Telepresence Robots in Healthcare

Integrating advanced robotics, AI, and communication technologies into telepresence robots redefines healthcare delivery boundaries. They represent a significant advancement in telemedicine, elevating remote care by enabling real-time interaction between patients and healthcare professionals, regardless of their geographic location. The numerous advantages of telepresence robots in healthcare include real-time patient interaction and monitoring, increased healthcare access, improved healthcare quality and efficiency, and a positive effect on patient outcomes.

4.1 Real-Time Patient Interaction and Monitoring

The ability to facilitate real-time communication between healthcare providers and patients is one of the most immediate benefits of telepresence robots in healthcare. These robots enable more interaction than conventional telemedicine platforms by providing a physical proxy for the provider at the patient's location.

This interaction's real-time nature is crucial for multiple reasons. First, it enables healthcare providers to respond quickly to changes in a patient's condition, which is vital in acute care settings and medical emergencies. Second, real-time interaction can improve the patient-provider relationship by enabling more engaging and personalised communication. Seeing the provider's face and hearing their voice can provide patients with comfort and foster a sense of connection, which can be especially important for isolated or remote individuals.

Telepresence robots can support real-time patient monitoring in addition to facilitating real-time communication. Depending on their capabilities and features, these robots can be outfitted with various medical devices and sensors to measure vital signs, conduct diagnostic tests, and even administer treatments. This information can be transmitted in real-time to the healthcare provider, enabling them to continuously monitor the patient's condition and adjust the treatment plan as necessary.

4.2 Potential for Increasing Healthcare Access

Telepresence robots have substantial potential to expand access to healthcare (Capello 2015), particularly for individuals in remote or underserved areas. By removing geographical barriers, these robots can provide healthcare services to individuals who would otherwise have limited or no access due to distance, lack of transportation, or a lack of local healthcare providers.

Patients in rural areas can access specialist care using telepresence robots, which is frequently concentrated in urban areas or academic medical centres. This can be especially advantageous for patients with complex or chronic conditions requiring ongoing speciality care.

In addition, telepresence robots can support home-based care and ageing in place, thereby increasing access to healthcare for older adults and individuals with limited mobility. By providing remote monitoring and care, these robots can allow individuals to receive the necessary care in the comfort of their own homes, thereby reducing the need for hospitalisation or institutional care.

Additionally, telepresence robots can assist in addressing healthcare workforce shortages, a global issue especially severe in developing nations and rural areas. These robots can increase the capacity of the healthcare workforce by allowing healthcare professionals to care for patients remotely.

4.3 Enhancement of Healthcare Quality and Efficiency

Telepresence robots can significantly contribute to the improvement of healthcare quality and productivity. They can facilitate timely access to care, facilitate patient-centred communication, and support the evidence-based practice by collecting and analysing data in real time.

Access to care promptly is a crucial determinant of healthcare quality. By facilitating instantaneous communication between patients and healthcare providers, telepresence robots can reduce care delays that can result in adverse outcomes. This is especially crucial in emergencies, where a prompt response can mean the difference between life and death.

Communication centred on the patient, involving patients as active participants in their care, is an additional crucial aspect of healthcare quality. Telepresence robots can facilitate face-to-face communication between patients and providers in real time. This can improve patients' comprehension of their condition and treatment, encourage shared decision-making, and boost patient satisfaction.

In addition, telepresence robots can support evidence-based practice (Naseer et al. 2023), an approach to care that integrates individual clinical expertise with the best external clinical evidence derived from systematic research. These robots can collect a vast array of patient data in real-time, which can be used to monitor the efficacy of treatments, identify patterns and trends, and inform clinical decisions.

Telepresence robots can help optimise the use of healthcare resources from an efficiency standpoint. These robots can contribute to cost savings by reducing the demand for patient transport and hospitalisation. They can also increase the efficiency of healthcare providers by allowing them to treat patients in multiple locations without the need for travel.

4.4 Impact on Patient Outcomes

Telepresence robots share the ultimate objective of all healthcare interventions: to enhance patient outcomes. These robots can positively influence patient outcomes by facilitating real-time patient interaction and monitoring, expanding access to care, and improving healthcare quality and efficiency.

For instance, timely access to care via telepresence robots can lead to earlier diagnosis and treatment, improving the prognosis for various conditions. Patients with complex or chronic conditions frequently require specialised knowledge and skills for effective management and can experience improved outcomes with increased access to specialised care.

Enhanced patient-provider communication can result in enhanced disease understanding and management, greater adherence to treatment plans, and improved self-care, all of which can contribute to improved health outcomes. In addition, real-time patient monitoring enables quick responses to changes in a patient's condition, thereby preventing complications and enhancing the efficacy of treatments. The influence of telepresence robots on patient outcomes is an expanding field of study with promising findings. Specifically, a 2022 study published in the Journal of Telemedicine and Telecare found that the use of telepresence robots in intensive care units reduced mortality rates and length of hospital stay, as depicted in Fig. 3 for the healthcare environment.

5 Case Studies: Telepresence Robots in Action

Globally, telepresence robots play a transformative role in healthcare delivery. Their utility is particularly striking in developing nations, where healthcare disparities are most pronounced. The following case studies illustrate the implementation and impact of telepresence robots in various healthcare settings in developing countries.

5.1 Case Study 1: Telepresence Robots in Rural India

India's vast rural areas present significant barriers to healthcare access (N. H. M. 2014). Due to the high patient-to-doctor ratio and the urban location of most specialists, it is difficult for rural patients to receive quality care.

The implementation of telepresence robots in several rural healthcare facilities in India has demonstrated remarkable promise. In one instance, a healthcare facility in a remote Rajasthan village utilised a telepresence robot to facilitate consultations with specialists in Jaipur and Delhi. Equipped with a high-definition camera and monitor, the robot enables physicians to interact with patients in real time, conduct physical examinations with the assistance of on-site nurses, and even direct medical procedures. Utilising the robot has significantly reduced the distance patients must travel for consultations with specialists.

Impact:

1. The telepresence robot has allowed hundreds of patients to receive care from specialists without leaving their village.
2. Patients no longer have to incur expensive and time-consuming travel expenses to reach urban areas for consultations.
3. Patients' health outcomes have improved because the telepresence robot facilitated early diagnosis and prompt treatment.

5.2 Case Study 2: Telepresence Robots in Brazil's Amazon Rainforest

Providing healthcare in the vast and difficult-to-navigate Amazon Rainforest presents a formidable challenge (Melo et al. 2022). Several remote clinics in the Amazon have deployed telepresence robots to bridge this healthcare gap.

These robots, outfitted with various medical devices, enable urban-based healthcare professionals to remotely conduct medical consultations, monitor patients' health, and administer treatments. The robots are also employed to provide health education to local communities, thereby assisting in preventing and managing common health conditions.

Impact:

1. Expanded Healthcare Access: Telepresence robots have made healthcare services accessible to previously inaccessible communities.
2. Telepresence robots have enabled remote communities to receive health education, improving health practices and disease prevention.
3. Enhanced patient monitoring It is now possible to monitor patients continuously, allowing for timely interventions and improved management of chronic conditions.

5.3 Case Study 3: Telepresence Robots in Kenyan Hospitals

In Kenya, where there is a severe shortage of healthcare professionals, particularly specialists, telepresence robots make a substantial difference. In several hospitals (K. M. o. Health 2014), these robots are used to connect patients with specialists in Nairobi and other metropolitan areas.

These robots enable specialists to conduct virtual rounds, consult with on-site medical personnel, and monitor patients' conditions in real time. In some cases, they have

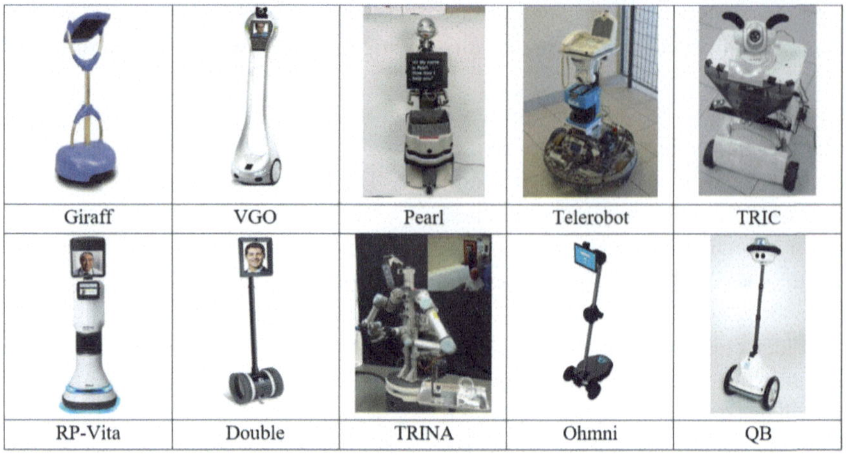

Fig. 3 Different telepresence robot in healthcare (Casiddu et al. 2015; VGo robotic telepresence for healthcare, education and business 2023; Koceska et al. 2017; Laniel et al. 2021; Tsai et al. 2007; RP-Vita Telepresence Robot | InTouch Vita | Vita Reviews 2023; Double Robotics - Telepresence Robot for the Hybrid Office 2023; Human-Inspired Robotics Lab » Tele-Robotic Intelligent Nursing Assistant (TRINA) 2023; Ohmni SuperCam 2023; Anybots | Telepresence Robots 2023)

been utilised to facilitate remote surgical procedures, with the remote specialist guiding the on-site surgeon during complex operations.

Impact:

1. Telepresence robots have assisted in mitigating the effects of workforce shortages by extending the reach of existing healthcare professionals.
2. The ability to consult with specialists has significantly improved the quality of care in these hospitals.
3. Telepresence robots have reduced the need to refer patients to urban centres, resulting in cost savings for both patients and the healthcare system.

5.4 Case Study 4: Telepresence Robots in Remote Areas of the Philippines

Geography presents the Philippines, an archipelago of over 7,000 islands, with unique healthcare delivery challenges (Marcelo 2019). Significant obstacles include the distance between islands, the lack of infrastructure, and the scarcity of healthcare professionals in remote areas.

Several outlying healthcare facilities in the Philippines have implemented telepresence robots. With telecommunication capabilities and medical sensors, these robots enable healthcare professionals in urban hospitals to care for patients in these remote areas.

Impact:

1. Bridging Geographical Gaps: Telepresence robots have helped bridge geographical gaps, allowing remote communities to receive much-needed healthcare services.
2. In emergencies, robots have proven invaluable, providing immediate care and stabilisation until patients can be transported to better-equipped facilities.
3. The early intervention and better access to care that the robots have made possible have improved healthcare outcomes for patients in these remote areas.

5.5 Case Study 5: Telepresence Robots in Paediatric Care in South Africa

In South Africa, where access to paediatric specialists is restricted, especially in rural areas, telepresence robots provide specialised paediatric care. Using these robots, a children's hospital in Cape Town connects with rural clinics to provide consultations, diagnosis, and treatment guidance for complex paediatric cases.

The robots enable paediatric specialists to interact with patients, perform examinations with the assistance of local nurses, and provide real-time guidance for treatment procedures.

Impact:

1. Access to Specialized Paediatric Care The use of telepresence robots has facilitated rural children's access to specialised paediatric care.
2. Through their interactions with the specialists, the local healthcare providers in these rural clinics have gained valuable knowledge and skills.
3. Improved Child Health Outcomes In these rural areas, telepresence robots have provided prompt and specialised care, which has improved child health outcomes.

Table 2 Summary of Case Studies

Case study	Country	Application	Impact
Rural healthcare centres	India	Remote consultations with specialists	Increased access to specialist care, reduced travel costs and time, improved health outcomes
Amazon rainforest clinics	Brazil	Remote consultations, health education, patient monitoring	Expanded healthcare access, enhanced health education, improved patient monitoring
Hospitals	Kenya	Remote consultations with specialists, remote surgical procedures	Addressed workforce shortages, enhanced quality of care, and reduced referral costs
Remote healthcare facilities	Philippines	Remote consultations, emergency response	Bridging geographical gaps, improved emergency response, improved healthcare outcomes
Paediatric care	South Africa	Remote consultations with paediatric specialists	Access to specialised paediatric care, capacity building, improved child health outcomes

The detail case studies illustrated in Table 2 with the transformative potential of telepresence robots in developing nations' healthcare delivery. While technological infrastructure, cost, and user acceptance remain obstacles, the benefits in terms of improved access to care, better health outcomes, and cost savings are substantial. As technology advances and becomes more affordable, it is likely that the use of telepresence robots in healthcare will increase, bringing us closer to the goal of universal health coverage.

6 Challenges in the Adoption of Telepresence Robots

Although the potential benefits of telepresence robots in healthcare are substantial, their implementation presents a few difficulties. Multiple obstacles can impede the adoption of these technologies, especially in developing nations. These obstacles include technological and infrastructure requirements, regulatory and policy constraints, societal acceptance and ethical concerns.

6.1 Technological and Infrastructural Requirements

Robots used for telepresence rely on advanced technology and a solid infrastructure. The capabilities for high-definition video conferencing, the navigation and mobility features, and the integration with other medical devices necessitate advanced and dependable technological support.

Internet connectivity availability and dependability are significant obstacles. Practical telepresence robots require high-speed, dependable Internet connections. Internet access may be intermittent, unreliable, or non-existent in many developing nations, particularly in rural or remote areas. In addition, even in regions with Internet access, the bandwidth may not be adequate to support the data-intensive operations of telepresence robots. The availability of a reliable electricity supply is another obstacle. Common in many developing nations, power outages can interfere with the operation of telepresence robots, jeopardising patient care.

Lastly, the complexity of the technology may also present a difficulty. Telepresence robot operation requires a certain level of technical expertise. Healthcare professionals and patients may require training to use these robots effectively, which can be a barrier in areas with low digital literacy.

6.2 Regulatory and Policy Constraints

In addition to regulatory and policy constraints, the adoption of telepresence robots in healthcare can be hindered by other factors. Regulations pertaining to telemedicine vary widely across nations and even within countries, and in many instances, they have not kept pace with technological advances.

The licensing of healthcare providers is a major regulatory issue. In several jurisdictions, healthcare professionals are licensed to practice in particular regions or nations. These regulations may prohibit the use of telepresence robots to provide care across geographic boundaries.

Another regulatory challenge involves patient confidentiality and data security. Telepresence robots collect and transmit sensitive patient data, raising concerns about data protection. This could be a significant barrier to the adoption of telepresence robots in nations where data security regulations are inadequate or non-existent. At the end, reimbursement policies can also be problematic. Telemedicine services are not reimbursed at the same rate as in-person services in many healthcare systems, if they are reimbursed at all. This can discourage healthcare providers' adoption of telepresence robots and other telemedicine technologies.

6.3 Societal Acceptance and Ethical Considerations

In healthcare, societal acceptance of telepresence robots can also present challenges. Patients and healthcare professionals may have reservations regarding the utilisation of these robots. These reservations among patients may result from worries about the impersonal nature of technology, the calibre of robot-provided care, and the privacy of their medical records. Concerns for healthcare providers may include the technical skills required to operate the robots, the possibility of human care being replaced by robots, and the impact on the doctor-patient relationship.

In addition to these concerns, there are also ethical factors to consider. There may be concerns regarding the accessibility of this technology, for instance. Existing health disparities may worsen if only a small portion of the population has access to telepresence robot-delivered care.

Despite these obstacles, the potential benefits of telepresence robots in healthcare are substantial. All stakeholders, including policymakers, healthcare providers, technology developers, and patients, must collaborate to address these challenges. It is possible to overcome these obstacles and realise the full potential of this promising technology with the application of suitable strategies and financial resources.

7 Strategies for Overcoming Challenges

The successful implementation and adoption of telepresence robots in healthcare in developing nations require a proactive and strategic approach to overcome the inherent obstacles. This includes a combination of policy recommendations, infrastructure development strategies, and initiatives for societal engagement.

7.1 Policy Recommendations for Facilitating Technology Adoption

For the adoption of telepresence robots in healthcare, a policy environment that is supportive and enabling is essential. Policymakers must align regulations with the realities of digital health technologies and ensure that these regulations facilitate the adoption of such technologies rather than hinder them.

First, licensing regulations must be reviewed and updated to accommodate the transnational nature of telepresence robot healthcare delivery. This could entail the introduction of reciprocal licensing agreements that permit healthcare providers licensed in one jurisdiction to provide services in another.

Secondly, policymakers must address patient privacy and data security concerns. This could involve the creation of comprehensive data protection laws that outline the responsibilities of various parties in collecting, storing, and transmitting patient data. These laws should also provide clear guidelines for using digital health technologies with informed consent.

Thirdly, reimbursement policies for the use of telepresence robots in healthcare should be revised. This could involve extending the definition of reimbursable services to include services provided by telepresence robots and ensuring that the reimbursement rates for these services are proportional to their value.

7.2 Infrastructure Development Strategies

Infrastructure development is essential for facilitating the adoption of telepresence robots in healthcare. This involves both the development of technological infrastructure and human capacity.

Regarding technological infrastructure, efforts should be made to increase internet access in underserved areas. This could involve investing in broadband infrastructure and promoting public–private partnerships to leverage the resources and expertise of the private sector. To reach remote and difficult-to-reach areas, policymakers should also investigate alternative connectivity solutions, such as satellite Internet and mobile data networks.

A reliable source of electricity is another crucial infrastructure requirement. This could involve investments in grid expansion and upgrade and the promotion of off-grid solutions, such as solar power, in regions where grid connectivity is impractical. The training programs should be implemented to equip healthcare professionals and patients with the skills necessary to use telepresence robots. Collaborations with technology providers, who can provide technical training and support, may be required.

7.3 Strategies for Societal Engagement and Acceptance

Successful adoption of telepresence robots in healthcare is contingent on societal acceptance. This involves addressing the concerns of patients and healthcare professionals and applying them in the technology adoption process.

Education and awareness campaigns can play an important role in fostering societal acceptance. These campaigns can educate the public on the advantages of telepresence robots in healthcare, dispel myths and address concerns. Additionally, they can highlight successful case studies to demonstrate the potential of this technology to enhance healthcare outcomes.

Furthermore, ethical considerations must be at the forefront of all engagement strategies. This includes addressing access to care equity issues and ensuring that telepresence robots do not exacerbate existing health disparities.

8 The Future of Healthcare with Telepresence Robots

Telepresence robots can potentially revolutionise the healthcare industry, particularly in developing nations with limited access to quality medical care. The future of healthcare with telepresence robots appears promising, with exciting opportunities for enhancing healthcare accessibility, efficiency, and outcomes. This future is shaped by potential advances in telepresence technology, the anticipated impact on the healthcare landscape, and the role these robots will play in achieving the goals of Society 5.0.

8.1 Potential Future Developments in Telepresence Technology

The capabilities of telepresence robots are expected to expand significantly as technological innovation continues to advance rapidly. Integration of AI into telepresence robots is a possible future development. AI enables these robots to perform more complex tasks (Nagar et al. 2021b; The Lancet Regional Health—Europe 2023; Chaddad et al. 2023; Jankowska et al. 2023; Malik 2023), such as analysing patient data to identify trends or potential health risks, providing personalised health advice, and even carrying out specific medical procedures.

In addition, sensory technology developments could improve telepresence robots' capabilities. For instance, incorporating haptic feedback technology could enable healthcare professionals to 'feel' what the robot 'feels,' thereby enhancing their capacity to perform remote physical examinations or procedures.

Additionally, improvements could be made to the mobility and autonomy of telepresence robots. Future robots will be able to navigate more complex environments, move more naturally, and perform tasks autonomously without needing constant remote control.

8.2 Impact on the Healthcare Landscape

The widespread use of telepresence robots in healthcare could profoundly affect the landscape of healthcare. By enabling remote healthcare delivery, these robots could significantly expand access to healthcare, especially in underserved areas. This could alleviate the strain on overburdened healthcare facilities, reduce waiting times, and provide more timely and proactive healthcare delivery.

Incorporating telepresence robots could also improve the effectiveness of healthcare delivery. These robots could allow healthcare professionals to focus on more complex tasks and patient interactions by performing specific tasks. Moreover, telepresence robots could facilitate more individualised and preventive medical care through real-time monitoring and data analysis.

However, the emergence of telepresence robots may also present obstacles. It could disrupt current healthcare practices and necessitate substantial healthcare policy, infrastructure, and workforce training modifications. In addition, it raises ethical and social concerns, including the potential impact on the doctor-patient relationship, the confidentiality of patient data, and the equitable distribution of healthcare resources.

8.3 Role in Achieving the Goals of Society 5.0

Society 5.0, a Japanese concept, envisions a human-centred society that integrates cyberspace and physical space to address social issues and enhance the quality of life. In healthcare, telepresence robots closely align with Society 5.0's objectives. Telepresence robots can help expand access to high-quality healthcare regardless of location by enabling remote healthcare delivery. This is consistent with the Society 5.0 vision of a society where all individuals have access to the services necessary to live a fulfilling life.

Telepresence robots can contribute to creating a more personalised and preventative healthcare model by integrating AI and data analysis. This is consistent with the Society 5.0 vision of a society that uses data and technology to meet individual needs and prevent problems beforehand. Telepresence robots can contribute to developing a more sustainable healthcare system by enhancing healthcare efficiency and reducing the workload of healthcare professionals. This is consistent with the Society 5.0 vision of a society that balances economic development and the resolution of social issues, including the sustainability of public services.

With disruptive technologies such as telepresence robots, the future of healthcare promises increased access, improved quality, and increased efficiency. In a world increasingly characterised by digital integration, these technologies align well with Society 5.0's goals of promoting a human-centred society where everyone can access quality healthcare.

To reach this future, however, requires ongoing effort, collaboration, and creativity. It is essential to focus on developing technologies and creating an environment that facilitates their adoption. Adopting disruptive technologies is not an end but a means to the ultimate objective of healthcare transformation: a system that is equitable, patient-centred, and able to provide high-quality care to all.

As we embark on this exciting journey, let us proceed with optimism, resolve, and a shared commitment to leveraging technology to better healthcare, especially in developing nations. The path ahead may be difficult, but the potential rewards—a transformed healthcare landscape that ensures the health and well-being of all—make the effort worthwhile.

References

"AncestryDNA® | DNA Tests for Ethnicity & Genealogy DNA Test." Ancestry® | Family Tree, Genealogy & Family History Records. https://www.ancestry.com/dna/ (accessed Aug. 4, 2023).

"Anybots | Telepresence Robots." Telepresence Robots | Remote Presence Robots , Virtual Presence Robots, Telebots. https://telepresencerobots.com/anybots/ (accessed Aug. 4, 2023).

"Augmented and Virtual Reality Environments for Healthcare," Brainiacs Journal of Brain Imaging and Computer Science, vol. 1, no. 1, 2020. https://doi.org/10.48085/gcf086af4.

"Building new cancer therapies atom by atom | Nanobiotix." Building new cancer therapies atom by atom | Nanobiotix. https://www.nanobiotix.com/ (accessed Aug. 4, 2023).

"DNA Genetic Testing For Ancestry & Traits - 23andMe International." DNA Genetic Testing For Ancestry & Traits - 23andMe International. https://www.23andme.com/ (accessed Aug. 4, 2023).

"Double Robotics - Telepresence Robot for the Hybrid Office." Double Robotics - Telepresence Robot for the Hybrid Office. https://www.doublerobotics.com/ (accessed Aug. 4, 2023).

"High Resolution SLA and SLS 3D Printers for Professionals." Formlabs. https://formlabs.com/asia/ (accessed Aug. 4, 2023).

"Home." Propeller Health. https://propellerhealth.com/ (accessed Aug. 4, 2023).

"Human-Inspired Robotics Lab » Tele-Robotic Intelligent Nursing Assistant (TRINA)." WPI Labs – Just another WPI Sites site. http://labs.wpi.edu/hiro/project-portfolio/tele-robotic-intelligent-nursing-assistant-trina/ (accessed Aug. 4, 2023).

"IBM Watson Health is now Merative." IBM - Deutschland | IBM. https://www.ibm.com/watson-health/merative-divestiture (accessed Aug. 4, 2023).

"Offizielle Website von Fitbit für Aktivitäts-Tracker und mehr." Offizielle Website von Fitbit für Aktivitäts-Tracker und mehr. https://www.fitbit.com/ (accessed Aug. 4, 2023).

"Ohmni SuperCam." Telepresence Robots | Remote Presence Robots , Virtual Presence Robots, Telebots. https://telepresencerobots.com/robots/ohmnilabs-ohmni-supercam/ (accessed Aug. 4, 2023).

"RP-Vita Telepresence Robot | InTouch Vita | Vita Reviews." Telepresence Robots | Remote Presence Robots , Virtual Presence Robots, Telebots. https://telepresencerobots.com/robots/intouch-health-rp-vita/ (accessed Aug. 4, 2023).

"VGo robotic telepresence for healthcare, education and business." VGo robotic telepresence for healthcare, education and business. https://www.vgocom.com/ (accessed Aug. 4, 2023).

"Virtual Care Solutions for Hospitals & Health Systems." Virtual Care Solutions for Hospitals & Health Systems. https://intouchhealth.com/ (accessed Aug. 4, 2023).

"VR Software for Mental Health Professionals' Therapy." Amelia Virtual Care. https://ameliavirtualcare.com/ (accessed Aug. 4, 2023).

"Watch." Apple. https://www.apple.com/watch/ (accessed Aug. 4, 2023).

"Wearable Device for Health Monitor," Int. J. Eng. Adv. Technol., vol. 9, no. 4, p. 595–598, Apr. 2020. Accessed: Aug. 4, 2023. [Online]. Available: https://doi.org/10.35940/ijeat.d7533.049420

"Whole-Person Care Delivered Virtually." Whole-Person Care Delivered Virtually. https://www.teladochealth.com/ (accessed Aug. 4, 2023).

A. A. Altalbe, A. Shahzad, and M. Nasir Khan, "Computing and Implementation of a Controlled Telepresence Robot," Intell. Automat. & Soft Comput., vol. 37, no. 2, p. 1569–1585, 2023. Accessed: Aug. 4, 2023. [Online]. Available: https://doi.org/10.32604/iasc.2023.039124

K. Alsalem, A. Steinmetz, N. Muhammad, D. Frierson, and M. Nashed, "Predicting Life Expectancy at Birth," in 2020 2nd International Conference on Computer and Information Sciences (ICCIS), Sakaka, Saudi Arabia, October 13–15, 2020, pp. 1–7. https://doi.org/10.1109/iccis49240.2020.9257630.

A. Altalbe, A. Shahzad, and M. N. Khan, "Parameterization and Design of Telepresence Robot to Avoid Obstacles," Appl. Sci., vol. 13, no. 4, pp. 2174, Feb. 2023. Accessed: Aug. 4, 2023. [Online]. Available: https://doi.org/10.3390/app13042174

R. Anupama, A. P. Shaji, N. George, S. Shihabudeen, A. Antony, and P. H. Rishikesh, "Telepresence Robot," SSRN, Feb. 2021. https://doi.org/10.2139/ssrn.3857800

J. Bass, D. Metcalf, V. Dhillon, M. Hooper, and A. Cahana, Blockchain in Healthcare. Boca Raton, FL, USA: CRC Press, 2021

E. A. Berseneva, S. V. Umnov, M. S. Umnov, and Z. K. Agamov, "Blockchain technology in healthcare digitalisation," Profilakticheskaya meditsina, vol. 26, no. 4, pp. 95, 2023. Accessed: Aug. 4, 2023. [Online]. Available: https://doi.org/10.17116/profmed20232604195

L. G. Biesecker and B. B. Biesecker, "Genome Sequencing and Individual Responses to Results," in Clinical Genome Sequencing, S. Richards, Ed. Academic Press, 2019, pp. 17–30. https://doi.org/10.1016/b978-0-12-813335-4.00002-7.

F. Capello, "Teleoncology in Developing Countries," in TELe-Health. Cham: Springer International Publishing, 2015, p. 51–61. Accessed: Aug. 4, 2023. [Online]. Available: https://doi.org/10.1007/978-3-319-16378-9_6

N. Casiddu et al., "Robot Interface Design: The Giraff Telepresence Robot for Social Interaction," in Biosystems & Biorobotics. Cham: Springer International Publishing, 2015, p. 499–509. Accessed: Aug. 4, 2023. [Online]. Available: https://doi.org/10.1007/978-3-319-18374-9_46

A. Chaddad, J. Peng, J. Xu, and A. Bouridane, "Survey of Explainable AI Techniques in Healthcare," Sensors, vol. 23, no. 2, pp. 634, Jan. 2023. Accessed: Aug. 4, 2023. [Online]. Available: https://doi.org/10.3390/s23020634

S. Chaudhry, "Appraising Telemedicine," IP Int. J. Comprehensive Adv. Pharmacol., vol. 5, no. 3, p. 138–142, Oct. 2020. Accessed: Aug. 4, 2023. [Online]. Available: https://doi.org/10.18231/j.ijcaap.2020.028

P. M. G. Emmelkamp and K. Meyerbröker, "Virtual Reality Therapy in Mental Health," Annu. Rev. Clin. Psychol., vol. 17, no. 1, p. 495–519, May 2021. Accessed: Aug. 4, 2023. [Online]. Available: https://doi.org/10.1146/annurev-clinpsy-081219-115923

N. Harikrishnan, S. A. Soni, A. M. Alex, V. Menon, and V. C. Nair, "Virtual Interactive Reality Telepresence Robot," SSRN, Feb. 2020. https://doi.org/10.2139/ssrn.3791104

S. M. A. Iqbal, I. Mahgoub, E. Du, M. A. Leavitt, W. Asghar, "Advances in healthcare wearable devices," NPJ Flexible

Electronics, vol. 5, no. 1, Jan. 2021. https://doi.org/10.1038/s41528-021-00107-x.

N. Herencsar, “Smart Consumer Healthcare Technologies,” *IEEE Consum. Electron. Mag.*, vol. 12, no. 4, p. 10–11, Jul. 2023. Accessed: Aug. 4, 2023. [Online]. Available: https://doi.org/10.1109/mce.2023.3271080

G. Huang and A. A. Foysal, “Blockchain in Healthcare,” Technol. Investment, vol. 12, no. 03, p. 168–181, 2021. Accessed: Aug. 4, 2023. [Online]. Available: https://doi.org/10.4236/ti.2021.123010

J. o. Healthcare Engineering, “Retracted: Critical Retrospection of Performance of Emerging Mobile Technologies in Health Data Management,” *J. Healthcare Eng.*, vol. 2023, pp. 1, May 2023. Accessed: Aug. 4, 2023. [Online]. Available: https://doi.org/10.1155/2023/9838676

Intuitive | Maker of Da Vinci & Ion Robotic Systems. https://www.intuitive.com/en-us (accessed Aug. 4, 2023).

A. Jankowska and J. Ngai, "I, Robot: Healthcare decisions made with AI," J. Cardiothoracic Vascular Anesthesia, Jul. 2023. Accessed: Aug. 4, 2023. [Online]. Available: https://doi.org/10.1053/j.jvca.2023.06.045

K. M. o. Health, Kenya HIV and AIDS research agenda: 2014/15–2018/19. Nairobi, Kenya: National AIDS Control Council, 2014.

N. Koceska, S. Koceski, V. Sazdovski, and D. Ciambrone, "Robotic Assistant for Elderly Care – Development and Evaluation," Int. J. Automat. Technol., vol. 11, no. 3, p. 425–432, Apr. 2017. Accessed: Aug. 4, 2023. [Online]. Available: https://doi.org/10.20965/ijat.2017.p0425

P. N. Kunchur, P. Pujar, K. Hiremath, A. Budnimath, S. Bangarashetti, and V. Pandurangi, “Blockchain Technology in Healthcare,” JNNCE J. Eng. Manage., vol. 5, no. 1, pp. 15, Sep. 2021. Accessed: Aug. 4, 2023. [Online]. Available: https://doi.org/10.37314/jjem.2021.050103

S. Laniel, D. Létourneau, F. Grondin, M. Labbé, F. Ferland, and F. Michaud, "Toward enhancing the autonomy of a telepresence mobile robot for remote home care assistance," Paladyn, J. Behav. Robot., vol. 12, no. 1, p. 214–237, Jan. 2021. Accessed: Aug. 4, 2023. [Online]. Available: https://doi.org/10.1515/pjbr-2021-0016

D. Li and Z. Xiong, “Bio-3D Printing,” Chin. J. Mech. Engineering: Additive Manuf. Frontiers, pp. 100027, Jun. 2022. Accessed: Aug. 4, 2023. [Online]. Available: https://doi.org/10.1016/j.cjmeam.2022.100027

D. Lu, "DeepMind's medical AI," New Scientist, vol. 243, no. 3242, pp. 15, Aug. 2019. Accessed: Aug. 4, 2023. [Online]. Available: https://doi.org/10.1016/s0262-4079(19)31464-2

J. Malik, "Development of new ai in healthcare," Int. j. health sci., vol. 7, S1, p. 1590–1599, Jun. 2023. Accessed: Aug. 4, 2023. [Online]. Available: https://doi.org/10.53730/ijhs.v7ns1.14379

A. B. Marcelo, "Telemedicine in developing countries: Perspectives from the Philippines," in Telehealth in the Developing World. CRC Press, 2019, p. 27–33. Accessed: Aug. 4, 2023. [Online]. Available: https://doi.org/10.1201/9781315272917-4

E. Mbunge, B. Muchemwa, S. Jiyane, and J. Batani, “Sensors and healthcare 5.0: transformative shift in virtual care through emerging digital health technologies,” *Global Health J.*, vol. 5, no. 4, p. 169–177, Dec. 2021. Accessed: Aug. 4, 2023. [Online]. Available: https://doi.org/10.1016/j.glohj.2021.11.008

M. de Melo et al., “The health and environment relationship of the peoples of the Amazon rainforest,” Revista Científica Multidisciplinar Núcleo do Conhecimento, vol. 5, no. 01, pp. 05–17, Jan. 2022. https://doi.org/10.32749/nucleodoconhecimento.com.br/health/health-and-environment

D. F. T. Morais, G. Fernandes, G. D. Lima, and J. J. P. C. Rodrigues, “IoT-Based Wearable and Smart Health Device Solutions for Capnography: Analysis and Perspectives,” Electronics, vol. 12, no. 5, pp. 1169, Feb. 2023. Accessed: Aug. 4, 2023. [Online]. Available: https://doi.org/10.3390/electronics12051169

N. H. M. (India), Rural health practitioners: Augmenting sub-center service delivery in Assam. New Delhi: Published on behalf of the National Health Mission by its technical support institution National Health Systems Resource Centre, 2014.

N. Nagar, P. Roy, S. Deswal, P. Pandya, A. Bhardwaj, and P. Naraei, “MEDICARE AI-ASSISTED AI IN HEALTHCARE,” Global Journal of Research Analysis, vol. 8, no. 4, pp. 40–44, 2021a. https://doi.org/10.36106/gjra/6311237

N. Nagar, P. Roy, S. Deswal, P. Pandya, A. Bhardwaj, and P. Naraei, "MEDICARE AI-ASSISTED AI IN HEALTHCARE," GLOBAL J. RES. ANAL., p. 40–44, Jul. 2021. Accessed: Aug. 4, 2023. [Online]. Available: https://doi.org/10.36106/gjra/6311237

F. Naseer, M. N. Nasir Khan, Z. Nawaz, and Q. Awais, “Telepresence Robots and Controlling Techniques in Healthcare System,” Computational Materials and Continua, vol. 74, no. 3, pp. 6623–6639, 2023. https://doi.org/10.32604/cmc.2023.035218.

F. Naseer, M. N. Khan, and A. Altalbe, “Telepresence Robot with DRL Assisted Delay Compensation in IoT-Enabled Sustainable Healthcare Environment,” Sustainability, vol. 15, no. 4, p. 3585, Feb. 2023. https://doi.org/10.3390/su15043585

F. Naseer, M. N. Khan, and A. Altalbe, “Intelligent Time Delay Control of Telepresence Robots Using Novel Deep Reinforcement Learning Algorithm to Interact with Patients,” Applied Sciences, vol. 13, no. 4, p. 2462, Feb. 2023. https://doi.org/10.3390/app13042462

F. Naseer, M. N. Khan, A. Rasool, and N. Ayub, “A novel approach to compensate delay in communication by predicting teleoperator behaviour using deep learning and reinforcement learning to control telepresence robot,” Electronics Letters, vol. 59, no. 9, pp. 1-3, May 2023. https://doi.org/10.1049/ell2.12806

T. J. A. Pacheco, A. C. A. Vieira, L. S. Menezes, V. P. Brandão, N. B. M. Costa, and D. G. d. Souza, “3D printing applied to health,” Research, Soc. Develop., vol. 12, no. 6, Jun. 2023, Art. no. e2512641975. Accessed: Aug. 4, 2023. [Online]. Available: https://doi.org/10.33448/rsd-v12i6.41975

D. Pathania, R. Bunger, and R. Pathak, “Telemedicine,” Int. j. health sci., p. 10726–10732, Jul. 2022. Accessed: Aug. 4, 2023. [Online]. Available: https://doi.org/10.53730/ijhs.v6ns4.10895

D. Putrino, T. Bijlani, J. M. Tosto-Mancuso, and L. Tabacof, “Remote Patient Monitoring,” in Telemedicine for the Musculoskeletal Physical Exam. Cham: Springer International Publishing, 2023, p. 1–15. Accessed: Aug. 4, 2023. [Online]. Available: https://doi.org/10.1007/978-3-031-16873-4_1

R. S. M, P. ThameezDeen, and P. Sudhakaran, “Wearable Health Status Monitoring Device Based on Wireless Sensor Network,” ECS Trans., vol. 107, no. 1, p. 12775–12782, Apr. 2022. Accessed: Aug. 4, 2023. [Online]. Available: https://doi.org/10.1149/10701.12775ecst

K. N. Ray, S. R. Wittman, J. Yabes, L. M. Sabik, A. Hoberman, and A. Mehrotra, “Telemedicine visits to children during the pandemic:Practice-based telemedicine vs. telemedicine-only providers,” Academic Pediatrics, May 2022. Accessed: Aug. 4, 2023. [Online]. Available: https://doi.org/10.1016/j.acap.2022.05.010

"Robotic Nurse Assistant Market Size & Growth Report, 2030." Market Research Reports & Consulting | Grand View Research, Inc. https://www.grandviewresearch.com/industry-analysis/robotic-nurse-assistant-market (accessed Aug. 6, 2023).

N. Rogozovs and I. Meirāns, “VIRTUAL REALITY,” HUMAN. ENVIRONMENT. TECHNOLOGIES. Proc. Students Int. Scientific Practical Conf., no. 24, p. 95–98, Apr. 2020. Accessed: Aug. 4, 2023. [Online]. Available: https://doi.org/10.17770/het2020.24.6757

F. Saunders, “3D Printing Medical Devices,” Amer. Scientist, vol. 110, no. 4, pp. 235, 2022. Accessed: Aug. 4, 2023. [Online]. Available: https://doi.org/10.1511/2022.110.4.235

R. Sheng, "3-D printing in healthcare," in 3D Printing, A. Erman, Ed. Elsevier, 2022, pp. 111–120. https://doi.org/10.1016/b978-0-323-99463-7.00013-x.

R. Singh, H. K. Sharma, T. Choudhury, A. Mor, S. Mohanty, and S. N. Mohanty, "Blockchain for IoT-enabled Healthcare," EAI Endorsed Trans. Pervasive Health Technol., vol. 9, Jun. 2023. Accessed: Aug. 4, 2023. [Online]. Available: https://doi.org/10.4108/eetpht.9.3348

V. Srivastav, "Smart Wearable Device," Int. J. Res. Appl. Sci. Eng. Technol., vol. 9, no. 5, p. 910–917, May 2021. Accessed: Aug. 4, 2023. [Online]. Available: https://doi.org/10.22214/ijraset.2021.34318

N. Surantha, P. Atmaja, David, and M. Wicaksono, "A Review of Wearable Internet-of-Things Device for Healthcare," Procedia Comput. Sci., vol. 179, p. 936–943, 2021. Accessed: Aug. 4, 2023. [Online]. Available: https://doi.org/10.1016/j.procs.2021.01.083

The Lancet Regional Health – Europe, "Embracing generative AI in health care," Lancet Regional Health - Europe, vol. 30, pp. 100677, Jul. 2023. Accessed: Aug. 4, 2023. [Online]. Available: https://doi.org/10.1016/j.lanepe.2023.100677

T.-C. Tsai, Y.-L. Hsu, A.-I. Ma, T. King, and C.-H. Wu, "Developing a Telepresence Robot for Interpersonal Communication with the Elderly in a Home Environment," Telemedicine e-Health, vol. 13, no. 4, p. 407–424, Aug. 2007. Accessed: Aug. 4, 2023. [Online]. Available: https://doi.org/10.1089/tmj.2006.0068

World Bank Group, Digital Government and Open Data Readiness Assessment. Independently Published, 2022.

Blockchain-Based Traceability in the Agricultural Sector: A Case Study on the Adoption of FPO

C. Ganeshkumar, A. Sivakumar, B. Venugopal, and Arokiaraj David

Abstract

Since the advent of the 4th Industrial Revolution technologies, considerable study on technology adoption in agriculture has been lacking. These agribusiness applications span several crops and sub-domains. Since there have been cases of food goods harming human life, traceability has gained relevance. This study aimed to comprehend how blockchain-based traceability technology is applied in farming. This case study-based study looked at the applicability of a company's traceability technology in several agriculture contexts. The consequences of creating favorable circumstances for more advanced technologies were discovered during the investigation using the UTAUT theory.

Keywords

Agribusiness · Case study · Blockchain · FPO · Traceability

1 Introduction

One of the newest information technologies, blockchain technology, offers a variety of uses in many fields and companies. While also being tamper-proof, it aids in transaction transparency. The digital archiving of all transactions allows for decentralized understanding, reference, and authentication of numerous changes in all organizations involved in transactions (Pachayappan et al., 2020). Blockchain technology is a part of the fourth industrial revolution technologies that have helped in the digital transformation of several industries, among the sectors that have the potential to use blockchain technology in agriculture. Blockchain technology is considered a crucial component of the fourth industrial revolution in agriculture, offering a range of benefits to the sector.

One of the primary advantages of blockchain in agriculture is increased transparency. By creating a secure and tamper-proof record of the product's journey from production to consumption, blockchain allows for full product traceability, providing greater transparency and visibility throughout the supply chain. This increased transparency can improve food safety and security, as any issues or concerns can be traced back to their source, allowing for rapid and effective action. Another benefit of blockchain in agriculture is improved efficiency. By reducing the number of intermediaries in the supply chain and streamlining processes, blockchain technology can help to eliminate inefficiencies, reduce costs, and increase productivity. It can also benefit farmers, increasing their control over the supply chain and giving them more direct access to consumers, helping to ensure they receive a fair price for their products (David et al., 2022).

Moreover, blockchain technology can enhance consumer trust, providing a transparent and secure record of a product's journey from farm to table. It can help to build consumer confidence in the quality and authenticity of the products they purchase, leading to increased demand for

C. Ganeshkumar
Associate Professor, University of Hyderabad, Telangana, India

A. Sivakumar
Professor, VIT Business School, Vellore, India
e-mail: sivakumar.a@vit.ac.in

B. Venugopal
Assistant Professor, Indian Institute of Plantation Management, Bengaluru, India

A. David (✉)
Associate Professor, ATMS, SBS Swiss Business School, Ras Al Khaimah, United Arab Emirates
e-mail: mbaarokiaraj@gmail.com

S. Arezki et al. (eds.), *Emerging Disruptive Technologies for Society 5.0 in Developing Countries*, Advances in Science, Technology & Innovation, https://doi.org/10.1007/978-3-031-63701-8_15

agricultural products. Integrating blockchain technology into agriculture can bring significant benefits to the sector, including increased transparency, improved efficiency, and enhanced consumer trust.

Agriculture has a long value chain that starts with the inputs involved in producing or growing a crop or an animal. These inputs transform the production process into products that are further processed for human consumption. Since the inputs directly get incorporated into the product, a key issue is to trace various inputs and outcomes before they transform into processed food for consumption. Food safety is, therefore, a key issue in human safety, resulting in the need for traceability (Ganeshkumar et al., 2022).

Traceability has several uses, including the need for regulatory authorities like the Food Safety Authority to take action in case of an incident involving food consumption. Moreover, the food processors and marketers in the food business are interested in traceability to ensure that the food they market adheres to regulations and is free from contaminants. Consumers are concerned with traceability to know food origins and changes processed food has undergone before they consume it (Panpatte & Ganeshkumar, 2021). Due to the significance and importance of traceability in agriculture, the use of blockchain technology in traceability has grown in its application worldwide (David et al., 2020). It can adopt blockchain technology for traceability at individual and organizational levels. In terms of farmers' organizations, farmers' producer organizations are gaining traction in India. These organizations help in aggregating farmers based on their crops, animals that they grow, or the geographical area they belong to. This consolidation of especially small and marginal farmers helps them to obtain inputs at a better price and sell their produce at a competitive price (Paul et al., 2019). Farmer Producer Organisations is a collective organization that runs like a business entity. It ensures that farmer shareholders get their profit share based on their share capital contribution and the produce they sell through the FPO (Ganeshkumar et al., 2021).

FPOs depend on agritech companies that develop technologies suitable for use in agriculture for their needs. FPOs, or Farmer Producer Organizations, are organizations in India formed by small-scale farmers to improve their bargaining power, market access, and resources such as credit and technology (Ganeshkumar et al., 2023_a). These organizations aim to empower small-scale farmers by providing them with a collective voice and enabling them to negotiate better prices for their products and access services that may be difficult for them to access as individuals. In India, FPOs have been promoted by the government to improve the livelihoods of small-scale farmers and address the challenges they face. They are established under the Companies Act and registered with the Registrar of Companies. FPOs can be involved in various activities, including procurement of inputs, collective marketing of produce, and providing credit and extension services to members. The formation of FPOs has been seen as a positive step towards improving the situation of small-scale farmers in India, as they provide farmers with a platform to negotiate better prices for their products and access resources that may otherwise be difficult to access. However, challenges are also associated with developing FPOs in India, including limited access to finance, technical expertise, and market access. Nevertheless, forming FPOs is seen as an important step towards improving the livelihoods of small-scale farmers in India and empowering them to improve their economic and social status.

Thus, the use of blockchain technology in agriculture requires the presence of these agritech companies that develop applications (Siddhartha et al., 2019). Traceability applications in agriculture require the adoption of this technology. FPOs' technology adoption, therefore, is crucial in ensuring traceability is achieved in agriculture. This study uses a case study to explore the adoption of 4th industrial revolution technology in agriculture with traceability applications in India (Ganeshkumar et al., 2020).

2 Literature Review

Literature on traceability and blockchain technology in agriculture is spread across multiple dimensions. Blockchain technology in agriculture can be used for supply chain management to increase the transparency and traceability of food products. It can improve data management, such as crop yields, weather patterns, and other production data. Decentralized marketplaces for farmers to sell crops directly to consumers. Additionally, it can reduce post-harvest losses by providing better storage and transportation solutions.

Further, to implement smart contracts for efficient contract management and payment processing. One of the dimensions is the study of its applications in different crops. Salah et al. (2019) studied traceability based on blockchain in the soybean supply chain. However, in the case of grapes, (Tescione et al., 2018) used isotopes in grapes rather than blockchain technology for geographic traceability. Cao et al. (2021) studied how a blockchain-based traceability mechanism bettered consumer trust in the beef supply chain (Madaan et al., 2021). Casino et al. (2021) studied the traceability dairy sector and the greenhouse seedling crops, respectively (González-Amarillo et al., 2018). In the case of greenhouse seedling crops, an IOT-based traceability system helped understand a different traceability application through a case study. Thapa et al. (2021) undertook a case study on the ginger traceability system in Nepal. They did similar work on Rice and Textiles (Yakubu et al., 2022, Carrières et al., 2022).

Another dimension of the work on blockchain-based traceability has been its use with other technologies. Blockchain-based traceability refers to using blockchain technology to create a secure and transparent record of a product's journey from production to consumption. This traceability system allows each supply chain step to be recorded and tracked from the farm to the retailer, providing a complete and transparent view of the product's history. The information stored on the blockchain network is secure, tamper-proof, and verifiable, making it an ideal solution for tracking the movement of products through the supply chain. It can greatly improve food safety, as any issues or concerns can be traced back to their source, allowing for rapid and effective action (Ganeshkumar et al., 2023_b).

Additionally, blockchain-based traceability can provide consumers with more information about the products they purchase, such as the origin, quality, and authenticity of the food they eat. Overall, blockchain-based traceability has the potential to revolutionize the way the agriculture sector operates, bringing increased transparency, security, and efficiency to the supply chain. Chang, Xu, & Ghafoor (2021) studied the use of IoT with Blockchain for Smart Water Management. RFID is another technology that can be used along with blockchain for different purposes. Counterfeit products are a menace in generic agricultural produce, and therefore (Wang & Qiao, 2020) analyzed the use of RFID and Blockchain for Anti-counterfeiting. In the case of organic produce, (Hu et al., 2021) researched how using edge computing technology in coordination with blockchain can reduce the trust deficit in the supply chain (Thummula et al., 2019). Chun-Ting et al. (2020) proposed a service platform for agricultural produce traceability using IoT sensors with blockchain technology in their paper. Smart contract-based traceability in agribusiness is another technology that can work in conjunction with the blockchain (Wang et al., 2021, David et al., 2019a, Kim et al., 2018) went one step further in integrating smart contract-tokens and IoT with blockchain for traceability solutions (Ganeshkumar et al., 2019).

Blockchain-based traceability research in agriculture has focused on several key areas: implementation, user adoption, and benefits. In terms of performance, studies have investigated the technical challenges and solutions in creating a blockchain-based traceability system, including selecting appropriate blockchain platforms, data management, and security concerns (Zheng et al., 2018). User adoption research has explored the factors that influence farmers, processors, and other actors in the agriculture sector to adopt blockchain-based traceability, including cost, technical knowledge, and the availability of supportive infrastructure (Liu et al., 2020). Additionally, research has analyzed the benefits of blockchain-based traceability, including increased transparency, improved food safety, and enhanced consumer trust (Tian et al., 2019). Overall, the body of research on blockchain-based traceability suggests that it has the potential to revolutionize the way the agriculture sector operates. Still, more research is needed to fully understand the challenges and opportunities in its implementation and adoption.

Blockchain-based traceability research has also extended to other dimensions, like using multiple methodologies in traceability. Patra et al. (2021) used a Queueing Model in their study. Web API technology is another technology that could be used in consonance with a smartphone and the web to achieve traceability (Dandage, 2018). Wang, Wang, & Liu (2019) used the analytic hierarchy process (AHP) to study factors that help set up successful product traceability systems in organic agriculture. In the context of consumers eating out, restaurants are where food consumption happens. Food traceability is important in the case of restaurants to convince their patrons of the quality of food. George et al. (2019) developed a food quality traceability prototype for restaurants. The intermediate location where food traceability is important is the warehouse where food and grains are stored. Banerjee et al. (2020) developed an IoT-based warehouse traceability system for farmers (Ahmed et al., 2022).

The various other agribusiness applications on which research has been done using blockchain and traceability in India include (Yadav et al., 2021) on the marketing information system, (Patel et al., 2021) on farmer's credit scheme (Manocha et al., 2021) on Land Ownership and Authorization of Services. Regarding consumer-based studies on blockchain-based traceability systems, recent research includes a consumer valuation study (Shew et al., 2022) and a paper on consumer perception (Asfarian et al., 2020).

The literature analysis above shows that FPOs and their use of blockchain-based traceability systems have not been studied. This paper attempts to fill this gap in the literature, as FPOs are being encouraged by the Government of India, and traceability is increasingly becoming significant in the agribusiness sector (Siddhartha et al., 2021).

3 Research Methodology

Case Research methodology is strongly recommended when the early stage research on a topic is attempted. In this case, case research looks appropriate since there is a shortage of research on using blockchain-based traceability systems in India among the FPOs. Another reason why case research is commonly used is when a contemporary phenomenon is studied in a real-life context. Since the current phenomenon studied is contemporary, case research is apt in the current context. In this study, the leading blockchain-based traceability organization in agribusiness organization, namely TraceX, is analyzed. In addition to the study of TraceX, this research is interested in using the agritech among FPOs and the issues related to its use (Ravi et al., 2018). Therefore, along with details of TraceX, interviews, and reviews of the use of TraceX's technology among FPOs, are also undertaken to understand the adoption of this technology among FPOs. The study, therefore, uses multiple sources of evidence to ensure the validity of the results.

4 Results and Discussion

TraceX is a blockchain-based traceability business service-providing organization in the agribusiness sector. Srivatsa Sreenivasarao and Anil Nadig founded TraceX in 2019. The company is in the business-to-business market that provides traceability solutions in the software as a service mode. Companies involved in agribusinesses across subsectors like livestock, poultry, seafood, and crops use TraceX's services to ensure the traceability of products across their supply chains. More than 30 agribusiness companies, 8000 farmers, and 5000 hectares of land are covered with TraceX solutions. Its solutions help farmers and agribusinesses in several aspects like boosting productivity, improving market linkages, enhancing product quality, regulatory compliance, loss reduction, inventory management, and product recalls. Supply chain digitization to ensure trust, transparency, and traceability is one of the key aspects the company has been achieving through blockchain technology. With the help of Amazon Web Services, they have been able to work towards ensuring that their digital traceability services are resilient and free from cyber-attacks.

Producers and consumers in the agribusiness value chain are interested in the product's journey from the farm to the plate. As agricultural development transforms at different levels before it reaches the leaves of the consumers, all the stakeholders involved, including the consumers, are interested in the product journey from the origin to the final consumption point. Digitization of this journey also helps connect the various stakeholders in the supply chain, ensuring a network of all the entities in the system (Arokiaraj et al., 2020). Using blockchain's hyper ledger concept, TraceX helps capture data for agribusinesses that exhibit product transformation details.

FPOs are a new set of organizations that have been encouraged by the government to help increase the bargaining power of small and medium farmers and their income levels. These organizations are also involved in the use of TraceX's solutions. One such FPO is Sahyadri Farmers Producer Company. This FPO took to traceability triggered by the requirements of ISO and Food Safety standards regulations of their export customers in Europe. One issue with foreign customers is their inability to physically verify the credentials of the products imported at their end. In this case, remote digital access to the supply chain data and transactions helps the smooth processing of exports and imports and therefore helps both the FPO and the foreign customer.

An important crop whose use is daily in cooking across the world is the tomato. TraceX joined hands with an FPO, managing tomato farmers to ensure the use of blockchain across the farm operations from crop management to post-harvest management. Centre of Excellence for Sustainable Agriculture & Farm Excellence (CSAFE) is a TATA-Rallis-promoted FPO commemorating 150 years of the Tata Group. They help tomato farmers grow, harvest, and post-harvest use tomatoes. More than 200 farmers in this FPO were introduced to TraceX using a vernacular language-based mobile application of TraceX to monitor all the activities of the tomato farm for each of them. It ensured that they digitized all the data at the farm level and helped in easy access to the further stages in the supply chain. The mobile application included multi-lingual and offline use capabilities (David et al., 2019_b). These characteristics ensure its effective use in the Indian context. A key benefit was the capture of tomatoes' grades after harvest and their sale in appropriate retail outlets based on their requirement and customers' preferences (Victer et al., 2020).

Kazhani Farmer Producer Company Ltd (KFPCL) is an FPO from Erode in Tamil Nadu, India, focusing on Red banana cultivation. Madurai Agribusiness Incubation Forum, supported by National Bank for Agriculture and Rural Development (NABARD) and Tamil Nadu Agricultural University (TNAU), encouraged KFPCL to adopt modern agribusiness practices. TraceX worked with more than 500 hectares of Red Banana farms of greater than 200 farmers in the FPO for their traceability solution. The key technology used was a QR code, which helps identify the batches of graded red bananas sold in domestic and export markets. Through their mobile application, TraceX ensured continuous monitoring of the farmers' practices to manage the red banana crop. They captured the user interface that the mobile application had also assured a dashboard that displayed the crop management and the harvest details as soon as all the data was on the same. Similarly, TechnoServe in Araku Valley of Andhra Pradesh for the Organic GI-tagged Araku Coffee and MTR Foods that used FPOs to source Byadgi Chilli, a special chilly variety grown in the northern part of Karnataka, used TraceX"s blockchain-based traceability service for their operations.

An analysis of the FPOs' experience using blockchain technology for traceability in all these instances shows that The Unified Theory of Acceptance and Use of Technology framework has an appropriate application here. This theory posits that technology adoption depends on Performance

Expectancy, Effort Expectancy, Social Influence, and Facilitating Conditions. In the case of performance expectancy, the key factor that can help many FPOs adopt technology is the use case development and the demonstrable results from technology use. TraceX, like organizations, needs to expand the application across multiple geographies and crops to ensure greater acceptance of blockchain technology. Effort expectancy is a crucial determinant of the users in embracing technology, as the lesser the effort greater the ease of use of technology. In the case of TraceX, the availability of a mobile application in multiple languages and a better user interface helps ensure positive effort expectancy. Social Influence and facilitating conditions are indirect influencers in the acceptance and use of technology. Social Influence happens with the creation of greater awareness, which is currently minimal in looking at the possible economic benefits of technology adoption. It is a form of peer pressure to press for greater adoption.

5 Conclusions and Recommendations

Blockchain-based traceability is increasing, becoming the fourth industrial revolution-based digital technology influencing agribusiness. However, its use in agribusiness and how farmer-producer organizations have adopted this technology have rarely been studied. Because of this research gap, the current study using the case research methodology utilized TraceX and its interaction with FPOs to understand the issues related to this technology adoption. The study used the UTAUT framework to analyze the FPO adoption factors. The four key factors that affect technology adoption are the possible gains from technology use, the ease with which the technology can be used, peer influence, and organizational/technical support for new technology use.

The FPOs and government act as facilitating mechanisms for technology adoption. It would mean that it would encourage FPO members to adopt new technologies with the government's support through various incentives. The studies showed that they varied the top management in FPOs regarding expertise and training and therefore required training before convincing their fellow members to accept new technology. Government and buyers can provide subsidies or concessions or both so that the individual farmer does not feel the burden of paying for the subscription services. Peer influence requires greater adoption and the development of demonstration sites to showcase advantages. Government, as well as FPOs, can work towards providing training on the new technology. Initial adoption requires payment of the initial charges or the inclusion of them in the overall package of services. To increase greater adoption, increased satisfaction, greater trust, and lowering perceived risk would be essential.

References

Ahmed, I., Mehta, S. S., Ganeshkumar, C., & Natarajan, V. (2022). Learning from failure to enhance performance: a systematic literature review of retail loss. *Benchmarking: An International Journal*, (ahead-of-print).

Arokiaraj, D., Ganeshkumar, C., & Paul, P. V. (2020). Innovative management system for environmental sustainability practices among Indian auto-component manufacturers. *Int J Bus Innov Res*, *23*(2), 168–182.

Asfarian, A., Hilmi, K. I., & Hermadi, I. (2020, September). Preliminary User Studies on Consumer Perception towards Blockchain-Based Livestock Traceability Platform in Indonesia: An Implication to Design. In 2020 International Conference on Computer Science and Its Application in Agriculture (ICOSICA) (pp. 1–6). IEEE.

Banerjee, S., Saini, A. K., Nigam, H., & Vijay, V. (2020, January). IoT instrumented food and grain warehouse traceability system for farmers. In 2020 international conference on artificial intelligence and signal processing (AISP) (pp. 1–4). IEEE.

Cao, S., Powell, W., Foth, M., Natanelov, V., Miller, T., & Dulleck, U. (2021). Strengthening consumer trust in beef supply chain traceability with a blockchain-based human-machine reconciliation mechanism—computers and electronics in agriculture, 180, 105886.

Carrières, V., Lemieux, A. A., Margni, M., Pellerin, R., & Cariou, S. (2022). Measuring the Value of Blockchain Traceability in Supporting LCA for Textile Products. Sustainability, 14(4), 2109.

Casino, F., Kanakaris, V., Dasaklis, T. K., Moschuris, S., Stachtiaris, S., Pagoni, M., & Rachaniotis, N. P. (2021). Blockchain-based food supply chain traceability: a case study in the dairy sector. International Journal of Production Research, 59(19), 5758–5770.

Chang, Y., Xu, J., & Ghafoor, K. Z. (2021). An IoT and Blockchain Approach for the Smart Water Management System in Agriculture. Scalable Computing: Practice and Experience, 22(2), 105–116.

Chun-Ting, P., Meng-Ju, L., Nen-Fu, H., Jhong-Ting, L., & Jia-Jung, S. (2020, January). Agriculture blockchain service platform for farm-to-fork traceability with IoT sensors. In 2020 international conference on information networking (ICOIN) (pp. 158–163). IEEE.

Coniglio, A., Mora, V., Puente, M., & Cassán, F. (2019). Azospirillum as biofertilizer for sustainable agriculture: Azospirillum brasilense AZ39 as a model of PGPR and field traceability. In Microbial Probiotics for Agricultural Systems (pp. 45–70). Springer, Cham.

Dandage, K. (2018). Food traceability through web and smartphone for farmer's agriculture products in India with the help of web API technology. AgroLife Scientific Journal, 7(2), 31–42.

David, A. (2020). Consumer purchasing process of organic food product: an empirical analysis. *Journal of Management System-Quality Access to Success (QAS)*, *21*(177), 128–132.

David, A., Kumar, C. G., & Paul, P. V. (2022). Blockchain technology in the food supply chain: Empirical analysis. *International Journal of Information Systems and Supply Chain Management (IJISSCM)*, *15*(3), 1–12.

David, A., Nagarjuna, K., Mohammed, M., & Sundar, J. (2019$_a$). Determinant Factors of Environmental Responsibility for the Passenger Car Users. *International Journal of Innovative Technology and Exploring Engineering, ISSN*, 2278–3075.

David, A., Thangavel, Y. D., & Sankriti, R. (2019$_b$). Recover, recycle and reuse: An efficient way to reduce the waste. *Int. J. Mech. Prod. Eng. Res. Dev*, *9*, 31–42.

Ganeshkumar, C., David, A., & Jebasingh, D. R. (2022). Digital Transformation: Artificial Intelligence Based Product Benefits and Problems of Agritech Industry. In *Agri-Food 4.0*. Emerald Publishing Limited.

Ganeshkumar, C., David, A., Sankar, J. G., & Saginala, M. (2023a). Application of Drone Technology in Agriculture: A Predictive Forecasting of Pest and Disease Incidence. In *Applying Drone Technologies and Robotics for Agricultural Sustainability* (pp. 50–81). IGI Global.

Ganeshkumar, C., Jena, S. K., Sivakumar, A., & Nambirajan, T. (2021). Artificial intelligence in the agricultural value chain: review and future directions. *Journal of Agribusiness in Developing and Emerging Economies*.

Ganeshkumar C, Meenakshi Sundaresan, Nitish Kumar Singh (2023b) Farmer Producer Organizations Behavioral Intentions towards Fourth Industrial Revolution Technologies Adoption, Academy of Marketing Studies Journal, 21(1), 1–20.

Ganeshkumar, C., Prabhu, M., & Abdullah, N. N. (2019). Business analytics and supply chain performance: partial least squares-structural equation modeling (PLS-SEM) Approach. *International Journal of Management and Business Research*, *9*(1), 91–96.

Ganeshkumar, C., Prabhu, M., Reddy, P. S., & David, A. (2020). Value Chain Analysis of Indian Edible Mushrooms. *International Journal of Technology*, *11*(3), 599–607.

George, R. V., Harsh, H. O., Ray, P., & Babu, A. K. (2019). Food quality traceability prototype for restaurants using blockchain and food quality data index. Journal of Cleaner Production, 240, 118021.

George, R. V., Harsh, H. O., Ray, P., & Babu, A. K. (2019). Food quality traceability prototype for restaurants using blockchain and food quality data index. Journal of Cleaner Production, 240, 118021.

González-Amarillo, C. A., Corrales-Muñoz, J. C., Mendoza-Moreno, M. Á., Hussein, A. F., Arunkumar, N., & Ramirez-González, G. (2018). An IoT-based traceability system for greenhouse seedling crops. IEEE Access, 6, 67528–67535.

Hate, M., Jadhav, S., & Patil, H. (2018, January). Vegetable traceability with smart irrigation. In 2018 International Conference on Smart City and Emerging Technology (ICSCET) (pp. 1–4). IEEE.

Hu, S., Huang, S., Huang, J., & Su, J. (2021). Blockchain and edge computing technology enabling organic agricultural supply chain: A framework solution to trust crisis. Computers & Industrial Engineering, 153, 107079.

Kim, M., Hilton, B., Burks, Z., & Reyes, J. (2018, November). Integrating blockchain, smart contract-tokens, and IoT to design a food traceability solution. In 2018 IEEE 9th annual information technology, electronics and mobile communication conference (IEMCON) (pp. 335–340). IEEE.

Liu, J., Ouyang, Y., & Zhang, Y. (2020). Blockchain-based traceability in food supply chain management: A review of challenges and opportunities. Food Research International, 135, 110836.

Madaan, G., Swapna, H. R., Kumar, A., Singh, A., & David, A. (2021). Enactment of sustainable technovations on healthcare sectors. *Asia Pacific Journal of Health Management*, *16*(3), 184–192.

Manocha, P., Som, S., & Manocha, K. (2021, September). Blockchain as an Instrument for Land Ownership and Authorization of Services. In 2021 9th International Conference on Reliability, Infocom Technologies and Optimization (Trends and Future Directions) (ICRITO) (pp. 1–6). IEEE.

Pachayappan, M., Ganeshkumar, C., & Sugundan, N. (2020). Technological implication and its impact in the agricultural sector: An IoT Based Collaboration framework. *Procedia Computer Science*, *171*, 1166–1173.

Panpatte, S., & Ganeshkumar, C. (2021). Artificial intelligence in agriculture sector: a case study of blue river technology. In *Proceedings of the Second International Conference on Information Management and Machine Intelligence* (pp. 147–153). Springer, Singapore.

Patel, N., Shukla, A., Tanwar, S., & Singh, D. (2021). KRanTi: blockchain-based farmer's credit scheme for the agriculture-food supply chain. Transactions on Emerging Telecommunications Technologies, e4286.

Patra, S. S., Misra, C., Singh, K. N., Gourisaria, M. K., Choudhury, S., & Sahu, S. (2021). qIoTAgriChain: IoT Blockchain Traceability Using Queueing Model in Smart Agriculture. In Blockchain Applications in IoT Ecosystem (pp. 203–223). Springer, Cham.

Paul, V., Ganeshkumar, C., & Jayakumar, L. (2019). Performance evaluation of population seeding techniques of permutation-coded GA traveling salesman problems-based assessment: performance evaluation of population seeding methods of permutation-coded GA. *International Journal of Applied Metaheuristic Computing (IJAMC)*, *10*(2), 55–92.

Ravi, S., David, A., & Imaduddin, M. (2018). Controlling & calibrating vehicle-related issues using RFID technology. *International Journal of Mechanical and Production Engineering Research and Development*, *8*(2), 1125–1132.

Salah, K., Nizamuddin, N., Jayaraman, R., & Omar, M. (2019). Blockchain-based soybean traceability in the agricultural supply chain. IEEE Access, 7, 73295–73305.

Shew, A. M., Snell, H. A., Nayga Jr, R. M., & Lacity, M. C. (2022). Consumer valuation of blockchain traceability for beef in the United States. Applied Economic Perspectives and Policy, 44(1), 299–323.

Siddhartha, T., Nambirajan, T., & Ganeshkumar, C. (2019). Production and retailing of self-help group products. *Global Business and Economics Review*, *21*(6), 814–835.

Siddhartha, T., Nambirajan, T., & Ganeshkumar, C. (2021). Self-help group (SHG) production methods: insights from the union territory of Puducherry community. *Journal of Enterprising Communities: People and Places in the Global Economy*.

Tescione, I., Marchionni, S., Casalini, M., Vignozzi, N., Mattei, M., & Conticelli, S. (2018). 87Sr/86Sr isotopes in grapes of different cultivars: A geochemical tool for geographic traceability of agriculture products. Food Chemistry, 258, 374–380.

Thapa, S., Piras, G., Thapa, S., Rimal, P., Thapa, A., & Adhikari, K. (2021). Blockchain-based secured traceability system for the agriculture supply chain of ginger in Nepal: A case study. Archives of Agriculture and Environmental Science, 6(3), 391–396.

Tian, Y., Li, J., Wei, Y., & Fan, W. (2019). Blockchain technology in agriculture and food supply chain management: A review. Biosystems Engineering, 180, 83–95.

Thummula, E., Yadav, R. K., & David, A. (2019). A cost-effective technique to avoid communication and computation overhead in vehicle insurance databases for online record monitoring. *International Journal of Mechanical and Production Engineering Research and Development (IJMPERD)*, *9*(2), 711–722.

Victer Paul, P., Ganeshkumar, C., Dhavachelvan, P., & Baskaran, R. (2020). A novel ODV crossover operator-based genetic algorithm for traveling salesperson problem. *Soft Computing*, *24*(17), 12855–12885.

Wang, H. W., & Qiao, Z. (2020). Anti-counterfeiting Traceability System for Agricultural Products Based on RFID and Blockchain. DEStech Transactions on Engineering and Technology Research, mcaee, 349–354.

Wang, J. S., Wang, J. S., & Liu, C. M. (2019). Based on the analytic hierarchy process (AHP) to discuss the key success factors in establishing product traceability systems for Eco-Agriculture. Ekoloji, 28(107), 3783-3789.

Wang, L., Xu, L., Zheng, Z., Liu, S., Li, X., Cao, L., & Sun, C. (2021). Smart contract-based agricultural food supply chain traceability. IEEE Access, 9, 9296–9307.

Xie, C., & Xiao, X. (2020, June). Traceability of agricultural product quality and safety based on blockchain–taking fresh e-commerce as an example. In International conference on applications and techniques in cyber security and intelligence (pp. 288–294). Springer, Cham.

Yadav, J., Misra, M., & Goundar, S. (2021). Autonomous agriculture marketing information system through blockchain: a case study of e-NAM adoption in India. In Blockchain Technologies, Applications, and Cryptocurrencies: Current Practice and Future Trends (pp. 115–138).

Yadav, V. S., Singh, A. R., Raut, R. D., & Cheikhrouhou, N. (2021). Blockchain drivers to achieve sustainable food security in the Indian context. Annals of Operations Research, 1–39.

Yakubu, B. M., Latif, R., Yakubu, A., Khan, M. I., & Magashi, A. I. (2022). RiceChain: secure and traceable rice supply chain framework using blockchain technology. PeerJ Computer Science, 8, e801.

Yang, X., Li, M., Yu, H., Wang, M., Xu, D., & Sun, C. (2021). A trusted blockchain-based traceability system for fruit and vegetable agricultural products. IEEE Access, 9, 36282–36293.

Zheng, L., Fan, W., & Zhang, J. (2018). Blockchain for traceability in food supply chain management: A review. Food Control, 93, 170–181.

Design and Development of an AI Agriculture System

El Hamlaoui Mahmoud, El Youssr Mohamed Amine, Abid Soukayna, Khalil Driss, Mejbar Meryeme, Messous Amine, and Nouhas Hasnae

Abstract

The agricultural sector consumes approximately 85% of the world's available freshwater resources. With population growth and increased food demand, this percentage is increasing exponentially. Therefore, the challenge of managing the growing demand becomes more difficult to address without applying modern agricultural methods. The smart irrigation system is the key factor that leads to improve productivity and reduce costs. The main objective of this work, is to create an intelligent system based on the combination of the Internet of Things and Artificial Intelligence in order to regulate irrigation depending on specific environmental conditions. The system is accessible through a web platform that retrieves different parameters such as soil moisture, temperature, humidity and luminosity, collected through sensors connected to the Raspberry PI. It provides also automated or remote access to a pumping engine.

Keywords

Agriculture • Irrigation management system • Plant evolution • Prediction • Recommendation • Internet of Things • Sensors • Kubernetes • POD • Microservices

1 Introduction

In order to improve the agricultural yield with fewer resources and labor efforts, substantial innovations have been made throughout human history. Nevertheless, the high population rate never lets the supply and demand match at all times. By the year 2050, the world population is expected to reach 9.8 billion. Additionally, income levels will surpass their current state, further driving food demand. Consequently, countries will be more careful about their food supply. Not only the food, but also crop production is becoming equally critical for industry indeed, crops like cotton, rubber, and gum are playing vital roles in the economies of many countries. Unfortunately, only a limited portion of the earth's surface is suitable for agricultural use due to various constraints, including climate, temperature, topography, and soil quality, and even within these suitable areas, homogeneity is far from being guaranteed. Further examination reveals that each field possesses distinct characteristics that can be measured separately in terms of both quality and quantity. Critical characteristics, such as soil type, irrigation flow, nutrient presence, and pest resistance, define its suitability and capability for a specific crop. Considering the standard of farming, farmers need to visit the agriculture sites frequently throughout the crop life to have a better idea about the crop conditions. For this, the need for smart modern agriculture arises, as 70% of farming time is spent on understanding and monitoring and the crop states, rather than engaging in actual fieldwork. Recent communication and sensing technologies provide a true remote "eye in the field" ability, enabling farmers to observe field activities without physical presence. Wireless sensors are facilitating the monitoring of crops permanently with higher accuracy, and the ability to detect early stages of undesirable state.

Automating irrigation represents an important development in managing water losses in agriculture, reducing water consumption by 9 to 20% (Mannini et al. 2013). Traditional agriculture requires a significant time and a huge effort to achieve satisfactory production. In this context, the integration of AI and IoT assists in reducing the necessary requirements by transitioning from situations necessitating human intervention to the use of autonomous systems.

For this reason, a system based on the Internet of Things and Artificial Intelligence is developed. This system offers the possibility to either remotely manage the water needs and the evolution state of the plant or automatically.

This system is composed of two phases. The first one involves reading the characteristics provided by the sensors

E. H. Mahmoud (✉) · E. Y. M. Amine · A. Soukayna · K. Driss · M. Meryeme · M. Amine · N. Hasnae
ENSIAS, Mohammed V University, Rabat, Morocco
e-mail: ElHamlaoui.Mahmoud@um5.ac.ma

S. Arezki et al. (eds.), *Emerging Disruptive Technologies for Society 5.0 in Developing Countries*, Advances in Science, Technology & Innovation, https://doi.org/10.1007/978-3-031-63701-8_16

and storing them. The second phase consists in a web platform that includes the irrigation mechanism and visualization of the measurement parameters to control the pumps. As well as a system to detect the growth activity of the plants.

This paper is organized as follows. Section 2, provides an overview on the recent works. Section 3 describes globally the system. Sections 4 and 5 delve into the design and implementation of the Web platform. Section 6 explains how AI has been used in order to automate plant watering. Section 7 presents a selection of the Web platform interfaces. Finally, Sect. 8 synthesizes the findings of this work.

2 Related Works

This section provides a detailed overview of various studies using IoT and artificial intelligence technologies in the context of smart agriculture.

Using a set of sensors, the plant's water requirements can be determined. Classification algorithms can be applied based on the stored characteristics, allowing for the creation of an optimal model for decision-making.

The selected characteristics, as presented in Shibani et al. [2020], include temperature and humidity. Nawandar and Satpute [2019] also incorporate crop evapotranspiration and soil moisture. However, the use of evapotranspiration to determine the amount of irrigation may lead to over- or under-irrigation, as noted in Pasha et al. [2020]. Whereas in Mahadevaswamy [2018], luminosity is taken into consideration, as well as precipitation weather forecasts in Sumathi et al. (2019).

In general, the majority of automatic irrigation systems are primarily based on soil moisture values. When the moisture value exceeds the threshold, the soil is considered wet. Conversely, when the value falls below the threshold, the soil is considered dry, and the motor is started, as discussed in Sumathi et al. (2019) and Mahadevaswamy (2018).

Regarding machine learning algorithms, the authors in Shibani et al. [2020] conducted a comparative study employing three classifiers: Support Vector Machine (SVM), Logistic Regression, and Random Forest. The approach proposed by authors in Nawandar and Satpute [2019], is supported by the neural network algorithm with a hidden layer, whereas the decision tree algorithm is selected by Reddy et al. [2020].

3 Overall System Description

The mock-up below (Fig. 1) provides a comprehensive overview of the specificities of our project. The components used in this project are categorized into three groups. Plant Characteristics Sensor, Irrigation Equipment and Plant Evolution Equipment.

The characteristics of the plant are measured by a Raspberry PI 3 model B. It's connected with:

- DHT11 temperature humidity sensor,
- MCP3008 Analog-to-digital converter; to read the values of DHT11,
- Soil moisture sensor to measure water content in the soil,
- LDR light sensor.

The components used for automatic irrigation are:

- 12V DC 60W 0.6Mpa water pump,
- 12V 7A battery,
- Relay module to control the pump.

To monitor the plant's growth progression, a V1.3 camera is installed in front of a plant in the field. At ten-day intervals, the camera captures an image, which is then transmitted to the server for comparative analysis with previous captures.

As seen in Fig. 2, the sensors are connected with the Raspberry Pi, and the soil moisture sensor is placed in the ground. The camera is positioned in front of the plant, even for the PIR motion sensor to detect the presence of animals. The hose is assembled with the pump as well as the water source. Then the Raspberry Pi is linked to the power supply.

The mock-up also encompasses the client side, affording the ability to monitor their plants via a SaaS (Software as a Service) platform. Additionally, users can remotely assess their plants' conditions and administer water pumping through a Web Platform.

4 Software Vision of the Platform

TThe architecture that can fulfill our application requirements and accommodate future developments is a microservices-oriented architecture, which distinctly separates BackEnd processing from the FrontEnd.

Figures 3 and 4 detail the components of the application architecture:

- Orchestrator service: the role of this service is the orchestration of the architecture, i.e. it receives requests from clients and redirects them to the requested service,
- Recommendation service: it's a content-based recommendation system, it uses the characteristics of an element to identify similar elements, in our case these characteristics are the living conditions of a plant (temperature, humidity, wind speed, etc.). After extracting the necessary data from the installed sensors, a score is calculated in order to measure the degree of similarity (with the data from the database), then the results are sorted according

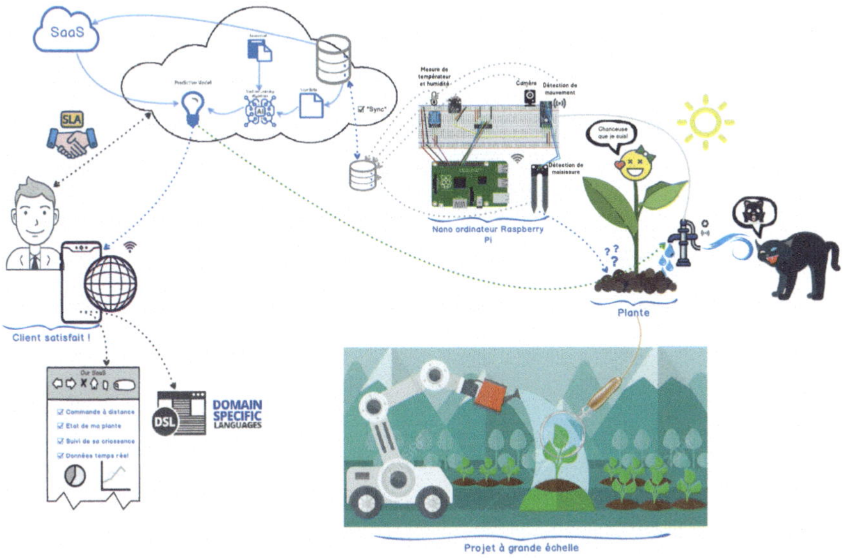

Fig. 1 Platform mockup

Fig. 2 The prototype of the proposed smart agricultural system

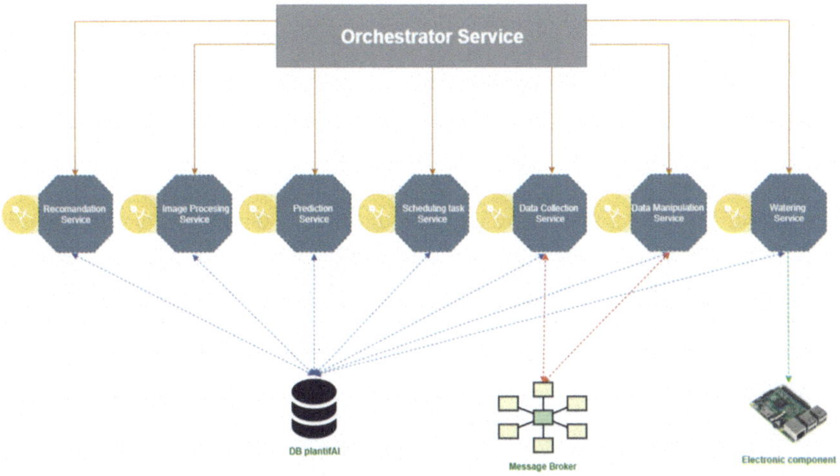

Fig. 3 Application components

Fig. 4 Component diagram

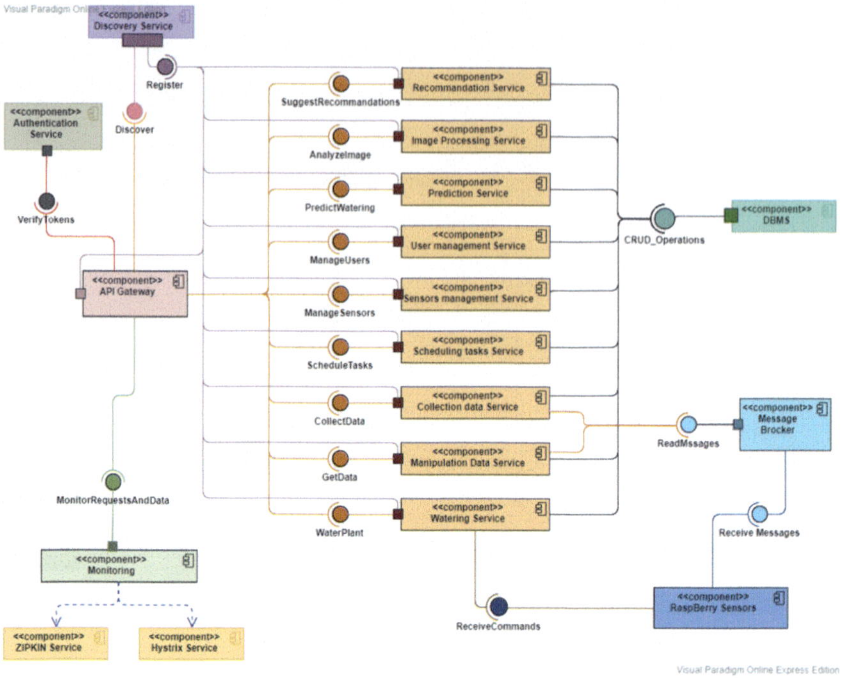

to this degree of similarity. For the technical part, we simulated this algorithm in a notebook (google collab), with the python language and the scikit-learn library,

- Image processing service: an intelligent service based on the CNN model Majid et al. [2022] which is part of deep learning models and which is a particular form of neural networks dedicated to image processing. In our case it's a question of analyzing the images of the plants in order to check whether they are healthy or not. To implement this model, we used the Python language and frameworks (OpenCV Bradski and Kaehler [2008], Keras Gulli and Pal [2017] and Tensorflow Abadi et al. [2016]),
- Prediction service: an intelligent service that takes as input the data provided by the installed sensors in order to decide whether the plant should be watered or not according to the preferences of the users (farmers) and the data of other users, the best model to implement this service is the logistic regression model, which is one of the best models used for classification. To implement this model, we used the Python language and the Tensorflow framework,
- Task planning service: a service that updates the plant statistics (average value of the temperature of each day, …) automatically without the intervention of the user, to implement these functionalities, we uses the java language and the Spring framework,
- Data collection service: allows real-time data to be retrieved on a periodic basis from a message service linked with the sensors, and to store this data in the cloud. This service is based on the Spring framework and AWS cloud services,
- Irrigation service: this service allows you to control the electronic cards installed in a user's farm to start the irrigation process. The technical implementation is carried out with Spring/Java,
- Data manipulation service: this service updates plant data automatically via a Kafka-type message broker, which remains one of the best messaging systems and allows data to be communicated with the application in an asynchronous way.

Figure 5 presents the detail of each component from a technical point of view:

1. The client is a Lightweight client-side application,
2. A request sent from the client to the server is accompanied by a token which ensures the security of the exchange by verifying the integrity of the data using a digital signature. For our case, we use the JWT (Json Web Token) Heffelfinger [2022] standard that allows the secure exchange of tokens (tokens) between several parties (services),
3. The API Gateway is the orchestrator service, this service makes it possible to redirect the request to the appropriate service after checking the token (4) and searching for the appropriate service (6),
4. The authentication service is used to verify the security information sent by the API Gateway,
5. For the monitoring of the application (server), we use 2 services: a Hystrix service Gu et al. [2020] which provides us with a dashboard on the requests received (requests in progress, requests well processed or erro-

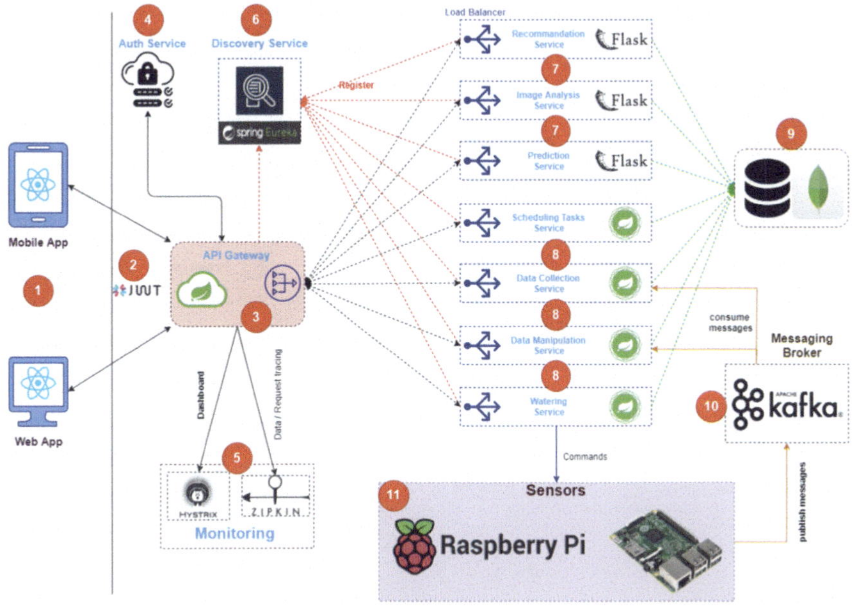

Fig. 5 Technical architecture

neous, ...), it implements the pattern Circuit Breaker that helps control collaboration between different services to provide high latency and failure tolerance. We also use another ZIPKIN service Mallanna and Devika [2020] that centralizes and organizes all traces of requests and data that pass through all levels of our application,

6. The Discovery service is the service registration directory of our application, it is based on the Eureka service offered by Netflix, it generally contains some service information (status, IP address, port number). Note that all services must register in this directory,
7. For business services, we have intelligent services that we described in the previous section. Generally, load balancing is used by creating several instances to overcome the problem of failures,
8. We have a 2nd category of business services that implements the reactive programming paradigm to make data exchange asynchronous,
9. As a database management system, a non-relational and document-oriented database is used,
10. We also add a messaging service in the form of a Message Broker Cluster which transmits data from a producer to a consumer. In our case, the producers are the physical sensors and the consumers are 2 microservices. The most appropriate solution is to use Kafka which allows communication with services based on any technology (NodeJs, Python, Java, ...),
11. Physical components (temperature, humidity, soil quality sensors, etc.) to be connected with a Raspberry Pi.

5 Architecture and Deployment

During the development phase, we deployed our application by creating the necessary containers and then orchestrating them. In the production phase, these containers were deployed in the cloud.

The deployment architecture is presented in Fig. 6. We first use Terraform (De Carvalho et al. 2020), a tool categorized under which the Infrastructure As Code category, which automates infrastructure configuration using scripts. When a user seeks to access the application, interaction takes place with the Amazon Route 53 service -an Amazon Cloud DNS web service that aids in routing users to their intended destinations.

The Amazon ELB (Elastic Load Balancer) (Kumari and Jha 2021) service enables load balancing by creating multiple instances for a resource (virtual machines, services, ...). The Amazon VPC (Virtual Private Cloud) (Sharma et al. 2020) service, in turn, makes it possible to create a virtual network for resources isolated from the Cloud. We create 2 subnets (public and private). In the public subnet, we put a scalable group of Amazon EC2 (Elastic Compute Cloud) (Wankhede et al. 2020) instances, EC2 is a service that allows us to rent servers on which we run our application and these components (Services).

In this subnet, we generally deploy the Kubernetes (Rejiba and Chamanara 2022) master nodes which is responsible for maintaining the desired state for the cluster, it is also a set of processes that run on a single node of the cluster: kube controller manager (Component of the master which runs the controllers), kube-apiserver (Component on the Master

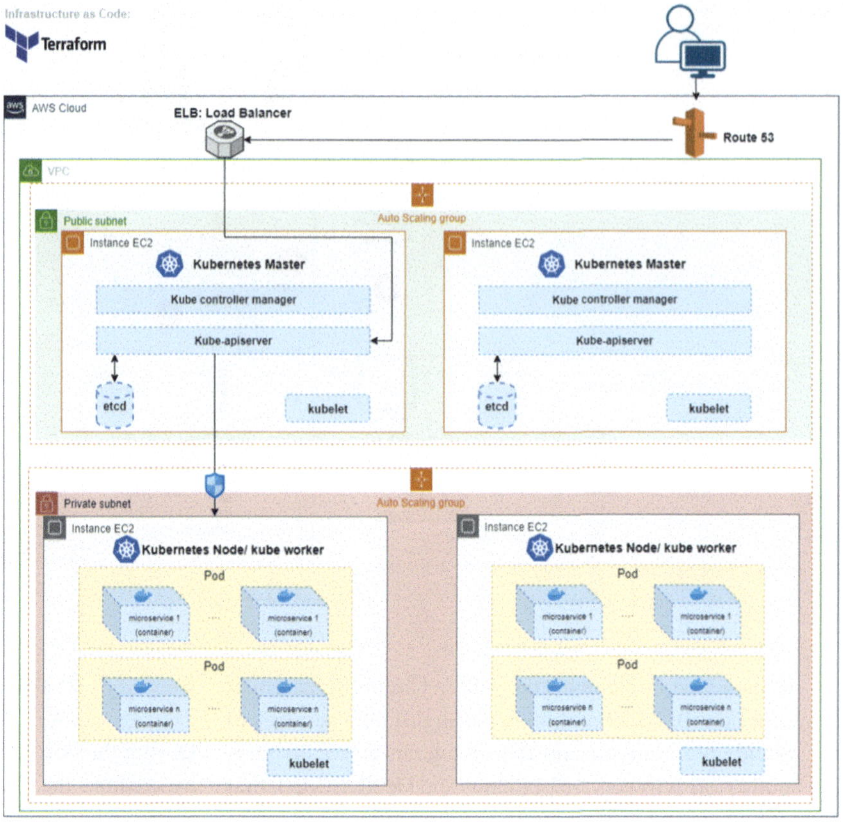

Fig. 6 Deployment architecture

which exposes the Kubernetes API, this is the front-end for the Kubernetes control plane). etcd memory (a consistent, highly available key value database used as backing memory for all cluster data).

Lastly, a kubelet agent operates on each node within the cluster. Its role involves ensuring proper container functioning within a pod, which may encompass one or more containers. Notably, this subnet accommodates multiple Kubernetes masters to ensure availability. In the private subnet, we establish a scalable group of Kubernetes nodes. Within these nodes, services are deployed, containers are created, and they are housed within pods.

6 Automatic Irrigation

To automate the irrigation process, we follow a three-step approach. The first step involves gathering the plant's characteristics at a specific time using sensors. These collected characteristics are used to construct a dataset, enabling the determination of whether the plant requires watering. The second step entails applying our model to this dataset to identify the optimal model. Finally, the last step involves transmitting the result (whether watering is needed or not) to the Raspberry Pi, triggering the activation of the pump in the affirmative scenario.

6.1 DataSet

The measurements collected to form the dataset vary based on the plant type. Plant characteristics are recorded, and a learning model is subsequently developed using these recordings to determine the plant's requirements. In instances where watering is necessary, the pump is automatically activated, but it can also be manually triggered by clicking an irrigation button within the web application. Once the pump starts, the decision cell within the data table is assigned a value of 1. Conversely, if the plant does not require water (value 0), a new entry is recorded. To train and evaluate the model, a database comprising 2674 records was used.

6.2 Learning Model

The output of the program will be binary (irrigated or not), so we will use a classification algorithm.

The data may be linearly separable or not. The idea is to consider that the data are inseparable and apply the algorithm.

To apply a linear transformation we need to see the structure of the data in space, to see if it is a circle or another shape to deduce the equation and after the application of the sign we will have the linear hypothesis. Unfortunately, we won't have this opportunity so we moved on to deep learning algorithms.

Table 1 Irrigation prediction model evaluation metrics

Accuracy (%)	Precision (%)	Recall (%)	F1 score (%)
98	98.38	94.09	96.18

image; then it is calculated and compared to see the adequacy of the plant's environment.

The sensors deployed in the plant measure environmental parameters including temperature, humidity, luminosity, and soil moisture. The parameters are visualized in the created application. The data is collected and stored in the Raspberry PI are accessible remotely. This application provides an intelligent monitoring solution; to observe the characteristics of the plant from anywhere and at any time, ensuring irrigation and development monitoring. The proposed machine learning model, provides an excellent evaluation measurement values as shown in Table 1 with the collected data set to detect the water requirement.

In this study, we demonstrated that Mask R-CNN can be used as a precise tool for plant identification and segmentation. As shown in Fig. 1, the extraction of the plant is well done, therefore the comparison of plant growth performed well.

7 Proof of Concept

In the dashboard, according to Fig. 9, the customer can follow the detailed watering history and the state of his plants in real time.

The Recommendation page (Fig. 10) is reserved for the recommendation of the plants proposed to the customer after the analysis of the information resulting from his environment.

The image processing functionality, Fig. 11, offers our customers the possibility of seeing the state of a plant (Greenery, Light, Growth and Insects) from an image.

8 Conclusion/Perspective

The main objective of the undertaken work within this project is the automation of crop management, particularly focusing on irrigation automation and plant evolution monitoring. A web application has been developed to enable remote control of the plant. Through this interface, plant characteristics are displayed, and the pump is automatically activated based on the plant's requirements, although manual activation is also possible. The plant's growth is assessed, and for red fruits, the plant's maturity is determined. Plant evolution is periodically evaluated by comparing images captured by the camera with previous ones. This comparison informs decisions about the plant's environmental suitability or the need to relocate it. The future work will be focused on the possibility of identifying the plant species and applying the appropriate learning model, as well as identifying the crop's disease.

References

Abadi, M., Barham, P., Chen, J., Chen, Z., Davis, A., Dean, J., Devin, M., Ghemawat, S., Irving, G., Isard, M., et al.: Tensorflow: a system for large-scale machine learning. In: Osdi. vol. 16, pp. 265–283. Savannah, GA, USA (2016)

Antognelli, S.: Agricolus: Ndvi and ndmi vegetation indices (2018)

Bradski, G., Kaehler, A.: Learning OpenCV: Computer vision with the OpenCV library. "O'Reilly Media, Inc." (2008)

De Carvalho, L.R., de Araujo, A.P.F.: Performance comparison of terraform and cloudify as multicloud orchestrators. In: 2020 20th IEEE/ACM International Symposium on Cluster, Cloud and Internet Computing (CCGRID). pp. 380–389. IEEE (2020)

Gu, H., Hu, J., Gu, M., Yuan, M.: Research and design of digital content management system based on microservice. In: Proceedings of the 2020 4th International Conference on Electronic Information Technology and Computer Engineering. pp. 865–869 (2020)

Gulli, A., Pal, S.: Deep learning with Keras. Packt Publishing Ltd (2017)

Heffelfinger, D.R.: Security with json web tokens. In: Payara Micro Revealed: Cloud-Native Application Development with Java, pp. 191–203. Springer (2022)

Huang, S., Tang, L., Hupy, J.P., Wang, Y., Shao, G.: A commentary review on the use of normalized difference vegetation index (ndvi) in the era of popular remote sensing. Journal of Forestry Research **32**(1), 1–6 (2021)

K. Sumathi, Kundhavai, Selvarani, K., K. Nagarajan: Irrigation alert system for farmers based on external intelligence and field sensors data. International Journal of Innovative Technology and Exploring Engineering (IJITEE) **8**, 121–131 (2019)

Kumari, R., Jha, V.K.: Performance analysis of load balancing algorithms in amazon cloud. In: Proceeding of Fifth International Conference on Microelectronics, Computing and Communication Systems: MCCS 2020. pp. 401–412. Springer (2021)

Mahadevaswamy, U., et al.: Automatic IoT based plant monitoring and watering system using raspberry pi. International Journal of Engineering and Manufacturing **8**(6), 55 (2018)

Majid, S., Alenezi, F., Masood, S., Ahmad, M., Gündüz, E.S., Polat, K.: Attention based cnn model for fire detection and localization in real-world images. Expert Systems with Applications **189**, 116114 (2022)

Mallanna, S., Devika, M.: Distributed request tracing using zipkin and spring boot sleuth. International Journal of Computer Applications **175**(12), 35–37 (2020)

Mannini, P., Genovesi, R., Letterio, T.: Irrinet: large scale dss application for on-farm irrigation scheduling. Procedia Environmental Sciences **19**(0), 823–829 (2013)

Nawandar, N.K., Satpute, V.R.: Iot based low cost and intelligent module for smart irrigation system. Computers and Electronics in Agriculture **162**, 979–990 (2019)

Pasha, M.F.K., Srinivasamurthy, N., Singh, D., Yeasmin, D., Valenzuela, G.: An artificial intelligence model to predict crop water requirement using weather, soil moisture, and plant health monitoring data. In: World Environmental and Water Resources Congress 2020: Water

Resources Planning and Management and Irrigation and Drainage. pp. 9–14. American Society of Civil Engineers Reston, VA (2020)
Reddy, K.S.P., Roopa, Y.M., Nandan, N.S.: Iot based smart agriculture using machine learning. In: 2020 Second International Conference on Inventive Research in Computing Applications (ICIRCA). pp. 130–134. IEEE (2020)
Rejiba, Z., Chamanara, J.: Custom scheduling in kubernetes: A survey on common problems and solution approaches. ACM Computing Surveys **55**(7), 1–37 (2022)
Ruck, D.W., Rogers, S.K., Kabrisky, M.: Feature selection using a multilayer perceptron. Journal of Neural Network Computing **2**(2), 40–48 (1990)
Sharma, V., Nigam, V., Sharma, A.K.: Cognitive analysis of deploying web applications on Microsoft windows azure and amazon web services in global scenario. Materials Today: Proceedings (2020)
Shibani, K., Kumar, K.S., Shanmugam, G.S.: An effective approach for plant monitoring, classification and prediction using IoT and machine learning. In: Artificial Intelligence and Evolutionary Computations in Engineering Systems, pp. 143–154. Springer (2020)
Tudela, J.A., Hernández, N., Pérez-Vicente, A., Gil, M.I.: Growing season climates affect quality of fresh-cut lettuce. Postharvest biology and technology **123**, 60–68 (2017)
Wankhede, P., Talati, M., Chinchamalatpure, R.: Comparative study of cloud platforms-microsoft azure, google cloud platform and amazon ec2. J. Res. Eng. Appl. Sci **5**(02), 60–64 (2020)

Blockchain for Collaborative and Integrated Supply Chain

Safia Nasih, Sara Arezki, and Taoufiq Gadi

Abstract

The supply chain is a sequence of processes that have ensured development in the insight of the logistics field, thanks to the methods and techniques adopted; the supply chain interacts with all stakeholders and deals with a considerable number of flows, financial, physical, or information. Blockchain technology is a pervasive technology that ensures transparency, validity, Immutability, and security of data. Tracking and tracing assets is one of the activities that preoccupies the attention of researchers and developers in the maritime scope, whether with the control of the supply chain or without. Tracking and tracing issue is a subject that has been treated in different forms with different technologies, in this chapter, we will have an overview of the Supply chain, the blockchain technology, the benefit of implementing Blockchain into the Supply chain, and the tracking and tracing operation as an application.

Keywords

Supply chain · Blockchain technology · Tracking and tracing

1 Introduction

The integration of the supply chain is highly significant in the way trade and delivery of goods are organized. In addition, the logistic methods have been turned upside down, and the customer–supplier-operator relationship has changed, as well as the modes of delivery of different types of products through different flows.

In the last few years, an international trend has emerged concerning the importance of competition by the deadlines, demanded by customers, which pushes companies to improve their products and to look for the most efficient services, and methods that favor their gains, thus the notion of supply chain appeared.

One of the most critical issues in supply chain management is the tracking of assets and products, and assuring the transparency of data access for all stakeholders.

During the last decade, researchers and maritime industry investors used different techniques and technologies to track and collect information related to the product concerned: location, geographic position, temperature, etc.

Pharmaceutical goods and food commerce are one of the most popular applications for tracking goods along the supply chain. One of the biggest global public trade problems is the counterfeiting of products in the medicinal supply chain, as well as manipulated food data.

This is one of the problems encountered with the supply chain, which is affected by many actors integrating into this process. This chapter is organized as follows:

In the first part, we will give an overview of the Supply chain, its origins, and history, the process of logistics that was the reason for establishing the supply chain notion, and the three flow types. The second part concerns Blockchain technology, definitions with general notions and characteristics, and properties that show that Blockchain fits Supply chain applications, the third part concerns an application in the Supply chain that suits Blockchain technology, it concerns the tracking and tracing assets operation. Finally, the paper ends with a general conclusion.

S. Nasih (✉) · S. Arezki · T. Gadi
Faculty of Sciences and Technologies Computer Science and Engineering Laboratory, Hassan First University of Settat, Settat, Morocco
e-mail: s.nasih@uhp.ac.ma

S. Arezki et al. (eds.), *Emerging Disruptive Technologies for Society 5.0 in Developing Countries*, Advances in Science, Technology & Innovation, https://doi.org/10.1007/978-3-031-63701-8_17

2 The Supply Chain Basis and Notions

2.1 Supply Chain Overview

Millions of products are distributed daily through a supply chain that spans the globe. Despite this, we have as much as researchers, limited knowledge about the origin, real-time location, and any parameter related to the goods along the way from their production to delivery. Between the cost of production and the cost of transport and storage, companies are forced to take into account the control of all their activities to reduce the overall cost. Thus, logistics appeared.

The word logistics comes from the Greek word "logistico" which means administrative and comes from the military field. It is the whole of the techniques implemented to ensure the supply and the maintenance of operational conditions of the armed troops in times of war (P. Médan et A. Gratacap 2007).

To define the supply chain, (Zeinbou 2014) proposes that the supply chain is the art of transferring material and information with a permanent watch on the safety of people and goods and the protection of the environment. (Mentzer, et al. 2001), in turn proposes another definition: the supply chain is a network of integrated entities into various processes and activities that produce value, delivered to the final consumer in the form of products and services (Zeinbou 2014).

The supply chain is not a sector of logistics, nor a service or an activity offered by companies, it is the result of a long process of evolution of the supply chain, it is an approach that aims to ensure the management of goods, and efficiency in production and delivery. The supply chain can be defined according to the English Collins Dictionary (2019), as "the entire process of providing goods from raw material and its manufacture to distribution and sale".

Another definition, (Ivanov et al. 2019) proposes: "Supply chain is a network of organization and processes, where a diverse number of companies (manufacturers, suppliers, wholesalers, and retailers) collaborate along the chain to acquire raw materials, convert them into specified finished products, and deliver the latter products to customers."

To clarify, the purpose is to ensure the performance of the entire process, and this is through:

- The guarantee of the quality of the product.
- The reduction of costs.
- Respect the deadlines.

Before two decades, the company's organizational structure was seen from a functional angle: marketing, R&D, purchasing, warehousing, production, sales, and finance.

The approach on which the vision of the supply chain is based on the global approach which links all the actors, from the source to the final consumer. Supply chain management (SCM) is an approach based on physical, informational, and financial integration combined and coordinated to transform and use resources. From raw material suppliers to customers, resources are allocated in the most efficient manner possible along the value chain. (SCM) is in charge of balancing supply and demand throughout the value chain, and integrates the procedures for production and logistics. Manufacturing, logistics, and (SCM) concerns are interconnected, they interact with one another in real-time.

SCM emerged around the 1980s when companies discovered they cannot effectively compete without better performance with minimal risk (Tan 2001). Three key trends—customer focus, market globalization, and the emergence of an information society—led to the development of SCM in the 1990s. These patterns prompted modifications to the competitive strategy of companies, hence the need for new concepts of value chain management (Ivanov et al. 2019).

2.2 Supply Chain Flows

The supply chain process is divided into three flows, as follows (Fig. 1).

a) Physical Flow

The physical flow concerns the production process, the supply, maintenance, inventory, and warehouse management functions, and the transportation of goods from the raw material to the market, including all phases of distribution. The overall goal of physical flow management in a supply chain is getting the right products to the right place, in the right quantities, at the right time, and in the right condition, while minimizing costs for the end user. The physical flow for a supply chain includes all goods and products of all types, fluid, bulk, containerized goods, etc.…

b) Financial Flow

It is restricted to the transmission of money in various forms between distinct recipients and payments. The financial flow constitutes monetary flows aiming to satisfy the actors who participated in the functioning of the supply chain. It can be broken down into four processes: The paid process (supplier), the invoiced process (products to customers), the cashed process (the money from the physical flow transaction), the budgeted process (forecasting variations and the level of the financial flow). The financial flow

Blockchain for Collaborative and Integrated Supply Chain

Safia Nasih, Sara Arezki, and Taoufiq Gadi

Abstract

The supply chain is a sequence of processes that have ensured development in the insight of the logistics field, thanks to the methods and techniques adopted; the supply chain interacts with all stakeholders and deals with a considerable number of flows, financial, physical, or information. Blockchain technology is a pervasive technology that ensures transparency, validity, Immutability, and security of data. Tracking and tracing assets is one of the activities that preoccupies the attention of researchers and developers in the maritime scope, whether with the control of the supply chain or without. Tracking and tracing issue is a subject that has been treated in different forms with different technologies, in this chapter, we will have an overview of the Supply chain, the blockchain technology, the benefit of implementing Blockchain into the Supply chain, and the tracking and tracing operation as an application.

Keywords

Supply chain · Blockchain technology · Tracking and tracing

1 Introduction

The integration of the supply chain is highly significant in the way trade and delivery of goods are organized. In addition, the logistic methods have been turned upside down, and the customer–supplier-operator relationship has changed, as well as the modes of delivery of different types of products through different flows.

In the last few years, an international trend has emerged concerning the importance of competition by the deadlines, demanded by customers, which pushes companies to improve their products and to look for the most efficient services, and methods that favor their gains, thus the notion of supply chain appeared.

One of the most critical issues in supply chain management is the tracking of assets and products, and assuring the transparency of data access for all stakeholders.

During the last decade, researchers and maritime industry investors used different techniques and technologies to track and collect information related to the product concerned: location, geographic position, temperature, etc.

Pharmaceutical goods and food commerce are one of the most popular applications for tracking goods along the supply chain. One of the biggest global public trade problems is the counterfeiting of products in the medicinal supply chain, as well as manipulated food data.

This is one of the problems encountered with the supply chain, which is affected by many actors integrating into this process. This chapter is organized as follows:

In the first part, we will give an overview of the Supply chain, its origins, and history, the process of logistics that was the reason for establishing the supply chain notion, and the three flow types. The second part concerns Blockchain technology, definitions with general notions and characteristics, and properties that show that Blockchain fits Supply chain applications, the third part concerns an application in the Supply chain that suits Blockchain technology, it concerns the tracking and tracing assets operation. Finally, the paper ends with a general conclusion.

S. Nasih (✉) · S. Arezki · T. Gadi
Faculty of Sciences and Technologies Computer Science and Engineering Laboratory, Hassan First University of Settat, Settat, Morocco
e-mail: s.nasih@uhp.ac.ma

S. Arezki et al. (eds.), *Emerging Disruptive Technologies for Society 5.0 in Developing Countries*, Advances in Science, Technology & Innovation, https://doi.org/10.1007/978-3-031-63701-8_17

2 The Supply Chain Basis and Notions

2.1 Supply Chain Overview

Millions of products are distributed daily through a supply chain that spans the globe. Despite this, we have as much as researchers, limited knowledge about the origin, real-time location, and any parameter related to the goods along the way from their production to delivery. Between the cost of production and the cost of transport and storage, companies are forced to take into account the control of all their activities to reduce the overall cost. Thus, logistics appeared.

The word logistics comes from the Greek word "logistico" which means administrative and comes from the military field. It is the whole of the techniques implemented to ensure the supply and the maintenance of operational conditions of the armed troops in times of war (P. Médan et A. Gratacap 2007).

To define the supply chain, (Zeinbou 2014) proposes that the supply chain is the art of transferring material and information with a permanent watch on the safety of people and goods and the protection of the environment. (Mentzer, et al. 2001), in turn proposes another definition: the supply chain is a network of integrated entities into various processes and activities that produce value, delivered to the final consumer in the form of products and services (Zeinbou 2014).

The supply chain is not a sector of logistics, nor a service or an activity offered by companies, it is the result of a long process of evolution of the supply chain, it is an approach that aims to ensure the management of goods, and efficiency in production and delivery. The supply chain can be defined according to the English Collins Dictionary (2019), as "the entire process of providing goods from raw material and its manufacture to distribution and sale".

Another definition, (Ivanov et al. 2019) proposes: "Supply chain is a network of organization and processes, where a diverse number of companies (manufacturers, suppliers, wholesalers, and retailers) collaborate along the chain to acquire raw materials, convert them into specified finished products, and deliver the latter products to customers."

To clarify, the purpose is to ensure the performance of the entire process, and this is through:

- The guarantee of the quality of the product.
- The reduction of costs.
- Respect the deadlines.

Before two decades, the company's organizational structure was seen from a functional angle: marketing, R&D, purchasing, warehousing, production, sales, and finance.

The approach on which the vision of the supply chain is based on the global approach which links all the actors, from the source to the final consumer. Supply chain management (SCM) is an approach based on physical, informational, and financial integration combined and coordinated to transform and use resources. From raw material suppliers to customers, resources are allocated in the most efficient manner possible along the value chain. (SCM) is in charge of balancing supply and demand throughout the value chain, and integrates the procedures for production and logistics. Manufacturing, logistics, and (SCM) concerns are interconnected, they interact with one another in real-time.

SCM emerged around the 1980s when companies discovered they cannot effectively compete without better performance with minimal risk (Tan 2001). Three key trends—customer focus, market globalization, and the emergence of an information society—led to the development of SCM in the 1990s. These patterns prompted modifications to the competitive strategy of companies, hence the need for new concepts of value chain management (Ivanov et al. 2019).

2.2 Supply Chain Flows

The supply chain process is divided into three flows, as follows (Fig. 1).

a) Physical Flow

The physical flow concerns the production process, the supply, maintenance, inventory, and warehouse management functions, and the transportation of goods from the raw material to the market, including all phases of distribution. The overall goal of physical flow management in a supply chain is getting the right products to the right place, in the right quantities, at the right time, and in the right condition, while minimizing costs for the end user. The physical flow for a supply chain includes all goods and products of all types, fluid, bulk, containerized goods, etc.…

b) Financial Flow

It is restricted to the transmission of money in various forms between distinct recipients and payments. The financial flow constitutes monetary flows aiming to satisfy the actors who participated in the functioning of the supply chain. It can be broken down into four processes: The paid process (supplier), the invoiced process (products to customers), the cashed process (the money from the physical flow transaction), the budgeted process (forecasting variations and the level of the financial flow). The financial flow

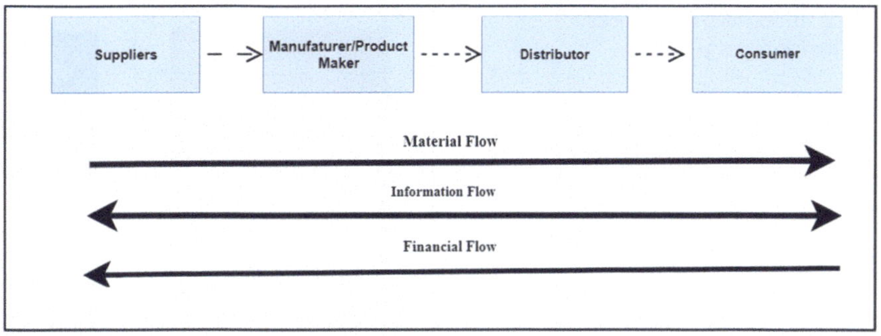

Fig. 1 The three flows in supply chain management

circulates in the opposite direction of the physical flow but in an unordered way.

c) Information Flow

All product-related information is included in the information flow, including the pricing, sales catalogs, sales history, and details on suppliers, transporters, and middlemen. The notion of information flow is associated with Big Data. The design and storage of a database which is considered important, requires tools and information systems that are efficient, servers that ensure better scalability. The database adopted is made up of all the information relating to customers, suppliers, and providers, for effective management of the supply chain (SupplyChainInfo 2022).

3 Blockchain Technology

Blockchain technology is a distributed decentralized ledger, that is built on peer to peer network with no need for central authority or third-party verification. This technology aims to avoid third parties trust which means to avoid transactions or control of treatments, and replace it with a trust on a programming code. Blockchain technology was introduced as the basic technology behind the Bitcoin currency edited in a scientific paper by Satoshi Nakamoto in 2008.

Blockchain technology, as mentioned, is implemented in a private or public network of computers that are called Nodes, these nodes hold a similar copy of the database, which is a distributed synchronized ledger.

The Blockchain is a peer-to-peer network, based on the transmission of transactions through a network of nodes. Before adding this transaction to the Blockchain, each new transaction is broadcast to the network so that the different nodes are aware of the time spent to receive the transaction to ensure that the system is resistant to the double spending problem.

Transactions are validated by nodes, accepted or rejected, before being added to the blockchain, and nodes can then aggregate multiple transactions into blocks and share them with other nodes in the network. Consensus algorithms are the technique adopted to decide which node should propose its block of transactions. It is necessary to specify that there are a multitude of consensus algorithms, we choose the algorithm according to the case study treated.

Blockchain is a sort of distributed ledger technology (DLT) that keeps an immutable record of all data on transactions and is immune to manipulation. Unlike traditional storage methods, DLT uses nodes and different computers to record, distribute, and synchronize transaction data. Following that, blockchain collects data into blocks that are linked together in a chain. This approach could be used in a distributed supply chain context where stakeholders share coordinated data (R. A. Rayan et M. A. M. Zubair 2021).

For protecting exposed data in transactions broadcasted over the network from manipulation, data should be secured in blocks. Blockchain maintains a secure environment by encrypting public data asymmetrically and using hashing techniques.

Hashing algorithms replace input data into hashes that represent uniquely their blocks, thus it prevents finding the original message without approval from all entities (R. A. Rayan and M. A. M. Zubair 2021).

Transparency offers all entities easy access to data regarding the source of elements and procedure parts, with variable levels of visibility (R. A. Rayan and M. A. M. Zubair 2021). As a result, all entities must accept social responsibility for their actions that affect consumer behavior while also allowing competitors to keep their credibility (Fig. 2).

3.1 Blockchain Properties

Blockchain is characterized by some properties, as mentioned below:

- Tamper resistance: for adding blocks to the blockchain, a consensus protocol is applied to validate these blocks, and having a similar copy with every Node, makes it difficult to tamper with data stored in the blockchain.

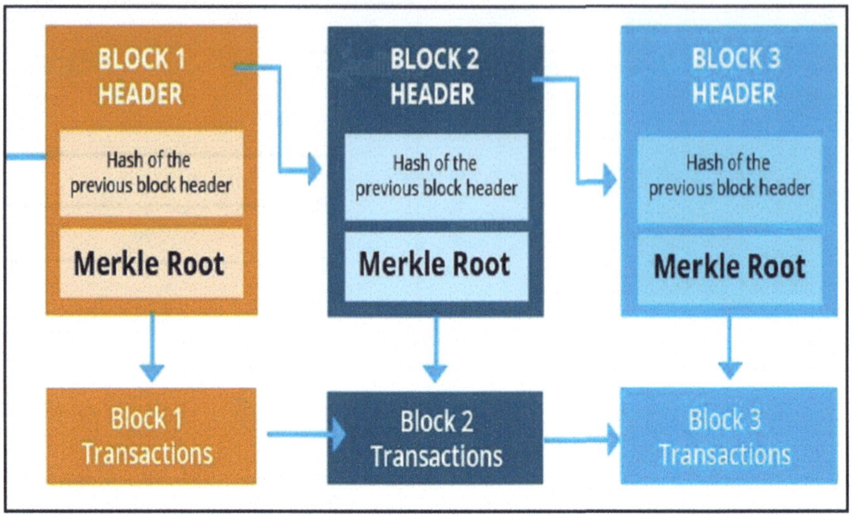

Fig. 2 Blockchain data structure and the block components

- Decentralization: Blockchain by nature is based on a decentralized network, data is replicated to all nodes participating, in consequence, any attack to one of these nodes doesn't affect the Blockchain data.
- Immutability: Data in the blockchain is immutable, once a transaction is added to the block and the block is validated and added to the chain, data cannot be deleted or modified. this property protects data from being tampered with.
- Security: Blockchain is a process of steps where data is verified then validated and controlled to avoid any risk, every user of the blockchain utilizes a private key to produce a signature for each transaction, which is done using digital signatures and a powerful cryptographic algorithm. This signature allows you to validate the transaction's legitimacy and prove that the specified user submitted it. Since the signature has already been updated, it cannot be altered (P. Tasca and C. J. Tessone 2019).

3.2 Implementing Blockchain in Supply Chain

The implementation of the blockchain in the supply chain is very important especially when it could enhance all procedures enabling better services.

According to Wang et al. (2019), several factors influence the application of blockchain in supply chains, but trust is the primary one that sparks interest in its SCM integration…

Some researchers in the systematic review done in Wang et al. (2019) acclaim that supply chain participants may become disconnected from one another and more complex due to geographically distant facilities and trading partners. It's crucial to maintain trustworthy data, and the purpose of blockchain is to offer seamless networks entire visibility, and symmetric information.

Consumers are Concerned about food safety (such as the horsemeat crisis in the UK and hazardous milk powder in China), they pay considerably greater attention to the authenticity and legitimacy of the products they buy. They want to know where, when, and how things are created (Tian, 2016, 2017) and environmental concerns (such as child labor and organic products) (S. Abeyratne et R. Monfared 2016).

Public safety and security are further motivations for blockchain usage. The installation of blockchain-based customs systems was suggested by Engelenburg et al. (2019) as a way to stop antisocial behaviors including terrorist assaults on ships and marine cargo. According to T. K. Mackey and G. Nayyar (2017), the grey market that allowed for the sale of counterfeit goods necessitates the use of blockchain technology.

Fraud and corruption are major issues in certain emerging economies. According to Y. Guo and C. Liang (2016), the blockchain is essential for resolving these legal difficulties by bringing forth much-needed openness.

According to Blossey et al. (2019), Blockchain technology has some key features that can enhance coordination and integration among the members of a Supply chain:

- Decentralization: Blockchain by nature is based on a decentralized network, data is replicated to all nodes participating, in consequence, any attack to one of these nodes doesn't affect the Blockchain data.
- Immutability: Data in the blockchain is immutable, once a transaction is added to the block and the block is validated and added to the chain, data cannot be deleted or modified. This property protects data from being tampered with.
- Transparency: relates to the shared ledger in the network where users participate, might add data, and have the right to get a similar copy of the ledger.

- Automation: operations in the Supply Chain bring several stakeholders together, and implement a great number of materials, documents, and money to be processed and carried with the minimum error. Automation is a way to deal with: the supply chain with better efficiency and rigor. In this way, Blockchain can provide the possibility to execute automatic programs called: Smart Contract based on verified information on the Blockchain.
- Immutability: In the supply chain, storing a history of transactions in a safe and secure system is a necessity. When the storage of data related to SC grows tremendously, the need for scalable databases or systems is a necessity. Immutability of records and consensus-based verification enables information validation (K. Christidis and M. Devetsikiotis 2016).
- Tamper resistance: for adding blocks to the blockchain, a consensus protocol is applied to validate these blocks, and having a similar copy with every Node, makes it difficult to tamper with data stored in the blockchain.
- Tokenization: The creation of tokens that reflect a specific claim on any valued item and their exchange amongst participants is made possible by blockchain technology (Blossey et al. 2019; Chen 2018).
- Security: Blockchain is a process of steps where data is verified then validated and controlled to avoid any risk, every user of the blockchain utilizes a private key to produce a signature for each transaction, which is done using digital signatures and a powerful cryptographic algorithm. This signature allows to validate of the transaction's legitimacy and proves that it was submitted by the specified user. Since the signature has already been updated, it cannot be changed (P. Tasca and C. J. Tessone 2019).

The use of Blockchain technology in the supply chain would result in better transaction management since these transactions will be validated and shared with all participants. One of Blockchain's advantages is the ability to track items, to store data history with no threat to lose data or to be tampered with. Transparency is the most noticed characteristic, that is crucial, especially in international trade. Tracking and tracing assets through supply chain is a recent and pervasive application domain for Blockchain technology in the supply chain sector.

4 The Tracking and Tracing Operation

Tracking and tracing are an issue that arises in supply chain processing, when shipping is integrated, especially with the exponential growth in the number of containers and items handled in different ports and vessels. Chain traceability, as stated by the ISO 9001:2000 standard, is the capacity to track the development, use, or location of an entity using documented identifications across the supply chain. In the real world, traceability is only possible if businesses keep track of their clients and vendors and share this data along the whole supply chain (Bechini et al. 2008).

4.1 Tracking and Tracing Definition

Traceability refers to the collection, consolidation, and archiving of all tracking and tracing data. The tracking information allows to know where an object is in the logistical chain at any time. The tracing data represents the history of the steps that this object has taken.

The notions of Tracking, whose sense of operation begins with origin to market, and tracing (from market to origin) conceptualize the path of a product and how it can be identified within a supply chain (Schwägele 2005). Traceability is a general concept, whereas tracking and tracing in theory defines the direction a good has traveled. Both tracking and tracing are employed by several businesses, including the food and pharmaceutical sectors, for various objectives. In certain situations, tracking may be used to detect non-conforming objects based on specified criteria, whereas tracing serves as a foundation for determining the reason why the item is non-conforming Bechini et al. 2008). Tracking is the capacity to follow a product through the supply chain, potentially using specified criteria. This is critical, for example, for an efficient recall of defective items (Bechini et al. 2008). On the other hand, tracing refers to the ability to identify the origin and qualities of a certain product. This is accomplished by making use of supply chain records that are kept upstream. Finding the root of problems related to quality is possible thanks to the tracing process (Bechini et al. 2008).

The tracing and tracking data is a subject of study that has been initiated from different angles, for example (Bechini et al. 2008) explored the use of tracking in the food industry and suggests that tracking is to enable the system to trace for identifying the source of an issue and preventing it to happen again, or to appropriately send a recall for potentially harmful foods, therefore preserving public health. As a result, developing a traceability system is a work that encompasses all stages of manufacturing, processing, and distribution. Traceability data must be stored for all assets and products. Processes act on products (movement, transformation, or combination), consequently, traceability requires support from appropriate architectural designs, technical solution implementation, and appropriate operational services. (Bechini et al. 2008) proposes an organic approach to managing the inter-organizational aspects of computer systems related to traceability (scalability, semantics, information management) to develop traceability systems. On the other hand, different articles and research have dealt with the subject of tracking in ports, they have proceeded from different points of view.

Cho et al. 2012) proposed an improved method for trajectory estimation for real-time localization systems, in the field of port logistics, the proposed method generates a virtual track when RTLS sends the track or location, and the uncertainty correction is realized by the Kalman filter.

In (Jain 2011), Real-time electronic tracking data is collected from the information systems. They found that the information obtained by simulation in a research conducted in Nagoya, Japan at the Nabeta Pier Container Terminal, by performing simulation, is effective in analyzing the performance of the portal. (Madleňák et al. 2016) dealt in their article with traceability, control of identification, and tracking of container movements by automatic data capture technologies by RFID technology. Using a web application, the authors identified and measured the time spent by the containers in the selected study center. The authors installed all modules in the selected distribution centers of the logistics provider, they placed RFID Tags on all rolling containers in selected centers. For a few days, the system recorded the data related to the containers. The result of this study was the determination of the conditions for implementing RFID technology in tracking and identifying containers.

In the article (Gnimpieba et al. 2015), the authors propose an architecture of a platform based on new technologies (IoT, CC, GPS/GPRPS), this platform must provide identification, traceability, and real-time tracking of products in the Supply chain.

4.2 Tracking and Tracing Problems

The traditional architecture of traceability systems in supply chain is often based on information collection primarily through EDI exchanges and, in some cases, web service calls. These exchanges and calls take place with transportation information systems, which are the primary or, in some cases, the only source of all transportation information. It is even possible that these details will be gathered through emails, phone calls, or text messages.

The following are the main limitations of these systems.

- The incapacity to have real-time tracking information is because information must be collected, captured, and made available by the transporter's information system before it can be accessed by the other participants in the logistics chain.
- The centralization of transportability information poses a significant risk to the availability and reliability of these data. The method used by the transporter to gather and transmit information has a significant effect on the quality of the data provided by his information system.
- The delay in obtaining information, which makes it impossible to address potential flaws in the transport chain. Even if online services are available, the logistics operator's information system gets it, which takes time before being notified of events or problems in the transportation chain.

The following issues must be resolved to provide reliable and responsive traceability systems for logistical chains.

- The availability of data for all participants in the supply chain, or the sharing of traceability data (Wattanakul et al. 2018), would increase the transparency of the operations and processes taking place inside this chain.
- The potential for having responsive systems that might respond to events occurring in logistical chains by receiving notices of them. The events might be, for instance, adjustments brought about by changes in customer needs or even an unexpected event that arises in the supply chain and necessitates quick action to prevent delays in the flow of goods.
- The possibility of having responsive systems that can respond to events that arise in logistical chains by receiving alerts of them. The events could be, for instance, adjustments brought about by changes in the customer's needs or even an unexpected event that arises in the logistical chain and necessitates quick action to prevent delivery delays or, at the very least, to keep them to a minimum. Setting up responses that would be activated in response to events occurring in the transport chain would be necessary to achieve this.
- Evaluating the accuracy and reliability of the information the system is transmitting (Ahmed Mohamed et al. 2019).

5 Conclusion

Through this research work, we made an overview of the supply chain, its different flows, as well as principal notions of Blockchain, special Blockchain properties that can affect supply chain collaboration and integration, and finally an example of Blockchain application in the supply chain, we took the tracking and tracing point as an example of applying the implementing of Blockchain technology in the supply chain.

Different issues can be discussed along with Blockchain integration in the supply chain, for example, the safety of products and material flow. Safety of the supply chain might be improved by integrating the right technology in the process of communication between devices, and information seeker programs.

As an example RFID, format labels can help to protect the security of the supply chain, The Internet of Things (IoT) can trace the flow of goods inventory at each checkpoint using two-dimensional barcodes and smart labels for packaging (R. A. Rayan and M. A. M. Zubair 2021).

The work in this paper is a part of a research work about tracking and tracing notions in a part of the Supply chain. In this paper we proved the importance of integrating Blockchain within the Supply Chain and the convenience of their properties, the result is building a collaborative and integrated Blockchain.

References

M. Ahmed Mohamed, C. Taconet, et M. Ould Mohamed Lemine, « La traçabilité dans les chaînes logistiques en utilisant l'IoT et la Blockchain », in Evolution des SI : vers des SI Pervasifs ?, Paris, France: Université Paris 1 Panthéon-Sorbonne, juin 2019, p. 1–10. Consulté le: 10 août 2023. [En ligne]. Disponible sur: https://hal.science/hal-02152725

A. Bechini, M. G. C. A. Cimino, F. Marcelloni, et A. Tomasi, « Patterns and technologies for enabling supply chain traceability through collaborative e-business », Information and Software Technology, vol. 50, n° 4, p. 342–359, mars 2008, https://doi.org/10.1016/j.infsof.2007.02.017.

G. Blossey, J. Eisenhardt, et G. Hahn, « Blockchain Technology in Supply Chain Management: An Application Perspective », présenté à Hawaii International Conference on System Sciences, 2019. https://doi.org/10.24251/HICSS.2019.824.

Y. Chen, « Blockchain tokens and the potential democratization of entrepreneurship and innovation », Business Horizons, vol. 61, n° 4, p. 567–575, juill. 2018, https://doi.org/10.1016/j.bushor.2018.03.006.

H. Cho, T. Kim, Y. Park, et Y. Baek, « Enhanced Trajectory Estimation Method for RTLS in Port Logistics Environment », in 2012 IEEE 14th International Conference on High-Performance Computing and Communication & 2012 IEEE 9th International Conference on Embedded Software and Systems, Liverpool, United Kingdom: IEEE, juin 2012, p. 1555–1562. https://doi.org/10.1109/HPCC.2012.227.

S. V. Engelenburg, M. Janssen, et B. Klievink, « Design of a software architecture supporting business-to-government information sharing to improve public safety and security: Combining business rules, Events, and blockchain technology », J Intell Inf Syst, vol. 52, n° 3, p. 595–618, juin 2019, https://doi.org/10.1007/s10844-017-0478-z.

Z. D. R. Gnimpieba, A. Nait-Sidi-Moh, D. Durand, et J. Fortin, « Using Internet of Things Technologies for a Collaborative Supply Chain: Application to Tracking of Pallets and Containers », Procedia Computer Science, vol. 56, p. 550–557, 2015, https://doi.org/10.1016/j.procs.2015.07.251.

D. Ivanov, A. Tsipoulanidis, et J. Schönberger, Global Supply Chain and Operations Management: A Decision-Oriented Introduction to the Creation of Value. in Springer Texts in Business and Economics. Cham: Springer International Publishing, 2019. https://doi.org/10.1007/978-3-319-94313-8.

S. Jain, American Statistical Association, Association for Computing Machinery, et IEEE Systems, Man, and Cybernetics Society, Éd., MODELING THE MATERIALS HANDLING IN A CONTAINER TERMINAL USING ELECTRONIC REAL-TIME TRACKING DATA. Piscataway, NJ: IEEE, 2011.

K. Christidis et M. Devetsikiotis, « Blockchains and Smart Contracts for the Internet of Things », IEEE Access, vol. 4, p. 2292–2303, 2016, https://doi.org/10.1109/ACCESS.2016.2566339.

R. Madleňák, L. Madleňáková, et Z. Kolarovszká, « System of Management and Traceability of Logistic Items through New Technologies », Procedia - Social and Behavioral Sciences, vol. 230, p. 128–135, sept. 2016, https://doi.org/10.1016/j.sbspro.2016.09.016.

J. T. Mentzer et al., « DEFINING SUPPLY CHAIN MANAGEMENT », Journal of Business Logistics, vol. 22, n° 2, p. 1–25, sept. 2001, https://doi.org/10.1002/j.2158-1592.2001.tb00001.x.

P. Médan et A. Gratacap, Logistique et supply chain management : intégration, collaboration et risques dans la chaîne logistique globale / Pierre Médan, Anne Gratacap. in Gestion sup (Paris). Dunod. Paris, 2007. Consulté le: 25 mars 2023. [En ligne]. Disponible sur: https://library.kedge.edu/Default/doc/SYRACUSE/50496/logistique-et-supply-chain-management-integration-collaboration-et-risques-dans-la-chaine-logistique

P. Tasca et C. J. Tessone, « A Taxonomy of Blockchain Technologies: Principles of Identification and Classification », ledger, vol. 4, févr. 2019, https://doi.org/10.5195/ledger.2019.140.

R. A. Rayan et M. A. M. Zubair, « IoT-Integrated Blockchain in the Drug Supply Chain », in Blockchain Applications in IoT Ecosystem, T. Choudhury, A. Khanna, T. T. Toe, M. Khurana, et N. Gia Nhu, Éd., in EAI/Springer Innovations in Communication and Computing. Cham: Springer International Publishing, 2021, p. 105–117. https://doi.org/10.1007/978-3-030-65691-1_7.

S. Abeyratne et R. Monfared, « Blockchain Ready Manufacturing Supply Chain Using Distributed Ledger », International Journal of Research in Engineering and Technology, vol. 05, sept. 2016.

F. Schwägele, « Traceability from a European perspective », Meat Science, vol. 71, n° 1, p. 164–173, sept. 2005, https://doi.org/10.1016/j.meatsci.2005.03.002.

« Quels sont les différents types de flux de la Supply Chain ? - SupplyChainInfo », 12 avril 2022. https://www.supplychaininfo.eu/faq/quels-differents-types-flux-supply-chain/ (consulté le 30 décembre 2022).

T. K. Mackey et G. Nayyar, « A review of existing and emerging digital technologies to combat the global trade in fake medicines », Expert Opinion on Drug Safety, vol. 16, n° 5, p. 587–602, Mai 2017, https://doi.org/10.1080/14740338.2017.1313227.

H.-T. Tan, « Methodological Issues in Measuring Knowledge Effects », International Journal of Auditing, vol. 5, n° 3, p. 215–224, nov. 2001, https://doi.org/10.1111/1099-1123.00337.

Y. Wang, J. H. Han, et P. Beynon-Davies, « Understanding blockchain technology for future supply chains: a systematic literature review and research agenda », SCM, vol. 24, n° 1, p. 62–84, janv. 2019, https://doi.org/10.1108/SCM-03-2018-0148.

S. Wattanakul, S. Henry, M. L. Bentaha, N. Reeveerakul, et Y. Ouzrout, « Improving risk management by using smart containers for real-time traceability », 2018, https://doi.org/10.48550/ARXIV.1810.13332.

Y. Guo et C. Liang, « Blockchain application and outlook in the banking industry », Financ Innov, vol. 2, n° 1, p. 24, déc. 2016, https://doi.org/10.1186/s40854-016-0034-9.

Zoubeir Zeinbou, « Vers un systeme d'aide à l'allocation des postes à quai dans un terminal à conteneur.pdf », these, Le Havre, 2014.

Intelligent Transportation and Engineering Applying to Society 5.0

Energy Supply Control for a Hybrid Microgrid Using an Artificial Neural Network with Integrating of an EV Charging Station: A Case Study of Smart University in a DC Hybrid Microgrid

Elmehdi Nasri, Tarik Jarou, and Abderrahmane Elkachani

Abstract

The article explores the integration of photovoltaic (PV) and wind energy systems, electric vehicle (EV) charging systems, and a hybrid DC microgrid within a smart university setting. The aim is to meet the energy demands of various loads by considering the power supplied by PV panels, wind turbines, and a battery storage system (BSS). To achieve this, an intelligent control model has been proposed to manage the BSS, ensuring a stable energy supply for all components within the hybrid microgrid and enabling voltage control. The research presents an exhaustive study of a microgrid energy management system (EMS), which integrates AC/DC loads, Li-ion batteries, backup electrical networks, and renewable energy sources like solar panels and wind turbines. The Maximum Power Point Tracking (MPPT) mode of the EMS is used to maximize the use of energy from renewable sources. Furthermore, by using artificial neural network controllers (ANNCs) for optimal regulation of battery charging and discharging, efficient management of the stored energy is accomplished. Maintaining power balance inside the DC microgrid is the primary aim of this system, which also provides resilient and adaptable control that provides for a variety of scenarios and alterations. Results from MATLAB simulations are used to verify the viability and efficacy of the suggested method and technique in microgrid control under various operating situations.

Keywords

ANN controller · DC micro-grid · Energy supply reliability · Renewable energy system · Electric vehicle EV · EV charging station · Smart University

1 Introduction

The use of electric vehicles (EVs) for transportation is a promising strategy being used by many countries to minimize greenhouse gas emissions. EVs employ electric motors and battery storage for propulsion, producing very little noise and no direct greenhouse gas emissions (Mahmud et al. 2018). Over the past decade, the deployment of EVs has seen significant growth, with the global number of electric passenger cars surpassing five million in 2018, marking a 63% higher than the prior year (Global EV Outlook 2022). However, the increasing prevalence of EVs can pose significant challenges to the power distribution system (Dang 2018). The frequent exploitation of the grid for EV charging can lead to issues with power quality and system stability (Gong et al. 2015). Additionally, the impact of the charging load is amplified if EV charging coincides with the local grid's peak demand. (Saldaña et al. 2019). The significant rise in electric vehicle (EV) adoption has resulted in a notable surge in electricity demand, prompting the exploration of various solutions to address this energy consumption escalation and voltage control challenges. Researchers have focused on several avenues in this domain, including the integration of EVs in microgrids (Liu et al. 2018; Bimenyimana et al. 2021), analyzing the impact of EVs on the grid (Wang et al. 2021; Stiasny et al. 2021), and studying charging infrastructure (Das et al. 2020).

E. Nasri (✉) · T. Jarou
Advanced Systems Engineering Laboratory, National School of Applied Sciences, Ibn Tofail University, Kenitra, Morocco
e-mail: elmehdi.nasri1@uit.ac.ma

T. Jarou
e-mail: Tarik.jarou@uit.ac.ma

A. Elkachani
Physics of Materials and Subatomics Laboratory, Ibn Tofail University, Kenitra, Morocco

S. Arezki et al. (eds.), *Emerging Disruptive Technologies for Society 5.0 in Developing Countries*, Advances in Science, Technology & Innovation, https://doi.org/10.1007/978-3-031-63701-8_18

Among these research directions, the integration of EVs into DC microgrid systems plays a crucial role in tackling the issues of high energy demand, voltage control within the DC microgrid, and ensuring the frequency stability of AC loads. This integration aims to optimize the incorporation of energy storage systems (ESS) and renewable energy systems (RES). In our study, we specifically examine the integration of EV charging in a smart university setting to address these concerns. This research paper introduces a model for an electric vehicle (EV) charging station incorporated within a direct current (DC) microgrid, specifically within the context of a smart university environment. The DC microgrid is designed to integrate various components, including Electric vehicles, a battery storage system, a connection to the public grid, photovoltaic (PV) panels, and a wind energy source, with the objective of achieving power balance within the system (Marcincin and Medvec 2014). The study presents a DC microgrid system that is interconnected with the electrical grid, featuring PV panels, an energy storage battery system, a wind energy system, an EV charging station, and a smart university as the primary AC load. To optimize energy utilization, the electrical grid serves as a backup source, while the PV and wind energy systems function as the primary sources, leveraging maximum power point tracking (MPPT) control. When the PV system generates its peak power, it supplies electricity to the DC microgrid, simultaneously charging the battery storage and the EV battery. Any surplus power generated by the PV system is redirected to the grid. Conversely, during periods of low power output from the PV system, the battery storage system provides electricity to the DC microgrid and the AC loads necessary for the smart university. This arrangement ensures efficient utilization of renewable energy sources while maintaining a stable power supply.

This work explores various scenarios considering different conditions such as energy generation from PV and wind systems, the demand for a DC hybrid microgrid, load from electric vehicles (EVs), and a smart university. When the power generated by the system's components is insufficient to meet the loads, the grid maintains stability. To ensure grid voltage and AC system frequency, as well as reliable energy supply in various cases involving DC components, control of battery storage is achieved through the implementation of an Artificial Neural Network Controller (ANNC). The article is presented into the following sections: Sect. 2 provides an explanation of microgrid modeling, which incorporates an electric vehicle charging station. Section 3 introduces the energy management system utilizing the ANNC. Section 4 provides the results of the simulator as well as a description of the main cases and functioning modes. After that, the conclusions are presented in Sect. 5.

2 Microgrid Modelling Integrating an Electric Vehicles Charging Station

The design of electric vehicle charging stations incorporates the implementation of a DC microgrid topology, as depicted. The proposed local DC microgrid technology encompasses the integration of a photovoltaic array (PVA), a connection to the public grid, electrochemical storage, and batteries from plug-in electric vehicles (PEVs), all interconnected within the DC grid. Moreover, this technology can seamlessly integrate with car parking areas, establishing a local grid connection where sun-shading roofs can be equipped with PV panels. The DC microgrid sources are typically interconnected through a shared DC bus, enabling efficient electricity distribution. The PV-generated power primarily caters to the charging requirements of electric vehicles. Alongside PV panels and the commun grid, energy storage serves as a backup power source that can be utilized for EV charging or for storing surplus electricity generated from solar sources. The public grid functions as an additional backup power supply, enabling the sale of excess electricity generated by the PV sources. In situations where the PV-generated electricity falls short of meeting the EV charging demands, the storage system provides most of the extra power, followed by the public grid. Conversely, any surplus energy is typically stored before being exported to the public grid, as indicated in the aforementioned studies (Locment and Sechilariu 2014; [PDF] 2023).

2.1 PV System

Figure 1 showcases a solar system comprising a boost converter, a panel of photovoltaic cells, and an MPPT (Maximum Power Point Tracking) controller.

In order to efficiently collect and transfer the maximum power generated by photovoltaic (PV) generators to the load, a DC/DC power converter, also referred to as a static converter, is employed as an interface. To make the most of the capacity of solar power systems, the MPPT method is utilized, specifically targeting the PV array's operating point at its maximum power point using the perturb and observe (P&O) algorithm. This approach ensures optimal utilization of available solar power resources (Thakran et al. 2018; Bhattacharyya et al. 2021). The boost converter is regulated by an MPPT controller to maintain maximum power efficiency at all times. The main objective of this strategy is to maintain the PV power generation at or near its highest peak power point. To achieve this, the output current (Ipv) and voltage (Vpv) of the PV generator are measured, and the power is calculated. By analyzing the variation of power (Ppv) and voltage (Vpv), the position of the point

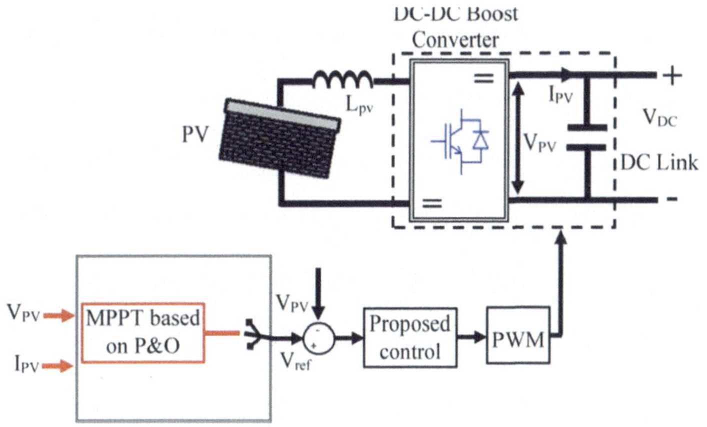

Fig. 1 Solar energy system with controller

(Vpv (t), Ppv (t)) on the PV curve is determined. When the power derivative is positive, it indicates that the operating point is approaching the MPPT. The voltage fluctuation is then evaluated to determine the search direction. Based on the direction of the search, the duty cycle of the pulse width modulation (PWM) control signals is adjusted either to increase or decrease. The program follows an iterative approach and follows a specific algorithmic procedure, as depicted in the Fig. 2.

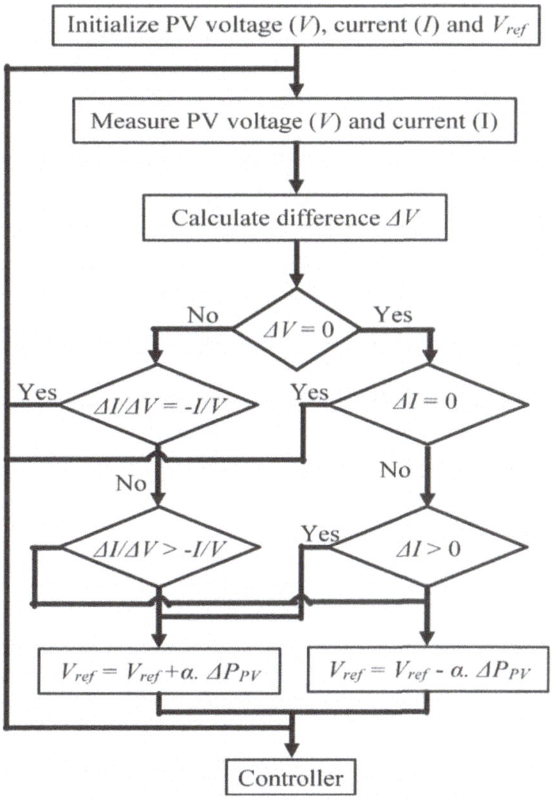

Fig. 2 Flowchart of MPPT algorithm

2.2 Wind System

Wind turbine systems offer a highly promising and readily available means of generating electricity. These systems harness mechanical energy through the rotation of turbines, which is subsequently converted into electrical power using generators. The overall energy output is directly impacted by the wind speed, while the maximum power point, determined by the wind speed, governs the functionality of the MPPT management unit (Kushwaha et al. 2020). Figure 3 illustrates a typical Wind Energy System (WES) comprising three main components, a wind turbine for capturing wind power, a synchronous permanent magnet power source, and a power converter that optimizes power extraction from the wind generator by using the Maximum Power Point Tracking (MPPT) method. The model of the wind energy converter is described in the paragraph that follows (Kumar et al. 2020):

$$\frac{dV_w}{dt} = \frac{T_w}{C_w} - \frac{I_{L_w}}{C_w} \tag{1}$$

$$\frac{dV_{dc}}{dt} = (1 - U_1)\frac{I_{Lw}}{C_{dc}} - \frac{I_{L_w}}{C_w} + D_1 \tag{2}$$

$$\frac{V_w}{L_w} = \frac{dI_w}{dt} + (1 - U_1)\frac{V_{dc}}{L_w} + D_2 \tag{3}$$

The rate of change of wind velocity V_w with respect to time (t), denoted as $\frac{dV_w}{dt}$, indicates how the wind velocity is changing over time. Similarly, the rate of change of the direct current (DC) voltage (V_{dc}) with respect to time (t), represented as $\frac{dV_{dc}}{dt}$, signifies how the DC voltage is changing over time. The third equation implies that the ratio of wind velocity (V_w) to the characteristic length (L_w) is equal to the sum of the rate of change of a certain parameter ($\frac{dI_w}{dt}$).

In the wind energy converter model, the symbol I_w represents the rectified wind current, while L_w denotes the

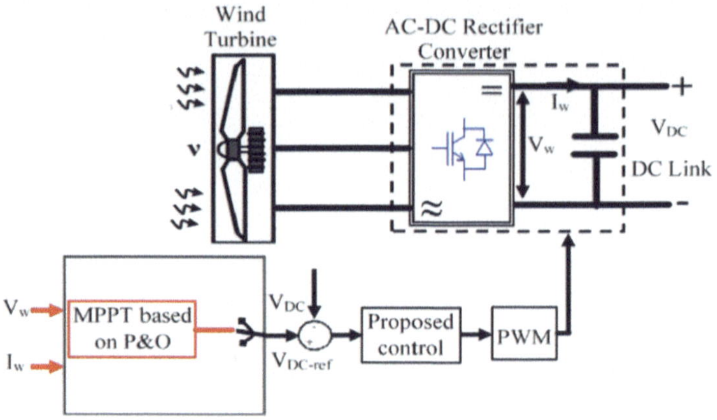

Fig. 3 System for generating wind power

inductance. I_{LW} represents the current flowing through the inductor, and V_w stands for the rectified input voltage. The control signal is represented by U_l, while V_{dc} represents the link voltage. T_w represents the wind torque acting on the wind energy converter (WEC), which measures the rotational force exerted by the wind on the WEC. C_w represents a constant or coefficient associated with the wind dynamics or characteristics, while C_{dc} represents a coefficient associated with the electrical dynamics or characteristics of the DC voltage. The dynamical variability of the energy stage parameters can be identified by the numerical values D_1 and D_2.

Wind energy is converted into electrical energy by the wind generator. The subsequent equations can be utilized to calculate the output voltage and current of the wind turbine. (Gajewski and Pieńkowski 2021):

$$V_{out} = \frac{(V_w \cdot C_p \cdot A \cdot 0.5 \cdot rho \cdot V_w)}{\left(\frac{1}{3} \cdot H \cdot (R + H)\right)} \tag{4}$$

$$I_{out} = \frac{P_{out}}{V_{out}} \tag{5}$$

The output voltage (V_{out}), output current (I_{out}), and output power (P_{out}) of the wind system are represented in Eq. (4). This equation indicates that the output voltage (V_{out}) is dependent on the following parameters:

- Wind Velocity or Speed (V_w): The speed of the wind directly influences the amount of energy that can be harnessed by the wind system.
- Power Coefficient (C_p): This coefficient indicates the effectiveness of the wind system in converting the kinetic energy of the wind into electrical power.
- Swept Area of the Blades (A): The total area covered by the rotating blades of the wind system. A larger swept area allows for capturing more wind energy.
- Air Density (rho): The density of the air through which the wind system operates. Higher air density provides more energy for conversion.
- Height of the Turbine (H): The vertical position at which the wind turbine is installed. Typically, higher heights enable access to stronger and more consistent winds.
- Radius of the Blades (R): The distance from the center of the turbine to the tip of the blades. Longer blades can capture more wind energy.

Equation (5) represents the relationship among these variables in the process of converting wind energy into electrical power.

2.3 Battery Storage System

In situations where renewable energy sources (RES) cannot meet the energy demand or when there is an excess of energy, BSS or battery storage system, is fundamental in maintaining system balance. The BSS, depicted in Fig. 4, consists of a lithium-ion battery, a charging and discharging management system, and a bidirectional DC-DC converter. These components work together to enable the storage and release of energy, ensuring equilibrium within the system.

Figure 4 showcases bidirectional DC/DC converters that enable the transfer of electricity between the battery and the microgrid. In this study, bidirectional converters with a half-bridge IGBT topology operating in continuous conduction mode were utilized. These converters are becoming more and more common to control the process by which batteries charge and discharge by varying the polarity of the flow of current, while maintaining constant voltage polarity at each position. The converter operates in boost mode to store excess energy on the DC bus, and in buck mode to supply power to the battery. During buck mode, energy is delivered to the battery through S1 and D_2, while in boost mode, current flows to the DC bus via S2 and D_1.

2.4 EV Charging Station System

The charging converter of a battery electric vehicle (BEV) incorporates constant-voltage and constant-current control mechanisms to facilitate battery charging. Fast charging is achieved through inner current loop control, while outer voltage loop control is used for constant-voltage charging, as shown in Fig. 5. Charging occurs when there is a positive current flowing into the battery (Ibatt > 0), while discharging takes place when the current is negative. The EMS controller generates the controlled power for the battery based on the direction of the battery current (Iref).

The operation of the charging converter is influenced by two variables: State of Charge (SOC) and reference current (Iref) Direction. The converter will function in constant-current or constant-voltage mode, depending on the control signal. The converter works in constant-voltage charging mode while the switch is closed, and in constant-current charging mode when the switch is opened.

Equation (8) presents the modeling equations for EV charging. In this equation v_{EVs} and I_{Lev} represent the voltage and current on the output side of the EV converter, respectively. L_{EVs} and C_{EVs} denote the inductor and capacitor of the EV, respectively. The input current for EVs is represented by i_EVs, while v'_{EVs} $i'_{L_{EVs}}$ indicate the voltage and current on the input side of the EV converter. The EVs are connected to the common DC bus through their dedicated static converters, which are controlled by a switching function f_{EVs}. The control variable for the electric vehicle energy supply is denoted as m_{EVs} (Wang et al. 2020).

$$\frac{dv_{EVs}}{dt} = \frac{i_{L_{EVs}} - i_{EVs}}{C_{EVs}} \tag{6}$$

$$\frac{di_{LEVs}}{dt} = \frac{v_{EVs}' - v_{EVs}}{L_{EVs}} \tag{7}$$

$$\begin{bmatrix} v'_{EVs} \\ i'_{L_{EVs}} \end{bmatrix} = f_{EVs} \begin{bmatrix} v_{EVs} \\ i_{L_{EVs}} \end{bmatrix} \tag{8}$$

$$=> \begin{bmatrix} v'_{EVs} \\ i'_{L_{EVs}} \end{bmatrix} = m_{EVs} \begin{bmatrix} v_{EVs} \\ i_{L_{EVs}} \end{bmatrix}$$

$$m_{EVs} = \int_0^T f_{EVs} dt \quad \text{with} \quad m_{EVs} \in [0; 1]$$

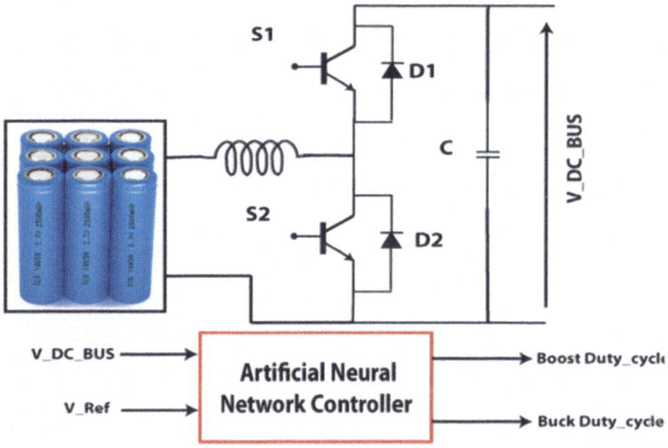

Fig. 4 Battery system based on a bi-directional inverter

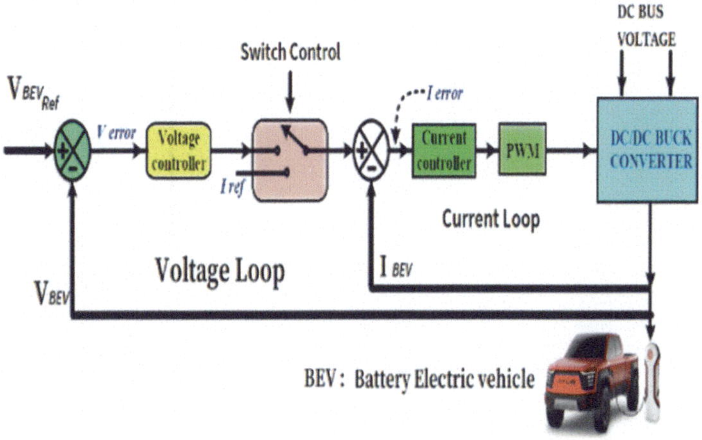

Fig. 5 Battery charging and discharge for BEVs

3 Energy Management System Using ANNC Artificial Neural Network Controller

3.1 ANNC Artificial Neural Network Controller

The utilization of an artificial neural network controller has demonstrated significant success in controlling engineering applications. The primary objective of this control approach is to linearize nonlinear processes. In this study, when the plant model follows a specific structure, the employed artificial neural network controller is referred to as feedback linearization control. Conversely, when the plant model is estimated using the same structure, it is referred to as NARMA-L2 control. This kind of control concentrates mainly on linearizing the nonlinear processes. Two neural networks compose up the NARMA-L2 controllers: the first network represents general discrete-time nonlinear systems, while the second network creates the control signal. The NARMA model is used to identify the systems that need to be regulated. This setup can be seen visually in Fig. 6 (Al Sumarmad et al. 2022).

Consequently, we may create the following controller using the NARMA-L2 model:

$$U(k+1) = \frac{Y(k+d) - f[y(k),\ldots,y(k-n+1),u(k),\ldots,u(k-n+1)]}{g[y(k),\ldots,y(k-n+1),u(k),\ldots,u(k-n+1)]} \tag{9}$$

To ensure that the constant DC voltage aligns with the reference voltage, this study employed an Artificial Neural Network Controller (ANNC) to regulate the bidirectional DC-DC converter. The ANNC generated the duty cycle for the Pulse Width Modulation (PWM). The inputs to the ANNC consisted of the reference voltage, DC voltage, and duty cycle values at the output. Multiple tests were conducted to establish a comprehensive database for the ANNC. During the experiments, the duty cycle and DC bus voltages were measured while simulating different load and irradiation power conditions (Al Sumarmad et al. 2022).

3.2 Energy Management System (EMS)

In this study, Fig. 7 illustrates the assortment of power sources incorporated into the microgrid. The proposed approach for managing the microgrid involves an Artificial Neural Network (ANN) controller. To optimize power output, a Maximum Power Point Tracking (MPPT) block governs a DC/DC converter that links the photovoltaic solar system to the DC bus. Additionally, multiple converters and an MPPT block are employed to harness the maximum available power from a wind turbine connected to the DC bus. In case of insufficient renewable energy, an AC/DC converter establishes a connection between the primary grid and the DC bus. However, its usage is limited to emergency situations when the battery's state of charge drops below 20%. The battery system is integrated into the microgrid through a bidirectional DC/DC converter, with its operation regulated by an ANN controller.

To meet the energy requirement, the proposed energy management system maintain a voltage level of 400 V, ensure a 50 Hz AC bus frequency for the smart university, and prevent overcharging or undercharging of the battery. The Flowchart for the energy management strategy is illustrated in Fig. 8.

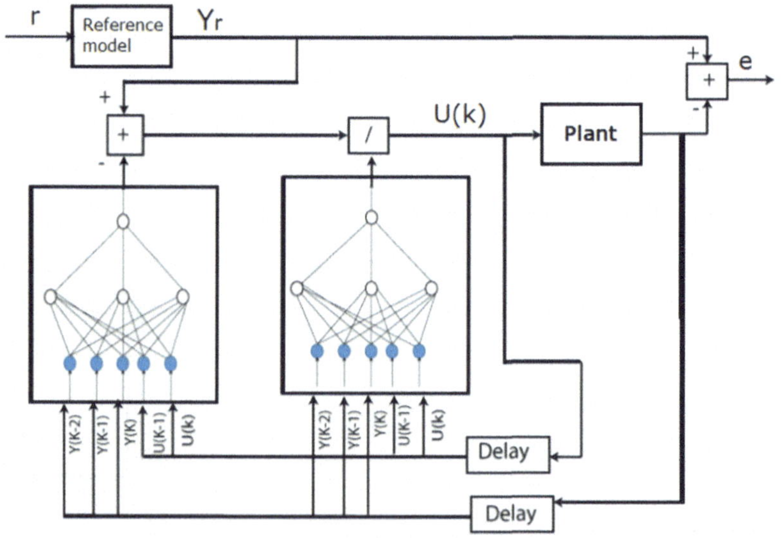

Fig. 6 Converter control under the ANNC controllers

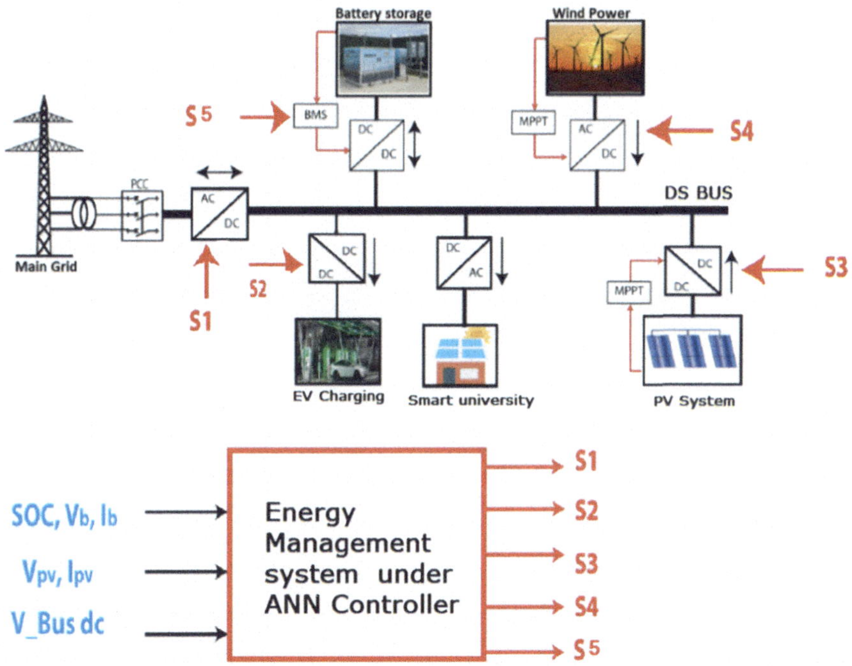

Fig. 7 Microgrid design

4 Simulation Results and Discussion

Figure 9 from the work shows a hybrid energy system integrated with a smart DC microgrid. Battery storage system (BSS) and an Hybrid energy sources, each outfitted with a unique converter and coupled to the DC-link, are the key elements of the system. The power converters try to get as much electricity as they can out of the renewable resources that are on hand. The second part consists of the loads, which include a variety of AC loads that may be found in a modern institution, such as experimentation benches, fans, and lights. The energy control unit plays a crucial role in calculating energy consumption and production, enabling the selection of appropriate control modes. The proposed system is simulated using Matlab/Simulink, allowing for the evaluation of its performance.

The photovoltaic (PV) system has a maximum power output of 50 KW, while the permanent magnet synchronous generator (PMSG) wind turbine can provide up to 45 KW. The reference voltage for the DC link is set at 300 V. The battery storage system's starting state of charge (SOC) is 80%. The AC bus load demand varies between 20 and 60 KW for a one-second duration, representing the energy requirements of the smart university. Meanwhile, the DC bus load demand is set at a constant 10 KW at a voltage of 300 V.

In order to evaluate the performance of each controller in maintaining microgrid balance under challenging conditions, a simulation was conducted for a duration of one second, with a sampling rate of 0.00001 s. Interface monitoring was employed to analyze the response of each component to the different variations. Figures 10 and 11 illustrate the fluctuations in power output from the solar panels and wind turbines, respectively, based on the suggested weather scenario. These [s provide valuable insights into how the renewable energy sources adapt and respond to changing environmental conditions.

During the initial period of the simulation, from t=0 s to t=0.2 s, the combined power generated by the renewable sources (5 KW from PV panels and 12 KW from wind turbines) fell short of meeting the demand of the DC and AC loads, which amounted to 30 KW. To address this imbalance and fulfill the load requirements, the battery discharged its stored energy. The battery's programming ensured that its state of charge remained within the range of 20–80%. As depicted in Figs. 12 and 13, the state of charge declined, and the battery supplied 20 KW of power to the system, resolving the power deficiencies in the DC bus and AC loads within the microgrid.

Furthermore, between t=0.2 s and t=0.5 s, the solar energy input increased by over 60 KW, while the wind power rose to 30 KW. This influx of energy caused a system imbalance and an energy shortage. However, thanks to the battery's critical role in balancing the system, it stored the excess energy while maintaining its state of charge within the safe zone. This equilibrium between power generation and consumption was essential for ensuring stable microgrid operation.

During the initial phase of the simulation, spanning from t=0 s to t=0.2 s, the total power generated by the renewable sources was insufficient to meet the demand of the DC

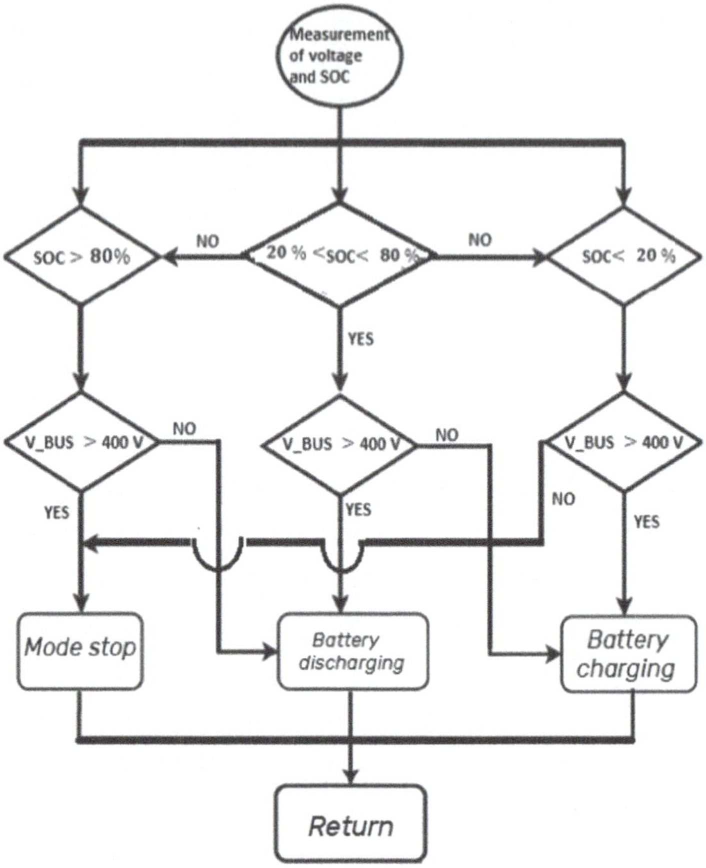

Fig. 8 Flowchart for the energy management plan

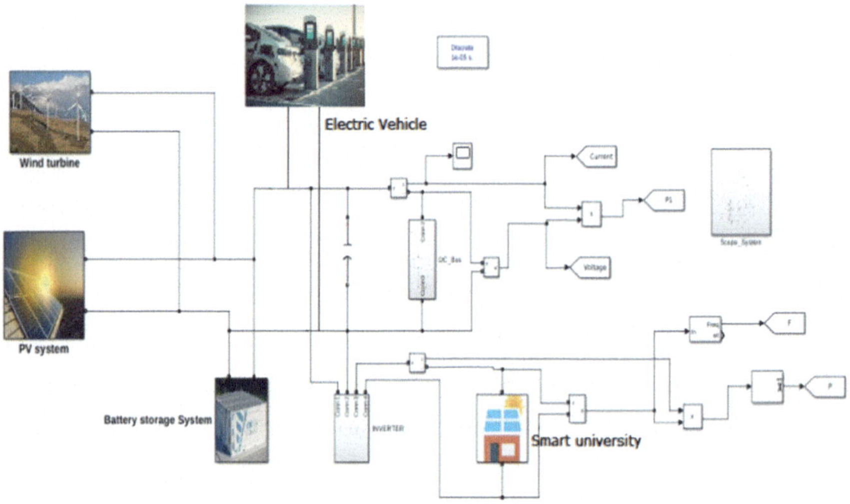

Fig. 9 Simulink model of the proposed hybrid Microgrid

and AC loads, which amounted to 30 KW. Specifically, the PV panels generated approximately 5 KW, while the wind turbines produced around 12 KW. Consequently, the battery had to discharge its stored energy in order to supply power to the microgrid, ensuring a balanced system and meeting the load requirements. The battery's programming aimed to maintain a state of charge ranging from 20 to 80%. The state of charge exhibited a decline, and the battery provided 20 KW of power to the system, as illustrated in Figs. 12 and 13. As a result, the issue of power shortages in the DC bus and AC loads was effectively resolved.

The energy consumption of both the AC and DC buses was measured during the time interval from t=0 s to t=1 s. From t=0 s to t=0.3 s, the AC load consumed 20 KW, while the DC load remained constant at 10 KW. Between t=0.3 s and t=0.5 s, the AC load increased to 50 KW, while the DC load

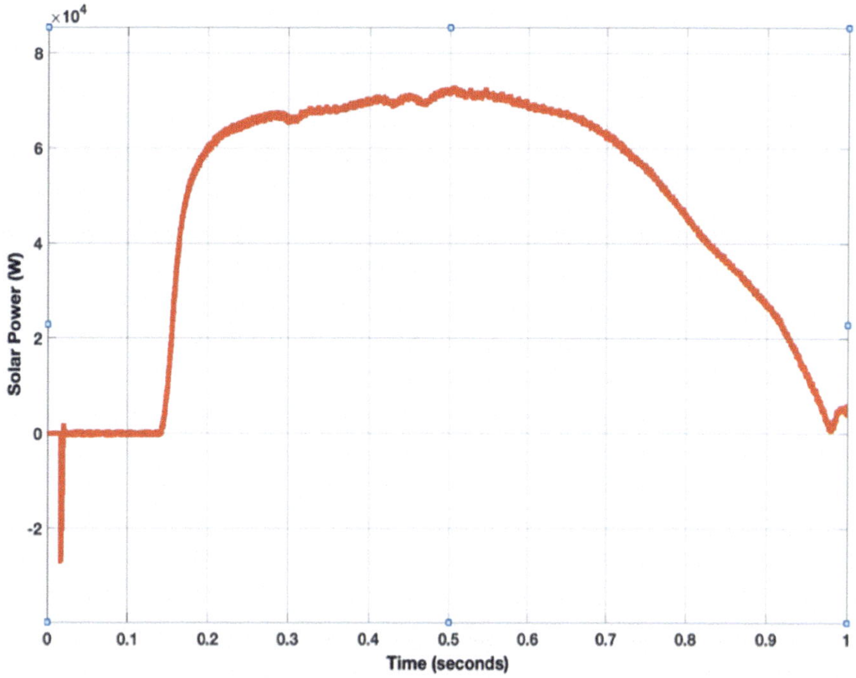

Fig. 10 Measured solar power (W)

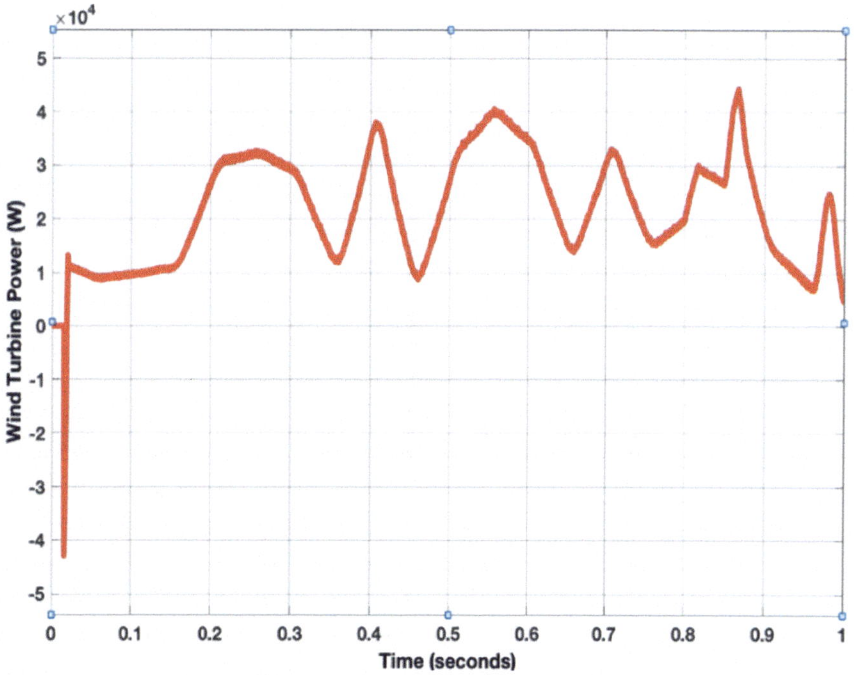

Fig. 11 Measured wind turbine power (W)

remained unchanged. Finally, from t=0.5 s to t=1 s, the AC load further increased to 60 KW. Throughout this entire duration, the DC bus voltage was maintained at a constant value of 300 V, as initially specified for simulation purposes. Upon examining Figs. 14, 15, it can be concluded that the ANN controller method offers significant advantages in maintaining both the voltage and power at their desired reference values, taking into consideration the AC loads required by the smart university as noted in the Fig. 16.

Based on the information presented in Fig. 17, the method demonstrated a frequency variation ranging from −0.02 to +0.02, with the exception of the initial phase of the test which was specifically designed to represent the temporary or initial regime.

The simulation findings indicate that the proposed energy management approach, employing an ANN controller, effectively maximizes and sustains the balance of the microgrid by utilizing renewable energy sources. The

Fig. 12 BES state of charge variants (%)

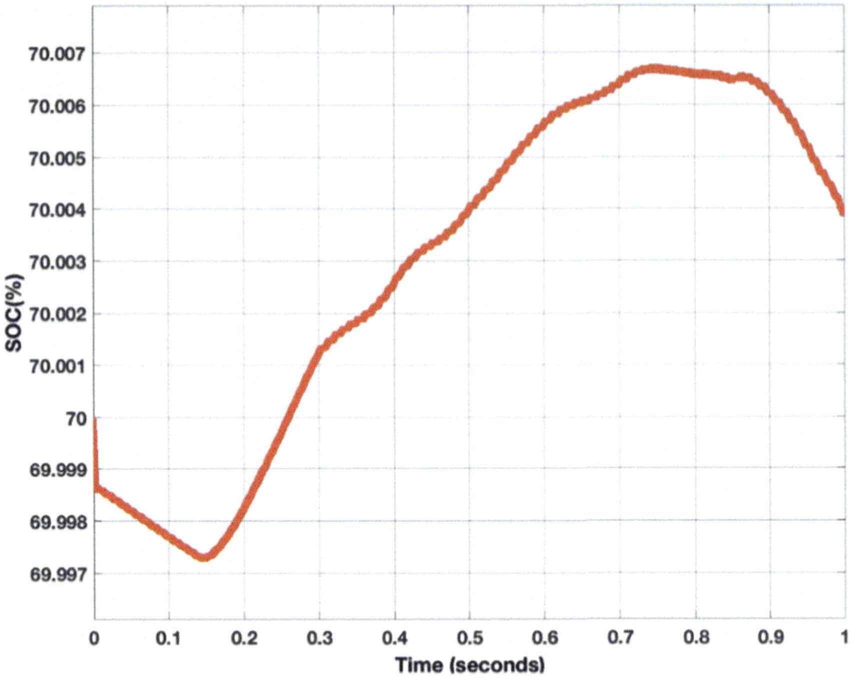

Fig. 13 BES power variants (W)

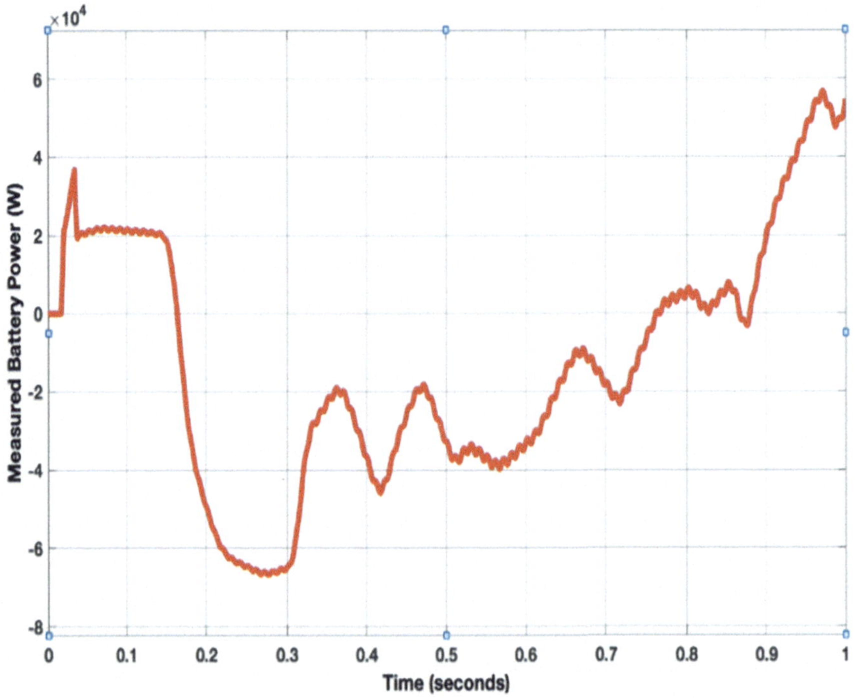

ANN controller demonstrates its ability to make intelligent decisions regarding battery charging and discharging, considering the varying energy demands of loads and the availability of renewable energy sources. Consequently, the microgrid consistently maintains a stable power supply throughout the simulation duration. Furthermore, the ANN controller showcases its adaptability and resilience in response to changing conditions, such as weather patterns and load demands. The simulation outcomes also reveal that the battery efficiently stores surplus energy during high renewable energy generation periods and discharges it during low generation periods, thus diminishing reliance on the utility grid. In summary, the proposed energy management strategy utilizing the ANN controller proves to be an efficient solution for optimizing the utilization of renewable energy sources and ensuring microgrid stability.

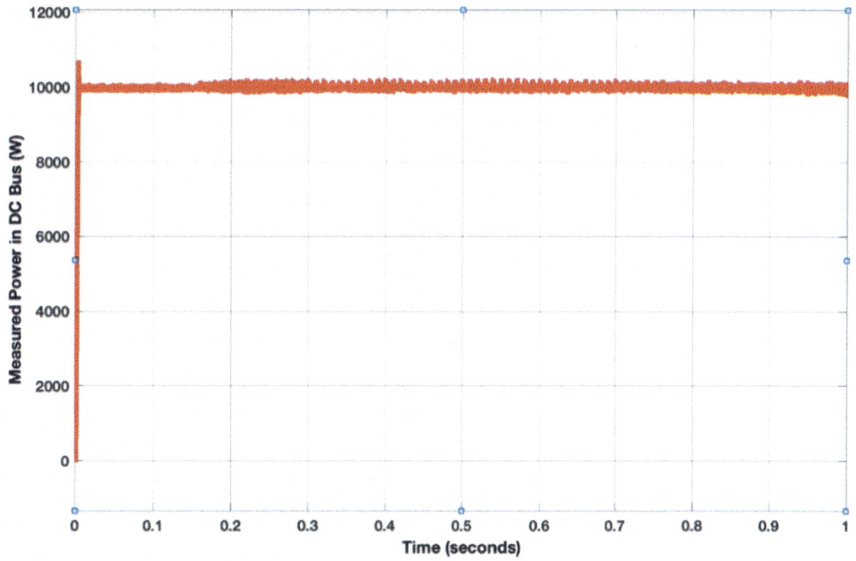

Fig. 14 Measured power in DC load (W)

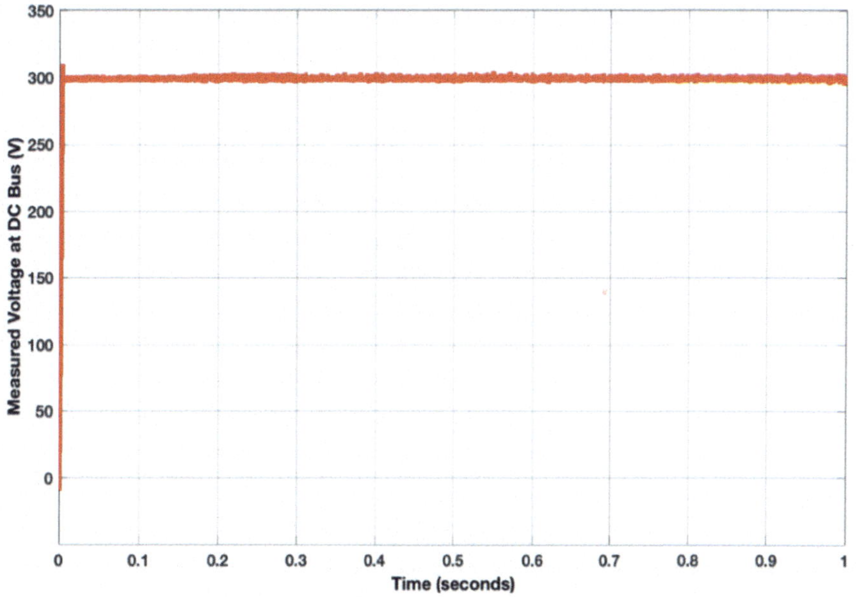

Fig. 15 DC bus observed voltage (V)

5 Conclusion

This study presents a novel energy management system that aims to optimize power generation from renewable sources while efficiently managing battery charging and discharging in a DC hybrid microgrid that integrates an EV charging station and a smart university. The system was implemented and simulated using Matlab/Simulink, demonstrating its effectiveness in maintaining microgrid balance and providing a stable power supply to the loads. The measured power output from solar and wind turbines closely matched the load demands, and the battery's state of charge and power were effectively managed. The DC bus voltage remained stable, with minimal frequency variation of less than 0.02. The proposed artificial neural network (ANN) controller successfully regulated battery operations for charging and discharging. In conclusion, the proposed energy management system proved to be a viable solution for microgrid energy management, maximizing the utilization of renewable energy sources and ensuring reliable power supply to the loads. Future research could focus on implementing the system in a real microgrid environment to assess its performance under various scenarios and conditions.

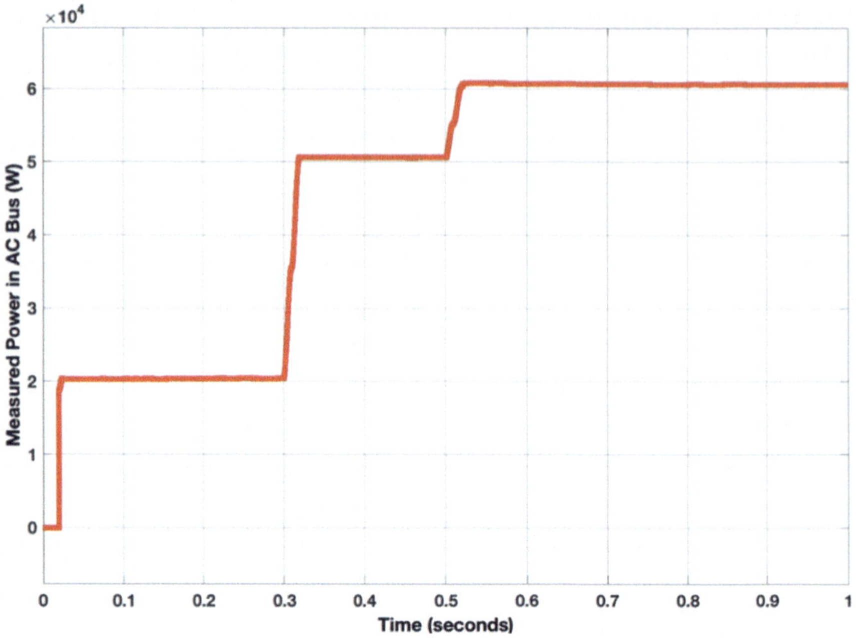

Fig. 16 Measured power in AC load required by the smart university (W)

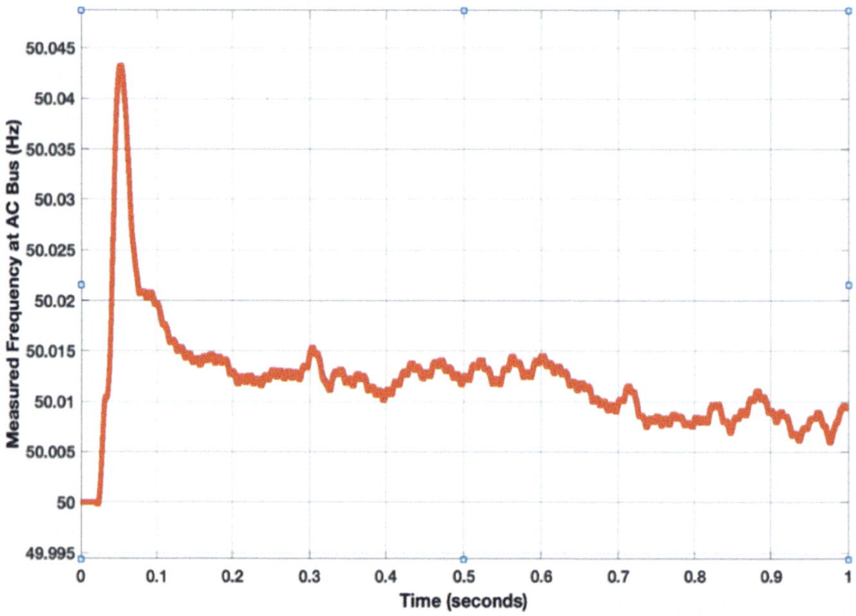

Fig. 17 Measured frequency at AC bus required by the smart university (Hz)

Acknowledgements I want to express my gratitude to my PhD project director M. Tarik Jarou and all of the personnel of the advanced systems engineering laboratory, as well as to everyone else with whom I have had the privilege to work on this and other similar projects.

References

"[PDF] Modeling and Simulation of DC Microgrids for Electric Vehicle Charging Stations | Semantic Scholar." https://www.semanticscholar.org/paper/Modeling-and-Simulation-of-DC-Microgrids-for-Locment-Sechilariu/41eaadaaa794bc9957e7d4f394e188acc6cab305 (accessed Apr. 09, 2023).

K. A. Al Sumarmad, N. Sulaiman, N. I. A. Wahab, and H. Hizam, "Energy Management and Voltage Control in Microgrids Using Artificial Neural Networks, PID, and Fuzzy Logic Controllers," Energies, vol. 15, no. 1, Art. no. 1, Jan. 2022, https://doi.org/10.3390/en15010303.

S. Bhattacharyya, D. S. Kumar P, S. Samanta, and S. Mishra, "Steady Output and Fast Tracking MPPT (SOFT-MPPT) for P&O and InC Algorithms," IEEE Trans. Sustain. Energy, vol. 12, no. 1, pp. 293–302, Jan. 2021, https://doi.org/10.1109/TSTE.2020.2991768.

S. Bimenyimana et al., "Integration of Microgrids and Electric Vehicle Technologies in the National Grid as the Key Enabler to the Sustainable Development for Rwanda," Int. J. Photoenergy, vol. 2021, pp. 1–17, Jul. 2021, https://doi.org/10.1155/2021/9928551.

Q. Dang, "Electric Vehicle (EV) Charging Management and Relieve Impacts in Grids," in 2018 9th IEEE International Symposium on Power Electronics for Distributed Generation Systems (PEDG), Jun. 2018, pp. 1–5. https://doi.org/10.1109/PEDG.2018.8447802.

H. S. Das, M. M. Rahman, S. Li, and C. W. Tan, "Electric vehicles standards, charging infrastructure, and impact on grid integration: A technological review," Renew. Sustain. Energy Rev., vol. 120, p. 109618, Mar. 2020, https://doi.org/10.1016/j.rser.2019.109618.

P. Gajewski and K. Pieńkowski, "Control of the Hybrid Renewable Energy System with Wind Turbine, Photovoltaic Panels and Battery Energy Storage," Energies, vol. 14, no. 6, Art. no. 6, Jan. 2021, https://doi.org/10.3390/en14061595.

"Global EV Outlook 2022: Securing supplies for an electric future | en | OECD." https://www.oecd.org/publications/global-ev-outlook-bdb28e12-en.htm (accessed Apr. 18, 2023).

Q. Gong, S. Midlam-Mohler, E. Serra, V. Marano, and G. Rizzoni, "PEV Charging Control Considering Transformer Life and Experimental Validation of a 25 kVA Distribution Transformer," IEEE Trans. Smart Grid, vol. 6, no. 2, pp. 648–656, Mar. 2015, https://doi.org/10.1109/TSG.2014.2365452.

P. S. Kumar, R. P. S. Chandrasena, V. Ramu, G. N. Srinivas, and K. V. S. M. Babu, "Energy Management System for Small Scale Hybrid Wind Solar Battery Based Microgrid," IEEE Access, vol. 8, pp. 8336–8345, 2020, https://doi.org/10.1109/ACCESS.2020.2964052.

A. Kushwaha, M. Gopal, and B. Singh, "Q-Learning based Maximum Power Extraction for Wind Energy Conversion System With Variable Wind Speed," IEEE Trans. Energy Convers., vol. 35, no. 3, pp. 1160–1170, Sep. 2020, https://doi.org/10.1109/TEC.2020.2990937.

Z. Liu, Y. Chen, R. Zhuo, and H. Jia, "Energy storage capacity optimization for autonomy microgrid considering CHP and EV scheduling," Appl. Energy, vol. 210, pp. 1113–1125, Jan. 2018, https://doi.org/10.1016/j.apenergy.2017.07.002.

F. Locment and M. Sechilariu, "DC microgrid for future electric vehicle charging station designed by Energetic Macroscopic Representation and Maximum Control Structure," in 2014 IEEE International Energy Conference (ENERGYCON), May 2014, pp. 1454–1460. https://doi.org/10.1109/ENERGYCON.2014.6850614.

K. Mahmud, G. E. Town, S. Morsalin, and M. J. Hossain, "Integration of electric vehicles and management in the internet of energy," Renew. Sustain. Energy Rev., vol. 82, pp. 4179–4203, Feb. 2018, https://doi.org/10.1016/j.rser.2017.11.004.

O. Marcincin and Z. Medvec, "Concept of charging stations for electric cars," in Proceedings of the 2014 15th International Scientific Conference on Electric Power Engineering (EPE), May 2014, pp. 169–172. https://doi.org/10.1109/EPE.2014.6839469.

G. Saldaña, J. I. San Martin, I. Zamora, F. J. Asensio, and O. Oñederra, "Electric Vehicle into the Grid: Charging Methodologies Aimed at Providing Ancillary Services Considering Battery Degradation," Energies, vol. 12, no. 12, Art. no. 12, Jan. 2019, https://doi.org/10.3390/en12122443.

J. Stiasny, T. Zufferey, G. Pareschi, D. Toffanin, G. Hug, and K. Boulouchos, "Sensitivity analysis of electric vehicle impact on low-voltage distribution grids," Electr. Power Syst. Res., vol. 191, p. 106696, Feb. 2021, https://doi.org/10.1016/j.epsr.2020.106696.

S. Thakran, J. Singh, R. Garg, and P. Mahajan, "Implementation of P&O Algorithm for MPPT in SPV System," 2018 Int. Conf. Power Energy Environ. Intell. Control PEEIC, pp. 242–245, Apr. 2018, https://doi.org/10.1109/PEEIC.2018.8665588.

D. Wang, F. Locment, and M. Sechilariu, "Modelling, Simulation, and Management Strategy of an Electric Vehicle Charging Station Based on a DC Microgrid," Appl. Sci., vol. 10, no. 6, Art. no. 6, Jan. 2020, https://doi.org/10.3390/app10062053.

L. Wang, Z. Qin, T. Slangen, P. Bauer, and T. van Wijk, "Grid Impact of Electric Vehicle Fast Charging Stations: Trends, Standards, Issues and Mitigation Measures - An Overview," IEEE Open J. Power Electron., vol. 2, pp. 56–74, 2021, https://doi.org/10.1109/OJPEL.2021.3054601.

IoT System for Smart Electric Car Charging Station Using Micro-CPV Unit

Sarah El Himer, Mariya Ouaissa, Mariyam Ouaissa, and Zakaria Boulouard

Abstract

The power supply of a smart station that employs Internet of Things technology to monitor concentrated solar production is the subject of this article. The first section of this study evaluates the general performance of two optical components that will be employed in photovoltaic micro-concentrator (MCPV) systems for electric vehicle charging stations: a Fresnel lens (FL) and two secondary optics (circular and square dome). The time needed to recharge the energy storage system of an electric vehicle is covered in the second section. The technological variations between quick DC chargers and traditional alternating current (AC) chargers are investigated. To examine the cost of charging a car by integrating IoT devices, the collected data is made available online to the original equipment manufacturers of each charging station. Although the two circular SOs have the highest intensity and best uniformity, the square dome has optimal homogeneity and maximum optical efficiency according to the first simulation findings. Therefore, to generate such a volume of electricity for fast charging, a solar system with a total output of approximately 120 kW is required. One hundred sixty-seven multi-junction cells are required for this energy to power an electric vehicle at any power level. As a result, 120.24 kW of power are generated. Therefore, 1.3 m^2 of the total surface is needed for our charging station. Unlike the stations in Morocco, our station does not need a big space or a lot of power. The optical system provides the best way for the system to equip EV users with an execution framework to deliver energy demand solutions to all entities operating in a charging smart station infrastructure.

Keywords

Fresnel lens · Micro-CPV · Flux homogeneity acceptance angle · Primary optic · Optical effectiveness · Dome · Intelligent electric vehicles · Secondary optic

1 Introduction

Wireless technologies such as smartphones and tablets are gaining popularity due to advances in wireless networks and mobile devices with access to the Internet. The Internet of Things (IoT) was developed as a novel concept and then produced. Recently, the IoT has attracted significant attention regarding wired and wireless networks. In general, the IoT is a network for sharing data of everyday businesses including consumer goods and appliances, intelligent transportation, healthcare, smart cities, smart homes, intelligent cars, energy systems, and workplace safety.

Electric charging stations with solar panels operate differently than conventional fast-charging systems. Indeed, the solar panels associated with the charging station will be affected by photons at the level of the photovoltaic cells. These push the electrons to move, producing a direct electric current.

Inverters will then transform the direct current into an alternating current, which the charging station will store. This electric current stored in the charging station will then be redistributed to the electric car when the motorist wishes to recharge it.

S. El Himer
Sidi Mohamed Ben Abdellah University, Fes, Morocco
e-mail: sarah.elhimer@usmba.ac.ma

M. Ouaissa (✉)
LISI, Cadi Ayyad University, Marrakech, Morocco
e-mail: m.ouaissa@uca.ac.ma

M. Ouaissa
LTI, Chouaib Doukkali University, El Jadida, Morocco
e-mail: ouaissa.mariyam@ucd.ac.ma

Z. Boulouard
LIM, Hassan II University, Casablanca, Morocco
e-mail: zakaria.boulouard@fstm.ac.ma

S. Arezki et al. (eds.), *Emerging Disruptive Technologies for Society 5.0 in Developing Countries*,
Advances in Science, Technology & Innovation, https://doi.org/10.1007/978-3-031-63701-8_19

Electric car owners choose charging stations equipped with photovoltaic panels because devices such as solar panels have many advantages.

The first advantage of charging stations equipped with photovoltaic panels is primarily economic. Indeed, installing a solar panel allows a consumer to reduce their electricity bills, or even to be both a consumer and a producer if the production covers all the household's needs. In general, installing solar panels usually pays for itself in 10 years.

The other advantages linked to charging stations equipped with solar panels are ecological. Indeed, by choosing to recharge their electric car using terminals equipped with photovoltaic panels, motorists who have already chosen to adopt more environmentally responsible mobility by switching to the electric car can continue their ecological approach by recharging their vehicle's battery using solar energy, a clean and entirely renewable energy.

This article proposes a study which includes a fast intelligent charging station (120 kW) of an electric vehicle powered by a micro-concentration photovoltaic system. This study is divided into two sections. The first section examines the general performance of two optical components (Fresnel lens [FL] and two secondary optics [circular and square dome]) to be used in photovoltaic micro-concentrator (MCPV) systems for electric car charging stations. The optical capabilities of the two developed micro-CPV systems are evaluated using ray-tracing modeling. The MCPV's performance in connecting the lens to the dome is evaluated. The second section addresses the differences between standard AC charging infrastructure facilities and IoT-enabled DC fast chargers. An analysis of the existing state of the electric vehicle infrastructure, techniques for designing a safe EV-charging infrastructure, use of pertinent theory, and risk assessment studies are discussed. Distinctions between conventional AC charging infrastructure and DC fast chargers with IoT capabilities are investigated, and the current condition of the EV charging infrastructure, strategies for creating a safe EV-charging system, application of pertinent theory, and risk assessment studies are discussed.

2 Related Work

A photovoltaic shade house is an independent, electric vehicle portable energy recharge station that is made accessible to consumers by local governments as well as for sites with private usage, including shopping malls, car rental businesses, or individuals (Fig. 1). Rechargeable batteries that use the power grid or other renewable energy sources serve as the vehicle's power source (solar, wind turbines, etc.). Heavy vehicles are parked in this location. Solar technologies including micro-CPV and concentrated photovoltaic (CPV) are excellent for this use. The shade house protects against the sun's beams and inclement weather while converting sunlight into energy. Among the most optimistic ways to use solar radiation to produce sustainable power are concentrated photovoltaic (CPV) systems which act as a very effective substitute for the typical flat plate module (Sanna et al. 2015). The quantity of space needed in the cells is significantly reduced by this method. To maximize a number of benefits, micro-CPV is used to achieve submillimeter cell size reduction, but doing so also presents some production challenges. The micro-CPV reduces the width since the volume, weight, and thickness of the CPV modules are related to the cell size. Technology has improved to the point that modules are approaching 40% efficiency in contrast to this commercial failure (Steiner et al. 2016).

Fig. 1 The photovoltaic shade

Concentration optics can be created using one or two optical components. Numerous authors have used parabolic mirrors (Trespidi and Timò 1881; Trespidi et al. 1881; Lokeswaran et al. 2020; Wang et al. 2020; Yazdanifard et al. 2017; Yew et al. 2015), Fresnel lenses (Yew et al. 2015; Himer et al. 2018a, 2016; Leutz et al. 1999; Akisawa and Hiramatsu 2012; Pham 2018; Languy et al. 2013; Vallerotto et al. 2017; Zhuang 2014; Wang et al. 2016; Ryu et al. 2006; Pham et al. 2019; El-Yahyaoui et al. 2017), and compound parabolic concentrators. The findings show that systems using CPV cannot satisfy the overall performance requirement when utilizing one stage. Either the mechanism is highly effective but the cell's flux dispersion is not uniform, or the opposite is true. Several-stage concentrators, which consist of optical elements called the primary optic (PO) and secondary optic (SO), can be more effective. Secondary systems based on Fresnel lenses that we found in the literature and that Rodriguez et al. (2017, 2018) researched included the dome, pyramid, and crossed compound parabolic concentrator and the hyperbole. According to modeling data, optical efficiency exists for the four concentrators at a level greater than 80% and at an acceptance angle of less than 1°. The best flux uniformity may be attained using the pyramid.

These conclusions are supported by experiments which showed that the optical efficiency level fell to 73%, and the acceptance angle fell to 0.8°. El Himer et al. (2018b) investigated four CPV systems with a 1000x concentration rate using just simulation. The systems were comprised of four auxiliary optical elements (CPC, cone, CCPC, and pyramid). Additionally, the authors demonstrated how the SO pyramid gives the widest acceptance angle (1.4°), the highest level of optical efficiency, and the most uniform lighting on the solar cell, regardless of the material used (83%). Numerous authors have researched the effectiveness of parabolic mirrors as a primary or secondary optic (Canavarro et al. 2013; Chen et al. 2009). The findings show that the usage of a parabolic mirror as the main optical element gives significant optical effects, particularly when paired with a flat mirror, resulting in optical efficiency of up to 85%. The CPV system works better when two optical components of concentration are utilized because it permits high optical efficiency, high concentration, and a wide acceptance angle.

An innovative approach to creating high-efficiency, low-cost PV systems is the use of micro-concentrator photovoltaic (MCPV) systems. They might be installed at low cost, similar to solar panels that are flat on rooftops, and in small spaces (Araki et al. 2019). Micro-CPV systems are predicated on the size of the system being reduced (cells and optics). The only difference between micro-CPV modules and CPV modules is their smaller size. The primary optic is similar in size to the thickness of the module, measuring a few centimeters per side, and the width of a multijunction solar cell is often less than one millimeter (Cruz-Campa et al. 2010). The back of a micro-concentrator may not always have a heat sink in addition to the variable size. The amount of heat that needs to be evacuated is reduced by the lenses' limited gathering area. The heat generated by the cell's conversion losses can be effectively dissipated by the metal tracks that join the cells in series (Cruz-Campa et al. 2010). This method avoids losses in Fresnel lenses since full lenses are employed to achieve good optical efficiency; draft angles or tip rounding may be present.

Sharp (Apostoleris et al. 2016) and IRDEP FR: 73x (Jutteau et al. 2016) are two micro-CPVs that operate at a rate of less than 400x and have module efficiencies of 32.7% and 12.x6%, respectively. Additionally, Semprius uses modules with an efficiency of 35.0% (Ghosal et al. 2016) and a concentration rate of 1111. Using micro-concentration, the Insight and Morgan solar firms were able to reach module efficiencies of 36.4% and 29.0%, respectively (Domínguez et al. 2017).

Making efficient energy use sustainable is one of the major concerns of smart city facilities. The two primary architectures created by EV manufacturers are plug-in hybrid electric cars (xEVs) and plug-in electric vehicles (EVs).

For the purpose of onboard use and range, two powertrains were first deployed. In nations that use EVs, EVs are charged using controlled and adapted circuits with battery pack capacity using AC and DC chargers. DC charging facilities have the potential to save time by 80% (Guide to EV Charging 2018) depending on battery capacity. A DC charger can bring the battery pack of an electric car from a completely discharged state to a full charge in 650 to 1850s (SOC). An Android smartphone app created in Bedogni et al. (2014) can offer a list of charging station (CS) locations that are physically closest to the location of an electric vehicle (EV), but the EV user may not be aware of whether the nearby CS is open or not, resulting in the selection of the incorrect CS. This tracking technology is also employed in Anuradha and Sendhilkumar (2011) to provide the accurate location of the vehicle. ETA and required distance for the vehicle are also provided to commuters through an online application. The concept is to employ ZigBee technology to replace the current wireless sensor network (WSN) and radio-frequency identification (RFID) system in parking garages, according to Patil and Bhonge (2013). Kuran et al. (2015) has created a system for scheduling the charging of electric vehicles (EVs) in parking lots. This approach is based on a sensible parking scheme that prioritizes individual parking spaces for vehicles. It categorizes electric vehicles into two groups based on how mobile they are. Using a two-layered PLRS algorithm, the proposed system recharges electric vehicles based on parking patterns. Khanna and Anand (2016) presents an IoT-based, cloud-integrated smart parking solution. The IoT modules made in-country are the foundation of this proposed smart parking system. One smart city concept is the Internet of Things. The Internet of Things concept monitors and reports parking space availability. In addition, it offers a smartphone application that informs users of available parking spots. By using this smartphone application, users can reserve a parking space. This technology provides real-time statistics on the number of parking spaces in the lot. Induction or magnetic coupling techniques are suitable WPT methods for the charging of electric vehicles, according to Sultanbek et al. (2017). The smart parking system technique is shown in Gupta and Kulkarni (2017). According to Niu et al. (2019), more infrastructures for charging are required due to the rise in electric vehicle (EV) use. Wireless charging is more efficient than plugs and wires for charging. It is crucial to deal with problems as the number of EVs rises. Resonant inductive power transfer is the fundamental theory underlying the widely utilized wireless charging technology. Battery swapping, conductive charging, and wire-to-conductor (WC) transfer are the three different charging methods. Because the global market for electric vehicles is growing swiftly, there are many different charging stations today.

3 Modeling of Electric Car Charging Station Using Micro-CPV System

8 to 12 h or at a charging station for electric vehicles, electric vehicles can be fully charged merely by plugging them into a protected household socket in 8–12 h. Depending on the type of charging station, the second approach cuts the charging time by at least 30% while providing improved charging security. Currently, this public charging infrastructure is most used.

Typically, charging stations have the shape of a fixed device that is directly connected to an electrical distribution board. There may be one or more charging points per charging station. These points form the structures that supply electricity and to which a user connects his car by using a movable connection or a cable fixed to the terminal. A user interface and a radio-identification reader (RFID) can be added to the terminals to manage service identification, charging, and billing. Currently, there are three different kinds of charging stations (see Fig. 2), each of which has unique specifications regarding the outlets, electrical power delivered (in kW), and charging rate.

To ensure that the batteries are fully charged in 6 to 8 h, "regular" or "standard" charging stations supply an electrical output of between 3 and 7 kW. They produce a power demand comparable to a water heater.

- With a power of 22 kW, "accelerated" charging stations (also known as semi-rapid charging stations) guarantee a complete charge of the batteries in 1 h. The power draw of a building is produced via accelerated charging.
- "Rapid" charging stations deliver power between 43 and 50 kW, enabling the battery to regain 80% of its autonomy in less than 30 min.
- Fast charging produces a power draw (120 kW) comparable to a metropolitan neighborhood. As a result, the local network is often strengthened in conjunction with the construction of fast charging stations. This requires substantial investment.

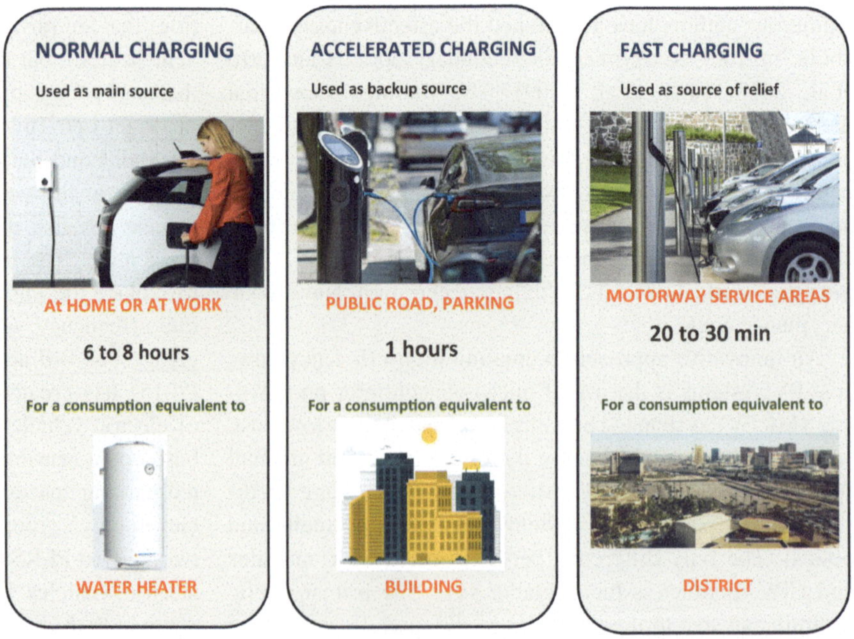

Fig. 2 Power levels for three different uses

3.1 Fundamental Ideas for Solar Concentrators

Figure 3 displays an example of an optical system that separates two media with n_1 and n_2 refractive indices for the environments at the entry and the exit, respectively.

The ratio of the total concentration of the system is defined as:

3.2 Optical Elements

Numerous small concentric grooves make up the Fresnel lens. In this section, we look at the situation of a two-dimensional Fresnel lens with inward grooves. We can create the following Eqs. (1–6) based on Fig. 4:

$$\mathbf{C} = \eta \times \mathbf{C_g} \tag{1}$$

where the optical efficiency η is indicated by:

$$\eta = \frac{\mathbf{P_{out}}}{\mathbf{P_{in}}} \tag{2}$$

The rate of the entry and exit surfaces determines the geometrical concentration Cg. This is provided by:

$$\mathbf{C_g} = \frac{\mathbf{A_{in}}}{\mathbf{A_{out}}} = \frac{\mathbf{n_2 sin\theta_{out}}}{\mathbf{n_2 sin\theta_{in}}} \tag{3}$$

$$\beta = r' + \theta_i \tag{4}$$

$$\theta_i = \mathrm{artg}\frac{d}{2f} \tag{5}$$

$$\tan r' = \frac{d}{2\left(n\sqrt{\left(\frac{d}{2}\right)^2 + f^2 - 1}\right)} \tag{6}$$

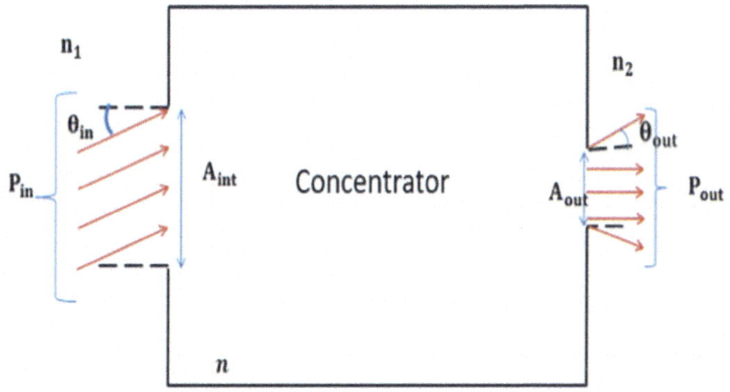

Fig. 3 General view of an optical system

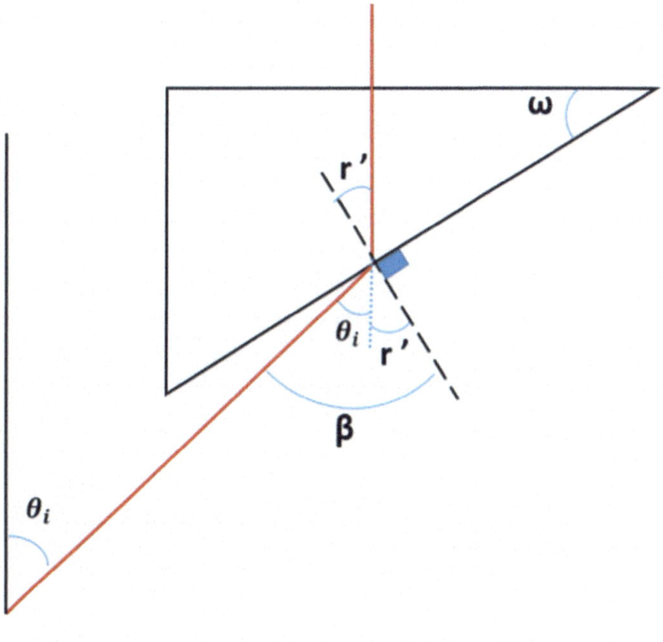

Fig. 4 The Fresnel lens's inward-facing prism

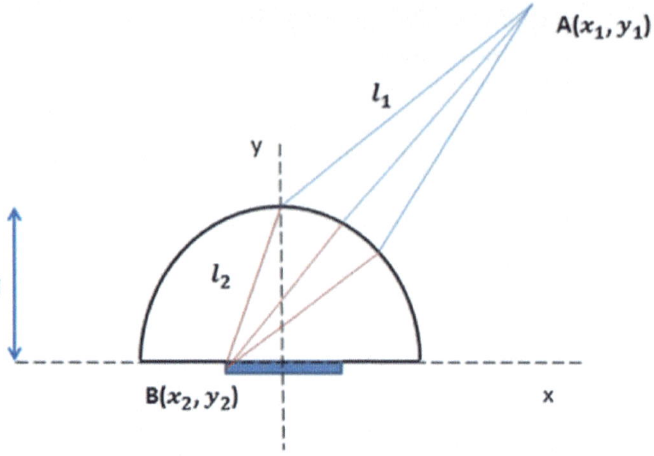

Fig. 5 Fermat's concept was used to create secondary optical element

Another optic is a dome with square and circular exits. Its goal (see Fig. 5) is to build the entry surface of the dome so that every ray from the primary lens A (x_1, y_1) strikes the opposite extreme point of the cell B (x_2, y_2). Additionally, regardless of the angle of incidence, all rays passing through points A and B must adhere to Fermat's conservation of optical path length (Eqs. 7–9) (Wei et al. 2018). The following is Fermat's premise under these conditions:

$$\mathbf{l_1 + n_{SOE}l_{21} = cst} \tag{7}$$

$$\mathbf{l_1 = \sqrt{(x - x_1)^2 + (y - y_1)^2}} \tag{8}$$

$$\mathbf{l_2 = \sqrt{(x - x_2)^2 + (y - y_2)^2}} \tag{9}$$

The dome's height, hSO (Eq. 10), serves as the foundation for constructing the profile. By imposing the tangent of the bidimensional profile, it is fixed, where F/# denotes the primary lens's f-number to be horizontal at the origin.

$$(x_0, y_0) = (0, h_{SO}) = \frac{x_0}{\tan\left[\boldsymbol{arcsin}\left(\frac{\sin\left(\boldsymbol{arctg}\left(\frac{1}{2F/\#}\right)\right)}{n_{SO}}\right)\right]} \tag{10}$$

3.3 Simulation Results and Discussion

To evaluate the performance significance of concentrators, we use a dome of various forms (circular and square), a 0.25×0.25 mm^2 solar cell, and a flat circular Fresnel lens with an 8-mm diameter, 16 prisms, and an 8-mm focal length.

Each SO's optical efficiency and output flux distribution is compared. The SO is always placed near the Fresnel lens's focal point. The simulations made use of a standard spectral light source (0.38–1.4 m) with a sun-like angular dispersion and an intensity of 1000 W/m^2.

Table 1 Micro-CPV module's optical performance and acceptance angle with a dome as SOs

	Circular dome	Square dome
Optical efficiency (%)	82.82	86.76
Angle of acceptance (°)	1	1.4
Power (W)	664	720

Despite the two round SOs having the highest intensity which exceeds 80%, specifying that the square dome presents the highest intensity (86.76%) and the largest acceptance angle (1.4°) as illustrated in Table 1, we learned that the two domes present respectable homogeneity as demonstrated in Fig. 6.

Although an electric car's battery is rarely completely empty when the owner gets home, a solar system made expressly for this purpose would need to produce between 24 and 100 kWh so that the battery can be recharged through the day. Therefore, to refuel a car battery on a sunny day, you would need a 6-kW solar system. Six and a half kilometers, or 150 Wh per kilometer, may be covered by an electric car using 1 kWh of battery energy or 1 kWh of battery-generated energy (note that this amount can change based on the kind of road and the season). For an electric vehicle to move, it must be provided with approximately 3000 kWh of electricity to travel 20,000 km annually using solar power.

Therefore, to achieve such a large amount of electricity, a solar system with a total output of approximately 120 kW is needed for fast charging. It takes 167 multi-junction cells to charge an electric vehicle at any power level with this electricity. Consequently, 120.24 kW of power are generated. Thus, the total surface area needed for our charging station is 1.3 m^2. Compared to stations placed in Morocco, our station does not need a large surface area or a lot of power.

Fig. 6 The dome's distribution of flux

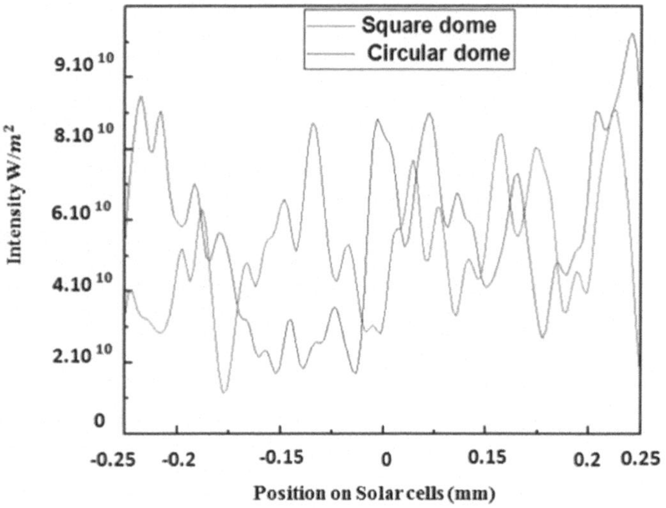

4 Iot Connectivity for a Smart Car Charging Station

4.1 Battery Charging

The most significant issues with EVs are charging and battery expense. Deep discharge and overcharging of batteries cause accelerated aging characteristics. The current generation of lithium-ion energy storage devices is more susceptible to a number of physical factors, including overcharging, temperature window, safety concerns, charge status, cycle life, shelf life, and cell balancing. Battery management systems (BMS), also known as sensors, estimators, and actuators with integrated battery management and supervisory control, are required to address these issues. These BMS contain a wide range of repairable components and significant difficulties, such as balancing cells, maintaining acceptable operating temperatures, detecting cell voltage to correlate charge state, and fault identification. A module is comprised of countless cells coupled in different combinations of parallel and series, and some integrate modules are referred to as vehicle battery packs. Battery packs and motor controllers make up the powertrain management systems for electric vehicles (EVs). According to credible literature, charging and discharging in an equivalent circuit of internal resistance Rint take comparable routes. Using the equivalent circuit model (ECM) and research on the Kalman filter, it is possible to determine the charge's condition. As shown in Fig. 7, the Coulomb counting Ampere-hour integral approach, which was used to calculate SOC, connected the battery pack's readings of the cell voltage and SOC.

The charge's state (SOC) and state of health (SOH) forecast of the xEVs battery pack serves as the input BMS for displaying the remaining charge and monitoring the constantly changing battery aging parameters. An enhanced adaptive Kalman filter (AEKF) is rated as the best solution regarding very non-linear systems by the vast majority of respondents to the survey. The Q-estimation algorithm determines the capacity estimation approach, as demonstrated by some research. Figure 8 depicts a double layer

Fig. 7 Adaptive extended Kalman filter

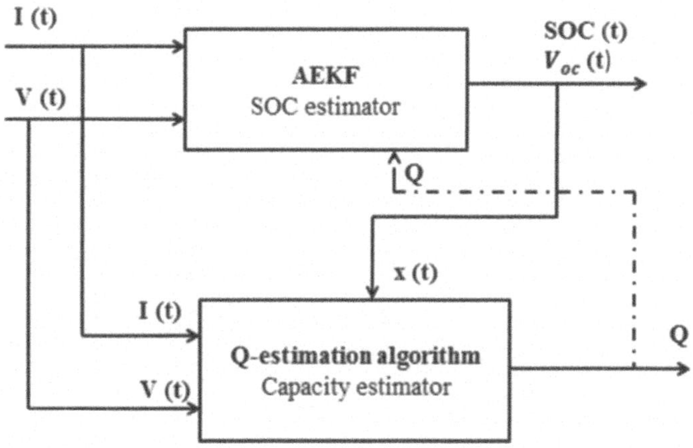

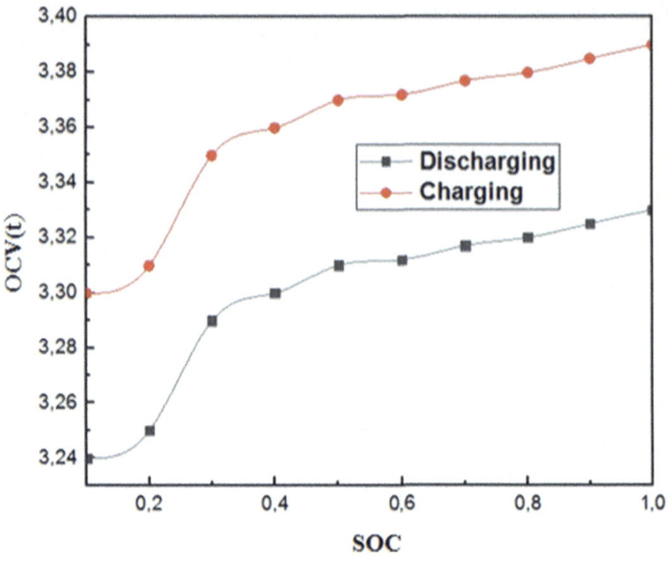

Fig. 8 State of charge versus charging and discharging profile for an 18,650 lithium-ion phosphate cell

estimation framework structure combined with an algorithm for evaluating both SOC and Q, with the SOC estimation coming from an extended adaptive Kalman filter (AEKF).

Given the actual degree of aging, the Q-estimation method gives the updated estimate of the AEKF filter for the battery capacity. The Q value factor tunes the charger to be set automatically based on aging while fast charging. The charging and discharging are shown in Fig. 7 by the behavior of a lithium-ion cell manufactured using the chemistry of ion phosphate (LFP). The hysteresis of the profile for charging and discharging is depicted on the plot. The Q algorithm forecasts the rate of aging at various operation temperatures. The user will receive information about the remaining usable life of the battery pack from the collected data on its usage history (Fig. 9). Regardless of the communication medium used by the sensors, the architecture makes assimilation easier because the block is equipped with mechanisms for encapsulating access to data from various communication protocols via wireless topology. The design elements are able to gather data from various system-connected sensors in this way. The choice of charging station is made using the information gathered from the car and the availability of nearby charging stations. Gathering data from any of the sensory networks is the task of the following layer.

Data access is pre-processed before it is acquired by the various sensors used in mobile architecture. Optimization algorithms are run to reflect the knowledge of demand forecast, and estimation as data from many sources receives information fusion. The operation of the optimization algorithms is dependent on how the information overlay is implemented in the data access. The optimization model incorporates data from generated routes, information about the physical locations of the routes, data from earlier intakes, and data from EV sensors for mobile navigation and instrument cluster devices.

The optimization models assist in classifying the levels of the route taken, the battery level, the user's physical exertion, and the traffic circumstances. A neural network coordinated specific optimization efforts on the particle swarm optimization (PSO) to improve a number of route limitations. The control approach with real-time optimization is

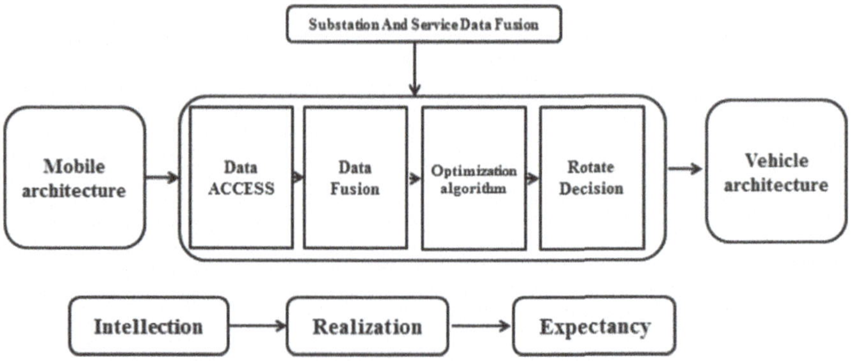

Fig. 9 IoT-based battery parameters observation system

anticipated to estimate and predict based on GPS data and drive cycle demand. The battery pack characteristics adopt the real torque from the powertrain's optimal torque by changing torque demand and restricting speed to the conditions on the road. However, a large amount of calculating effort is needed to achieve the real-time requirement. The design uses the most popular fused sensor network for electric vehicles, which charges the battery according to the best route location. For the cost structure of intelligent systems, optimizing battery stacking results based on battery SOC, temperature, trip distance, and network concerns in the battery pack will be essential.

4.2 IoT-Based Battery Management for Electric Vehicle

An intelligent vehicle instrument cluster, an interface protocol for mobile architecture, data collecting, cloud storage, and components include an IoT-based EV battery conditioning system. Communication between the various data flow nodes is facilitated via an integrated IoT-embedded architecture. All battery system parameters are connected via the Internet gateway as encapsulated data, making it possible to back up, analyze, and regulate the crucial parameters using cloud computing systems.

The built-in Internet of Things battery cooling system uses digital TCP/IP communication via MAT-file (MATLAB) format for data collection. The battery monitoring data are taken from the mobile architecture for use in other applications. Specifically, in the D2S pattern, integrated protocols are optimal for connecting devices to vehicle operators because vehicles are connected to servers through the Internet. Data is shared with the web server, the database, and cloud system clients via the Internet entry point. Operators receive a judgment via the xEVs's touchscreen instrument cluster panel that is based on the processing and analysis of data in the cloud system. The Internet of Things (IoT) architecture regarding the battery pack observation systems will include an embedded system that can be used as an IoT to make proposals through hardware integration, as the principal data collector, and as a data access gateway for the Internet.

The configuration shown in Fig. 10 entails processing the obtained data into an optimum method estimation and proposing a prediction using a Kalman filter. The automotive instrument cluster runs the software which was created utilizing an interface with graphics to the data server. Data-gathering procedures are carried out using the web-based GUI to obtain parameters for battery measurement in the MAT-file format. The information that was moved utilizing cloud computing stations and structured query language will be kept.

4.3 Integration Requirements for IoT Charging Stations

The following safety and security requirements must precede the design phase of IoT-integrated xEV charger systems.

Guidelines and technical measures expose threats in the current chargers. The extortions, liabilities, and risks associated with IoT-driven EV charging are intended to be reduced by these methods and technological inspection (Table 2).

Fig. 10 Kalman fiber method

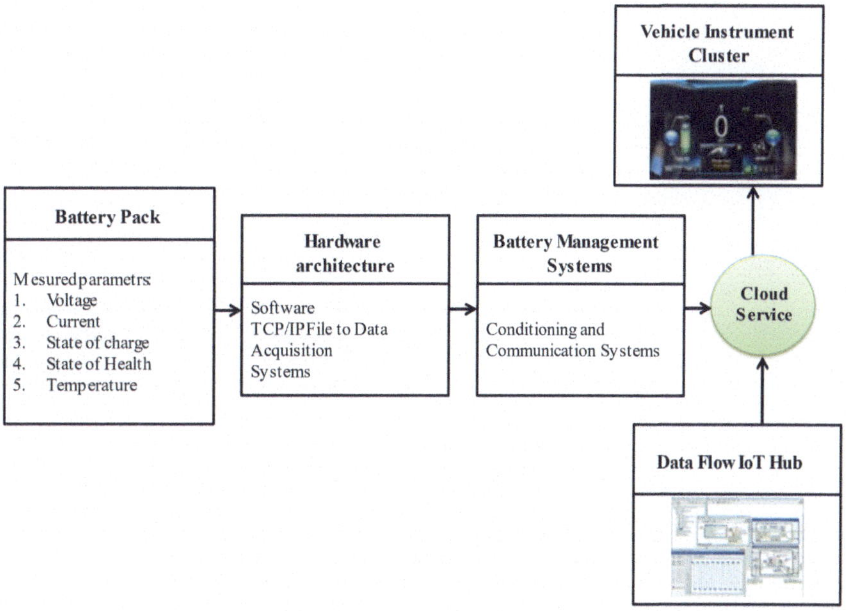

Table 2 Comparison of several station charging proposals

Reference paper	Merits	Demerits
Wei et al. (2018) Charging and Parking System	Use of charging management system (CMS)	No mobile application
Panchal et al. (2018) Charging System	Wireless charging is simpler and more efficient than plug-in charging Used for high power application	Efficient to use only in stationary modes
Kesler (2018) Charging System	It offers an efficient, flexible means of charging electric vehicles	Lack of standardization in wireless charging
Niu et al. (2019) Charging System	Wireless charging has more advantages than plug-in charging	–
Anusha et al. 2019) 2019 Parking System	Facility for booking parking slots	GPS is not used. There is no data uploading
Our study	Use of mobile application Secure Use of micro-CPV system for alimentation Small space Does not take up a lot of space	–

Figure 11 illustrates the communication and power lines for the quick DC chargers as well as connections between IoT modems and the cloud service. The user device for the xEVs has mobile applications installed that guarantee the safety and identification of the charging process. In this schematic, the service provider can determine the demand for vehicles by determining the users' positions via navigation systems with charger ID in addition to a user's request to enter the charging station ID.

Initiating a payment exchange with an outside provider of online payment services utilizing an RFID-based detecting device, a wallet, a credit card, a debit card, or net banking is what a cloud payment service does if the user ID matches. The cloud service instructs the fast DC chargers. There is an IoT hub to authorize the linked EV of the user and permit use of the charging station after the payment transaction has been approved by the payment service. Only the initial quantity of energy used—as measured by the battery's SOC—is paid for. Bidirectional links between cloud computing and vehicles are established via user display devices and the user, according to DIN SPEC 70,121 and ISO 15118 (smartphone app). For cost deduction authentication, the payment service also uses a bank account that is connected to a cloud service. If a user wants to go a shorter distance and just needs a partial charge to charge the battery, a DC quick charger is a transaction that returns money to the user's account. In comparing our research with other studies (Panchal et al. 2018; Kesler 2018; Niu et al. 2019), we can say that ours contains a charging station powered by the micro photovoltaic concentration. More discussions of the

Fig. 11 Integration of a standard IoT charging station

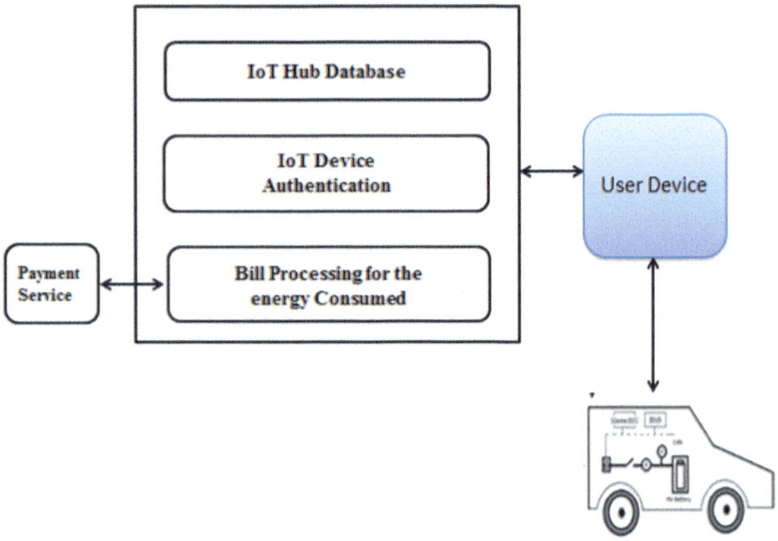

chapter relate to the analysis of the current scenario of the infrastructure of charging of electric vehicles, the methods of designing a safe charging system for electric vehicles, the use of the risk assessment research, and pertinent theory.

Based on a literature review, Table 2 compares various research papers to present the merits and demerits. As the table shows, our proposal presents an intelligent charging station using a mobile application and a secure station with a micro-CPV system for power supply.

Finally, conclusions and some limitations of IoT-driven smart charging infrastructure installations are discussed. IoT technology is rapidly developing, creating chances for xEV manufacturers to prioritize their robust market presence. IoT still faces malware risks and lack of interoperability, privacy, platform standards, and network standard protocols. In response, manufacturers of IoT devices have offered ideas and considered the design and development of extremely secure authentication.

Additionally, the integrated IoT should have security information on vulnerable locations evaluated thoroughly before integration. Architectural checkpoints that are crucial to the design process are carefully examined for dangers to the setup. Additionally, the standard protocol will be used by the charging infrastructure of xEVs connected to various xEV manufacturers.

Recognition, detection, access control, encryption, flexibility, and safe bill payment transactions are the main components in demonstrating a successful implementation. These components are applied to the IoT-driven charging infrastructure. Users can monitor and regulate EV parameters for knowledge and information about the use of the charging systems by testing a smart application on a user interface display or mobile device. The cloud data from each EV database will be useful to EV producers for research and development information. The same information will also give a detailed picture of the batteries' usage history and charge/discharge cycles.

Energy suppliers can examine energy consumption during periods of high and low demand. Additionally, IoT-derived data on energy use and charging times gives buyers information on the best EVs so they may select the best vehicle.

Information for specific vehicles that have not been driven for a few days or more can be forecasted using the IoT self-discharge and aging characteristics of the energy storage devices.

5 Conclusion

This article discusses the general performance of two optical components to be utilized in micro concentrator photovoltaic (MCPV) systems for electric car charging stations employing the same basic optic: the Fresnel lens (FL). This lens involves circular and square dome imaging optics. The performance of each concentrator system is evaluated by comparing the exact concentrations attained, the acceptance angles, as well as the power distribution of the light output. This article covers the second half, which deals with the use of Internet of Things technology to monitor concentrated photovoltaic generation. The second part deals with data on how long it takes to recharge an electric vehicle's energy storage system. In addition, the technological variations between quick DC chargers and conventional alternating current (AC) chargers are examined. To examine the cost of charging a car by integrating IoT devices, the gathered data is shared online with the original equipment manufacturers of each charging station. Additionally, DC rapid charging stations offer electric vehicle users a perfect way to exchange power between all integrated components and related elements. At every charging station, the EV metering architecture gathers real-time data to provide up-to-date information about operations and behaviors on the power distribution network. The square dome has the best homogeneity and optical efficiency despite the two circular SOs having the highest intensity and best uniformity, according to the first simulation findings. Therefore, to generate such a volume of electricity for fast charging, a solar system with a total output of approximately 120 kW is required. Furthermore, 167 multijunction cells are required if this energy can power an electric vehicle at any power level. As a result, 120.24 kW of power is generated. Therefore, 1.3 m2 of total surface area will be needed for our charging station. Unlike the stations in Morocco, our station does not need a lot of space or power. The platform provides the best way for the system to provide EV users with an execution framework to deliver energy demand solutions to all entities operating in a charging smart station infrastructure.

Acknowledgements The heading should be treated as a 3rd level heading and should not be assigned a number.

References

Akisawa, M. Hiramatsu, K. Ozaki, Design of dome-shaped non-imaging Fresnel lenses 3 taking chromatic aberration into account, Solar Energy 86 (2012) 877–885. https://doi.org/10.1016/j.solener.2011.12.017

Anuradha, P. and Sendhilkumar, R. (2011) Design and Implementation of Zigbee-RFID Based Vehicle Tracking. International Conference on Sustainable Energy and Intelligent Systems, Chennai, 20–22 July 2011, 689–694. https://doi.org/10.1049/cp.2011.0451

Anusha, Arshita M S, Anushri, Geetanjali Bishtannavar, Ms. Megha D Hegde, Review Paper on Smart Parking System, International Journal of Engineering Research and Technology, Vol. 7, 2019 IJERT

Apostoleris, H.; Stefancich, M.; Chiesa, M. Tracking-integrated systems for concentrating photovoltaics. Nat. Energy 2016, 1, 16018.

Araki, K.; Sato, D.; Masuda, T.; Lee, K.H.; Yamada, N.; Yamaguchi, M. Why and how does car-roof PV create 50 GW/year of new installations? Also, why is a static CPV suitable to this application? AIP Conf. Proc. 2019, 2149, 050003.

Bedogni, L., Bononi, L., D'Elia, A., Di Felice, M., Rondelli, S. and Cinotti, T.S. (2014) A Mobile Application to Assist Electric Vehicles' Drivers with Charging Services. 2014 8th International Conference on Next Generation Mobile Applications, Services and Technologies, Oxford, UK, 10–12 September 2014, 78–83. https://doi.org/10.1109/NGMAST.2014.49

Canavarro, D.; Chaves, J.; Collares-Pereira, M. New second-stage concentrators (XX SMS) for parabolic primaries; Comparison with conventional parabolic trough concentrators. Sol. Energy 2013, 92, 98–105

Chen, C.F.; Lin, C.H.; Jan H.T.; Yang, Y.L. Design of a solar concentrator combining paraboloidal and hyperbolic mirrors using ray tracing method. Opt. Commun. 2009, 282, 360–366

Cruz-Campa, J.L.; Okandan, M.; Busse, M.L.; Nielson, G.N. Microlens rapid prototyping technique with capability for wide variation in lens diameter and focal length. Microelectron. Eng. 2010, 87, 2376–2381

Domínguez, C.; Jost, N.; Askins, S.; Victoria, M.; Antón, I. A review of the promises and challenges of micro-concentrator photovoltaics. AIP Conf. Proc. 2017, 1881, 080003

S. El Himer, A. Ahaitouf, Sara El-yahyaoui, Abdellah Mechaqrane, Performance analysis of non-imaging Fresnel lens as a primary stage for CPV units, IOP Conference Series: Earth and Environmental Science (2018) 012029. https://doi.org/10.1088/1755-1315/161/1/012029

S. El Himer, A. Ahaitouf, S. El-yahyaoui, A. Mechaqrane, Parametric optimization and performances analysis of four secondary optical elements for concentrator photovoltaic systems, International Journal of Renewable Energy Research-IJRER 8 (2018) 4. https://doi.org/10.1063/1.5053502

El-Yahyaoui, S.; El Himer, S.; Mechaqrane, A.; Ahaitouf, A. Optimal design of inverted truncated pyramid with Fresnel lens for concentrated photovoltaic Units. IOP Conf. Ser. Mater. Sci. Eng. 2017, 186

Ghosal, K.; Fisher, B.; Lilly, D.; Gabriel, J.; Seel, S.; Burroughs, S. Ultrahigh Efficiency HCPV Modules and Systems. IEEE J. Photovolt. 2016, 6, 1360–1365

Guide to EV charging Jun-2018. https://www.zap-map.com/charge-points/

Gupta, A., Kulkarni, S., et al. (2017) Smart Car Parking Management System Using IoT. American Journal of Science, Engineering and Technology, 2, 112–119

Himer, S.E.; El-yahyaoui, S.; Mechaqrane, A.; Ahaitouf, A. Performance Comparison of Two Optical Elements. In Proceedings of the 2016 International Renewable and Sustainable Energy Conference (IRSEC), Marrakech, Morocco, 14–17 November 2016

Jutteau, S.; Guillemoles, J.-F.; Paire, M. Study of a micro-concentrated photovoltaic system based on Cu(In,Ga)Se2 microcells array. Appl. Opt. 2016, 55, 6656–6661

Morris Kesler, Wireless Charging of Electrical Vehicles, WiTricity Corporation, Watertown, MA, USA, 2018. IEEE

Khanna, A. and Anand, R. (2016) IoT Based Smart Parking System. 2016 International Conference on Internet of Things and Applications, Pune, India, 22–24 January 2016, 266–270. https://doi.org/10.1109/IOTA.2016.7562735

Kuran, M.S., Carneiro Viana, A., Iannone, L., Kofman, D., Mermoud, G. and Vasseur, J.P. (2015) A Smart Parking Lot Management System for Scheduling the Recharging of Electric Vehicles. IEEE Transactions on Smart Grid, 6, 2942-2953. https://doi.org/10.1109/TSG.2015.2403287

F. Languy, C. Lenaerts, J. Loicq, T. Thibert, S. Habraken, Performance of solar concentrator made of an achromatic Fresnel doublet measured with a continuous solar simulator and comparison with a singlet, Solar Energy Materials and Solar Cells (2013) 70–76. https://doi.org/10.1016/j.solmat.2012.10.008

R. Leutz, A.Suzuki A. Akisawa, T. Kashiwagi, Design of a nonimaging Fresnel lens for solar concentrators, Solar energy 65 (1999) 379–387. https://doi.org/10.1016/b978-008043895-5/50228-9

Lokeswaran, S.; Mallick, T.K.; Reddy, K.S. Design and analysis of dense array CPV receiver for square parabolic dish system with CPC array as secondary concentrator. Sol. Energy 2020, 199, 782–795

Niu, S., Xu, H., Sun, Z., Shao, Z.Y. and Jian, L. (2019) The State-of-the-Arts of Wireless Electric Vehicle Charging via Magnetic Resonance: Principles, Standards and Core Technologies. Renewable and Sustainable Energy Reviews, 114, Article ID: 109302. https://doi.org/10.1016/j.rser.2019.109302

Songyan Niu, Haiqi Xu, Zhirui Sun, Z. Y. Shao, Linni Jian, The State of The Arts of Wireless Electrical Vehicle Charging via Magnetic Resonance: Principles, Standards and Core Technologies, Journal of Renewable and Sustainable Energy Reviews, 2019

Chirag Panchal, et al, Review of static and dynamic wireless electric vehicle charging system, Engineering Science and Technology, an International Journal, pp. 922–937, 21 June 2018

Patil, M. and Bhonge, V. (2013) Wireless Sensor Network and RFID for Smart Parking System. International Journal of Emerging Technology and Advanced Engineering, 3, 188–192. http://citeseerx.ist.psu.edu/viewdoc/download?doi=10.1.1.413.7821&rep=rep1&type=pdf

T. T. Pham, Ngoc Hai Vu, and S. Shin, Design of curved fresnel lens with high performance creating competitive price concentrator photovoltaic, Energy Procedia 144 (2018) 16–32. https://doi.org/10.1016/j.egypro.2018.06.004

T. T. Pham, N. H. Vu and S. Shin, Novel Design of Primary Optical Elements Based on a Linear Fresnel Lens for Concentrator Photovoltaic Technology, Energies 12 (2019) 1209. https://doi.org/10.3390/en12071209

J. P. F.Rodríguez, H. Baig, E. F.Fernández, F. Almonacid, T. Mallick, P.P. Higueras, Optical modeling of four Fresnel-based high-CPV units, Solar Energy 155 (2017) 805-815. https://doi.org/10.1016/j.solener.2017.07.027

J. P.F.Rodríguez, E. F.Fernández, H. Baig, F. Almonacid, T. Mallick, P.P.Higueras, Development, indoor characterisation and comparison to optical modelling of four Fresnel-based high-CPV units equipped with refractive secondary optics. Solar Energy Materials and Solar Cells 186 (2018) 273–283. https://doi.org/10.1016/j.solmat.2018.06.050

K. Ryu, J.G. Rhee, K.M. Parkc, J. Kim. Concept and design of modular Fresnel lenses for concentration solar PV system, Solar energy 80 (2006) 1580–1587. https://doi.org/10.1016/j.solener.2005.12.006

JC. Sanna; M. Gawronska; A. Damiano, "Energy Performance of Concentrator and Flat Plate Photovoltaics in the Mediterranean Area", 2015 IEEE International Conference on Renewable Energy Research and Applications (ICRERA), Palermo, Italy, pp 760–765, 22–25 Nov. 2015

M. Steiner, G. Siefer, T. Schmidt, M. Wiesenfarth, F. Dimroth, and A. W. Bett, "43 % Sunlight to Electricity Conversion Efficiency Using CPV," IEEE J. Photovolt., vol. 6, no. 4, pp. 1020–1024, Jul. 2016

Sultanbek, A., Khassenov, A., Kanapyanov, Y., Kenzhegaliyeva, M. and Bagheri, M. (2017) Intelligent Wireless Charging Station for Electric Vehicles. 2017 International Siberian Conference on Control and Communications, Astana, 29–30 June 2017, 1–6. https://doi.org/10.1109/SIBCON.2017.7998497

F. Trespidi and G. Timò, Optical Design of an Off-axis Mirror Based Solar Concentrator, in: AIP Conference Proceedings 1881 (2017) 030008. https://doi.org/10.1063/1.5001419

F. Trespidi, E. Malvisi, and R. Parmesani, Shape characterization of the primary mirror of a mirror based solar concentrator, in: AIP Conference Proceedings 1881 (2017) 030009. https://doi.org/10.1063/1.5001420

G. Vallerotto, M Victoria, S Askins, I Antón, and G Sala, Experimental characterization of achromatic doublet on glass (ADG) Fresnel lenses, AIP Conference Proceedings 1881 (2017) 030010. https://doi.org/10.1063/1.5001421

G. Wang, Z. Chen, P. Hu, X. F. Cheng, Design and optical analysis of the band-focus Fresnel lens solar concentrator, Applied Thermal Engineering 102 (2016) 695–700. https://doi.org/10.1016/j.applthermaleng.2016.04.030

Wang, G.;Wang, F.; Shen, F.; Jiang, T.; Chen, Z.; Hu, P. Experimental and optical performances of a solar CPV device using a linear Fresnel reflector concentrator. Renew. Energy 2020, 146, 2351–2361.

Zhe Wei, Yue Li, Yongmin Zhang, Lin Cal, Intelligent Parking Garage EV Charging Scheduling Considering Battery Charging Characteristic, IEEE Transaction on Industrial Electronics, Vol 65, 3 March 2018

Yazdanifard, F.; Ebrahimnia-Bajestan, E.; Ameri, M. Performance of a parabolic trough concentrating photovoltaic/thermal system: Effects of flow regime, design parameters, and using nanofluids. Energy Conver. Manag. 2017, 148, 1265–1277

Yew, T.K.; Chong, K.K.; Lim, B.H. Performance study of crossed compound parabolic concentrator as secondary optics in non-imaging dish concentrator for the application of dense-array concentrator photovoltaic system. Sol. Energy 2015, 120, 296–309

Z. Zhuang, F.eihong Yu, Optimization design of hybrid Fresnel-based concentrator for generating uniformity irradiance with the broad solar spectrum, Optics & Laser Technologys 60 (2014) 27. https://doi.org/10.1016/j.optlastec.2013.12.021

The Role of Software-Defined Vehicular Networks in Society 5.0

Meryem Chouikik, Mariyam Ouaissa, Mariya Ouaissa, Zakaria Boulouard, and Mohamed Kissi

Abstract

Software-Defined Vehicular Network (SDVN) plays a pivotal role in realizing the vision of Society 5.0. This emerging societal concept seeks to seamlessly integrate technology into all aspects of human life. In this context, Software-Defined Network (SDN) enhances vehicular networks by providing centralized control and dynamic resource allocation, optimizing communication between vehicles and infrastructure. Vehicular networks, empowered by SDN, become a cornerstone of digital transformation, enabling smoother traffic flow, reduced accidents, and improved urban mobility management. Society 5.0 emphasis on technological integration aligns with the potential of vehicular networks and SDN to create innovative solutions, addressing complex challenges such as environmental sustainability and enhanced safety. Together, they drive the shift towards a society where technology catalyzes social and economic progress, aligning individual and collective aspirations with an increasingly interconnected world. In this chapter, we present a comprehensive review of Vehicular Ad-Hoc Network (VANET) architecture, the SDN technology and the integration of SDN in the architecture of VANET. Also, we discuss the role of VANET in the context of Society 5.0.

Keywords

SDVN · VANET · SDN · Society 5.0

1 Introduction

Vehicular Ad-Hoc Network (VANET) (Liu et al. 2019) and Software-Defined Network (SDN) (Chouikik et al. 2022) integration is a cutting-edge technical convergence that fully reflects the aspirational Society 5.0 vision. This social vision aims to establish an ecosystem where technology is smoothly incorporated into all facets of daily life, significantly enhancing both environmental sustainability and quality of life. By intelligently fusing together mobile devices, road infrastructure, and automobiles, VANETs have already started to play a significant part in accomplishing these goals. They encourage safer and more effective urban movement, lessen traffic jams and automobile accidents, and help cut down on carbon emissions (Sheikh et al. 2019).

The dynamic and centralized network management provided by SDN networks, on the other hand, enables VANETs to swiftly adjust to shifting traffic requirements, improve the connection between cars and infrastructure, and guarantee high-quality service. Due to its ability to provide seamless communication and intelligent coordination, this pairing of VANETs with SDN constitutes an important development in urban mobility. As a result, trip times, greenhouse gas emissions, and transportation costs are all reduced (Nobre et al. 2019).

Incorporating these cutting-edge technologies into the Society 5.0 ecosystem will help society transition to a time when intelligent transportation networks are the norm and provide real advantages like decreased urban congestion,

M. Chouikik · Z. Boulouard · M. Kissi
LIM, Hassan II University, Casablanca, Morocco
e-mail: meryem.chouikik-etu@etu.univh2c.ma

Z. Boulouard
e-mail: zakaria.boulouard@fstm.ac.ma

M. Kissi
e-mail: mohamed.kissi@fstm.ac.ma

M. Ouaissa (✉)
LTI, Chouaib Doukkali University, El Jadida, Morocco
e-mail: ouaissa.mariyam@ucd.ac.ma

M. Ouaissa
LISI, Cadi Ayyad University, Marrakech, Morocco
e-mail: m.ouaissa@uca.ac.ma

S. Arezki et al. (eds.), *Emerging Disruptive Technologies for Society 5.0 in Developing Countries*,
Advances in Science, Technology & Innovation, https://doi.org/10.1007/978-3-031-63701-8_20

improved road safety, and the development of a cleaner, more sustainable urban environment. This interaction between VANETs and SDN is a practical illustration of how technology may spur social advancement by bringing individual and group goals into line with the opportunities presented by a society that is becoming more linked (Shaghaghi et al. 2020a).

The structure of this paper is organized as follows: The subsequent section provides a description of the architecture of VANET. Section 3 presents an overview of SDN technology. Section 4 describes the integration of SDN in VANET architecture. We discuss the role of VANET in the context of Society 5.0 in Sect. 5. Conclusions are drawn in Sect. 6.

2 Vehicular Communications

Vehicle-specific wireless networks called Vehicular Ad Hoc Networks link moving cars. They have become an essential technology for enhancing the security and effectiveness of transportation. Vehicles can interact with one another and the nearby road infrastructure thanks to VANETs. Real-time communication enables the transmission of crucial information, like traffic situations, accidents, emergency braking, and many more things. Through sharing information, drivers can better foresee possible problems, which helps to increase road safety. Additionally, VANETs are crucial to the advancement of automatic driving. They make it possible for cars to work together intelligently, resulting in a more peaceful and secure driving environment. Furthermore, by enhancing traffic management and raising the overall energy efficiency of the transportation system, these networks have the potential to lessen traffic congestion. VANETs open the door for a significant change in the way we think about, handle, and experience road mobility (Ouaissa et al. 2022).

Vehicular Ad Hoc Networks are built with communication between moving cars and the local road infrastructure in mind. Here is a broad outline of a VANET network's usual architecture (Houmer and Ouaissa 2022) (Fig. 1):

- Each vehicle connected to the VANET network has an On-Board Unit (OBU), also known as an OBU. Information is collected, processed, and sent by this device. OBUs may feature sensors to keep an eye on the state of the road, wireless communication tools such Wi-Fi, LTE, or Dedicated Short Range Communications (DSRC), and data processing capabilities.
- Road Side Units (RSUs): RSUs are pieces of equipment that are installed beside roadways and frequently match existing roadside features like traffic signals, signs, and lampposts. They function as network entry points and serve as a conduit for data between moving vehicles and network management servers.
- Vehicle-to-Vehicle communication (V2V): This element allows for direct communication between cars. Through specialized wireless connections, the OBUs of cars communicate information such as warnings of impending collisions and speed and direction data.
- RSUs and other road infrastructures can be reached by Vehicle-to-Infrastructure communication (V2I). This makes it possible to gather real-time road data, send safety alerts, and optimize traffic by changing traffic signals.
- Network Management Servers: The VANET network is coordinated and managed by these servers. They maintain data storage, control RSU access, and provide information to vehicles as required. They are essential for managing network efficiency and security.

Fig. 1 VANET architecture

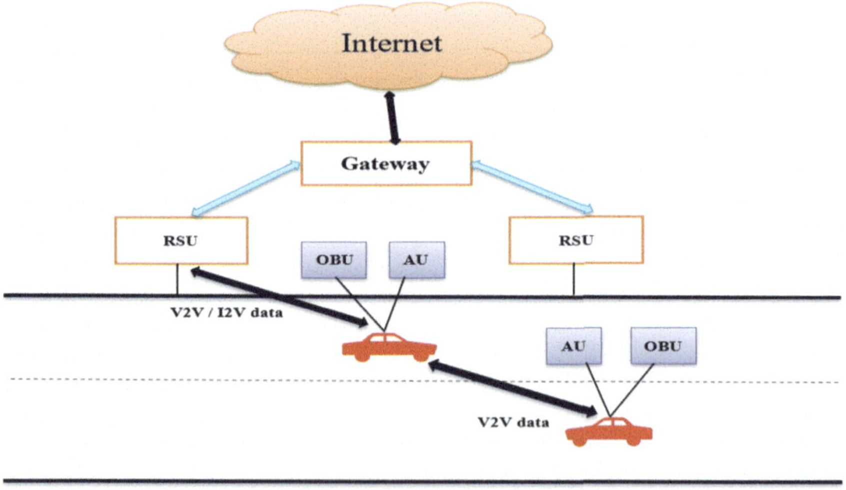

- Cloud and Data Centers: VANET data may be processed and stored in the cloud or data centers, enabling in-depth analysis and the delivery of cutting-edge services like real-time navigation, weather warnings, and more.

Three communication modalities may be distinguished in vehicle networks:

- Infrastructure Mode: In this mode, cars use V2I communication to interact with the RSUs that make up the fixed network infrastructure. This form of communication improves passenger services connected to traffic and allows for better use of shared resources. The biggest disadvantage of this communication method is the expensive and time-consuming process of deploying RSUs along the highways, not to mention the maintenance expenditures that go along with it.
- Ad Hoc Mode: This mode depicts an ad hoc architecture in which V2V communication is used between vehicles. When operating in this mode, a car can connect with another vehicle either directly if it is within its radio coverage area or indirectly through other nearby vehicles using a multi-hop protocol. This form of communication relies on a decentralized infrastructure to provide low-latency, cost-effective, and adaptable communication. In fact, V2V communications are quite successful in spreading notifications for services relevant to road safety. However, because of the increased mobility of cars, they do not ensure constant connectivity and frequently experience disconnections.
- Combining the first two modes is the hybrid mode. It employs V2V communications to increase the roadside infrastructure's meager coverage area. The cost of deploying units along the roadways is decreased by this technique, which has major economic significance. Additionally, minimal latency in V2V communications is an advantage it offers. Because it combines the benefits of the two earlier modalities, this kind of communication is the most widely employed.

3 Software Defined Networking: An Overview

The Software Defined Networking paradigm introduces a centralized and programmable method of designing networks and was created to address the shortcomings of traditional networks, including their high latency in path-recovery due to a distributed approach, manual configuration, and maintenance of each and every device in the network, etc. SDN divides the control plane from the data plane. improving the network's ability to be programmed by outside applications (Chouikik et al. 2023). In an SDN-based network, the intelligence is concentrated in a network controller, which defines how traffic flows will be carried throughout the network; whereas network devices (switches, routers) merely forward the packets, following the per-flow rules imposed by the controller. Through a Southbound The control plane can communicate with the data plane and application plane using a Southbound Interface (SBI) and a Northbound Interface (NBI), respectively. SDN streamlines network administration by achieving this. More specifically, it allows for extremely dynamic, adaptable, and automatic network reconfiguration, more effective utilization of network resources, and simpler troubleshooting and debugging (Shaghaghi et al. 2020b).

The network architecture known as SDN separates the control plane from the data plane in networking devices and enables centralized management and programmability of network resources. More adaptable, effective, and dynamic network administration is made possible by the separation of the control and data planes. The following are the main elements and ideas of SDN network architecture (Karmakar et al. 2019; Xia et al. 2014) (Fig. 2).

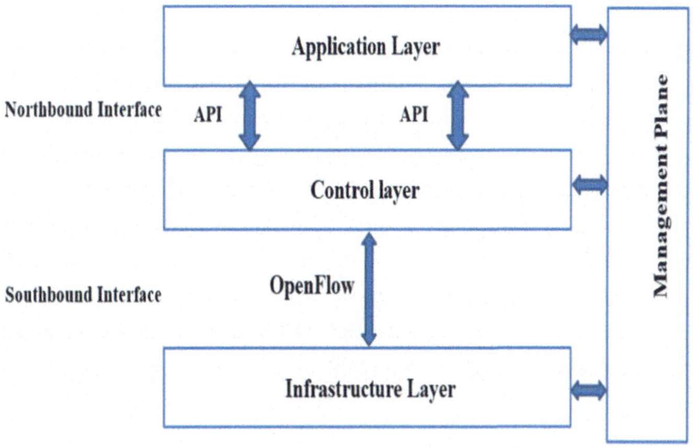

Fig. 2 SDN architecture

Data Plane: Also referred to as the forwarding plane, the data plane is in charge of directing network traffic from one device to another. Switches and routers in SDN are largely responsible for packet forwarding based on instructions from the control plane.

Control Plane: The control plane is in charge of selecting the best course of action for network traffic forwarding. Network managers may manage network policies and routing selections from a central controller thanks to SDN's abstracted and centralized control plane. To implement network policies, this controller connects with the data plane hardware.

SDN Controller: A crucial element of the SDN architecture is the SDN controller. It serves as the centralized brain of the SDN network, deciding how traffic should be routed by the needs of the network and the requirements of the applications. OpenDaylight, ONOS, and OpenFlow-based controllers are examples of common SDN controllers.

Southbound APIs: These communication channels link the data plane devices with the SDN controller. OpenFlow, which enables the controller to advise network switches on how to route packets, is one of the most frequently used southbound APIs.

Northbound APIs: Northbound APIs are used to interface with apps or network management systems from the SDN controller. In order to create network regulations and services, other applications can communicate with the SDN controller using these APIs. For this purpose, RESTful APIs are frequently employed.

Network Applications: That operate on top of the SDN controller make up the application layer. These programs can be created to offer particular network functions and services, like load balancing, traffic optimization, security, and others. To connect with the controller, they do so via the northbound APIs.

Network Virtualization: SDN makes it possible to build several virtual network segments (commonly referred to as overlays) on top of an existing physical network architecture. For cloud settings and multi-tenancy, this is very helpful.

Network administrators may design and dynamically enforce network regulations using SDN. Adapting the network to changing requirements is simpler when policies are based on variables like application kind, user identification, or real-time network circumstances.

Programmability: Because SDN networks are highly programmable, administrators may use scripts, APIs, or orchestration tools to automate network configuration and administration activities. Because of this programmability, networks are more agile and require fewer human setup modifications.

Traffic Engineering and Optimization: SDN enables real-time traffic routing and load balancing optimization depending on network circumstances, enhancing the effectiveness and performance of the network.

Monitoring and Analytics: Monitoring and analytics features are frequently incorporated into SDN. Administrators may learn more about network performance, security risks, and general network health by collecting and analyzing network data in real-time.

OpenFlow: Communication protocol OpenFlow is essential to Software-Defined Networking. Separating decision-making (Control Plane) from actual data forwarding (Data Plane) in network devices like switches and routers enables centralized network control. With OpenFlow, network managers may dynamically design and manage network traffic, boosting modern network infrastructures' flexibility, automation, and adaptability. With the help of this open standard, network management has undergone a revolutionary change, allowing more effective and flexible networks ideal for data centers, cloud environments, and expansive business networks (Flauzac et al. 2015; Hoang and Pham 2019).

4 Software-Defined Vehicular Networks

The SDN model, originally created for wired networks, is also well-known. as a desirable and encouraging method for enhancing wireless and mobile networks. These can profit in many ways from the programmability, flexibility, and centralized control wireless resource optimization services SDN provides, such as channel allocation and interference efficient mobility and network performance, packet routing in multi-hop multi-path settings, and heterogeneity management. It is possible because it is only an approach rather than a strict design (Truong et al. 2015). Apply SDN in a situation other than the one it was intended for. The adoption of SDN is particularly difficult in VANETs, for instance, where node mobility is considerable and network architecture changes regularly. The reference SDN-enabled architecture for VANETs taken into consideration in this study is shown in Fig. 3. The architecture is vulnerable to the well-known flaws of

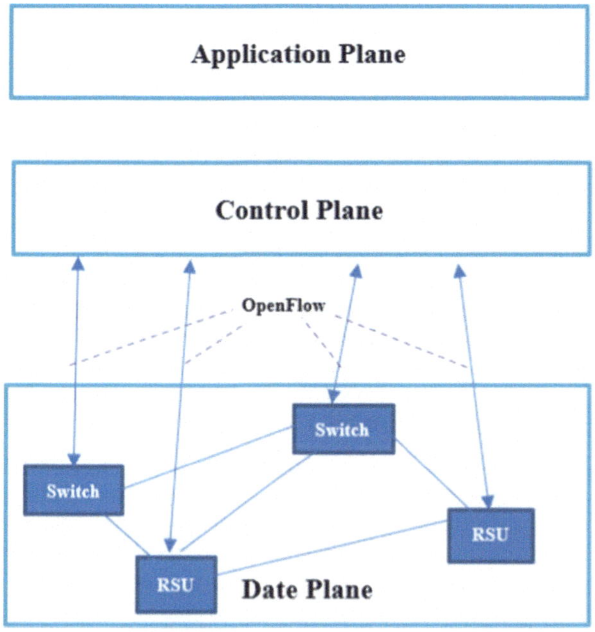

Fig. 3 SDVN architecture

classic wired SDN in a fully-centralized mode of operation, such as the existence of single points of failure and loss of communication between the Data plane and RSUC, etc. A hybrid operating mode, in which the RSUC and the local SDN agents that are deployed in specific RSUs and cars share network control, is preferred due to its higher dependability (Trivedi et al. 2019). In this scenario, cars are outfitted with two different interfaces for data channel exchanges and communication on control channels. While IEEE 802.11p (a Wi-Fi-based standard) has been determined to be the protocol for V2V and V2I communication in the data plane, however, it is yet unknown which technology (among 4G, LTE, WiFi, etc.) will be most effective for Southbound communication between the RSUC and the other network elements. Effective spectrum management solutions are required due to the small number of reserved channels compared to the numerous applications that must be supported. Channel usage might rise with an SDN-enabled architecture while maintaining. little likelihood of a collision. Liu et al. offer the first contribution in this field by creating a cooperative data distribution system for VANETs. The cars inside the RSU's coverage area can receive scheduling choices from an SDN agent that has been deployed, telling them which channel to tune to and what data to broadcast and receive. An RSUC may also predict the number and length of connections between cars and RSUs, as well as the volume of data they can share (Adbeb et al. 2020).

5 The Role of VANET in Society 5.0

VANETs, or vehicular ad hoc networks, are crucial to achieving the goals of Society 5.0. In this era of social change, when it is necessary to seamlessly integrate technology into daily life, VANETs stand out as a key element in the development of transportation systems. They play a variety of roles. First and foremost, by allowing cars to interact with one another and with road infrastructure, VANETs advance smarter and safer transportation. Through real-time communication, traffic congestion may be reduced and transportation resources are used most effectively. It nicely complements Society 5.0's objective to increase efficiency and safety in transportation. Additionally, the development of autonomous cars, a key element of Society 5.0, is based on VANET networks. They anticipate future transportation demands by providing the connection and data these cars require to function independently (Gaur and Grover 2019; Arif et al. 2018).

Finally, VANETs make it possible to manage transportation resources more sustainably and efficiently, supporting environmental sustainability, a key component of Society 5.0. They make it easier for electric vehicle coordination, traffic congestion reduction, and route optimization, which reduces emissions and makes better use of the transportation infrastructure. In conclusion, VANET networks play a crucial role in creating a Society 5.0 where technology, particularly intelligent connection, improves mobility, safety, and sustainability while putting people at the heart of this transition (Prajapati et al. 2018; Kadhim and Seno 2019).

6 Conclusion

In this study, we looked at how SDN (Software-Defined Networking) and VANETs (Vehicular Ad Hoc Networks) may operate together to realize the "Society 5.0" vision. In addition to helping to solve pressing societal challenges like traffic congestion, road safety, and carbon footprint reduction, this confluence presents intriguing prospects to improve connection, mobility, and security in both urban and rural settings. We can improve communication between cars, infrastructures, and intelligent transportation systems by utilizing the centralized administration and programmability aspects of SDN networks. This will increase transportation efficiency as well as pave the way for new intelligent applications including intelligent traffic signal control, navigation supported by autonomous vehicles, and real-time data collecting for urban planning. The social, ethical, and legal ramifications must be taken into account for this convergence to succeed. Three crucial issues that need to be addressed are public confidence, data security, and privacy protection. Furthermore, tight cooperation among researchers, decision-makers, businesses, and civil society should be the cornerstone of the effective deployment of new technologies. In the end, the combination of SDN networks with VANETs provides an important step toward realizing "Society 5.0" by building surroundings that are smarter, more sustainable, and more connected. To solve the technological, social, and ethical problems involved, a comprehensive and interdisciplinary approach is needed, but the potential advantages for our society and quality of life make it worthwhile.

References

Tesfanesh Adbeb, Wu Di, Muhammad Ibrar, "Software-Defined Networking (SDN) based VANET Architecture: Mitigation of Traffic Congestion," International Journal of Advanced Computer Science and Applications, 2020; pp 1–9.

Arif, M.; Wang, G.; Wang, T.; Peng, T. SDN based secure VANETs communication with fog computing. In Proceedings of the International Conference on Security, Privacy and Anonymity in Computation, Communication and Storage, Melbourne, NSW, Australia, 11 September 2018; pp. 46–59.

M. Chouikik, M. Ouaissa, M. Ouaissa, Z. Boulouard, and M. Kissi, "Software-Defined Networking Security: A Comprehensive Review," Big Data Analytics and Computational Intelligence for Cybersecurity, pp. 91–108, 2022.

M. Chouikik, M. Ouaissa, M. Ouaissa, Z. Boulouard, and M. Kissi, "Impact of DoS attacks in software defined networks," in AIP Conference Proceedings, AIP Publishing, vol. 2814, no.1, Jul. 2023.

O. Flauzac, C. González, A. Hachani, F. Nolot, SDN based architecture for IoT and improvement of the security, in 2015 IEEE 29th international conference on advanced information networking and applications workshops, IEEE, (2015), pp. 688–693.

Gaur, K.; Grover, J. Exploring VANET Using Edge Computing and SDN. In Proceedings of the 2019 Second International Conference on Advanced Computational and Communication Paradigms (ICACCP), Gangtok, India, 25 February 2019; pp. 1–4.

Hoang, H.D.; Pham, V.-H. A Security-Enhanced Monitoring System for Northbound Interface in SDN using Blockchain. In Proceedings of the Tenth International Symposium on Information and Communication Technology (SoICT), Hanoi-Ha long Bay, Vietnam, 4–6 December 2019; pp. 197–204.

M. Houmer, M. Ouaissa, M. Ouaissa, Secure authentication scheme for 5G-based v2x communications. Procedia Computer Science, 2022, vol. 198, p. 276–281.

A. J. Kadhim and S. A. H. Seno, "Energy-efficient multicast routing protocol based on sdn and fog computing for vehicular networks," Ad Hoc Networks, vol. 84, pp. 68–81, 2019.

Karmakar, K.K.; Varadharajan,V.; Tupakula, U. Mitigating attacks in software defined networks. Clust. Comput. 2019, 22, 1143–1157.

K. Liu, X. Xu, M. Chen, B. Liu, L. Wu, and V. C. Lee, "A hierarchical architecture for the future internet of vehicles," IEEE Communications Magazine, vol. 57, no. 7, pp. 41–47, 2019.

J. C. Nobre, A. M. de Souza, D. Ros´ario, C. Both, L. A. Villas, E. Cerqueira, T. Braun, and M. Gerla, "Vehicular software-defined networking and fog computing: Integration and design principles," Ad Hoc Networks, vol. 82, pp. 172–181, 2019.

M. Ouaissa, M. Ouaissa, M. Houmer, et al. A Secure Vehicle to Everything (V2X) Communication Model for Intelligent Transportation System. In: Computational Intelligence in Recent Communication Networks. Cham: Springer International Publishing, 2022. p. 83–102.

A. Prajapati, A. Sakadasariya, J. Patel, (2018, January). Software-defined network: Future of networking, in 2018 2nd International Conference on Inventive Systems and Control (ICISC), IEEE, (2018), pp. 1351–1354.

A. Shaghaghi, M.A. Kaafar, R. Buyya, S. Jha, Software-defined network (SDN) data plane security: issues, solutions, and future directions. Handbook of Computer Networks and Cyber Security, 341–387, (2020).

A. Shaghaghi, M.A. Kaafar, R. Buyya, S. Jha, Software-defined network (SDN) data plane security: issues, solutions, and future directions, in: Handbook of Computer Networks and Cyber Security, Springer, 2020, pp.341–387.

Sheikh, M.S.; Liang, J.; Wang,W. A Survey of Security Services, Attacks, and Applications for Vehicular AdHoc Networks (VANETs). Sensors 2019, 19, 3589.

Trivedi, H.; Tanwar, S.; Thakkar, P. Software Defined Network-Based Vehicular Adhoc Networks for Intelligent Transportation System: Recent Advances and Future Challenges. In Proceedings of the International Conference on Futuristic Trends in Network and Communication Technologies, Chandigarh, India, 22 November 2019; pp. 325–337.

N. B. Truong, G. M. Lee, and Y. Ghamri-Doudane, "Software defined networking-based vehicular adhoc network with fog computing," in 2015 IFIP/IEEE International Symposium on Integrated Network Management (IM). IEEE, 2015, pp. 1202–1207.

W. Xia, Y. Wen, C.H. Foh, D. Niyato, H. Xie, A survey on software-defined networking, IEEE Commun. Surv. Tutor. 17 (2014) 27–51.

Dilute Magnetic III–V Semiconductors for Spintronic Applications in the Digital Society 5.0 Era

Ilyas Bouziani, Ismail Essaoudi, and Abdelmajid Ainane

Abstract

The future trend in the microelectronic technologies is to exploit the fundamental degrees of freedom, spin and charge of electron for enhancing the operational speed, transfer efficiency, and storage capacity of the electronic devices in the digital society 5.0 era. Herein, within the density functional theory, we have studied the electronic- and magnetic-characteristics of bulk diluted magnetic semiconductor materials based on the III-V compound GaN, using the ab-initio full potential method and the generalized gradient approximation. We have shown that (Ga, Cr)N and (Ga, Cr, V)N compounds have half-metallic nature with a total spin-polarization at the Fermi level E_F. Furthermore, we have found that these systems exhibit a ferromagnetic behavior, whose stability is ensured by the double-exchange and ferromagnetic super-exchange mechanisms. In addition, we have used Monte Carlo simulation to extend the study of the ground state to finite temperatures. We have found that the studied diluted magnetic semiconductors show second-order phase transition with high Curie temperatures, well above room temperature. These results indicate that the three-dimensional diluted magnetic semiconductors of III-V type, namely GaN doped and co-doped with transition metals, are desirable for spintronic applications.

I. Bouziani (✉) · I. Essaoudi · A. Ainane
Physics Department, Faculty of Sciences, Laboratoire de Physique des Matériaux et Modélisation des Systèmes, (LP2MS), Unité Associée Au CNRST-URAC 08, Moulay Ismail University of Meknes, Meknes, Morocco
e-mail: i.bouziani@edu.umi.ac.ma

I. Bouziani
Laboratory of Inorganic Materials for Sustainable Energy Technologies (LIMSET), Mohammed VI Polytechnic University (UM6P), Benguerir, Morocco

A. Ainane
Max-Planck-Institut für Physik Complexer Systeme, Dresden, Germany

Keywords

Society 5.0 · Diluted magnetic semiconductors · Spintronic applications · III-V compound · Density functional theory · KKR approach

1 Introduction

The technological progress, which we are currently living without precedent, has only become possible thanks to the progress of semiconductor technology, continuously increasing the number of transistors in electronic devices, packed by the milliards into small integrated circuits or chips. This evolution is governed by the famous Moore's Law (Moore 1965); "the transistors number in a dense integrated circuit doubles almost every two years", and today reaches a cap, in which the conventional electronic materials are brought beyond their functional limits.

Contemporary electronic devices are based on semiconductor materials, which exploit the charge of the electron by manipulating it in various solid-state devices, e.g., random access memories (RAMs), computer processing units (CPUs), and more recently, solid-state drives (SSDs). In other words, we store and process information in our devices through complex control of electronic charges by electric current or potential. Spintronics, as a new path to technological progress in the digital society 5.0 era, overcome the limitations of controlling the electronic charge alone by introducing the spin of electron as another freedom degree. With complete control of both fundamental properties of the electron, Spintronic technology offers a next generation of devices with many advantages compared to standard electronic one, such as non-volatility and faster operation, increased integration densities and reduced power consumption, and even new avenues for combining information processing and storage (Bader and Parkin 2010).

S. Arezki et al. (eds.), *Emerging Disruptive Technologies for Society 5.0 in Developing Countries*, Advances in Science, Technology & Innovation, https://doi.org/10.1007/978-3-031-63701-8_21

From 1988 onwards, Fert and Grünberg (Baibich et al. 1988; Binasch et al. 1989) made a major contribution to the discovery of the giant magnetoresistance effect (GMR) in spin valve structures, which revolutionized data storage technology and earned them the 2007 Nobel Prize in Physics. Integrated into our living environment in the form of hard disk read heads, spin valves based on the GMR effect were later replaced by magnetic tunnel junctions based on the magnetoresistance effect. While this first generation of spintronics, also known as magnetoelectronics, radicalized data storage technology, it also created a bottleneck when combined with increasingly integrated conventional von-Neuman architectures for information processing and storage: data are stored in metal-based magnetic devices and processed in semiconductor-based electronic ones. As the exchange of data between these two units becomes more and more time consuming and energy inefficient, an increasingly attractive approach has emerged, attempting to combine both functionalities within a single device, the in-memory processing approach (Umesh and Mittal 2019). In other words, this has caused a redirection of the field from metal-based spintronics to semiconductor-based spintronics, requiring new materials where the tunability of semiconductors is combined with the spin contrast characteristic of ferromagnetic materials (ferromagnets).

Conventional Non-magnetic semiconductors such as Silicon, Gallium Arsenide and Gallium Nitride find use in integrated circuits transistors and lasers; while ferromagnetic materials such as Iron, Cobalt and Nickel, which are non-semiconductors, are used in digital storage devices. The development of spin-biased semiconductors operating above room temperature (RT) has been one of the most promising avenues to combine semiconductor tunability with the spin contrast of ferromagnets into functional spintronic materials (Dietl and Ohno 2014).

Diluted magnetic semiconductors (DMSs) are a prototypical example of such materials, a pioneering development in semiconductor-based spintronics, introducing magnetic ions into non-magnetic semiconductors resulting in simultaneous charge carrier spin polarization and ferromagnetic properties. Thus, two conditions are of crucial importance in the practical implementation of DMSs in spintronic devices, which are closely related to their fundamental electronic- and magnetic-characteristics: (i) the charge carriers in the semiconductors must be spin-polarized; and (ii) the localized magnetic moments must achieve ferromagnetic order through a long-range mechanism, up to typical Curie temperatures T_C, above room temperature. The combination of these two conditions lays the foundation for carrier-mediated ferromagnetism in DMSs, which require efficient coupling between spin-polarized charge carriers and localized ferromagnetic moments, in other words, the charge carriers participate in the ferromagnetic ordering mechanism (Awschalom et al. 2002).

With over thirty years of exciting history and various generations of Curie temperature increases and functionalities, DMSs have attracted the attention of the semiconductor and magnetics community, becoming one of the most propitious research topics in materials science and engineering today. An encouraging moment came in 1992, when Hideo Ohno and colleagues discovered ferromagnetism in Indium Arsenide with only 1.3% of Manganese (Ohno et al. 1992). In 1996, they also reported ferromagnetic order in Mn-doped GaAs, with a transition temperature of 110 K (Ohno et al. 1996). Recently, significant efforts have been deployed for finding magnetic semiconductors based on III-V compounds to meet the challenge of practical implementation of DMSs in spintronic applications. In this regard, GaN doped with transition metals (TMs) exhibits ferromagnetic behavior at room temperature (Dietl et al. 2000; Prellier et al. 2003; Huang et al. 2005; Kang et al. 2009). More importantly, Hashimoto et al. demonstrated that (Ga,Cr)N compounds present ferromagnetic character with T_C around 400 K using the electron cyclotron resonance plasma assisted molecular beam growth technique (Hashimoto et al. 2002). Incited by these results, Souissi et al. showed that Vanadium-doped GaN thin films have a ferromagnetic character with Curie temperatures T_C identified in the vicinity of 350 K using chemical vapor deposition (Souissi et al. 2012). Despite these efforts, the magnetism of these materials continues to be a subject of controversy, and the main objective is to overcome Curie temperatures well above room temperature.

In this chapter we aim to study, theoretically, the effect of doping and codoping by low concentrations of magnetic impurities on the electronic- and magnetic-characteristics of the type III-V compound GaN. Our results mainly indicate that (Ga,Cr,V)N and (Ga,Cr,V)N compounds show a half-metallic behavior with a full spin polarization at the Fermi level E_F and a ferromagnetic behavior above room temperature. Thus, thanks to the doping and codoping techniques, the three-dimensional diluted magnetic semiconductors based on the III-V compound are powerful candidates for spintronic applications.

2 Methods and Calculation Details

The results presented in this chapter for the study of the electronic- and magnetic-characteristics of bulk DMSs are obtained using ab-initio computations based on the total potential KKR approach (Kohn and Rostoker 1954; Korringa 1947), in the general framework of density functional theory. The exchange–correlation effect is described by the generalized-gradient approximation (GGA) (Perdew and Wang 1992).

The KKR approach is based on the multiple-scattering theory which presents an adequate framework for the disorder description provided by magnetic impurities, randomly distributed on the cationic sites of semiconductor compounds, i.e. on the III sites in compound III-V. The disorder issue can be well described by the coherent-potential approximation (CPA) (Akai and Dederichs 1993; Shiba 1971; Soven 1967; Taylor 1967; Velický et al. 1968), in which a substitutional alloy A_xB_{1-x} (where $x = x_A$ designates the concentration of atoms A and $x_B = 1 - x_A$ that of atoms B) is replaced by a periodic system of the same coherent potential which represents a global average of all possible configurations, determining an effective medium similar to the original alloy. If we note the matrices "t" of the atoms (A; B) and of the effective medium CPA respectively by (t_A; t_B) and t_{CPA}, then the self-consistency condition CPA, which determines t_{CPA}, leads in the description of multiple-scattering KKR approach to:

$$x_A T_A + x_B T_B = 0, \tag{1}$$

with $T_{A,B}$ indicates the total single-site T-matrix of A or B atom incorporated in the CPA medium at site 0,

$$T_{A,B} = \left(t_{A,B} - t_{CPA}\right)\frac{1}{1 - G^0_{CPA}\left(t_{A,B} - t_{CPA}\right)}, \tag{2}$$

where the G^0_{CPA} are the elements of the Green CPA function (G_{CPA}) at site 0. These elements can be obtained from the t_{CPA} by integration over the Brillouin zone (BZ):

$$G_{CPA} = \frac{1}{\Omega_{BZ}}\int_{ZB}\frac{g(K)}{1 - t_{CPA}g(K)}dk, \tag{3}$$

with g(K) denotes the structure constants in free space.

In accordance with the Eq. (2), the CPA medium, i.e., the scattering matrix t_{CPA}, must be chosen such that the insertion of the A and B atoms at the site under consideration remains unchanged the scattering, which is the condition in Eq. (1). For this study, we utilized 512 K-points in the irreducible part of the BZ.

The previous points can easily be extended to the case of a spin-polarized system where two types of the charge densities $n^\uparrow(r)$ and $n^\downarrow(r)$ must be distinguished, with $n(r) = n^\uparrow(r) + n^\downarrow(r)$ representing the total charge density. Then, all other quantities (G, t_A, t_B, T_A, T_B, ...) have supplementary spin-index.

For DMSs, it is crucial to differentiate between the ferromagnetic (FM) state, where all magnetic element moments are aligned in the same direction (ordered phase below the Curie temperature T_c), and the disordered local moment (DLM) state (Gyorffy et al. 1985; Hasegawa 1979; Hubbard 1979), where the directions of all local moments are distributed in a random manner (disordered phase above the Curie temperature T_c), so that spontaneous magnetization disappears. The DLM state models the system in paramagnetic phase (Otrokov et al. 2011).

Within the framework of CPA approximation, while the ferromagnetic state is represented by (A_xB_{1-x}) alloy where the cationic sites of concentration x are occupied by magnetic impurities with spins aligned parallel to each other, The DLM state can be assimilated to ($A^\uparrow_{x/2}A^\downarrow_{x/2}B_{1-x}$) alloy where the magnetic impurities spins are antiparallel, that is, the cationic sites of concentration x are occupied by one part of magnetic atoms with "up" local momentum ($A^\uparrow$) and another part with "down" momentum ($A^\downarrow$). Both parts have concentrations equal to x/2 (Akai and Dederichs 1993).

In this context, the energy difference ΔE_state $\Delta E_{état}\left(A_xB_{1-x}\right)$ between the local disordered-momentum state and the ferromagnetic state of dilute magnetic semiconductors of type A_xB_{1-x} is defined by the expressions below (Akai and Dederichs 1993):

$$\Delta E^{A_xB_{1-x}}_{état} = E^{A_xB_{1-x}}_{DLM} - E^{A_xB_{1-x}}_{FM} = E\left(A^\uparrow_{x/2}A^\downarrow_{x/2}B_{1-x}\right) - E\left(A_xB_{1-x}\right), \tag{4}$$

where x is the magnetic impurities concentration.

So as to extend the investigation of the magnetic characteristics of DMSs from the ground state (T = 0 K) to finite temperatures (T > 0 K), we use Monte Carlo simulation based on five principles, namely: (i) Markov chain where the evolution of the system is temporal, (ii) ergodicity; i.e., all possible states of the system during its evolution are accessible, (iii) detailed balance which describes the equilibrium of the system, (iv) acceptance rate, and (v) importance sampling; i.e., the states considered are those with a significant Boltzmann factor $p = \exp\left(-\frac{\Delta E}{K_BT}\right)$, where ΔE can be defined as the energy disparity between two configurations, K_B is the Boltzmann constant, and T is the absolute temperature (Bortz et al. 1975; Metropolis and Ulam 1949; Newman and Barkema 1999).

The Ising model is particularly suitable for studying DMSs systems due to the limited magnetic impurities concentration in semiconductors and the low magnetic moments interaction. In the Ising model, The Hamiltonian describing diluted magnetic semiconductor system $\left(A_{x/2}A_{x/2'}\right)B_{1-x}$ is expressed as follows (Blood 1970; Sato et al. 2010):

$$H_{DMS} = -J_{A-A}\sum_{ij} S^A_{i,z}S^A_{j,z} - J_{A'-A'}\sum_{nm} S^{A'}_{n,z}S^{A'}_{m,z} - J_{A-A'}\sum_{in} S^A_{i,z}S^{A'}_{n,z}, \tag{5}$$

where ⟨i, j⟩, ⟨n, m⟩ and ⟨i, n⟩ denote the sum over all nearest-neighbor magnetic impurity pairs. The parameters $S^A_{i,z}$, $S^A_{j,z}$, $S^{A'}_{n,z}$ and $S^{A'}_{m,z}$ denote the spins at the i, j, n, and m sites of the magnetic impurities A and A' respectively. As for the terms J_{A-A}, $J_{A'-A'}$ and $J_{A-A'}$, which Refer to the exchange coupling coefficients existing between the nearest neighbor magnetic impurities, obey the relations:

$$J_{A-A} = \frac{2\Delta E_{\text{état}}^{A_xB_{1-x}}}{Z_1(S_z^A)^2} = \frac{2\left\{E_{DLM}^{A_xB_{1-x}} - E_{FM}^{A_xB_{1-x}}\right\}}{Z_1(S_z^A)^2}, \quad (6)$$

$$J_{A'-A'} = \frac{2\Delta E_{\text{é tat}}^{A'_xB_{1-x}}}{Z_1(S_z^{A'})^2} = \frac{2\left\{E_{DLM}^{A'_xB_{1-x}} - E_{FM}^{A'_xB_{1-x}}\right\}}{Z_1(S_z^{A'})^2}, \quad (7)$$

$$J_{A-A'} = \frac{2\Delta E_{\text{é tat}}^{(A_{x/2}A'_{x/2})B_{1-x}}}{Z_2(S_z^A S_z^{A'})} = \frac{2\left\{E_{DLM}^{(A_{x/2}A'_{x/2})B_{1-x}} - E_{FM}^{(A_{x/2}A'_{x/2})B_{1-x}}\right\}}{Z_2(S_z^A S_z^{A'})}, \quad (8)$$

where ($E_{DLM}^{A_xB_{1-x}}$, $E_{DLM}^{A_x\prime B_{1-x}}$, $E_{DLM}^{(A_{x/2}A_{x/2}\prime)B_{1-x}}$) and ($E_{FM}^{A_xB_{1-x}}$, $E_{FM}^{A_x\prime B_{1-x}}$, $E_{FM}^{(A_{x/2}A_{x/2}\prime)B_{1-x}}$) are the computed energies of the DLM-state and the FM-state of the compounds A_xB_{1-x}, $A_x\prime B_{1-x}$ and $(A_{x/2}A_{x/2}\prime)B_{1-x}$. The terms Z_1 et Z_2 are the number of first-nearest neighbor impurities of the same and different types, respectively. The factor of 2 is added because the interaction is shared by two magnetic atoms.

To implement the Monte Carlo simulation, we have used the heat-bath algorithm which is a one-spin flipping algorithm (Krauth 2006; Metropolis et al. 1953). In our calculations, we applied the periodic boundary conditions in the x-, y-, and z-orientations. Since the investigation of DMSs systems necessitates a high number of atoms, we used a total number of sites $N = L_x \times L_y \times L_z$, with $L = L_x = L_y = L_z = 15$, where the magnetic elements replace less than 15% of the sites that are distributed randomly. Interestingly, the Monte Carlo step per site has been used to calculate the averages of the magnetic magnitudes after discarding the initial 2×10^5 for each temperature to reach equilibrium.

3 Results and Discussion

3.1 Pure Gallium Nitride

In our study we have chosen Gallium Nitride as a type III-V semiconductor, which can crystallize in different forms. Specifically, our focus lies on the zinc blende phase for which the associated space group is F-43 m (n° 216). This compound consists of Ga and N atoms of electronic configurations [Ar]$3d^{10}4s^24p^1$ and [He]$2s^22p^3$, respectively. Figure 1 shows the cubic structure of GaN where the Ga elements are located in (0 0 0); (0 0.5 0.5); (0.5 0 0.5); (0.5 0.5 0) and the N atoms in (0.25 0.25 0.25); (0.25 0.75 0.75); (0.75 0.25 0.75); (0.75 0.75 0.25).

Before starting the study of the electronic- and magnetic-characteristics of GaN doped with single- and double-impurities, we determined the ground state of the pure GaN system and its associated electronic structure.

As a means to optimize the structure of the GaN compound, we performed a self-consistent calculation of the total energy for various lattice parameter values a in the vicinity of the experimentally measured value $a_{exp} = 4.50$ Å (Lei et al. 1992). Figure 2 shows the total energy versus volume (a^3) for the GaN cubic system. The minimum of the curve corresponding to the theoretical value of the lattice constant is $a_{th} = 4.506$ Å, which aligns remarkably well with the experimental results finding (Lei et al. 1992).

The electronic structure of GaN can be obtained from the calculation of the total density of states (TDOS) per mesh and the local densities of states (LDOSs) per atom. Figure 3 shows the total electronic density of states of the GaN cubic system and the local electronic densities of states of 2p-N and 3d-Ga, in the energy range of −0.6 Ry to 0.6 Ry, using the GGA functional. It appears that the valence-band is predominantly dominated by the 2p-state of the N atom while the conduction-band is essentially formed by the 3d-state of the Ga atom and the 2p-state of the N atom. These two bands are also separated by a gap of width $E_{gap} = 2.97$ eV, which is coherent with experimental observations (Levinshtein et al. 2001). Note also that the two spin-up and spin-down electronic parts of the TDOS are symmetric, which means that the GaN compound is non-magnetic. These results confirm the non-magnetic semiconductor behavior of the GaN cubic system.

3.2 Chromium-Doped Gallium Nitride

Motivated by the ferromagnetism, with high T_c, experimentally shown in the (Ga,Cr)N compound (Hashimoto et al. 2002), we first carried out the study the electronic- and magnetic-characteristics of the GaN semiconductor doped

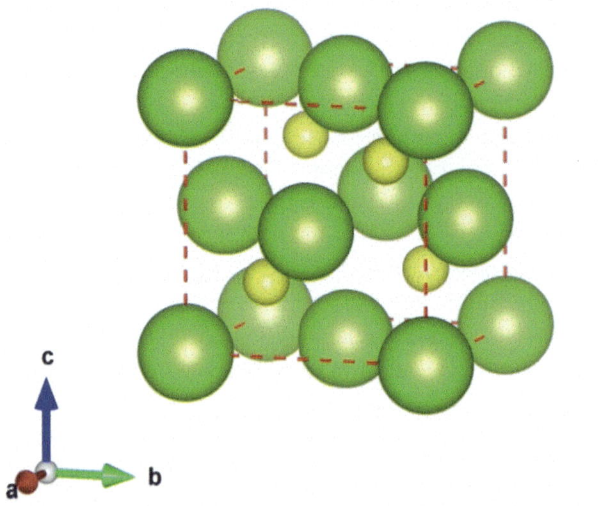

Fig. 1 Crystal structure of the GaN compound in zinc blende phase. Ga and N are indicated by green and yellow balls, respectively

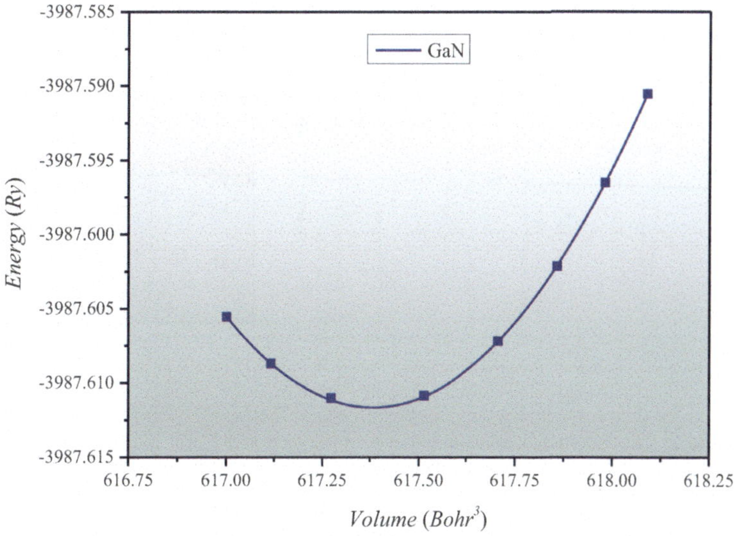

Fig. 2 Total energy versus volume for the GaN cubic system

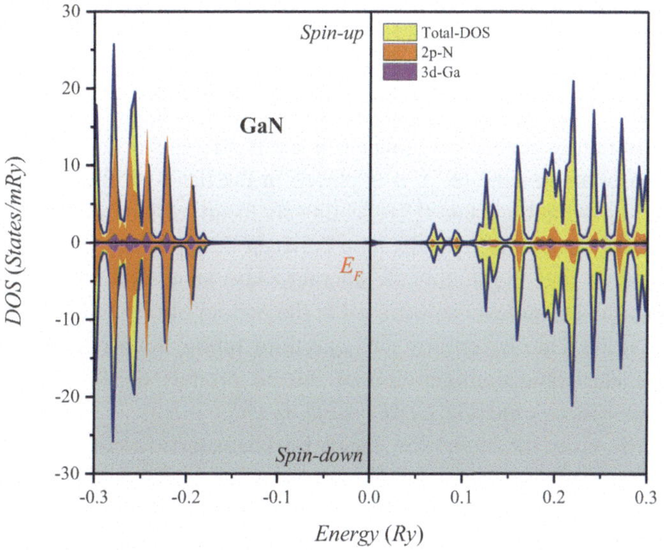

Fig. 3 Total and local densities of electronic states of the GaN compound. The E_F is taken as the energy origin

with the transition metal-like magnetic Chromium impurities and having the electronic configuration [Ar]$3d^5 4s^1$. In the energy range of -0.3 Ry to 0.3 Ry, Fig. 4 shows the total densities of states per mesh and the local densities of states per atom of the compound $\left(Ga_{1-x}Cr_x\right)N$ for $x = 0.04$ and 0.06. We observe the emergence of impurity states in the spin-up channel of the band-gap which are produced by the 3d-orbitals of the Cr atom, giving rise to a metallic nature in the spin-up part while retaining the semiconducting character in the other spin part, this implies that the compound (Ga, Cr)N exhibits a half-metallic behavior with a total spin polarization at E_F.

According to the general discussion of Zunger and Katayama-Yoshida on the electronic structure of TM-impurities in semiconductor compounds (Katayama-Yoshida 1987; Zunger 1986), the degenerate d-states of the magnetic impurities are divided into doubly degenerate (dγ) and triply degenerate (dε) states in a tetrahedral symmetry (T_d) environment. The three levels of dε states, which have xy-, yz-, and zx-symmetries, hybridize strongly with the p states of the semiconductor anion (strong p- dε hybridization) so that they form a binding state (t_b) in the valence band, while the antibinding state (t_a) is pushed toward the band-gap. However, the two levels of the dγ states, which have the $3z^2 - r^2$ and $x^2 - y^2$ symmetries, form a highly localized non-bonding state (e) owing to the weak p-dγ hybridization. This characteristic of the impurity states is clearly evident in the 3d-Cr LDOS as shown in Fig. 4, where the binding state t_b^{Cr} is localized in the valence band due to the presence of strong p-dε hybridization between the 2p state of the N atom and the threefold degenerate (3dε) state of the Cr atom, on the other hand, the

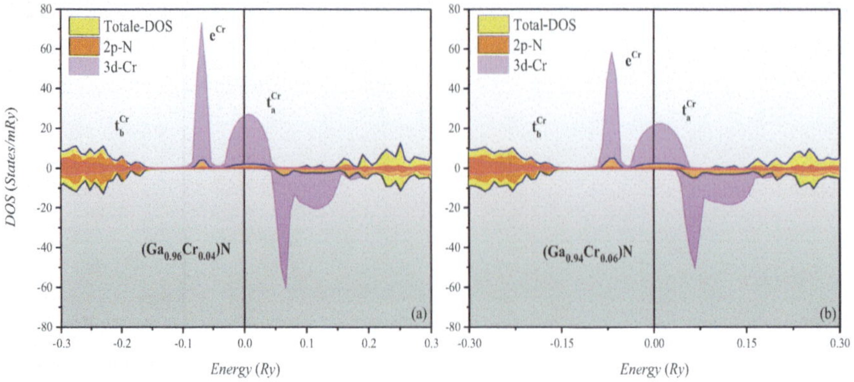

Fig. 4 Total and local densities of states of the compound $(Ga_{1-x}Cr_x)N$ for x = 0.04 (**a**) and 0.06 (**b**)

Table 1 The calculated magnetic energy difference and Curie temperature of $Ga_{1-x}Cr_xN$ compound (from x = 0.04–0.06) using Monte Carlo method (Bouziani et al. 2019)

$(Ga_{1-x}Cr_x)N$	x		
	0.04	0.05	0.06
$\Delta E(mRy)$	0.205	0.261	0.322
$T_c(K)$	535	545	560

antibinding state t_a^{Cr} is situated in the band-gap. As for the non-bonding state (e^{Cr}), it is placed in the band-gap below the anti-bonding state t_a^{Cr} reflecting its localized nature due to the weak p-dγ hybridization between the 2p state of the N atom and the doubly degenerate (3dγ) state. Note also that the Fermi level is localized at the bottom of the t_a^{Cr} anti-bonding state by ensuring its one-third filling. As a result, the electronic configuration of the 3d orbitals of the Cr impurities, in the (Ga, Cr)N system, is $e^2t_a^1$.

In order to study the magnetic characteristics of the (Ga, Cr)N system in the ground state, we calculated the magnetic energy difference per unit-cell between its DLM and FM states. The magnetic energy difference per-unit cell (ΔE_{state}) of the compound $(Ga_{1-x}Cr_x)N$ for different doping concentrations, from 0.04 to 0.06, are illustrated in Table 1. It is evident that the ΔE_{state} is positive and increases with the increase of Chromium impurities concentration, indicating that the DLM-state is less stable than the FM-one. Thus, the (Ga, Cr)N system exhibits ferromagnetic character in the ground state.

To understand the mechanism responsible for the ferromagnetic stability in the (Ga, Cr)N system in the ground state, we present in Fig. 5 the LDOS of the 3d-Cr state of the compound $(Ga_{1-x}Cr_x)N$ for x varies from 0.04 to 0.06 in the spin-up channel. We clearly see that with increasing Cr concentration, the 3d impurity state broadens in energy and reduces in amplitude, and it is only the widening of the incompletely saturated t_a^{Cr} state that leads to the ferromagnetic stability, due to the fact that the electrons in the e^{Cr} state are less itinerant than those in the t_a^{Cr} state due to the non-bonding nature of the e^{Cr} state. This indicates that ferromagnetic stability is provided by the double-exchange mechanism (Akai 1998; Kanamori 2001), where itinerant 3d electrons can jump between the t_a^{Cr} states of neighboring Cr impurities to lower their kinetic energy. This type of hopping only occurs when the magnetic ions have parallel magnetic moments (Katayama-Yoshida et al. 2007; Sato et al. 2003; Sato and Katayama-Yoshida 2002a, 2002b).

To conduct a more in-depth exploration of the magnetic characteristics of the (Ga, Cr)N system beyond the ground state, we have made use of the Ising model, whose Hamiltonian of the system is defined by:

$$H = -J_{Cr-Cr}\sum_{ij} S_{i,z}^{Cr} S_{j,z}^{Cr}, \tag{9}$$

where the symbol i, j denotes the sum over all nearest-neighbor pairs of magnetic Cr impurities. The parameters $S_{i,z}^{Cr}$ and $S_{j,z}^{Cr}$ denote the spins at i and j sites, respectively, which can be given the values (±3/2; ± 1/2) at each site. The term J_{Cr-Cr} is the exchange coupling constant between the local moments of the Cr impurities at sites i and j, which is written from the magnetic energy difference $\Delta E_{état}^{(Ga,Cr)N}$ of the (Ga, Cr)N compound in the ground state as:

$$J_{Cr-Cr} = \frac{2\Delta E_{état}^{(Ga,Cr)N}}{Z(S_z^{Cr})^2} = \frac{2\left\{E_{DLM}^{(Ga,Cr)N} - E_{FM}^{(Ga,Cr)N}\right\}}{Z(S_z^{Cr})^2}, \tag{10}$$

where $E_{DLM}^{(Ga,Cr)N}$ and $E_{FM}^{(Ga,Cr)N}$ are the energies of the DLM-state and the FM-state of the compound (Ga, Cr)N, respectively. The term Z denotes the number of the first nearest neighbor Cr impurities.

By performing the Monte Carlo calculations based on the heat-bath algorithm, the Curie temperature obtained from the magnetization and the magnetic-susceptibility data of $(Ga_{1-x}Cr_x)N$ for (x = 0.04–0.06) is illustrated in Table 1. It is seen that T_c is higher than 400 K. This is in accordance

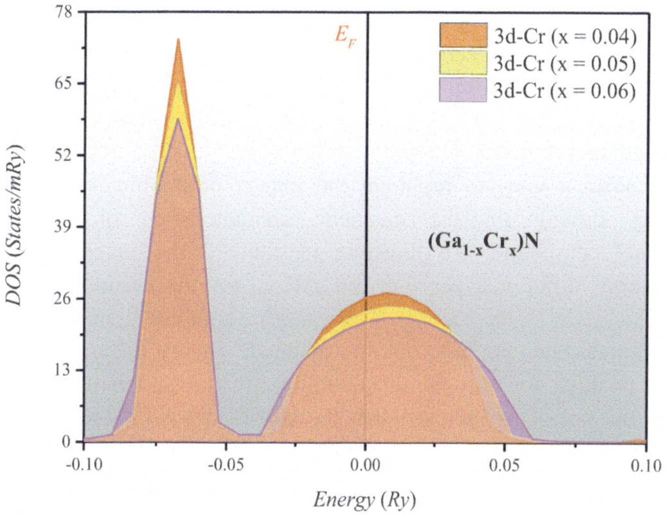

Fig. 5 Variation of the 3d-Cr density of state in the (Ga, Cr)N system for different concentrations of Cr impurities (x = 0.04 to 0.06)

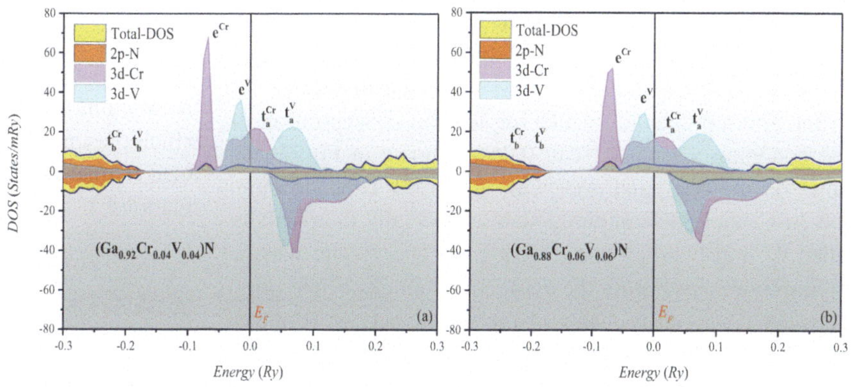

Fig. 6 Total and local densities of state of the compound $\left(Ga_{1-2x}Cr_xV_x\right)N$ for the codoping concentrations x = 0.04 (a) and 0.06 (b)

with the experimental data (Hashimoto et al. 2002). Note also that with the variation of the doping concentration from 0.04 to 0.06, the Curie temperature T_c increases from 535 to 560 K (Bouziani et al. 2019), indicating that the ferromagnetic stability area of the (Ga, Cr)N compound increases with the increase of the doping concentration.

3.3 Gallium Nitride Codoped with Chromium and Vanadium

The codoping technique is another way to increase the ferromagnetic stability area and to free critical temperatures T_c beyond those obtained by simple doping (Chen et al. 2008; Dinh et al. 2003; Xu et al. 2009). In this sense, we opted for codoping GaN with Chromium and Vanadium, having the electronic configurations $[Ar]3d^5 4s^1$ and $[Ar]3d^3 4s^2$, respectively, in order to make our system more competitive for spintronic applications. In this new system, where each of the two impurities contributes three electrons to the bond with the N atom, we expect the electronic configurations of the 3d orbitals of the Cr- and V-impurities to be $e^2 t_a^1$ and $e^2 t_a^0$, respectively, in the absence of charge transfer between them.

In order to highlight the effect of codoping on the electronic characteristics of the GaN compound, we have calculated the total electron densities per mesh and local electron densities per atom of the $\left(Ga_{1-2x}Cr_xV_x\right)N$ system, for x = 0.04 and 0.06. From the results shown in Fig. 6, in the energy range from -0.3 Ry to 0.3 Ry, we note that the compound (Ga, Cr, V)N shows a half-metallic nature with full spin polarization at E_F, due to the appearance of impurity states in the spin-up part of the band-gap, which are generated by the 3d orbitals of the Cr and V atoms. Note also that the binding states (t_b^{Cr},t_b^V) are localized in the valence band because of the strong p-dε hybridization, yet the antibinding states (t_a^{Cr},t_a^V) are pushed toward the band-gap. For the non-bonding states (e^{Cr},e^V), they are placed in the band-gap below the anti-bonding states (t_b^{Cr},t_b^V) because of the weak p-dγ hybridization. Interestingly, the Fermi-level is situated at the top of the anti-bonding state t_a^{Cr} and in the middle of the non-bonding one e^V ensuring the filling of two thirds of the former and half of the latter, respectively. As a result, the electronic configurations of the 3d orbitals of the Cr- and V-impurities, in the (Ga, Cr, V)N compound, are $e^2t_a^2$ and $e^1t_a^0$, respectively. This indicates the existence of a charge transfer from V to Cr because of the low electronegativity of V (1.63) compared to Cr (1.66) (Allred 1961; Pauling 1960).

With a view to highlight the impact of double impurity doping on the magnetic characteristics of the GaN compound, we illustrate in Table 2 the magnetic energy difference per unit-cell ΔE_{state} for the compound $(Ga_{1-2x}Cr_xV_x)N$ (x = 0.04 to 0.06), computed in the ground state. We note that the magnetic energy difference is positive for various concentrations of the understudied impurities. This indicates that the DLM-state is less stable than the FM-one. Therefore, the new (Ga, Cr, V)N compound also demonstrates ferromagnetic nature in the ground state.

For the purpose of understanding the origin of the ferromagnetic stability in the present system $(Ga_{1-2x}Cr_xV_x)N$ in the ground state, we studied the behavior of its 3d-Cr (a) and 3d-V (b) states, from the local densities of states in the spin-up channel, while varying the concentration of the codoping x from 0.04 to 0.06 as shown in Fig. 7. We note, on the one hand, that with increasing concentration, the 3d-Cr and 3d-V impurity states, especially the partially filled t_a^{Cr} anti-bonding state, broaden in energy and narrow in amplitude, indicating the existence of an electronic jump between t_a^{Cr} impurity states of the same energies (double-exchange mechanism). On the other hand, the t_a^{Cr} and e^V states move to lower and higher energies, respectively, due to the transfer of electrons from the fully filled e^V state to the partially filled t_a^{Cr} state (ferromagnetic super-exchange mechanism) (Belhadji et al. 2007). Thus, these two mechanisms are at the origin of the ferromagnetic stability in the (Ga, Cr, V)N system. It should also be noted that, the double-exchange resulting from the broadening of the e^V state, i.e. the electronic jump e^V-e^V, is very small and practically negligible due to the non-bonding nature of the e^V state.

Table 2 The calculated magnetic energy difference and Curie temperature of $Ga_{1-2x}Cr_xV_xN$ compound (from x = 0.04–0.06) using Monte Carlo method (Bouziani et al. 2019)

$(Ga_{1-2x}Cr_xV_x)N$	x		
	0.04	0.05	0.06
$\Delta E(mRy)$	0.42	0.53	0.65
$T_C(K)$	540	555	565

For further information on the magnetic characteristics of the compound (Ga, Cr, V)N from zero temperature (T = 0 K) to finite temperatures (T > 0 K), we performed the Monte Carlo calculations on the Hamiltonian of the system given by:

$$H = -J_{Cr-Cr}\sum_{ij} S^{Cr}_{i,z}S^{Cr}_{j,z} - J_{V-V}\sum_{nm} S^{V}_{n,z}S^{V}_{m,z} - J_{Cr-V}\sum_{in} S^{Cr}_{i,z}S^{V}_{n,z}, \qquad (11)$$

where the symbols i, j, n, m and i, n denote the sum over all nearest-neighbor pairs of magnetic impurities Cr and V. The parameters $S^{Cr}_{i,z}$, $S^{Cr}_{j,z}$, $S^{V}_{n,z}$ and $S^{V}_{m,z}$ denote the spins at the i, j, n, and m sites, respectively, which can be given the values (±3/2; ± 1/2) for the Cr atom and (±1; 0) for the V atom at each site. The terms J_{Cr-Cr}, J_{V-V} and J_{Cr-V}, which present the exchange coupling constants between the local moments of the nearest neighbor impurities, obey the relations:

$$J_{Cr-Cr} = \frac{2\Delta E^{(Ga,Cr)N}_{état}}{Z_1(S^{Cr}_z)^2} = \frac{2\left\{E^{(Ga,Cr)N}_{DLM} - E^{(Ga,Cr)N}_{FM}\right\}}{Z(S^{Cr}_z)^2}, \qquad (12)$$

$$J_{V-V} = \frac{2\Delta E^{(Ga,V)N}_{état}}{Z_1(S^{V}_z)^2} = \frac{2\left\{E^{(Ga,V)N}_{DLM} - E^{(Ga,V)N}_{FM}\right\}}{Z(S^{V}_z)^2}, \qquad (13)$$

$$J_{Cr-V} = \frac{2\Delta E^{(Ga,Cr,V)N}_{état}}{Z_2(S^{Cr}_zS^{V}_z)} = \frac{2\left\{E^{(Ga,Cr,V)N}_{DLM} - E^{(Ga,Cr,V)N}_{FM}\right\}}{Z(S^{Cr}_zS^{V}_z)}, \qquad (14)$$

where $(E^{(Ga,Cr)N}_{DLM}, E^{(Ga,V)N}_{DLM}, E^{(Ga,Cr,V)N}_{DLM})$ and $(E^{(Ga,Cr)N}_{FM}, E^{(Ga,V)N}_{FM}, E^{(Ga,Cr,V)N}_{FM})$ are the energies of the DLM-state and FM-state of the compounds (Ga, Cr)N, (Ga, V)N and (Ga, Cr, V)N respectively. The terms Z_1 and Z_2 denote the

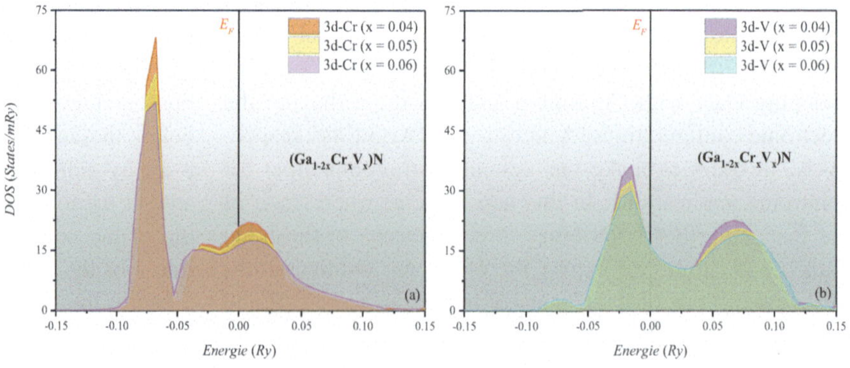

Fig. 7 Variation of 3d-Cr (**a**) and 3d-V (**b**) densities of states in the $(Ga_{1-2x}Cr_xV_x)N$ compound, for different concentrations of the codoping (x = 0.04–0.06)

numbers of the first-nearest neighboring Cr and V impurities of the same and different types, respectively.

The Curie temperature reached from the magnetization and the magnetic susceptibility results of the $(Ga_{1-2x}Cr_xV_x)N$ system (x = 0.04–0.06) are shown in Table 2. It is seen that the Curie temperature T_c, is well above room temperature and increases from 540 to 565 K while varying the concentration of codoping from 0.04 to 0.06, which means that the ferromagnetic stability area of the (Ga, Cr, V)N compound rises with increasing the cooping concentration.

4 Conclusion

The current investigation focuses on the electronic- and magnetic-characteristics of dilute magnetic semiconductors based on type III-V compounds (GaN) in the ground state using ab-initio computations based on the full potential method and the generalized gradient approximation, within the DFT.

From the calculations of the total and local electronic densities of states of GaN semiconductors doped by double magnetic impurities, we have shown that the $(Ga_{1-x}Cr_x)N$ and $(Ga_{1-2x}Cr_xV_x)N$ systems (x = 0.04 to 0.06) have a half-metallic nature with a total spin polarization at E_F. Also, based on the calculations of the magnetic energy difference per unit-cell for the (Ga,Cr)N and (Ga,Cr,V)N systems, we have found that these systems exhibit ferromagnetic behavior in the ground state whose stability is ensured by the ferromagnetic double-exchange and super-exchange mechanisms.

Furthermore, we have extended this ground state study to finite temperatures using Monte Carlo simulation. We have found that the considered system exhibits high Curie temperatures T_c well above room temperature.

These findings indicate that the doping and codoping techniques of type III-V semiconductors with transition metals allows to obtain massive dilute magnetic semiconductors with full spin polarization at E_F and ferromagnetism above room temperature, which is strongly desirable for spintronic applications in the digital society 5.0 era.

Acknowledgements The present work has been initiated with the support of the project PPR2: (MESRSFC-CNRST) and the Swedish Research Links program dnr-348-2011-7264.

References

Akai, H.: Ferromagnetism and Its Stability in the Diluted Magnetic Semiconductor (In, Mn)As. Physical Review Letters, 81 (1998), 3002–3005.

Akai, H., & Dederichs, P. H.: Local moment disorder in ferromagnetic alloys. Physical Review B, 47 (1993), 8739–8747.

Allred, A. L.: Electronegativity values from thermochemical data. Journal of Inorganic and Nuclear Chemistry, 17 (1961), 215–221.

Awschalom, D. D., Loss, D., & Samarth, N.: Semiconductor spintronics and quantum computation. Springer Science & Business Media (2002).

Bader, S. D., & Parkin, S. S. P.: Spintronics. Annu. Rev. Condens. Matter Phys., 1 (2010), 71–88.

Baibich, M. N., Broto, J. M., Fert, A., Van Dau, F. N., Petroff, F., Etienne, P., Creuzet, G., Friederich, A., & Chazelas, J.: Giant magnetoresistance of (001) Fe/(001) Cr magnetic superlattices. Physical review letters, 61 (1988), 2472.

Belhadji, B., Bergqvist, L., Zeller, R., Dederichs, P. H., Sato, K., & Katayama-Yoshida, H.: Trends of exchange interactions in dilute magnetic semiconductors. Journal of Physics: Condensed Matter, 19 (2007), 436227.

Binasch, G., Grünberg, P., Saurenbach, F., & Zinn, W.: Enhanced magnetoresistance in layered magnetic structures with antiferromagnetic interlayer exchange. Physical review B, 39 (1989), 4828.

Blood, F. A.: Approximate calculations for the two-dimensional Ising model. Journal of Statistical Physics, 2 (1970), 301–304.

Bortz, A. B., Kalos, M. H., & Lebowitz, J. L.: A new algorithm for Monte Carlo simulation of Ising spin systems. Journal of Computational Physics, 17 (1975), 10–18.

Bouziani, I., Benhouria, Y., Essaoudi, I., Ainane, A., & Ahuja, R.: Half metallic ferromagnetic behavior in (Ga, Cr) N and (Ga, Cr, V) N compounds for spintronic technologies: Ab initio and Monte Carlo methods. Journal of Magnetism and Magnetic Materials, 477 (2019), 220–225.

Chen, J., Liu, J., West, A., Yan, Y., Yu, M., & Zhou, W.: Room Temperature Ferromagnetism of FeCoCodoped ZnO Nanorods Prepared by Chemical Vapor Deposition. IEEE Transactions on Magnetics, 44 (2008), 2681–2683.

Dietl, T., Ohno, o H., Matsukura, a F., Cibert, J., & Ferrand, e D.: Zener model description of ferromagnetism in zinc-blende magnetic semiconductors. Science, 287 (2000), 1019–1022.

Dietl, T., & Ohno, H.: Dilute ferromagnetic semiconductors: Physics and spintronic structures. Reviews of Modern Physics, 86 (2014), 187.

Dinh, V. A., Sato, K., & Katayama-Yoshida, H.; Tc-Enhanced Codoping Method for GaAs-Based Dilute Magnetic Semiconductors. Japanese Journal of Applied Physics, 42 (2003), L888.

Gyorffy, B. L., Pindor, A. J., Staunton, J., Stocks, G. M., & Winter, H.: A first-principles theory of ferromagnetic phase transitions in metals. Journal of Physics F: Metal Physics, 15 (1985), 1337–1386.

Hasegawa, H.: Single-Site Functional-Integral Approach to Itinerant-Electron Ferromagnetism. Journal of the Physical Society of Japan, 46 (1979), 1504–1514.

Hashimoto, M., Zhou, Y.-K., Kanamura, M., & Asahi, H.: High temperature (> 400 K) ferromagnetism in III–V-based diluted magnetic semiconductor GaCrN grown by ECR molecular-beam epitaxy. Solid state communications, 122 (2002), 37–39.

Huang, R.-T., Hsu, C.-F., Kai, J.-J., Chen, F.-R., & Chin, T.-S.: Room-temperature diluted magnetic semiconductors p-(Ga, Ni) N. Applied Physics Letters, 87 (2005), 202507.

Hubbard, J.: Magnetism of iron. II. Physical Review B, 20 (1979), 4584–4595.

Kanamori, J.: Principal Mechanisms Underlying Magnetic Order in Transition Metals and Compounds. Transactions of the Magnetics Society of Japan, 1 (2001), 1–10.

Kang, T., Sung, J., Shim, W., Moon, H., Cho, J., Jo, Y., Lee, W., & Kim, B.: Synthesis and magnetic properties of single-crystalline Mn/Fe-doped and Co-doped ZnS nanowires and nanobelts. The Journal of Physical Chemistry C, 113 (2009), 5352–5357.

Katayama-Yoshida, H.: SPIN-POLARIZED ELECTRONIC STRUCTURE OF INTERSTITIAL 3d TRANSITION ATOM IMPURITIES IN SILICON. International Journal of Modern Physics B, 01 (1987), 1207–1247.

Katayama-Yoshida, H., Sato, K., Fukushima, T., Toyoda, M., Kizaki, H., Dinh, V. A., & Dederichs, P. H.: Theory of ferromagnetic semiconductors. Physica Status Solidi (a), 204 (2007), 15–32.

Kohn, W., & Rostoker, N.: Solution of the Schrödinger equation in periodic lattices with an application to metallic lithium. Physical Review, 94 (1954), 1111.

Korringa, J.: On the calculation of the energy of a Bloch wave in a metal. Physica, 13 (1947), 392–400.

Krauth, W.: Statistical mechanics : Algorithms and computations. OUP Oxford 13 (2006).

Lei, T., Moustakas, T. D., Graham, R. J., He, Y., & Berkowitz, S. J.: Epitaxial growth and characterization of zinc-blende gallium nitride on (001) silicon. Journal of Applied Physics, 71 (1992), 4933–4943.

Levinshtein, M. E., Rumyantsev, S. L., & Shur, M. S.: Properties of Advanced Semiconductor Materials : GaN, AIN, InN, BN, SiC, SiGe. John Wiley & Sons (2001)

Metropolis, N., & Ulam, S.: The Monte Carlo method. Journal of the American statistical association, 44 (1949), 335–341.

Metropolis, N., Rosenbluth, A. W., Rosenbluth, M. N., Teller, A. H., & Teller, E.: Equation of state calculations by fast computing machines. The Journal of Chemical Physics, 21 (1953), 1087–1092.

Moore, G. E.: Cramming more components onto integrated circuits. McGraw-Hill New York (1965).

Newman, M., & Barkema, G.: Monte Carlo methods in statistical physics chapter 1–4. New York, USA (1999).

Ohno, H., Munekata, H., Penney, y T., Von Molnar, S., & Chang, L. L.: Magnetotransport properties of p-type (In, Mn)As diluted magnetic type (In, Mn)As diluted magnetic III-V semiconductors. Physical Review Letters, 68 (1992), 2664.

Ohno, H., Shen, n A., Matsukura, F., Oiwa, A., Endo, A., Katsumoto, S., & Iye, Y.: (Ga, Mn)As: A new diluted magnetic semiconductor based on GaAs. Applied Physics Letters, 69 (1996), 363–365.

Otrokov, M. M., Ernst, A., Ostanin, S., Fischer, G., Buczek, P., Sandratskii, L. M., Hergert, W., Mertig, I., Kuznetsov, V. M., & Chulkov, E. V.: Intralayer magnetic ordering in Ge/Mn digital alloys. Physical Review B, 83 (2011), 155203.

Pauling, L.: The Nature of the Chemical Bond.... Cornell university press Ithaca, NY 260 (1960).

Perdew, J. P., & Wang, Y.: Pair-distribution function and its coupling-constant average for the spinpolarized electron gas. Physical Review B, 46 (1992), 12947

Prellier, W., Fouchet, A., Mercey, B., Simon, C., & Raveau, B.: Laser ablation of Co: ZnO films deposited from Zn and Co metal targets on (0001) Al2O3 substrates. Applied physics letters, 82 (2003), 3490–3492.

Sato, K., Dederichs, P. H., Katayama-Yoshida, H., & Kudrnovsky, J.: Magnetic impurities and materials design for semiconductor spintronics. Physica B: Condensed Matter, 340 (2003), 863–869.

Sato, K., Bergqvist, L., Kudrnovský, J., Dederichs, P. H., Eriksson, O., Turek, I., Sanyal, B., Bouzerar, G., Katayama Yoshida, H., Dinh, V. A., Fukushima, T., Kizaki, H., & Zeller, R.: First-principles theory of dilute magnetic semiconductors. Reviews of Modern Physics, 82 (2010), 1633–1690.

Sato, K., & Katayama-Yoshida, H.: Ab initio Study on the Magnetism in ZnO-, ZnS-, ZnSe- and ZnTeBased Diluted Magnetic Semiconductors. Physica Status Solidi (b), 229 (2002), 673–680.

Sato, K., & Katayama-Yoshida, H.: First principles materials design for semiconductor spintronics. Semiconductor Science and Technology, 17 (2002), 367–376.

Shiba, H.: A Reformulation of the Coherent Potential Approximation and Its Applications: Progress of Theoretical Physics, 46 (1971), 77–94.

Souissi, M., Schmerber, G., Derory, A., & El Jani, B.: Effects of high-temperature annealing on magnetic properties of V-doped GaN thin films grown by MOCVD. Journal of Magnetism and Magnetic Materials, 324 (2012), 2539–2542.

Soven, P.: Coherent-Potential Model of Substitutional Disordered Alloys. Physical Review, 156 (1967), 809–813.

Taylor, D. W.: Vibrational Properties of Imperfect Crystals with Large Defect Concentrations. Physical Review, 156 (1967), 1017–1029.

Umesh, S., & Mittal, S.: A survey of spintronic architectures for processing-in-memory and neural networks. Journal of Systems Architecture, 97 (2019), 349–372.

Velický, B., Kirkpatrick, S., & Ehrenreich, H.: Single-Site Approximations in the Electronic Theory of Simple Binary Alloys. Physical Review, 175 (1968), 747–766.

Xu, H., Zhao, Q., Yang, H., & Chen, Y.: Study of magnetic properties of ZnO nanoparticles codoped with Co and Cu. Journal of Nanoparticle Research, 11 (2009), 615–621.

Zunger, A.: Electronic Structure of 3d Transition-Atom Impurities in Semiconductors. In H. Ehrenreich & D. Turnbull (Éds.), Solid State Physics, 39 (1986), 275–464.